Cracknell's
Law Students' Companion

Real Property

Cracknell's
Law Students' Companion

Real Property

Second Edition

CEDRIC D BELL LLB, LLM, PhD
*Barrister, Head of Professional and
Postgraduate Studies, Holborn College,
Visiting Professor of Legal Practice,
University of Hertfordshire*

Series Editor
D G Cracknell, LLB
of the Middle Temple, Barrister

OLD BAILEY PRESS

OLD BAILEY PRESS LIMITED
200 Greyhound Road, London, W14 9RY

First published 1968
Second Edition 1997

ISBN 1 85836 039 0

British Library Cataloguing-in-Publication.

A CIP Catalogue record for this book is available from the British Library.

Printed and bound in Great Britain.

Contents

Preface
to the Second Edition

In preparing this new edition it has been necessary to carry out a comprehensive overhaul of material because of the time gap between editions and to reflect the proliferation of statutory and case law developments during that period.

The aim of the new edition, like its predecessor, is to bring together in a clear and concise format the more important cases and statutory provisions to which students of Real Property Law are likely to be referred during their studies. The book is designed as a valuable supplement to, not a replacement for, an appropriate textbook.

The cases section features a number of important recent rulings of the Court of Appeal including *Cheltenham & Gloucester Building Society* v *Norgan* [1996] 1 All ER 449 (on mortgage arrears), *Drake* v *Whipp* (1995) The Times 19 December (on the differences between constructive and resulting trusts), *National & Provincial Building Society* v *Lloyd* [1996] 1 All ER 630 (on the exercise by a court of its discretion under s36 of the Administration of Justice Act 1970, as amended) and *Woolwich Building Society* v *Dickman* [1996] 3 All ER 204 (on overriding interests). In recent years one of the most dynamic areas of Real Property Law has concerned the enforceability of mortgages in situations of undue influence/misrepresentation – in particular the circumstances in which a court will set aside a mortgage signed by a wife along with her husband to secure a loan which is for the husband's sole benefit. Accordingly, considerable coverage has been afforded to the recent case law developments in this field, including the key House of Lords rulings in *Barclays Bank plc* v *O'Brien* [1993] 3 WLR 786 and *CIBC Mortgages plc* v *Pitt* [1993] 3 WLR 802 and a number of post *O'Brien* Court of Appeal decisions.

Developments up to 1 September 1996 have been taken into account. Statutory provisions in force on that date have been covered, but the coming into force of the Trusts of Land and Appointment of Trustees Act 1996 has been anticipated in the statutes section. Amongst other things, this important Act makes provisions for the phasing out of the Settled Land Act 1925: it is at present expected that it will come into force on 1 January 1997. There have also been included certain provisions of the Disability Discrimination Act 1995 and the Housing Act 1996 which will have come into force before the end of 1996.

Finally, I should like to express my thanks to Doug Cracknell, the Series Editor, for his invaluable help and guidance, and to my wife Vera and young daughters Elizabeth and Victoria for their encouragement, support and understanding.

CEDRIC D BELL
September 1996

Preface
to the First Edition

The first problem facing any contributor to this series is one of selection. Certainly, it has been difficult to decide what to omit from this particular volume in view of the enormous number of cases and amount of legislation to be found in the field of Real Property, but I trust that in general all the essential materials have been included. I have, however, deliberately omitted the Law of Property Act 1925 and the Settled Land Act 1925. Their inclusion would have increased the length of this volume out of all proportion. As it is, this volume is the largest yet published in the series, and the assumption has been made that those studying this branch of law will automatically arm themselves with copies of these Acts. Apart from these, and the rent restriction legislation which has recently been consolidated and is now conveniently available in the form of the Rent Act 1968, as space has allowed I have included statutory provisions, covering some 49 statutes, to which students of Real Property will wish to refer.

The aim is again to make available to students basic information in the form of statutory provisions and case summaries and so to provide a companion to correspondence course, lecture notes and textbooks. Of course, students are wise to avail themselves of every opportunity to read the full reports, but not every student has ready access to a law library and it is believed that even those who have may find this book useful when working at home or revising for examinations.

With regard to cases, emphasis has been placed on more recent decisions, although many older ones have been included. Real Property over-laps other subjects, and some of the topics receive fuller treatment in other volumes in the series.

I gladly record my thanks to Mr M L S Passey MA (Cantab), Solicitor, who has again prepared a glossary, and to the publishers whose help has been invaluable in so many ways.

D G CRACKNELL
June 1968

Cases

Abbey National Building Society v Cann [1990] 1 All ER 1085   **[1]**
(House of Lords)

Mrs Cann (second defendant) and her husband (third defendant) lived in 7 Hill View, a leasehold house purchased as a home for them by Mrs Cann's son (first defendant) in his own name for £34,000 with the aid of a mortgage of £25,000 provided by the plaintiff building society. This property was the third in a succession of properties bought for the second and third defendants by the first defendant. As to the first of these purchases, the mother (who was a sitting tenant) had been given the chance to purchase the freehold at a price below the market one. Her son helped her to make this purchase and in doing so he promised his mother that she would have a roof over her head for the rest of her life (that promise applied to the subsequent properties). The balance of the purchase price for 7 Hill View (ie the £9,000) came from the proceeds of sale of the two earlier properties. When the son completed the mortgage application form in respect of 7 Hill View he fraudulently declared that the house was for his sole occupation. In fact he never lived in it. Contracts were exchanged on 7 Hill View on 19 July 1984 with completion on 13 August. Prior to that date the son executed a legal charge in favour of the plaintiffs. The mother was out of the country on holiday on the day of completion. However, carpet layers began to lay her carpets and her son and husband started to bring her furniture into the house from about 11.45am on that day. Completion took place at about 12.20pm on 13 August. On 13 September 1984, the son was registered as proprietor with simultaneous registration of the plaintiffs as proprietors of the charge. Subsequently, the son defaulted in paying the mortgage instalments to the plaintiffs who brought proceedings against all three defendants claiming possession of the property. The son did not defend and took no part in the proceedings. However, the mother resisted the plaintiffs' claim. She contended that by virtue of an equitable interest in the two earlier properties and the aforementioned assurance given to her by her son she had acquired either on or immediately prior to completion, an equitable interest in 7 Hill View which was an overriding interest, and which by reason of her actual occupation at the date of registration took priority over the plaintiffs' charge under s70(1)(g) of the Land Registration Act 1925. As to the establishment of her equitable interest, the mother in particular argued that her status as a sitting tenant of the first property had contributed to her son's purchase of it. The judge rejected the claim of the second and third defendants and that decision was upheld by the Court of Appeal. Mrs Cann and her husband appealed to the House of Lords. *Held*, the appeal would be dismissed. The relevant date for ascertaining the existence of an overriding interest under ss23(1) and 70(1) of the Land Registration Act 1925 affecting the estate transferred or created was the date of registration of the transfer or interest created. However, the relevant date for determining whether an interest in registered land was protected by actual occupation and had priority over the holder of a legal estate by virtue of s70(1)(g) of the 1925 Act was the date when the legal estate was transferred or created (ie completion) and not the date when it was registered. Accordingly, a person with a beneficial interest in the

1

property who entered into occupation of it after the creation of a charge (ie after completion of the transaction) but before it was registered could not claim the benefit of s70(1)(g) of the 1925 Act. Here the appellants were not in actual occupation of the property at the date of completion of the purchase which was when the building society's charge was created and accordingly they were not entitled to claim the benefit of s70(1)(g). Further, the acts of moving in the mother's furniture and laying her carpets prior to completion were not sufficient to amount to 'actual occupation' for the purpose of s70(1)(g). Rather they were acts preparatory to occupation. (See also *Lloyds Bank plc* v *Rosset*.)

Abbey National plc v Moss [1994] 1 FLR 307 (Court of Appeal) [2]

M (first defendant) owned the property in question outright. She was persuaded by her daughter, L (second defendant), to transfer the property into their joint names in order to simplify the passing of the property on the mother's death. However, the transfer was on condition that the house would never be sold during M's lifetime without her consent. Subsequently, L borrowed £30,000 from the plaintiff on the security of the house. M and L then fell out. L left the country and defaulted on the mortgage, and the plaintiff sought possession of the house under s30 of the Law of Property Act 1925. The mortgage documents showed the signatures of both the mother and the daughter. However, the county court judge found that M had not known of the mortgage until some time after the loan had been advanced. Relying on *Re Citro* he concluded that the bargain between M and L was not a factor which could inhibit him in making an order for sale as between the plaintiff and M. Accordingly, he ordered L and her husband (third defendant) to pay the plaintiff £45,624 due from them as mortgagor and guarantor respectively under the mortgage in question on the house which was owned by M and L as joint tenants. Since the plaintiff was a 'person interested' in the property for the purposes of s30 of the Law of Property Act 1925 he further ordered the house to be sold under that provision. M (first defendant) appealed against the sale order. *Held*, the appeal would be allowed. The position in law created by the transfer of the house subject to the aforementioned condition was that the trust for sale thereby brought into being could not be implemented without M's consent. In such circumstances, in proceedings apart from s30 of the 1925 Act, the court would not allow the trustees for sale to ignore the consent requirement. Further, it could not have been within the contemplation of either M or L that the assignment (whether voluntary or involuntary) by L of her interest could lead to the house being sold against M's wishes. Again, apart from s30 of the 1925 Act, an assignee of the donee was not in any better position than the donee to ignore the requirement of the mother's consent to a sale. The court then examined the current state of case law on the exercise of its discretion in s30 proceedings when consent was refused. They noted that *Jones* v *Challenger* was clear authority for the principle that so long as a secondary purpose was still subsisting necessitating the retention of the property, the trust for sale would not be enforced, but that once the secondary purpose came to an end one beneficial owner could not insist on the property being retained against the wishes of another who wanted it sold. Here it was impossible to conclude that the secondary purpose (that M should remain in the property during her lifetime) had come to an end just because L had lost her beneficial interest through the mortgage, because the secondary purpose was completely unaffected by that event. However, it would have been different if the secondary purpose had been that both mother and daughter were to have lived together in the house. Finally, the court considered *Re Citro*. The conclusion of the county court judge, that the latter case decided that a court would not usually take a subsisting secondary purpose into account when one of the original parties to that purpose had parted with his share, was wrong. PETER GIBSON LJ continued: 'On the contrary *Re Citro* only establishes that the collateral [secondary] purpose would not be treated as subsisting when that purpose is to provide a matrimonial home and one of the parties ceases through bankruptcy or the like to own his share. It does not purport to apply where a different collateral purpose continues to subsist and where such purpose is not affected by the alienation by a party to that purpose of his share.' In the court's view *Re Citro* was limited to cases where one of the parties ceased to have an interest by reason of bankruptcy or insolvency. The present case was quite distinct from *Re Citro*. The court refused, in the exercise of its discretion under s30, to order a sale.

Acklom, Re, Oakeshott v Hawkins [1929] 1 Ch 195   [3]

A testator provided in his will that his sister could reside in his leasehold house for her life and directed his trustees that 'if and when she shall not wish to reside or continue to reside' in the house they should sell the same and divide the proceeds amongst certain charities. The sister sold the house as the tenant for life or the person having the powers of a tenant for life. *Held*, these powers were properly exercised by her and, by virtue of s106 of the Settled Land Act 1925, she had not forfeited her interest in the proceeds of sale. 'By parity of reasoning ... she was entitled to let Wiseton Court without incurring any forfeiture even if she ceased thereupon to reside or to continue to reside [therein]' (*per* MAUGHAM J). (See also *Re Patten, Westminster Bank Ltd v Carlyon.*)

Ackroyd v Smith (1850) 10 CB 164   [4]

Assignees of land sought to rely upon a right of way granted to the assignor for purposes wholly unconnected with the land conveyed to them. *Held*, they were not entitled to do so. 'If a way be granted in gross, it is personal only, and cannot be assigned ... It is not in the power of a vendor to create any rights not connected with the use or enjoyment of the land, and annex them to it, nor can the owner of land render it subject to a new species of burthen, so as to bind it in the hands of an assignee' (*per* CRESSWELL J). (See also *Bailey v Stephens.*)

Adler v Blackman [1952] 2 All ER 945 (Court of Appeal)   [5]

A weekly tenant entered into an agreement with his landlord for a tenancy for one year at a rent of £3 a week. At the end of the year the tenant held over at the same rent. *Held*, the tenancy was a weekly one as it was essential to the presumption of a yearly tenancy on the determination of a letter for a year or for a term of years that the rent should be expressed as an annual sum; here, that presumption was rebutted as the rent was expressed to be paid as a weekly rent and not as an instalment of the rent fixed for the one year's tenancy.

AG Securities v Vaughan [1988] 3 WLR 1205 (House of Lords)   [6]

AG (the plaintiffs) owned a flat which comprised six living rooms, a kitchen and a bathroom. Of the six living rooms they furnished four as bedrooms, one as a lounge and the final one as a sitting-room. AG granted the right to occupy this flat to four individual flat-sharers (the defendants) under separate short-term agreements termed 'licences' which were made at different times and on different terms but were usually for six months' duration with renewal provisions. Each agreement provided for the payment of a different monthly rent and no occupant was responsible for the payments of the others. Each agreement further provided that each occupant had 'the right to use (the flat) in common with others who have or may from time to time be granted the like right ... but without the right to exclusive possession of any part of the ... flat'. When one occupant left a new occupant was mutually agreed by AG and the remaining occupants. In 1985, AG served notices to quit on the four occupants. The occupants applied to a rent officer to have a fair rent registered for the flat on the ground that they were tenants of the flat. AG sought and obtained a declaration that the defendants occupied the flat as licensees and not as tenants. Three of the occupants appealed to the Court of Appeal which allowed their appeal. AG appealed to the House of Lords. *Held*, the appeal would be allowed. The agreements entered into by AG with the four occupants whereby each occupant had exclusive possession of one bedroom and shared the rest of the accommodation did not have the effect of creating a collective joint tenancy among the occupants for the time being of the flat by virtue of their having between them exclusive possession of the flat, because the agreements were independent of one another, started on different dates, covered different periods and provided for different payments for that occupation. There was nothing artificial in the agreements. 'The arrangement seems to have been a sensible and realistic one to provide accommodation for a shifting population of individuals who were genuinely prepared to share the flat with others introduced from time to time who would, at least initially, be strangers to them. There was no artificiality in the contracts concluded to give effect to this arrangement. On the contrary, it seems to me to require the highest degree of artificiality to force these contracts into the mould of a joint tenancy' (*per* LORD BRIDGE OF HARWICH). LORD TEMPLEMAN stated that if the four occupants had been jointly entitled to exclusive possession of the flat then when one of them died the remaining three would have been entitled to joint and exclusive occupation. But in reality they could not exclude a fourth person nominated by AG. LORD OLIVER OF AYLMERTON focused on the four unities necessary for there to be a joint tenancy. He concluded as follows: 'For my part I [find] no unity of interest, no unity of title, certainly no unity of time and, as I think, no unity of possession.' There was no joint tenancy of the flat to give the occupants the protection of the Rent Acts (a tenancy was essential for such protection). Rather the agreements constituted licences. (Distinguished: *Street* v *Mountford*; see also *Antoniades* v *Villiers*.)

Ailesbury's (Marquis) Settled Estates, Re [1892] 1 Ch 506   **[7]**
(Court of Appeal)

The Marquis of Ailesbury, tenant for life of the Savernake estate, sought the sanction of the court (see now s65 of the Settled Land Act 1925) to the sale of Savernake House, the principal mansion house and principal residence of the Ailesbury family since 1675. The proposed sale was opposed by the remaindermen who desired that the property be preserved within the family. *Held*, the court should have regard to all the circumstances, not merely to the wishes of the remaindermen and the tenant for life and, in the light of those circumstances, the sale would be sanctioned as 'in all human probability everybody connected with [the estate] will be ruined unless it is sold' (*per* LINDLEY LJ). His Lordship added that in what is now s107(1) of the Settled Land Act 1925 'the expression "have regard to the interests" means ... that he is to consider all the interests in the widest sense – not merely pecuniary interests, but wishes and sentimental feelings, and so on'.

Alefounder's Will Trusts, Re, Adnams v Alefounder   **[8]**
[1927] 1 Ch 361

Before 1 January 1926, Alefounder was entitled to settled estates as adult legal tenant in tail in possession, with remainders over, but without any overriding trusts or incumbrances. When the new property legislation came into force on that day he automatically became estate owner, holding the legal fee simple in trust for himself as equitable tenant in tail with remainders over, but still without any overriding trusts or incumbrances. *Held*, if he barred his equitable entail, and so put an end to the settlement, he could make a valid disposition of the property as absolute legal owner in fee simple, without first obtaining a vesting deed pursuant to s13 of the Settled Land Act 1925 which section having regard to s112(2) of the Act, applies only to dispositions under that Act.

Allen, Re, Faith v Allen [1953] 2 All ER 898 (Court of Appeal) [9]

Subject to certain prior limited interests a testator devised real property to the eldest of the sons of his nephew Francis 'who shall be a member of the Church of England and an adherent to the doctrine of that church' and, in the event of there being no son who was 'a member of the Church of England or an adherent to the doctrine of that church', to William Allen. *Held*, the formula used by the testator amounted to a condition precedent or qualification (as opposed to a condition subsequent) and, as such, it should not be declared void for uncertainty 'unless the terms of the condition or qualification are such that it is impossible to give them any meaning at all or such that they involve repugnancies or inconsistencies in the possible tests which they postulate as distinct, for example, from mere problems of degree' (*per* SIR R EVERSHED MR). Here the expressions used by the testator were capable of a sensible and definite meaning and a claimant should be allowed the opportunity of showing that he fulfilled the condition or qualification. (But see *Clayton* v *Ramsden*.)

Allen v Greenwood [1970] 1 All ER 819 (Court of Appeal) [10]

A owned a house and garden. The rear garden contained a greenhouse which for at least the last 20 years had been used as a normal domestic greenhouse. It was built alongside the boundary with the neighbouring property. G, the owner of the adjoining property, erected a fence on his property which stood 18 inches above the eaves of A's greenhouse and then he parked a caravan next to the fence alongside the greenhouse. The effect of the fence and the caravan was to reduce the amount of direct sunlight falling on the greenhouse and, although sufficient light was left for working in the greenhouse, there was insufficient light for growing plants. A sought an injunction and a declaration that he had acquired an easement under s3 of the Prescription Act 1832 contending that he had enjoyed the access and use of light to and for the greenhouse for 20 years without interruption and therefore had an absolute and indefeasible right to that light. The judge held that a greenhouse was a building which required special light and as there was no evidence that G knew of the precise purpose being made of the greenhouse the action would be dismissed. A appealed. *Held*, the appeal would be allowed. The amount of light which could be acquired by prescription was to be measured according to the nature of the building and the purposes for which it was normally used. The normal use of a greenhouse was to promote the growth of plants. Since that use required a high degree of light A had acquired as part of his prescriptive right to ordinary light the right to that degree of light and to the benefits of that light including the rays of the sun required to grow plants in the greenhouse and not just the amount of light required for illumination. Alternatively, a right to an exceptional amount of light for a given purpose could be acquired by prescription provided it was enjoyed for the full 20-year period to the knowledge of the servient owners and, as G must have known how the greenhouse was being used, A had acquired a right to an exceptionally high degree of light by known enjoyment of that degree of light over 20 years. Since G was blocking the light to the greenhouse A was entitled to the injunction and declaration sought. (See also *Ough* v *King* and *Carr-Saunders* v *Dick McNeil Associates Ltd*.)

Alliance Building Society v Pinwill [1958] 2 All ER 408 [11]

A legal charge of a dwelling-house provided that the mortgagor attorned tenant to the mortgagees at a yearly rent of a peppercorn if demanded, but in the event of their power of sale becoming exercisable the mortgagees could determine the tenancy by giving 'at least seven days' notice to quit'. Did such notice contravene s16 of the Rent Act 1957, by which a notice giving less than four weeks' notice to quit any premises let as a dwelling was invalid? *Held*, it did not as 'the Rent Act 1957 s16, protects a real tenant against a real landlord under a real "residential letting" and is not intended to, and does not, benefit a mortgagor to the detriment of his mortgagee. I should add that although this decision may apply to many cases in which attornment clauses appear in mortgages, it may not necessarily apply to all such cases; it might, for instance, be inapplicable to a case where the rent reserved was not a peppercorn but a full rackrent, or to a case in which the terms of the mortgage obliged the mortgagor to reside personally on the premises' (*per* VAISEY J).

Allied Irish Bank v Byrne See **TSB Bank plc v Camfield**

Andrews v Partington (1791) 3 Bro CC 401 [12]

The rule in *Andrews* v *Partington* has been stated to be: 'Where there is a bequest of an aggregate fund to children as a class, and the share of each child is made payable on attaining a given age, or marriage, the period of distribution is the time when the first child becomes entitled to receive his share, and children coming into existence after that period are excluded' (*Hawkins on Wills*). In *Re Wernher's Settlement Trusts* [1961] 1 All ER 184 BUCKLEY J found that the rule applies equally to a settlement inter vivos. (See also *Re Bleckly*.)

Antoniades v Villiers [1988] 3 WLR 1205 (House of Lords) [13]

A (the plaintiff) converted the attic of his house into a furnished flat (there was only one bedroom). A granted to V and his girlfriend (the defendants) the right to use the flat under separate but identical agreements called 'licences'. These agreements which were executed at the same time emphasised that V and his girlfriend were not to have exclusive possession. In particular, clause 16 of the agreements provided as follows: 'The licensor shall be entitled at any time to use the rooms together with the licensee and permit other persons to use all of the rooms together with the licensee.' The agreements also stated that the real intention of the parties was to create a licence not coming under the Rent Acts. The cost of occupancy was £174 a month. Each agreement placed upon each occupant an individual but not a joint responsibility for paying half of the sum of £174. The agreements were determinable by one month's notice by either party. A never attempted to use any of the rooms in the flat or to have them used by others. In 1986, A gave the defendants notice to quit and applied to the court for a possession order. However, his claim was dismissed on the ground that the defendants were tenants who were entitled to the protection of the Rent Acts. A successfully appealed to the Court of Appeal and thereafter V and his girlfriend appealed to the House of Lords. *Held*, the appeal would be allowed. Their Lordships emphasised that an express statement of intention was not decisive of the matter (ie whether there was a lease or a licence) and that they would pay attention to the facts, the surrounding circumstances and to what the parties did as well as to what they said. Here the two agreements were interdependent on one another and were therefore to be read together as forming a single transaction. Since it was the intention of the young couple to occupy the flat as man and wife, and since A knew of this intention, the true nature of the arrangement was to create a joint tenancy. Clause 16 was designed to disguise the grant of a tenancy and to deprive the young couple of the protection of the Rent Acts. '... the provisions of the joint agreement purporting to retain the right in the respondent [A] to share the occupation of the flat with the young couple himself or to introduce an indefinite number of third parties to do so could be seen, in all the relevant circumstances, to be repugnant to the true purpose of the agreement. No one could have supposed that those provisions were ever intended to be acted on. They were introduced into the agreement for no other purpose than as an attempt to disguise the true character of the agreement which it was hoped would deceive the court and prevent the appellants [V and his girlfriend] enjoying the protection of the Rent Acts' (*per* LORD BRIDGE OF HARWICH). Accordingly, the agreement created a joint tenancy and not a licence. (See also *AG Securities* v *Vaughan*.)

## Appah v Parncliffe Investments Ltd [1964] 1 All ER 838			[14]
(Court of Appeal)

The plaintiff hired a residential room in the defendants' house at 15s a day or £5 a week. The defendants reserved the right to enter the room, there was a notice requiring visitors to be out by 10.30pm and the plaintiff was told that she would not have to give notice to leave provided the rent was not in arrear. Certain of the plaintiff's belongings were stolen from the room. *Held*, the plaintiff was a licensee for reward, as opposed to a tenant, and it followed that the defendants were under an obligation to use reasonable care to see that she and her property suffered no loss. Since, on the facts, the defendants were in breach of this duty and such breach was the probable cause of the plaintiff's loss, the plaintiff was entitled to damages.

## Armory v Delamirie (1721) 1 Stra 505				[15]

A chimney sweeper's boy found a jewel set in a socket. He took his find to a goldsmith who refused to return the jewel. The boy brought an action for trover. *Held*, he would succeed as he had such a property in the jewel as would enable him to keep it against all but the rightful owner. By way of damages, he should recover the value of the best jewel that would fit the socket. (Applied in *Parker* v *British Airways Board*.)

## Ashburn Anstalt v Arnold [1988] 2 All ER 147 (Court of Appeal)		[16]

The first defendant held the headlease and A Co (second defendant) the sublease of shop premises which were part of a block which the landlords C Ltd wanted to develop. By agreements entered into on 28 February 1973 the first defendant sold the headlease to M Ltd and A Co sold the sublease to M Ltd. On the same day the benefit of these agreements was assigned by M Ltd to C Ltd (ie the headlease and sublease were merged in the freehold). Clause 5 of the agreement between A Co and M Ltd provided that A Co could remain in possession of the premises as 'licensees' without payment of rent subject to giving up possession to M Ltd if M Ltd gave one quarter's notice in writing certifying that they were ready to proceed with the redevelopment. Clause 6 of that agreement provided that on redevelopment M Ltd would grant A Co a lease of a shop in the new development. In 1985 the plaintiffs (AA) purchased the freehold of the premises from C Ltd expressly subject to the 1973 agreement between A Co and M Ltd. Subsequently, the plaintiffs purported to terminate A Co's occupation and sought possession. A Co refused to vacate and the plaintiffs brought possession proceedings claiming that A Co were only licensees. A Co claimed that the 1973 agreement created a tenancy which took effect as an overriding interest under s70(1)(g) of the Land Registration Act 1925. The judge dismissed the plaintiffs claim for possession and the plaintiffs appealed. *Held*, the appeal would be dismissed. The reservation of a rent was not necessary for the creation of a tenancy. Lord Templeman's speech in *Street* v *Mountford* was not to be read as laying down a 'no rent no lease' principle. The need for rent was negatived by the definition of 'term of years absolute' in s205(1)(xxvii) LPA 1925 as '... a term of years (taking effect either in possession or in reversion *whether or not at a rent)*'. Accordingly, the fact that clause 5 did not require A Co to pay rent for their occupancy of the shop pending the redevelopment did not prevent that occupation being pursuant to a lease rather than a licence. Clause 5 gave A Co exclusive possession. Further, A Co's possession was for a term which was not uncertain because the circumstances which would determine the agreement could be clearly identified. The reservation created a tenancy. The tenancy was not from year to year but for a term which would continue until M Ltd certified that it was ready to proceed with the development or until A Co gave a quarter's notice or vacated the property without giving notice. (On this point – that the term was certain – but only on this point, the case was overruled by the House of Lords in *Prudential Assurance Co Ltd* v *London Residuary Body*.) It followed that clause 5 created a lease, and since A Co was in actual occupation it was an overriding interest under s70(1)(g) of the Land Registration Act 1925 and was therefore binding on the plaintiffs. Clause 6 of the agreement was sufficiently clear to be enforceable as a contract and so was likewise an overriding interest notwithstanding that it had not been registered as an estate contract. The fact that A Co was in possession was sufficient. A Co could compel the plaintiffs to offer it a lease of a shop on the redeveloped site if shop premises were included in the redevelopment. However, A Co could not prevent the plaintiffs from proceeding with a redevelopment which did not provide suitable shop premises. Per incuriam: a contractual licence did not create an interest in land capable of binding third parties – even a third party with notice (*Errington* v *Errington* disapproved on this point). (Distinguished: *Lace* v *Chandler*.)

Asher v Whitlock (1865) LR 1 QB 1 [17]

One Thomas Williamson enclosed some land which, on his death, passed to his wife and daughter. His wife remarried but soon afterwards first she and then her daughter died and left her second husband in possession of the land. The daughter's heir-at-law brought an action for ejectment. *Held*, she was entitled to succeed as she had a good title against all but the true owner.

Attwood v Llay Main Collieries Ltd [1926] Ch 444 [18]

The defendant colliery owners abstracted water from a river through a seven-inch main and converted the water into steam for working the colliery machinery: at least 600,000 gallons of water a week were used in this way. *Held*, on the assumption that the defendants were riparian owners, their use of the water could not be justified as they took 'the water for extraordinary purposes without returning it to the river' (*per* LAWRENCE J). His Lordship summarised the law as follows: 'For the purposes of this judgment, it is sufficient to state that a riparian owner may take and use the water for ordinary purposes connected with the riparian tenement (such as domestic purposes or the wants of his cattle), and that in the exercise of his rights he may exhaust the water altogether; that he may also take and use the water for extraordinary purposes, if such user be reasonable and be connected with the riparian tenement, provided that he restores the water so taken and used substantially undiminished in volume and unaltered in character;

and lastly, that he has no right whatever to take the water and use it for purposes unconnected with the riparian tenement.' It should be noted that His Lordship believed the occupation by the defendants of a strip of land carrying a railway line did not have the effect of converting the site of the defendants' works, which was at least a mile away from the river, into a riparian tenement, 'an expression which … connotes, in addition to contact with the river, a reasonable proximity to the river bank'.

Austerberry v Corporation of Oldham See Rhone v Stephens

Australian Blue Metal Ltd v Hughes [1962] 3 All ER 335   **[19]** (Privy Council)

By an agreement in writing the respondents granted the appellants 'the right to mine for magnesite' on certain land in return for a royalty of, at first, 10s per ton, and later (after the appellants had told the respondents that they would have to pull out unless they could decrease costs) 6s per ton. The agreement did not expressly define the period of the mining licence thus granted, provide for its termination or expressly or impliedly oblige the appellants to do any mining on their land: it was a non-exclusive licence, therefore entitling the respondents to grant other licences to mine the land or to resume work there themselves. Shortly after the reduction in royalty the appellants found that work on part of the land would be very profitable and the respondents thereupon contested the appellants' right to mine this area and by letter asked them to 'cease operations [on the land] immediately'. *Held*, the agreement had been properly terminated by the letter, and the respondents were entitled to an injunction to restrain the appellants from working on the land. The agreement had merely given permission to mine revocable at will subject to allowing the appellants a reasonable period to quit the land (the parties agreed that such a period had already expired), and no provision for termination only on reasonable notice would be implied. 'The agreement … was … nothing more than an ad hoc arrangement whereby the labour and equipment which the appellants had available might be employed on the respondents' land to their mutual advantage so long as it suited both parties' (*per* LORD DEVLIN). (See also *Winter Garden Theatre (London) Ltd v Millennium Productions Ltd.*)

Bailey v Stephens (1862) 12 CB (NS) 91   **[20]**

The occupier of a close called Bloody Field, which was owned by the defendant, claimed a right to go upon the adjoining close of the plaintiff (Short Cliffe Wood) and take all the wood that was growing there on the ground that such right had been exercised 'from time whereof the memory of man runneth not to the contrary'. *Held*, the claim could not be upheld as it was a claim of a right appurtenant to the defendant's land, to take all the profits of the plaintiff's land, wholly unconnected with the defendant's land, and such 'was not an incident which can be annexed by law to the ownership, much less to the occupation of land' (*per* WILLES J). (See also *Hill v Tupper.*)

Ballard's Conveyance, Re [1937] 2 All ER 691   **[21]**

In 1906 about 18 acres of land was sold and the purchaser covenanted with the vendor, her heirs and assigns and successors that he, his heirs and assigns would perform and observe certain conditions and stipulations for the benefit of the 1,700 acre Childwickbury Estate retained by the vendor. Could the successors in title of the vendor obtain relief in respect of a breach, or threatened breach, of this covenant by the purchaser? *Held*, they could not as, although a breach of the stipulations might affect part of the Childwickbury Estate, far the largest part could not possibly be affected by any such breach. 'I asked in vain for any authority which would justify me in severing the covenant, and treating it as annexed to or running with such part of the land as is touched by or concerned with it, though, as regards the remainder of the land, namely, such part as is not touched by or concerned with the covenant, the covenant is not, and cannot be, annexed to it, and accordingly does not, and cannot, run with it. Nor have I been able, through my own researches, to find anything in the books which seems to justify any such course' (*per* CLAUSON J). (See also *Zetland (Marquess) v Driver.*)

Banco Exterior Internacional v Mann [1995] 1 All ER 936 [22]
(Court of Appeal)

H, the first defendant, wanted to charge the matrimonial home as security for a loan to be granted by the plaintiff bank to a company owned and controlled by him. The bank sent the relevant documents to the company in question marked for the attention of H to enable W (his wife) to sign a declaration that her rights would be postponed to the bank's charge over the matrimonial home. In a covering letter, the bank required W's declaration to be signed by her in the presence of a solicitor who would certify that he had explained its effect to her (the purpose of this requirement was to bring home to the wife the risk she was running in signing the documents and advise her to take independent legal advice and so rebut the presumption of undue influence by the husband in such cases). However, nothing was said about the need for the solicitor to be acting only for W. In fact, the documents were sent to a solicitor who for some time had acted for both H and his company. This solicitor explained the declaration to W who stated that she had no real choice but to sign. The solicitor then certified that he had explained the nature and effect of the declaration to W. The bank itself never communicated with W and never gave her any advice. Subsequently the company went into liquidation and the bank sought a possession order. At first instance the judge found that W was entitled to a beneficial interest in the property and that a presumption of undue influence by H over W in respect of the transaction had arisen which had not been rebutted. He further found that the bank had constructive notice of this undue influence. Accordingly, W's beneficial interest was binding on the bank and constituted a defence to the possession claim. The bank appealed. *Held*, the appeal would be allowed. The bank had taken reasonable steps to ensure that the undue influence of H had been counteracted. They had required W to sign the declaration in the presence of a solicitor who was required to certify that before it was executed its nature and effect had been explained to her. As to the independent legal advice aspect, the bank had received the warranty of a solicitor that he had explained to W the nature and effect of the declaration. It was for the solicitor to consider whether he was able to do this without any conflict of interest. The bank could rely on the fact that the solicitor undertook the task as demonstrating that he was sufficiently independent for that purpose. Further, the bank was entitled to consider that it would not have been possible for the solicitor to have satisfactorily explained the effect of the declaration to W without making it clear to her the risks she would be running if she signed the declaration and thereafter the company defaulted. Accordingly, the bank had taken reasonable steps to avoid being fixed with constructive notice of W's right to set aside the declaration as having been entered into by her in consequence of H's undue influence. (Applied: *Barclays Bank plc v O'Brien*; followed: *Massey v Midland Bank plc.*)

Barclays Bank plc v O'Brien [1993] 3 WLR 786 (House of Lords)   [23]

A matrimonial home was in the joint names of a husband and wife. The husband but not the wife had an interest in a company. In order to raise capital for this company the husband negotiated a loan from the bank, with the bank taking a legal charge over the matrimonial home as security. He misrepresented the transaction to his wife by telling her that she would be signing a mortgage for a fixed amount of £60,000 that would only last for three weeks and would enable him to increase his shareholding in the company in question. In actual fact, they were guaranteeing the company's debt to the bank which granted the company a £135,000 overdraft secured on the matrimonial home. The bank prepared the security documents and sent them to the local branch for execution with instructions that branch staff were to explain the deal to the wife and advise her to take independent advice before she signed. The husband signed the relevant documents in the absence of his wife. When the wife went to sign the legal charge the effect of the deal was not explained to her nor was she advised to obtain independent legal advice. Rather, she signed the documents without reading them. Subsequently, when the company got into financial difficulty the husband was called upon to honour the guarantee. When he failed to pay the sums owing to the bank it sought to realise its security by seeking a possession order in respect of the matrimonial home. The county court granted the bank a possession order. The wife appealed. The Court of Appeal ruled that because the wife mistakenly believed her liability was restricted to £60,000 the bank was only entitled to that sum. The bank appealed. *Held*, the appeal would be dismissed. Where a wife, as here, signed a mortgage as surety for the debts of her husband four main legal principles were to be applied. First, the surety would be enforceable by the creditor unless the wife was induced to enter into the agreement by undue influence, misrepresentation or other legal wrong on the part of her husband, the principal debtor. In particular, the wife could not be released from her obligations just because she had misunderstood the nature of the security. Second, in the event of there being such undue influence, etc that undue influence, etc would be attributed to the creditor/mortgagee if the latter had actual or constructive notice of the undue influence, misrepresentation, etc. Third, a creditor would have constructive notice of the undue influence, etc if the transaction was on its face not to the financial advantage of the claimant (the wife) and it was of such a kind that there was a substantial risk that undue influence, etc might have been exercised. Accordingly, the bank had constructive notice of the wife's right to set this transaction aside because it met the aforementioned criteria (wife signing a mortgage as surety for her husband's debts). Fourth, a creditor would avoid being fixed with constructive notice if he warned the surety (wife) in the absence of the principal debtor (husband) of the risks involved and advised the surety to seek independent legal advice. Here since the bank had failed to explain the full implications of the transaction to the wife and to recommend that she took independent legal advice, the legal charge was unenforceable against her. In dealing with undue influence, the law treated married women tenderly. LORD BROWNE-WILKINSON justified this approach on the ground that although the idea that a wife was subservient to her husband in the management of family finance was outmoded 'yet in a substantial proportion of marriages it is still the husband who has the business experience and the wife is willing to follow his advice without bringing a truly independent mind and will to bear'. Finally, their Lordships said the ruling would also apply to unmarried couples, heterosexual or homosexual, in a relationship where there was a risk of one of them exploiting the other's emotional involvement and trust. (Applied: *Kingsnorth Trust Ltd* v *Bell*; see also *CIBC Mortgages plc* v *Pitt*, *Banco Exterior Internacional* v *Mann* and *TSB Bank plc* v *Camfield*; applied in *Massey* v *Midland Bank plc*.)

Barclays Bank Ltd v Stasek [1956] 3 All ER 439 [24]

A bank became mortgagee of certain premises subject to a weekly tenancy and on different dates the tenants subsequently entered into two further tenancies of different parts of the same house as a result of which they still occupied only one of the rooms originally let to them. It was a term of the mortgage that leases (which term included tenancies) could only be granted with the bank's consent, but the bank did not give its consent to the granting of the two subsequent tenancies. The bank sought to recover possession from the tenants. *Held*, although the second and third lettings were effective against the mortgagor (the landlord) and, being effective lettings, by operation of law created a surrender of the then existing tenancy, as against the bank the original tenancy remained and the tenants were entitled to occupy their old rooms because there was no surrender save through the new tenancies and, as far as the bank was concerned, these were not effective because they are granted without its consent. 'When a lease is granted, with the result of effecting a surrender of an existing lease and the second lease is not effective in law because it exceeds the powers which the lessor had, then the surrender, whether it appears that it was an express surrender or a surrender through operation of law, is ineffective, and consequently the original term remains effective' (*per* DANCKWERTS J). (See also *Lever Finance Ltd* v *Trustee of Property of Needleman*.)

Bathavon Rural District Council v Carlile [1958] 1 All ER 801 [25]
(Court of Appeal)

A weekly tenancy of a council house ran from a Monday to midnight the following Sunday and on Friday 14 June 1957 the council gave a notice to quit 'by noon on Monday 1 July 1957'. *Held*, the notice to quit was bad as it did not expire at the proper time, viz the end of a current week's tenancy. 'While "Monday" without more can be construed ... as meaning the first moment of the day (the preceding midnight), "by noon on Monday" cannot be so construed' (*per* HODSON LJ).

Baxter v Four Oaks Properties Ltd [1965] 1 All ER 906 [26]

Lord Clanrikarde owned certain land at Sutton Coldfield and beginning in 1891 he sold building plots, of varying sizes, to purchasers as they came along. There was no evidence that Lord Clanrikarde laid out the estate in lots before the first sale took place but all purchasers and those who claimed under them were expressly bound by a deed of mutual covenant to observe certain covenants, including a covenant that no dwelling-house shall be used otherwise than as a private residence. The defendants purchased one of the plots in 1963 with notice of the existence of the covenants and derived their title from a conveyance by Lord Clanrikarde in 1894; the plaintiffs, some of whom derived their title from purchasers from Lord Clanrikarde before and some after 1894, sought to enforce the covenants against the defendants who had demolished the house on their plot and built thereon a block of flats. *Held*, by building the flats upon their land the defendants were in breach of covenant and this covenant could be enforced by all the plaintiffs because, in all the circumstances, and especially because of the execution of the deed of mutual covenant, it could properly be inferred that Lord Clanrikarde and the purchasers from him had in fact intended a building scheme. The plaintiffs' claim was not defeated by the fact that Lord Clanrikarde had not laid out his estate in lots before he began to sell it off. (See also *Re Dolphin's Conveyance*; but see *Elliston* v *Reacher*.)

Beckett (Alfred F) Ltd v Lyons [1967] 1 All ER 833 **[27]**
(Court of Appeal)

It was alleged that there was a right (justified by a prescription from time immemorial either by common law or by custom or by lost grant or declaration of trust) in favour of the inhabitants of the county of Durham to enter on the foreshore, with or without animals or vehicles, to collect and remove sea coal, ie small coals washed up by the tide. Witnesses said that coal had been thus taken since 1895. *Held*, no such right had been established as the evidence of removal extended in substance only to the poorer inhabitants of villages near the foreshore and not also of the inland area of the county. Further, the practice was sufficiently explained by the tolerance of the foreshore owner (ie the taking was not necessarily of right), the commercial exploitation by lorries was quite different from the old practice and a fluctuating body such as the inhabitants of a county could not acquire by custom a profit à prendre. 'I cannot find any clear decision that the public has the right to walk on the foreshore when the tide is out, nor of landing from boats or embarking except in cases of emergency. It seems also clear enough that there is no public highway along the foreshore' (*per* HARMAN LJ). 'It has never been established in English law that beachcombing can give rise to a legal right to frequent the foreshore for the purpose of beachcombing or require a presumption of a legal origin; and the early evidence in this case to my mind amounts to no more than beachcombing ... it does not seem to me that the only reasonable conclusion from the evidence is that the practice [of taking sea coal] must have had a legal origin; here the factual contrast with *Goodman* v *Saltash Corporation* (1882) 7 App Cas 633 is most marked. I think that the only reasonable conclusion is mere tolerance of the unimportant' (*per* RUSSELL LJ).

Bedson v Bedson [1965] 3 All ER 307 (Court of Appeal) **[28]**

When the husband retired from the army he bought a freehold draper's shop with a flat above, the money coming from his savings. On solicitor's advice, the property was conveyed to the husband and wife as joint tenants. The parties lived in the flat, the husband managed and the wife helped in the shop, and the business accounts were drawn up on the basis that the property belonged to husband and wife in equal shares. When the wife left, she brought proceedings under s17 of the Married Women's Property Act 1882 for a half share in the property, and for an order of sale. *Held*, the wife was entitled to a half share because of the joint tenancy, and because on the evidence it seemed that the parties intended to share the property equally. RUSSELL LJ further held that as the property had been conveyed to the parties on trust for themselves as joint tenants, 'there was no jurisdiction by virtue of s17 of the Act of 1882 to find or assert in the wife any beneficial interest other than one equal to that of the husband'. The court in its discretion refused to order a sale, because the property was bought as the matrimonial home, and for business purposes, and to have ordered a sale would have defeated both those purposes. (But see *Harris* v *Goddard*.)

Belgravia Insurance Co Ltd v Meah [1963] 3 All ER 828 **[29]**
(Court of Appeal)

A Mr Sorenti was lessee of a shop in Kings Cross and he assigned his lease to a Mr Meah and, as Mr Meah could not find all the purchase money, £1,000 was left on mortgage to Mr Sorenti. Mr Meah fell into arrears with his rent, the plaintiff landlords claimed forfeiture for non-payment of rent and Mr Sorenti applied for relief against forfeiture. *Held*, such relief would be granted under s146(4) of the Law of Property Act 1925 on payment by Mr Sorenti of the arrears of rent and certain of the costs of the application and upon his making good the breaches of the lessee's covenants. 'It seems to me that ... the court will, in the ordinary way, grant relief to an underlessee on the terms of paying the rent in arrear, performing the covenants, and paying all the costs ... the court may always refuse relief, if the conduct of the applicant is such as to make it inequitable that relief should be given to him' (*per* LORD DENNING MR). (See also *Grangeside Properties Ltd* v *Collingwoods Securities Ltd* and *Segal Securities Ltd* v *Thoseby*.)

Benn v Hardinge (1992) 66 P & CR 246 (Court of Appeal)   [30]

B claimed a right of way over a carriageway on land owned by H. The right claimed arose from an enclosure award in 1818. H contended that the right had been impliedly abandoned as there was no evidence that either B or his predecessors in title had ever endeavoured to use it. The country court dismissed B's claim on the basis that there had been no grant of a right of way and therefore it could not have been abandoned. B appealed. *Held*, the appeal would be allowed. On the true construction of the enclosure award a right of way had been granted. As to abandonment, the court emphasised that there had to be a clear intention to abandon. Non-user of a right of way, even as here, for a very long period of time (175 years), was not by itself enough to indicate an intention in the proprietor of the right to abandon it. There was a simple explanation for the non-user – B and his predecessors had alternative access to the fields served by the right of way (ie there was no need for them to use the disputed right of way). Accordingly, on the facts the court was not prepared to infer abandonment. The court emphasised that a right of way was a piece of property of latent value whose abandonment should not readily be inferred.

88 Berkeley Road London NW9, Re, Rickwood v Turnsek   [31]
[1971] 1 All ER 254

In 1955, R (the plaintiff) and Miss G bought 88 Berkeley Road providing the purchase money in equal shares. The property was transferred to them as joint tenants both at law and in equity. In 1968, Miss G decided to sever the beneficial joint tenancy. She consulted solicitors who prepared and had signed by Miss G a notice in writing under s36(2) of the Law of Property Act 1925. The notice was then sent to R at the house by recorded delivery together with a covering letter from the solicitors asking R to accept service and acknowledge receipt. R was not at home when the letter arrived and it was taken and signed for by Miss G herself who claimed that she used to put letters for R either on the table or on the mantelpiece. However, R never received the letter. After Miss G died in 1969, the letter and notice came to light because R found it among Miss G's papers and she brought it to the notice of her own solicitors and those of Miss G's personal representatives. R claimed to be entitled to the entire beneficial interest under the principle of survivorship. She contended that the beneficial joint tenancy had not been severed because she had never received the notice of severance. *Held*, the joint tenancy had been severed during Miss G's lifetime. By virtue of s36(2) of the 1925 Act a joint tenant could sever the beneficial joint tenancy by giving notice in writing to the other joint tenants. Section 196(4) of the Law of Property Act 1925 provided that 'any notice required or authorised by the Act to be served shall be sufficiently served' if sent by registered post to a proper address unless returned through the post office undelivered and service was deemed to be made when the registered letter would ordinarily be delivered. The Recorded Delivery Service Act 1962 equated recorded delivery with registered post for most purposes including service under s196(4) of the 1925 Act. PLOWMAN J accepted R's evidence that she had never received the letter. The words 'if the letter is not returned through the post office undelivered' in s196(4) referred to the ordinary case of the post office being unable to effect delivery at the address on the letter because, eg, the addressee had gone away or the house was shut or empty and it did not apply to a case where the letter was delivered by the postman at the address to which it was sent. The onus of proof on the defendant (executor of Miss G's will) here was no higher than proof that on the balance of probabilities Miss G's solicitors had put the notice of severance in the envelope with the covering letter before it was sent. '... I feel no difficulty in reaching the conclusion that, on the balance of probabilities, it was in fact done' (*per* PLOWMAN J). Despite never being received by R the notice of severance had been sufficiently served for the purposes of s36(2) of the 1925 Act.

Bernstein (Lord) v Skyviews and General Ltd [32]
[1977] 2 All ER 902

The defendant company used an aircraft to fly over the plaintiff's country house for the purpose of photographing it. *Held*, the plaintiff's action for trespass would fail, since the rights of a landowner in the air space above his land are restricted to such height as is necessary for the ordinary use and enjoyment of his land and the structures upon it, and the defendant's flight was hundreds of feet above the ground. Apart from common law, the defendant was protected by s40(1) of the Civil Aviation Act 1949, which exempted certain flights by aircraft from actions in trespass or nuisance. The taking of photographs cannot of itself make an act a trespass. (But see *Kelsen* v *Imperial Tobacco Co (of Great Britain and Ireland) Ltd.*)

Berry v Geen [1938] AC 575 (House of Lords) [33]

A testator directed his trustees to accumulate income until the death of the last of several annuitants, and subject thereto, and to the payment of certain legacies, he gave the whole of his property to the Congregational Union of England and Wales. The church, which wanted immediate possession of the fund, argued that as the estate was amply sufficient to satisfy all the annuities and legacies, they were entitled at once to call a halt to the accumulation. *Held*, the church was not entitled to immediate possession. As the testator died in 1925, the trust for accumulation could not legally continue beyond the expiry of the statutory period in 1964. The surplus income, from then until the death of the last surviving annuitant, realised by the operation of s164 of the Law of Property Act 1925 must pass according to the rules of intestacy, and the estate could, therefore, only be handed over to the church authority at the expense of a violation of the rights of those entitled under those rules.

Beswick v Beswick [1967] 2 All ER 1197 (House of Lords) [34]

By an agreement in writing PB assigned his business as a coal merchant to his nephew, JB. In consideration JB agreed to employ PB as a consultant at £6 10s 0d a week for the rest of his life; and, further, to pay PB's wife after his death an annuity of £5 a week for her life. PB's wife was not a party to the agreement. After PB's death, JB paid one sum of £5 to the widow, but refused to pay any further sum. The widow sought an order for specific performance of the agreement in her capacity as administratrix of her husband's estate and in her personal capacity. *Held*, although s56 of the Law of Property Act 1925 did not apply to this agreement and so enable the widow to enforce the agreement in her personal capacity, the widow as administratrix was entitled to enforce the agreement by an order for specific performance in her own personal favour. (But see *White* v *Bijou Mansions Ltd.*)

Birmingham Citizens Permanent Building Society v Caunt [35]
[1962] 1 All ER 163

A legal charge provided that if the mortgagor made default in payment of a monthly instalment the whole of the loan became immediately repayable and the mortgagees were entitled to eject the mortgagor from the mortgaged property. The mortgagor failed to pay certain instalments. *Held*, 'where, as here, the legal mortgagee under an instalment mortgage under which, by reason of default, the whole money has become payable, is entitled to possession, the court has no jurisdiction to decline to make the order or to adjourn the hearing, whether on terms of keeping up payments or paying arrears, if the mortgagee cannot be persuaded to agree to this course. The sole exception to this is that the application may be adjourned for a short time to afford to the mortgagor a chance of paying off the mortgagee in full or otherwise satisfying him; but this should not be done if there is no reasonable prospect of this occurring' (*per* RUSSELL J). As the mortgagees did not agree to an adjournment and there was no reasonable prospect of the mortgagor being able to discharge the mortgage in full within a short time, an order was made for possession within 28 days after service of the order. (See also *Quennell v Maltby* and *Cheltenham and Gloucester Building Society v Norgan*.)

Blades v Higgs (1865) 11 HL Cas 621 (House of Lords) [36]

Some poachers started, chased and killed wild rabbits on the land of Lord Exeter. *Held*, the rabbits belonged to his Lordship and his servants were justified in forcibly taking them from the plaintiff, a licensed dealer in game, to whom they had been sold. Discussing the views expressed by HOLT CJ in *Sutton v Moody*, after accepting without question the first proposition advanced by his Lordship, LORD CHELMSFORD said: 'It would appear to me to be more in accordance with principle, to hold that if the trespasser deprived the owner of the land where the game was started, of his right to claim the property by unlawfully killing it on the land of another to which he had driven it, he converted it into a subject of property for the other owner and not for himself.'

Bland v Yates (1914) 58 SJ 612 [37]

The defendant, a market gardener, piled an unusual and excessive quantity of manure on a spot immediately adjoining the plaintiffs' garden. Because they objected to the smell and the abnormal number of house flies which bred in the manure, the plaintiffs sought an injunction to restrain the defendant from causing a nuisance by depositing manure on his land. *Held*, the injunction would be granted.

Bleckly, Re, Bleckly v Bleckly [1951] 1 All ER 1064 [38]
(Court of Appeal)

By a codicil to his will a testator, who died in 1925, gave £10,000 to his executors 'upon trust to invest the same ... and to pay the income thereof to my daughter-in-law Gette ... the wife of my son Herbert ... during so much of her life as she shall remain the wife or widow of my said son ... Subject to the interest of my daughter-in-law therein my executors shall hold the said sum of £10,000 ... upon trust for all or any the children or child of my son Herbert ... who shall attain the age of twenty-one years'. In 1927 Herbert's marriage to Gette, of which there was no issue, was dissolved and shortly afterwards he married his present wife and the only child of that marriage to survive more than a few days, a daughter, was born in 1929 and had now attained the age of twenty-one years. Herbert was now in his fifties and, although it was unlikely that his present wife would have any more children, there was the possibility that his marriage would be terminated, by death or otherwise, and that he would have further children by a third wife. *Held*, applying the rule in *Andrews* v *Partington*, the class of remaindermen closed on the attainment of the age of twenty-one by the daughter who was, therefore, entitled to the whole fund. Although the rule, a rule of construction, could be excluded by sufficiently clear language, the fact that the daughter was not born until after the cesser of the life interest in favour of Gette was not sufficient to exclude it.

Borman v Griffith [1930] 1 Ch 493   **[39]**

James agreed to demise The Gardens (a dwelling-house situate in a large park) to the plaintiff for seven years without expressly reserving any right of way to the plaintiff and three years later demised The Hall (including the park) to the defendant for fourteen years. A carriage drive ran from the public highway to The Hall and passed the front door of The Gardens, and at the time of the granting of the lease of The Gardens James was constructing and later completed an unmetalled way from the public highway to the back of The Gardens. *Held*, although an agreement for a lease exceeding a term of three years was not an 'assurance of property or of an interest therein' within s205(1)(ii) of the Law of Property Act 1925, and therefore could not be deemed to include the general words of s62 of that Act, the plaintiff was in the same position as if the court had granted specific performance of the agreement and a demise to the plaintiff of a right to use the drive would be implied. 'The authorities are sufficient to show that a grantor of property, in circumstances where an obvious, ie, visible and made road is necessary for the reasonable enjoyment of the property by the grantee, must be taken prima facie to have intended to grant a right to use it' (*per* MAUGHAM J). (See also *Wright* v *Macadam*, *Goldberg* v *Edwards* and *Walsh* v *Lonsdale*.)

Boston's (Lord) Will Trusts, Re, Inglis v Boston   **[40]**
[1956] 1 All ER 593

Lord Boston devised and bequeathed to his executors and trustees his residuary real and personal estate on trusts for sale and conversion (with the usual power to postpone sale and conversion) and for investment. Included in the residuary estate were certain agricultural properties and the question arose as to the extent to which the trustees were entitled, as persons having the powers of a tenant for life under the Settled Land Act 1925, to pay for repairs out of capital and whether they, as trustees for sale, having regard to the terms of s75(2) of the Settled Land Act 1925, had a discretion to apply capital moneys for the payment of repairs without regard to the interest of the persons entitled to the capital of the estate in remainder. *Held*, 'the trustees of the testator's will, notwithstanding para 23 of Schedule 3 to the Agricultural Holdings Act 1948, have a duty to preserve the capital value of the testator's residuary estate in exercising the discretionary powers conferred on them by the joint effect of the Law of Property Act 1925, s28, the Settled Land Act 1925, s73(1)(iv) and the Agricultural Holdings Act 1948, s96(1), and ought not to lay out capital moneys in any manner authorised by the joint effect of those sections without regard to such duty' (*per* VAISEY J). (See also *Re Lord Brougham and Vaux's Settled Estates*.)

Bourne's Settlement Trusts, Re, Bourne v Mackay   **[41]**
[1946] 1 All ER 411 (Court of Appeal)

£7,000 was settled upon trust for the benefit, in the first instance, of seven of the settlor's grandchildren (at the date of the settlement the youngest was seven months old) and, subject to the paying of £52 a year to each grandchild on attaining 18, the income of the fund was, from the date of the settlement, to be accumulated in a separate fund. The date of final distribution of both funds (the trustees had an absolute discretion as to which member or members of defined classes, which included the grandchildren living at that time, should take and in what proportions) was the date on which the youngest surviving grandchild attained 23 and, before that date, the trustees were empowered (ie had a discretion) to give each grandchild on or after attaining 23 that grandchild's share of the £7,000 together with £500 out of the income fund. *Held*, as the accumulation was to take effect from the date of the settlement, the appropriate period during which it could be allowed was defined in s164(1)(a) of the Law of Property Act 1925, ie the life of the settlor. Notwithstanding the power to make payments of £500 out of the income fund, the direction to accumulate was not a provision for 'raising portions' within s164(2)(ii)(a) of the 1925 Act and because the grandchildren were not 'entitled to the income directed to be accumulated' s164(1)(d) did not apply. (See also *Re Robb's Will Trusts*.)

Bridgett and Hayes' Contract, Re [1928] 1 Ch 163 [42]

Under the will of Caroline Stoneley her niece Thornley was on 1 January 1926, and at the date of her (Thornley's) death, tenant for life of settled land, and one Jackson was the sole surviving trustee of the settlement. Thornley died on 17 January 1926, by her will appointing Bridgett to be the sole executor thereof, and a general grant of probate of her will was duly made to him. On the death of Thornley the settlement came to an end, and Bridgett contracted to sell part of the land to Hayes. *Held*, Bridgett could, without the concurrence of Jackson, give a good title to the land contracted to be sold.

Bristol and West Building Society v Ellis [43]
(1996) The Times 2 May (Court of Appeal)

In 1987, BWBS lent E and her husband £40,000 on mortgage secured on their matrimonial home. The mortgage was to be repaid in one sum at the end of 25 years on the maturity of an endowment assurance policy (ie the borrowers' monthly payments were of interest only). Subsequently, the mortgage loan was increased to £60,000. In 1990, E's husband moved out of the home leaving substantial arrears with the interest payments. BWBS was granted an order for possession suspended if E paid an immediate lump sum of £5,000 and thereafter £200 a month in addition to the usual payment of interest. E failed to comply with this initial order. By early 1995, the interest arrears stood at over £16,000 which with the mortgage debt of £60,000 left £76,000 owed to BWBS. The lender was granted a warrant for possession. E sought to suspend the order. She gave evidence that she could pay the lump sum, meet the interest payments but thereafter she would only be able to make a token payment of £10 a month to reduce the arrears of interest. She further gave evidence that she intended to sell the house after her children had completed their university education (a period of three to five years) and that the property value would cover the redemption figure. In this regard, she relied on two estate agents' estimates (challenged by BWBS) that the property was worth between £80,000 and £85,000 which would be sufficient to cover the redemption figure of over £77,000 plus costs. The district judge suspended execution on terms that E should pay arrears then amounting to £16,805 by way of a lump sum of £5,000 within a month and the balance at the rate of £10 per month in addition to the monthly instalments of interest. He did not impose any term as to the sale of the property. BWBS unsuccessfully appealed on the ground that it would take E 98 years to pay of the arrears (the judge considered that the period of three to five years before sale was relevant). BWBS further appealed submitting that the suspension order was contrary to s36 of the Administration of Justice Act 1970 (as amended) which provided that the period of repayment should be 'reasonable'. *Held*, the appeal would be allowed. The district judge – whatever his expectation – had not suspended the order for a period within which E was required to sell. It was difficult to see how BWBS could rely on the expectation of sale to secure immediate possession if, after five years, E refused to sell while continuing to pay the interest and monthly instalments of £10. As to what constituted a reasonable period under s36 of the 1970 Act for bringing payments up to date the court noted that in *Cheltenham and Gloucester Building Society* v *Norgan* an earlier Court of Appeal had stated that the court should take the full term of the mortgage as its starting point. However, that starting point was not available to a mortgagor like E who could not discharge the arrears by periodic payments and whose only prospect of repaying the entire loan and accrued and accruing interest was from the sale of the property. In such a case, the reasonableness of the order was a matter for the court in the circumstances of the case. The most important factors in most cases were likely to be the extent to which the mortgage debt and arrears were secured by the value of the property and the effect of time on that security. Here there was insufficient evidence for the district judge to have exercised his discretion under s36 of the 1970 Act and find that the property could be sold at a high enough price to discharge E's overall debt to BWBS within a three to five year period. Even if the district judge had made an order defining a specific period for the sale within five years the evidence before him was not sufficient to enable him to fix on it as reasonable within s36 of the 1970 Act. The appropriate order was an order for immediate possession. (See also *Cheltenham and Gloucester Building Society* v *Norgan*.)

British Railways Board v Glass [1964] 3 All ER 418   **[44]**
(Court of Appeal)

Under the terms of a conveyance of land to a railway company there was excepted to the owner of adjoining farm land (the former owner of the land conveyed to the railway company) 'a right of crossing the railway ... with all manner of cattle'. In 1938 the defendant, the then and the present owner of the adjoining land, allowed a few caravans to be put on part of it and six of these caravans had been there for at least 20 years. The plaintiffs, successors to the railway company, maintained that the right of crossing was restricted under the terms of the conveyance to the agricultural and domestic purposes of the farm and that the right of crossing which had been acquired by prescription was restricted to use for the purposes of the six caravans. *Held*, this was not the case since the exception conferred a general right of way, ie not one limited to the user contemplated when the grant was made, and the mere increase in the number of caravans using the site did not give rise to an excessive user of the right of crossing to and from the caravan site acquired by prescription. 'A right to use a way for this purpose or that has never been to my knowledge limited to a right to use the way so many times a day or for such and such a number of vehicles so long as the dominant tenement does not change its identity. If there be a radical change in the character of the dominant tenement, then the prescriptive right will not extend to it in that condition' (*per* HARMAN LJ).

Brougham and Vaux's (Lord) Settled Estates, Re   **[45]**
[1953] 2 All ER 655

In 1932, by a deed of family arrangement, the tenant for life assigned his equitable life interest to the trustees of the settlement to be held on specified trusts and in 1948 he directed the execution on agricultural land, which was subject to the settlement and had been leased to a tenant, certain works including improvements to a Dutch barn, repairs to doors, gates and gutters and painting. *Held*, although the tenant of the farm was responsible for repairs (the repairs mentioned in para 23, Sched 3, of the Agricultural Holdings Act 1948, were incorporated into s73(1)(iv) of the Settled Land Act 1925 without the qualification 'other than repairs which the tenant is under an obligation to carry out') and although the tenant for life was not at the material time entitled to receive the rents and profits of the property (he was nevertheless a 'landlord' within s73(1)(iv) of the 1925 Act as a person having the statutory powers), the works were properly authorised by the tenant for life as improvements within s73(1) of the Act of 1925 and the cost should be met out of capital moneys. It should be noted that VAISEY J acknowledged the error which he had made in *Re Duke of Northumberland* [1950] 2 All ER 181 which had been pointed out by HARMAN J in *Re Sutherland Settlement Trusts* [1953] 2 All ER 27 regarding expenditure incurred before 1948. (See also *Re Boston's (Lord) Will Trusts.*)

Buchanan-Wollaston's Conveyance, Re, Curtis v Buchanan-Wollaston [1939] 2 All ER 302 (Court of Appeal) [46]

In order to protect the amenities of their houses four owners purchased land adjoining as joint tenants upon trust for sale (see ss35 and 36 of the Law of Property Act 1925) and subsequently executed a deed which provided, inter alia, that the land could not be sold without the unanimous agreement of the parties. One of the parties withheld his consent to a proposed sale. *Held*, in the present circumstances the court would not make an order under s30 of the Law of Property Act 1925 compelling the dissentient to concur in the proposed sale. 'The court of equity, when asked to enforce the trust for sale, whether one created by a settlement or a will or one created by the statute, must look into all the circumstances of the case and consider whether or not, at the particular moment and in the particular circumstances when the application is made to it, it is right and proper that such an order shall be made' (*per* SIR WILFRED GREENE MR). (See also *Re Mayo, Mayo v Mayo* and *Jones v Challenger.*)

Buckland v Butterfield (1820) 2 Brod & Bing 54 [47]

A tenant purchased a conservatory, erected it on a brick foundation and attached it to the house by cantilevers let nine inches into the wall. *Held*, it had become part of the freehold, and could not be removed by the tenant or his assignees. (But see *Spyer v Phillipson.*)

Bull v Bull [1955] 1 All ER 253 (Court of Appeal) [48]

In 1949 a son and his mother together purchased a freehold house as a home for them both, the son providing the greater part of the money and taking the conveyance in his name: the mother did not intend her contribution to be gift to the son. The mother and son lived together in the house until 1953 and then, on the son's marriage, it was arranged that the mother should occupy two rooms and the son and his wife the remainder. Differences arose between the mother and her daughter-in-law and the son told his mother to leave and, as she failed to do so, the son sought her eviction. *Held*, his action would fail. The mother and son were equitable tenants in common subject to the statutory trusts for sale under s35 of the Law of Property Act 1925 and, until the property was sold, each was entitled concurrently with the other to the possession of the house and to the use and enjoyment of it in a proper manner. (See also *Re Kempthorne, Charles v Kempthorne*; but see *Inwards v Baker.*)

Burgess v Rawnsley [1975] 3 All ER 142 (Court of Appeal)   **[49]**

H, a widower, was the sitting tenant of a house. In 1966, the owner of the house offered to sell the freehold to him for £850. H told his friend R (a widow) and she agreed to buy the house with him. At the time, H contemplated marrying R and intended that the house would be their matrimonial home. However, he had never mentioned marriage to her and she had no intention of marrying H. Her reason for joining in the purchase was to live in the upstairs flat in the house while H occupied the lower flat. In 1967, the house was conveyed to H and R jointly as joint tenants with an express declaration of trust for themselves as joint tenants; each contributed half the purchase price of £850 (ie there was a joint tenancy in equity). The expectations of neither party were fulfilled – R would not marry H and he refused to allow her to occupy the upstairs flat. In 1968, H attempted to buy R's share from her. She orally agreed to sell her share to H for £750, but subsequently changed her mind saying she was not satisfied with £750 and wanted £1,000. Matters there rested. H continued to live in the house and paid all the outgoings until his death three years later. The house was sold and the plaintiff (H's administratrix and daughter) claimed that she was entitled to a half share in the proceeds of sale either because there was a resulting trust or alternatively that the joint tenancy had been severed in equity. R (the defendant) claimed that the house was hers by survivorship. The county court judge declared that the house was held by R on trust for the plaintiff and herself in equal shares. R appealed. *Held*, the appeal would be dismissed. A resulting trust could only arise where, in making a disposition of property, both parties had had a common purpose which had failed. Here since H alone had entered into the conveyance in contemplation of marriage and had not communicated that purpose to R there was no common purpose which had failed so as to give rise to a resulting trust. However, the oral agreement by R to sell her share to H had operated to sever the beneficial joint tenancy. Although the agreement was not enforceable under s40 of the Law of Property Act 1925 in the absence of a memorandum in writing, it established that the parties themselves no longer intended the tenancy to operate as a joint tenancy and they had automatically effected a severance. 'I think there was evidence that Mr Honick and Mrs Rawnsley did come to an agreement that he would buy her share for £750. That agreement was not in writing and it was not specifically enforceable. Yet it was sufficient to effect a severance' (*per* LORD DENNING MR). There had been a mutual agreement between both the joint tenants evidencing an intention to sever. The fact that the agreement was subsequently repudiated was immaterial. Alternatively (*per* LORD DENNING MR) even if there was no firm agreement between the parties, the course of dealing between them had clearly evinced an intention by both of them that henceforth the house would be held in common and not jointly. Since the joint tenancy had been severed the house was not R's by survivorship. Rather she held it on trust for herself and H's estate in equal shares.

Buttle v Saunders [1950] 2 All ER 193   **[50]**

The defendants were the trustees of certain premises in Montpelier Square which they held on the statutory trusts for sale under the Law of Property Act 1925, and, when negotiations for the sale of the property for £6,000 had reached an advanced stage, although contracts had not actually been exchanged, a third party offered £6,500. The defendants felt bound by considerations of commercial morality to complete with the original purchaser. *Held*, they had an overriding duty to obtain the best price for their beneficiaries and they should have probed the later offer and agreed to it on condition that the person making it bound himself immediately to complete the purchase at the higher price.

Carr-Saunders v Dick McNeil Associates Ltd [51]
[1986] 1 WLR 922

In 1968, C-S purchased 2 Neal's Yard Covent Garden, the second floor of which was occupied by a tenant who used it as an office. That floor was lighted naturally through windows at the front and two at the rear. The property situated opposite the two rear windows was owned by DMA Ltd (the defendants). All these windows had been in place for over 20 years. In 1976, C-S obtained possession of the second floor and converted it into a single open space which he used as living accommodation. In about 1981, C-S added two storeys to the building for his own occupation and converted the second floor into a suite of six consulting rooms with four rooms at the front of the building and two at the rear. The two rear rooms were still lighted by the relevant rear windows facing DMA Ltd's premises. C-S obtained planning permission to use all six rooms as medical consulting rooms. Subsequently, DMA Ltd erected two storeys onto their premises and this building work significantly reduced the amount of light received through the two rear windows on the second floor of C-S's property. Accordingly, C-S sought damages from DMA Ltd for actionable nuisance on the ground that he enjoyed a right to light under s3 of the Prescription Act 1832 and that DMA Ltd had interfered with that right. DMA Ltd contended that while the windows in question had been in place for 20 years the rooms behind the windows had not – they were of recent construction. Accordingly, they argued that C-S was not entitled to claim a prescriptive right to light under s3 of the 1832 Act. *Held*, C-S had established an actionable nuisance and damages were assessed at £8,000. The right acquired under s3 of the 1832 Act was an easement for the access of light to a building and not to a particular room within it. The dominant owner's right to light was not to be measured by the given use to which the dominant tenement had been put in the past. Rather, he was entitled to such access of light as would render his premises adequately lit for all ordinary purposes for which they were used or might reasonably be expected to be used in the future – this principle included an alteration in the internal arrangements of the premises. Accordingly, it followed that even before the subdivision of the second floor had taken place it would have been necessary to consider the effect of DMA Ltd's two additional storeys, not only on the second floor as it was then used (ie as a single open space) but on any other arrangement of that space which might reasonably be expected to be adopted in the future. MILLETT J was satisfied that here some subdivision, even if not the present one, of the second floor of C-S's property was an ordinary and reasonable use to which that space might be put. He continued as follows: 'In my judgment, therefore, the raising of the height of the defendant's premises has caused a substantial interference with the plaintiff's enjoyment of his property 2 Neal's Yard, since the space on the second floor can no longer comfortably be used for any purpose which requires the sub-division of that space … on this basis the plaintiff has established an actionable nuisance; not because the … rooms are no longer adequately lit (though they are not), but because the second floor can no longer (as it formerly could) conveniently be subdivided in such a way that the subdivided areas each receive an adequate amount of light.' (See also *Allen* v *Greenwood*.)

Cartwright, Re, Cartwright v Smith [1938] 4 All ER 209 [52]
(Court of Appeal)

The testator effected a settlement of real property and during his lifetime the real property was sold and the proceeds invested. His wills were valid to pass personalty but not realty. *Held*, by virtue of s75(5) of the Settled Land Act 1925, the investments would be regarded as land (ie realty) and it followed that they could not pass under his wills. 'Where you are dealing with a settled freehold which is sold, the capital money would be treated as freehold, and, where you have a settled leasehold which is sold, the capital money would be treated as leasehold, and so forth' (*per* SIR WILFRID GREENE MR)

Chalmers v Pardoe [1963] 3 All ER 552 (Privy Council)   **[53]**

Two close friends made an arrangement whereby the one, Chalmers, would build on the other's, Pardoe's, leasehold land, provided he (Chalmers) got the consent of the Native Land Trust Board, the lessors. Pardoe was originally willing gratuitously to sub-let to Chalmers the land on which he built or to surrender his lease with a view to a new lease being granted to Chalmers. With Pardoe's approval Chalmers built some houses on the land, but Chalmers did not get the Board's consent and without this the building was not lawful. Chalmers claimed an equitable charge on Pardoe's land for the cost of the buildings which he had erected. *Held*, as the work was unlawful the court could not lend its aid to Chalmers but, apart from this, equity would have intervened to prevent Pardoe from going back on his word and taking the buildings for nothing. 'There can be no doubt on the authorities that where an owner of land has invited or expressly encouraged another to expend money on part of his land on the faith of an assurance or promise that that part of the land will be made over to the person so expending his money a court of equity will prima facie require the owner by appropriate conveyance to fulfil his obligation; and when, for example by reasons of title, no such conveyance can effectively be made, a court of equity may declare that the person who had expended the money is entitled to an equitable charge or lien for the amount so expended' (*per* SIR TERENCE DONOVAN). (See also *Inwards* v *Baker*.)

Chandler v Bradley [1897] 1 Ch 315   **[54]**

A tenant for life granted to the defendant a lease of a dwelling-house forming part of the trust property after receiving from the defendant an inducement of 20 guineas to execute the lease. *Held*, having regard to the payment, the lease was void because the 'best rent' had not been obtained (see now s42(1)(ii) of the Settled Land Act 1925), and the law did not permit such a payment to be made. 'No rule is clearer than that a trustee may not derive a personal benefit from his trust; and it was therefore improper on [the tenant for life's] part to accept, and on the part of the defendant to make, any such payment' (*per* STIRLING J). (See now s107(1) of the Settled Land Act 1925.)

Chardon, Re, Johnston v Davies [1928] Ch 464   **[55]**

A testator bequeathed £200 to trustees on trust to invest the money and to pay the income to a cemetery company for as long as the company maintained two specified graves. The testator directed that if the company failed to maintain the graves, the trustees should pay the income to the persons entitled to the residuary estate. *Held*, 'the cemetery company and the persons interested in the legacy ... could combine tomorrow and dispose of the whole legacy. The trust does not, therefore, offend the rule against alienability. The interest of the cemetery company is a vested interest; the interests of the residuary legatee ... are also vested; all the interests therefore created in this £200, legal and equitable, are vested interests and, that being so, the trusts do not offend the rule against perpetuity' (*per* ROMER J). The trust was therefore valid. (See also *Re Tyler, Tyler* v *Tyler*; but see s12(1)(b) of the Perpetuities and Accumulations Act 1964.)

Chasemore v Richards (1859) 7 HL Cas 349 (House of Lords)   **[56]**

The plaintiff's mill had been worked by a stream for upwards of 60 years, and the stream was chiefly supplied by water which percolated underground. The defendants, the Croydon Local Board of Health, sank on their own land a well to supply water to the local inhabitants, but it drew off much of the water which would have found its way into the stream, to the detriment of the plaintiff's mill. *Held*, the plaintiff was without a remedy. (See also *Race* v *Ward*.)

Chatham Empire Theatre (1955) Ltd v Ultrans Ltd   **[57]**
[1961] 2 All ER 381

A lessee failed to pay the rent due under the head lease and the landlords claimed, inter alia, possession of the whole of the premises. Sub-lessees of part of the premises applied for relief against forfeiture under s146(4) of the Law of Property Act 1925. *Held*, the sub-lessees were entitled to relief against forfeiture on payment of that proportion of the total arrears of rent which the rent payable under their sub-lease bore to the rent payable under the head lease, since the landlords were only entitled to be put back into the same position as they were in before the forfeiture qua that part of the premises let to the sub-lessees. (See also *Segal Securities Ltd* v *Thoseby*.)

Cheltenham and Gloucester Building Society v Grant   **[58]**
(1994) The Times 9 May (Court of Appeal)

A county court judge had upheld a decision of a district judge in favour of G (the mortgagor) that a possession order in respect of his home should not be enforced without the leave of the court while G continued to make his mortgage payments to the plaintiffs. The plaintiffs appealed against this order on the ground that a court could only be satisfied that it could exercise its discretion to suspend a possession order under s36 of the Administration of Justice Act 1970, as amended by s8 of the Administration of Justice Act 1973, on hearing evidence by or on behalf of the mortgagor. Here the judge had acted on the basis of information given to him informally by those representing G (the defendant). *Held*, the appeal would be dismissed. The court concluded that it was not its function to prescribe strict rules for district and circuit judges as to the procedural aspects of the matter in question. If a plaintiff argued that the truth of what the court was told by a defendant ought not to be accepted without formal evidence then it would be necessary for the defendant to file affidavit evidence. However, in the absence of such a submission it was for the judge to determine whether or not to act on the basis of informal evidence or material. The judicial discretion under s36 of the 1970 Act, as amended, could only be exercised in favour of a mortgagor if the court concluded that the mortgagor had the ability within a reasonable period of time of paying both his arrears and current instalments. Here, the way in which the judge had exercised his discretion could not be interfered with. (See also *National and Provincial Building Society* v *Lloyd*.)

Cheltenham and Gloucester Building Society v Norgan   **[59]**
[1996] 1 All ER 449 (Court of Appeal)

Since 1974, N, her husband and family lived in a period farmhouse. N became sole owner of the farmhouse (said to be worth about £225,000) when she bought out her husband's half share. In 1986, £90,000 was borrowed by way of mortgage from the Guardian Building Society using the farmhouse as security. Under the terms of the mortgage if at any time any monthly instalment was in arrears and unpaid for one month after becoming due the mortgagee would be entitled to take possession of the property. N fell into arrears with the interest payments on the mortgage after her husband's business ran into difficulties. By April 1990 when the Guardian Building Society was taken over by the Cheltenham and Gloucester Building Society N owed about £7,000. The Cheltenham and Gloucester was a member of the Council of Mortgage Lenders whose statement of current practice provided means of helping some borrowers in difficulty, including lengthening the term of a repayment loan, deferring interest payments for a period and capitalising interest. The building society obtained a county court order for possession but execution was suspended as N made strenuous efforts to pay off her arrears. In September 1993 a district judge refused to block the possession order any longer. In June 1994 that decision was upheld by O'MALLEY J in Shaftesbury County Court. He estimated that N's arrears were £20,000 and decided that a period of two to four years was the maximum that would normally be allowed for clearing arrears (even though here the mortgage had 13 years still to run). He concluded that it would be impossible for N to meet that target and therefore the building society was entitled to have its possession order enforced unless it decided to give N more time. N appealed. *Held*, the appeal would be allowed. At common law the court had only a very limited jurisdiction to grant relief to a borrower in default under a mortgage. It could only adjourn the application for a short time to give the borrower the chance to pay up in full: *Birmingham Citizens Permanent Building Society* v *Caunt*. However, the rigour of the common law position had been mitigated by the Administration of Justice Acts 1970 and 1973. Under the Acts the court had a discretion to treat the sum due under the mortgage as being only the arrears of instalments or interest and to allow a reasonable period for the borrower to pay off the arrears if it appeared he was likely to be able to do so. The question was what exactly constituted a 'reasonable period' for bringing payments up to date? The court unanimously agreed that 'the logic and spirit of the legislation' required, especially in cases where the parties were proceeding with the type of arrangement provided for in the statement of current practice, that the court should take the full term of the mortgage as its starting point and pose at the outset the following question: 'Would it be possible for the borrower to maintain payment-off of the arrears by instalments over that period?' The court identified a number of considerations which were likely to be relevant in establishing a reasonable period, including the following: (1) how much could the borrower reasonably afford to pay both now and in the future?; (2) if the borrower had a short term problem in meeting his mortgage commitments, how long was the difficulty likely to last?; (3) why had the arrears accumulated?; (4) how much remained of the original term?; and (5) were there any reasons affecting the security which should influence the length of the period for payment? Accordingly, the case would be remitted to the county court to work out a new repayment scheme over the remaining 13 years of the loan. Finally, the building society would be ordered to pay the costs of the case. (See also *Cheltenham and Gloucester Building Society* v *Grant* and *Bristol and West Building Society* v *Ellis*.)

CIBC Mortgages plc v Pitt [1993] 3 WLR 802 (House of Lords) [60]

A matrimonial home (valued at £270,000 in 1986) was in the joint names of a husband and wife. The only encumbrance on it was a mortgage in favour of a building society for £16,700. In 1986, the husband told the wife that he wanted to borrow some money on the security of the matrimonial home and then use the money so raised to buy shares on the stock market. The wife was unhappy with this idea but eventually agreed to it as a result of pressure from her husband. The husband and wife signed a mortgage application form for a loan of £150,000 from the plaintiff company in which the purpose of the loan was stated to be to pay off the existing mortgage and use the balance to buy a holiday home. The husband

and wife signed the mortgage offer and the legal charge. Before signing these documents the wife did not read them, nor did she receive any legal advice about the transaction, nor did anyone suggest that she should seek such advice. Further, she did not know how much was being borrowed. After discharging the existing mortgage the rest of the loan was paid into the joint account of the husband and wife. The husband used it to speculate on the stock market. However, when the stock market crashed in October 1987 the husband was unable to keep up the mortgage payments, and the plaintiffs applied for a possession order in respect of the matrimonial home. The wife contested the application on the basis that she had been induced to sign the relevant documents by undue influence on her husband's part. At first instance the judge held that the plaintiffs' legal charge was valid against her (in particular the judge stressed that the transaction in question was an advance to a husband and wife by way of loan for their joint benefit rather than one of a wife standing surety for her husband's debts). The wife's appeal to the Court of Appeal was dismissed. She further appealed to the House of Lords. *Held*, the appeal would be dismissed. A claimant who proved undue influence was not under the additional burden of showing that the transaction induced by undue influence was manifestly disadvantageous to him but was entitled as of right to have it set aside as against the person exercising the undue influence. Although here the wife had established undue influence by her husband, the plaintiffs would not be affected by it unless the husband had acted as their agent in procuring the wife's agreement or they had notice (actual or constructive) of the undue influence. Here, the husband had not acted as the lender's agent in procuring the wife's consent. Further, the lender had no actual or constructive notice of the undue influence. The loan had been advanced to the husband and wife jointly and there was nothing to suggest to the plaintiffs that it was anything other than a normal advance to a married couple for their joint benefit. The mere fact that there was a risk of undue influence because one of the borrowers was the wife of the other was not, in itself, enough to put the plaintiffs on inquiry. (See also *Barclays Bank plc* v *O'Brien*.)

Citro (Domenico) (a bankrupt), Re; Citro (Carmine)   [61]
(a bankrupt), Re [1990] 3 WLR 880 (Court of Appeal)

D and C were brothers, both of whom were adjudicated bankrupt. Both brothers were married with children. D was separated from his wife who lived in the matrimonial home together with their three children, the youngest of whom was 12. C lived in the matrimonial home with his wife and their three children, the youngest of whom was 10. In both cases, the matrimonial home was owned in equal shares in equity by the bankrupt and his wife. The only assets of each bankrupt was their half share of the beneficial interest in their respective matrimonial home. The debts of each bankrupt exceeded the value of their respective half share. The trustee in bankruptcy of the joint and several estates applied to the court by notice of motion for declarations as to the beneficial interests in the two properties and for orders under s30 of the Law of Property Act 1925 for possession and sale of the homes. At first instance HOFFMANN J declared that in each case the beneficial interest in the property was owned by the bankrupt and his wife in equal shares and he made orders for possession and sale. However, after taking into account all the problems which would have affected the children he postponed the orders until the younger child in each case attained 16 years of age. The trustee in bankruptcy appealed. *Held*, the appeal would be allowed. For the purposes of making an order for sale in favour of a trustee in bankruptcy under s30 of the Law of Property Act 1925 no distinction was to be made between a case where a property was being enjoyed as a matrimonial home and one where it had ceased to be so used. Where a spouse having a beneficial interest in a matrimonial home went bankrupt, and where the debts of the bankrupt could not be met without selling the matrimonial home, a sale of the property within a short period would usually be ordered unless there were exceptional circumstances (ie the interests of the creditors would usually prevail over the interests of the other spouse). Although the circumstances of the wives and children were distressing (a sale would result in their eviction) they were not exceptional. The ordinary consequences of debt and improvidence did not constitute an exceptional circumstance. However, where postponement of a sale would not cause hardship to the creditors that could be an exceptional circumstance. The order sought by the trustee in bankruptcy would be made and a period of postponement not to exceed six months substituted. (Applied: *Jones* v *Challenger*; but see *Abbey National plc* v *Moss*.)

City of London Building Society v Flegg [1987] 2 WLR 1266   [62]
(House of Lords)

In 1977 a house known as 'Bleak House' was purchased for £34,000. Mr and Mrs F (the defendants) provided £18,000 of the purchase price. The balance was provided by their daughter and son-in-law Mr and Mrs Maxwell-Brown who raised their share by a mortgage. In consequence of the mortgage, the house was conveyed into the names of Mr and Mrs M-B on trust for sale for themselves and the Fleggs as tenants in common, in the proportions which they had contributed to the purchase price. Mr and Mrs M-B were registered as the proprietors in the Land Registry. From the time of conveyance the two couples occupied the property in common. In 1982, the M-B's mortgaged the house to the City of London Building Society (the plaintiffs) as security for an advance of £37,500. They used the money so raised to pay off the existing mortgage and other debts. The plaintiffs were unaware that Mr and Mrs F were in occupation of the property and made no inquiries to ascertain who was in occupation before making the advance. Mr and Mrs F were unaware of the mortgage. Mr and Mrs M-B subsequently defaulted on the mortgage repayments and the plaintiffs brought an action for possession of the property. The possession order was granted at first instance. The judge held that the overriding interest of Mr and Mrs F arising under s70(1)(g) of the Land Registration Act 1925 because of their actual occupation of the house had been overreached by the plaintiffs' mortgage by virtue of s2(1)(ii) of the Law of Property Act 1925 which provided that a conveyance of a legal estate to a purchaser overreached any equitable interests in that estate, whether or not the purchaser had notice of the equitable interests, if 'the conveyance is made by trustees for sale and the equitable interest ... is ... capable of being overreached by such trustees'. On an appeal by Mr and Mrs F, the Court of Appeal held, applying *Williams & Glyn's Bank Ltd* v *Boland*, that Mr and Mrs F had an overriding interest in the house which was protected by s70(1)(g) of the 1925 Act and therefore binding on the plaintiffs and was also protected by s14 of the Law of Property Act 1925 which provided, inter alia, that Part I of that Act (which included s2) was not prejudicially to affect the interest of any person in actual occupation of land to which he was entitled in right of such occupation. The building society appealed to the House of Lords. *Held*, the appeal would be allowed. The rights which Mr and Mrs F had by reason of their occupation of the house and as beneficiaries under the trust for sale were no more than the rights to enjoy in specie the rent and profits of the land held in trust for them and were referable to and derived from the trust for sale. When Mr and Mrs M-B, exercising as registered proprietors the powers conferred on them as trustees for sale, created the legal mortgage the advancement of the capital moneys by the building society to them *overreached* Mr and Mrs F's interest because it was an advancement to two trustees. The interest of Mr and Mrs F transferred from the land to the capital moneys raised by the charge and to the equity of redemption held by the trustees and thereafter Mr and Mrs F no longer had *any interest in the land* which their occupation could protect as an overriding interest under s70(1)(g) (ie their beneficial interest had been overreached by the legal charge). The enjoyment of occupation of the property did not give rise to any separate right from those enjoyed under the trust for sale. The payment to the two trustees (Mr and Mrs M-B) distinguished the case from *Williams & Glyns Bank Ltd v Boland*. That case on which the Court of Appeal had relied covered a different situation. There the husband was sole proprietor who was trustee for himself and his wife as tenants in common. 'The wife's beneficial interest coupled with actual occupation constituted an overriding interest to which the husband's mortgagee took subject. But in that case the interest of the wife was not overreached or overridden because the mortgagee advanced capital moneys to a sole trustee' (*per* LORD TEMPLEMAN). Further, the position of Mr and Mrs F was not saved by s14 of the Law of Property Act 1925 because s14 could not enlarge or add to their beneficial interest in the equity of redemption by preserving it as an equitable interest in the land or by bringing it on to the title. Accordingly, the interest of Mr and Mrs F had been overreached by the legal charge executed in favour of the building society by Mr and Mrs M-B and the building society was entitled to a possession order.

Cityland and Property (Holdings) Ltd v Dabrah   [63]
[1967] 2 All ER 639

D had been the tenant for 11 years of a house of which C & P Ltd (the plaintiffs) were the registered proprietors. When his lease expired, D purchased the freehold from C & P Ltd for £3,500. He provided £600 from his own resources with the balance of the purchase money (£2,900) being raised by way of a mortgage of the house to C & P Ltd. The mortgage deed provided that (a) in return for the loan of £2,900 D charged the land with the payment of £4,553 (the additional £1,653 being a premium) to C & P Ltd to be paid by 72 equal monthly instalments, and (b) in the event of default in paying an instalment the whole of the principal and the premium would become due. The mortgage made no provision for the payment of interest on the capital sum. The premium represented 57 per cent of the loan and had it represented interest the rate would have been 19 per cent per annum. After a year, D fell into arrears and C & P Ltd took out a summons seeking possession and claiming payment of all moneys due with interest at 5 per cent, even though the original mortgage made no provision as to interest. D claimed relief against the premium on the ground that it was an unreasonable and unconscionable collateral advantage. *Held*, C & P Ltd were only entitled to repayment of the £2,900 with interest at 7 per cent from the date of the advance minus the repayments already made by D. The premium was a collateral advantage and that in the circumstances (in particular its size, the fact that the whole balance of both it and the loan became instantly repayable on default in paying instalments and the high rate of interest which complete payment over the instalment period would represent) the premium was oppressive and unreasonable. A mortgagee was only entitled to a reasonable sum by way of interest. There had been a clear lack of equality of bargaining power between the parties. This was not a case involving two large commercial concerns. Rather it involved D, a sitting tenant of limited means, buying his own house (in the court's view he possibly agreed to the mortgage terms to prevent himself becoming homeless at the expiry of the lease) and C & P Ltd, a property company experienced in these matters and fully aware of the effect of this particular transaction. Accordingly, C & P Ltd would not be allowed to take advantage of D's circumstances. Thus, the mortgage would be varied to secure payment of the loan (£2,900) together with interest at 7 per cent. (See also *Multiservice Bookbinding Ltd v Marden*.)

Clark v Chief Land Registrar [1994] 4 All ER 96 (Court of Appeal)   [64]

The plaintiffs, who were judgment creditors, obtained a charging order against a house jointly owned under a statutory trust for sale by their debtors. They protected that order by entering cautions on the register in August and November 1990. Subsequently, the second defendant advanced a sum of money to the debtors secured by way of legal charge on the property. The second defendant sought registration of the legal charge in December 1990. At that point the Land Registry ought to have informed the plaintiffs (the cautioners) of the proposed registration of this charge so that they could object. However, they failed so to act and the legal charge was registered. Subsequently, when the debtors' property was sold the sale proceeds were insufficient to satisfy the claims of the cautioners and the legal chargee. At first instance the judge declared that the plaintiffs were entitled to an indemnity from the Chief Land Registrar (first defendant) under s83 of the Land Registration Act 1925 for failing to give them notice of a charge over the land subsequently registered by the second defendant. The first defendant appealed. Two substantive points fell to be considered: first, whether registration of a charging order against property held on trust for sale was over an interest in land (the 'charging order' point). It was argued on behalf of the Chief Land Registrar that it only created a charge over interests in the proceeds of sale of the land (which if correct would have created no interest capable of being protected on the register). Second, assuming that it was over an interest in land, whether the registration of the caution protected that interest or simply gave the cautioner the opportunity to gain protection by the entry of a notice when a subsequent dealing with the land was proposed (the 'caution' point). Here the Chief Land Registrar was arguing in the alternative that the caution lodged in respect of the order gave the plaintiffs' charge priority over that of the second defendant (if this was correct then the plaintiffs had suffered no damage in consequence of the Land Registry's failure to warn them of the second defendant's legal charge and thus there was no need for an indemnity). *Held*, the appeal of the first defendant would be dismissed. As to the 'charging order' point, such an order held on trust for sale registered under s2(1)(b) of the Charging Orders Act 1979 was effective to create a charge over the legal estate in the land and not simply over interests in the sale proceeds of the land. In relation to the 'caution' point, the court examined ss54 to 56 of the Land Registration Act 1925 which described the nature and effect of cautions. There was no support in these provisions for the view that the lodging of a caution against dealings automatically achieved priority for the interest in respect of which it was lodged. Rather they set up a procedure whereby a person interested in the land could ensure that he was warned of any proposed dealings and given an opportunity to assert the priority of his interest. Accordingly, the registration of the caution by the plaintiffs simply gave them a right to be given notice of any proposed dealing. It did not entitle them to assert the priority of their interest over the second defendant's subsequently registered land charge.

Clarke v Grant [1949] 1 All ER 768 (Court of Appeal)   [65]

A yearly tenant of a dwelling-house received a valid notice to quit and, after the notice had expired, the landlord's agent accepted one month's rent, mistakenly believing that it was in respect of the month before the expiration of the notice to quit. *Held*, such acceptance did not operate as a waiver of the notice to quit. Where a tenancy is 'brought to an end by a notice to quit [as opposed to notice that an act of forfeiture has been committed], a payment of rent after the termination of the tenancy would only operate in favour of the tenant if it could be shown that the parties intended that there should be a new tenancy' (*per* LORD GODDARD CJ). In this case it was impossible to say that the parties intended that there should be a new tenancy. (But see *Segal Securities Ltd* v *Thoseby*.)

Clayton v Ramsden [1943] 1 All ER 16 (House of Lords)   [66]

By his will a testator bequeathed a large sum upon trust for his daughter and declared that if she should at any time after his death marry 'a person who is not of Jewish parentage and of the Jewish faith' her interest under his will should determine. *Held*, the condition subsequent was void for uncertainty and it followed that the daughter, who had married an English Wesleyan, did not thereby forfeit her interest under her father's will. It was impossible to say precisely and distinctly what was meant by 'of Jewish parentage' and the requirement that a person should be 'of the Jewish faith' was too vague to enable it to be said with certainty whether a particular person complied with it. (See also *Sifton* v *Sifton*; but see *Re Allen, Faith* v *Allen*.)

Clifton v Viscount Bury (1887) 4 TLR 8   [67]

The line of fire of the 12th Middlesex Volunteer Corps on their range on Wimbledon Common passed over the plaintiff's land. There was evidence that the bullets ordinarily passed over at 75 ft above the surface. *Held*, although this was not technically a trespass, the plaintiff, by reason of the risk involved, had 'a legal grievance' which entitled him to an injunction. (But see *Kelsen* v *Imperial Tobacco Co (of Great Britain and Ireland) Ltd*.)

Clore v Theatrical Properties Ltd [1936] 3 All ER 483   [68]
(Court of Appeal)

An indenture stipulated that the lessor demised unto the lessee the 'front of the house rights' ('the free and exclusive use of all the refreshment rooms bars cloak rooms and wine cellars', etc) of the Prince of Wales Theatre for a term of 21 years at a rental of £25 a week. *Held*, this document did not convey any interest in land but was merely a personal contract embodying a licence. It followed that the assignees of the 'front of the house rights' could not assert any rights against the present lessee of the theatre as there was no contractual nexus between them. 'This is not a document which creates an estate in land, but merely one which is a personal contract between the parties named therein and is only enforceable among parties between whom there is privity of contract' (*per* LORD WRIGHT MR). (See also *Minister of Health* v *Bellotti*.)

Coleman's Will Trusts, Re, Public Trustee v Coleman   [69]
[1936] 2 All ER 225

A testator gave his estate to trustees upon trust for sale and conversion and directed the proceeds to be divided among five sons of whom Walter was one, but Walter's share was settled upon discretionary trusts for Walter during his life and after his death the income of the share was to be held on discretionary trusts for any widow he might leave and all or any of his children: after the death of such widow the share was to be held on trust for Walter's sons attaining 21 and daughters attaining 21 or marrying. *Held*, the trust for the widow was void as she might be a person born after the death of the testator and the discretion would then be exercisable at a date beyond that allowed by the perpetuity rule. However, the trust for the son's children, which was not contingent or dependent on the void trust, became vested in interest (though not in possession) within the period allowed by the rule, and was therefore good.

Commission for the New Towns v Cooper (GB) Ltd [70]
[1995] 2 All ER 929 (Court of Appeal)

In 1986, EHL (C's predecessor in title) became a tenant of commercial premises on an underlease for MK (CNT's predecessor). An agreement was reached between the parties whereby MK was to do certain building work to be paid for by the underlessee. The parties made three other agreements by deed which gave EHL a variety of options. The first was a 'put option' which was a covenant by MK to take an assignment of the underlease from EHL under certain conditions. The second was a 'larger premises option' allowing EHL to opt to transfer to larger premises. The third was a 'side land option' allowing EHL to acquire land alongside the existing premises. Both the put option and the larger premises option were expressed to be personal to EHL. In 1988, C (the defendant) acquired the unexpired residue of the term of the underlease by assignment. However, the business made losses and in 1990 C's American parent company analysed the cost of closing the business, including the penalty payable on the surrender of the underlease. In 1991 C decided instead to try to obtain from MK the put option that had previously been enjoyed by C's predecessor (EHL) without MK realising it (C's intention was to use that option to enable it to reduce its liquidation costs by avoiding the penalty payment for termination of the underlease). The parties met on 11 January 1991 with no formal agenda. The negotiation centred upon a dispute concerning the building work. C did not mention the put option at all but indicated that as part of a comprehensive settlement it expected to obtain the rights previously enjoyed by EHL and specifically mentioned the side land option (they did this merely to raise a reference to the separate deeds which existed – they had no interest in the side land option). A provisional agreement was reached at the meeting under which C agreed to pay £45,000 in full resolution of the dispute over the building work and MK agreed to treat C 'in all respects as having the same rights and benefits under the original documentation' as its predecessors had had and to grant C a new side land option. At the end of the negotiation C, the same day, sent a faxed letter confirming the provisional agreement. In particular the letter included the following sentence: 'You confirmed at our meeting that you will treat CoopInd (UK) Ltd in all respects as having the same rights and benefits under the original documentation as Edison Halo Limited.' On 14 January, MK by way of response sent a copy of the recommendation to confirm the agreement which was to be put to MK's executive management committee for its approval. The executive committee approved the agreement. On 16 January, C by faxed letter sought written confirmation from MK of the accuracy of the 11 January letter. Later that day MK gave C the written confirmation required. As soon as agreement had been reached, C immediately sought to exercise the put option so as to require MK to take an assignment of the underlease. MK denied that it had granted a put option and sought rectification of the agreement. The judge held that (i) C had acquired the put option and that the plaintiff was not entitled to rectification because it had not been shown that C knew of the plaintiff's mistake; and (ii) the correspondence between the parties did not satisfy the requirements of s2 of the Law of Property (Miscellaneous Provisions) Act 1989 (contracts for the sale or disposition of an interest in land should be in writing) so the plaintiff was not bound by the agreement (ie there was no enforceable agreement to grant the put option). C appealed from the judge's decision on the second issue and the plaintiff cross-appealed against his decision on the first issue. The issue on C's appeal was whether an exchange of correspondence concerning an oral agreement concerning land could satisfy s2 of the 1989 Act. *Held*, the appeal would be dismissed and the cross-appeal would be allowed. The contract did not include the put option. Where one party to a contract intended the other to be mistaken as to the terms of their agreement and made false and misleading statements to divert the other's attention from discovering the mistake he could not insist on performance of the contract to the letter but might be bound by the agreement which the other party mistakenly thought was being made. The other party might be entitled to rectification of the contract even where it could not be shown that his mistake was induced by any misrepresentation. As to the s2 issue, a contract to grant a put option in the form enjoyed by C's predecessor in title was a disposition of an interest in land within the meaning of s2 of the 1989 Act. Accordingly, it was required to be evidenced in writing either in one document recording the agreement signed by both parties or by an exchange of contracts (C contended that the exchange of letters of 16 January was a sufficient exchange of contracts within the meaning of s2). STUART SMITH LJ drew a distinction between the formal 'exchange of contracts' and simple letters of offer and acceptance. Here the letters relied upon did not record all the express terms of the agreement already reached. Rather they were the final offer and acceptance which concluded the negotiation. The closing stages of correspondence by which an agreement was reached, ie the final offer or counter offer and an unqualified acceptance of it, could not also constitute the 'exchange of contracts' which was required by s2 before a contract could be made. An additional exchange of documents setting out or incorporating all 'the terms which the parties have agreed' must take place or the parties must sign a simple document which sets them out. Although the correspondence would have amounted to a sufficient note or memorandum under s40 of the Law of Property Act 1925 it did not constitute an exchange of contracts and therefore could not satisfy the more stringent requirements of s2 of the 1989 Act. (But see *Hooper* v *Sherman.*)

Commissioners of Crown Lands v Page [1960] 2 All ER 726   [71]
(Court of Appeal)

In 1937 the Commissioners of Crown Lands granted a 25-year lease of premises in Cornwall Terrace and in 1945 the premises were requisitioned by the Ministry of Works on behalf of the Crown under powers conferred by the Defence (General) Regulations 1939. The premises remained in requisition until 1955 and the landlords claimed rent for the period 1945–1955 during which time compensation was payable for the requisition. *Held*, the landlords were entitled to succeed: in order to constitute an eviction of the tenant at law the landlords' act must have the characteristics of permanence, of having been done with the intention of depriving the tenant of enjoyment of the premises, and of wrongfulness.

Cooke, Re, Beck v Grant [1948] 1 All ER 231   [72]

In 1924 a freehold property was conveyed by deed for valuable consideration to the testatrix and her husband 'in fee simple as joint tenants' and on 1 January 1926, by virtue of s36(1) of the Law of Property Act 1925, there was imposed on this beneficial tenancy a trust for sale whereby the two joint tenants became trustees of the proceeds of sale for themselves jointly. The husband died in 1944 and two months later, shortly before her death, by her will the testatrix gave her 'personal estate' to her nieces and nephew. *Held*, the statutory trust for sale came to an end on the husband's death and thereafter the testatrix was the absolute owner free from the trust. It followed that the freehold property was real estate at the time of the testatrix's will and death and that it devolved as on an intestacy. (But see *Re Kempthorne, Charles* v *Kempthorne.*)

Copeland v Greenhalf [1952] 1 All ER 809   [73]

For upwards of fifty years the defendant and his father before him had carried on business as wheelwrights and had placed vehicles and other articles awaiting repair or collection on a strip of the plaintiff's land, some 150ft by 15ft to 35ft, adjoining their premises: from time to time they had also repaired vehicles there.

Was the defendant entitled to an easement so to use the strip by virtue of s2 of the Prescription Act 1832? *Held*, although it was no objection that the right claimed related to his business, he was not so entitled as he was really claiming a joint user of the land, and such a wide and undefined right could not be the proper subject-matter of an easement. 'It seems to me that for this claim to succeed it must really amount to a right of possession by long adverse possession' (*per* UPJOHN J). (Distinguished in *Miller* v *Emcer Products Ltd* and *Ward* v *Kirkland*; see also *Gardner* v *Hodgson's Kingston Brewery Co Ltd* and *London and Blenheim Estates Ltd* v *Ladbroke Retail Parks Ltd*.)

Cornish v Brook Green Laundry Ltd [1959] 1 All ER 373   [74]
(Court of Appeal)

A lease expired and the freeholders offered the lessees, Brook Green, who had continued to occupy the premises, a fresh lease, at a higher rent, subject to the carrying out by the lessees of certain works. A form of acceptance was sent to the lessees and they sealed and returned it: they paid the increased rent, but no lease was granted and the specified works were not carried out. *Held*, the lessees were not equitably entitled to a new tenancy by virtue of the doctrine of *Walsh* v *Lonsdale* as the agreement to grant a new lease was subject to a condition not yet fulfilled. 'Brook Green were not in a position to sue ... for specific performance of an agreement to grant them a new lease, for the only agreement which ... subsisted ... was subject to the fulfilment by Brook Green of a condition which they had not performed. From this it follows that one of the basic features of the *Walsh* v *Lonsdale* equity was wanting' (*per* ROMER LJ).

Cotterell v Price [1960] 3 All ER 315   [75]

One Mantle created a first mortgage on Malvern Cottage in March 1930, and a second mortgage on the same property in May 1930. The legal date for redemption under the second mortgage was on or about 13th August 1930, and no interest was ever paid thereunder. *Held*, on the second mortgagee's rights of action against Mantle becoming statute-barred in 1942, the second mortgagee lost all estate and interest in the mortgaged property and with it his status as mortgagee, and the equity of redemption, being incidental to that status, could not survive in gross the demise of the second mortgage: it followed that the second mortgagee had no right to redeem the first mortgage.

Crabb v Arun District Council [1975] 3 All ER 865   [76]
(Court of Appeal)

In 1946, A purchased 5.5 acres of land bounded on the north by a public highway called Hook Lane. He divided the land by a north-south line into two areas of 3.5 acres and 2 acres. The 2 acre plot was further subdivided by an east-west line into a northern portion and a southern portion. He erected commercial premises on the 2 acre plot. The northern portion of the 2 acre plot was adjacent to Hook Lane but the southern portion had no separate access to the highway. In 1962, the then owners (A's executors) obtained planning permission to develop the 3.5 acre plot and to make a new north-south road along the boundary between the 3.5 acre plot and the 2 acre plot. In 1965, the executors sold the 2 acre plot to C (the plaintiff). In the conveyance, they covenanted to erect a fence along the boundary line between the two plots and granted C a right of access at a point (point A) in the northern portion of the 2 acre plot and a right of way from that point along the proposed new road to Hook Lane. In 1966, the executors sold the 3.5 acre plot to the local district council (the defendants) expressly reserving the rights of access and way granted to C. The council undertook to erect the fence on the boundary line except for a gap at point A. In 1967, C decided to sell the northern and southern parts of the 2 acre plot separately. In July of that year C and his architect had a meeting with a representative of the council and after explaining his plans C pointed out that he would need access to the proposed new road at another point (point B) in order to serve the southern portion. The council gave him an assurance that this would be acceptable. No details were settled. However, in 1967 the council erected the new fence with gaps at both points A and B, and early in 1968 the council constructed gates at points A and B. In September 1968, C sold the northern portion of his 2 acre plot without reserving for himself as owner of the southern portion any right of way over the northern portion to point A – believing he had access from the southern portion at point B. In 1969, the council removed the gate at point B and closed up the access by extending the fence across the gap. The council offered to grant a right of access and an easement on payment by C of £3,000. C sought a declaration that he was entitled to a right of way from point B, an injunction to restrain interference therewith and damages. At first instance the judge dismissed C's action against the council. C appealed. *Held*, the appeal would be allowed. The council were estopped from denying that C had a right of access at point B and a right of way from that point to Hook Lane since by their words and conduct (ie by the assurance made by their representative at the July 1967 meeting, by the erection of gates at point B and by their failure over a period in excess of one year to give any indication that they might resile from their assurance) they had led C to act to his detriment by selling the northern portion of the 2 acre plot without reserving for himself a right of way over it to point A from the southern portion. If the matter had been finally settled in 1967 it would have been reasonable for C to pay something towards the cost of constructing the access. However, the damage suffered by C in having the southern part of the 2 acre plot rendered useless for a period of years as a result of the council's conduct exceeded any sum he could reasonably be expected to pay towards the cost of providing access. Accordingly, C was entitled to have the right of access free of charge and would be granted the declaration and injunction sought. (Applied: *Inwards* v *Baker*, see also *Pascoe* v *Turner*.)

Cricklewood Property and Investment Trust Ltd v Leighton's [77] Investment Trust Ltd [1945] 1 All ER 252 (House of Lords)

A building lease was entered into in 1936 for a term of 99 years whereby the tenants were to erect a number of shops to form a shopping centre. War came before the work was completed and the tenants refused to pay the rent reserved by the lease on the ground that the lease had been frustrated by restrictions imposed by the government on building and the supply of materials. *Held*, the tenants' view would not be supported as the interruption of building did not destroy the identity of the arrangement or make it unreasonable to carry out the work as soon as the restrictions were lifted. (See also *National Carriers Ltd* v *Panalpina (Northern) Ltd.*)

Cuckmere Brick Co Ltd v Mutual Finance Ltd [1971] [78] 2 WLR 1207 (Court of Appeal)

C Co borrowed £50,000 from M Co on the security of a mortgage of 2.6 acres of land on the outskirts of Maidstone for which C Co had planning permission for development by the erection of 100 flats. Subsequently in 1964 C Co told M Co that it would be more profitable to develop the site with houses. With the consent of M Co they obtained planning permission to erect 33 detached houses. When by 1966 C Co had not commenced building M Co gave notice calling in the mortgage and took possession of the site. M Co sought to exercise their power of sale in respect of the land and the plot was advertised for sale by auction as having planning permission for the erection of 33 detached houses. However, the advertisements made no mention of the planning permission for flats. When this omission was discovered by C Co they wrote to M Co seeking a postponement of the sale to enable particulars of the planning permission for flats to be circulated. However, M Co refused to postpone the sale but they did undertake to instruct the auctioneers to mention at the sale the existence of the planning permission for the flats. At auction the plot realised £44,000 which was insufficient to cover the mortgage debt of £50,000. C Co brought a negligence action against M Co claiming that the land would have realised far more than £44,000 but for M Co's default and failure to take reasonable precautions in relation to the sale (in particular failing to make clear in the advertisements that planning permission for flats was also in existence). At the request of both parties, the trial judge determined (based on the evidence given at the trial) the price which the site would have realised (if correctly advertised) at £65,000. The judge found M Co negligent, and even reckless, in failing to advertise the land as having planning permission for the erection of flats and in failing to postpone the sale. Accordingly, he awarded damages against them on the basis that, but for that failure, the site would have realised £65,000 instead of £44,000. M Co appealed. *Held*, the appeal would be allowed in part and the case remitted for enquiry as to damages. A mortgagee was not a trustee of the power of sale for the mortgagor and, where there was a conflict of interests, the mortgagee was entitled to give preference to his own interest over that of the mortgagor, particularly in deciding on the timing of the sale. 'It matters not that the moment may be unpropitious and that by waiting a higher price could be obtained' (*per* SALMON LJ). However, in exercising the power of sale the mortgagee was not just under a duty to act in good faith (ie honestly and without reckless disregard for the mortgagor's interest) but also *owed a duty to the mortgagor to take reasonable care to obtain a proper price* (described by SALMON LJ as the 'true market value' of the mortgaged property at the moment he chose to sell it). M Co had been in breach of that duty by failing adequately to publicise the planning permission for flats and by refusing to postpone sale. C Co had suffered from the omission of the planning permission for flats from the particulars of sale because the inference to be drawn from the evidence of C Co's witnesses, which the trial judge accepted, was that if it had been included persons interested in development for flats would have attended the auction and on that basis a bid would have been made in excess of the £44,000 actually realised. Finally, although both parties had asked the trial judge to assess the damages on the basis of the evidence given at the trial, the judge should not have acceded to that request (SALMON LJ dissenting), and therefore the case would be remitted for an enquiry as to damages on the basis that the price at which the land could probably have been sold was at large. Although C Co's valuer could not be criticised for using the residual method of valuation in the absence of evidence of recent local sales of land for flats the deficiencies of that method made the assessment of £65,000 unreliable.

Curryer's Will Trusts, Re, Wyly v Curryer [1938] 3 All ER 574   [79]

In respect of his residuary estate the testator made a gift to take effect 'upon the decease of my last surviving child or the death of the last surviving widow or widower of my children as the case may be whichever shall last happen'. The gift to a class to be ascertained on the decease of the testator's last surviving child would not infringe the rule against perpetuities: the gift to a class to be ascertained on the death of the last surviving widow or widower would infringe the rule as a child might have married a person who was not a life in being at the testator's death. *Held,* notwithstanding the use of the words 'as the case may be whichever shall last happen', the testator had referred to two distinct events and the gift would be valid if the event which happened was the decease of the last surviving child, and not the death of the last surviving widow or widower.

Davies v Du Paver [1952] 2 All ER 991 (Court of Appeal)   [80]

In 1949 the defendant purchased and occupied a hill farm in Wales which, for some 60 years, had been occupied by a succession of tenants. In May 1950 he began to fence the land whereupon an adjoining owner, the plaintiff, wrote through his solicitors claiming that he had a prescriptive right to graze his sheep on part of it. The fencing proceeded and the plaintiff's solicitors continued to write letters of complaint, and on 1 August 1950 they stated that their client was compelled to take the necessary steps to assert his right. On 9 August 1950 the fencing was completed and the plaintiff's sheep entirely excluded from the defendant's land, but no other step was taken by or on behalf of the plaintiff until 28 September 1951, when he instituted proceedings. Although the tenants up to 1949 might have been aware of the use of the land by the plaintiff's sheep, there was no evidence that the defendant was himself aware of it. *Held,* although failure to make any complaint or take any further step between 9 August 1950 and 28 September 1951 was not conclusive evidence of submission or acquiescence for more than one year within s1 of the Prescription Act 1832 (a question of fact), as there was no evidence that the defendant was aware of the plaintiff's use of the land, the user could not be said to be as of right within s5 of the 1832 Act and the plaintiff's claim to an injunction and damages failed both under the Act and at common law. (See also *Reilly* v *Orange.*)

Dennis (a bankrupt), Re [1995] 3 All ER 171 (Court of Appeal)   [81]

D and his wife owned two properties as beneficial joint tenants. In September 1982, D committed an act of bankruptcy (he failed to comply with a bankruptcy notice) as a consequence of which a bankruptcy petition was presented against him. D's wife died in February 1983 leaving her estate to her two children in her will. In May 1983 a receiving order was made against D and in November 1983 he was adjudicated bankrupt. The question arose whether the vesting of D's property in the trustee which severed the joint tenancies occurred at the date of the act of bankruptcy by retrospective effect of the adjudication or at the date of adjudication of bankruptcy. If the former, the joint tenancies were severed before the wife's death and her share as a tenant in common would devolve under her will. If the latter, the joint tenancies were not severed before the wife's death and the wife's share would pass on her death to D as survivor, with the result that on adjudication the whole interest in the properties vested in the trustee and was available to D's creditors. The judge held that under s38(a) of the Bankruptcy Act 1914 title to the bankrupt's property only vested in the trustee when the adjudication order was made. The wife's personal representatives appealed. *Held,* the appeal would be allowed. Where a joint tenant of property was adjudged bankrupt under the Bankruptcy Act 1914, the title of the trustee in bankruptcy to that property related back to the first available act of bankruptcy even though the debtor was not adjudged bankrupt until some later date. Consequently, the joint tenancies had been severed in September 1982 (date of bankruptcy) and not in November 1983 (date of adjudication). Since the relation back of the trustee's title to the act of bankruptcy was an automatic statutory consequence he could not then lay claim to the property and at the same time deny that it had vested in him at that earlier date. Just as the trustee could elect to rely on the doctrine of relation back to base a claim to property formerly belonging to the debtor and to claim that a joint tenancy had been severed where it was the debtor who had died in the intervening period, the personal representatives of a deceased joint tenant could also rely on the doctrine to deprive the trustee of his claim to an interest which had accrued to the debtor under the principle of survivorship. Here the joint tenancies had been severed on D's act of bankruptcy in September 1982 (ie before the wife's death) and therefore the wife's share devolved under her will. Accordingly, the court declared that a one-half share in the properties formed part of the wife's estate. (But see *Re Palmer (deceased) (a debtor).*)

Doherty v Allman (1878) 3 App Cas 709 (House of Lords) [82]

The lessee of certain premises which were held for terms of 999 years from 1798 and 988 years from 1824 respectively and had been used for storing corn proposed to convert the premises from their dilapidated state into dwelling-houses. There were no covenants by the lessee not to turn the buildings to any other use. *Held*, an injunction to restrain the lessee from so converting the premises had properly been refused as 'the waste, if waste there be, is ameliorating waste, and the injury to the property produced by the waste is not merely trivial but absolutely non-existent' (*per* LORD O'HAGAN).

Dolphin's Conveyance, Re, Birmingham Corporation v [83]
Boden [1970] 2 All ER 664

D was the fee simple owner of a 30 acre estate known as the Selly Hill Estate. On his death in 1870 the land passed under his will to his sisters A and M as tenants in common. They sold four parcels of land in 1871 to four different purchasers. All the conveyances were identical in form, reciting the title of the vendors to the Selly Hill Estate and containing covenants by the purchasers for themselves, their heirs and assigns with the vendors, their heirs, executors, administrators and assigns to the effect that every house built on the land conveyed had to cost at least £400, be detached, have at least one-quarter of an acre of ground and be not less than 21 feet from the road. The vendors covenanted that on a sale or lease of any other part of the estate it would be sold or leased subject to the same stipulations and with covenants to the like effect. In 1873 A died leaving her share to W, her nephew. Subsequently in 1876 he acquired the rest of the estate from M by deed of gift. W then sold off the rest of the estate in six parcels on the same terms as his aunts had sold the earlier four parcels of land, except for the last parcel. It was sold by W in 1893 with the purchaser covenanting in the terms set out above but as there was no land remaining unsold there was no covenant by the vendor. Birmingham Corporation (the plaintiffs) acquired a parcel of land which had formerly belonged to the estate. Part of the land held by the Corporation had been originally acquired in 1871 from A and M and part of it had been acquired from W in 1877. They were planning as part of their housing programme to redevelop their land in a manner inconsistent with the restrictive covenants. Accordingly, they took out a summons seeking a declaration that they were no longer subject to or affected by the restrictive covenants. There was no annexation or assignment and the only way in which the covenants could be enforced was if there was a scheme of development. The Corporation argued that there was no such scheme because the land had not been divided into plots before sale and there was no common vendor as required by *Elliston* v *Reacher*. Rather there had been two vendors with the later purchasers taking from the nephew of the original vendors. The defendants as owners of other parts of the Selly Hill Estate claimed to be entitled to enforce the covenants against the Corporation. *Held*, the land was subject to a scheme of development and the covenants were binding on the Corporation. As a matter of construction of the various conveyances, the covenants were imposed for the common benefit of the vendors and purchasers of the estate who all had a common interest in their enforcement. There was an equity in the owner of each parcel of land to enforce the covenants against the owners of the other parcels of land and that this was so where the intention was found on the face of several conveyances just as much as in a deed of mutual covenant or deduced from the necessary concomitants of a binding scheme. 'Here the equity ... arises not by the effect of an implication derived from the existence of a deed of mutual covenant, but by the existence of the common interest and the common intention actually expressed in the conveyances themselves ...' (*per* STAMP J). Accordingly, the fact that the land had not been divided into plots before sale and there was no common vendor did not preclude there being a scheme of development. (See also *Baxter* v *Four Oaks Properties Ltd*; but see *Elliston* v *Reacher*.)

Drake v Gray [1936] 1 All ER 363 (Court of Appeal)   [84]

By a deed of partition certain unsold land subject to a trust for sale was partitioned between the testator's five children, three sons, who took absolutely, and two daughters, whose shares were settled. There was no building scheme, but in the partition deed all the land was subjected to certain restrictions and it provided that the trustees (to whom the daughters' land was conveyed) 'for themselves and their assigns to the intent and so that the covenants hereinafter contained shall be binding on the lands and premises hereby assured into whosoever hands the same may come ... covenant with the respective parties hereto ... and other the owner or owners for the time being of the remaining hereditaments so agreed to be partitioned as aforesaid ...' The plaintiff bought a small part of the land conveyed to one of the sons and the defendant purchased with notice of the covenants a small part of the land conveyed to the trustees on behalf of one of the daughters. *Held*, as it was clearly intended that the three sons were severally to have the benefit of the restrictive covenants, that benefit enured to the owner at any time of any part, however small, of the remaining hereditaments, and it followed that the plaintiff was entitled to enforce the covenants against the defendant. 'Where on a conveyance of land the purchaser enters into a restrictive covenant with the vendor, his heirs and assigns, or other the owners or owner for the time being of certain land, that is sufficient to show that the restrictive covenant is to enure for the benefit of the land so referred to' (*per* ROMER LJ). (But see *Re Jeffs' Transfer (No 2)*.)

Drake v Whipp (1995) The Times 19 December   [85]
(Court of Appeal)

Mrs D (plaintiff) and Mr W (defendant) were a cohabiting couple who had been living together for three years when in 1988 they purchased for £61,254 a barn for conversion. Mrs D provided £25,000 of the purchase price (40 per cent) and Mr W the rest. The barn was conveyed into Mr W's sole name. A further £129,536 was spent on conversion works to the property; of that Mrs D paid £13,000 and Mr W the rest (ie Mrs D provided only just over 10 per cent of the conversion costs). In 1989, the couple moved into the barn. However, in 1991 Mr W formed a relationship with another woman. Eventually Mrs D left the barn and sought a declaration that Mr W held the property in trust for both of them in equal shares or such shares as the court might think fit. It was suggested to the court that it did not matter whether the terminology used was concerned with a constructive trust or a resulting trust. The county court judge assessed Mrs D's share on the basis of her percentage contribution to the purchase price – a simple resulting trust based on her contributions to the initial purchase and conversion costs. The judge ruled that Mrs D was entitled to a 19.4 per cent share in the barn and ordered Mr W to pay her £43,650. Mrs D appealed. *Held*, the appeal would be allowed. A potent source of confusion in such property disputes was caused by the suggestion that it was irrelevant whether the terminology used was that of a constructive trust or that of a resulting trust. There was a difference between acquiring a beneficial interest under a resulting trust as opposed to a constructive trust. In a resulting trust, the claimant's share was directly related to the cost of acquisition. In a constructive trust what was needed was a common intention that the party not on the legal title would have a beneficial interest and that that party had acted to his or her detriment in reliance on that intention. That was the case here. There was clear evidence of a common intention between the parties that they were to share beneficially which had been relied upon by Mrs D, and her payments constituted the detriment. Accordingly, it was wrong to decide the appeal on the false footing that the parties' shares were to be determined in accordance with the law on resulting trusts. In a constructive trust case like this the court could adopt a broad brush approach to determining the respective shares of the parties. Their Lordships took into account not only the money Mrs D had contributed but also that she had paid for food and other household expenses and taken care of housekeeping. They rejected the contention of the county court judge that for a constructive trust there had to be a common intention as to the respective shares to be taken by the individual beneficial owners. In the circumstances, Mrs D's fair share would be one-third. This ruling meant that Mr W would have to pay £75,000 to buy out Mrs D and the court also ordered that if he did not the barn should be sold so that Mrs D could get her money. Finally, their Lordships welcomed the recent announcement by the Law Commission that they were to examine the property rights of homesharers.

Draper's Conveyance, Re, Nihan v Porter [1967] 3 All ER 853   **[86]**

A husband and wife were the legal and beneficial joint tenants of a dwelling-house which was their matrimonial home. In November 1965, W was granted a decree nisi of divorce which was made absolute in March 1966. In February 1966, W applied under s17 of the Married Women's Property Act 1882, by summons, to which H was respondent for an order that the house should be sold and the proceeds distributed between them. In her supporting affidavit W asked that the 'property may be sold and that the proceeds may be distributed equally' (between them). At the hearing of the summons it was declared that W had a half share in the property and an order for sale was made. H died intestate before possession was obtained or the house sold. W claimed to be entitled to the entire beneficial interest in the house by survivorship. Some of the children of the marriage who were entitled on H's intestacy claimed that the beneficial joint tenancy had been severed by virtue of the divorce proceedings taken by W and the orders that had been made. *Held*, W held the legal estate on trust for herself and her former husband's estate as tenants in common in equal shares. The beneficial joint tenancy had been severed in February 1966 by the issue of the summons and by W's supporting affidavit – this constituted sufficient notice in writing for the purposes of s36(2) of the Law of Property Act 1925. (But see *Harris* v *Goddard*.)

Eccles v Bryant [1947] 2 All ER 865 (Court of Appeal)   **[87]**

The parties agreed to the sale and purchase of a house, subject to contract, and the vendor's solicitors wrote to the purchaser's solicitors: 'Our clients have now signed their part of the contract herein and we are ready to exchange.' The purchaser's solicitors sent their client's part of the contract, duly signed, to the vendor's solicitors but the vendors changed their minds and did not send their part in exchange. *Held*, in transactions conducted in this way (ie by the customary method of exchanging the two parts of the contract), until such exchange took place, notwithstanding that both parts were signed, there was no contract. (But see *Property and Bloodstock Ltd v Emerton.*)

Ellenborough Park, Re, Powell v Maddison [1955] 2 All ER 38;   [88]
affd [1955] 3 All ER 667 (Court of Appeal)

In 1855 Davies and Whereat owned Ellenborough Park, Weston-super-Mare, and surrounding land and in subsequent years they sold plots of the surrounding land for building purposes. By these conveyances Davies and Whereat granted, inter alia, the full enjoyment 'at all times hereafter in common with the other persons to whom such easements may be granted of ... Ellenborough Park ... but subject to the payment of a fair and just proportion of the costs ... of keeping in good order and condition the said pleasure ground'. The purchasers covenanted for themselves and jointly with the other purchasers to pay a fair proportion of such costs and Davies and Whereat covenanted each for himself and his executors administrators and assigns to keep the park as an ornamental pleasure ground. Had the present owners of the plots any enforceable rights over the park against the trustees of the purchaser from Davies and Whereat who had bought the park subject to the rights still subsisting of all persons to whom the enjoyment of the park had been granted? *Held*, the conveyances of the plots for building conferred on the purchasers and their successors in title legal easements to use Ellenborough Park, subject to the obligation to pay a fair proportion of the costs of keeping the park in good condition. 'The essential qualities of an easement are (i) there must be a dominant and a servient tenement; (ii) an easement must accommodate the dominant tenement, ie be connected with its enjoyment and for its benefit; (iii) the dominant and servient owners must be different persons; and (iv) the right claimed must be capable of forming the subject-matter of a grant' (*per* DANCKWERTS J). Although a new species of burden could not be brought into being and given the status and legal effect of an easement, his Lordship found 'there are authorities binding on me which lead me to the conclusion that the right to use a pleasure ground is a right known to the law and an easement'.

Elliston v Reacher [1908] 2 Ch 665 (Court of Appeal)   [89]

In 1860 a building society bought the Felixstowe Estate. In the same year, the land was plotted out for sale in numbered lots shown on a sale plan exhibited in the society's office. The conditions on which it was proposed to sell the plots were printed on this plan. In early January 1861, the estate was conveyed to two trustees for the society. Shortly afterwards an engrossment was prepared, dated 16 January 1861, of an indenture (outmoded term for a deed) and stamped. It purported to be made between the purchasers whose names were set out in the Second Schedule and the trustees. It contained covenants by the purchasers with each other and the trustees to observe the restrictions contained in the First Schedule to the engrossment (they were the same as those on the sale plan). One of the restrictions was that on no lot should any hotel, tavern, public house or beer house be built or any house used as such without the vendor's consent. Further, the vendors reserved to themselves a power to deal with any part of the estate not disposed of without reference to the restrictions. To this document a plan of the estate was annexed showing part of the estate plotted out for sale in numbered lots as on the sale plan and the rest marked as reserved. This document was never executed either by the trustees or any purchaser. However, it was referred to in the following conveyances. By two deeds executed in December 1861 and April 1866 the trustees conveyed two of the numbered lots to R's predecessors in title subject to a covenant by the purchaser to observe and perform the restrictions contained in an indenture dated 16 January 1861. By two deeds executed in December 1861 containing an identical covenant other numbered lots were conveyed by the trustees to E's predecessors in title. All four conveyances were in identical printed forms (ie they contained a covenant by the purchasers to observe and perform the restrictions contained in the indenture dated 16 January 1861). Further, copies of the 1861 document were shown to the various purchasers. R in breach of the restrictive covenant started to use buildings on his land as an hotel (the relevant consent had not been obtained). E relying upon the covenant sought an injunction to restrain R from so acting. At first instance PARKER J held that the existence of a building scheme intended for the benefit of all the lots sold was proved, that the covenant not to use the land as an hotel was binding on R and could be enforced by way of an injunction by E. He stated that the requirements of a building scheme were as follows: '... it must be proved: (1) that both the plaintiffs and defendants derive title under a common vendor; (2) that previously to selling the lands to which the plaintiffs and defendants are respectively entitled the vendor laid out his estate, or a defined portion thereof (including the lands purchased by the plaintiffs and defendants respectively) for sale in lots subject to restrictions intended to be imposed on all the lots and which, though varying in details as to particular lots, are consistent and consistent only with some general scheme of development; (3) that these restrictions were intended by the common vendor to be and were for the benefit of all the lots intended to be sold, whether or not they were also intended to be and were for the benefit of other land retained by the vendor; and (4) that both the plaintiffs and the defendants, or their predecessors in title, purchased their lots from the common vendor upon the footing that the restrictions subject to which the purchases were made were to enure for the benefit of other lots included in the general scheme whether or not they were also to enure for the benefit of other lands retained by the vendor.' R appealed. *Held*, the appeal would be dismissed. Notwithstanding the reservation of a dispensing power to the vendors and the non-execution of the deed of covenant (the engrossment of 16 January 1861) there was a general building scheme for the benefit of the purchasers inter se as well as the vendors and the covenant could be enforced by E. There was not a purchaser of any of the lots who had not completed his purchase on the footing that he was bound by, and that the other parties were bound by, the stipulations in the engrossment. As to the reservation of a dispensing power to the vendors, it was altogether exceptional *not* to see some power reserved to the vendors to abstract certain property from a building scheme. As to the non-execution of the deed of covenant, if as here the document referred to in the conveyances could be identified the mere fact that it was wrongly described as an indenture was immaterial. Finally, PARKER J's statement of the requisites for a building scheme would be approved. (But see *Baxter v Four Oaks Properties Ltd* and *Re Dolphin's Conveyance*.)

Elwes v Brigg Gas Co (1886) 33 Ch D 562   **[90]**

A gas company took a 99-year lease of certain land for the purpose of erecting a gasholder. In the course of excavations they discovered a prehistoric boat six feet below the surface. *Held*, the boat was the property of the lessor. (But see *Parker v British Airways Board*.)

Elwes v Maw (1802) 3 East 38   **[91]**

The tenant of a farm erected thereon at his own expense a beast-house, a carpenter's shop, a fuel-house, a cart-house and pump-house and fold-yard. The buildings were of brick and mortar and their foundations were about one and a half feet in the ground. *Held*, the tenant was not entitled to remove these buildings, even during the term of the lease and although he might leave the premises in the same state as when he entered.

Errington v Errington [1952] 1 All ER 149 (Court of Appeal)   [92]

With the help of a mortgage from a building society a father bought a house for his son and daughter-in-law in his (the father's) own name and told the daughter-in-law, to whom he handed the building society book, that if and when she and her husband had paid all the instalments due under the mortgage the house would be their property. The daughter-in-law paid the instalments regularly out of moneys given to her by her husband, but when the father died by his will he left the house to his widow: shortly after the father's death the son left his wife. The widow sought to recover possession from the daughter-in-law. *Held*, her action could not succeed as the son and daughter-in-law were licensees with a contractual or equitable right to remain in possession so long as they paid the instalments. 'They have acted on the promise and neither the father nor his widow, his successor in title, can eject them in disregard of it' (*per* DENNING LJ). (But see *Ashburn Anstalt* v *Arnold*.)

Esso Petroleum Co Ltd v Harper's Garage (Stourport) Ltd   [93]
[1967] 1 All ER 699 (House of Lords)

The respondents, the owners of Corner garage, charged the same by way of legal mortgage to the appellants to secure the repayment of a principal sum of £7,000 and covenanted to repay the £7,000 with interest by quarterly instalments over 21 years and during the continuance of the mortgage to purchase exclusively from the appellants all motor fuels which they might require for consumption or sale at Corner garage. The mortgage further provided that the respondents were not entitled to redeem the security otherwise than in accordance with the covenant as to repayment. *Held*, the mortgage stipulation relating to the purchase of fuel was within the ambit of the legal doctrine relating to covenants in restraint of trade, it was unenforceable as being an unreasonable restraint of trade and the respondents were entitled to redeem the mortgage. (But see *Knightsbridge Estates Trust Ltd* v *Byrne*.)

Facchini v Bryson (1952) 96 SJ 395 (Court of Appeal)   [94]

Although an agreement between an ice-cream manufacturer and one of his employees provided 'the employer will permit [the employee] during the continuance of this agreement ... to occupy [a dwelling-house] but nothing in this agreement shall be construed to create a tenancy' between the parties, the operative clauses of the agreement indicated that the employee had the rights of a lessee, eg the employee undertook that he would 'not assign underlet or part with possession of the premises'. *Held*, the agreement constituted a service tenancy and not a licence. 'In recent cases where the occupier had been held to be a licensee there had been something in the nature of a family arrangement, an act of friendship or generosity which negatives the idea of a tenancy' (*per* DENNING LJ). (See also *Street* v *Mountford*; but see *Marcroft Wagons Ltd* v *Smith*.)

Fay v Miller, Wilkins & Co [1941] 2 All ER 18 (Court of Appeal)   [95]

The memorandum of a contract for the sale of a house incorporated certain conditions of sale in which it was stated: 'The vendor will convey as personal representative'. *Held*, this was a sufficient description of the vendor to satisfy the requirements of s40 of the Law of Property Act 1925. 'If the vendor's name does not appear on the face of the contract, the contract will not suffer from insufficiency on that score if it indicates the vendor by a description sufficient to preclude any fair dispute as to identity' (*per* CLAUSON LJ). (See now s2 of the Law Reform (Miscellaneous Provisions) Act 1989.)

Federated Homes Ltd v Mill Lodge Properties Ltd [96]
[1980] 1 WLR 594 (Court of Appeal)

In 1970 M Ltd, the owner of a site which included three areas of land, the red, green and blue land, obtained outline planning permission to develop the site by the erection of a specified number of dwellings. In 1971 M Ltd sold the blue land to D Co (the defendants). The conveyance contained a restrictive covenant whereby D Co covenanted with M Ltd that in developing the blue land they would not build 'at a greater density than a total of 300 dwellings so as not to reduce the number of units which the vendor [M Ltd] might eventually erect on the retained land under the existing planning consent'. The 'retained land' was described as 'any adjoining or adjacent property' retained by M Ltd (ie the red and green land). P Co (the plaintiffs) ultimately became the owners of both the red and the green land after various intermediate purchasers. The green land carried an unbroken chain of express assignments of the benefit of the restrictive covenant. However, in the case of the red land, the transfer to P Co did not contain any express assignment of the benefit of the covenant. In 1977 P Co obtained planning permission to develop the red and green land. They then discovered that D Co had obtained planning permission to develop the blue land to a higher density than 300 dwellings and that that density was likely to prejudice development of the red and green land. Accordingly, P Co sought to restrict D Co from building on the blue land and at a density which would be in breach of the restrictive covenant. The judge held that the benefit of the covenant had not been annexed to the retained land because the 1971 conveyance to D Co had not expressly or impliedly annexed it and because s78 of the Law of Property Act 1925 did not have the effect of annexing the benefit of the covenant to the retained land. In respect of the green land, he concluded that the unbroken chain of assignments of the benefit of the covenant vested the benefit of it in P Co as the owners of that land. In respect of the red land he held that the benefit of the covenant had *not* passed by assignment but that under s62 of the 1925 Act (which implied general words into a conveyance of land) the benefit of the covenant had been carried to P Co as owners of that land. Accordingly, the judge granted P Co an injunction restraining breach of the restrictive covenant by D Co who appealed. The issue on appeal was whether the benefit of the covenant had passed to P Co as the owners of the red land. *Held*, the appeal would be dismissed. Where there was a restrictive covenant which touched and concerned the covenantee's land s78(1) of the 1925 Act had the effect of annexing the benefit of the covenant to the covenantee's land and was not just a statutory shorthand for shortening a conveyance. The language of s78(1) implied that such a restrictive covenant was enforceable at the suit of (1) the covenantee and his successors in title; (2) a person deriving title under him or them; and (3) the owner or occupier of the benefited land and therefore under s78(1) such a covenant ran with the covenantee's land and was annexed to it. Here since the covenant was for the benefit of the retained land and that land was sufficiently described in the 1971 conveyance for the purpose of annexation, the covenant touched and concerned the land of the covenantee (M Ltd) and s78(1) had the effect of annexing the benefit of the covenant to the retained land for the benefit of M Ltd, its successors in title and the persons deriving title under it or them including the owners for the time being of the retained land. It followed that s78(1) had caused the benefit of the restrictive covenant to run with the red land and be annexed to it. Accordingly, P Co as owners both of the green and red land were entitled to enforce the covenant against D Co. (Applied: *Smith* and *Snipes Hall Farm Ltd v River Douglas Catchment Board*; see also *Roake v Chadha*.)

Feversham Settled Estate, Re [1938] 2 All ER 210 [97]

The tenant for life of a settled estate would dearly have liked to live in the principal mansion house containing some ten reception rooms and some 52 bedrooms, but for financial reasons he felt compelled to let it as a school for a term of 30 years. At a cost of over £13,000 he then adopted another house on the estate as his residence and the question arose whether this house had become the principal mansion house within the meaning of the Settled Land Act 1925. *Held*, it had. 'The question whether or not a particular house is the principal mansion house is a question of fact, which the court has to determine on the proper evidence at the time when the application is made, and it is quite impossible to lay down any sort of general principle as to when a mansion house may cease to be mansion house and when some other residence may become a principal mansion house' (*per* FARWELL J).

Fison's Will Trusts, Re, Fison v Fison [1950] 1 All ER 501 [98]

A testator died in 1920 and by his will gave his son the option of purchasing certain properties which were subject to a mortgage and an equitable charge. *Held*, if the son exercised the option, he elected to become a purchaser and was not a devisee under the will and, therefore, s1 of the Real Estate Charges Act 1854 (now s35 of the Administration of Estates Act 1925) did not apply: it followed that the son would be entitled to a conveyance of the properties free from any encumbrances. (But see *Re Wakefield*.)

Fitzwalter, Re, Wright v Plumptre [1943] 2 All ER 328 [99]
(Court of Appeal)

Acting under their Settled Land Act powers previous tenants for life had granted certain mining leases of the settled property. The present tenant for life was not unimpeachable for waste. *Held*, nevertheless, he was entitled under s47 of the Settled Land Act 1925, to receive as rents and profits of the settled estates the residue of the rents payable under the leases after one-fourth part only has been set aside as capital money as a tenant for life, though not declared by the settlement unimpeachable for waste, is not as regards open mines 'impeachable for waste in respect of minerals' within s47 of the 1925 Act.

Gaite's Will Trusts, Re, Banks v Gaite [1949] 1 All ER 459 [100]

By her will a testatrix made gifts to Mrs Gaite for life and thereafter to the grandchildren of Mrs Gaite 'living at [the date of the testatrix's] death or born within five years therefrom who shall attain the age of 21 years or being female marry under that age'. Did these bequests infringe the rule against perpetuities? *Held*, they did not as a child born to Mrs Gaite after the death of the testatrix must have been under 16 years of age at the expiration of the five-year period and therefore could not have been lawfully married and have had lawful children within the period of five years.

Gape's Will Trusts, Re, Verey v Gape [1952] 2 All ER 579 [101]
(Court of Appeal)

By her will the testatrix directed that her residuary estate should be held on trust for various people in succession provided each person entitled 'shall within six months from the date of becoming ... entitled take up permanent residence in England and in default ... the trusts hereinbefore declared in favour of such person ... shall determine'. *Held*, 'the phrase "take up permanent residence in

England" embodies a conception which is clear and precise' (*per* MORRIS LJ) and it followed that the defeasance clause was valid. (Distinguished: *Sifton* v *Sifton*.)

Gardner v Hodgson's Kingston Brewery Co Ltd [1903] AC 229   [102]
(House of Lords)

For more than 40 years without interruption the plaintiff, the owner of a house, crossed the yard of the Red Lion in order to pass from her stables to and from the public highway. For the greater part of the time, if not for all of it, the plaintiff or her predecessors in title had paid to the owners of the Red Lion 15s a year. *Held*, it would be inferred that the payment was made for leave to use the way across the yard; there had therefore been no enjoyment as of right within s2 of the Prescription Act 1832, and there was no ground for presuming a lost grant. (See also *Copeland* v *Greenhalf*.)

Glass v Kencakes Ltd [1964] 3 All ER 807   [103]

The tenants of certain premises in Bayswater sub-let flats therein to Dean who used them for the purposes of prostitution, but the tenants had no cause to suspect the immoral user. The lease provided that the flats were to be used 'as residential flats and for no other purpose or purposes' and the landlord served notice of forfeiture on the tenants alleging a breach of this covenant and that the breach was incapable of remedy. Three weeks later the tenants served a notice of forfeiture on Dean, but by this time Dean had caused the prostitutes to leave the flats. *Held*, the landlord's action for forfeiture would fail. A breach of covenant as to user was normally capable of being remedied and, indeed, in this case had been remedied within a reasonable time: it followed that her notice was bad as it had not required the tenants to remedy the breach of covenant: see s146(1)(b) of the Law of Property Act 1925. 'The fact that the business user involves immorality does not in itself render the breach incapable of remedy provided that the lessees neither knew nor had any reason to know of the fact that the flat was being so used. The remedy in such a case, however, must involve not only that immediate steps are taken to stop such a user so soon as the user is known, but that an action for a claim for forfeiture of the sub-tenant's lease must be started within a reasonable time. If therefore the lessee had known of such a breach for a reasonable time before the notice is served, the breach is incapable of remedy unless such steps have been taken' (*per* PAULL J). (But see *Grangeside Properties Ltd* v *Collingwoods Securities Ltd* and *Hoffman* v *Fineberg*.)

Goldberg v Edwards [1950] Ch 247 (Court of Appeal)   [104]

The first defendant let to the plaintiff for two years an annexe at the back of his house: access to the annexe was permitted to the plaintiff through the house, though there was other access to it from waste land at the back. The first defendant then let the house to the second defendant who barred the plaintiff's access through it to the annexe: the plaintiff sought an injunction. *Held*, the plaintiff's claim apart from s62 of the Law of Property Act 1925, could not be sustained as a way through the house was not even prima facie necessary for the reasonable or convenient enjoyment of the annexe (but see *Borman* v *Griffith*), but a right of ingress and egress through the house was conferred on the plaintiff himself by s62 of the 1925 Act with effect from the date on which the annexe was let to him. (See also *Wright* v *Macadam*; but see *Phipps* v *Pears*.)

Goodman v Saltash Corporation See Beckett (Alfred F) Ltd v Lyons

Gough v Wood & Co [1894] 1 QB 713 (Court of Appeal) [105]

The defendants agreed to supply a tenant with a boiler and piping for the purpose of his trade, on hire-purchase terms, and the tenant afterwards mortgaged the premises to the plaintiff who had no notice of the hire-purchase agreement but allowed the tenant to remain in possession of the premises. The tenant defaulted in the payment of an instalment and the defendants entered and carried away the boiler and pipes, which had been fixed in the brickwork, in accordance with the terms of the hire-purchase agreement. *Held*, they were entitled so to do as the plaintiff, having allowed the mortgagor (the tenant) to remain in possession, would be taken to have acquiesced in his making agreements for fixing and removing fixtures for the purposes of his trade. (But see *Reynolds* v *Ashby & Son*.)

Grand Junction Co Ltd v Bates [1954] 2 All ER 385 [106]

Contrary to the terms of the lease an assignee permitted the premises to be used as a brothel, and in an action for possession the question arose whether a Mr Bennett, with whom the assignee had entered into a mortgage by way of legal charge, was entitled to claim relief under s146(4) of the Law of Property Act 1925. *Held*, although Mr Bennett had no estate or term in the property, he was entitled to claim relief as the effect of s87(1) of the 1925 Act is to give a mortgagee by way of legal charge the same protection, powers and remedies as though he had a sub-demise, and a mortgagee by sub-demise undoubtedly had the right to protect his mortgage, where it was a term of years, by applying for relief under s146(4) of the 1925 Act.

Grangeside Properties Ltd v Collingwoods Securities Ltd [107]
[1964] 1 All ER 143 (Court of Appeal)

Eastern Trades Ltd obtained a loan of £3,000 from the defendants and, in order to secure the advance, by a homemade document expressed as an out-and-out assignment, assigned their lease of certain premises to the defendants. The lease contained a covenant against assignment without first obtaining the landlords' written consent, and such consent was not sought. *Held*, although not expressed to be so made, the assignment was an 'assignment ... by way of mortgage' within s86(2) of the Law of Property Act 1925, and it took effect by way of sub-demise: 'Section 86(2) cannot have intended to alter the ancient law, which has always been that Chancery would treat as a mortgage that which was intended to be a conveyance by way of security between A and B. Once a mortgage, always a mortgage and nothing but a mortgage, has been a principle for centuries' (*per* HARMAN LJ). Further, the defendants, as under-lessees, were entitled to relief against forfeiture under s146(4) of the Act of 1925, especially because they were in a sound financial position to stand in the shoes of the lessees and if the landlords had been asked to agree to a mortgage at the time of the 'assignment' consent could not reasonably have been refused. (But see *Glass* v *Kencakes Ltd*.)

Green v Ashco Horticulturist Ltd [1966] 2 All ER 232 [108]

By leases made in 1931, 1945 and 1959 (for 21 years) certain landlords successively leased a shop adjoining their premises to one Green. A passageway on the landlords' premises gave access to the rear of the shop: although Green made considerable use of the passageway from 1931 onwards the leases did not expressly confer on Green any right to use the back entrance and it was found that such use was by consent of the landlords and subject to the exigencies of their own business and to the requirements of tenants and their neighbouring garages. Green and the persons to whom his lease was assigned in 1964 claimed a right of way to and from the back entrance to the shop. *Held*, they were not entitled to succeed as the intermittent consensual privilege enjoyed by Green was not user that could have been the subject of a grant of a legal right and, accordingly, had not been converted by s62 of the Law of Property Act 1925 into a legal easement on the occasion of the grant of either the second or the third lease. (Distinguished: *International Tea Stores Co* v *Hobbs*; applied: *Wright* v *Macadam*; see also *Wheeldon* v *Burrows*.)

Halsall v Brizell See Rhone v Stephens

Hambro v Duke of Marlborough [1994] 3 All ER 332   [109]

The case concerned the Blenheim settlement which had been constituted by the combined effect of a public Act of Parliament of 1704, certain letters patent of 1705 and a further public Act of Parliament of 1706. It settled upon the first Duke of Marlborough and his issue the Manor of Woodstock and other property as a reward for his services to the nation, particularly his victory at Blenheim. The 1706 Act set out how the estate and the Palace of Blenheim (then in the course of erection) were to devolve to the first Duke's issue. In particular, it prohibited any Duke from any act which would hinder, bar or disinherit a successor from possessing and enjoying the land in kind (the entrenching provision). The plaintiffs were the trustees of the settlement which was a strict settlement within the Settled Land Act 1925. The first defendant was the eleventh Duke. He was the tenant in tail in possession and had all the powers of a tenant for life under the 1925 Act. The second defendant was the Marquess of Blandford, the Duke's eldest son. He was the heir apparent and the tenant in tail in remainder. If and when he succeeded his father he would be entitled to all the powers of a tenant for life. Owing to the irresponsible behaviour of the Marquess, the plaintiffs sought an order under s64(2) of the Settled Land Act 1925 which in effect would have limited his right to manage the Blenheim estate. Section 64 gave the court power to order any transaction which would be for the benefit of the settled land. The trustees and the Duke had reluctantly concluded that the Marquess was not capable of managing the estate. Accordingly, they prepared a scheme in order to provide for the proper management of the estate in the future. Under the scheme the trust fund was to be held to pay the income to the eleventh Duke for life and subject thereto on protective trusts for the Marquess for his life and capital on the trusts of the existing settlement. The Duke was to execute a conveyance of substantially all the land comprised in the settlement to the trustees of the new trust to be held by them on trust for sale. The aim was to protect the relevant assets for the beneficiaries generally. Under the scheme, the land would be taken out of the Settled Land Act by the creation of a trust for sale and the beneficial interest of the Marquess would be varied without his consent. The application of the trustees was opposed by the Marquess. The question before the court was not whether the scheme should be approved but whether the court had jurisdiction under s64 of the Settled Land Act 1925 to do so. *Held*, the court could, under s64 of the 1925 Act, approve any transaction which was for the benefit of the settled land, even if thereafter the land would cease to be settled land within the Settled Land Acts 1882 and 1925. Although s64 of the 1925 Act was most frequently used to sanction a transaction on behalf of beneficiaries who could not consent for themselves, the court had jurisdiction, under the provision, to approve a transaction which varied the beneficial interest of an ascertained beneficiary, of full age and capacity, who did not consent, provided that the variation was for the benefit of the settled land or all the beneficiaries under the settlement. Accordingly, the person whose beneficial interest was affected (unless it was so remote as to be de minimis) would obtain some countervailing advantage either as one of the beneficiaries or as someone interested in the settled land which was being benefited. The entrenching provision in the 1706 Act was incompatible with the powers of the tenant for life under the Settled Land Acts 1882 and 1925. Accordingly, the latter Acts impliedly repealed the former and the Duke, as tenant for life of the settled estate, could effect a transaction which would deprive the Marquess of Blandford of the right to live in and manage Blenheim Palace and the estate. (See also *Re Simmons' Trusts, Simmons* v *Public Trustee*.)

Hannah v Peel [1945] 2 All ER 288   **[110]**

The plaintiff, a lance-corporal in the Royal Artillery, was stationed in a house which was owned by, but had never been actually occupied by, the defendant. During his stay the plaintiff accidentally discovered a valuable brooch in a wall crevice in an upstairs room. The real owner of the brooch could not be traced and the parties disagreed as to which of them should have it. *Held*, the plaintiff was entitled to the brooch as the defendant had never been in physical possession of the house and had no knowledge of the existence of the brooch until it was found by the plaintiff.

Harker's Will Trust, Re, Harker v Bayliss [1938] 1 All ER 145   **[111]**

The tenant for life of certain settled property in Cumberland and Westmorland sold some larch plantations and trees, which were ripe for cutting, were duly felled and carried away. Larch was not timber either at common law or by the custom of Cumberland or Westmorland and the will creating the settlement provided that the trustees were to cultivate and manage the estate according to the custom of the district, and gave them full discretionary powers to cut timber and underwood for sale, repairs, or otherwise. *Held*, the trees having been felled in the ordinary course of management of the property, the whole of the purchase money was payable to the tenant for life, and she was under no obligation to plant fresh trees. 'If larch is not timber, and it is not, then it appears to me to follow as a matter of law that, in the absence of any special provision in the will or other disposition affecting the property, a tenant for life who cuts it in due course of management of the estate is entitled to retain for his own use the whole of the proceeds of sale ... Of course, if a tenant for life improperly cuts wood which is not timber – that is to say, cuts it before it is ripe for felling – then no doubt he is liable to an action in the nature of waste, for he has not done that which is right and proper as between himself and the persons entitled to the inheritance of the estate. Also, ... if some accident intervenes – that is to say, if there is a great storm by reason of which a plantation is laid low before the time has come for felling – or if, again, by an accident of any kind such as a great war, there are created peculiar exigencies in the timber trade, so that it becomes desirable to cut and sell wood at a time at which it is not ordinarily ripe for cutting, then equity will intervene, and will decree that some part of the proceeds of the wood thus fortuitously sold should be retained for the benefit of the inheritance' (*per* SIMONDS J).

Harris v Goddard [1983] 3 All ER 242 (Court of Appeal)   **[112]**

A husband and his second wife were equitable joint tenants of a property which they used partly as the matrimonial home and partly as shop premises. The marriage broke down and W petitioned for divorce. Her petition included a prayer asking 'That such order may be made by way of transfer of property and/or settlement of property and/or variation of settlement in respect of the former matrimonial home ... and otherwise as may be just.' Subsequently H was seriously injured in a car accident and he died a few weeks later before the hearing of the petition. H's executors and the children of his first marriage (the plaintiffs) sought a declaration that the equitable joint tenancy had been severed under s36(2) of the Law of Property Act 1925 by the prayer in W's divorce petition and that therefore they were entitled to one-half of the proceeds of sale of the property as tenants in common in equity. W counterclaimed seeking a declaration that she was entitled to the entire proceeds of sale under the principle of survivorship on H's death. The judge dismissed the plaintiffs' claim and allowed W's counterclaim. The plaintiffs appealed. *Held*, the appeal would be dismissed. A notice in writing of a desire to sever an equitable joint tenancy served under s36(2) of the 1925 Act took effect forthwith and therefore a desire to sever had to evince an intention to bring about the severance immediately. Here the prayer in W's divorce petition was merely an invitation to the court to decide *at some future time* whether or not to exercise its jurisdiction in one or more of three different ways in relation to the property (ie it did not demonstrate an intention to sever immediately). Accordingly, it did not operate as a notice in writing to sever the equitable joint tenancy and W was entitled to the entire proceeds of sale of the property by survivorship. (But see *Re Draper's Conveyance* and *Bedson v Bedson*.)

Harvey v Pratt [1965] 2 All ER 786 (Court of Appeal)   **[113]**

The parties came to an agreement which they put into writing whereby the defendant would take a lease of garage premises known as Broadway Service Station, but the document did not specify any date from which the lease was to commence. *Held*, in the light of authority it could not now be said that it was an implied term that the lease was to commence within a reasonable time or that it should be inferred that the lease was to commence at the date of the written agreement, and it followed that there was no binding contract. 'It is settled beyond question that, in order for there to be a valid agreement for a lease, the essentials are that there shall be determined not only the parties, the property, the length of the term and the rent, but also the date of its commencement' (*per* LORD DENNING MR).

Herbert, Re, Herbert v Lord Bicester [1946] 1 All ER 421   **[114]**

By his will the testator settled the Boyton Manor estate and created a 'maintenance fund', the income of which was to be applied in payment of certain outgoings of the settled estate and any of the income not required for this purpose was given to the tenant for life. On the sale of the manor house, the maintenance fund was to become part of the testator's residuary estate. Acting under his statutory powers, the tenant for life sold the settled estate. *Held*, the income of the maintenance fund remained payable to the tenant for life as the provision of the testator's will directing that the fund should become part of his residuary estate should the manor house be sold tended to induce the tenant for life not to exercise his statutory power of sale and was therefore void by virtue of s106 of the Settled Land Act 1925. (See also *Re Acklom, Oakeshott v Hawkins*.)

Hill v Tupper (1863) 2 H & C 121 (Court of Exchequer)   **[115]**

A canal company granted to the plaintiff, who occupied premises on the bank of the canal, the sole and exclusive right of putting or using pleasure boats on the canal for hire. The defendant landlord of an inn, which also abutted on the canal, began to put boats on the canal for hire, and the plaintiff alleged that his rights had been infringed. *Held*, his action would fail. 'This grant merely operates as a licence or covenant on the part of the grantors, and is binding on them as between themselves and the grantee, but gives him no right of action in his own name for any infringement of the supposed exclusive right' (*per* POLLOCK CB). (See also *Ackroyd v Smith*.)

Hoffman v Fineberg [1948] 1 All ER 592 [116]

Gambling was conducted in the Somerset Hall Social Working Men's Club in breach of a covenant contained in their lease and the manager was convicted of an offence in connection with those activities. The landlord served a notice under s146(1) of the Law of Property Act 1925, alleging the conviction of the manager and that the club had been carried on in breach of covenant, but the notice did not require the tenants to remedy the breach. *Held*, even if the premises were no longer used for gambling, the landlord was entitled to be protected from the slur involved in being said to be the landlord of a gaming house, although he had suffered no monetary damage, and, therefore, the breach was one which was not capable of remedy within s146(1) of the 1925 Act and the notice was valid. In the circumstances of the case the tenants were not entitled to relief against forfeiture under s146(2) of the Act of 1925. (Distinguished in *Glass* v *Kencakes Ltd.*)

Holland v Hodgson (1872) LR 7 CP 328 [117]

Certain looms in a worsted mill were attached to the stone floors of the mill (and therefore steadied and kept in a true position) by nails driven through holes in the feet of the looms. Although it was impossible to remove the looms without withdrawing the nails, the nails could be withdrawn without difficulty and without any serious damage to the flooring. *Held*, the looms passed by a mortgage of the mill as part of the realty. 'There is no doubt that the general maxim of the law is, that what is annexed to the land becomes part of the land; but it is very difficult, if not impossible, to say with precision what constitutes an annexation sufficient for this purpose. It is a question which must depend on the circumstances of each case, and mainly on two circumstances, as indicating the intention, viz the degree of annexation and the object of the annexation ... Perhaps the true rule is, that articles not otherwise attached to the land than by their own weight are not to be considered as part of the land, unless the circumstances are such as to show that they were intended to be part of the land, the onus of showing that they were so intended lying on those who assert that they have ceased to be chattels, and that, on the contrary, an article which is affixed to the land even slightly is to be considered as part of the land, unless the circumstances are such as to show that it was intended all along to continue a chattel, the onus lying on those who contend that it is a chattel' (*per* BLACKBURN J). (But see *Lyon & Co* v *London City and Midland Bank.*)

Hollington Brothers Ltd v Rhodes [1951] 2 All ER 578 [118]

In 1945 the terms of an underlease for seven years were agreed between the parties and, although both parts of the underlease were executed and one part was delivered to the defendants' solicitor, the counterpart was never delivered to the plaintiffs. Nevertheless, the plaintiffs were allowed to take possession and they paid the rent agreed. In 1947 the defendants assigned their head lease to Daymar Estates Ltd, who were aware of the plaintiffs' 'underlease', and on the same day they gave the plaintiffs notice to quit. *Held*, on the facts, there was no contract between the plaintiffs and the defendants for the grant of an underlease for seven years but, even if there had been, by virtue of s13(2) of the Land Charges Act 1925, and s199(1) of the Law of Property Act 1925 (the contract coming within Class C(iv) as a 'charge or obligation affecting land' and not having been registered as such), there was no breach by the defendants. 'The fact is that it was the policy of the framers of the legislation of 1925 to get rid of equitable rights of this kind unless registered ... I do not see how that which is void and which is not to prejudice the purchaser can be valid by some equitable doctrine' (*per* HARMAN J). (See also *Sharp* v *Coates.*)

Hopper v Liverpool Corporation (1944) 88 SJ 213   **[119]**

In 1805 Liverpool Corporation conveyed certain land, on which there was a building called the Lyceum containing a newsroom and library, to the trustees of the Liverpool Library, their heirs and assigns, 'during such time and so long as the building called the Lyceum or any other building erected on the site thereof shall be used and enjoyed for the use and purposes of the said institution'. *Held*, fees determinable (such as that created by the conveyance of 1805) can still exist, but they are subject to the rule against perpetuities and, in this case, any possibility of a reverter to the Corporation was defeated by that rule. Further, in this case the condition subsequent was void for uncertainty, and the trustees were entitled to the land in fee simple free from any right or claim vested in the Corporation. 'Conditions subsequent which cause a forfeiture must, in order to be valid, be so framed that the persons affected (or the court if they seek its guidance) can from the outset know with certainty the exact event on the happening of which their interests are to be divested' (*per* SIR JOHN BENNETT VC). (See also *Re Leach, Leach v Leach*, and s12 of the Perpetuities and Accumulations Act 1964.)

Hooper v Sherman [1994] NPC 153 (Court of Appeal)   **[120]**

H and S lived together for several years in a house which was in their joint names but in unequal shares with S having the greater share. The property was subject to a mortgage in respect of which each was jointly liable. The relationship between the couple deteriorated and culminated in S applying for an ouster and non-molestation order. However, before the application was heard a compromise agreement was reached by the parties. Under the agreement (which was *not* expressed to be subject to contract), H would transfer all his interest in the house to S in return for her assuming sole responsibility for the mortgage. Further, H undertook not to assault S and to vacate the house. The next day S's solicitor wrote a letter to H's solicitor confirming the fact of an agreement and detailing its terms. H's solicitor replied in a letter marked 'without prejudice'. This letter confirmed the fact of agreement and stated that H was prepared to transfer his share in the house to S provided the mortgagee agreed to release him from all his obligations under the mortgage. Difficulties arose when the mortgagee would not agree to release H until there had been a period of six months satisfactory payments by S. Faced with this delay, H said the arrangement was unsatisfactory and applied under s30 of the Law of Property Act 1925 for an order that the house be sold. A preliminary issue arose as to whether there was any contract in existence between the parties. The issue was whether the two letters satisfied the requirements of s2(1) of the Law of Property (Miscellaneous Provisions) Act 1989. At first instance there was a preliminary ruling that H and S had made a legally valid contract to transfer H's share of the property and mortgage liability to S by an exchange of letters. H appealed contending that the letter from his solicitors did not contain all the terms of the agreement and emphasising that it had been marked 'without prejudice'. *Held*, the appeal would be dismissed (MORRITT LJ dissenting). H's counsel made two important concessions. First, that 'exchange of contracts' was not a term of art. Second, that in accordance with Law Commission Report No 164 (which formed the basis of the 1989 Act) it was still possible to make a contract by correspondence. The majority accepted that these concessions had been rightly made and concluded that the letters which the parties' solicitors wrote to each other (ie exchanged) after the oral agreement was entered into amounted to an 'exchange of contracts' within s2 of the 1989 Act. Since the letters both dealt with all the essentials, the parties, the subject matter and the consideration they amounted to an exchange of contracts and constituted a valid agreement under s2 of the 1989 Act even though one letter referred to undertakings which the other did not mention. Finally, marking the letter from H's solicitors 'without prejudice' did not prevent a contract from being formed because 'without prejudice' did not have the same effect as 'subject to contract'. (But see *Commission for the New Towns* v *Cooper (GB) Ltd.*)

### Hurst v Picture Theatres Ltd [1915] 1 KB 1 (Court of Appeal)			[121]

The plaintiff paid 6d for a seat in the defendants' Kensington cinema. The manager mistakenly believed that he had not paid and had him wrongfully and forcibly ejected. The plaintiff brought an action for assault. *Held*, he would succeed as, since the Judicature Act 1873, it could be said that he had an irrevocable right to remain in the theatre until the conclusion of the performance although his licence to do so, which was coupled with an interest or grant, was not granted under seal. (But see *Clore* v *Theatrical Properties Ltd* and *Wood* v *Leadbitter*.)

### Hutton v Watling [1948] 1 All ER 803 (Court of Appeal)			[122]

An agreement relating to the sale of the goodwill, stock and fixtures of a business was found to provide: 'In the event of purchaser wishing at any future date to purchase property in which the business is situated, she has the option of purchase at a price not exceeding £450', and it was also found that the purchaser had validly exercised the option. *Held*, the purchaser was entitled to an order for specific performance against the vendor of the business and present owner of the premises, and it should be noted that no appeal was made against the decision of JENKINS J at first instance that 'the rule against perpetuities affords no bar to the relief by way of specific performance here claimed'. (See also ss9 and 10 of the Perpetuities and Accumulations Act 1964.)

### International Tea Stores Co v Hobbs [1903] 2 Ch 165			[123]

The defendant was the owner of two houses, one in his own occupation and the other leased to the plaintiff company. The houses were separated by a roadway leading to and forming part of the defendant's yard, and with the defendant's permission the plaintiffs had used this roadway to gain access to the back part of their premises. The defendant sold to the plaintiffs the house leased to them, and conveyed it by a deed containing no general words or reference to any right of way. *Held*, such a right of way as the plaintiffs had actually enjoyed at the date of the deed passed to them by virtue of the general words inserted in the deed by virtue of s6 of the Conveyancing and Law of Property Act 1881 (see now s62(1) of the Law of Property Act 1925), and it made no difference that such enjoyment was wholly permissive and precarious. (Distinguished in *Green* v *Ashco Horticulturist Ltd*; see also *Schwann* v *Cotton*.)

### Inwards v Baker [1965] 1 All ER 446 (Court of Appeal)			[124]

In 1931 a father suggested to his son, who wanted a piece of land on which to build a bungalow, that the son should build the bungalow on a piece of his, the father's land. The son gave up the idea of purchasing other land and built the bungalow on the father's land. The father made no contractual arrangement or promise as to the terms on which the son should occupy the land or for how long he should remain in occupation, but the son believed that he would be allowed to remain there for his lifetime or for so long as he wished. The father died in 1951. Under his will, made in 1922, the land vested in trustees for the benefit of persons other than the son. In 1963 the trustees sought possession of the bungalow. *Held*, where a person spends money on the land of another in the expectation, induced or encouraged by the owner of the land, that he will be allowed to remain in occupation, equity will protect his occupation of the land in such manner as the court will determine. The son was permitted to remain in occupation of the bungalow for so long as he desired. (Applied in *Ward v Kirkland, Crabb v Arun District Council* and *ER Ives Investments Ltd v High*; see also *Chalmers v Pardoe*; but see *Bull v Bull*.)

Ives (ER) Investments Ltd v High [1967] 1 All ER 504 **[125]**
(Court of Appeal)

The plaintiffs' predecessor in title, one Westgate, and the defendant bought adjoining building sites, and the foundations of Westgate's block of flats encroached at least 12 inches into the defendant's land. The defendant objected to the trespass, but he and Westgate agreed (evidence of the agreement was contained in letters which passed between them) in 1949 that the foundations could remain and that the defendant could have a right of way across the yard of the block of flats. Westgate sold his land in 1950 to a Mr and Mrs Wright and in 1959 the defendant built a garage on his land so positioned that access to it could only be gained over the yard. The Wrights watched the garage being built and complimented the defendant on it. In 1960 the defendant contributed one-fifth of the cost of re-surfacing the yard and in 1963 the Wrights conveyed their land to the plaintiffs subject 'to the right (if any) of the owners and occupiers of [the defendant's property] as now enjoyed to pass and repass with or without vehicles over the open yard'. The right of way was never registered as a land charge. *Held*, the defendant had in equity a good right of way across the yard by virtue of the principle qui sentit commodum sentire debet et onus and by virtue of equitable estoppel or acquiescence of the plaintiffs' immediate predecessors in title, and neither of these rights was an estate contract or equitable easement within Class C(iv) or Class D(iii) of s10(1) of the Land Charges Act 1925, with the consequence that neither right was invalidated for want of registration. (Applied: *Inwards v Baker*.)

Jeffs' Transfer, Re, Rogers v Astley (No 2) [1966] 1 All ER 937 **[126]**

Jeffs purchased an estate in 1928 and by 1939 had sold off about half of it in 70 plots for development. In May 1939 he conveyed a plot to a Mr Frankel who covenanted, as regards that land, 'for the benefit of the remainder of [the estate] belonging to the vendor to observe and perform' certain restrictive covenants. There being no building scheme, could those who purchased plots on the estate after May 1939, without express assignments of the benefit of the covenants, enforce them against Mr Frankel's successor in title? *Held*, they could not since the benefit of the covenants was not annexed to each and every part of the estate. (But see *Drake v Gray*.)

Johnstone v Holdway [1963] 1 All ER 432 (Court of Appeal) **[127]**

A vendor agreed to sell certain land to a company and by a conveyance reciting this agreement the vendor as trustee and the company as beneficial owner conveyed part of the land to a purchaser excepting and reserving to the company a right of way 'for all purposes (including quarrying)' shown on a plan drawn on the conveyance. Although the vendor and the company were owners of land adjoining the land conveyed, the dominant tenement was not identified precisely in the conveyance. *Held*, this fact did not defeat the exception and reservation of the right of way as it was a question of the construction of the deed by which it was created (ie the conveyance) and, in all the circumstances, and especially because at the time of the conveyance the purchaser would have been aware of the original agreement and the plan annexed thereto showing that the vendor and the company retained land adjoining including a quarry, the dominant tenement was sufficiently identified. Further, the easement created by the reservation to the company, which operated by way of re-grant, was a legal easement, although at the date of the conveyance the company had only an equitable title to the dominant tenement. (See also *Todrick* v *Western National Omnibus Co Ltd*.)

Jones v Challenger [1960] 1 All ER 785 (Court of Appeal)   **[128]**

A husband and wife bought a lease of a house, and provided the purchase money in equal shares; they held on trust for sale, with power to postpone sale and to hold the proceeds on trust for themselves as joint tenants. The marriage broke up, the husband divorced the wife on the ground of her adultery, and the wife remarried. He remained in the former matrimonial home, and she applied under s30 of the Law of Property Act 1925 for an order for sale of the house and equal division of the proceeds. *Held*, different considerations arose on applications under s30 of the Law of Property Act 1925 and s17 of the Married Women's Property Act 1882 as in the latter case the marriage still subsisted. Here, the house had been bought as the matrimonial home, and that purpose had ended; the duty to sell under the trust for sale accordingly prevailed. The house would be ordered to be sold, and the proceeds divided equally. 'The true question is whether it is inequitable for the wife, once the matrimonial home has gone, to want to realise her investment ... in my judgment it clearly is not' (*per* DEVLIN LJ). (Applied in *Re Citro*; see also *Re Buchanan-Wollaston's Conveyance*, *Waller* v *Waller* and *Abbey National plc* v *Moss*.)

Jordan v May [1947] 1 All ER 231 (Court of Appeal)   **[129]**

The plaintiff let to the defendant certain premises which included a shed containing an electricity generating plant and, on a table in the shed, some storage batteries connected to the generator by wires. The generator was bolted down to a concrete bed and it was not disputed that it was a fixture. *Held*, the batteries were not an essential or integral part of the generator and, for this reason, they were not fixtures and part of the shed. 'As regards the law, a criterion laid down in some recent cases ... is that the test is whether the article in question is an integral or essential part of a machine which is itself admittedly a fixture' (*per* ASQUITH LJ). (See also *Poole's Case*.)

Kelly v Battershell [1949] 2 All ER 830 (Court of Appeal)   **[130]**

In 1937 Foster became tenant of a house in Lancaster Gate and covenanted to use the premises as a private dwelling-house only, subject to two licences which permitted use as a residential club. Foster used the ground floor and basement as a club and the remaining floors (apart from the top floor) were let off as flats, subject to covenants requiring user as private dwellings only in order that the terms of the head lease might not be infringed. The plaintiff became tenant of the top floor, without a written agreement, and she alleged that Foster told her that it was his intention to maintain the flats as private dwellings. In 1949 Foster sold his interest to the defendants, who were running a hotel next door, and they incorporated the whole of the premises, except the top floor, as part of their hotel, at some inconvenience to the plaintiff. *Held*, in all the circumstances, Foster's alleged statement (even if made) could not amount to a covenant implied in the plaintiff's tenancy agreement that the rest of the premises (apart from the ground floor and basement) would be used only as private dwellings and a letting scheme could not be inferred in relation to the whole house which was originally built as one dwelling and had never been physically divided into separate dwellings;

further, as the user of the remainder of the house as a hotel was merely an interference with the plaintiff's convenience, amenity or privacy, the fact of the incorporation of the premises in a hotel did not amount to a derogation from the grant made to the plaintiff. 'The question whether particular circumstances amount to a derogation from a grant, as distinct from mere interference of amenities, seems to me to be a question of fact' (*per* COHEN LJ). (But see *Newman v Real Estate Debenture Corporation Ltd*.)

Kelsen v Imperial Tobacco Co (of Great Britain and Ireland)   [131]
Ltd [1957] 2 All ER 343

The plaintiff was lessee of a ground floor room in Islington which he used as a tobacconist's shop. The premises had a flat roof and the plaintiff's landlords gave to the owners of the adjoining building consent to the defendants', who were wholesale tobacconists, erecting a large 'Players Please' sign which projected into the air space above the plaintiff's shop a distance of some eight inches. *Held*, the invasion of the plaintiff's air space by the sign amounted to a trespass on the part of the defendants, and not merely a nuisance, and he was entitled to a mandatory injunction requiring the defendants to remove such portion of the sign as projected over his premises. 'Prima facie, the lease of the land includes the lease of the air space above, and ... prima facie ... the lease of a single storey ground floor premises would include the lease of the air space above' (*per* MCNAIR J) and the landlords could not derogate from their demise of the air space. (But see *Bernstein (Lord) v Skyviews and General Ltd* and *Clifton v Viscount Bury*.)

Kempthorne, Re, Charles v Kempthorne [1930] 1 Ch 268   [132]
(Court of Appeal)

By his will a testator devised to his brother 'all my freehold ... property'. When he died in 1928 the question arose whether the testator's interest in certain undivided shares in freehold land passed under this gift. *Held*, it did not, as it was subjected to a trust for sale on 1 January 1926, and thereby converted into personalty: see Law of Property Act 1925, s35 and Schedule I, Part IV, para 1. (See also *Bull v Bull*; but see *Re Cook, Beck v Grant*.)

Kingsnorth Trust Ltd v Bell [1986] 1 All ER 423 (Court of Appeal)   [133]

B ran his own business and several small businesses in partnership with his son. He was the sole legal owner of the matrimonial home but it was accepted that his wife had made a contribution to the purchase price and therefore had a beneficial interest in the house and a right to occupy it. B wanted to expand the partnership activities by buying another business. In order to finance this expansion he arranged to borrow £18,000 from K Ltd (the plaintiffs) on the security of, inter alia, a second mortgage of the matrimonial home. K Ltd's solicitors asked B's solicitors to arrange for the execution of the mortgage deed and to act as their agents on completion, and B's solicitors in turn entrusted B with obtaining his wife's signature. K Ltd had no knowledge of the arrangement for B to obtain his wife's signature. B fraudulently misrepresented the purpose of the loan to Mrs B in order to obtain her signature. She did not instruct solicitors to act on her behalf nor did she receive any independent advice before signing the deed. In the mortgage deed, Mrs B was expressed to concur to charge all her interest in the property and release her rights of occupation to K Ltd. K Ltd made their advance to B. Mrs B secured no personal benefit from the advance – she was not involved in B's businesses. Subsequently B was unable to pay off the mortgage and K Ltd sought to enforce the mortgage and obtain possession against B and his wife. The county court judge made a possession order against both of them holding that although Mrs B had been misled as to the purpose of the loan she had signed the mortgage knowing that it created a charge on her home and it was therefore enforceable against her. Mrs B appealed. *Held*, the appeal would be allowed. Where a wife under her husband's influence executed a mortgage of the matrimonial home without knowing his true intention in wanting the loan her rights in the property retained their priority to the lender's rights. Here Mrs B came within that principle. She had signed the mortgage deed under B's influence (being induced to do so by his fraudulent misrepresentation), had been misled as to the purpose of the loan and had received no independent advice. Further, K Ltd had through the two firms of solicitors entrusted to B the execution of the mortgage deed by Mrs B. B had in effect been acting as their agent in this regard and they were bound by the fraudulent misrepresentation made by B to his wife and K Ltd could not enforce against Mrs B the mortgage that she had been induced to sign (ie they were in no better a position than B was). Accordingly, the possession order against Mrs B would be set aside. (Applied in *Barclays Bank plc v O'Brien*.)

Knightsbridge Estates Trust Ltd v Byrne [1940] 2 All ER 401   [134]
(House of Lords)

Under the terms of a mortgage the appellant mortgagors were not entitled to pay off the loan otherwise than by 80 half-yearly instalments and it followed that they would not be entitled to the free enjoyment of their property for 40 years except by a voluntary concession from the respondent mortgagees. One of the questions which arose was whether any of the provisions of the mortgage were invalidated by the rule against perpetuities. *Held*, they were not as the rule has never applied and did not now apply to mortgages. It should be noted that the Court of Appeal ([1938] 4 All ER 618) had also held that a provision whereby a mortgage is made irredeemable for a period of 40 years is not merely by reason of the length of the period unreasonable and that the postponement of redemption for 40 years, having regard to the provisions of the mortgage deed, was not a clog upon the equity of redemption, as the provision was not unfair or unconscionable nor inconsistent with, nor repugnant to, the contractual or the equitable right to redeem. It followed that the mortgagors were not entitled to redeem otherwise than in accordance with the terms of the mortgage deed. (Applied in *Multiservice Bookbinding Ltd v Marden*; but see *Lewis v Frank Love Ltd*.)

Lace v Chandler [1944] 1 All ER 305 (Court of Appeal)   [135]

A house in Barrow-in-Furness was let for the duration of the war. *Held*, such a term was uncertain and no valid tenancy was created. 'A term created by a leasehold tenancy agreement must be a term which is either expressed with certainty and specifically, or is expressed by reference to something which can, at the time when the lease takes effect, be looked to as a certain ascertainment of what the term is meant to be. In the present case, when the tenancy agreement took effect, the term was completely uncertain ... It is important to observe that where the term is capable of being rendered certain, it must be so "before the lease takes effect"' (*per* LORD GREENE MR). (**NB** By the Validation of War-Time Leases Act 1944, such leases were converted into terms of ten years determinable after the end of the war by a month's notice.) (Distinguished in *Ashburn Anstalt v Arnold*; see also *Prudential Assurance Co Ltd v London Residuary Body*.)

Leach, Re, Leach v Leach [1912] 2 Ch 422   **[136]**

Certain freeholds were devised upon trust to pay the annual income therefrom to Robert 'until he shall assign charge or otherwise dispose of the same or some part thereof or become bankrupt ...' *Held*, Robert took an equitable estate in fee simple determinable on the happening of any of the specified events, which estate would on his death without the happening of any of those events become an absolute estate in fee simple. 'This limitation to Robert of a determinable fee simple appears to be free from objection in every respect, notwithstanding what may have been said in any book as to the effect of the Statute of Quia Emptores' (*per* JOYCE J). (See also *Hopper* v *Liverpool Corporation*.)

Leakey v National Trust for Places of Historic Interest or   **[137]**
Natural Beauty [1980] 1 All ER 17 (Court of Appeal)

The defendants owned and occupied a hill which was peculiarly liable to crack and slip as a result of weathering; the plaintiffs owned houses at the foot of it. After a large fall, the plaintiffs asked the defendants to remove the earth and debris from their land, but they refused, saying they were not responsible for what had occurred. The judge held that the defendants were liable in nuisance. *Held*, their appeal would be dismissed. 'The duty is a duty to do that which is reasonable in all the circumstances, and no more than what, if anything, is reasonable, to prevent or minimise the known risks of damage or injury to one's neighbour or to his property. The criteria of reasonableness include the factor of what the particular man, not the average man, can be expected to do, having regard, amongst other things, where a serious expenditure of money is required to eliminate or reduce the danger, to his means' (*per* MEGAW LJ).

Leek and Moorlands Building Society v Clark   **[138]**
[1952] 2 All ER 492 (Court of Appeal)

A husband and wife were joint tenants of certain premises in Birmingham and the husband contracted to purchase the reversion 'subject to the existing tenancy' and to sell the premises to one Clark with vacant possession on completion. Clark mortgaged the property to the plaintiffs and fell into arrear with his payments under the mortgage deed, but the wife had no knowledge of the terms of the sale to Clark or of the mortgage and she had not authorised the termination of her joint tenancy. *Held*, the joint tenancy had not been terminated and, as against the husband and wife, the plaintiffs were not entitled to possession as 'one of two joint lessees cannot, in the absence of express words or authority, surrender the rights held jointly' (*per* SOMERVELL LJ).

Legh's Resettlement Trusts, Re, Public Trustee v Legh   **[139]**
[1937] 3 All ER 823 (Court of Appeal)

The testator by his will exercised a special power of appointment conferred upon him by a deed of 1891, and the relevant provision of his will, by which he appointed a sixth part of the settled funds in favour of two grandchildren, was as follows: 'Upon trust during the joint lives of my said [grandchildren] to pay the income thereof to them in equal shares as tenants in common and after the death of either of them to pay the whole of the income thereof to the survivor of them during the residue of his or her life.' There followed a disposition of the capital upon the death of the surviving grandchild and, as neither of the two grandchildren was alive at the date of the deed which conferred the power, the question arose whether the gift of the whole income to the survivor of them was void for perpetuity. *Held*, it was as the reversionary life interest in the whole income appointed to the surviving grandchild was a contingent interest. 'In a gift upon trust to pay the income to A during his life and after his death to transfer the capital to B, if he shall be then living, B's interest is contingent, and will fail if A's death is an event falling outside the limit permitted by the rule. On the other hand, if the gift to B is in terms absolute with a gift over in the event of his predeceasing A, his interest will be a vested one, and the rule will not apply, notwithstanding that the practical result in the two cases will be the same' (*per* SIR WILFRED GREENE MR). (But see s3 of the Perpetuities and Accumulations Act 1964.)

Leigh v Taylor [1902] AC 157 (House of Lords)   **[140]**

The tenant for life of the Luton Hoo estates hung valuable tapestries in the mansion-house by nailing strips of wood to the drawing-room walls, nailing canvas to the strips of wood and tacking the tapestries to the canvas and wood. The tapestries could be removed without causing any real damage to the walls. *Held*, the tapestries formed part of the estate of the tenant for life and were removable by her executor: in other words, the tapestries had not become part of the house. 'It never was intended [that the tapestries should] remain a part of the house; the contrary is evident from the very nature of the attachment, the extent and degree of which was as slight as the nature of the thing attached would admit of' (*per* EARL OF HALSBURY LC). (See also *Wiltshear v Cottrell* and *Re Whaley*.)

Lever Finance Ltd v Trustee of Property of Needleman   **[141]**
[1956] 2 All ER 378

Certain premises were let for a term of 63 years and on the day on which the lease was granted the lessees charged the property by way of legal mortgage, clause 8 of the charge providing: 'The mortgagors shall not except with the consent in writing of the mortgagees exercise the powers of leasing ... conferred by the Law of Property Act 1925, on a mortgagor while in possession but it shall not be necessary to express such consent in any such lease ... nor shall any lessee be concerned to see that any such consent has been given.' The mortgagors granted a 21-year lease of the first floor without first obtaining the consent of the mortgagees. *Held*, the mortgagees were estopped from denying that the lease had been granted with their consent because, in view of the terms of clause 8 of the charge, a lessee was entitled to assume that such consent had been given. It followed that the mortgagees could not recover possession of the first floor from the lessee of that floor. (See also *Barclays Bank Ltd v Stasek*.)

Leverhulme, Re, Cooper v Leverhulme (No 2)   **[142]**
[1943] 2 All ER 274

Viscount Leverhulme died in 1925 and by his will directed his trustees to set aside certain shares and hold them upon the trusts declared until the date of distribution, ie 'the day on which shall expire the period of 21 years (less the last two days thereof) calculated from the death of the last survivor of the following persons ... (1) my executors and trustees ... (2) my descendants living at my death and (3) the descendants living at my death of Her late Majesty Queen Victoria'. *Held*, the trusts, which were created in 1925, were valid but, because of the increased difficulty in establishing the date of death of the descendants of Queen Victoria, MORTON J discouraged the use of the formula. (See also *Re Villar, Public Trustee v Villar*.)

Lewis v Frank Love Ltd [1961] 1 All ER 446 [143]

The plaintiff mortgaged his land in Southwark to one Aikin to secure an advance of £6,000 but, after the death of Aikin, his personal representatives called in the sum of £6,000 which remained outstanding. As the plaintiff was unable to pay, the personal representatives instituted proceedings and recovered judgment for the total amount due on the security. The plaintiff arranged with the defendants that they would lend him £6,500 to enable the debt to the judgment creditors to be repaid and to enable him to meet certain other expenses on terms which included giving the defendants an option to purchase part of the property comprised in the mortgage. The transaction was carried out by a transfer of the existing mortgage to the defendants for £6,070 and by a contemporaneous written agreement between the plaintiff and the defendants granting them the option on condition that they did not require payment of the principal sum secured by the mortgage for two years. *Held*, looking at the substance of the transaction and not at the form in which it was carried out, the defendants' option to purchase was a clog on the plaintiff's equity of redemption and was therefore void. 'The option to purchase was in fact a clog on the equity because ... if it is exercised it will prevent the plaintiff from getting back the piece of land to which it applies' (*per* PLOWMAN J). (See also *Esso Petroleum Co Ltd* v *Harper's Garage (Stourport) Ltd.*)

Lloyds Bank plc v Rosset [1990] 2 WLR 867 (House of Lords) [144]

In 1982 a married couple decided to buy a semi-derelict house, title to which was registered, for £57,000. The purchase money was given to H by the trustees of a family trust who insisted that the house was purchased in his name alone. This was duly done. Contracts for the purchase were exchanged on 23 November 1982. However, from the beginning of November (ie prior to completion) the vendors allowed H and W to enter on the property together with their builders to start carrying out the necessary renovation work to make the house habitable. During a five-to six-week period from the beginning of November 1982, W spent nearly every day at the property helping the builders. She supervised and encouraged them, went to builders' merchants and obtained materials for them, removed light rubbish from the site and undertook extensive decorating work (she was a skilled interior decorator). H, without W's knowledge, secured a loan of £15,000 from the bank for the renovation. The purchase was completed on 17 December 1982 and on the same day H executed a charge in favour of the bank. W knew nothing of the grant of the charge to the bank. Further, she made no financial contribution to the acquisition of the property. The transfer and the bank's charge were registered at the Land Registry on 7 February 1983. By mid-February the renovation work was almost completed and H and W moved into the house. Subsequently, there were matrimonial difficulties and H left (W continued to reside in the house with the children). Further, the amount owing on H's overdraft continued to rise and the bank demanded payment of the amount outstanding (which by then was nearly £23,000). When H was unable to repay the amount owing the bank started proceedings for the possession and sale of the property. W resisted the bank's claim on the ground that she had a beneficial interest in the property under a constructive trust that qualified as an overriding interest under s70(1)(g) of the Land Registration Act 1925 to which the bank's interest was subject because she had been in actual occupation of the land both on the date of creation and on the date of registration of the charge. The judge found that up to the exchange of contracts H and W had not decided whether W should have any interest in the property. He then reached two conclusions. First, he found that it was the common intention of H and W that the renovation of the house ought to be a joint venture after which the house was to become a family home. Second, he based his inference of a common intention that W ought to have a beneficial interest in the property under a constructive trust on W's activities in connection with the renovation work. However, the judge held that W was not in actual occupation of the property on 17 December 1982 when the bank's charge was created (for him the date of creation of the charge, not its registration, was the crucial date for the purpose of a s70(1)(g) overriding interest). Accordingly, although the judge found that W had a beneficial interest in the property he upheld the bank's claim for possession because W was not in actual occupation of the property on the date when the charge was created and therefore W's equitable interest was not protected as a s70(1)(g) overriding interest so as to prevail over the bank's legal charge. W appealed to the Court of Appeal and succeeded. They held that the relevant date on which W had to show that she was in actual occupation in order to establish a s70(1)(g) overriding interest was the date of creation of the bank's charge (ie 17 December 1982) and concluded that W had been in 'actual occupation' then (they took the view that she had been in actual occupation vicariously through the builders). The bank appealed. *Held*, the appeal would be allowed. The relevant date for ascertaining whether an interest in registered land was protected by actual occupation so as to prevail against the holders of a legal estate as an overriding interest under s70(1)(g) was that of completion of the transaction not its registration. W's activities in relation to the renovation of the property between the beginning of November 1982 and completion, on which the judge had, in essence, based his inference of a common intention that W should have a beneficial interest in it, had been insufficient to support that inference and therefore the judge's finding that H held the house on constructive trust for himself and W in equity could not be supported (ie W had no beneficial interest in the house). W had been extremely anxious that the house would be ready by Christmas. In such circumstances, their Lordships decided that it was only natural for W to have spent her spare time trying to accelerate the progress of the renovation work (given that H was abroad at the time) irrespective of any expectation that she might have had of enjoying a beneficial interest in the property. In the absence of an express intention, it was very doubtful whether anything less than direct contributions to the purchase price by the non-owning partner would be sufficient to create a constructive trust. Neither a common intention by spouses that a house was to be renovated as a joint venture nor a common intention that it was to be shared by them and their children as the family home threw any light on their intention with respect to the beneficial ownership of the property. (See also *Abbey National Building Society* v *Cann*; but see *Midland Bank plc* v *Cooke*.)

London and Blenheim Estates Ltd v Ladbroke Retail [145]
Parks Ltd [1993] 4 All ER 157 (Court of Appeal)

In 1987 L Ltd the owner of a parcel of land (the transferor) sold part of it to L & B (the plaintiffs). The transfer contained an express grant of a right of way over and the right to park cars on the part of the land retained by the transferor. These rights were to be exercised for the benefit of the transferred land and 'future land' (ie other land capable of benefiting from the rights so long as notice was given to the transferor within five years that such land was to be included in the transferred land and that at the date of the notice L & B or a subsidiary company still owned the transferred land). Later on in 1987 L & B contracted to buy two parcels of leasehold land, and this was completed in 1989. However, in February 1988 ownership of the retained (servient) land passed from the transferor L Ltd to W Ltd who, several months later, sold it to LRP (the defendants). In March 1988, L & B gave notice requiring the land they had contracted to buy to be brought within the transferred land. LRP submitted that the rights in question did not amount to interests in land and were not binding on the transferor's successors in title. L & B sought a declaration that the land could have the benefit of the easements contained in the 1987 transfer, and LRP counterclaimed for a declaration that no right to park on the retained/servient land existed in favour of the 'future'/additional land. At first instance, the judge declared that a right to park could amount to an easement provided it was not a right to park in a defined space. In each case it was a question of degree whether the dominant rights were so extensive as to destroy the very nature of an easement. He further declared that rights contained in the grant of an easement could be exercised in relation to leasehold as well as freehold land. However, he found for LRP on the ground that no easement could exist for the benefit of the 'future' land. For an easement to exist there had to be in existence a dominant and a servient tenement in separate ownership or occupation. Here, however, at the time the easement was said to have been granted (when L & B served their notice on LRP) the servient land was no longer owned by the person who promised to grant the easement. L & B appealed. *Held*, the appeal would be dismissed. The dominant tenement had to be specified (or at least ascertainable) at the time of the grant. Here the grant of a right to nominate unspecified land as the dominant tenement of an easement was not in itself enough to create an interest in land binding upon successors in title of the servient land because land could not be encumbered with burdens of uncertain extent. Further, no interest in land had been created because before there was a dominant tenement the servient tenement had been disposed of by the person who promised to grant the easement. (See also *Copeland* v *Greenhalf*.)

Long v Tower Hamlets London Borough Council   [146]
[1996] 2 All ER 683

On 4 September 1975, agents acting for one of THLBC's predecessors in title wrote a letter to L, then a prospective tenant, confirming that he would be granted a quarterly tenancy of shop premises with a maisonnette above. The letter stated what the rent would be and that the tenancy would commence on 29 September 1975 on a quarterly basis. On 8 September 1975, L returned a copy of the letter (the tenancy document) to the landlord endorsed with his signature and a statement to the effect that he agreed to abide by the terms and conditions of the tenancy. Three weeks later, L moved in. A notice to quit was served on L by the local authority in September 1983. Although the notice expired on 25 March 1984, L remained in possession. No further action was taken. Then in 1995 L issued an originating summons claiming title to the premises by adverse possession. The deputy master granted THLBC's application to have L's application struck out. L appealed. It was common ground between the parties that L had not paid rent for many years. However, the parties disagreed as to when L stopped paying rent. L claimed he had not paid rent since 1977 and contended that THLBC's right of action to recover the premises had accrued at the latest by 1 January 1978, and that in consequence any claim by THLBC to recover the premises became statute-barred in accordance with s15(1) of the Limitation Act 1980 (which prescribed a 12-year limitation period) at the latest by 1 January 1990 some five years before the present proceedings were commenced. THLBC argued that L last paid rent in March 1984 less than 12 years before the proceedings were commenced on 13 January 1995 (ie its claim to recover the premises was not yet statute-barred). However, the basis on which THLBC sought to strike out L's claim was that whatever might be the eventual resolution of the factual dispute as to when rent was last paid they could establish on another ground that time could not on any view have begun to run in L's favour until 1984 at the earliest. The other ground was that the tenant's endorsed letter (the tenancy document) was a 'lease in writing' within para 5 of Schedule 1 to the 1980 Act. If this was correct then time did not begin to run when L ceased to pay rent (whenever that was) but only when his tenancy was brought to an end by notice to quit, and the only relevant notice to quit here was the one which expired on 25 March 1984 (ie less than 12 years before the current proceedings commenced). L denied that the letter created a 'lease in writing' because it was not dispositive and took effect, if at all, as a reversionary lease. The issue was whether L had obtained title to the premises by adverse possession. *Held*, the appeal would be allowed. A written document was not a 'lease in writing' for the purposes of para 5(1) of Schedule 1 to the 1980 Act if the writing simply evidenced the existence of a lease and this was so even if as here the terms were comprehensive and clearly referred to the existence of a lease. The document had to be dispositive, ie it created at law a leasehold estate in land. Since the tenancy document had not been executed as a deed it could only take effect as a lease creating a legal estate in land if it came within s54(2) of the Law of Property Act 1925 as a 'lease *taking effect in possession* for a term not exceeding three years' (because such a lease could be made in writing without the need for a deed). Here the tenancy document was executed on 8 September 1975. However, the tenancy was not to commence immediately but rather on a future date, 29 September 1975 and L had no right to take possession until that later date. Accordingly, the lease did not 'take effect in possession'. Rather it took effect, if at all, as a reversionary lease. Such a lease did not come within s54(2) of the 1925 Act (ie a reversionary lease could only take effect if made by deed). Here there was obviously a tenancy but it had not been created by the tenancy document (the letter). Rather it had arisen by operation of law by the payment and receipt of rent. Since the tenancy document was not a 'lease in writing' L was entitled to have his claim determined at trial.

Lyon & Co v London City and Midland Bank [1903] 2 KB 135   **[147]**

Chairs were hired from the plaintiffs for use in the Brighton Hippodrome and, in compliance with the council's requirements, the chairs were fastened to the floor by screws. The Hippodrome and 'all fixtures' were mortgaged to the defendants and the defendants entered into possession under the terms of the mortgage deed. *Held*, the chairs did not cease to be chattels on being screwed to the floor and, therefore, as against the plaintiffs the property in them did not pass to the defendants. (But see *Vaudeville Electric Cinema Ltd* v *Muriset*.)

McCarrick v Liverpool Corporation [1946] 2 All ER 646   **[148]**
(House of Lords)

There was evidence on which the court could find that the house in question, to which s2 of the Housing Act 1936 applied, had not been kept by the landlord in all respects reasonably fit for human habitation. Was the landlord obliged to keep the premises fit for human habitation even though no notice had been given to him that they were not so fit? *Held*, he was not. 'It is an implied term, resulting only from the comprehensiveness of the statutory term and the circumstances necessarily involved in the tenancy, that, in a case where the tenant knows the defect and the landlord does not, the obligation to do a specific act directed to the reparation of that defect does not arise until at least the landlord becomes aware of the need for it' (*per* LORD UTHWATT). (See also *Pembery* v *Lamdin* and *Summers* v *Salford Corporation*.)

McHardy and Sons v Warren [1994] 2 FLR 338 (Court of Appeal)   **[149]**

H and W bought their first matrimonial home with the help of a deposit of £650 towards the purchase price paid by H's father as a wedding present to the couple. The legal title to the matrimonial home was in H's sole name as were the couple's two subsequent homes which in each case were bought by way of mortgage finance and the proceeds of sale of the previous house. Subsequent to moving into the current (ie third) matrimonial home, H, who was heavily in debt to the plaintiffs for the supply of goods to his business, executed an all moneys charge over the house in their favour. The plaintiffs did not take the precaution of seeking W's concurrence to the charge and getting her agreement to postpone her interest in the house to the charge. Subsequently the plaintiffs (trading creditors of H) sought a declaration that W had no beneficial interest in the matrimonial home as they were seeking to enforce the charge against the property in question. Alternatively, they argued that her beneficial interest amounted to only 8.97 per cent (the proportion that half the £650 deposit bore to the total purchase price). Since W was in occupation of the matrimonial home with H if she had a beneficial interest then the plaintiffs were deemed to have notice of her interest and thus it had priority over them. Further, if W did have a beneficial interest then the plaintiffs could only enforce their charge against H's share of the property. W's claim to a beneficial interest arose because her father-in-law had paid the deposit on the first matrimonial home as a wedding present to H and W. Counsel for the plaintiffs argued that the fact that H's father had so acted did not cast any light on the beneficial interest W had in the property. The county court declared that H held the matrimonial home upon trust for himself and W as beneficial tenants in common in equal shares. The plaintiffs appealed. *Held*, the appeal would be dismissed. Where a parent paid the deposit on his child's first matrimonial home as a wedding present the bride and groom were to have equal interests in the home and not an interest by reference to the percentage which the deposit bore to the full price. There was no intention that W should have no interest merely because the property was in H's sole name. Accordingly, the home was held by H on an implied trust for sale for himself and W in equal shares.

McManus v Cooke (1887) 35 Ch D 681   [150]

The parties, who owned adjoining houses, orally agreed that they would pull down and rebuild a party wall and that each of them would be entitled to build a lean-to resting on the new wall and inclining upwards and outwards to the respective houses. The plaintiff carried out his part of the agreement but the defendant erected a lean-to which did not comply with its provisions as to height. *Held*, the oral agreement had given each party an easement of light over the other's land and the plaintiff was entitled to have it enforced. While the agreement was one to which s4 of the Statute of Frauds (replaced by s40 of the Law of Property Act 1925) applied, the doctrine of part-performance also applied and 'the defendant having obtained all the advantages which this agreement was intended to give him, it would be a fraud on his part to refuse to carry out his part of the agreement, and to resist an attempt to compel him to do so by insisting on the Statute of Frauds' (*per* KAY J). (But see s2 of the Law of Property (Miscellaneous Provisions) Act 1989 replacing s40 of the Law of Property Act 1925.)

Maddison v Alderson (1883) 8 App Cas 467 (House of Lords)   [151]

Thomas Alderson induced the appellant to serve him for many years without wages as his housekeeper by making an oral promise to leave her a life estate in his land. Alderson did in fact make a will which purported to carry out his promise but it was of no effect as it was not properly attested. The appellant sought a decree of specific performance in respect of the intestate's oral promise. *Held*, her plea would be rejected as her acts in serving the intestate until his death were not unequivocally, and in their own nature, referable to some such agreement as that alleged and therefore would not constitute such part performance as to take the case beyond the provisions of s4 of the Statute of Frauds. The fact that the Statute had not been complied with rendered the contract unenforceable but not void. (But see s2 of the Law of Property (Miscellaneous Provisions) Act 1989 replacing s40 of the Law of Property Act 1925 which in turn replaced s4 of the Statute of Frauds.)

Marcroft Wagons Ltd v Smith [1951] 2 All ER 271 [152]
(Court of Appeal)

From 1901 until his death in 1938 one Aris occupied a dwelling-house within the Rent Acts which belonged to the plaintiffs and at his death he was a statutory tenant thereof. Aris's widow and daughter continued to occupy the house until the widow's death in 1950 and, although the plaintiffs refused to transfer the tenancy to the daughter as they wanted the house for one of their employees, they said that they did not wish to disturb her and she remained in possession, paying rent, for about six months. *Held*, the plaintiffs had merely intended that the daughter should remain for the time being in occupation of the premises for a consideration, but without becoming a tenant, and no new tenancy had been created in her favour. (But see *Facchini* v *Bryson*.)

Marten v Flight Refuelling Ltd [1961] 2 All ER 696 [153]

The first plaintiff was the present owner in fee simple of a large agricultural estate known as Crichel Estate. By a conveyance dated 25 March 1943, the second plaintiffs, who were at that time the owners in fee simple of the Crichel Estate as the special executors of the first plaintiff's father (the first plaintiff being then an infant) conveyed a part of the estate called Crook Farm to a purchaser. The conveyance contained a covenant by the purchaser with 'the vendor and its successors in title' that no part of the land conveyed should at any time thereafter be used for other than agricultural purposes without the previous consent of 'the vendor or its agent'. In 1958 a part of Crook Farm which, since 1942, had been requisitioned by the Air Ministry under statutory powers for an aerodrome, was conveyed to the Ministry by the purchaser's executors, subject to the restrictive covenant so far as it was valid, and this land was occupied by the defendant company, under licence from the Ministry, and, in addition to maintaining the airfield for the Ministry, used part of the land for industrial purposes. In 1950 the first plaintiff having attained her majority, the second plaintiffs assented to the vesting of the Crichel Estate in her in fee simple, but the assent contained no reference to the restrictive covenant. *Held*, the plaintiffs were entitled to the benefit of the restrictive covenant because an intention that it should be for the benefit of the Crichel Estate could and should be found from the surrounding circumstances (it was not necessary that the intention should be expressly stated or that the land to be benefited should be specifically identified) and the Crichel Estate was capable of being benefited by the covenant. Although the first plaintiff was not an express assignee of the benefit of the restrictive covenant, she, as the person for whose benefit in equity the covenant was made, and the second plaintiffs, as the original covenantees, were entitled together to enforce it, but not so as to restrict the use of the land by the Ministry or the defendants for the statutory purposes for which it had been compulsorily acquired, ie an aerodrome for the Royal Air Force.

Massey v Midland Bank plc [1995] 1 All ER 929 (Court of Appeal) [154]

M owned a house and was persuaded by misrepresentations by her lover, P, to charge her house to the plaintiff bank as security for an overdraft granted to a business venture in which P was involved. The bank indicated to P that M had to be independently advised by a solicitor before it would proceed with the transaction. P arranged for his own solicitors to advise M and the bank sent the charge to them. M was advised by P's solicitor who explained the nature of the bank's charge to her in the presence of P. M signed the charge and the solicitors confirmed to the bank that they had advised her and explained the charge to her. Thereafter, the bank lent the money to P. Subsequently the company went into liquidation and the bank sought possession of M's house. M resisted on the ground that she had been induced to sign the charge by P's misrepresentations (in particular he fraudulently exaggerated the prospects of the new business) and undue influence and that the bank was affected by P's wrongdoing. The deputy judge held that the bank was unaffected by P's dishonesty and granted them an order of possession. M appealed. *Held*, the appeal would be dismissed. The bank was put on inquiry by the circumstances in which M had agreed to provide the security. However, its actions (taking reasonable steps to ensure that M's agreement to the charge had been properly obtained and receiving confirmation from the solicitors that they had explained the charge to her) prevented it from being fixed with constructive notice of P's misrepresentations. The bank was entitled to conclude that M had received independent advice from the firm of solicitors and to assume that the solicitor dealing with the matter had acted honestly and given proper advice. The bank was under no duty to enquire into what had happened at the interview between M and the solicitors. (Applied: *Barclays Bank plc* v *O'Brien*; followed in *Banco Exterior Internacional* v *Mann*.)

Mayo, Re, Mayo v Mayo [1943] 2 All ER 440 **[155]**

A trustee sought an order under s30 of the Law of Property Act 1925, directing his co-trustees to concur with him in effecting a statutory trust for sale arising under s36 of the Settled Land Act 1925. *Held*, the order would be made as the judicial discretion under s30 of the Law of Property Act must be exercised in favour of the statutory trust for sale and a sale must be ordered unless there is mala fides or the trustees unanimously agree to exercise their power to postpone the sale. (See also *Re Buchanan-Wollaston's Conveyance, Curtis* v *Buchanan-Wollaston*.)

Mercer v Denne [1905] 2 Ch 538 (Court of Appeal) **[156]**

The fishermen of Walmer sought to establish an immemorial custom for fishermen of the parish to spread their nets to dry on the defendant's land near the sea and within the parish, at all times necessary or proper for the purposes of their trade or business. *Held*, it was a valid legal custom, and where imperceptible accretion to the land had occurred, the land so added was also subject to the custom. In a judgment affirmed by the Court of Appeal FARWELL J said: 'A defendant may no doubt defeat a custom by showing that it could not have existed in the time of Richard I, but he must demonstrate its impossibility, and the onus is on him to do so if the existence of the custom has been proved for a long period.'

Midland Bank plc v Cooke [1995] 4 All ER 562 **[157]**
(Court of Appeal)

After their marriage in 1971, C and his wife moved into a house which C had purchased just before they married in his sole name. The house cost £8,500 and it was financed by way of a mortgage of £6,450 with the balance coming out of C's savings and a wedding gift of £1,100 from C's parents. In 1978, the mortgage was replaced by a general mortgage in favour of the plaintiff bank granted to C to secure repayment of the business overdraft of C's company, and his wife (W) signed a form of consent postponing any rights she might have in the property to the bank's security. In 1984, the property was transferred by conveyance into the joint names of C and his wife with them holding as tenants in common. In 1987, the bank commenced county court proceedings against C and his wife claiming payment of £52,491 due under the mortgage and possession in default of payment. W filed a defence asserting that her signature to the consent form had been obtained to the knowledge of the bank by C's undue influence and counterclaimed for a declaration that she was entitled to a one-half beneficial interest in the property overriding any interests of the bank under the mortgage. During the proceedings C and W testified that they had made no agreement as to the proportions of their beneficial interest in the home. The judge held that the bank had known of C's undue influence and that the consent was not binding on W and that her equitable interest took priority over the bank's claims. He further held that W's beneficial interest depended on her monetary contributions and accordingly she was entitled to a beneficial interest of 6.47 per cent in the property, being the proportion represented by her half-share of the wedding gift from C's parents (£550) to the total purchase price of the property (£8,500). W appealed contending that the judge had adopted the wrong approach to the quantification of her beneficial interest. From almost the outset of their marriage, both C and W had worked and while W did not make any contribution to the mortgage payments she had discharged other household outgoings and made a contribution to the improvement of the property. Further, W had remained in work throughout the marriage – with brief spells of part-time work when each of their children were born (ie W argued that the judge should have taken into account her 'maintenance and improvement' contribution). *Held*, the appeal would be allowed. Where a partner in a matrimonial home not on the legal title established an equitable interest through direct contribution to the purchase price of the property, the court would (in the absence of express evidence of intention) assess the proportions the parties were to be assumed to have intended for their beneficial ownership. The court would do this by looking at the whole course of dealing between the parties relevant to their ownership and occupation of the property and would not be confined *solely* to the financial contributions of the parties where the circumstances suggested that some other agreement as to shares in the property was appropriate. Positive evidence, as here, that the parties had neither discussed nor intended any agreement as to the proportions of their beneficial interest did not preclude the court from inferring one on general equitable principles. The judge had erred in treating W's cash contribution to the purchase price as wholly determinative of the issue of the current proportion of beneficial entitlement without regard to the other factors emerging from the whole course of dealing between C and W. Applying the correct approach as to quantification of beneficial interest to the instant facts it was clear that the parties presumed intention was to share the beneficial interest in the property in equal shares. 'One could hardly have a clearer example of a couple who had agreed to share everything equally: the profits of the business while it prospered and the risks of indebtedness suffered through its failure; the upbringing of their children; and a home into which over the years Mrs Cooke gave the benefit of the maintenance and improvement contribution' (*per* WAITE LJ). W was entitled to a beneficial half interest in the home and a declaration to that effect would be granted. (But see *Lloyds Bank plc v Rosset*).

Midleton's (Earl) Will Trusts, Re, Whitehead v Midleton (Earl) See Re St Albans' (Duke) Will Trusts, Coutts & Co v Beauclerk

Miller v Emcer Products Ltd [1956] 1 All ER 237   [158]
(Court of Appeal)

Four rooms on the ground floor of a house were demised for a term of years together with the right to use 'in common with the landlords and superior landlords and all persons authorised by them and the other tenants ... the lavatories on the first and second floors'. *Held*, the right to use the lavatories could be regarded as an easement which the landlords were professing to grant for a term of years, and such an easement would rank as an interest in or over land capable of being created at law by virtue of s1(2)(a) of the Law of Property Act 1925. 'It is true that during the times when the dominant owner exercised the right, the owner of the servient tenement would be excluded, but this in greater or less degree is a common feature of many easements (eg rights of way) and does not amount to such an ouster of the servient owner's rights as was held by UPJOHN J, to be incompatible with the legal easement in *Copeland* v *Greenhalf*' (*per* ROMER LJ).

Minister of Health v Bellotti [1944] 1 All ER 238   **[159]**
(Court of Appeal)

Evacuees from Gibraltar occupied premises at an evacuees' centre under licences from the Minister of Health. Differences arose between the evacuees, who were licensees for valuable consideration, and officials of the Ministry, and the evacuees were each given a week's notice to quit the premises they occupied. *Held*, a notice determining a licence revokes the licence immediately on service and the notice becomes operative on the expiration of a reasonable time from the date of service, even though the notice states a period of time for the vacation of the premises which is held to be too short. What is a 'reasonable time' for these purposes depends on the circumstances of a particular case and, in this case, the time limit was insufficient. (See also *Hurst* v *Picture Theatres Ltd*.)

Moody v Steggles (1879) LR 12 Ch D 261   **[160]**

The plaintiffs, the owners of the Grosvenor Arms, claimed the right to affix a sign-board, bearing the name of their public house, to the wall of the defendants' house. The sign-board had been so affixed for upwards of 40 years. *Held*, the easement claimed was a legal one, and a grant by the defendants' predecessors in title to the plaintiffs' predecessors in title would be presumed.

Mortgage Corporation Ltd v Nationwide Credit   **[161]**
Corporation Ltd [1993] 4 All ER 623 (Court of Appeal)

The registered proprietors of a residential property executed a legal charge (dated 10 July 1989) in favour of the plaintiffs (MCL) to secure an advance of £367,500 – the plaintiffs' charge. They then executed a second legal charge (dated 31 July 1989) in favour of the defendants (NCC) to secure an advance of £60,000 – the defendants' charge. The defendants entered a notice under s49 of the Land Registration Act 1925 on 14 August 1989 in the Charges Register of title. The plaintiffs took no steps to protect their mortgage. Crucially, neither mortgage was a registered charge (the defendants' charge was protected by notice under s49 but not registered). The plaintiffs subsequently obtained an order for possession against the registered proprietors and sold the property for £300,000. In view of the fact that the sale proceeds were insufficient to repay both parties in full, the defendants agreed to withdraw their s49 notice to facilitate completion of the sale and that the question of priority between the plaintiffs' and the defendants' charges would be determined post-completion by application to the court. The issue was whether the plaintiffs had priority as first in time or whether it was the defendants by virtue of the s49 notice. The judge at first instance held that the plaintiffs' charge had priority. The defendants appealed. *Held*, the appeal would be dismissed. There was no difficulty as to priority between registered charges because s29 of the Land Registration Act 1925 provided that such charges ranked in order of registration not order of creation. However, here neither mortgage was a registered charge. Rather, both mortgages were equitable minor interests. By virtue of s106 of the Land Registration Act 1925 (as substituted by the Administration of Justice Act 1977) a charge protected by a s49 notice, but not registered, was no longer capable of being overridden as a minor interest. However, it only took effect in equity unless and until it became a registered charge. Accordingly, the equitable rule as to priorities applied. The court then considered s52(1) of the Land Registration Act 1925. The aim of that subsection was to preserve the priority of a minor interest protected by a notice against a subsequent registered disposition. In particular it did not have the effect of creating priority over an earlier unprotected minor interest (ie it did not apply on these facts). Accordingly, the defendants' charge was overridden by the plaintiffs' charge by virtue of s106 of the 1925 Act.

Multiservice Bookbinding Ltd v Marden [1978] 2 All ER 489   [162]

In 1966, MB Ltd (the plaintiffs) borrowed £36,000 from M on a mortgage of their business premises to enable them to buy larger premises so that they could expand their business. Each side instructed separate solicitors who agreed a form of mortgage which was executed on 7 September 1966. The mortgage deed provided (1) that MB Ltd would pay interest at 2 per cent above bank rate on the full capital sum (ie £36,000) for the full duration of the mortgage notwithstanding capital repayments; (2) that arrears of interest would be capitalised after 21 days; (3) that the loan could not be called in or redeemed within the first ten years; and (4) in clause 6 that sums payable by way of principal or interest were to be increased or decreased proportionately if at the close of business of the day preceding the day on which payment was made the rate of exchange between the Swiss franc and the pound sterling should vary by more than 3 per cent from the rate of the Swiss franc to the pound sterling prevailing on 7 September 1966 (then there were 12 Swiss francs to the pound). Clause 6 meant that the value of the capital and interest would be index-linked to the Swiss franc. Unfortunately for MB Ltd in the decade which followed the pound greatly depreciated in value against the Swiss franc and in 1976 when MB Ltd wanted to redeem the mortgage there were just over four Swiss francs to the pound sterling (in 1966 the Swiss franc was worth less than 9p whereas in 1976 it was worth 25p). The effect of the mortgage provisions on the capital position was as follows – although just over £24,000 had by 1976 been repaid on capital account the repayments had operated to reduce the nominal amount of the debt by only £15,000 leaving £21,000 still to be discharged which, after adding the Swiss franc uplift, meant that an additional payment of just over £63,000 would be required with the result that M, who had advanced £36,000, would receive just over £87,500 in repayment of capital. The amount payable as interest over the ten years under the provisions of the mortgage (high minimum lending rate plus clause 6) amounted to £45,380, including £14,319 under the Swiss franc index-linking clause, which meant that the average rate of interest over the ten year period was 16.01 per cent. MB Ltd contended that clause 6 was void either on the ground that it was contrary to public policy or that it was unconscionable and a clog on the equity. *Held*, MB Ltd were bound to comply with all the terms of the mortgage. There was nothing contrary to public policy in the index-linking arrangement. The test of the enforceability of the terms of the mortgage was not whether they were reasonable but whether they were unfair and unconscionable. A bargain would only be held to be unfair and unconscionable where it was shown that one of the parties to it had imposed objectionable terms in a morally reprehensible way. Here there was nothing oppressive or morally reprehensible in the terms of the mortgage and the parties were of equal bargaining strength. M had struck a hard bargain but he had done nothing that he was not entitled to do. 'The parties made a bargain which the plaintiffs, who are businessmen, went into with their eyes open, with the benefit of independent advice, without any compelling necessity to accept a loan on these terms and without any sharp practice by the defendant. I cannot see that there was anything unfair or oppressive or morally reprehensible in such a bargain entered into in such circumstances' (*per* BROWNE-WILKINSON J). MB Ltd did not have to accept the £36,000 on the terms offered. Finally, the court noted that the value of the property in question had more than doubled during the term of the mortgage and MB Ltd's growth had been considerable. (Applied: *Knightsbridge Estates Trust Ltd* v *Byrne*; see also *Cityland & Property (Holdings) Ltd* v *Dabrah*.)

National and Provincial Building Society v Lloyd   **[163]**
[1996] 1 All ER 630 (Court of Appeal)

In 1992, L (the defendant) borrowed £280,000 by way of mortgage from N & P (the plaintiffs) on the security of a farm in Cardigan and another property in Dorset. He soon fell into arrears with his mortgage repayments and N & P sought possession of both charged properties. By the date of the hearing in March 1995 L owed about £335,000 including the principal debt. He gave evidence that he had sold part of the farm property for £155,000 and had an offer of £44,000 for the Dorset property, and that it was likely that what he would raise from the sale of the rest of his farmland would more than cover his debts. Nevertheless the deputy district judge made an order for possession. L applied to have the order suspended. At the hearing in May 1995, L gave evidence that of his mortgaged land that remained unsold the main portion (including four barns) could be sold for at least £100,000, that he had received an offer of £57,500 in respect of another portion which was expected to reach completion in a little over a year, and that the purchaser of the farm had an option to buy more land for £13,000. Section 36 of the Administration of Justice Act 1970 (as amended) empowered the court in the exercise of its discretion to suspend an order for the possession of mortgaged property (consisting of or including a dwelling-house) if there was sufficient evidence to enable it to conclude that the borrower was likely to be able to pay any sums due under the mortgage within a reasonable period. MCKINNEY J sitting in Bournemouth county court found that s36 of the 1970 Act applied and the possession order was suspended. N & P appealed arguing that (1) an order for possession of mortgaged property could only be suspended if the sale was to take place within a short period of time; and (2) on the facts here there was insufficient evidence about the three unsold portions of land to have entitled the judge to make the finding that she did. *Held*, the appeal would be allowed. There was no rule of law to the effect that an order for possession of mortgaged property would only be suspended if the sale would take place within a short period of time. If there was clear evidence that the completion of a property sale, perhaps by piecemeal disposal, could take place within six months to a year there was no reason why a court could not conclude in the exercise of its discretion under s36 of the 1970 Act that the borrower was 'likely to be able within a reasonable period to pay any sums due under the mortgage'. However, the sale need not be in the immediate future provided the terms of s36 were satisfied. The question of what was a 'reasonable period' to wait for the sale (and thus payment of the moneys due) would be a question for the court in each individual case (ie it would depend upon the facts of each case). Here, however, the evidence adduced by L had been insufficient to entitle the judge to make the suspension order. Much of the evidence was nothing more than a mere expression of hope. On the facts the only way in which L would be able to pay the money which was owing under the mortgage would be if the £100,000 or more which could be secured from the sale of the barns was taken into account. However, there was insufficient specific evidence about the barns to have enabled the judge to conclude that it was likely that L would be able within a reasonable period to pay the moneys due under the mortgage. Accordingly, the suspension order would be revoked. (See also *Birmingham Citizens Permanent Building Society* v *Caunt.*)

National Carriers Ltd v Panalpina (Northern) Ltd   **[164]**
[1981] 1 All ER 161 (House of Lords)

On 1 January 1974, NC Ltd let a warehouse in Hull to P Ltd for a term of ten years (ie the term was to expire on 31 December 1983) at an annual rent of £6,500 for the first five years and £3,300 for the second five years. The only access to the warehouse was along Kingston Street, a public highway, along which NC Ltd purported to grant a right of way for all purposes connected with the occupation of the premises. On 18 May 1979, the local authority closed Kingston Street because a derelict warehouse opposite the leased warehouse was in a dangerous condition. Since the derelict warehouse was a 'listed' building the local authority was required to apply to the Secretary of State for the Environment for consent to demolish it. After a public inquiry the Secretary of State gave his consent in March 1980. The estimated date for completion of the demolition was late December 1980 or early January 1981 when Kingston Street would be re-opened. The closure of Kingston Street prevented P Ltd from using the warehouse for the only purpose contemplated by the lease, viz as a warehouse. From 18 May 1979, P Ltd ceased to pay rent (ie from the time Kingston Street was closed). In July 1979, NC Ltd issued a writ for two quarters' rent due and unpaid. P Ltd filed a defence claiming that they were not liable to pay the rent because the closure of Kingston Street had frustrated the lease. NC Ltd applied for summary judgment under RSC Order 14. The Master gave judgment for them and the judge dismissed P Ltd's appeal holding that the doctrine of frustration could not apply to a lease. However, leave was given to P Ltd to appeal directly to the House of Lords under s12 of the Administration of Justice Act 1969. *Held*, the appeal would be dismissed. The doctrine of frustration was capable of applying to a lease so as to bring the lease to an end if a frustrating event (ie an event such that no substantial use permitted by the lease and in the contemplation of the parties remained possible to the tenant) occurred during the term. There was no class of lease to which the doctrine was 'inherently inapplicable'. However, the circumstances in which the doctrine of frustration could apply to a lease were exceedingly rate ('hardly ever rather than never'). Here the loss of under two years out of a total of ten years, though severe for P Ltd, was not sufficient to frustrate the lease. There would be a further three years of the lease remaining after access was re-established. The loss of the two years did not alter significantly the nature of the rights and obligations that had been contemplated by the parties at the time when the lease was granted. Accordingly, P Ltd, had no defence to the action. (See also *Cricklewood Property and Investment Trust Ltd* v *Leighton's Investment Trust Ltd.*)

Neeld, Re, Carpenter v Inigo-Jones [1962] 2 All ER 335   **[165]**
(Court of Appeal)

Certain farms and parcels of land specifically devised by clause 3 of the testator's will were all part of the Neeld or Grittleton estates, the residue of which were by express description included in the residuary devise and bequest in clause 14 of the will which devise and bequest was 'subject to and after payment out of my personal estate or in the case of deficiency thereof out of my real estate of my funeral and testamentary expenses and debts and the legacies and annuities bequeathed by this my will'. At the date of the will the Grittleton estate was not subject to any substantial charge, but subsequently the testator created a charge on the whole of the estate in the sum of £25,000. This charge was outstanding at the testator's death: should repayment of the sum secured be borne entirely by residue or should the part of the Grittleton estate specifically devised by clause 3 bear its rateable proportion? *Held*, on a true construction of the will and of s35 of the Administration of Estates Act 1925, the testator had not 'signified a contrary ... intention' for the purposes of that section, and it followed that the properties specifically devised by clause 3 of the testator's will should bear a proportionate part of the charge of £25,000. (See also *Re Wakefield, Gordon* v *Wakefield*.)

Newman v Real Estate Debenture Corporation Ltd   [166]
[1940] 1 All ER 131

A building was let off in flats and, with the exception of the ground floor, the tenant of each flat covenanted that he would use the flat for residential purposes only. The landlord leased the whole of the building to another company, subject to the lease in favour of the tenant of the fourth and fifth floors, for business purposes, and the making of necessary structural alterations, and the way in which the business was carried on, caused much annoyance and inconvenience to the tenant of the fourth and fifth floors. *Held*, it had been established that there was a scheme which imposed, inter alia, an obligation on the landlord not to let the other parts of the premises for purposes other than residential, nor to permit any other tenant to do anything which might cause annoyance to the tenant of the fourth and fifth floors and, by letting the remainder of the building for business purposes, and because of the nuisance created during alterations, the landlord was in breach of his implied covenant not to derogate from the grant to the tenant of the fourth and fifth floors as, in view of his act, those parts of the premises had become materially less fit for the purposes for which they were let, ie residential purposes. The other company was similarly in breach of the same implied covenant because of the nuisance created by the way in which its business was conducted. (But see *Kelly* v *Battershell*.)

Nisbet and Potts' Contract, Re [1906] 1 Ch 386   [167]
(Court of Appeal)

In 1872 K entered into a restrictive covenant with a neighbour providing that no buildings other than private houses should be erected on K's land. H obtained title to K's land by adverse possession and in 1878 sold the land to N. In 1903 N agreed to sell the land to P. P agreed not to require any evidence of N's title to the land beyond his conveyance from H. This conveyance did not disclose the existence of the covenant, but if P had made enquiry as to title for the full statutory period (then 40 years) he would have discovered the existence of the covenant. P wished to build shops on the land. The question arose whether the covenant could be enforced against him. *Held*, a restrictive covenant can be enforced against any subsequent owner of the land except a bona fide purchaser for value of the legal estate without notice. Such a covenant is enforceable against a squatter, both before and after he has acquired a statutory title by adverse possession. If a purchaser from a person who has acquired such a statutory title chooses to accept evidence of title for a shorter period than the statutory period he is fixed with constructive notice of all equitable interests which he would have discovered if he had made enquiries for the full period. P was therefore bound by the covenant.

Northumberland (Duke), Re See Brougham and Vaux's (Lord)
Settled Estates, Re

Orlebar, Re, Orlebar v Orlebar [1936] 1 Ch 147 [168]

A strict settlement of the Crawley Estate provided that if the tenant for life should fail to reside at Crawley House for at least six months (either continuous or discontinuous) in every year his 'estate ... shall cease and determine'. *Held*, if the tenant for life sold Crawley House under his Settled Land Act powers the condition of residence would be inoperative: see s106 of the 1925 Act. (See also *Re Herbert, Herbert* v *Lord Bicester.*)

Ough v King [1967] 3 All ER 859 (Court of Appeal) [169]

The plaintiff was entitled to rights of light ('ancient lights') in respect of a room on the ground floor of her house where she worked as a minister of the United Fundamentalist Church: the defendant extended his house (it was separated from the plaintiff's by a passage six feet wide) and thereby diminished the amount of light to the plaintiff's ground floor room by about one-fifth. Half the room remained adequately lit, but the trial judge found that the room received less light after the defendant's alteration than was sufficient according to the ordinary notions of mankind. The learned judge awarded the plaintiff £300 damages in lieu of an injunction, assessing the damages as the difference in the value of the house before and after the infringement. *Held*, the amount of damages was assessed on the right basis and should not be disturbed. In determining whether there was an infringement of the plaintiff's right to light the court was entitled to have regard to the locality and to the higher standard of lighting at the present day and was not confined to a rule that so long as half a room was adequately lit there was no infringement. 'It is not every diminution of light which gives an action. It is only when it is so diminished as to be a nuisance. It means that the defendant was not allowed to build next door in such a way as to deprive the plaintiff of the light coming to her room so as to make it uncomfortable according to the ordinary notions of mankind' (*per* LORD DENNING MR). (See also *Allen* v *Greenwood.*)

Owen v Gadd [1956] 2 All ER 28 (Court of Appeal) [170]

A lease of a lock-up shop contained a covenant by the lessors that the lessee 'shall and may peaceably and quietly hold and enjoy the ... premises ... without any lawful interruption or disturbance from or by the lessors'. The lessors erected scaffold poles immediately in front of the shop in order to carry out necessary repairs to the upper part of the premises which they occupied: the poles remained in position for 11 days and interfered with the lessee's trade. *Held*, the lessee was entitled to damages for breach of the covenant for quiet enjoyment.

Palk v Mortgage Services Funding plc [1993] 2 All ER 481 [171]
(Court of Appeal)

In 1990 a husband borrowed £300,000 from the defendants which was secured by way of mortgage over a house which he jointly owned with his wife. After the husband's company failed, the couple decided to sell the house. They negotiated a sale of it for £283,000. However, the defendants refused to agree to this sale because the aforementioned price would not pay off the debt (the amount needed to redeem the mortgage, including arrears, was just over £358,000). Further, the defendants had secured a suspended order for possession and were hoping to let the property in order to generate income pending an upturn in the housing market, when they would sell it. Of central significance to the case was the fact that the sum due under the mortgage was rising by about £43,000 per year whereas the projected income from letting was between £13,000 to £14,000 a year. The plaintiffs applied for a sale order. Their application was dismissed at first instance. The wife appealed. *Held*, the appeal would be allowed. The court had an unfettered discretion under s91(2) of the Law of Property Act 1925 to order a sale of mortgaged property (at the instance of any interested person) even against the wishes of the mortgagee. The fact that the mortgagee was not in breach of any duty owed by it to the mortgagor was only one of the factors to have regard to. In the exceptional circumstances of the case, it was just and equitable to order a sale (even though a significant amount of the debt would remain outstanding and unsecured) because otherwise unfairness and injustice would ensue. (See also *Target Homes Loans Ltd v Clothier.*)

Palmer (deceased) (a debtor), Re [1994] 3 All ER 835   **[172]**
(Court of Appeal)

In 1989 P, a solicitor, together with his wife bought a property as joint tenants. Following allegations of serious misconduct the Law Society commenced inquiries into the conduct of P's practice, but before these inquiries were completed P died on 22 November 1990. At his death there were substantial claims against his estate by former clients of the deceased's firm and the Inland Revenue which could only be met if P's share of the jointly owned property devolved as part of his estate rather than passing to his wife under the principle of survivorship. In consequence of the deceased's indebtedness his executor obtained in 1991 an insolvency administration order under the Administration of Insolvent Estates of Deceased Persons Order 1986 (the Order was made under s421 of the Insolvency Act 1986). The respondent was appointed trustee of the estate and he sought a declaration under s283 of the Insolvency Act 1986 as modified by Schedule 1 of the 1986 Order that his title to P's estate operated retrospectively so as to take effect before P died (if correct this would have severed the joint tenancy before P died thus creating a tenancy in common with the result that the deceased's share would devolve to the estate and thus provide assets for the creditors). Under s283 of the 1986 Act as modified a deceased debtor's estate comprised 'all property belonging to [him] or his personal representative ... at the date of the insolvency administration order', while under para 12 of Schedule 1 to the 1986 Order the administration order was to be taken as being made 'on the date of death of the deceased debtor'. VINELOTT J granted the declaration sought. He concluded that (1) the insolvency administration order was to be treated as being made on the date of death (legislative fiction); and (2) according to judicial fiction the order was to be taken as being made on the first moment of that day. By combining the legislative fiction and the judicial fiction he concluded that the order had been made before P died and thus the joint tenancy had been severed before death so that an undivided half share devolved as part of P's estate. P's widow appealed. *Held*, the appeal would be allowed. The rule that a judicial act was presumed to have been made on the first moment of the day when it was done and took precedence over other non-judicial acts on the same day (judicial fiction) could not be allowed to operate so as to render a statutory instrument ultra vires primary legislation. Here the judge had wrongly combined the judicial fiction and the legislative fiction to reach the conclusion that the insolvency order had been made before P died. That construction rendered the 1986 Order ultra vires because the administration order would then go beyond what was sanctioned by s421 of the 1986 Act – namely making an order dealing with the insolvent estate of a deceased person. The 1986 Act clearly referred to the estate of a 'deceased person'. Nothing in the 1986 Act altered the ordinary meaning of the 'estate of a deceased person' which in the case of the estate of a deceased joint tenant did not include his unsevered interest under a beneficial joint tenancy since that passed by the principle of survivorship to the surviving joint tenant and did not pass to his personal representative or form part of his estate. It was not possible to use the

1986 Order in combination with the judicial fiction to make an insolvency administration order applicable to the property of a person who had not yet died. On the proper application of the 1986 Act and the 1986 Order the insolvency administration order took effect at the moment when P died and not on the first moment of the day he died. This meant that when P died the joint tenancy had not been severed because the insolvency administration order only became effective then. Accordingly, since P's interest in the joint tenancy had passed by survivorship at the moment of his death to his widow it never formed part of his estate and was not affected by the insolvency administration order. (But see *Re Dennis (a bankrupt)*.)

Parker v British Airways Board [1982] 1 All ER 834   [173]
(Court of Appeal)

P was in the international executive lounge at London airport as a passenger waiting for a British Airways flight. The lounge was leased by the airline from the British Airports Authority. P found a gold bracelet on the floor of the lounge. He handed it to an employee of the airline, gave his name and address and asked for the bracelet to be returned to him if it was not claimed by the owner. The bracelet was not claimed. However, instead of returning it to P, British Airways sold it for £850 and retained the proceeds. P sued BAB for the value of the bracelet. The county court judge awarded him the amount of the proceeds of sale (£850) as damages plus interest. BAB appealed. *Held*, the appeal would be dismissed. A finder of a chattel who was not a trespasser acquired a right to keep it against all but the true owner if the chattel had been lost or abandoned and if he took it into his care and control. Here P had acted honestly and discharged his obligations as a finder. He had acquired rights of possession except as against the true owner. His rights could only be replaced by those of BAB if they could show as occupiers an obvious intention to exercise such control over the passenger lounge and all articles in it so as to acquire rights of possession over the bracelet *before* P found it (ie land would only include a chattel found on it when the occupier was exercising rights of possession over it). On the facts they had not done so. BAB had shown neither an intention to exercise control over lost chattels in their lounge nor an intention that permission to enter granted to travelling members of the public was, on the basis, that the commonly understood maxim 'finders keepers' would not apply. Accordingly, P's right as finder of the bracelet against all but the true owner prevailed over the airline's rights as occupiers of the premises where the bracelet was found. (Applied: *Armory v Delamirie*; but see *Elwes v Brigg Gas Co*.)

Parker's Settled Estates, Re, Parker v Parker [1928] 1 Ch 247   [174]

A legal estate in fee simple in land was vested in trustees upon trust to sell, but subject to a wife's jointure rent-charge, which was not yet an interest in possession, and subject to a term of 1,000 years to secure portions not yet raisable, and the land was accordingly subject to a compound settlement. What was the position after the coming into force of the Settled Land Act 1925 and the Law of Property Act 1925? *Held*, notwithstanding the trust for sale and s1(7) of the Settled Land Act 1925, as amended, the land was settled land under a compound settlement within s1(1)(i) of the 1925 Act. 'The words "trust for sale", when used in reference to land that is subject to a prior equitable interest, are not confined to cases where that equitable interest can be overreached by the trustees ... the word ['binding'] may quite conceivably have been inserted to meet the case of a revocable trust for sale, ... and even if this be not so I should prefer to treat the word as mere surplusage' (*per* ROMER J).

Pascoe v Turner [1979] 2 All ER 945 (Court of Appeal) **[175]**

In the early 1960s P, a businessman of some substance, met and became friendly with T, a widow. In 1963 T moved into P's home as his housekeeper and also began helping him with his business. Subsequently, they lived as man and wife. In 1965 P bought another house for himself and T to live in. P alone paid for the house and its contents and the house was conveyed into his name alone. T bought her own clothes and various small things for the house and continued to help P in his business. In 1973 P began a relationship with another woman with whom he subsequently went to live. T remained in the house bought in 1965. P assured T that she had nothing to worry about and told her on several occasions that 'the house is yours and everything in it'. Further, he repeated this assurance about the house and its contents to others. However, no conveyance was ever drawn up nor was there anything in writing. Relying on P's assurance and with his full knowledge and encouragement T spent money on redecorations, improvements and repairs to the house. In particular she purchased a gas fire and a cooker, installed a new sink, fitted carpets and bought curtains. In 1976 P and T quarrelled and his solicitor wrote to T giving her two months' notice 'to determine her licence to occupy' the house. T refused to leave the house and P brought proceedings to recover possession. T counterclaimed for a declaration that the house and its contents were hers and that P held the house on trust for her or that P had given her a licence to occupy the house for life and claimed that P was estopped from denying the trust or the licence. A possession action in the county court was dismissed. The judge found both that P had made a gift of the house contents to T and that the beneficial interest in the house had passed under a constructive trust inferred from the words and conduct of the parties. P appealed. *Held*, the appeal would be dismissed. There had been a complete gift of the contents of the house because T was already in possession of them as bailee when P declared the gift. However, the gift of the house was incomplete because of the absence of writing to satisfy the formality requirements of ss52–54 of the Law of Property Act 1925. T could not claim a constructive trust because there was no common intention. However, P had given an assurance to T and as a result of it she had spent money doing substantial work in or about the property between 1973 and 1976 with P's encouragement and acquiescence. Accordingly, P would be *estopped* from asserting his legal rights to the property. The court had to decide what was the minimum equity to do justice to T. Their Lordships felt that they had two alternatives: either they could declare that T had a licence to occupy the house for life or they could order P to transfer the fee simple of the house to her. In all the circumstances the equity to which the facts gave rise could only be satisfied by requiring P to give effect to his promise and T's expectations and perfect the gift by conveying the fee simple of the house to her. Such a remedy would obviously give T security of tenure which was important here because of T's age and P's determination to evict her if at all possible. Accordingly, the judge's order would be varied by declaring that the fee simple of the house was vested in T. (See also *Crabb* v *Arun District Council*.)

Patten, Re, Westminster Bank Ltd v Carlyon [1929] 2 Ch 276 **[176]**

A testator set aside £3,000 to maintain and pay outgoings in respect of his house which his aunt (the person having the powers of a tenant for life under s20(1)(iv) of the Settled Land Act 1925) could occupy during her life or so long as she might require it 'but without the power to sublet the same or any part thereof; on the termination of her occupation the house is to be sold' and the proceeds of sale added to certain charitable bequests. *Held*, the provision forbidding subletting was void by virtue of s106(1) of the Settled Land Act 1925 and the gift over of the proceeds of sale could take effect only on her ceasing to reside in the premises for any reason other than the exercise of her powers of leasing as a tenant for life. (See also *Re Orlebar, Orlebar* v *Orlebar.*)

Pembery v Lamdin [1940] 2 All ER 434   [177]

A landlord let certain premises for 16 years 4 months and 10 days and covenanted to 'keep the external part of the premises in good tenantable repair and condition'. The tenant maintained that, under the covenant, the landlord was liable to waterproof the outside walls, and so render the premises dry. *Held*, this was not the case as the obligation on the landlord was only to keep the premises in repair in the condition in which they were demised and, as they were old premises, he was not liable to do more than point the brickwork. 'The obligation of the landlord is to repair that which is demised, and not to give [the tenant] something much drier in its nature than that which was demised' (*per* SLESSER LJ). (But see *Summers* v *Salford Corporation.*)

Pennell v Payne [1995] 2 All ER 592 (Court of Appeal)   [178]

In 1971 the tenant entered into an agreement for the tenancy of a farm. One of the terms of the tenancy (which was an agricultural holding within the Agricultural Holdings Act 1986) prohibited the tenant from subletting the land without the landlord's consent. In 1991 the tenant entered into a transaction (a sub-lease) with a company for the working of the farm without the landlord's consent. Thereafter the landlord served a notice to quit on the tenant relying on s26(2) of and Case E in Part I of Schedule 3 to the 1986 Act (this allows a notice to quit to have effect without the consent of an agricultural land tribunal where the landlord's interest in the holding has been materially prejudiced by the tenant committing an irremediable breach of covenant). The notice to quit was referred to arbitration. An arbitrator found that the sub-tenancy had caused material prejudice to the landlord. The Recorder upheld the arbitrator's decision. Further, in respect of the issue of material prejudice, he ruled that the landlord might at some future date be forced into a direct relationship with the sub-tenant if the tenant served an upwards notice to quit on the landlord thereby bringing the head lease to an end at which point the sub-lease (albeit unlawful) would become binding on the landlord. The tenant appealed on the basis that the Recorder's decision was wrong in law and that there was no material prejudice for the purposes of Case E. *Held*, the appeal would be allowed. The sole issue on appeal was whether if a head tenant served an upwards notice to quit on the landlord would this automatically bring the sub-tenancy to an end or would it force the landlord into a relationship with the sub-tenant? The general rule was that upon a head lease coming to an end, a sub-lease deriving from it would also come to an end, ie the landlord was entitled to possession of the land and was not bound by any sub-leases. The remedy of the sub-tenant in such a situation was in damages against the tenant. A notice to quit did not create a direct relationship of landlord and tenant between the occupying sub-tenant and the landlord and as a result the head tenant's breach of covenant (in sub-letting the farm without the landlord's consent) had caused no material prejudice to the landlord for the purpose of Case E of the 1986 Act. Accordingly, it followed that the landlord's notice to quit required the tribunal's consent to its operation.

Petrie, Re, Lloyds Bank Ltd v Royal National Institute for the Blind [1961] 3 All ER 1067 (Court of Appeal)   [179]

The testatrix gave the residue of her estate on trust, after payment of her debts and funeral and testamentary expenses, for her two brothers absolutely and she directed her trustees that if both brothers should predecease her without leaving issue they should realise and divide the residue of her estate among certain charities, including, as part thereof, 'any national appeal to the public which may exist in the United Kingdom at the time when the residue of my estate is realised … for contributions for research into … rheumatoid arthritis'. The will did not contain an express power to postpone conversion; both brothers predeceased the testatrix without leaving issue and the estate consisted of cash, money on deposit with a building society and investments. It was contended that the gift in favour of 'any national appeal' was void since the beneficiary might not have to be ascertained until a date after the expiration of 21 years from the testatrix's death; in other words, that the realisation of the testatrix's estate might be held up for an indefinite period. *Held*, the gift did not infringe the rule against perpetuities as the words 'at the time when the residue of my estate is realised' were to be construed, having regard to the facts of the testatrix's estate, as referring to the date of completion of the administration of the estate in the ordinary course or the expiration of the executor's year (see s44 of the Administration of Estates Act 1925), whichever should first happen.

Phillips v Lamdin [1949] 1 All ER 770   **[180]**

After contracts had been exchanged for the sale of the defendant's house to the plaintiff the defendant removed an ornate door matching a mantelpiece which was attributed to the design of one of the brothers Adams, and replaced it by one of plain white wood. *Held*, the defendant was in breach of his duty to take reasonable care to preserve the property pending completion and, as damages could not be an adequate remedy, he should return the door and pay the expenses of so doing.

Phipps v Pears [1964] 2 All ER 35 (Court of Appeal)   **[181]**

Two houses, 14 and 16 Market Street, Warwick, were owned by a Mr Field and in about 1930 he pulled down No 16 and built a new house with its flank wall flat up against and touching the wall of No 14, although the two walls were not bonded together. In 1962 the then owners of No 14, the defendants, demolished the property and thus left exposed the flank wall of the new No 16 which, because of the position in which it was built, had never been pointed, rendered or plastered. As the wall was not weatherproof, rain got in and during the winter froze and caused cracks and the then owner of No 16, the plaintiff, sought damages maintaining that the defendants had infringed his right of protection from the weather. *Held*, his claim would fail as there was no such easement known to the law as an easement to be protected from the weather. Further, protection from the weather was not one of the 'advantages' which passed to the plaintiff under s62 of the Law of Property Act 1925, because any such advantage must be one which is known to the law in the sense that it is capable of being granted at law so as to be binding on all successors in title, even those who take without notice, and protection from the weather was not such an advantage. (Applied: *Wright* v *Macadam*; but see *Goldberg* v *Edward* and *Ward* v *Kirkland*.)

Poole's Case (1703) 1 Salk 368   **[182]**

A tenant of a house in Holborn, a soap-boiler by trade, for the convenience of his trade installed vats and other equipment. *Held*, 'during the term the soap-boiler might well remove the vats … and … he might do it by the common law … But after the term they become a gift in law to him in reversion, and are not removable' (*per* HOLT CJ). (See also *Smith* v *City Petroleum Co Ltd*; but see *Buckland* v *Butterfield*.)

Property and Bloodstock Ltd v Emerton [1967] 3 All ER 321   **[183]**
(Court of Appeal)

Was a mortgagee's duly made contract for sale of mortgaged leasehold premises
(the mortgagee's power of sale having arisen) prevented from terminating the
mortgagor's right of redemption by a condition under its special conditions of sale
that 'the sale is subject to the vendor obtaining the consent of the' lessor to the
assignment of the lease to the purchaser? *Held*, the obtaining of the landlord's
consent was not a condition precedent to the formation of a contract of sale and
creation of the relation of vendor and purchaser between the mortgagee and the
purchaser (the landlord's consent had to be obtained by the date at which title had
in fact to be established) and, as an unconditional contract for sale by a mortgagee
precluded the mortgagor's right of redemption, the lessee had been precluded
since the date of the contract from exercising the right of redemption. (But see
Eccles v *Bryant*.)

Prudential Assurance Co Ltd v London Residuary Body   **[184]**
[1992] 3 WLR 279 (House of Lords)

Prior to 1930 the plaintiffs' predecessor in title owned land with a street frontage
on which there were commercial premises. In 1930 the then London County
Council in its capacity as a highway authority purchased a strip of the land along
the street frontage for future road widening. The LCC then purported to lease it
back to the plaintiffs' predecessor in title at a yearly rent of £30 under an
agreement which in clause 6 stated that 'the tenancy shall continue until ... the
land is required by the Council for the purposes of ... [road widening]'. Over 60
years later the highway had still not been widened and the reversion was now
vested in the first defendant, the London Residuary Body (the successor in title to
the LCC). The LRB agreed to sell the strip of land in question to the second, third
and fourth defendants (a company and two private individuals) and their freehold
title was subsequently vested in these defendants. None of the defendants was a
highway authority with road-widening powers. Prior to the sale, LRB served a six
months' notice to quit on the plaintiffs purporting to end the tenancy. The rental
value of the land was estimated to be over £10,000 per annum. The plaintiffs
sought a declaration that the notice to quit was null and void because they argued
that the tenancy could only be determined if the land was required for road-
widening purposes in accordance with clause 6 of the agreement. The judge held
that the tenancy had been brought to an end by the notice to quit. The Court of
Appeal reversed his decision on appeal and granted the declarations sought. The
second to fourth defendants appealed to the House of Lords. *Held*, the appeal
would be allowed. All leases must be certain in duration. Here the 1930 agreement
did not create an estate in land because it purported to grant a term of uncertain
duration (until the land was required by the Council for the purposes of widening
the road). However, because the tenant had entered into possession pursuant to
the agreement and paid the yearly rent reserved by the agreement they had
become a tenant from year to year and only those terms in the 1930 agreement
which were consistent with a yearly tenancy would apply (ie a tenant who entered
under a void lease became by virtue of possession and the payment of a yearly
rent a yearly tenant). A yearly tenancy was determinable by either party at the end
of the first or any subsequent year of the tenancy by six months' notice. A tenancy
from year to year (a periodic tenancy) was saved from being *uncertain* because
each party had the power by notice to determine at the end of any year. 'The term
continues until determined as if both parties made a new agreement at the end of
each year for a new term for the ensuing year' (per LORD TEMPLEMAN). Accordingly,
the rule that a lease must be certain or capable of being made certain at the outset
of the term did apply to periodic tenancies. Here the term relating to road

widening was inconsistent with the ability of either party to determine a yearly tenancy on six months' notice and, as a result, the plaintiffs' tenancy had been lawfully determined by the notice to quit served by LRB. (See also *Lace v Chandler* and *Ashburn Anstalt v Arnold*.)

Quennell v Maltby [1979] 1 WLR 318 (Court of Appeal)   [185]

Q owned a house worth more than £30,000. In 1973 he let it to M and another student for one year expiring on 31 December 1974. In August 1974, Q mortgaged the house to his bank to secure a loan of £2,500. The mortgage prohibited the creation of any lettings during the continuance of the security without the written consent of the bank. On 1 December 1974, without the bank's consent, Q relet the house for another year to two other students. On the expiration of that year, Q again without the bank's consent let the house for another year to M and L (the defendants). From 1 December 1976 onwards M and L became statutory tenants under the Rent Acts. Q wanted to sell his house with vacant possession. Accordingly, he asked the bank to bring possession proceedings against M and L because the tenancy was not binding on the bank. The bank refused to do so having ample security. After Q consulted his lawyers, his wife paid off the bank and the benefit of the mortgage was transferred to her by the bank. Q's wife then, as successor in title of the bank, brought an action for possession against M and L. The judge made a possession order. M and L appealed. *Held*, the appeal would be allowed. The court was entitled to look behind the formal legal relationship of the parties since a mortgagee would not be granted possession unless it was sought bona fide and reasonably for the purpose of enforcing the security. Here Q's wife had not brought the action to enforce payment of any amount due under the mortgage or to protect her security. Rather she had an ulterior motive – to help her husband obtain vacant possession and thus defeat the protection enjoyed by the tenants under the Rent Acts. In such circumstances, she was to be regarded as Q's agent and since Q as landlord could not obtain a possession order against M and L as they had a statutory tenancy protected by the Rent Acts his wife was not entitled to a possession order. (See also *Birmingham Citizens Permanent Building Society v Caunt*.)

Race v Ward (1855) 4 E & B 702   [186]

The defendants sought to rely on an immemorial custom for the inhabitants of a township to take water from a well or spring on the plaintiff's land to their houses to be used there for domestic purposes. *Held*, the custom would be upheld: water from a spring was not 'part of the soil, like sand, or clay, or stones, nor the produce of the soil, like grass, or turves, or trees. A right to take these by custom, claimed by all the inhabitants of the district, would clearly be bad; for they all come under the category of profit à prendre, being part of the soil or the produce of the soil ... But the spring of water is supplied and renewed by nature ... While it remains in the field where it issues forth (ie until contained in a cistern or vessel in which the owner of the land has placed it for his private use], in the absence of any servitude or custom giving a right to others, the owner of the field, and he only, has a right to appropriate it ... but when it has left his field, he has no more power over it, or interest in it, than any other stranger' (*per* LORD CAMPBELL CJ). (See also *Chasemore v Richards*.)

Regis Property Co Ltd v Dudley [1958] 3 All ER 491   [187]
(House of Lords)

In an agreement in writing for a monthly tenancy the tenant undertook to keep 'the interior of the flat together with all the fixtures and fittings ... in good and substantial repair and clean sanitary condition (fair wear and tear ... excepted)'. *Held*, this exception did not except the tenant from responsibility for taking steps to avoid further damage deriving from a defect of repair which itself was originally due to fair wear and tear. 'If a slate falls off through wear and tear and in consequence the roof is likely to let through the water, the tenant is not responsible for the slate coming off but he ought to put in another one to prevent further damage' (*per* LORD DENNING MR). (But see *Warren* v *Keen*.)

Reilly v Orange [1955] 2 All ER 369 (Court of Appeal)   **[188]**

In 1934 (the exact date was uncertain) the parties owned adjoining plots of land and the plaintiff allowed the defendant a means of access to his garage over his (the plaintiff's) land until such time as the defendant made a new access over his own land. The defendant having constructed such new access in 1953 the plaintiff gave him notice purporting to terminate the right over the plaintiff's land and in 1954 commenced proceedings for a declaration that the defendant's right had been determined. *Held*, as the defendant had not proved uninterrupted enjoyment of the right for a full period of 20 years before action brought he had failed to establish a title by prescription to the right of way and the plaintiff was entitled to his declaration. The commencement of the action was not an interruption within s4 of the Prescription Act 1832 which, if it were to be effective under that section to interrupt a period of enjoyment, would have to be submitted to or acquiesced in for one year. (See also *Swan* v *Sinclair*.)

Renals v Cowlishaw (1879) 11 Ch D 866 (Court of Appeal)   **[189]**

In 1845 the fee simple owners of a residential estate (the Mill Hill Estate) and adjoining land sold part of the adjoining land to S who entered into covenants restricting his right to build on and use the purchased land. The covenants were made with 'the vendors their heirs executors administrators and assigns'. In 1854 the same fee simple owners sold and conveyed the Mill Hill Estate to B. However, the latter conveyance contained no reference to the restrictive covenants, nor was there any contract or representation that B was to have the benefit of them. Subsequently B died and his devisees in trust in 1870 sold and conveyed the Mill House Estate to R. Ultimately the adjoining land initially bought by S became vested in C who wanted to build in contravention of the restrictive covenants entered into by S. R sought to restrain C from so acting. HALL VC concluded that the benefit of the restrictive covenants had not been annexed to the Mill Hill Estate. R appealed. *Held*, the appeal would be dismissed. The wording of the conveyance by which the adjoining land was passed to S was not sufficient to bring about an annexation of the benefit to the vendor's retained land (ie the Mill Hill Estate) because no reference had been made in the covenants to the land which was intended to receive the benefit. 'There was nothing in the deed of conveyance defining the property for the benefit of which the restrictive covenants were entered into' (*per* JAMES LJ). (But see *Rogers* v *Hosegood*.)

Reynolds v Ashby & Son [1904] AC 466 (House of Lords)   **[190]**

Some heavy carpenter's tools, the subject of a hire-purchase agreement, were put on the ground floor of a factory on a bed of concrete prepared for them and fastened down to the concrete bed by nuts and bolts. By unscrewing the nuts each machine could be raised up and removed without injury to the building, and without injury to its concrete bed and the bolts embedded in it. *Held*, the machines were so affixed to the building as to pass to the hirer's mortgagee as being a portion of the factory. 'I was disposed to think that the question of chattel or fixture, being one of fact, ought necessarily to have been submitted to the jury, but apparently the course taken by the learned judge in treating the question as one of law, or as one of fact upon which the jury were bound to accept his directions and apply the law as declared by him, was correct' (*per* LORD JAMES). (But see *Gough* v *Wood & Co.*)

Rhone v Stephens [1994] 2 All ER 65 (House of Lords)   **[191]**

In 1960 a vendor sold part of his land known as Walford Cottage to a purchaser and remained in occupation of the rest of his land known as Walford House. Clauses 2 and 3 of the conveyance were relevant to the litigation. Clause 2 imposed reciprocal benefits and burdens of support. By virtue of clause 3, the vendor covenanted '... for himself and his successors in title ... to maintain to the reasonable satisfaction of the purchasers and their successors in title such part of the roof of Walford House [the retained land] ... as lies above the property conveyed [Walford Cottage] in wind and watertight condition'. Subsequently, Walford House was conveyed to B and Walford Cottage to R and his wife (the plaintiffs). The roof which was the subject of the repairing covenant fell into disrepair and the attempts of B to repair it were inadequate. Accordingly, R and his wife commenced proceedings to enforce the repairing covenant (by the time of the litigation B had died and S – the defendant – was her executrix). The county court judge found that S was bound by the repairing covenant entered into by the predecessor in title of B and ordered S to pay damages to R and his wife for breach of covenant. In allowing S's appeal, the Court of Appeal applied the rule in *Austerberry* v *Corporation of Oldham* and held that the burden of a positive covenant could not run with freehold land and was not enforceable against a successor in title of the vendor. R and his wife appealed. *Held*, the appeal would be dismissed. Their Lordships accepted that upon a true construction of the 1960 conveyance the owner of Walford House was in breach of the covenant to repair. The appellants contended that the effect of *Austerberry* v *Corporation of Oldham* (1885) 29 Ch D 750 had been blunted by the pure principle of benefit and burden distilled by MEGARRY VC from the case law in *Tito* v *Waddell (No 2)* [1977] Ch 106 (ie that any party deriving any benefit from a conveyance had to accept any burden in the same conveyance). They submitted in essence that if the vendor's successor in title took the benefit of clause 2 they had to accept the burden of clause 3. LORD TEMPLEMAN rejected the appellants' contention in the following terms: 'The condition must be relevant to the exercise of the right. In *Halsall* v *Brizell* [1957] 1 All ER 371 there were reciprocal benefits and burdens enjoyed by the users of the road and sewers. In the present case clause 2 of the 1960 conveyance imposes reciprocal benefits and burdens of support but clause 3 which imposed an obligation to repair the roof is an independent provision. In *Halsall* v *Brizell* the defendant could at least, in theory, choose between enjoying the right and paying his proportion of the cost or alternatively giving up the right and saving his money. In the present case the owners of Walford House could not in theory or in practice be deprived of the benefit of the mutual rights of support if they fail to repair the roof.' Accordingly, the rule in *Austerberry* v *Corporation of Oldham* that the burden of a positive covenant did not run with freehold land at law was affirmed. Further, the rule that the burden of restrictive but not positive covenants could run with freehold land in equity so as to bind successors in title of the servient land was also affirmed. (Applied: *Tulk* v *Moxhay*.)

Rhyl Urban District Council v Rhyl Amusements Ltd   **[192]**
[1959] 1 All ER 257

The defendants were lessees from the plaintiffs of a lake and pleasure ground for a term of 24 years from 1 February 1921, but in June 1932 by deed they surrendered the property to the plaintiffs to the intent that the plaintiffs would forthwith grant the defendants a new lease for a term of 31 years from May 1932. The consent of the Minister of Health to the new lease was required but withheld and the defendants remained in possession and paid rent twice yearly in accordance with the new lease. *Held*, the surrender of the 1921 lease was effective as it was by deed notwithstanding the fact that the lease of 1932 was void ab initio because the Minister's consent had not been obtained, and the council, having acted ultra vires, could not be estopped from denying the validity of the 1932 lease. However, the defendants had held over as yearly tenants, and such tenancy was brought to an end when a proper notice, by reference to the dates on which the rent was paid, expired.

Ridley v Taylor [1965] 2 All ER 51 (Court of Appeal)   **[193]**

A lease for 90 years granted in 1897 contained a covenant by the lessee not to make alterations in the structure, but to keep and use the premises as a private dwelling-house only. In 1950 the landlord and tenant (an assignee of the lease) entered into a licence under seal by which the tenant was permitted, subject to the payment of additional rents, to convert the premises into five flats (the necessary works had at that date already been completed) and, from 1956, to convert the premises into three private residential self-contained maisonettes: the licence also declared that the covenants in the lease should remain in full force and effect, subject only to the terms of the licence, and be deemed to be incorporated therein. From 1961 the tenant used the premises only as a private residence for his family, although he continued to pay the additional rent agreed for use as five flats, and this, it was found, he was entitled to do. It was also found that the tenant could not, under the terms of the licence, be compelled to convert the premises into three self-contained maisonettes, although he could not, after 1956, use them for letting as five flats. The tenant applied under s84(1) of the Law of Property Act 1925 for modification of the restrictive covenants affecting the property to permit the same to be used as five self-contained private residential flats. *Held*, although he was not precluded from so applying merely because he was a party to the licence of 1950 by which the restrictive covenants were expressly incorporated (the court would, however, be slow to relieve an applicant of covenants which he himself had entered into) his application would be refused because the landlord would be injured thereby, ie he would lose the power to negotiate an additional rent (see s84(1)(c) of the Act of 1925). Even if he would not have been so injured, by analogy with s84(12) as amended by s52 of the Landlord and Tenant Act 1954, the court should exercise its discretion against modification because less than 25 years had elapsed since, in 1950, by the terms of the licence, the tenant had undertaken to observe the restrictive covenants, subject only to the terms of the licence.

Roake v Chadha [1984] 1 WLR 40   **[194]**

In 1930 an estate was conveyed to W Ltd who laid out the land in plots and proceeded to sell them using in each case a standard form of transfer. In 1934, L bought one of these plots and in the transfer he covenanted with W Ltd 'so as to bind (so far as practicable) the land hereby transferred into whosoever hands the same may come but so that this covenant shall not enure for the benefit of any owner or subsequent purchaser of [W Ltd's] land unless the benefit of this covenant shall be *expressly assigned*' that he and his successors in title would observe all the stipulations detailed in the schedule to the transfer. One of these stipulations was a prohibition on erecting more than one private dwelling-house on any plot. W Ltd sold a further plot of land, adjoining that of L, to X but did not expressly assign to him the benefit of the covenant with L. Some time later X transferred the plot to R (plaintiff). In turn L transferred his plot to C (defendant). R discovered that C was proposing to build an additional house on his plot contrary to the terms of the 1934 transfer. R brought an action against C seeking a declaration that his plot was entitled to the benefit of the covenant given to W Ltd by his (ie C's) predecessor in title and an injunction restraining C from erecting the additional house. R maintained that he was so entitled because the benefit of the covenant had been annexed to his plot by s78 of the Law of Property Act 1925 and the operation of that section could not be excluded by the expression of a contrary intention in the covenant (ie he was relying on *Federated Homes Ltd* v *Mill Lodge Properties Ltd*) or alternatively because, even if there had not been annexation of the benefit of the covenant to the land, it had passed to him by virtue of s62(1) of the 1925 Act as 'a right appertaining or reputed to appertain to the land'. *Held*, R was not entitled to the relief sought. It did not follow just because s78 of the 1925 Act provided that a covenant relating to land of the covenantee was deemed to be made with the covenantee and his successors in title, that the benefit of the covenant ran with the land. The covenant still had to be construed according to its own terms. Where the covenant was not qualified in any way annexation could readily be inferred. However, here the covenant itself provided that its benefit was not to enure for a subsequent purchaser unless it had been expressly assigned and due weight had to be given to that. It followed that, in view of the express terms of the covenant given by L, the benefit of it was *not* annexed to R's land. Nor given the express terms of the covenant, could it be said to be a right appertaining or reputed to appertain to the land within the meaning of s62 of the 1925 Act. (See also *Federated Homes Ltd* v *Mill Lodge Properties Ltd.*)

Robb's Will Trusts, Re, Marshall v Marshall [195]
[1953] 1 All ER 920

By his will a testator directed that his residuary estate be invested and annuities paid to his wife and daughter and, after their deaths, that his residuary estate be held in trust for his grandchildren who might attain the age of 25 years or marry under that age within 21 years of the death of the survivor of his wife and daughter. The testator also empowered his trustees to accumulate surplus income. *Held*, although the will contained only a power, as opposed to a direction, to accumulate, accumulation after the expiration of 21 years from the testator's death was prohibited by s164(1) of the Law of Property Act 1925. Further, as the grandchildren were given nothing until the death of the survivor of the wife and daughter, the surplus income which could not be lawfully accumulated passed under the testator's partial intestacy. (See also *Re Bourne's Settlement Trusts* and s13 of the Perpetuities and Accumulations Act 1964.)

Rodwell v Phillips (1842) 9 M & W 501 [196]

There was an agreement for the sale of 'all the crops of fruit ... from the large pear trees'. *Held*, it was a contract for the sale of an interest in land.

Rogers v Hosegood [1900] 2 Ch 388 (Court of Appeal) [197]

In May 1869 the owners of building land conveyed a plot of land to the Duke of Bedford who covenanted that no more than one dwelling-house was to be erected on the plot and that it was to be used for private residential purposes only. The conveyance stated that the covenant was entered into 'with intent that the covenant may enure to the benefit of the vendors their successors and assigns and others claiming under them to all or any of their lands adjoining'. In 1872 the same vendors sold a plot to Sir John Millais which was separated from the Duke's plot by an intervening plot. At the date of his conveyance, Sir John had no knowledge of the covenants contained in the deed of May 1869. Further, there was no assignment in the 1872 conveyance to Sir John of the benefit of the restrictive covenant taken from the Duke in the 1869 conveyance. In 1896 Sir John died and his plot passed under his will to his executors. A developer, H, bought the Duke of Bedford's plot and proposed to erect a block of residential flats on it. The executors of Sir John's estate (the plaintiffs) sought to enforce the covenants. The question was whether the benefit of the covenant entered into in 1869 had passed to Sir John's executors as owners of the plot purchased by him in 1872. FARWELL J concluded that the benefit ran with the land vested in Sir John's executors. Further, he said that for a covenant to touch and concern land it 'must either affect the land as regards mode of occupation or it must be such as per se, and not merely from collateral circumstances, affects the value of the land'. He decided that the covenant here satisfied this test. H appealed. *Held*, the appeal would be dismissed. The covenant touched and concerned land. Further the benefit of it had been annexed by the express declaration on the face of the 1869 conveyance to 'all or any of the vendor's land next or adjoining the plot sold' and that included the plot acquired by Sir John Millais. The fact that Sir John had no knowledge of the covenant did not prevent him or his successors from taking the benefit of it. '... authorities establish the proposition that, when the benefit has been once clearly annexed to one piece of land, it passes by assignment of that land, and may be said to run with it ... In such a case it [the benefit] runs not because the conscience of either party is affected, but because the purchaser has bought something which inhered in or was annexed to the land bought' (*per* COLLINS LJ). Accordingly, Sir John's executors were entitled to enforce the restrictive covenant against the developer. (But see *Renals v Cowlishaw*.)

Russel v Russel See **United Bank of Kuwait plc v Sahib**

Rye v Rye [1962] 1 All ER 146 (House of Lords) [198]

Two brothers in partnership agreed orally to grant themselves a yearly tenancy of the premises in which the partnership business was carried on and of which they were freeholders having purchased the premises in equal shares. One brother died, and the other claimed to be entitled to exclusive possession of the premises on the ground that he was the surviving tenant under the yearly tenancy granted to the partnership. *Held*, his action could not succeed as the purported grant was ineffective because the word 'convey' in s72(3) of the Law of Property Act 1925, does not extend to an oral disposition and that provision does not enable a man to grant a lease to himself, nor several persons to grant a lease to themselves. Further, s72(4) of the 1925 Act does not apply to a conveyance made by two or more persons to themselves; 'I read the subsection literally as meaning that where property is vested in two persons they may convey it to one of themselves and where it is vested in three persons they may convey it to one or two of themselves. I see no reason for giving a more extended meaning to this subsection' (*per* VISCOUNT SIMONDS).

St Albans' (Duke) Will Trusts, Re, Coutts & Co v Beauclerk [199]
[1962] 2 All ER 402

By his will the tenth Duke of St Albans, who died in 1898, gave certain estates to the use of his trustees during the life of his eldest son, with remainder to the sons of his eldest son in tail male. He then gave those estates to the use of every successive son for his life with remainder to the sons of that son in tail male and continued 'and on failure of such issue to the use of the person who on my death or the failure of any male issue (whichever shall last happen) shall become Duke of St Albans in tail male'. The testator's second son, the twelfth Duke, had no issue and was aged 87, and a disentailing assurance was executed by the presumptive successor to the dukedom on the death of the twelfth Duke, one Beauclerk. Did this disentailing assurance have any effect? *Held*, Beauclerk's interest was a contingent interest in property, not a mere expectancy: he was an 'actual tenant in tail ... in ... contingency' within s15 of the Fines and Recoveries Act 1833, and the disentailing assurance was effective under s15 of the Act to bar the entail if the contingency of Beauclerk's succeeding to the dukedom occurred. (It should be noted that in *Re Earl of Midleton's Will Trusts, Whitehead* v *Earl of Midleton* [1967] 2 All ER 834 STAMP J said: 'I am unable to accept ... the distinction between a gift to the heir of a living person, which is, or was, no more no less than a gift to him who on the death of that person succeeds to his undevised freehold estate of inheritance, and a gift to him who on the death of that person succeeds to his title. Such distinction as there may be is in my judgment a distinction without a difference'.)

Saunders v Vautier (1841) 4 Beav 115 [200]

A testator left property on trust to accumulate the income until a sole beneficiary should reach the age of 25, and then transfer to him the principal and accumulated income. When the beneficiary was 21 he claimed to have the fund transferred to him. *Held*, the beneficiary was entitled to have the fund transferred to him. (The 'rule in *Saunders* v *Vautier*' is that where all the beneficiaries are sui juris and between them absolutely entitled they may by unanimous direction put an end to the trust, and direct the trustees to hand over the trust property as they direct.) (See also s14 of the Perpetuities and Accumulations Act 1964.)

Schar, Re, Midland Bank Executor and Trustee Co Ltd v [201] Damer [1950] 2 All ER 1069

A bank and two other persons proved the testator's will and the court held that certain legacies and a share of residue were payable to them beneficially. In order to relieve itself of the embarrassment it felt the bank executed a deed, to which the other two executors were made parties but which they did not execute, whereby the bank recited that it 'does not intend and has never intended to accept or take advantage of any interests to which it is entitled beneficially under the will and codicil of the testator and is desirous of executing such release as is hereinafter contained' and did 'disclaim all that the share and interest of the bank of and in the legacies and share of residue'. *Held*, the bank and the two other executors were beneficial joint tenants under the testator's will and, although no disclaimer could be made by one of several joint tenants (unless, perhaps, there had been a prior severance of the joint tenancy), the deed, which the bank thought was going to be a release, operated as a release to the other two joint tenants of the bank's beneficial interests. 'I think that the only disclaimer which can be made by joint tenants is a disclaimer which is made by them all' (*per* VAISEY J).

Schnabel v Allard [1966] 3 All ER 816 (Court of Appeal) [202]

A flat was let at a weekly rent, the tenancy beginning on a Saturday. It was inferred that a notice to quit on Friday 1 April 1966 was served on Friday 4 March 1966. *Held*, the notice was valid at common law and it complied with the requirements of s16 of the Rent Act 1957, that it should have been given 'not less than four weeks before the date on which' it was to take effect. (See also Protection from Eviction Act 1977, ss3A, 5, and the Housing Act 1988, ss31, 32.)

Schwann v Cotton [1916] 2 Ch 459 (Court of Appeal)   **[203]**

Under a testator's will Braxton Cottage passed to the plaintiff's predecessor in title and Malta Cottage passed to the defendants' predecessor in title: the two properties adjoined one another and at the time of the testator's death Braxton Cottage was supplied with water by means of a pipe under the grounds of Malta Cottage. *Held*, the effect of the will was to devise Braxton Cottage with the right of passage of such water as might flow through the pipe, and to devise Malta Cottage subject to that right.

Segal Securities Ltd v Thoseby [1963] 1 All ER 500   **[204]**

A sub-lease of a maisonette contained a covenant by the tenant 'to use the ... premises for the purpose of a private residence in the occupation of one household only'. The tenant allowed a Miss Walker to reside in the maisonette as a paying guest and a Miss Whitehouse on a sharing basis. On 8 June the landlords served a notice under s146 of the Law of Property Act 1925, requiring the tenant to remedy the alleged breach of covenant within 28 days and on 25 June by a letter headed 'Without prejudice' the landlords demanded a quarter's rent payable in advance and due on 24 June. The rent was tendered but not accepted. *Held*, the tenant was in breach of covenant by reason only of Miss Walker's residence in the maisonette, but this was a continuing breach which was waived (notwithstanding the use of the words 'Without prejudice') by the demand for rent only until the notice under s146 of the 1925 Act expired as the landlords had not been shown to have had knowledge on 25 June that the breach would be continuing after the expiration of the notice on 6 July. However, in all the circumstances SACHS J believed that the landlords' action was unreasonable and so exercised his discretion as to grant the tenant unconditional relief against forfeiture. (See also *Belgravia Insurance Co Ltd v Meah* and *Chatham Empire Theatre (1955) Ltd v Ultrans Ltd*; but see *Clarke v Grant*.)

Sharp v Coates [1948] 2 All ER 871 (Court of Appeal)   **[205]**

By an agreement in writing dated 13 April 1944, Racey, the tenant from year to year of certain land of which his mother was freeholder, sub-let the land to the defendant on a yearly tenancy. The agreement provided that should the freehold become vested in Racey during the defendant's tenancy, Racey would grant the defendant a lease for a term of ten years from 11 October 1943, but this provision was not registered as a land charge under the Land Charges Act 1925. Racey became the freeholder in 1945 and later that year he sold the freehold to the plaintiff. *Held*, in 1944 Racey was an 'estate owner' within the meaning of the Land Charges Act 1925, s10(1), Class C(iv) and, therefore, the undertaking by Racey to grant a ten-year lease to the defendant was capable of registration as a land charge. As the undertaking has not been so registered under s13(2) of the 1925 Act it was void against a purchaser and it followed that the plaintiff was entitled to give the defendant notice to quit. (See also *Hollington Brothers Ltd v Rhodes*.)

Shayler v Woolf [1946] 2 All ER 54 (Court of Appeal)   **[206]**

Mr Shayler bought Pear Tree Cottage from Mrs Lawton who, in 1938, had purchased the land on which it was built from Mrs Woolf and on the same day Mrs Woolf entered into an agreement with Mrs Lawton to supply water from a pump on other land owned by Mrs Woolf to the bungalow to be built upon the land sold, ie Pear Tree Cottage. A clause of the agreement provided that Mrs Woolf would 'do all things as may be necessary to insure a constant supply of water', but the agreement was not in terms expressed to extend to bind assigns.

When in 1944 Pear Tree Cottage was conveyed to Mr Shayler Mrs Lawton assigned to him, so far as assignable, the benefit of the agreement relating to the supply of water. Was the benefit of the contract now vested in Mr Shayler and was he entitled to sue Mrs Woolf upon it? *Held*, it was so vested and he could sue upon it as there was nothing in the nature of personal services concerned in the agreement and there could be no suggestion that, in the case of an assignee of Pear Tree Cottage, the burden on Mrs Woolf would have been any greater than it would have been in the case of Mrs Lawton herself. 'Looking at the whole nature of the subject-matter, it seems to me impossible that any sensible persons could have intended in the circumstances that the right to this supply should be personal to [Mrs Lawton] herself' (*per* LORD GREENE MR). (See also *Smith and Snipes Hall Farm Ltd* v *River Douglas Catchment Board*.)

Sifton v Sifton [1938] 3 All ER 435 (Privy Council) [207]

By his will the testator declared trusts in favour of his daughter and stipulated that the payments to be made to her should continue 'only so long as she shall continue to reside in Canada'. *Held*, the condition laid down by the testator was a condition subsequent and it was void for uncertainty: it was impossible to say what constituted a ceasing on the part of the daughter to reside in Canada and the clause did not therefore satisfy the requirement that it should be seen from the beginning precisely and distinctly upon the happening of what events the payments to the daughter were to be discontinued. (Distinguished in *Re Gape's Will Trusts*; see also *Clayton* v *Ramsden*.)

Simmons' Trusts, Re, Simmons v Public Trustee [208]
[1955] 3 All ER 818

The settlor asked that the trustees of the settlement might be authorised to give effect to a scheme whereby she would receive one half of the capital of her share absolutely and would release her power of appointment over the other half. Under the trusts relating to her share the settlor had a protected life interest in the income which was to be held on trusts after her death for her children, and subject to those trusts she had a general power of appointment over her share, in default of appointment her share to accrue to the other shares. The trust fund included certain land which was vested in the trustees of the settlement on trust for sale. *Held*, the power conferred on a tenant for life by s64(1) of the Settled Land Act 1925, was among the powers conferred on trustees for sale by s28(1) of the Law of Property Act 1925; the scheme was a 'transaction' within s64(2) of the Settled Land Act and as, in the opinion of the court, the transaction was one which would be for the benefit of the persons interested under the settlement, the court would authorise it under s64(1) of the Settled Land Act. (Applied: *Re Wellsted's Will Trusts*; see also *Hambro* v *Duke of Marlborough*.)

Smith v City Petroleum Co Ltd [1940] 1 All ER 260 [209]

Smith let certain premises to one Ridge who placed upon them petrol pumps and tanks of the type usually found at roadside filling stations. Ridge's tenancy came to an end in October 1937, when the defendants became the tenants, but at that time nothing was said or done about the pumps and tanks, which were used by the defendants for the purposes of their business. It was admitted that the tanks were fixtures and passed to the landlord. *Held*, the pumps should be regarded as a separate entity and, as trade fixtures which were capable of being severed without injury to the land, were not part of the land. It followed that they were tenant's fixtures, and not landlord's fixtures, and that Ridge could have removed the pumps within a reasonable time after the end of his tenancy agreement. However, as he had not so removed them, the property in the pumps had passed to the landlord Smith and the defendants had no interest in them and therefore could not remove them when their tenancy agreement expired. (See also *Jordan* v *May*.)

Smith and Snipes Hall Farm Ltd v River Douglas Catchment Board [1949] 2 All ER 179 (Court of Appeal) [210]

In 1938 a catchment board, the defendants, covenanted with a Mrs Smith and ten other owners of land through which a river ran that they, the defendants, would 'widen and deepen and make good the banks of the river ... and maintain for all time the work when completed'. In 1940 the first plaintiff, one Smith, took a conveyance of Mrs Smith's land with the benefit of the agreement of 1938 and in 1944 Smith let the land to the second plaintiffs, Snipes Hall Farm Ltd. Two years later, owing to faulty work by the board, the banks burst and flooded the plaintiffs' land. The plaintiffs claimed damages for breach of contract and the defendants maintained that, if there was a breach, there was no privity of contract between the parties. *Held*, the defendants were liable as the covenant affected the use and value of the land and the benefit of the covenant was obviously intended to attach to the land and extend to any subsequent owners: it followed that the covenant was binding on the defendants although they were strangers to the conveyance to the first plaintiff who was able to enforce the covenant against the defendants as successor in title to Mrs Smith. The second plaintiffs were able to enforce the covenant against the defendants under s78(1) of the Law of Property Act 1925, as persons deriving title under the first plaintiff. (Applied in *Federated Homes Ltd* v *Mill Lodge Properties Ltd*; see also *Shayler* v *Woolf*; but see *Beswick* v *Beswick*.)

Spyer v Phillipson [1931] 2 Ch 183 (Court of Appeal) [211]

A lessee of a flat erected valuable antique panelling therein by inserting into the walls wooden plugs to which the panelling was attached by screws. He also installed ornamental chimney pieces and 'period' fireplaces, and this work involved some slight structural alteration. The lessee died during the currency of the term: could these things be removed by his executors as tenant's fixtures? *Held*, they could as, on the facts, an intention on the part of the lessee that they should become part of the demised premises could not be inferred, the proper inference being that the lessee intended himself to enjoy the fixtures and not to benefit the demised premises. (See also *Jordan* v *May*; but see *Buckland* v *Butterfield*.)

Strand and Savoy Properties Ltd, Re, DP Development Co Ltd v Cumbrae Properties Ltd [1960] 2 All ER 327 [212]

A lease for a term of 35 years from 24 June 1926 provided: 'The lessors will at the written request of the lessee made 12 months before the expiration of the term hereby created ... grant to him a lease of the demised premises for the further term of 35 years from the expiration of the said term hereby granted' at the same rent and subject to the same covenants 'with the exception of the present provision for renewal'. *Held*, the provision for renewal was valid, notwithstanding s149(3) of the Law of Property Act 1925. '[Section 149(3)] is confined, as far as contracts are concerned, to contracts to create terms which, when created, will only take effect more than 21 years from the dates of the instruments creating them; that is to say, it invalidates contracts for the granting of leases which will, when granted, be reversionary leases, the postponement of the commencement of the term being for more than 21 years from the date of the lease' (*per* BUCKLEY J). (See also *Weg Motors Ltd* v *Hales*.)

Street v Mountford [1985] 2 WLR 877 (House of Lords)   [213]

By a written agreement, described as a licence, S granted M the right to occupy two furnished rooms 'at a licence fee of £37 per week' subject to 14 days written notice of termination. The agreement provided that 'this personal licence is not assignable'. It concluded with a declaration that M understood and accepted that the agreement did not and was not intended to give her a tenancy protected under the Rent Acts. M had exclusive possession of the rooms. Several months after signing the agreement, M applied to have a fair rent registered in respect of the rooms. After a fair rent had been registered, S applied to the county court for a declaration that M's occupancy was a licence and not a tenancy. The Recorder made a declaration that M was a tenant entitled to the protection of the Rent Acts. However, on appeal by S the Court of Appeal held that M was a mere licensee. M appealed to the House of Lords. *Held*, the appeal would be allowed. Except in cases where occupancy was made under a contract for the sale of land or pursuant to a contract of employment or referable to the holding of an office, where residential accommodation was granted for a term at a rent with exclusive possession the landlord providing neither attendance nor services, the grant was a tenancy. Exclusive possession would lead to a presumption of a tenancy which had to be rebutted by the landlord. The use of the word 'licence' in the agreement and the concluding declaration were irrelevant (ie whatever label the parties used was not conclusive of the matter). Here the effect of the agreement between M and S was to grant M exclusive possession for a fixed term at a stated rent and no circumstances existed to negative the presumption of a tenancy. Accordingly, it was clear that M was a tenant. (See also *Ashburn Anstalt* v *Arnold, AG Securities* v *Vaughan* and *Antioniades* v *Villiers*.)

Stroud Building Society v Delamont [1960] 1 All ER 749   [214]

A mortgage provided that no lease of the premises was to be granted by the mortgagor without the written consent of the mortgagee, but the mortgagor granted Mrs Waller a tenancy at £5 5s a week without first obtaining the mortgagee's written consent. The mortgagor became bankrupt, the mortgagee appointed a receiver of the income of the property under s109 of the Law of Property Act 1925, and the receiver notified Mrs Waller of his appointment and requested her to pay her rent to him. In answer to her inquiry, the mortgagee's solicitors informed Mrs Waller that the terms and conditions of her tenancy were the same as between Mrs Waller and the mortgagor, and the mortgagee subsequently sent Mrs Waller a notice to quit the premises 'which you hold as tenant of' the mortgagee. If there was a tenancy between Mrs Waller and the mortgagee the notice was void as it did not comply with the statutory requirements. *Held*, although the receipt of rent by a receiver appointed under s109 of the 1925 Act did not create a tenancy between the tenant and the mortgagee because the receiver was the agent of the mortgagor, such a tenancy could be created by a mortgagee consenting to accept the mortgagor's tenant as his own. On the facts, the mortgagee had accepted Mrs Waller as its tenant, notwithstanding the receivership, and it followed that Mrs Waller was not a trespasser and the mortgagee was not entitled to possession. (But see *Taylor* v *Ellis*.)

Summers v Salford Corporation [1943] 1 All ER 68   [215]
(House of Lords)

The appellant was the tenant of the respondent corporation of premises to which s2 of the Housing Act 1936 applied, so that the respondents impliedly undertook that during the tenancy the premises would be kept in all respects reasonably fit for human habitation. In February 1940 one of the sash cords of the only window in one of the rooms broke and, although the appellant notified the respondents, the necessary repair was not carried out. About two months later, the other cord broke and, as a result, the appellant's hands were crushed. *Held*, she was entitled to damages as the house was not in all respects reasonably fit for human habitation. LORD ATKIN affirmed that the test was: 'If the state of repair of a house is such that by ordinary user damage may naturally be caused to the occupier, either in respect of personal injury to life or limb or injury to health, then the house is not in all respects reasonably fit for human habitation'. (But see *McCarrick* v *Liverpool Corporation* and s11 of the Landlord and Tenant Act 1985.)

Sutherland Settlement Trusts, Re See Brougham and Vaux's (Lord) Settled Estates, Re

Sutton v Moody (1697) 1 Ld Raym 250   [216]

In an action for trespass, HOLT CJ said: 'If A starts a hare in the ground of B and hunts it, and kills it there, the property continues all the while in B. But if A starts a hare in the ground of B and hunts it into the ground of C and kills it there, the property is in A the hunter; but A is liable to an action of trespass for hunting in the grounds as well of B as of C.' (See also *Blades* v *Higgs*.)

Swan v Sinclair [1925] AC 227 (House of Lords)   [217]

The plaintiff claimed to be entitled to a right of way over a strip of land at the back of houses owned by the defendant. The right alleged was created by conveyances made in 1871, but for the period of 50 years or thereabouts no person had sought to enforce it and no steps had been taken to provide a roadway over the land as was anticipated (and required of the various property owners concerned) at the time of the conveyances (indeed, existing fences and a wall remained and the level of the land at one point had been changed to make use of the way totally impracticable). *Held*, the inevitable inference was that the arrangements made in 1871 had been abandoned by common consent, and the plaintiff's action could not succeed. (See also *Davies* v *Du Paver*.)

Swans, The Case of (1592) 7 Co Rep 15b   [218]

The court resolved: 'A man hath not absolute property in any thing which is ferae naturae ... Property qualified and possessory a man may have in those which are ferae naturae; and to such property a man may attain by two ways ... by industry as by taking them, or by making them mansueta, ... so long as they remain tame, for if they do attain to their natural liberty, and have not animum revertendi, the property is lost, [secondly] ratione impotentiae et loci; as if a man has young shovelers or goshawks, or the like, which are ferae naturae, and they build in my land, I have possessory property in them, for if one takes them when they cannot fly, the owner of the soil shall have an action of trespass.'

Target Home Loans Ltd v Clothier [1994] 1 All ER 439   [219]
(Court of Appeal)

C and his wife (the defendants) borrowed £225,000 from THL by way of an instalment mortgage secured on their home. In 1990 they stopped making repayments. In October 1991, when the arrears were over £46,000, THL applied to the county court for a possession order. However, the district judge granted the defendants a stay under s36 of the Administration of Justice Act 1970 as amended by s8 of the Administration of Justice Act 1973 on the ground that they would be 'likely to be able within a reasonable time to pay any sums due under the mortgage'. THL appealed against the decision to adjourn their application. At the time of the hearing, the arrears exceeded £64,000 and the defendants had made no further payments. During the hearing, the defendants produced a draft for £10,000 in favour of THL and evidence of a prospective sale (subject to planning permission) of part of their property for around £48,000. The judge, using the aforementioned statutory powers adjourned the application for four months to enable planning permission to be obtained and the sale completed. THL appealed against this further adjournment. By the time of the appeal hearing the proposed sale of part of the defendants' land had not taken place despite planning permission being obtained. However, at the hearing the defendants indicated that they had put the mortgaged property in its entirety on the market for £495,000 and that an early sale was anticipated. *Held*, the appeal would be dismissed. Although there had been no evidence before the judge that the defendants at that point in time were likely to be able to pay the sums due under the mortgage within a reasonable time, the court concluded on the evidence before it that it was very unlikely that the defendants would meet their mortgage obligations without selling their home. The court *did* have power under s36 of the 1970 Act, as amended, when the proposed means of dealing with the arrears was a sale by the borrowers in order to discharge the entire debt rather than a scheme which would only repay the arrears. Here a sale of the home by the borrowers was to the advantage of all sides, not least because its market value greatly exceeded that of the mortgage debt and the arrears. Further, since a sale of the defendants' home would be more likely to be achieved if it was occupied rather than repossessed, the court deferred the possession order for three months. The court emphasised that if the defendants did not discharge their entire indebtedness to THL within the latter period THL would then be entitled to possession. The judge's order would be varied accordingly. (See also *Palk* v *Mortgage Services Funding plc*.)

Taylor v Ellis [1960] 1 All ER 549   [220]

A mortgage of certain premises provided 'that no lease made by the borrowers ... during the continuance of this security shall have effect by force or virtue of s18 of the Conveyancing and Law of Property Act 1881 [now s99 of the Law of Property Act 1925] unless the lender shall consent thereto in writing'. In 1940 the mortgagor granted a monthly tenancy, no interest was paid under the mortgage after 1950 and the mortgagee died in 1957 having had knowledge of the tenancy and having allowed the tenant to remain in possession. There was no evidence of written consent to the tenancy. *Held*, the mortgagee's executrix was entitled to possession because the onus of proving written consent lay on the tenant, and this onus he could not discharge. Further, knowledge by the mortgagee of the tenant's occupation of the property and the fact that the mortgagee had refrained from taking possession himself for many years did not preclude the mortgagee from treating the tenant as a trespasser when the mortgagee chose to do so, neither did the mere fact that for some years the mortgagee had been content to go without interest. (But see *Stroud Building Society* v *Delamont*.)

Tito v Waddell (No 2) See Rhone v Stephens

Todrick v Western National Omnibus Co Ltd [1934] Ch 561   [221]
(Court of Appeal)

The plaintiff maintained that the defendants did not have a right of way over a certain roadway as (it was said) it did not give direct access to the dominant tenements (ie the defendants' land on which they had erected a garage) as it passed over other land before it reached there. *Held*, this plea would be rejected:

physical contiguity was not essential, and the test was whether the alleged easement had some natural connection with the dominant tenement as being for its benefit – in this case it had. (See also *Johnstone* v *Holdway*.)

TSB Bank plc v Camfield [1995] 1 All ER 951 (Court of Appeal)   [222]

A husband and wife entered into a transaction in order to secure a loan for H's company from the plaintiff bank. The security for the loan was the matrimonial home over which the bank took a legal charge. The bank wrote to its solicitors requesting that W be given independent advice. The solicitors replied confirming that this had been done. In fact W was not seen on her own but together with H. W was induced to stand as surety by an innocent misrepresentation by H that their maximum liability for the loan was limited to £15,000, when in fact it was unlimited. H's business failed and the bank brought proceedings against H and W. The county court judge held that the case came within the principles laid down in *Barclays Bank plc* v *O'Brien* so that the legal charge had prima facie to be set aside against W. The bank was tainted by the misrepresentation because it had not taken reasonable steps to ensure that W was independently advised. However, he went on to give judgment for the bank against W for £15,000 and made an order for possession of the home subject to W making payment in full within six months (ie the charge was valid to the extent that W thought it was valid). W appealed claiming that she was entitled to have the charge set aside in toto. *Held*, the appeal would be allowed. The case came within the principles laid down in *Barclays Bank plc* v *O'Brien* (there their Lordships set out the circumstances in which a wife who had stood as surety for her husband's debts could rely on undue influence/ misrepresentation by the husband to resist liability to the lender pursuant to a charge or guarantee). Here the bank was fixed with constructive notice of H's misrepresentation (ie it was not tainted by the misrepresentation). The court recognised the morality and possible justice in an abstract sense of the partial enforcement solution put forward on behalf of the bank – namely that the court could set aside the charge on terms that W had acknowledged that it was a valid security for £15,000 (ie it was valid to the extent that the chargor thought the charge was valid). However, they preferred the view expressed by FERRIS J in the first instance case of *Allied Irish Bank* v *Byrne* [1995] 1 FCR 430 that the wife's right to set aside the transaction was 'an all or nothing process'. In the absence of anything to the contrary, there was no basis in principle for saying that a mortgagee in this type of case was in any better position than any other party who took subject to equitable rights of which he had notice. Accordingly, the bank was not entitled to an order that the charge be partially enforceable against W (ie the transaction could be set aside by W in its entirety). (See also *Barclays Bank plc* v *O'Brien*.)

Tulk v Moxhay (1848) 2 Ph 774   [223]

The plaintiff, who owned several houses in Leicester Square, sold the garden in the centre of the square to one Elms who covenanted, for himself, his heirs, and assigns, that he would keep the gardens and railings around them in their present condition and continue to allow the inhabitants of the square to have the use and enjoyment of the gardens. The land in question was sold to the defendant and the conveyance to him did not contain a covenant in similar terms, although he knew of the restriction contained in the deed to which the plaintiff and Elms were parties. The defendant announced that he intended to build on the land and the plaintiff, who still remained the owner of several adjacent houses, sought an injunction to restrain him from doing so. *Held*, the injunction would be granted as the covenant would be enforced in equity against all subsequent purchasers with notice. (Applied in *Rhone* v *Stephens*; see also *Re Nisbet and Potts' Contract*.)

Turton v Turton [1987] 2 All ER 641 (Court of Appeal)   [224]

In 1972 T and T an unmarried couple purchased a property in their joint names. The conveyance contained a declaration of trust that the couple held the property on trust for sale for themselves as beneficial joint tenants. Mr T provided £3,000 of the purchase price with the remainder being raised on a mortgage of the property. Mr T paid all the mortgage instalments. The couple lived in the property until August 1975 when Ms T left following the breakdown of their relationship. Mr T remained in occupation. In 1981 the mortgage was redeemed and in September 1982 Ms T served a notice of severance of the beneficial joint tenancy on Mr T. In August 1983 Ms T issued an originating summons in the county court seeking a declaration that the property was held by herself and Mr T on trust for sale for themselves as beneficial tenants in common in equal shares and an order for sale of the property. In 1986 the judge found for Ms T and made a sale order. She further held that the purpose of the trust ended when the parties separated in August 1975 and that that was the relevant date for valuing the parties' shares in the property. On that basis Ms T's half share was worth about £2,500. However, the house had considerably increased in value between 1975 and 1986 and Ms T appealed arguing that the proper date for valuing the parties' shares was the date of sale of the property (in which case she would receive £15,000). *Held*, the appeal would be allowed. The interest of a beneficiary under a trust for sale gave rise to an absolute and indefeasible right to share in the proceeds of sale. Where there was an express declaration of trust regarding an unmarried couple's beneficial interests in property, that declaration was conclusive and excluded any discretionary jurisdiction to value the interests at some date other than that on which, under the express declaration of trust, they fell to be valued, namely the date they were realised. Accordingly, the judge had erred in holding that Ms T's interest was to be valued as at the date of the parties' separation. *Per curiam*. Where there was no express declaration of trust in relation to an unmarried couple's beneficial interests in the property in which they lived together and their beneficial interests fell to be determined by inferring a constructive trust based on their common intention, such beneficial interests were to be valued at the date when the property was sold and not at the date when the relationship ended.

Tyler, Re, Tyler v Tyler [1891] 3 Ch 252   [225]

A testator bequeathed £42,000 in stock to the trustees for the time being of the London Missionary Society, with a gift over to the Blue Coat School, London, if the Society failed to keep the family vault in good repair. *Held*, the condition for the repair of the vault was valid and binding on the Society, and the gift over, on failure to comply with the condition, to the School was valid, on the principle that the rule against perpetuities had no application to a transfer, on the occurrence of a certain event, of property from one charity to another. (See also *Re Chardon*.)

United Bank of Kuwait plc v Sahib [1996] 3 All ER 215   [226]
(Court of Appeal)

In 1991, UBK (the plaintiff bank) obtained judgment against S for sums owed by him in respect of banking facilities which it had granted to him. In 1992, UBK was granted a charging order over S's interest in freehold property which he jointly owned with his wife in order to secure and enforce the judgment debt. SGA (the defendant bank) claimed to have an *equitable mortgage* over S's interest in the same property. S had received an advance of £130,000 from SGA. No legal mortgage was executed by S and his wife in respect of the advance. However, in 1990 S's solicitors had written to SGA confirming that the land certificate relating to the property in question was being held to SGA's order as security for the monies which it had advanced to S. UBK brought proceeding against S, his wife and SGA seeking, inter alia, a declaration that SGA did not hold any equitable mortgage or charge over the freehold property in question or if it did, that SGA's mortgage or charge did not take priority over its own charging order. SGA claimed to have an equitable mortgage over S's interest in the property by virtue of the deposit of the land certificate ranking in priority to UBK's charge under the charging order. It submitted that s2 of the Law of Property (Miscellaneous Provisions) Act 1989 had not altered the long established rule (applicable since *Russel* v *Russel* (1783) 1 Bro CC 269) that the deposit of title deeds to a property by way of security created an equitable mortgage of the property notwithstanding s4 of the Statute of Frauds 1677 and its successor, s40 of the Law of Property Act 1925. The judge declared that SGA did not hold an equitable mortgage over S's undivided share in the proceeds of sale of the property in question. SGA appealed. The main issue on appeal was whether the rule applicable since *Russel* v *Russel*, and relied upon by SGA, had survived the coming into force of s2 of the 1989 Act. *Held*, the appeal would be dismissed. Section 2 of the 1989 Act provided that a contract for sale or other disposition of an interest in land had to be in writing in a document incorporating all the terms of the agreement and signed by both parties. Here the deposit of the land certificate took effect as a contract to mortgage and fell within s2 of the 1989 Act. It followed that since there was no written document here the mere deposit of title deeds/ land certificate by way of security could not create a mortgage or charge (ie the old rule that had existed since *Russel* v *Russel* had been abolished). To create a valid equitable charge by a deposit of the land certificate there had to be a written mortgage agreement meeting the requirements of s2 of the 1989 Act.

Vaudeville Electric Cinema Ltd v Muriset [1923] 2 Ch 74 [227]

The plaintiffs' cinema was mortgaged to the defendants 'together ... with its fixtures'. In the cinema there were tip-up seats attached to the floor by iron standards 'in very much the same way in which the seats were secured in *Lyon & Co* v *London City and Midland Bank'* (*per* SARGANT J). *Held*, the seats were included in the mortgage and his Lordship distinguished this case from *Lyon & Co* v *London City and Midland Bank* because here the plaintiffs owned the seats as well as the cinema and the seats were affixed for the permanent benefit and equipment of the cinema. In other words, no inference could be drawn from anything that was done by the parties that there was an intention to prevent the annexation of the seats to the freehold. (See also *Holland* v *Hodgson*.)

Villar, Re, Public Trustee v Villar [1929] 1 Ch 243 [228]
(Court of Appeal)

A testator who died in 1926 gave his property to his trustees on certain trusts for his issue and provided that the capital was not to vest until the expiration of 'the period ending at the expiration of 20 years from the day of the death of the last survivor of all the lineal descendants of Her Late Majesty Queen Victoria who shall be living at the time of my death'. *Held*, although the existing lives selected were very numerous and it might be extremely difficult and expensive to ascertain the date of the last survivor's death, the trust did not offend against any rule of law and was therefore valid. (See also *Re Leverhulme, Cooper* v *Leverhulme (No 2)*.)

Wakefield, Re, Gordon v Wakefield [1943] 2 All ER 29 [229]
(Court of Appeal)

At a time when he owned no disposable real estate a testator devised his real estate (if any) to his nephew. After making his will the testator contracted to purchase a freehold property and, on selling some stock, asked his broker to let him have two cheques, one for £4,927 10s which was the amount of the balance of the purchase price of the freehold property. This cheque the testator forwarded to his solicitors with a covering letter in which he said, after referring to the property: 'Cheque enclosed for balance of purchase money'. The testator died before completion. *Held*, the letter contained no 'contrary or other intention' within the meaning of s35 of the Administration of Estates Act 1925 and it followed that the nephew took the property subject to the vendor's lien for the unpaid purchase money. 'In the present case a cheque was sent to the solicitors for the purpose of paying the purchase money. That seems to me to make no difference. It merely shows an intention on the part of the testator to pay the unpaid balance of the purchase money in his lifetime and it had no reference as to what the position would be after his death as regards the administration and distribution of his estate' (*per* LORD GREENE MR). (See also *Re Neeld, Carpenter* v *Inigo-Jones*; but see *Re Fison's Will Trusts*.)

Waller v Waller [1967] 1 All ER 305   [230]

Railway Cottage was bought in 1965, as a matrimonial home, and was conveyed to the husband alone although the wife contributed a substantial part of the purchase price. *Held*, 'had the parties not been husband and wife, the husband would on completion of the purchase have been an equitable tenant in common with the wife, of the house. He would have become a trustee of the property, holding it on trust for sale, but since it is the policy of the law for obvious reasons ... not to allow a single trustee to sell land which he is holding on trust for sale, and in the proceeds of sale of which other persons are interested in equity, he could not have sold the property and given a good receipt for the proceeds without first appointing an additional trustee (see the Trustee Act 1925, s14(2)). He would also have committed a breach of the trust if, having appointed an additional trustee, he had then proceeded to sell the property without ascertaining the wishes of the other beneficiary, the wife (see the Law of Property Act 1925, s26(3)) as substituted [by the Law of Property Amendment Act 1926, s7, Schedule] ... Neither the authorities nor the submissions satisfy me, however, that a tenant in common in equity who is the wife of the other tenant in common in equity is in any worse position to prevent a sale of the property by the husband, who is the sole trustee, than would be the position if the parties were complete strangers to each other' (*per* STAMP J). As the husband had agreed to sell the property without appointing an additional trustee and without ascertaining the wife's wishes, the wife would be granted an injunction. (See also *Jones* v *Challenger*.)

Walsh v Lonsdale (1882) 21 Ch D 9 (Court of Appeal)   [231]

W entered into possession of a cotton mill, under a written agreement with L for a seven years' lease. It was part of the agreement that a deed should be executed containing, inter alia, a provision that rent should be payable one year in advance upon L's demand. In the event no deed was executed. W paid rent, quarterly, in arrear, for a year and a half. L then demanded a year's rent in advance. When W refused to pay L distrained for the amount. W thereupon brought an action against L for illegal distress. W claimed that as he had been let into possession and had paid rent upon a yearly basis, he was in the position of a tenant from year to year. As a tenancy of this kind was determinable upon six months' notice, L's proposal that rent should be payable a year in advance was, he claimed, inconsistent with his position as a tenant from year to year. For this reason, W claimed L's distress was illegal. *Held*, since the agreement under which W entered into possession was capable of specific performance, and since equity looked on that as done which ought to be done, the position was just the same as it would have been if the formal lease had actually been executed. W thus held upon the full terms of the agreement to execute the lease. L was therefore entitled to demand that rent should be payable one year in advance and his distress was lawful. (See also *Borman* v *Griffith*, *Cornish* v *Brook Green Laundry Ltd* and s2 of the Law of Property (Miscellaneous Provisions) Act 1989.)

Ward v Kirkland [1966] 1 All ER 609 [232]

For many years prior to 1928 a cottage and a plot of land, and a farmhouse and lands, were part of a parson's glebe, and the farmyard adjoined the cottage along one wall of the cottage. In 1928 the rector conveyed the cottage and plot of land to the plaintiff's predecessors in title, together with the right to use the farmyard for unloading coal into the premises. In 1942 the defendant occupied the farmhouse and lands as tenant of the rector, and in 1954 the cottage and plot of land were conveyed to the plaintiff. In 1955 the plaintiff installed in the cottage a bathroom and two water closets, draining them through a pipe in the farmyard. The rector gave permission for the drain pipe to be laid and to drain the bath-water through it, the permission being indefinite in point of time, but he did not give express permission to drain the water closets through the pipe although he was aware of their installation. In 1958 the rector conveyed the farmhouse and lands to the defendant subject to the express rights conveyed by the conveyance of 1928. Maintenance of the wall of the cottage adjoining the farmyard was carried out from time to time by entry on the farmyard, which provided the only possible means of access, but there was no evidence of the freeholder's permission prior to 1958. In the period 1942 to 1954 work to the wall was done with the defendant's permission as tenant, but between 1954 and 1958 the plaintiff did not ask permission when he wished to do such work. *Held*, the plaintiff was entitled to an easement to go onto the defendant's land to maintain the wall because (1) assuming that such a right could subsist as an easement, it would not be defeated on the ground that it would amount to the possession or joint possession of the defendant's property, and (2) although such a right was not created by implication of law because it was not a continuous and apparent easement within the requirements of *Wheeldon* v *Burrows*, yet the advantage had in fact been enjoyed and, whether the enjoyment of it was by permission or not, it was transformed by s62 of the Law of Property Act 1925 into an easement on the occasion of the conveyance of 1928. However, as permission had been given by the tenant between 1942 and 1954 for the plaintiff to maintain the wall, no easement to do so had arisen by prescription. The plaintiff was also entitled to use the drain for the passage of bath-water (but not sewerage) and to have the drain there permanently – because he had put the drain in at his own expense believing that he had the rector's permission properly granted to put it there for an indefinite time there had arisen 'an equity of a permanent nature' (*per* UNGOED-THOMAS J). (Distinguished: *Copeland* v *Greenhalf*; applied: *Inwards* v *Baker*; but see *Green* v *Ashco Horticulturist Ltd*.)

Warren v Keen [1953] 2 All ER 1118 (Court of Appeal) [233]

A landlord maintained that her weekly tenant was liable for the cost of works arising from damp and stained plaster on internal walls, cracked and broken rendering on external walls, leaking window-sills with decayed paintwork and a leak in a hot-water boiler. *Held*, her action would fail: the defects were due to fair wear and tear for which a weekly tenant was not liable, his only obligation being to use the premises in a tenantlike manner. 'Apart from express contract, a tenant owes no duty to the landlord to keep the premises in repair. The only duty of the tenant is to use the premises in a husbandlike, or what is the same thing, a tenantlike, manner ... But what does it mean "to use the premises in a tenantlike manner"? It can, I think, best be shown by some illustrations. The tenant must take proper care of the premises. He must, if he is going away for the winter, turn off the water and empty the boiler; he must clean the chimneys, when necessary, and also the windows; he must mend the electric light when it fuses; he must unstop the sink when it is blocked by his waste. In short, he must do the little jobs about the place which a reasonable tenant would do. In addition, he must not, of course, damage the house wilfully or negligently; and he must see that his family and guests do not damage it – if they do he must repair it' (*per* DENNING LJ). His Lordship added that a weekly tenant was not liable for permissive waste. (But see *Regis Property Co Ltd* v *Dudley*.)

Watson's Settlement Trusts, Re, Dawson v Reid   [234]
[1959] 2 All ER 676

A settlement provided that the trustees (ie the original trustees or their successors) 'may from time to time by deed revocable or irrevocable ... at their absolute and uncontrolled discretion ... revoke all or any of the trusts powers and provisions hereinbefore declared ... and may direct that the shares to which such revocation extends shall thenceforth be held upon such other trusts ... for the benefit of such person or persons ... as they may think proper'. The trustees exercised the power of revocation in a way which at that time did not disclose any invalidity. *Held*, nevertheless the power of revocation was void ab initio because it was capable of being exercised beyond the period allowed by the rule against perpetuities, and it followed that the purported exercise of the power was also void.

Webb, Re, Sandom v Webb [1951] 2 All ER 131   [235]
(Court of Appeal)

The landlord was head lessee of certain business premises and during the period 1939 to 1949 when the tenant had occupied two upper floors under tenancy agreements the landlord had maintained two advertisements on the outer walls with the full knowledge of the tenant and without any claim or complaint on his part. By a lease made in 1949 the landlord let the two floors to the tenant for 21 years but, although the tenancy included the outer walls, there was no reservation in the landlord's favour of advertising or other rights as regards the use of the exterior surfaces. *Held*, prima facie the landlord could not assert against the tenant any right which was not expressly reserved to him in the lease and, as the maintenance of the advertisements was not a necessary incident of the landlord's user of the ground floor for his business and as the bare circumstance of the presence of the advertisements since 1939 was not sufficient to raise the inference that at the date of the lease it was the common intention of the parties to reserve to the landlord the right to continue to display the advertisements, the landlord had failed to discharge the onus of showing that a reservation of the right must be implied.

Weg Motors Ltd v Hales [1961] 3 All ER 181 (Court of Appeal)   [236]

By a lease certain land with garages thereon was demised to the plaintiff company for a term of 21 years from 25 December 1938 and by an agreement made on the same date and between the same parties, but signed before the execution of the lease, it was provided: 'In consideration of the lessees taking a lease of even date with but executed after these presents ... the lessees shall have the option of taking a further lease of the premises demised by the ... lease for a term of 21 years'. *Held*, the lease and the option agreement were contemporaneous and intimately related and their execution formed a single transaction: it followed that the right and obligation of the option agreement were properly incidents of the demise, were for the renewal of the lease and, as such, were excepted from the scope of the rule against perpetuities. Further, the option agreement was not, when it was entered into, a contract to create a term of years and it was not, therefore, rendered void by s149(3) of the Law of Property Act 1925: it was not until the option was exercised (30 April 1959) that the option agreement could be said to create a term of years. (See also *Re Strand and Savoy Properties Ltd*.)

Wellsted's Will Trusts, Re, Wellsted v Hanson   [237]
[1949] 1 All ER 577 (Court of Appeal)

By his will the testator gave his residuary estate to trustees on trust for sale, the said residue and the investments for the time being representing the same to be held on certain trusts for his widow and issue. The trustees proposed to sell realty, and to realise some of the trustee securities representing the proceeds of sale of realty, and to apply these sums, together with moneys in hand arising from the sale of realty, in the purchase of realty. *Held*, they were entitled so to do because the powers given by s28(1) of the Law of Property Act 1925 included all the powers conferred by s73 of the Settled Land Act 1925, and the proceeds of sale of trust realty remained 'proceeds of sale' within the meaning of s28(1) so long as they could be traced. (Applied in *Re Simmons' Trust*.)

Wernher's Settlement Trusts, Re See Andrews v Partington

Westripp v Baldock [1939] 1 All ER 279 (Court of Appeal)   [238]

The parties owned adjoining houses in Gillingham included within a building scheme and there was a restriction, enforceable by either of the parties against the other, that 'no trade or manufacture be carried on or any operative machinery be placed or fixed'. The defendant, a jobbing builder, placed ladders, planks and sand against the wall of the plaintiff's house, and erected a shed for storing builders' fittings in his (the defendant's) back garden, and it was found that he sold materials and fittings apart from the building works which he carried out. *Held*, the defendant was carrying on a trade (ie he was buying and selling) within the meaning of the covenant and the plaintiff was entitled to an injunction. Further, the covenant remained binding as the neighbourhood was still mainly residential and had not suffered such a change as would release the covenant: in other words, the defendant had failed to show so complete a change in the character of the neighbourhood as to render the covenant valueless to the plaintiff, so that an action to enforce it would be unmeritorious and useless.

Whaley, Re, Whaley v Roehrich [1908] 1 Ch 615   [239]
Whaley bought a house in which there was an Elizabethan room and the purchase price included tapestry fixed to the walls by nailing to wooden frames held in place by screws, and a picture of Queen Elizabeth similarly fixed over the fireplace. Whaley bequeathed his furniture and chattels to his wife and devised the house upon trust. *Held*, the tapestry and picture passed to his trustees. 'I cannot see any ground for supposing that when he devises the house he does not intend the house to pass as he bought it, and as he has used it with regard to the fixed ornaments which were used with it' (*per* NEVILLE J). (See also *Leigh v Taylor*.)

Wheeldon v Burrows (1879) 12 Ch D 31 (Court of Appeal)   **[240]**

A workshop and an adjacent piece of land belonging to the same owner were put up for sale by auction. The piece of land only was sold and conveyed to Wheeldon and some five weeks later Burrows contracted to buy the workshop, and it was conveyed to him in due course. The workshop had windows overlooking and receiving their light from the piece of land first sold. *Held*, as the vendor had not when he conveyed the piece of land reserved the right of access of light to the windows, no such right passed to the purchaser of the workshop, and Wheeldon could build so as to obstruct the windows of the workshop. 'In the case of a grant you may imply a grant of such continuous and apparent easements or such easements as are necessary to the reasonable enjoyment of the property conveyed, and have in fact been enjoyed during the unity of ownership, but ..., with the exception ... of easements of necessity, you cannot imply a similar reservation in favour of the grantor of land' (*per* THESIGER LJ). (See also *Green v Ashco Horticulturist Ltd, Ward v Kirkland, International Tea Stores Co v Hobbs* and *Wheeler v J J Saunders Ltd*.)

Wheeler v Mercer [1956] 3 All ER 631 (House of Lords)   **[241]**

A quarterly tenant of business premises held over after the termination of her tenancy in 1953 and in 1955, after protracted negotiations between the parties for a new lease had proved inconclusive, the landlord instituted proceedings for possession and the tenant claimed the protection of the Landlord and Tenant Act 1954. *Held*, the tenant was a tenant at will and the landlord was entitled to possession as a tenancy at will was not a 'tenancy' within the meaning of the 1954 Act. 'A tenancy at will can only arise with the consent, express or implied, of the landlord ... there is much to be said for the view that the [landlord] never consented to the [tenant's] occupation ... but took no active steps to recover possession, on the principle that "what cannot be cured must be endured" ... If this were the true view, the [tenant] would be a tenant on sufferance' (*per* LORD MORTON OF HENRYTON).

Wheeler v J J Saunders Ltd [1995] 2 All ER 697   **[242]**
(Court of Appeal)

W owned a farmhouse adjacent to farmland let to S Ltd. Originally the farmhouse and farmland were in common ownership. The common owner sold the house (quasi dominant land) to W and also disposed of the farm (quasi servient land). There were two ways of gaining access to the house. First, there was direct access from a road (the east entrance). Second, there was access across part of the farmland (the south entrance). However, the conveyance of the house to W did not contain an express grant of a right of way over the farmland in favour of the house. S Ltd took the view that W was not entitled to cross the farmland to reach the house and blocked the access strip with a wall of breeze blocks. W commenced proceedings against S Ltd on several matters, including the latter obstruction of the right of way to the house. At first instance, W obtained damages for the obstruction and a mandatory injunction requiring S Ltd to demolish the wall. S Ltd appealed. The appeal concerned several issues. The 'easement issue' was whether an implied easement had been granted to W under the rule in *Wheeldon v Burrows*. *Held*, the appeal would be allowed in part (S Ltd succeeded on the easement point but not on another ground of appeal). Under the doctrine of *Wheeldon v Burrows* easements were implied in favour of a grantee which were continuous and apparent or necessary for the reasonable enjoyment of the property granted and which had been and were at the time of the grant used by the common owner for the benefit of the part granted. While recognising that there had been some doubt as to whether the requirement that the easement should be continuous and apparent was an alternative to the requirement that the easement be necessary for the reasonable enjoyment of the property granted, the court on reviewing *Wheeldon v Burrows* concluded that the court on that occasion had treated the first requirement as synonymous with the second. The test of what was necessary for the reasonable enjoyment of land was not the same as the test for a way of necessity (one without which the property could not be used at all). PETER GIBSON LJ noted that in *Cheshire and Burn's Modern Law of Real Property* 'necessary' in the context of the doctrine of *Wheeldon v Burrows* indicated that the way 'conduces to the reasonable enjoyment of the property'. Here on the facts the south entrance (access across S Ltd's land) was not necessary for the reasonable enjoyment of the house since the east entrance would do just as well. The fact that the latter was four inches narrower than the south entrance was not critical. The court noted that the gate at the south entrance was usually shut and this led STAUGHTON LJ to conclude that it was 'not the main entrance and was probably only used on rare occasions'. Here access over the farmland was not necessary for the reasonable enjoyment of the house – not least because there was another means of access. Accordingly, W did not have an implied easement of way. The mandatory injunction requiring S Ltd to remove the wall would be discharged and the award of damages for the obstruction would be reversed.

White v Bijou Mansions Ltd [1938] 1 All ER 546   **[243]**
(Court of Appeal)

In 1886 the Davidsons entered into an agreement to sell the Shaftesbury House Estate to the Daws for development and the Davidsons undertook to grant leases as soon as houses were built, or to convey plots of land in fee simple, such leases or conveyances to contain covenants restricting the use of the premises to private residence. One Fellows purchased a plot in 1886: the conveyance was made between the Davidsons of the first part, the Daws of the second part and Mr Fellows of the third part and it contained a covenant by Mr Fellows to use the premises to be built thereon as a private residence and by the Daws that every building lease or other assurance of the estate should contain covenants by the lessees or purchasers with the Daws, their heirs or assigns, inter alia, to use any buildings as and for private dwelling-houses only, subject to certain powers of modification, and the conveyance to Mr Fellows also contained covenants by the Daws that the same restrictions should apply to any land retained and buildings erected by them and that at Mr Fellows' request they (the Daws) would enforce the covenants against future lessees or purchasers. In 1890 land was conveyed by the Davidsons and the Daws as vendors to one Nicholson who covenanted with the Davidsons and the Daws their heirs and assigns for himself his heirs executors administrators and assigns to use any premises erected thereon as a private residence but, although the conveyance recited the agreement for sale by the Davidsons to Daws and the stipulations and covenants set out therein, there was no restrictive covenant by the Daws and no restrictive covenant by the Davidsons with regard to that portion of the estate which at that date remained unsold. The plaintiff, an assign of Fellows, sought to restrain the defendants, who derived their title from Nicholson with notice of the restrictive covenant as to user, from using their premises as 'flatlets'. Only the conveyances to Fellows and Nicholson were in evidence. *Held*, the action would fail as it was 'quite impossible to draw any inference as to any intention on the part of anybody to apply to this estate some common regulations, which would be, and were, brought to the notice of all purchasers in such circumstances that each purchaser was entitled to infer that all other purchasers would be bound by them, and was willing to accept the liability towards every other purchaser' (*per* SIR W GREENE MR). Further, the plaintiff could not rely upon s56(1) of the Law of Property Act 1925, as the 'assigns' to which reference was made in the conveyance to Nicholson were those who would thereafter take from the Davidsons, not those (such as Fellows) who had already taken from them at the time of Nicholson's conveyance. (See also *Smith and Snipes Hill Farm Ltd* v *River Douglas Catchment Board.*)

White v Richards [1993] RTR 318 (Court of Appeal) [244]

R purchased agricultural land with the benefit of a right to pass and repass on foot and with or without motor vehicles over a dirt track just under nine feet wide and some 300 yards long owned by W and his wife (the plaintiffs) on their land. The plaintiffs' home faced onto the track and was just under ten feet away from it. A dispute arose between the parties as to R's use of the track. The plaintiffs claimed that R's use of the right was unlawful and they sought an injunction to restrict that use and damages for trespass. The county court judge found that R had committed 'acts of arrogant disregard for anybody's rights except his own' and that his use of the track was excessive (on average he took 15 juggernaut lorries daily over the track). The judge awarded damages and made declarations that: (1) use of the track was for pedestrians and vehicles but not livestock except horses led by someone on foot; (2) vehicles were to be restricted in size and weight (width not to exceed nine feet and laden weight not to exceed ten tons); and (3) user was not to interfere unreasonably with the plaintiffs' enjoyment of their land. R appealed. *Held*, the appeal would be allowed in part. Notwithstanding a right of way was granted in wide terms, the nature and extent of it so far as motor vehicles were concerned had to be assessed in the light of the physical characteristics of the track at the time the right was granted. Here the physical characteristics of the track were such as to require the words 'motor vehicles' to be restricted to those of limited dimensions and weight. R's use of the track by both authorised and unauthorised vehicles was, having regard to its physical characteristics and its proximity to the plaintiffs' home, clearly excessive. Accordingly, the plaintiffs were entitled to damages for trespass and to a declaration that R's use of the track should not unreasonably interfere with their rights. However, the grant of a right to use the track 'with or without motor vehicles' included a right of way with horse-drawn carriages and carts and such had to include a right to ride or lead horses and cattle but not to drive cattle or other animals along the track (in this regard the judge's order was reversed).

White v Taylor [1967] 3 All ER 349 [245]

An owner of a right of common of pasture for a certain number of sheep purchased part of the land over which the right extended. The right of pasturage was a right of common appurtenant, not appendant, and arose by grant of the right. *Held*, the purchase of part of the land over which the right of common appurtenant extended extinguished the right in relation to the whole of that land.

Wightwick's Will Trusts, Re, Official Trustees of [246]
Charitable Funds v Fielding-Gould [1950] 1 All ER 689

The testatrix bequeathed £2,000 to trustees on trust to invest and pay the dividends to the treasurer for the time being of the International Association for the Total Suppression of Vivisection for the purposes of the Association until such time as the practice of vivisection be made penal in the United Kingdom, Europe and elsewhere and from and after such time the trustees were directed to pay the dividends to the Royal Society for Prevention of Cruelty to Animals. The residue of the estate was given to one Anne Thacker absolutely. The income had been paid to the successors of the Association, the National Anti-Vivisection Society, and it had been held that this latter body was not established for charitable purposes only. *Held*, the gift to the Association was void as a perpetuity or as tending to a perpetuity. 'A trust of income for an indefinite period for a purpose not being charitable is void as a perpetuity because it involves rendering the capital inalienable. Turning to the language of the will, by which a limit is sought to be set on the period of payment to the Association, it appears to me that it can be no over-statement to say that it tends to a perpetuity, because it is hardly possible to imagine that the court could ever be satisfied on evidence that the condition on which the payment is to determine had been satisfied' (*per* WYNN-PARRY J). Further, the gift over was contingent and failed as it was not possible to postulate a dies certus when the primary gift would determine, and it followed that the investments fell into the residuary estate.

Williams & Glyn's Bank Ltd v Boland [1981] AC 487   [247]
(House of Lords)

A husband and wife bought a house together. Even though W had made a substantial contribution to the purchase of the house only H's name appeared as the registered proprietor on the register at the Land Registry. W did not protect her interest by any entry on the register (she could have protected it by registering a caution against dealings). The couple lived together in the house. Some time after the acquisition of the house, H formed a company which borrowed money from the bank. As collateral security for the loan to the company, H gave a personal guarantee of repayment and without W's knowledge mortgaged the matrimonial home by way of a legal mortgage to the plaintiff bank. Before taking the mortgage, the bank made no enquiry of H or W whether W had any interest in the property. The company got into financial difficulties and the bank called on H to repay the loan under his personal guarantee. H was unable to repay and accordingly the bank brought proceedings for and were granted a possession order in respect of the house. W appealed claiming that she was entitled to remain in possession of the house by virtue of her beneficial interest, notwithstanding that her interest had not been registered, contending that under s20(1) of the Land Registration Act 1925 a disposition of a freehold for valuable consideration took effect subject to '(b) ... the overriding interests, if any, affecting the estate transferred or created' and that her rights were an overriding interest within s70(1)(g) of the 1925 Act since she was in 'actual occupation' of the land. The Court of Appeal allowed W's appeal and the order for possession was discharged. The bank appealed to the House of Lords contending that (1) W was not a person in actual occupation of the house within the meaning of s70(1)(g) of the 1925 Act; and (2) that her beneficial interest in the house was a minor interest under s3(xv) of the 1925 Act. *Held*, the appeal would be dismissed. W had an equitable interest in the house under a trust for sale. Since H was the sole holder of the legal estate there could be no overreaching (two trustees were required for overreaching). Further, as W had not protected her interest by any entry on the register she had to establish an overriding interest in order to resist the bank's claim. W was a person 'in actual occupation' within the meaning of s70(1)(g). The question was one of fact not law. What was required was physical presence on the land. Since W was physically present in the house, with all the rights that occupiers had, including the right to exclude all others except those having comparable rights and the house was a matrimonial home occupied by both spouses both of whom had an interest in it, W was in actual occupation. Actual occupation was not necessarily confined to one person – the fact that the mortgagor (H) was also in occupation did not exclude the possibility of occupation by others. Accordingly, W's interest was capable of conferring protection as an overriding interest. By virtue of s3(xv) of the 1925 Act the interests of co-owners under the statutory trusts were minor interests. However, even though W's interest (in so far as it existed under a trust for sale) was an equitable interest capable of being overreached and therefore a minor interest it was also capable of being an overriding interest if it was protected by 'actual occupation', especially if it was a house bought jointly by spouses to be lived in as a matrimonial home. In such circumstance it would be 'a little unreal' to describe the spouses' interests as simply an interest in the proceeds of sale until sale and there was every reason why, in that event, such an interest should acquire the status of an overriding interest. W's interest subsisting as it did 'in reference to the land' within the opening words of s70(1) of the 1925 Act was by virtue of her occupation made into an overriding interest and thus protected by s70(1)(g) (ie the bank's charge was subject to her overriding interest). Their Lordships emphasised that the doctrine of notice had no part to play in the land registration system. (See also *City of London Building Society* v *Flegg*.)

Wiltshear v Cottrell (1853) 1 E & B 674 [248]

The defendant, an out going tenant, removed some staddles, a threshing machine and a granary which had been erected by his father (a previous owner) and he (the outgoing tenant) had been a party to a conveyance whereby the land 'and all fixtures' were conveyed to the plaintiff. *Held*, the staddles (stone pillars let into the earth and mortared to a foundation of brick erected to support ricks) passed under the conveyance either as part of the land or as fixtures and the threshing machine, which was fixed by bolts and screws to posts let into the ground, also passed under the conveyance. However, the granary, a wooden structure with a tile roof, which was supported by staddles and lay upon them in the same manner that the ricks lay upon the rick staddles, was a mere chattel and neither a part of the land nor affixed to the freehold. (See also *Leigh* v *Taylor* and s62(1) of the Law of Property Act 1925.)

Winter Garden Theatre (London) Ltd v Millennium [249]
Productions Ltd [1947] 2 All ER 331 (House of Lords)

The appellants granted the respondents a licence for the use of their theatre for two periods of six months and thereafter the appellants agreed that the respondents were 'to have the option of further continuing the licence of the theatre on the payment each week of a flat rental of £300 per week and you will give us one month's notice of your intention of then terminating the licence'. The licence made no provision for its termination by the appellants but after more than three years from the date of the original licence they purported to give the respondents one month's notice to withdraw from the premises. *Held*, the notice was valid and effectual as the licence was not perpetual and could be determined by the appellants by giving sufficient notice, and in these circumstances notice of one month was sufficient. (See also *Australian Blue Metal Ltd* v *Hughes*.)

Wong v Beaumont Property Trust Ltd [1964] 2 All ER 119 [250]
(Court of Appeal)

Under the terms of a lease the tenant was required to 'develop extend and improve' the business of a 'popular restaurant' carried on in three cellars: he was also required to 'control and eliminate all smells and odours' and 'to comply with the health regulations for the time being in force'. The Food Hygiene Regulations 1955 provided that 'suitable and sufficient means of ventilation shall be provided in every good room'. When the lease was made the existing ventilation was insufficient, although the parties did not appreciate this at the time, and the landlord, who owned the whole of the building, later refused consent to the erection of a duct outside the building, the only way in which an adequate system of ventilation could be provided. *Held*, in view of the terms of the lease, an easement of necessity to erect an outside duct had been impliedly granted by the landlord on the demise of the premises and it was immaterial that the duct required for the present tenant would be larger than that required for the original tenant as the larger duct would not impose any substantial additional burden on the servient tenement. 'In order to use this place as a restaurant, there must be implied an easement, by the necessity of the case, to carry a duct up this wall' (*per* LORD DENNING MR).

Wood v Leadbitter (1845) 13 M & W 838   **[251]**

The plaintiff bought from the defendant a guinea ticket which entitled him to go into the stand and enclosure at Doncaster races. In the course of the meeting, because of alleged malpractices on a previous occasion, the defendant asked the plaintiff to leave and when he refused to do so he was removed without the use of unnecessary violence. The plaintiff brought an action for assault. *Held*, he could not succeed as his licence to remain on the course, which was not coupled with an interest and in any case had not been given under seal, had been validly revoked. (But see *Hurst v Picture Theatres Ltd*.)

Woolwich Building Society v Dickman   **[252]**
[1996] 3 All ER 204 (Court of Appeal)

In 1984, D purchased a leasehold flat title to which was registered. In 1985, he installed his parents in law (the Todds) in the flat as his tenants. They were to refurbish it at their own expense and pay him £200 a month rent on the basis that they would enjoy a tenancy for their lives. In 1986, D applied to WBS for a mortgage advance on the property and in so doing he made it clear that the property was occupied by others. WBS failed to realise that the occupiers were tenants: they wrongly treated the application as one coming within the familiar category where the borrower shared rights of occupation with members of his family who might be able to establish a beneficial interest in the mortgaged property carrying rights of occupancy binding on a lender having notice of their occupation. Accordingly, as a condition of the mortgage advance WBS required the Todds to sign written consents stating that their rights of occupancy were subordinated to the rights and powers of WBS (as lender). The Todds duly signed the consent forms. Subsequently when D defaulted on the mortgage payments and was adjudicated bankrupt WBS brought possession proceedings. However, the Todds defended the action on the ground that their tenancy was binding on WBS. The district judge held that the consent forms were effective to subordinate all rights of occupation to the rights of WBS and granted the possession order sought. On appeal the judge ruled that the consents were inoperative and refused the possession order. WBS appealed. *Held*, the appeal would be dismissed. Where a protected tenancy was in existence at the date of the grant of the mortgage, written consents were not effective to subordinate the rights of the tenants to the rights of the mortgagee since it was inescapable that the mortgagee (WBS) derived its right to claim possession of the flat from the mortgage and was not therefore able to deny any contractual rights of the tenants which bound it or any interest of the tenants which affected its title. Further, the case concerned registered land and overriding interests within s70(1)(g) of the Land Registration Act 1925. No matter how effective the consents might otherwise have been to override the rights of the Todds as persons in actual occupation of the flat, they could have no effect upon the mandatory rights they enjoyed under s70(1)(g) unless a provision to that effect was 'expressed on the register'. However, no such provision was there expressed.

Accordingly, the Todds' tenancy remained an overriding interest under s70(1)(g) of the 1925 Act notwithstanding the letters of consent and WBS's charge took effect subject to it. WBS's application for possession came within s98(1) of the Rent Act 1977 (provides that a court shall not make a possession order in respect of a dwelling-house 'which is for the time being let on a protected tenancy ... unless the court considers it reasonable to make such an order ...'). Here there were no reasonable grounds for making a possession order and the application would be refused.

Wright v Macadam [1949] 2 All ER 565 (Court of Appeal)   **[253]**

In 1940 Mrs Wright became tenant of two rooms on the top floor of the defendant's house for one week and, by virtue of the Rent Restriction Acts, she remained in possession after the expiration of that week on the same terms until 28 August 1943. Early in 1941 the defendant permitted Mrs Wright to use a shed in the garden for the storage of her coal. On 28 August 1943, the defendant granted a new tenancy (including an extra room) for one year to Mrs Wright and her daughter and, at the expiration of the year, they remained in occupation of the flat on the same terms. The 1943 agreement, which was under hand, made no reference to the coal shed, but the tenants continued to use it until 1947 when the defendant denied them the use of it. *Held*, by virtue of ss52(2)(d) and 54(2) of the Law of Property Act 1925, the 1943 agreement passed to the tenants the legal estate in the property for the term contemplated and, therefore, there was a 'conveyance of land' within s62(1) of the 1925 Act. As the right to use the coal shed was a right capable of being granted at law (ie was a right known to the law) and it was not merely a temporary right (no time limit had been set on the time for which the shed could be used for the storage of coal) and as the right was being enjoyed with the property at the date of the 1943 agreement, and no contrary intention was expressed in that document, the right would be regarded as having passed under the 1943 letting by virtue of s62(1) of the Act of 1925. (Applied in *Phipps* v *Pears* and *Green* v *Ashco Horticulturist Ltd*; see also *Goldberg* v *Edwards*.)

Wyld v Silver [1962] 3 All ER 309 (Court of Appeal)   **[254]**

A private Act of Parliament of 1799 empowered certain named commissioners to appoint a parcel of waste land in the village of Wraysbury for the purpose of holding an annual fair on it, that the inhabitants should forever after have this right and that no building should be erected on the appointed parcel. The commissioners so appointed a parcel of land, and their award was enrolled in the Court of Common Pleas, but the defendant had now obtained planning permission for the erection of five bungalows. There was no evidence that a fair had been held in the village during the twentieth century and two held in the previous hundred years had been held on other sites. The plaintiffs sued on behalf of themselves and all the other inhabitants of the parish (in truth they represented only a minority) for a declaration of the right to hold a fair and for an injunction. *Held*, they were entitled to the declaration for which they asked and to an injunction as they had established either a statutory right to hold a fair, which could not be waived by the inhabitants nor lost by disuse, or a franchise which could not be abandoned, and the right was not, by virtue of being a right to hold a fair, too vague or uncertain to be valid.

Zetland (Marquess) and Zetland Estates Company v   [255]
Driver [1938] 2 All ER 158 (Court of Appeal)

A conveyance of shop premises in Redcar, being a small portion of a large area of settled land, provided that the purchaser, to the intent and so as to bind so far as practicable the property so conveyed into whosoever hands it might come and to benefit and protect such part or parts of the settled land as should for the time being remain unsold or as should have been sold by the vendor or his successors in title with the benefit of the covenants, covenanted, inter alia, 'that no act or thing shall be done or permitted thereon which ... may be a public or private nuisance or prejudicial or detrimental to the vendor and the owners or occupiers of any adjoining property or to the neighbourhood'. The respondent, subsequent purchaser of the premises, with notice of the covenant, opened a fried fish shop and the person then entitled under the settlement, the appellant, sought an injunction to restrain this use of the premises. At all material times portions of the land at Redcar were unsold and remained subject to the settlement. Was the covenant enforceable by the appellant? *Held*, it was as it was a covenant imposed by a vendor as owner of other land of which that sold formed a part, and intended to protect or benefit such unsold land. 'Such covenants can only be validly imposed if they comply with certain conditions. First, they must be negative covenants. No affirmative covenant requiring the expenditure of money, or the doing of some act can ever be made to run with the land. Secondly, the covenant must be one that touches or concerns the land, by which is meant that it must be imposed for the benefit, or to enhance the value, of the land retained by the vendor, or some part of it, and no such covenant can ever be imposed if the sale comprises the whole of the vendor's land. Further, the land retained by the vendor must be such as to be capable of being benefited by the covenant at the time when it is imposed. Thirdly, the land which is intended to be so benefited must be so defined as to be easily ascertainable, and the fact that the covenant is imposed for the benefit of that particular land should be stated in the conveyance, and the persons or the class of persons entitled to enforce it should also be stated ... Finally, it must be remembered that those covenants can only be enforced so long as the covenantee or his successor in title retains some part of the land for the benefit of which the covenant was imposed ... *Re Ballard's Conveyance* ... is clearly distinguishable ... if only on the ground that in that case the covenant was expressed to run with the whole estate, whereas in the present case ... the covenant is expressed to be for the benefit of the whole or any part or parts of the unsold settled property' (*per* FARWELL J).

Statutes

FIRES PREVENTION (METROPOLIS) ACT 1774
(14 Geo 3 c 78)

83 Money insured on houses burnt: how to be applied   [256]

And in order to deter and hinder ill-minded persons from wilfully setting their house or houses or other buildings on fire with a view of gaining to themselves the insurance money, whereby the lives and fortunes of many families may be lost or endangered: Be it further enacted by the authority aforesaid, that it shall and may be lawful to and for the respective governors or directors of the several insurance offices for insuring houses or other buildings against loss by fire, and they are hereby authorised and required, upon the request of any person or persons interested in or intitled unto any house or houses or other buildings which may hereafter be burnt down, demolished or damaged by fire, or upon any grounds of suspicion that the owner or owners, occupier or occupiers, or other person or persons who shall have insured such house or houses or other buildings have been guilty of fraud, or of wilfully setting their house or houses or other buildings on fire, to cause the insurance money to be laid out and expended, as far as the same will go, towards rebuilding, reinstating or repairing such house or houses or other buildings so burnt down, demolished or damaged by fire, unless the party or parties claiming such insurance money shall, within sixty days next after his, her or their claim is adjusted, give a sufficient security to the governors or directors of the insurance office where such house or houses or other buildings are insured, that the same insurance money shall be laid out and expended as aforesaid, or unless the said insurance money shall be in that time settled and disposed of to and amongst all the contending parties, to the satisfaction and approbation of such governors or directors of such insurance office respectively.

86 No action to lie against a person where the fire   [257]
accidentally begins

And no action, suit or process whatever shall be had, maintained or prosecuted against any person in whose house, chamber, stable, barn or other building, or on whose estate any fire shall accidentally begin, nor shall any recompence be made by such person for any damage suffered thereby, any law, usage or custom to the contrary notwithstanding: provided that no contract or agreement made between landlord and tenant shall be hereby defeated or made void.

[As amended by the Statute Law Revision Acts 1888, 1948 and 1958.]

PRESCRIPTION ACT 1832
(2 & 3 Will 4 c 71)

1 Claims to right of common and other profits à prendre,   [258]
(except tithes, etc), not to be defeated after thirty years
enjoyment by merely showing the commencement of the
right – after sixty years enjoyment the right to be absolute,
unless shown to be had by consent or agreement

No claim which may be lawfully made at the common law, by custom, prescription, or grant, to any right of common or other profit or benefit to be taken and enjoyed from or upon any land of our sovereign lord the King, or any land being parcel of the duchy of Lancaster or of the duchy of Cornwall, or of any ecclesiastical or lay person, or body corporate, except such matters and things as are herein specially provided for, and except tithes, rent, and services, shall, where such right, profit, or benefit shall have been actually taken and enjoyed by any person claiming right thereto without interruption for the full period of thirty years, be defeated or destroyed by showing only that such right, profit, or benefit was first taken or enjoyed at any time prior to such period of thirty years, but nevertheless such claim may be defeated in any other way by which the same is now liable to be defeated; and when such right, profit, or benefit shall have been so taken and enjoyed as aforesaid for the full period of sixty years, the right thereto shall be deemed absolute and indefeasible, unless it shall appear that the same was taken and enjoyed by some consent or agreement expressly made or given for that purpose by deed or writing.

2 In claims of rights of way or other easements the   [259]
periods to be twenty years and forty years

No claim which may be lawfully made at the common law, by custom, prescription, or grant, to any way or other easement, or to any watercourse, or the use of any water, to be enjoyed or derived upon, over, or from any land or water of our said lord the King, or being parcel of the duchy of Lancaster or of the duchy of Cornwall, or being the property of any ecclesiastical or lay person, or body corporate, when such way or other matter as herein last before mentioned shall have been actually enjoyed by any person claiming right thereto without interruption for the full period of twenty years, shall be defeated or destroyed by showing only that such way or other matter was first enjoyed at any time prior to such period of twenty years, but nevertheless such claim may be defeated in any other way by which the same is now liable to be defeated; and where such way or other matter as herein last before mentioned shall have been so enjoyed as aforesaid for the full period of forty years, the right thereto shall be deemed absolute and indefeasible, unless it shall appear that the same was enjoyed by some consent or agreement expressly given or made for that purpose by deed or writing.

3 Right to the use of light enjoyed for twenty years,   [260]
indefeasible, unless shown to have been by consent

When the access and use of light to and for any dwelling house, workshop, or other building shall have been actually enjoyed therewith for the full period of twenty years without interruption, the right thereto shall be deemed absolute and indefeasible, any local usage or custom to the contrary notwithstanding, unless it shall appear that the same was enjoyed by some consent or agreement expressly made or given for that purpose by deed or writing.

4 The periods to be those next before the suit or action – what shall constitute an interruption [261]

Each of the respective periods of years herein-before mentioned shall be deemed and taken to be the period next before some suit or action wherein the claim or matter to which such period may relate shall have been or shall be brought into question; and no act or other matter shall be deemed to be an interruption, within the meaning of this statute, unless the same shall have been or shall be submitted to or acquiesced in for one year after the party interrupted shall have had or shall have notice thereof, and of the person making or authorising the same to be made.

5 What claimant may allege [262]

In all actions upon the case and other pleadings, wherein the party claiming may now by law allege his right generally, without averring the existence of such right from time immemorial, such general allegation shall still be deemed sufficient, and if the same shall be denied, all and every the matters in this Act mentioned and provided, which shall be applicable to the case, shall be admissible in evidence to sustain or rebut such allegation; and in all pleadings to actions of trespass, and in all other pleadings wherein before the passing of this Act it would have been necessary to allege the right to have existed from time immemorial, it shall be sufficient to allege the enjoyment thereof as of right by the occupiers of the tenement in respect whereof the same is claimed for and during such of the periods mentioned in this Act as may be applicable to the case, and without claiming in the name or right of the owner of the fee, as is now usually done; and if the other party shall intend to rely on any proviso, exception, incapacity, disability, contract, agreement, or other matter herein-before mentioned, or on any cause or matter of fact or of law not inconsistent with the simple fact of enjoyment, the same shall be specially alleged and set forth in answer to the allegation of the party claiming, and shall not be received in evidence on any general traverse or denial of such allegation.

6 Restricting the presumption to be allowed in support of claims herein provided for [263]

In the several cases mentioned in and provided for by this Act, no presumption shall be allowed or made in favour or support of any claim, upon proof of the exercise or enjoyment of the right or matter claimed for any less period of time or number of years than for such period or number mentioned in this Act as may be applicable to the case and to the nature of the claim.

7 Proviso where any person capable of resisting a claim is an infant, etc [264]

Provided also, that the time during which any person otherwise capable of resisting any claim to any of the matters before mentioned shall have been or shall be an infant, idiot, non compos mentis, feme covert, or tenant for life, or during which any action or suit shall have been pending, and which shall have been diligently prosecuted, until abated by the death of any party or parties thereto, shall be excluded in the computation of the periods herein-before mentioned, except only in cases where the right or claim is hereby declared to be absolute and indefeasible.

8 What time to be excluded in computing the term of forty years appointed by this Act [265]

Provided always, that when any land or water upon, over or from which any such way or other convenient watercourse or use of water shall have been or shall be enjoyed or derived hath been or shall be held under or by virtue of any term of life, or any term of years exceeding three years from the granting thereof, the time of the enjoyment of any such way or other matter as herein last before mentioned, during the continuance of such term, shall be excluded in the computation of the said period of forty years, in case the claim shall within three years next after the end or sooner determination of such term be resisted by any person entitled to any reversion expectant on the determination thereof.

[As amended by the Statute Law Revision (No 2) Act 1888; Statute Law Revision Act 1890.]

WILLS ACT 1837
(7 Will 4 & 1 Vict c 26)

3 All property may be disposed of by will [266]

It shall be lawful for every person to devise, bequeath, or dispose of, by his will executed in manner herein-after required, all real estate and all personal estate which he shall be entitled to, either at law or in equity, at the time of his death, and which, if not so devised, bequeathed, and disposed of, would devolve upon his executor or administrator; and the power hereby given shall extend to all contingent, executory or other future interests in any real or personal estate, whether the testator may or may not be ascertained as the person or one of the persons in whom the same respectively may become vested, and whether he may be entitled thereto under the instrument by which the same respectively were created, or under any disposition thereof by deed or will; and also to all rights of entry for conditions broken, and other rights of entry; and also to such of the same estates, interests, and rights respectively, and other real and personal estate, as the testator may be entitled to at the time of his death, notwithstanding that he may become entitled to the same subsequently to the execution of his will.

23 A devise not to be rendered inoperative by any subsequent conveyance or act [267]

No conveyance or other act made or done subsequently to the execution of a will of or relating to any real or personal estate therein comprised, except an act by which such will shall be revoked as aforesaid, shall prevent the operation of the will with respect to such estate or interest in such real or personal estate as the testator shall have power to dispose of by will at the time of his death.

26 A general devise of the testator's lands shall include leasehold as well as freehold lands, in the absence of a contrary intention [268]

A devise of the land of the testator, or of the land of the testator in any place or in the occupation of any person mentioned in his will, or otherwise described in a general manner, and any other general devise which would describe a leasehold estate if the testator had no freehold estate which could be described by it, shall be construed to include the leasehold estates of the testator, or his leasehold estates, or any of them, to which such description shall extend, as the case may be, as well as freehold estates, unless a contrary intention shall appear by the will.

27 A general gift of realty or personalty shall include [269] property over which the testator has a general power of appointment

A general devise of the real estate of the testator, or of the real estate of the testator in any place or in the occupation of any person mentioned in his will, or otherwise described in a general manner, shall be construed to include any real estate, or any real estate to which such description shall extend (as the case may be), which he may have power to appoint in any manner he may think proper, and shall operate as an execution of such power, unless a contrary intention shall appear by the will; and in like manner a bequest of the personal estate of the testator, or any bequest of personal property described in a general manner, shall be construed to include any personal estate, or any personal estate to which such description shall extend (as the case may be), which he may have power to appoint in any manner he may think proper, and shall operate as an execution of such power, unless a contrary intention shall appear by the will.

28 A devise of real estate without any words of limitation [270] shall pass the fee, etc

Where any real estate shall be devised to any person without any words of limitation, such devise shall be construed to pass the fee simple, or other the whole estate or interest which the testator had power to dispose of by will in such real estate, unless a contrary intention shall appear by the will.

[As amended by the Statute Law Revision (No 2) Act 1888; Statute Law (Repeals) Act 1969.]

COMMON LAW PROCEDURE ACT 1852
(15 & 16 Vict c 76)

210 Proceedings in ejectment by landlord for [271] nonpayment of rent

In all cases between landlord and tenant, as often as it shall happen that one half year's rent shall be in arrear, and the landlord or lessor, to whom the same is due, hath right by law to re-enter for the nonpayment thereof, such landlord or lessor shall and may, without any formal demand or re-entry, serve a writ in ejectment for the recovery of the demised premises, which service shall stand in the place and stead of a demand and re-entry; and in case of judgment against the defendant for non-appearance, if it shall be made appear to the court where the said action is depending, by affidavit, or be proved upon the trial in case the defendant appears, that half a year's rent was due before the said writ was served, and that no sufficient distress was to be found on the demised premises, countervailing the arrears then due, and that the lessor had power to re-enter, then and in every such case the lessor shall recover judgment and execution, in the same manner as if the rent in arrear had been legally demanded, and a re-entry made; and in case the lessee or his assignee, or other person claiming or deriving under the said lease, shall permit and suffer judgment to be had and recovered on such trial in ejectment, and execution to be executed thereon, without paying the rent and arrears, together with full costs, and without proceeding for relief in equity within six months after such execution executed, then and in such case the said lessee, his assignee, and all other persons claiming and deriving under the said lease, shall be barred and foreclosed from all relief or remedy in law or equity, other than by bringing error for reversal of such judgment, in case the same shall be erroneous, and the said landlord or lessor shall from thenceforth hold the said demised premises discharged from such lease; provided that nothing herein contained shall extend to bar the right of any mortgagee of such lease, or any part thereof, who shall not be in possession, so as such mortgagee shall and do, within six months after such judgment obtained and execution executed pay all rent in arrear, and all costs and damages sustained by such lessor or person entitled to the remainder or reversion as aforesaid, and perform all the covenants and agreements which, on the part and behalf of the first lessee, are and ought to be performed.

211 Lessee proceeding in equity not to have injunction   [272]
or relief without payment of rent and costs

In case the said lessee, his assignee, or other person claiming any right, title, or interest, in law or equity, of, in, or to the said lease, shall, within the time aforesaid, proceed for relief in any court of equity, such person shall not have or continue any injunction against the proceedings at law on such ejectment, unless he does or shall, within forty days next after a full and perfect answer shall be made by the claimant in such ejectment, bring into court, and lodge with the proper officer such sum and sums of money as the lessor or landlord shall in his answer swear to be due and in arrear over and above all just allowances, and also the costs taxed in the said suit, there to remain till the hearing of the cause, or to be paid out to the lessor or landlord on good security, subject to the decree of the court; and in case such proceedings for relief in equity shall be taken within the time aforesaid, and after execution is executed, the lessor or landlord shall be accountable only for so much and no more as he shall really and bona fide, without fraud, deceit, or wilful neglect, make of the demised premises from the time of his entering into the actual possession thereof; and if what shall be so made by the lessor or landlord happen to be less than the rent reserved on the said lease, then the said lessee or his assignee, before he shall be restored to his possession, shall pay such lessor or landlord what the money so by him made fell short of the reserved rent for the time such lessor or landlord held the said lands.

212 Tenant paying all rent, with costs, proceedings to cease   [273]

If the tenant or his assignee do or shall, at any time before the trial in such ejectment, pay or tender to the lessor or landlord, his executors or administrators, or his or their attorney in that cause, or pay into the court where the same cause is depending, all the rent and arrears, together with the costs, then and in such case all further proceedings on the said ejectment shall cease and be discontinued; and if such lessee, his executors, administrators, or assigns, shall, upon such proceedings as aforesaid, be relieved in equity, he and they shall have, hold, and enjoy the demised lands, according to the lease thereof made, without any new lease.

[As amended by the Statute Law Revision Act 1892.]

BODIES CORPORATE (JOINT TENANCY) ACT 1899
(62 & 63 Vict c 20)

1 Power for corporations to hold property as joint tenants   [274]

(1) A body corporate shall be capable of acquiring and holding any real or personal property in joint tenancy in the same manner as if it were an individual; and where a body corporate and an individual, or two or more bodies corporate,

become entitled to any such property under circumstances or by virtue of any instrument which would, if the body corporate had been an individual, have created a joint tenancy, they shall be entitled to the property as joint tenants:

Provided that the acquisition and holding of property by a body corporate in joint tenancy shall be subject to the like conditions and restrictions as attach to the acquisition and holding of property to a body corporate in severalty.

(2) Where a body corporate is joint tenant of any property, then on its dissolution the property shall devolve on the other joint tenant.

LAW OF PROPERTY ACT 1922
(12 & 13 Geo 5 c 16)

145 Conversion of perpetually renewable leaseholds   [275]

For the purpose of converting perpetually renewable leases and underleases (not being an interest in perpetually renewable copyhold land enfranchised by Part V of this Act, but including a perpetually renewable underlease derived out of an interest in perpetually renewable copyhold land) into long terms, for preventing the creation of perpetually renewable leasehold interests and for providing for the interests of the persons affected, the provisions contained in the Fifteenth Schedule to this Act shall have effect.

190 Special definitions applicable to Part VII   [276]

In Part VII of this Act –

...

(iii) 'A perpetually renewable lease or underlease' means a lease or underlease the holder of which is entitled to enforce (whether or not subject to the fulfilment of any condition) the perpetual renewal thereof, and includes a lease or underlease for a life or lives or for a term of years, whether determinable with life or lives or not, which is perpetually renewable as aforesaid, but does not include copyhold land held for a life or lives or for years, whether or not determinable with life, where the tenant had before the commencement of this Act a right of perpetual renewal subject or not to the fulfilment of any condition;

(iv) 'Underlease', unless the context otherwise requires, includes a subterm created out of a derivative leasehold interest.

FIFTEENTH SCHEDULE   [277]

PROVISIONS RELATING TO PERPETUALLY RENEWABLE LEASES
AND UNDERLEASES

1. *Conversion of perpetually renewable leases into long terms*

(1) Land comprised in a perpetually renewable lease which was subsisting at the commencement of this Act shall, by virtue of this Act, vest in the person who at such commencement was entitled to such lease, for a term of two thousand years, to be calculated from the date at which the existing term or interest commenced, at the rent and subject to the lessees' covenants and conditions (if any) which under the lease would have been payable or enforceable during the subsistence of such term or interest.

(2) The rent, covenants and conditions (if any) shall (subject to the express provisions of this Act to the contrary) be payable and enforceable during the

subsistence of the term created by this Act; and that term shall take effect in substitution for the term or interest created by the lease, and be subject to the like power of re-entry (if any) and other provisions which affected the term or interest created by the lease, but without any right of renewal ...

5. *Dispositions purporting to create perpetually renewable leaseholds*

A grant, after the commencement of this Act, of a term, subterm, or other leasehold interest with a covenant or obligation for perpetual renewal, which would have been valid if this Part of this Act had not been passed, shall (subject to the express provisions of this Act) take effect as a demise for a term of two thousand years or in the case of a subdemise for a term less in duration by one day than the term out of which it is derived, to commence from the date fixed for the commencement of the term, subterm, or other interest, and in every case free from any obligation for renewal or for payment of any fines, fees, costs, or other money in respect of renewal ...

10. *Powers and covenants implied in leases and underleases affected*

(1) Every lease or underlease which, by virtue of this Part of this Act, takes effect for a term of two thousand years or for a derivative term of two thousand years less one or more days (as the case may require) shall be deemed to contain –

(i) A power (exerciseable only with the consent of the person, if any, interested in any derivative interest which might be prejudicially affected) for the lessee or underlessee by giving notice in writing to the lessor at least ten days before the lease or underlease would (but for this Act) have expired if it had not been renewed after the commencement of this Act, to determine the lease or underlease at the date on which (but for this Act) it would have expired if it had not been renewed as aforesaid; also a like power (exerciseable with the like consent if any) to determine subsequently by notice as aforesaid the lease or underlease at the time at which, if this Act had not been passed and all renewals had in the meantime been made in due course, the lease or underlease would have expired if it had not been further renewed after the date of the notice:

Provided that if any such notice be given all uncommuted additional rent attributable to a fine or other money which, if this Act had not been passed, would have been payable on a renewal made after the date of the notice, shall cease or not become payable:

(ii) A covenant by the lessee or underlessee to register every assignment or devolution of the term or subterm, including all probates or letters of administration affecting the same, with the lessor or his solicitor or agent, within six months from the date of the assignment, devolution, or grant of probate or letters of administration, and to pay a fee of one guinea (which shall be accepted in satisfaction of all costs) in respect of each registration; and the covenant so deemed to be contained shall be in substitution for any express covenant to register with the lessor or his solicitor or agent, assignments or devolutions of the term or subterm, and to pay fees or costs in respect of such registration:

(iii) A covenant by the lessee or underlessee within one year from the commencement of this Act to produce his lease or underlease or sufficient evidence thereof (including an assignment of part of the land comprised in the lease or underlease) with any particulars required to show that a perpetual right of renewal was subsisting at the commencement of this Act, to the lessor or his solicitor or agent, who shall, subject to the payment of his costs, if the right of renewal is admitted or proved, endorse notice of that fact on the lease, underlease, assignment, or copy thereof, at the expense of the lessee or underlessee; and such endorsement signed by or on behalf of the lessor shall, in favour of a purchaser, be sufficient evidence that the right of renewal was subsisting as aforesaid, either in respect of the whole or part of the land as the case may require:

and the power of re-entry (if any) contained in the lease or underlease shall apply and extend to the breach of every covenant deemed to be contained as aforesaid.

(2) If any dispute arises respecting the date on which a notice is authorised to be served by this section, or whether or not a lease or underlease or assignment or a copy thereof ought to be endorsed as aforesaid, the matter shall be submitted to the Minister for determination in the manner provided by this Act.

[As amended by the Law of Property (Amendment) Act 1924, s2, Schedule 2.]

SETTLED LAND ACT 1925
(15 Geo 5 c 18)

PART I

GENERAL PRELIMINARY PROVISIONS

1 What constitutes a settlement [278]

(1) Any deed, will, agreement for a settlement or other agreement, Act of Parliament. or other instrument, or any number of instruments, whether made or passed before or after, or partly before and partly after, the commencement of this Act, under or by virtue of which instrument or instruments any land, after the commencement of this Act, stands for the time being –

(i) limited in trust for any persons by way of succession; or
(ii) limited in trust for any person in possession –

(a) for an entailed interest whether or not capable of being barred or defeated;
(b) for an estate in fee simple or for a term of years absolute subject to an executory limitation, gift, or disposition over on failure of his issue or in any other event;
(c) for a base or determinable fee (other than a fee which is a fee simple absolute by virtue of section 7 of the Law of Property Act 1925) or any corresponding interest in leasehold land;
(d) being an infant, for an estate in fee simple or for a term of years absolute; or

(iii) limited in trust for any person for an estate in fee simple or for a term of years absolute contingently on the happening of any event; or ...
(v) charged, whether voluntarily or in consideration of marriage or by way of family arrangement, and whether immediately or after an interval, with the payment of any rentcharge for the life of any person, or any less period, or of any capital, annual, or periodical sums for the portions, advancement, maintenance, or otherwise for the benefit of any persons, with or without any term of years for securing or raising the same;

creates or is for the purposes of this Act a settlement and is in this Act referred to as a settlement, or as the settlement, as the case requires: provided that, where land is the subject of a compound settlement, references in this Act to the settlement shall be construed as meaning such compound settlement, unless the context otherwise requires.

(2) Where an infant is beneficially entitled to land for an estate in fee simple or for a term of years absolute and by reason of an intestacy or otherwise there is no instrument under which the interest of the infant arises or is acquired, a settlement shall be deemed to have been made by the intestate, or by the person whose interest the infant has acquired.

(3) An infant shall be deemed to be entitled in possession notwithstanding any subsisting right of dower (not assigned by metes and bounds) affecting the land, and such a right of dower shall be deemed to be an interest comprised in the subject of the settlement and coming to the dowress under or by virtue of the settlement. Where dower has been assigned by metes and bounds, the letters of administration or probate granted in respect of the estate of the husband of the dowress shall be deemed a settlement made by the husband.

(4) An estate or interest not disposed of by a settlement and remaining in or reverting to the settlor, or any person deriving title under him, is for the purposes of this Act an estate or interest comprised in the subject of the settlement and coming to the settlor or such person under or by virtue of the settlement.

(5) Where –

(a) a settlement creates an entailed interest which is incapable of being barred or defeated, or a base or determinable fee, whether or not the reversion or right of reverter is in the Crown, or any corresponding interest in leasehold land; or

(b) the subject of a settlement is an entailed interest, or a base or determinable fee, whether or not the reversion or right of reverter is in the Crown, or any corresponding interest in leasehold land;

the reversion or right of reverter upon the cesser of the interest so created or settled shall be deemed to be an interest comprised in the subject of the settlement, and limited by the settlement.

(6) Subsections (4) and (5) of this section bind the Crown.

(7) This section does not apply to land held upon trust for sale.

2 What is settled land [279]

Land not held upon trust for sale which is or is deemed to be the subject of a settlement is for the purposes of this Act settled land, and is in relation to the settlement referred to in this Act as the settled land.

3 Duration of settlements [280]

Land which has been subject to a settlement which is a settlement for the purposes of this Act shall be deemed for the purposes of this Act to remain and be settled land, and the settlement shall be deemed to be a subsisting settlement for the purposes of this Act so long as –

(a) any limitation, charge, or power of charging under the settlement subsists, or is capable of being exercised; or

(b) the person who, if of full age, would be entitled as beneficial owner to have that land vested in him for a legal estate is an infant.

4 Authorised method of settling land inter vivos [281]

(1) Every settlement of a legal estate in land inter vivos shall, save as in this Act otherwise provided, be effected by two deeds, namely, a vesting deed and a trust

instrument and if effected in any other way shall not operate to transfer or create a legal estate.

(2) By the vesting deed the land shall be conveyed to the tenant for life or statutory owner (and if more than one as joint tenants) for the legal estate the subject of the intended settlement: provided that, where such legal estate is already vested in the tenant for life or statutory owner, it shall be sufficient, without any other conveyance, if the vesting deed declares that the land is vested in him for that estate.

(3) The trust instrument shall –

(a) declare the trusts affecting the settled land;
(b) appoint or constitute trustees of the settlement;
(c) contain the power, if any, to appoint new trustees of the settlement;
(d) set out, either expressly or by reference, any powers intended to be conferred by the settlement in extension of those conferred by this Act;
(e) bear any ad valorem stamp duty which may be payable (whether by virtue of the vesting deed or otherwise) in respect of the settlement.

5 Contents of vesting deeds [282]

(1) Every vesting deed for giving effect to a settlement or for conveying settled land to a tenant for life or statutory owner during the subsistence of the settlement (in this Act referred to as a 'principal vesting deed') shall contain the following statements and particulars, namely –

(a) A description, either specific or general, of the settled land;
(b) A statement that the settled land is vested in the person or persons to whom it is conveyed or in whom it is declared to be vested upon the trusts from time to time affecting the settled land;
(c) The names of the persons who are the trustees of the settlement;
(d) Any additional or larger powers conferred by the trust instrument relating to the settled land which by virtue of this Act operate and are exercisable as if conferred by this Act on a tenant for life;
(e) The name of any person for the time being entitled under the trust instrument to appoint new trustees of the settlement.

(2) The statements or particulars required by this section may be incorporated by reference to an existing vesting instrument, and, where there is a settlement subsisting at the commencement of this Act, by reference to that settlement and to any instrument whereby land has been conveyed to the uses or upon the trusts of that settlement, but not (save as last aforesaid) by reference to a trust instrument nor by reference to a disentailing deed.

(3) A principal vesting deed shall not be invalidated by reason only of any error in any of the statements or particulars by this Act required to be contained therein.

6 Procedure in the case of settlements by will [283]

Where a settlement is created by the will of an estate owner who dies after the commencement of this Act –

(a) the will is for the purposes of this Act a trust instrument; and
(b) the personal representatives of the testator shall hold the settled land on trust, if and when required so to do, to convey it to the person who, under the will, or by virtue of this Act, is the tenant for life or statutory owner, and, if more than one, as joint tenants.

7 Procedure on change of ownership   [284]

(1) If, on the death of a tenant for life or statutory owner, or of the survivor of two or more tenants for life or statutory owners, in whom the settled land was vested, the land remains settled land, his personal representatives shall hold the settled land on trust, if and when required so to do, to convey it to the person who under the trust instrument or by virtue of this Act becomes the tenant for life or statutory owner and, if more than one, as joint tenants.

(2) If a person by reason of attaining full age becomes a tenant for life for the purposes of this Act of settled land, he shall be entitled to require the trustees of the settlement, personal representatives, or other persons in whom the settled land is vested, to convey the land to him.

(3) If a person who, when of full age, will together with another person or other persons constitute the tenant for life for the purposes of this Act of settled land attains that age, he shall be entitled to require the tenant for life, trustees of the settlement, personal representatives or other persons in whom the settled land is vested to convey the land to him and the other person or persons who together with him constitute the tenant for life as joint tenants.

(4) If by reason of forfeiture, surrender, or otherwise the estate owner of any settled land ceases to have the statutory powers of a tenant for life and the land remains settled land, he shall be bound forthwith to convey the settled land to the person who under the trust instrument, or by virtue of this Act, becomes the tenant for life or statutory owner and, if more than one, as joint tenants.

(5) If any person of full age becomes absolutely entitled to the settled land (whether beneficially, or as personal representative, or as trustee of land, or otherwise) free from all limitations, powers, and charges taking effect under the settlement, he shall be entitled to require the trustees of the settlement, personal representatives, or other persons in whom the settled land is vested, to convey the land to him, and if more persons than one being of full age become so entitled to the settled land they shall be entitled to require such persons as aforesaid to convey the land to them as joint tenants.

8 Mode and costs of conveyance, and saving of rights of   [285]
personal representatives and equitable chargees

(1) A conveyance by personal representatives under either of the last two preceding sections may be made by an assent in writing signed by them which shall operate as a conveyance.

(2) Every conveyance under either of the last two preceding sections shall be made at the cost of the trust estate.

(3) The obligations to convey settled land imposed by the last two preceding sections are subject and without prejudice –

(a) where the settlement is created by a will, to the rights and powers of the personal representatives for purposes of administration; and
(b) in any case, to the person on whom the obligation is imposed being satisfied that provision has been or will be made for the payment of any unpaid death duties in respect of the land or any interest therein for which he is accountable, and any interest and costs in respect of such duties, or that he is otherwise effectually indemnified against such duties, interest and costs.

(4) Where the land is or remains settled land a conveyance under either of the last two preceding sections shall –

(a) if by deed, be a principal vesting deed; and
(b) if by an assent, be a vesting assent, which shall contain the like statements

and particulars as are required by this Act in the case of a principal vesting deed.

(5) Nothing contained in either of the last two preceding sections affects the right of personal representatives to transfer or create such legal estates to take effect in priority to a conveyance under either of those sections as may be required for giving effect to the obligations imposed on them by statute.

(6) A conveyance under either of the last two preceding sections, if made by deed, may contain a reservation to the person conveying of a term of years absolute in the land conveyed, upon trusts for indemnifying him against any unpaid death duties in respect of the land conveyed or any interest therein, and any interest and costs in respect of such duties.

(7) Nothing contained in either of the last two preceding sections affects any right which a person entitled to an equitable charge for securing money actually raised, and affecting the whole estate the subject of the settlement, may have to require effect to be given thereto by a legal mortgage, before the execution of a conveyance under either of those sections.

9 Procedure in the case of settlements and of instruments [286] deemed to be trust instruments

(1) Each of the following settlements or instruments shall for the purposes of this Act be deemed to be a trust instrument, and any reference to a trust instrument contained in this Act shall apply thereto, namely –

(i) An instrument executed, or, in case of a will, coming into operation, after the commencement of this Act which by virtue of this Act is deemed to be a settlement;
(ii) A settlement which by virtue of this Act is deemed to have been made by any person after the commencement of this Act;
(iii) An instrument inter vivos intended to create a settlement of a legal estate in land which is executed after the commencement of this Act, and does not comply with the requirements of this Act with respect to the method of effecting such a settlement; and
(iv) A settlement made after the commencement of this Act (including a settlement by the will of a person who dies after such commencement) of any of the following interests –

(a) an equitable interest in land which is capable, when in possession, of subsisting at law; or
(b) an entailed interest; or
(c) a base or determinable fee or any corresponding interest in leasehold land,

but only if and when the interest settled takes effect free from all equitable interests and powers under every prior settlement (if any).

(2) As soon as practicable after a settlement, or an instrument which for the purposes of this Act is deemed to be a trust instrument, takes effect as such, the trustees of the settlement may, and on the request of the tenant for life or statutory owner shall, execute a principal vesting deed, containing the proper statements and particulars, declaring that the legal estate in the settled land shall vest or is vested in the person or persons therein named, being the tenant for life or statutory owner, and including themselves if they are the statutory owners, and such deed shall, unless the legal estate is already so vested, operate to convey or vest the legal estate in the settled land to or in the person or persons aforesaid and, if more than one, as joint tenants.

(3) If there are no trustees of the settlement, then (in default of a person able and willing to appoint such trustees) an application under this Act shall be made to the court for the appointment of such trustees.

(4) The provisions of the last preceding section with reference to a conveyance shall apply, so far as they are applicable, to a principal vesting deed under this section.

10 Procedure on acquisition of land to be made subject   [287] to a settlement

(1) Where after the commencement of this Act land is acquired with capital money arising under this Act or in exchange for settled land, or a rentcharge is reserved on a grant of settled land, the land shall be conveyed to, and the rentcharge shall by virtue of this Act become vested in, the tenant for life or statutory owner, and such conveyance or grant is in this Act referred to as a subsidiary vesting deed: Provided that, where an instrument is subsisting at the commencement of this Act, or is made or comes into operation after such commencement, by virtue of which any money or securities are liable under this Act, or the Acts which it replaces, or under a trust or direction contained in the instrument, to be invested in the purchase of land to be conveyed so as to become settled land, but at the commencement of this Act, or when such instrument is made or comes into operation after such commencement, as the case may be, there is no land in respect of which a principal vesting deed is capable of being executed, the first deed after the commencement of this Act by which any land is acquired as aforesaid shall be a principal vesting deed and shall be framed accordingly.

(2) A subsidiary vesting deed executed on the acquisition of land to be made subject to a settlement shall contain the following statements and particulars, namely –

(a) particulars of the last or only principal vesting instrument affecting land subject to the settlement;
(b) a statement that the land conveyed is to be held upon and subject to the same trusts and powers as the land comprised in such last or only principal vesting instrument;
(c) the names of the persons who are the trustees of the settlement;
(d) the name of any person for the time being entitled to appoint new trustees of the settlement.

(3) A subsidiary vesting deed reserving a rentcharge on a grant of settled land shall contain the following statements and particulars –

(a) a statement that the rentcharge is vested in the grantor and is subject to the settlement which, immediately before the grant, was subsisting with respect to the land out of which it was reserved;
(b) particulars of the last or only principal vesting instrument affecting such land.

(4) A subsidiary vesting deed shall not be invalidated by reason only of any error in any of the statements or particulars by this Act required to be contained therein.

(5) The acquisition of the land shall not operate to increase or multiply charges or powers of charging.

11 As to contracts for the settlement of land   [288]

(1) A contract made or other liability created or arising after the commencement of this Act for the settlement of land –

(i) by or on the part of an estate owner; or

(ii) by a person entitled to –

(a) an equitable interest which is capable when in possession of subsisting at law; or

(b) an entailed interest; or

(c) a base or determinable fee or any corresponding interest in leasehold land;

shall, but in cases under paragraph (ii) only if and when the interest of the person entitled takes effect free from all equitable interests and powers under every prior settlement, if any, be deemed an estate contract within the meaning of the Land Charges Act 1925 and may be registered as a land charge accordingly, and effect shall be given thereto by a vesting deed and a trust instrument in accordance with this Act.

(2) A contract made or other liability created or arising before the commencement of this Act to make a settlement of land shall be deemed to be sufficiently complied with if effect is given thereto by a vesting deed and a trust instrument in accordance with this Act.

12 Power to make vesting orders as to settled land [289]

(1) If –

(a) any person who is bound under this Part of this Act to execute a conveyance, vesting deed or vesting assent or in whom settled land is wrongly vested refuses or neglects to execute the requisite conveyance, vesting deed or vesting assent within one month after demand in writing; or

(b) any such person is outside the United Kingdom, or cannot be found, or it is not known whether he is alive or dead; or

(c) for any reason the court is satisfied that the conveyance, vesting deed or vesting assent cannot be executed, or cannot be executed without undue delay or expense;

the court may, on the application of any person interested, make an order vesting the settled land in the tenant for life or statutory owner or person, if any, of full age absolutely entitled (whether beneficially or as personal representative or trustee of land or otherwise), and, if the land remains settled land, the provisions of this Act relating to a principal vesting deed or a subsidiary vesting deed, as the case may be, shall apply to any order so made and every such order shall contain the like statements and particulars.

(2) No stamp duty shall be payable in respect of a vesting order made in place of a vesting or other assent.

13 Dispositions not to take effect until vesting instrument is made [290]

Where a tenant for life or statutory owner has become entitled to have a principal vesting deed or a vesting assent executed in his favour, then until a vesting instrument is executed or made pursuant to this Act in respect of the settled land, any purported disposition thereof inter vivos by any person, other than a personal representative (not being a disposition which he has power to make in right of his equitable interests or powers under a trust instrument), shall not take effect except in favour of a purchaser of a legal estate without notice of such tenant for life or statutory owner having become so entitled as aforesaid but, save as aforesaid, shall operate only as a contract for valuable consideration to carry out the transaction after the requisite vesting instrument has been executed or made, and a purchaser of a legal estate shall not be concerned with such disposition unless the contract is registered as a land charge. Nothing in this section affects the creation or transfer of a legal estate by virtue of an order of the court or the Minister or other competent authority.

14 Forfeiture and stamps   [291]

(1) Any vesting effected under the powers conferred by this Act in relation to settled land shall not operate as a breach of a covenant or condition against alienation or give rise to a forfeiture.

(2) Nothing in this Act shall operate to impose any stamp duty on a vesting or other assent.

15 Examples of instruments   [292]

Examples of instruments framed in accordance with the provisions of this Act are contained in the First Schedule to this Act.

16 Enforcement of equitable interests and powers   [293]
against estate owner

(1) All equitable interests and powers in or over settled land (whether created before or after the date of any vesting instrument affecting the legal estate) shall be enforceable against the estate owner in whom the settled land is vested (but in the case of personal representatives without prejudice to their rights and powers for purposes of administration) in manner following (that is to say) –

(i) The estate owner shall stand possessed of the settled land and the income thereof upon such trusts and subject to such powers and provisions as may be requisite for giving effect to the equitable interests and powers affecting the settled land or the income thereof of which he has notice according to their respective priorities;

(ii) Where any person of full age becomes entitled to require a legal estate in the settled land to be vested in him in priority to the settlement, by reason of a right of reverter, statutory or otherwise, or an equitable right of entry taking effect, or on the ground that his interest ought no longer to be capable of being over-reached under the powers of this Act, the estate owner shall be bound, if so requested in writing, to transfer or create such legal estate as may be required for giving legal effect to the rights of the person so entitled;

(iii) Where –

(a) any principal sum is required to be raised on the security of the settled land, by virtue of any trust, or by reason of the exercise of an equitable power affecting the settled land, or by any person or persons who under the settlement is or are entitled or together entitled to or has or have a general power of appointment over the settled land, whether subject to any equitable charges or powers of charging subsisting under the settlement or not; or

(b) the settled land is subject to any equitable charge for securing money actually raised and affecting the whole estate the subject of the settlement;

the estate owner shall be bound, if so requested in writing, to create such legal estate or charge by way of legal mortgage as may be required for raising the money or giving legal effect to the equitable charge:

Provided that so long as the settlement remains subsisting, any legal estate or charge by way of legal mortgage so created shall take effect and shall be expressed to take effect subject to any equitable charges or powers of charging subsisting under the settlement which have priority to the interests or powers of the person or persons by or on behalf of whom the money is required to be raised or legal effect is required to be given to the equitable charge, unless the persons entitled to the prior charges or entitled to exercise the powers consent in writing to the same being postponed, but it shall not be necessary for such consent to be expressed in the instrument creating such legal estate or charge by way of legal mortgage.

(2) Where a mortgage or charge is expressed to be made by an estate owner pursuant to this section, then, in favour of the mortgagee or chargee and persons deriving title under him, the same shall take effect in priority to all the trusts of the settlement and all equitable interests and powers subsisting or to arise under the settlement except those to which it is expressly made subject, and shall so take effect, whether the mortgagee or chargee has notice of any such trusts, interests, or powers, or not, and the mortgagee or chargee shall not be concerned to see that a case had arisen to authorise the mortgage or charge, or that no more money than was granted was raised.

(3) Nothing contained in paragraph (iii) of subsection (1) of this section affects the power conferred by this Act on a tenant for life of raising money by mortgage or of directing capital money to be supplied in discharge of incumbrances.

(4) Effect may be given by means of a legal mortgage to an agreement for a mortgage, or a charge or lien, whether or not arising by operation of law, if the agreement charge or lien ought to have priority over the settlement.

(5) Save as hereinbefore expressly provided, no legal estate shall, so long as the settlement is subsisting, be transferred or created by the estate owner for giving effect to any equitable interest or power under the settlement.

(6) If a question arises or a doubt is entertained whether any and what legal estate ought to be transferred or created pursuant to this section, an application may be made to the court for directions as hereinafter provided.

(7) If an estate owner refuses or neglects for one month after demand in writing to transfer or create any such legal estate, or if by reason of his being outside the United Kingdom, or being unable to be found, or by reason of the dissolution of a corporation, or for any other reason, the court is satisfied that the transaction cannot otherwise be effected, or cannot be effected without undue delay or expense, the court may, on the application of any person interested, make a vesting order transferring or creating the requisite legal estate.

(8) This section does not affect a purchaser of a legal estate taking free from any equitable interest or power.

17 Deed of discharge on termination of settlement [294]

(1) Where the estate owner of any settled land holds the land free from all equitable interests and powers under a trust instrument, the persons who in the last or only principal vesting instrument or the last or only endorsement on or annex thereto are declared to be the trustees of the settlement or the survivors of them shall, save as hereinafter mentioned, be bound to execute, at the cost of the trust estate, a deed declaring that they are discharged from the trust so far as regards that land: Provided that, if the trustees have notice of any derivative settlement, trust of land or equitable charge affecting such land, they shall not execute a deed of discharge until –

    (a) in the case of a derivative settlement, or trust of land, a vesting instrument or a conveyance has been executed or made for giving effect thereto; and

    (b) in the case of an equitable charge, they are satisfied that the charge is or will be secured by a legal mortgage, or is protected by registration as a land charge, or by deposit of the documents of title, or that the owner thereof consents to the execution of the deed of discharge.

Where the land is affected by a derivative settlement or trust of land, the deed of discharge shall contain a statement that the land is settled land by virtue of such vesting instrument as aforesaid and the trust instrument therein referred to, or is subject to a trust of land by virtue of such conveyance as aforesaid, as the case may require.

(2) If, in the circumstances mentioned in subsection (1) of this section and when the conditions therein mentioned have been complied with, the trustees of a settlement on being requested to execute a deed of discharge –

(a) by the estate owner; or

(b) by a person interested under, or by the trustees of, a derivative settlement; or

(c) by the trustees of land;

refuse to do so, or if for any reason the discharge cannot be effected without undue delay or expense, the estate owner, person interested, or trustees may apply to the court for an order discharging the first mentioned trustees as respects the whole or any part of the settled land, and the court may make such order as it may think fit.

(3) Where a deed or order of discharge contains no statement to the contrary, a purchaser of a legal estate in the land to which the deed or order relates shall be entitled to assume that the land has ceased to be settled land, and is not subject to a trust of land.

18 Restrictions on dispositions of settled land where [295] trustees have not been discharged

(1) Where land is the subject of a vesting instrument and the trustees of the settlement have not been discharged under this Act, then –

(a) any disposition by the tenant for life or statutory owner of the land, other than a disposition authorised by this Act or any other statute, or made in pursuance of any additional or larger powers mentioned in the vesting instrument, shall be void, except for the purpose of conveying or creating such equitable interests as he has power, in right of his equitable interests and powers under the trust instrument, to convey or create; and

(b) if any capital money is payable in respect of a transaction, a conveyance to a purchaser of the land shall only take effect under this Act if the capital money is paid to or by the direction of the trustees of the settlement or into court; and

(c) notwithstanding anything to the contrary in the vesting instrument, or the trust instrument, capital money shall not, except where the trustee is a trust corporation, be paid to or by the direction of fewer persons than two as trustees of the settlement.

(2) The restrictions imposed by this section do not affect –

(a) the right of a personal representative in whom the settled land may be vested to convey or deal with the land for the purposes of administration;

(b) the right of a person of full age who has become absolutely entitled (whether beneficially or as trustee of land or personal representative or otherwise) to the settled land, free from all limitations, powers, and charges taking effect under the trust instrument, to require the land to be conveyed to him;

(c) the power of the tenant for life, statutory owner, or personal representative in whom the settled land is vested to transfer or create such legal estates, to take effect in priority to the settlement, as may be required for giving effect to any obligations imposed on him by statute, but where any capital money is raised or received in respect of the transaction the money shall be paid to or by the direction of the trustees of the settlement or in accordance with an order of the court.

19 Who is tenant for life [296]

(1) The person of full age who is for the time being beneficially entitled under a settlement to possession of settled land for his life is for the purposes of this Act the tenant for life of that land and the tenant for life under that settlement.

(2) If in any case there are two or more persons of full age so entitled as joint tenants, they together constitute the tenant for life for the purposes of this Act.

(3) If in any case there are two or more persons so entitled as joint tenants and they are not all of full age, such one or more of them as is or are for the time being of full age is or (if more than one) together constitute the tenant for life for the purposes of this Act, but this subsection does not affect the beneficial interests of such of them as are not for the time being of full age.

(4) A person being tenant for life within the foregoing definitions shall be deemed to be such notwithstanding that, under the settlement or otherwise, the settled land, or his estate or interest therein, is incumbered or charged in any manner or to any extent, and notwithstanding any assignment by operation of law or otherwise of his estate or interest under the settlement, whether before or after it came into possession, other than an assurance which extinguishes that estate or interest.

20 Other limited owners having powers of tenant for life [297]

(1) Each of the following persons being of full age shall, when his estate or interest is in possession, have the powers of a tenant for life under this Act, (namely) –

(i) A tenant in tail, including a tenant in tail after possibility of issue extinct, and a tenant in tail who is by Act of Parliament reinstated from barring or defeating his estate tail, and although the reversion is in the Crown, but not including such a tenant in tail where the land in respect whereof he is so restrained was purchased with money provided by Parliament in consideration of public services;

(ii) A person entitled to land for an estate in fee simple or for a term of years absolute with or subject to, in any of such cases, an executory limitation, gift, or disposition over on failure of his issue or in any other event;

(iii) A person entitled to a base or determinable fee, although the reversion or right of reverter is in the Crown, or to any corresponding interest in leasehold land;

(iv) A tenant for years determinable on life, not holding merely under a lease at a rent;

(v) A tenant for the life of another, not holding merely under a lease at a rent;

(vi) A tenant for his own or any other life, or for years determinable on life, whose estate is liable to cease in any event during that life, whether by expiration of the estate, or by conditional limitation, or otherwise, or to be defeated by an executory limitation, gift, or disposition over, or is subject to a trust for accumulation of income for any purpose;

(vii) A tenant by the curtesy;

(viii) A person entitled to the income of land under a trust or direction for payment thereof to him during his own or any other life, whether or not subject to expenses of management or to a trust for accumulation of income for any purpose, or until sale of the land, or until forfeiture, cesser or determination by any means of his interest therein, unless the land is subject to a trust of land;

(ix) A person beneficially entitled to land for an estate in fee simple or for a term of years absolute subject to any estates, interests, charges, or powers of charging, subsisting or capable of being exercised under a settlement.

(2) In every such case as is mentioned in subsection (1) of this section, the provisions of this Act referring to a tenant for life, either as conferring powers on him or otherwise, shall extend to each of the persons aforesaid, and any reference in this Act to death as regards a tenant for life shall, where necessary, be deemed to refer to the determination by death or otherwise of the estate or interest of the person on whom the powers of a tenant for life are conferred by this section.

(3) For the purposes of this Act the estate or interest of a tenant by the curtesy shall be deemed to be an estate or interest arising under a settlement made by his wife.

(4) Where the reversion or right of reverter or other reversionary right is in the Crown, the exercise by a person on whom the powers of a tenant for life are conferred by this section of his powers under this Act, binds the Crown.

21 Absolute owners subject to certain interests to have [298] the powers of tenant for life

(1) Where a person of full age is beneficially entitled in possession to a legal estate subject to any equitable interests or powers, then, for the purpose of overreaching such interests or powers, he may, notwithstanding any stipulation to the contrary, by deed (which shall have effect as a principal vesting deed within the meaning of this Act) declare that the legal estate is vested in him on trust to give effect to all equitable interests and powers affecting the legal estate, and that deed shall be executed by two or more individuals approved or appointed by the court or a trust corporation, who shall be stated to be the trustees of the settlement for the purposes of this Act. Thereupon so long as any of the equitable interests and powers are subsisting the following provisions shall have effect –

(a) The person so entitled as aforesaid and each of his successors in title being an estate owner shall have the powers of a tenant for life and the land shall be deemed to be settled land;

(b) The instrument (if any) under which his estate arises or is acquired, and the instrument (if any) under which the equitable interests or powers are subsisting or capable of taking effect shall be deemed to be the trust instrument: provided that where there is no such instrument as last aforesaid then a deed (which shall take effect as a trust instrument) shall be executed contemporaneously with the vesting deed, and shall declare the trusts affecting the land;

(c) The persons stated in the principal vesting deed to be the trustees of the settlement for the purposes of this Act shall also be the trustees of the trust instrument for those purposes; and

(d) Capital money arising on any disposition of the land shall be paid to or by the direction of the trustees of the settlement or into court, and shall be applicable towards discharging or providing for payment in due order of any principal money payable in respect of such interests or charges as are overreached by such disposition, and until so applied shall be invested or applied as capital money under the trust instrument, and the income thereof shall be applied as the income of such capital money, and be liable for keeping down in due order any annual or periodical sum which may be overreached by the disposition.

(2) The following equitable interests and powers are excepted from the operation of subsection (1) of this section, namely –

(i) an equitable interest protected by a deposit of documents relating to the legal estate affected;

(ii) the benefit of a covenant or agreement restrictive of the user of land;

(iii) an easement, liberty or privilege over or affecting land and being merely an equitable interest;

(iv) the benefit of a contract to convey or create a legal estate, including a contract conferring either expressly or by statutory implication a valid option of purchase, a right of pre-emption, or any other like right;

(v) any equitable interest protected by registration under the Land Charges Act 1925 other than –

(a) an annuity within the meaning of Part II of that Act;

(b) a limited owner's charge or a general equitable charge within the meaning of that Act.

(3) Subject to the powers conferred by this Act on a tenant for life, nothing contained in this section shall deprive an equitable chargee of any of his rights or of his remedies for enforcing those rights.

22 Provisions applicable where interest in settled land is restored [299]

(1) Where by a disentailing assurance settled land is expressed to be limited (whether subject or not to any estates, interests, charges or powers expressly created or conferred thereby) upon the trusts subsisting with respect thereto immediately before the execution of such disentailing assurance, or any of such trusts, then, for the purposes of this Act and otherwise, a person entitled to any estate or interest in the settled land under any such previously subsisting trust is entitled thereto after the execution of such disentailing assurance as of his former estate or interest.

(2) Where by a resettlement of settled land any estate or interest therein is expressed to be limited to any person (whether subject or not to any estate, interest, charge or power expressly created or conferred by the resettlement) in restoration or confirmation of his estate or interest under a prior settlement, then, for the purposes of this Act and otherwise, that person is entitled to the estate or interest so restored or confirmed as of his former estate or interest, and in addition to the powers exercisable by him in respect of his former estate or interest, he is capable of exercising all such further powers as he could have exercised by virtue of the resettlement, if his estate or interest under the prior settlement had not been so restored or confirmed, but he had been entitled under the resettlement only.

23 Powers of trustees, etc, when there is no tenant for life [300]

(1) Where under a settlement there is no tenant for life nor, independently of this section, a person having by virtue of this Act the powers of a tenant for life then –

(a) any person of full age on whom such powers are by the settlement expressed to be conferred; and

(b) in any other case the trustees of the settlement;

shall have the powers of a tenant for life under this Act.

(2) This section applies to trustees of settlements of land purchased with money provided by Parliament in consideration of public services where the tenant in tail is restrained from barring or defeating his estate tail, except that, if the tenant in tail is of full age and capacity, the powers shall not be exercised without his

consent, but a purchaser shall not be concerned to see or inquire whether such consent has been given.

24 As to a tenant for life who has parted with his interest   [301]

(1) If it is shown to the satisfaction of the court that a tenant for life, who has by reason of bankruptcy, assignment, incumbrance, or otherwise ceased in the opinion of the court to have a substantial interest in his estate or interest in the settled land or any part thereof, has unreasonably refused to exercise any of the powers conferred on him by this Act, or consents to an order under this section, the court may, on the application of any person interested in the settled land or the part thereof affected, make an order authorising the trustees of the settlement, to exercise in the name and on behalf of the tenant for life, any of the powers of a tenant for life under this Act, in relation to the settled land or the part thereof affected, either generally and in such manner and for such period as the court may think fit, or in a particular instance, and the court may by the order direct that any documents of title in the possession of the tenant for life relating to the settled land be delivered to the trustees of the settlement.

(2) While any such order is in force, the tenant for life shall not, in relation to the settled land or the part thereof affected, exercise any of the powers thereby authorised to be exercised in his name and on his behalf, but no person dealing with the tenant for life shall be affected by any such order, unless the order is for the time being registered as an order affecting land.

(3) An order may be made under this section at any time after the estate or interest of the tenant for life under the settlement has taken effect in possession, and notwithstanding that he disposed thereof when it was an estate or interest in remainder or reversion.

25 Married woman, how to be affected   [302]

(1) The foregoing provisions of this Act apply to a married woman of full age, whether or not she is entitled to her estate or interest for her separate use or as her separate property, and she, without her husband, may exercise the powers of a tenant for life under this Act.

26 Infants, how to be affected   [303]

(1) Where an infant is beneficially entitled in possession to land for an estate in fee simple or for a term of years absolute or would if of full age be a tenant for life of or have the powers of a tenant for life over settled land, then, during the minority of the infant –

(a) if the settled land is vested in a personal representative, the personal representative, until a principal vesting instrument has been executed pursuant to the provisions of this Act; and
(b) in every other case, the trustees of the settlement;

shall have, in reference to the settled land and capital money, all the powers conferred by this Act and the settlement on a tenant for life, and on the trustees of the settlement.

(2) If the settled land is vested in a personal representative, then, if and when during the minority the infant, if of full age, would have been entitled to have the legal estate in the settled land conveyed to or otherwise vested in him pursuant to the provisions of this Act, a principal vesting instrument shall, if the trustees of the settlement so require, be executed, at the cost of the trust estate, for vesting the legal estate in themselves, and in the meantime the personal representatives shall,

during the minority, give effect to the direction of the trustees of the settlement, and shall not be concerned with the propriety of any conveyance directed to be made by those trustees if the conveyance appears to be a proper conveyance under the powers conferred by this Act or by the settlement, and the capital money, if any, arising under the conveyance is paid to or by the direction of the trustees of the settlement or into court, but a purchaser dealing with the personal representative and paying the capital money, if any, to him shall not be concerned to see that the money is paid to trustees of the settlement or into court, or to inquire whether the personal representative is liable to give effect to any such directions, or whether any such directions have been given.

(3) Subsection (2) of this section applies whether the infant becomes entitled before or after the commencement of this Act, and has effect during successive minorities until a person of full age becomes entitled to require the settled land to be vested in him.

(4) This section does not apply where an infant is beneficially entitled in possession to land for an estate in fee simple or for a term of years absolute jointly with a person of full age (for which case provision is made in the Law of Property Act 1925), but it applies to two or more infants entitled as aforesaid jointly, until one of them attains full age.

(5) This section does not apply where an infant would, if of full age, constitute the tenant for life or have the powers of a tenant for life together with another person of full age, but it applies to two or more infants who would, if all of them were of full age, together constitute the tenant for life or have the power of a tenant for life, until one of them attains full age.

(6) Nothing in this section affects prejudicially any beneficial interest of an infant.

30 Who are trustees for purposes of Act   [304]

(1) Subject to the provisions of this Act, the following persons are trustees of a settlement for the purposes of this Act, and are in this Act referred to as the 'trustees of the settlement' or 'trustees of a settlement', namely –

(i) the persons, if any, who are for the time being under the settlement, trustees with power of sale of the settled land (subject or not to the consent of any person), or with power of consent to or approval of the exercise of such a power of sale, or if there are no such persons; then

(ii) the persons, if any, for the time being, who are by the settlement declared to be trustees thereof for the purposes of the Settled Land Acts 1882 to 1890 or any of them, or this Act, or if there are no such persons; then

(iii) the persons, if any, who are for the time being under the settlement trustees with a power or duty to sell any other land comprised in the settlement and subject to the same limitations as the land to be sold or otherwise dealt with, or with power of consent to or approval of the exercise of such a power of sale, or, if there are no such persons; then

(iv) the persons, if any, who are for the time being under the settlement trustees with a future power or duty to sell the settled land, or with power of consent to or approval of the exercise of such a future power of sale, and whether the power or duty takes effect in all events or not, or, if there are no such persons; then

(v) the persons, if any, appointed by deed to be trustees of the settlement by all the persons who at the date of the deed were together able, by virtue of their beneficial interests or by the exercise of an equitable power, to dispose of the settled land in equity for the whole estate the subject of the settlement.

(2) Paragraphs (i) (iii) and (iv) of the last preceding subsection take effect in like

manner as if the powers therein referred to had not by this Act been made exercisable by the tenant for life or statutory owner.

(3) Where a settlement is created by will, or a settlement has arisen by the effect of an intestacy, and apart from this subsection there would be no trustees for the purposes of this Act of such settlement, then the personal representatives of the deceased shall, until other trustees are appointed, be by virtue of this Act the trustees of the settlement, but where there is a sole personal representative, not being a trust corporation, it shall be obligatory on him to appoint an additional trustee to act with him for the purposes of this Act, and the provisions of the Trustee Act 1925 relating to the appointment of new trustees and the vesting of trust property shall apply accordingly.

33 Continuance of trustees in office, and as to certain compound settlements [305]

(1) Where any persons have been appointed or constituted trustees of a settlement, whether by an order of the court or otherwise, or have by reason of a power or duty to sell, or by reason of a power of consent to, or approval of, the exercise of a power of sale, or by compound virtue of this Act, or otherwise at any time become trustees of a settlement for the purposes of the Settled Land Acts 1882 to 1890 or this Act, then those persons or their successors in office shall remain and be trustees of the settlement as long as that settlement is subsisting or deemed to be subsisting for the purposes of this Act. In this subsection 'successors in office' means the persons who, by appointment or otherwise, have become trustees for the purposes aforesaid ...

34 Appointment of trustees by court [306]

(1) If at any time there are no trustees of a settlement, or where in any other case it is expedient, for the purposes of this Act, that new trustees of a settlement be appointed, the court may, if it thinks fit, on the application of the tenant for life, statutory owner, or of any other person having, under the settlement, an estate or interest in the settled land, in possession, remainder or otherwise, or, in the case of an infant, of his testamentary or other guardian or next friend, appoint fit persons to be trustees of the settlement.

(2) The persons so appointed, and the survivors and survivor of them, while continuing to be trustees or trustee, and, until the appointment of new trustees, the personal representatives or representative for the time being of the last surviving or continuing trustee, shall become and be the trustees or trustee of the settlement.

35 Procedure on appointment of new trustees [307]

(1) Whenever a new trustee for the purposes of this Act is appointed of a trust instrument or a trustee thereof for the purposes aforesaid is discharged from the trust without a new trustee being appointed, a deed shall be executed supplemental to the last or only principal vesting instrument containing a declaration that the persons therein named, being the persons who after such appointment or discharge, as the case may be, are the trustees of the trust instrument for the purposes aforesaid, are the trustees of the settlement for those purposes; and a memorandum shall be endorsed on or annexed to the last or only principal vesting entitlement in accordance with the Trustee Act 1925.

(2) Every such deed as aforesaid shall, if the trustee was appointed or discharged by the court, be executed by such person as the court may direct, and, in any other case, shall be executed by –

(i) the person if any, named in the principal vesting instrument as the person for the time being entitled to appoint new trustees of the settlement, or if no person is so named, or the person is dead or unable or unwilling to act, the persons who if the principal vesting instrument had been the only instrument constituting the settlement would have had power to appoint new trustees thereof;

(ii) the persons named in the deed of declaration as the trustees of the settlement; and

(iii) any trustee who is discharged as aforesaid or retires.

(3) A statement contained in any such deed of declaration as is mentioned in this section to the effect that the person named in the principal vesting instrument as the person for the time being entitled to appoint new trustees of the settlement is unable or unwilling to act, or that a trustee has remained outside the United Kingdom for more than twelve months, or refuses or is unfit to act, or is incapable of acting, shall in favour of a purchaser of a legal estate be conclusive evidence of the matter stated.

36 Undivided shares to take effect behind a trust of land   **[308]**

(1) If and when, after the commencement of this Act, settled land is held in trust for persons entitled in possession under a trust instrument in undivided shares, the trustees of the settlement (if the settled land is not already vested in them) may require the estate owner in whom the settled land is vested (but in the case of a personal representative subject to his rights and powers for purposes of administration), at the cost of the trust estate, to convey the land to them, or assent to the land vesting in them as joint tenants, and in the meantime the land shall be held on the same trusts as would have been applicable thereto if it had been so conveyed to or vested in the trustees.

(2) If and when the settled land so held in trust in undivided shares is or becomes vested in the trustees of the settlement, the land shall be held by them (subject to any incumbrances affecting the settled land which are secured by a legal mortgage, but freed from any incumbrances affecting the undivided shares or not secured as aforesaid, and from any interests, powers and charges subsisting under the trust instrument which have priority to the trust for the persons entitled to the undivided shares) in trust for the persons interested in the land.

(3) If the estate owner refuses or neglects for one month after demand in writing to convey the settled land so held in trust in undivided shares in manner aforesaid, or if by reason of his being outside the United Kingdom or being unable to be found, or by reason of the dissolution of a corporation, or for any other reason, the court is satisfied that the conveyance cannot otherwise be made, or cannot be made without undue delay or expense, the court may, on the application of the trustees of the settlement, make an order vesting the settled land in them in trust for the persons interested in the land.

(4) An undivided share in land shall not be capable of being created except under a trust instrument or under the Law of Property Act 1925 and shall then only take effect behind a trust of land.

(5) Nothing in this section affects the priority inter se of any incumbrances whether affecting the entirety of the land or an undivided share ...

(6) In subsections (2) and (3) of this section references to the persons interested in the land include persons interested as trustees or personal representatives (as well as persons beneficially interested).

PART II

POWERS OF A TENANT FOR LIFE

38 Powers of sale and exchange   [309]

A tenant for life –

(i) May sell the settled land, or any part thereof, or any easement, right or privilege of any kind over or in relation to the land; and

(iii) May make an exchange of the settled land, or any part thereof, or of any easement, right, or privilege of any kind, whether or not newly created, over or in relation to the settled land, or any part thereof, for other land, or for any easement, right or privilege of any kind, whether or not newly created, over or in relation to other land, including an exchange in consideration of money paid for equality of exchange.

39 Regulations respecting sales   [310]

(1) Save as hereinafter provided every sale shall be made for the best consideration in money that can reasonably be obtained.

(2) A sale may be made in consideration wholly or partially of a perpetual rent, or a terminable rent consisting of principal and interest combined, payable yearly or half yearly to be secured upon the land sold, or the land to which the easement, right or privilege sold is to be annexed in enjoyment or an adequate part thereof. In the case of a terminable rent, the conveyance shall distinguish the part attributable to principal and that attributable to interest, and the part attributable to principal shall be capital money arising under this Act: provided that, unless the part of the terminable rent attributable to interest varies according to the amount of the principal repaid, the trustees of the settlement shall, during the subsistence of the rent, accumulate the income of the said capital money in the way of compound interest by investing it and the resulting income thereof in securities authorised for the investment of capital money and shall add the accumulations to capital.

(3) The rent to be reserved on any such sale shall be the best rent that can reasonably be obtained, regard being had to any money paid as part of the consideration, or laid out, or to be laid out, for the benefit of the settled land, and generally to the circumstances of the case, but a peppercorn rent, or a nominal or other rent less than the rent ultimately payable, may be made payable during any period not exceeding five years from the date of the conveyance.

(4) Where a sale is made in consideration of a rent, the following provisions shall have effect –

(i) The conveyance shall contain a covenant by the purchaser for payment of the rent, and the statutory powers and remedies for the recovery of the rent shall apply;

(ii) A duplicate of the conveyance shall be executed by the purchaser and delivered to the tenant for life or statutory owner, of which execution and delivery the execution of the conveyance by the tenant for life or statutory owner shall be sufficient evidence;

(iii) A statement, contained in the conveyance or in an indorsement thereon, signed by the tenant for life or statutory owner, respecting any matter of fact or of calculation under this Act in relation to the sale, shall, in favour of the purchaser and of those claiming under him, be sufficient evidence of the matter stated ... .

(6) A sale may be made in one lot or in several lots, and either by auction or by private contract, and may be made subject to any stipulations respecting title, or evidence of title, or other things.

(7) On a sale the tenant for life may fix reserve biddings and may buy in at an auction.

40 Regulations respecting exchanges [311]

(1) Save as in this Part of this Act provided, every exchange shall be made for the best consideration in land or in land and money that can reasonably be obtained.

(2) An exchange may be made subject to any stipulations respecting title, or evidence of title, or other things.

(3) Settled land in England or Wales shall not be given in exchange for land out of England and Wales.

41 Power to lease for ordinary or building or mining [312] or forestry purposes

A tenant for life may lease the settled land, or any part thereof, or any easement, right, or privilege of any kind over or in relation to the land, for any purpose whatever, whether involving waste or not, for any term not exceeding –

(i) In case of a building lease, nine hundred and ninety-nine years;
(ii) In case of a mining lease, one hundred years;
(iii) In case of a forestry lease, nine hundred and ninety-nine years;
(iv) In case of any other lease, fifty years.

42 Regulations respecting leases generally [313]

(1) Save as hereinafter provided, every lease –

(i) shall be by deed, and be made to take effect in possession not later than twelve months after its date, or in reversion after an existing lease having not more than seven years to run at the date of the new lease;
(ii) shall reserve the best rent that can reasonably be obtained, regard being had to any fine taken, and to any money laid out or to be laid out for the benefit of the settled land, and generally to the circumstances of the case;
(iii) shall contain a covenant by the lessee for payment of the rent, and a condition of re-entry on the rent not being paid within a time therein specified not exceeding thirty days.

(2) A counterpart of every lease shall be executed by the lessee and delivered to the tenant for life or statutory owner, of which execution and delivery the execution of the lease by the tenant for life or statutory owner shall be sufficient evidence.

(3) A statement, contained in a lease or in an indorsement thereon, signed by the tenant for life or statutory owner, respecting any matter of fact or of calculation under this Act in relation to the lease, shall, in favour of the lessee and of those claiming under him, be sufficient evidence of the matter stated.

(4) A fine received on the grant of a lease under any power conferred by this Act shall be deemed to be capital money arising under this Act.

(5) A lease at the best rent that can be reasonably obtained without fine, and whereby the lessee is not exempted from punishment for waste, may be made –

(i) Where the term does not exceed twenty-one years –

(a) without any notice of an intention to make the lease having been given under this Act; and

(b) notwithstanding that there are no trustees of the settlement; and

(ii) Where the term does not extend beyond three years from the date of the writing, by any writing under hand only containing an agreement instead of a covenant by the lessee for payment of rent.

43 Leasing powers for special objects   [314]

The leasing power of a tenant for life extends to the making of –

(i) a lease for giving effect (in such manner and so far as the law permits) to a covenant of renewal, performance whereof could be enforced against the owner for the time being of the settled land; and

(ii) a lease for confirming, as far as may be, a previous lease being void or voidable, but so that every lease, as and when confirmed, shall be such a lease as might at the date of the original lease have been lawfully granted under this Act or otherwise, as the case may require.

44 Regulations respecting building leases   [315]

(1) Every building lease shall be made partly in consideration of the lessee, or some person by whose direction the lease is granted, or some other person, having erected or agreeing to erect buildings, new or additional, or having improved or repaired or agreeing to improve or repair buildings, or having executed or agreeing to execute on the land leased, an improvement authorised by this Act for or in connection with building purposes.

(2) A peppercorn rent or a nominal or other rent less than the rent ultimately payable, may be made payable for the first five years or any less part of the term.

(3) Where the land is contracted to be leased in lots, the entire amount of rent to be ultimately payable may be apportioned among the lots in any manner: provided that –

(i) the annual rent reserved by any lease shall not be less than 50p; and

(ii) the total amount of the rents reserved on all leases for the time being granted shall not be less than the total amount of the rents which, in order that leases may be in conformity with this Act, ought to be reserved in respect of the whole land for the time being leased; and

(iii) the rent reserved by any lease shall not exceed one-fifth part of the full annual value of the land comprised in that lease with the buildings thereon when completed.

45 Regulations respecting mining leases   [316]

(1) In a mining lease –

(i) the rent may be made to be ascertainable by or to vary according to the acreage worked, or by or according to the quantities of any mineral or substance gotten, made merchantable, converted, carried away, or disposed of, in or from the settled land, or any other land, or by or according to any facilities given in that behalf; and

(ii) the rent may also be made to vary according to the price of the minerals or substances gotten, or any of them, and such price may be the saleable value, or the price or value appearing in any trade or market or other price list or return from time to time, or may be the marketable value as ascertained in any manner prescribed by the lease (including a reference to arbitration), or may be an average of any such prices or values taken during a specified period; and (iii) a fixed or minimum rent may be made payable, with or without power for the lessee, in case the rent, according to acreage or quantity or otherwise, in any specified period does not produce an amount equal to the fixed or minimum rent, to make up the deficiency in any subsequent specified period, free of rent other than the fixed or minimum rent.

(2) A lease may be made partly in consideration of the lessee having executed, or agreeing to execute, on the land leased an improvement authorised by this Act, for or in connexion with mining purposes.

46 Variation of building or mining lease according to circumstances of district [317]

(1) Where it is shown to the court with respect to the district in which any settled land is situate, either –

(i) that it is the custom for land therein to be leased for building or mining purposes for a longer term or on other conditions than the term or conditions specified in that behalf in this Act; or
(ii) that it is difficult to make leases for building or mining purposes of land therein, except for a longer term or on other conditions than the term and conditions specified in that behalf in this Act;

the court may, if it thinks fit, authorise generally the tenant for life or statutory owner to make time to time leases of or affecting the settled land in that district, or parts thereof for any term or on any conditions as in the order of the court expressed, or may, if it thinks fit, authorise the tenant for life or statutory owner to make any such lease in any particular case.

(2) Thereupon the tenant for life or statutory owner, and, subject to any direction in the order of the court to the contrary, each of his successors in title being a tenant for life or statutory owner, may make in any case, or in the particular case, a lease of the settled land, or part thereof, in conformity with the order.

47 Capitalisation of part of mining rent [318]

Under a mining lease, whether the mines or minerals leased are already opened or in work or not, unless a contrary intention is expressed in the settlement there shall be from time to time set aside, as capital money arising under this Act, part of the rent as follows, namely – where the tenant for life or statutory owner is impeachable for waste in respect of minerals, three fourth parts of the rent, and otherwise one fourth part thereof, and in every such case the residue of the rent shall go as rents and profits.

48 Regulations respecting forestry leases [319]

(1) In the case of a forestry lease –

(i) a peppercorn rent or a nominal or other rent less than the rent ultimately payable, may be made payable for the first ten years or any less part of the term;
(ii) the rent may be made to be ascertainable by, or to vary according to the value of the timber on the land comprised in the lease, or the produce thereof, which may during any year be cut, converted, carried away, or otherwise disposed of;
(iii) a fixed or minimum rent may be made payable, with or without power for the lessee, in case the rent according to value in any specified period does not

produce an amount equal to the fixed or minimum rent, to make up the deficiency in any subsequent specified period, free of rent other than the fixed or minimum rent; and

(iv) any other provisions may be made for the sharing of the proceeds or profits of the user of the land between the reversioner and the Forestry Commissioners.

(2) In this section the expression 'timber' includes all forest products.

49 Powers on dispositions to impose restrictions and   [320] make reservations and stipulations

(1) On a sale or other disposition or dealing under the powers of this Act –

(a) any easement, right, or privilege of any kind may be reserved or granted over or in relation to the settled land or any part thereof or other land, including the land disposed of, and in the case of an exchange, the land taken in exchange; and

(b) any restriction with respect to building on or other user of land, or with respect to mines and minerals, or with respect to or for the purpose of the more beneficial working thereof, or with respect to any other thing, may be imposed and made binding, as far as the law permits, by covenant, condition or otherwise, on the tenant for life or statutory owner and the settled land or any part thereof, or on the other party and any land disposed of to him; and

(c) the whole or any part of any capital or annual sum (and in the case of an annual sum whether temporary or perpetual) charged on or payable out of the land disposed of, or any part thereof, and other land subject to the settlement, may as between the tenant for life or statutory owner and his successors in title, and the other party and persons deriving title under or in succession to him (but without prejudice to the rights of the person entitled to such capital or annual sum) be charged exclusively on the land disposed of, or any part thereof, or such other land as aforesaid, or any part thereof, in exoneration of the rest of the land on or out of which such capital or annual sum is charged or payable.

(2) A sale of land may be made subject to a stipulation that all or any of the timber and other trees, pollards, tellers, underwood, saplings and plantations on the land sold (in this section referred to as 'timber') or any articles attached to the land (in this section referred to as 'fixtures') shall be taken by the purchaser at a valuation, and the amount of the valuation shall form part of the price of the land, and shall be capital money accordingly.

(3) Where on a sale the consideration attributable to any timber or fixtures is by mistake paid to a tenant for life or other person not entitled to receive it, then, if such person or the purchaser or the persons deriving title under either of them subsequently pay the aforesaid consideration, with such interest, if any, thereon as the court may direct, to the trustees of the settlement or other persons entitled thereto or into court, the court may, on the application of the purchaser or the persons deriving title under him, declare that the disposition is to take effect as if the whole of the consideration had at the date thereof been duly paid to the trustees of the settlement or other persons entitled to receive the same. 'The person, not entitled to receive the same, to whom the consideration is paid, and his estate and effects shall remain liable to make good any loss attributable to the mistake.

50 Separate dealing with surface and minerals, with [321]
or without wayleaves, etc

A sale, exchange, lease or other authorised disposition, may be made either of land, with or without an exception or reservation of all or any of the mines and minerals therein, or of any mines and minerals, and in any such case with or without a grant or reservation of powers of working, wayleaves or rights of way, rights of water and drainage, and other powers, easements, rights, and privileges for or incident to or connected with mining purposes, in relation to the settled land, or any part thereof, or any other land.

51 Power to grant options [322]

(1) A tenant for life may at any time, either with or without consideration, grant by writing an option to purchase or take a lease of the settled land, or any part thereof, or any easement, right, or privilege over or in relation to the same at a price or rent fixed at the time of the granting of the option.

(2) Every such option shall be made exercisable within an agreed number of years not exceeding ten.

(3) The price or rent shall be the best which, having regard to all the circumstances, can reasonably be obtained and either –

(a) may be a specified sum of money or rent, or at a specified rate according to the superficial area of the land with respect to which the option is exercised, or the frontage thereof or otherwise; or
(b) in the case of an option to purchase contained in a lease or agreement for a lease, may be a stated number of years' purchase of the highest rent reserved by the lease or agreement; or
(c) if the option is exercisable as regards part of the land comprised in the lease or agreement, may be a proportionate part of such highest rent;

and any aggregate price or rent may be made to be apportionable in any manner, or according to any system, or by reference to arbitration.

(4) An option to take a mining lease may be coupled with the grant of a licence to search for and prove any mines or minerals under the settled land, or any part thereof, pending the exercise of the option.

(5) The consideration for the grant of the option shall be capital money arising under this Act.

52 Surrenders and regrants [323]

(1) A tenant for life may accept, with or without consideration, a surrender of any lease of settled land, whether made under this Act or not, or a regrant of any land granted in fee simple, whether under this Act or not, in respect of the whole land leased or granted, or any part thereof, with or without an exception of all or any of the mines and minerals therein, or in respect of mines and minerals, or any of them, and with or without an exception of any easement, right or privilege of any land over or in relation to the land surrendered or regranted.

(2) On a surrender of a lease, or a regrant of land granted in fee simple, in respect of part only of the land or mines and minerals leased or granted, the rent or rentcharge may be apportioned.

(3) On a surrender or regrant, the tenant for life may in relation to the land or mines and minerals surrendered or regranted, or of any part thereof, make a new or other lease, or grant in fee simple, or new or other leases, or grants in fee simple, in lots.

(4) A new or other lease, or grant in fee simple, may comprise additional land or mines and minerals, and may reserve any apportioned or other rent or rentcharge.

(5) On a surrender or regrant, and the making of a new or other lease, whether for the same or for any extended or other term, or of a new or other grant in fee simple, and whether or not subject to the same or to any other covenants, provisions, or conditions, the value of the lessee's or grantee's interest in the lease surrendered, or the land regranted, may be taken into account in the determination of the amount of the rent or rentcharge to be reserved, and of any fine or consideration in money to be taken, and of the nature of the covenants, provisions, and conditions to be inserted in the new or other lease, or grant in fee simple.

(6) Every new or other lease, or grant in fee simple, shall be in conformity with this Act.

(7) All money, not being rent or a rentcharge, received on the exercise by the tenant for life of the powers conferred by this section, shall, unless the court, on an application made within six months after the receipt thereof or within such further time as the court may in special circumstances allow, otherwise directs, be capital money arising under this Act.

(8) A regrant shall be made to the tenant for life or statutory owner, and shall be deemed a subsidiary vesting deed, and the statements and particulars required in the case of subsidiary vesting deeds shall be inserted therein.

(9) In this section 'land granted in fee simple' means land so granted with or subject to a reservation thereout of a perpetual or terminable rentcharge which is or forms part of the settled land, and 'grant in fee simple' has a corresponding meaning.

53 Acceptance of leases   [324]

(1) A tenant for life may accept a lease of any land, or of any mines and minerals or of any easement, right, or privilege, convenient to be held or worked with or annexed in enjoyment to the settled land, or any part thereof, for such period, and upon such terms and conditions, as the tenant for life thinks fit: Provided that no fine shall be paid out of capital money in respect of such lease.

(2) The lease shall be granted to the tenant for life or statutory owner, and shall be deemed a subsidiary vesting deed, and the statements and particulars required in the case of subsidiary vesting deeds shall either be inserted therein or endorsed thereon.

(3) The lease may contain an option to purchase the reversion expectant on the term thereby granted.

54 Power to grant water rights to statutory bodies   [325]

(1) For the development, improvement, or general benefit of the settled land, or any part thereof, a tenant for life may make a grant in fee simple or absolutely, or a lease for any term of years absolute, for a nominal price or rent, or for less than the best price or rent that can reasonably be obtained, or gratuitously, to any statutory authority, of any water or streams or springs of water in, upon, or under the settled land, and of any rights of taking, using, enjoying and conveying water, and of laying, constructing, maintaining, and repairing mains, pipes, reservoirs, dams, weirs and other works of any kind proper for the supply and distribution of water, and of any part of the settled land required as a site for any of the aforesaid works, and of any easement, right or privilege over or in relation to the settled land or any part thereof in connexion with any of the aforesaid works.

(2) This section does not authorise the creation of any greater rights than could have been created by a person absolutely entitled for his own benefit to the settled land affected.

(3) In this section 'statutory authority' means an authority or company for the time being empowered by any Act of Parliament, public general, or local or private, or by any order or certificate having the force of an Act of Parliament, to provide with a supply of water any town, parish or place in which the settled land or any part thereof is situated.

(4) All money, not being rent, received on the exercise of any power conferred by this section shall be capital money arising under this Act.

55 Power to grant land for public and charitable purposes [326]

(1) For the development, improvement, or general benefit of the settled land, or any part thereof, a tenant for life may make a grant in fee simple, or absolutely, or a lease for any term of years absolute, for a nominal price or rent, or for less than the best price or rent that can reasonably be obtained, or gratuitously, of any part of the settled land, with or without any easement, right or privilege over or in relation to the settled land or any part thereof, for all or any one or more of the following purposes, namely –

(i) For the site, or the extension of any existing site, of a place of religious worship, residence for a minister of religion, school house, town hall, market house, public library, public baths, museum, hospital, infirmary, or other public building, literary or scientific institution, drill hall, working-men's club, parish room, reading room or village institute, with or without in any case any yard, garden, or other ground to be held with any such building; or
(ii) For the construction, enlargement, or improvement of any railway, canal, road (public or private), dock, sea-wall, embankment, drain, watercourse, or reservoir; or
(iii) For any other public or charitable purpose in connection with the settled land, or any part thereof, or tending to the benefit of the persons residing, or for whom dwellings may be erected, on the settled land, or any part thereof.

Not more than one acre shall in any particular case be conveyed for any purpose mentioned in paragraphs (i) and (iii) of this subsection, nor more than five acres for any purpose mentioned in paragraph (ii) of this subsection, unless the full consideration be paid or reserved in respect of the excess.

(2) All money, not being rent, received on the exercise of any power conferred by this section shall be capital money arising under this Act.

56 Dedication for streets, open spaces, etc [327]

(1) On or after or in connexion with a sale or grant for building purposes, or a building lease, or the development as a building estate of the settled land, or any part thereof, or at any other reasonable time, the tenant for life, for the general benefit of the residents on the settled land, or on any part thereof –

(i) may cause or require any parts of the settled land to be appropriated and laid out for streets, roads, paths, squares, gardens, or other open spaces, for the use, gratuitously or on payment, of the public or of individuals, with sewers, drains, watercourses, fencing, paving, or other works necessary or proper in connexion therewith; and
(ii) may provide that the parts so appropriated shall be conveyed to or vested in the trustees of the settlement, or other trustees, or any company or public

body, on trusts or subject to provisions for securing the continued appropriation thereof to the purposes aforesaid, and the continued repair or maintenance of streets and other places and works aforesaid, with or without provision for appointment of new trustees when required; and

(iii) may execute any general or other deed necessary or proper for giving effect to the provisions of this section (which deed may be inrolled in the Central Office of the Supreme Court), and thereby declare the mode, terms, and conditions of the appropriation, and the manner in which and the persons by whom the benefit thereof is to be enjoyed, and the nature and extent of the privileges and conveniences granted.

(2) In regard to the dedication of land for the public purposes aforesaid, a tenant for life shall be in the same position as if he were an absolute owner.

(3) A tenant for life shall have power –

(a) to enter into any agreement for the recompense to be made for any part of the settled land which is required for the widening of a highway under the Highways Act 1980 or otherwise;

(b) to consent to the diversion of any highway over the settled land under the Highways Act 1980 or otherwise;

and any agreement or consent so made or given shall be as valid and effectual, for all purposes, as if made or given by an absolute owner of the settled land.

(4) All money, not being rent, received on the exercise of any power conferred by this section shall be capital money arising under this Act.

57 Provision of land for small dwellings, small holdings   [328] and dwellings for working classes

(1) Where land is sold, or given in exchange or leased –

(a) for the purpose of the erection on such land of small dwellings; or

(b) to the council of a county or county borough for the purposes of small holdings;

the sale, exchange, or lease may, notwithstanding anything contained in this Act, be made for such consideration in money, or land, or in land and money, or may reserve such rent, as having regard to the said purposes and to all the circumstances of the case, is the best that can reasonably be obtained, notwithstanding that a better consideration or rent might have been obtained if the land were sold, exchanged, or leased, for another purpose.

(2) Notwithstanding anything contained in, and in addition to the other powers conferred by this Act, a tenant for life may at any time –

(a) for the purpose of the erection of dwellings for the working classes, or the provision of gardens to be held therewith; or

(b) for the purpose of the Small Holdings and Allotments Acts 1908 to 1919;

make a grant in fee simple or absolutely, or a lease for any term of years absolute of any part of the settled land, with or without any easement, right or privilege of any kind over or in relation to the settled land or any part thereof, for a nominal price or rent, or for less than the best price or rent that can reasonably be obtained or gratuitously: provided that, except under an order of the court, not more than two acres in the case of land situate in an urban district, or ten acres in the case of land situate in a rural district, in any one parish shall be granted or leased under the powers conferred by this subsection, unless the full consideration be paid or reserved in respect of the excess.

(3) All money, not being rent, received on the exercise of any power conferred by this section shall be capital money arising under this Act.

58 Power to compromise claims and release restrictions, etc [329]

(1) A tenant for life may with the consent in writing of the trustees of the settlement, either with or without giving or taking any consideration in money or otherwise, compromise, compound, abandon, submit to arbitration, or otherwise settle any claim, dispute, or question whatsoever relating to the settled land, or any part thereof, including in particular claims, disputes or questions as to boundaries, the ownership of mines and minerals, rights and powers of working mines and minerals, local laws and customs relative to the working of mines and minerals and other matters, easements, and restrictive covenants, and for any of those purposes may enter into, give, execute, and do such agreements, assurances, releases, and other things as the tenant for life may, with such consent as aforesaid, think proper.

(2) A tenant for life may, with the consent in writing of the trustees of the settlement, at any time, by deed or writing, either with or without consideration in money or otherwise, release, waive, or modify, or agree to release, waive, or modify, any covenant, agreement, or restriction imposed on any other land for the benefit of the settled land, or any part thereof, or release, or agree to release, any other land from any easement, right or privilege, including a right of pre-emption, affecting the same for the benefit of the settled land, or any part thereof ...

59 Power to vary leases and grants and to give licences [330]
and consents

(1) A tenant for life may, at any time, by deed, either with or without consideration in money or otherwise, vary, release, waive or modify, either absolutely or otherwise, the terms of any lease whenever made of the settled land or any part thereof, or any covenants or conditions contained in any grant in fee simple whenever made of land with or subject to a reservation thereout of a rent which is or forms part of the settled land, and in either case in respect of the whole or any part of the land comprised in any such lease or grant, but so that every such lease or grant shall, after such variation, release, waiver or modification as aforesaid, be such a lease or grant as might then have been lawfully made under this Act if the lease had been surrendered, or the land comprised in the grant had never been so comprised, or had been regranted.

(2) Where land is or has been disposed of subject to any covenant requiring the licence, consent, or approval of the covenantee or his successors in title as to –

(a) the user of the land in any manner; or

(b) the erection construction or alteration of or addition to buildings or works of any description on the land; or

(c) the plans or elevations of any proposed buildings or other works on the land; or

(d) any other act, matter, or thing relating to the land, or any buildings or works thereon; or

(e) any assignment, underletting or parting with the possession of all or any part of the property comprised in any lease affecting the settled land;

and the covenant enures for the benefit of settled land (including, where the disposition is a lease, the reversion expectant on the determination thereof), the licence, consent or approval may be given by the tenant for life of the settled land affected.

60 Power to apportion rents [331]

(1) A tenant for life may, at any time, by deed, either with or without consideration in money or otherwise, agree for the apportionment of any rent reserved or created by any such lease or grant as mentioned in the last preceding section, or any rent being or forming part of the settled land, so that the apportioned parts of such rent shall thenceforth be payable exclusively out of or in respect of such respective portions of the land subject thereto as may be thought proper, and also agree that any covenants, agreements, powers, or remedies for securing such rent and any other covenants or agreements by the lessee or grantee and any conditions shall also be apportioned and made applicable exclusively to the respective portions of the land out of or in respect of which the apportioned parts of such rent shall thenceforth be payable.

(2) Where the settled land, or any part thereof, is held or derived under a lease, or under a grant reserving rent, or subject to covenants, agreements or conditions, whether such lease or grant comprises other land or not, the tenant for life may at any time by deed, with or without giving or taking any consideration in money or otherwise, procure the variation, release, waiver, or modification, either absolutely or otherwise, of the terms, covenants, agreements, or conditions contained in such lease or grant, in respect of the whole or any part of the settled land comprised therein, including the apportionment of any rent, covenants, agreements, conditions, and provisions reserved, or created by, or contained in, such lease or grant.

(3) This section applies to leases or grants made either before or after the commencement of this Act.

61 Provisions as to consideration [332]

(1) All money, not being rent, payable by the tenant for life in respect of any transaction to which any of the three last preceding sections relates shall be paid out of capital money arising under this Act, and all money, not being rent, received on the exercise by the tenant for life of the powers conferred by any of those sections, shall, unless the court, on an application made within six months after the receipt thereof or within such further time as the court may in special circumstances allow, otherwise directs, be capital money arising under this Act.

(2) For the purpose of the three last preceding sections 'consideration in money or otherwise' means –

    (a) a capital sum of money or a rent;
    (b) land being freehold or leasehold for any term of years whereof not less than sixty years shall be unexpired;
    (c) any easement, right or privilege over or in relation to the settled land, or any part thereof, or any other land;
    (d) the benefit of any restrictive covenant or condition; and
    (e) the release of the settled land, or any part thereof, or any other land, from any easement, right or privilege, including a right of pre-exemption, or from the burden of any restrictive covenant or condition affecting the same.

62 Special provisions as to manorial incidents, etc [333]

(4) In reference to the conversion of a perpetually renewable lease or underlease into a long term, a tenant for life may enter into such agreements and do such acts and things as the lessor or lessee or underlessee, as the case may require, is, by any enactment authorised to enter into or do.

63 Power to complete predecessor's contracts [334]

A tenant for life may make any disposition which is necessary or proper for giving effect to a contract entered into by a predecessor in title, and which if made by that predecessor would have been valid as against his successors in title.

64 General power for the tenant for life to effect any [335] transaction under an order of the court

(1) Any transaction affecting or concerning the settled land, or any part thereof, or any other land (not being a transaction otherwise authorised by this Act, or by the settlement) which in the opinion of the court would be for the benefit of the settled land, or any part thereof, or the persons interested under the settlement, may, under an order of the court, be effected by a tenant for life, if it is one which could have been validly effected by an absolute owner.

(2) In this section 'transaction' includes any sale, exchange, assurance, grant, lease, surrender, reconveyance, release, reservation, or other disposition, and any purchase or other acquisition, and any covenant, contract, or option, and any application of capital money and any compromise or other dealing, or arrangement; and 'effected' has the meaning appropriate to the particular transaction; and the references to land include references to restrictions and burdens affecting land.

65 Power to dispose of mansion [336]

(1) The powers of disposing of settled land conferred by this Act on a tenant for life may be exercised as respects the principal mansion house, if any, on any settled land, and the pleasure grounds and park and lands, if any, usually occupied therewith: provided that those powers shall not be exercised without the consent of the trustees of the settlement or an order of the court –

(a) if the settlement is a settlement made or coming into operation before the commencement of this Act and the settlement does not expressly provide to the contrary; or
(b) if the settlement is a settlement made or coming into operation after the commencement of this Act and the settlement expressly provides that these powers or any of them shall not be exercised without such consent or order.

(2) Where a house is usually occupied as a farmhouse, or where the site of any house and the pleasure grounds and park and lands, if any, usually occupied therewith do not together exceed twenty-five acres in extent, the house is not to be deemed a principal mansion house within the meaning of this section, and may accordingly be disposed of in like manner as any other part of the settled land.

66 Cutting and sale of timber, and capitalisation of part of proceeds [337]

(1) Where a tenant for life is impeachable for waste in respect of timber, and there is on the settled land timber ripe and fit for cutting, the tenant for life, on obtaining the consent of the trustees of the settlement or an order of the court, may cut and sell that timber, or any part thereof.

(2) Three fourth parts of the net proceeds of the sale shall be set aside as and be capital money arising under this Act, and the other fourth part shall go as rents and profits.

67 Sale and purchase of heirlooms under order of court   [338]

(1) Where personal chattels are settled so as to devolve with settled land, or to devolve therewith as nearly as may be in accordance with the law or practice in force at the date of the settlement, or are settled together with land, or upon trusts declared by reference to the trusts affecting land, a tenant for life of the land may sell the chattels or any of them.

(2) The money arising by the sale shall be capital money arising under this Act, and shall be paid, invested, or applied and otherwise dealt with in like manner in all respects as by this Act directed with respect to other capital money arising under this Act, or may be invested in the purchase of other chattels of the same or any other nature, which, when purchased, shall be settled and held on the same trusts, and shall devolve in the same manner as the chattels sold.

(3) A sale or purchase of chattels under this section shall not be made without an order of the court.

(4) Any reference in any enactment to personal chattels settled as heirlooms shall extend to any chattels to which this section applies.

68 Provision enabling dealings with tenant for life   [339]

(1) In the manner mentioned and subject to the provisions contained in this section –

(a) a sale, grant, lease, mortgage, charge or other disposition of settled land, or of any easement, right, or privilege over the same may be made to the tenant for life; or
(b) capital money may be advanced on mortgage to him; or
(c) a purchase may be made from him of land to be made subject to the limitations of the settlement; or
(d) an exchange may be made with him of settled land for other land; and
(e) any such disposition, advance, purchase, or exchange as aforesaid may be made to, from, or with any persons of whom the tenant for life is one.

(2) In every such case the trustees of the settlement shall, in addition to their powers as trustees, have all the powers of a tenant for life in reference to negotiating and completing the transaction, and shall have power to enforce any covenants by the tenant for life, or, where the tenant for life is himself one of the trustees, then the other or others of them shall have such power, and the said powers of a tenant for life may be exercised by the trustees of the settlement in the name and on behalf of the tenant for life.

(3) This section applies, notwithstanding that the tenant for life is one of the trustees of the settlement, or that an order has been made authorising the trustees to act on his behalf, or that he is suffering from mental disorder, or a defective, but does not apply to dealings with any body of persons which includes a trustee of the settlement, not being the tenant for life, unless the transaction is either previously or subsequently approved by the court.

69 Shifting of incumbrances   [340]

Where there is an incumbrance affecting any part of the settled land (whether capable of being over-reached on the exercise by the tenant for life of his powers under this Act or not), the tenant for life, with the consent of the incumbrancer, may charge that incumbrance on any other part of the settled land, or on all or any part of the capital money or securities representing capital money subject or to become subject to the settlement, whether already charged therewith or not, in exoneration of the first mentioned part, and, by a legal mortgage, or otherwise, make provision accordingly.

70 Power to vary provisions of an incumbrance and to charge by way of additional security [341]

(1) Where an incumbrance affects any part of the settled land, the tenant for life may, with the consent of the incumbrancer, vary the rate of interest charged and any of the other provisions of the instrument, if any, creating the incumbrance, and with the like consent charge that incumbrance on any part of the settled land, whether already charged therewith or not, or on all or any part of the capital money or securities representing capital money subject or to become subject to the settlement, by way of additional security, or of consolidation of securities, and by a legal mortgage or otherwise, make provision accordingly.

(2) 'Incumbrance' in this section includes any annual sum payable during a life or lives or during a term of years absolute or determinable, but in any such case an additional security shall be effected so as only to create a charge or security similar to the original charge or security.

71 Power to raise money by mortgage [342]

(1) Where money is required for any of the following purposes namely –

(i) Discharging an incumbrance on the settled land or part thereof;
(ii) Paying for any improvement authorised by this Act or by the settlement;
(iii) Equality of exchange; ...
(vii) Commuting any additional rent made payable on the conversion of a perpetually renewable leasehold interest into a long term;
(viii) Satisfying any claims for compensation on the conversion of a perpetually renewable leasehold interest into a long term by any officer, solicitor, or other agent of the lessor in respect of fees or remuneration which would have been payable by the lessee or under-lessee on any renewal;
(ix) Payment of the costs of any transaction authorised by this section or either of the two last preceding sections;

the tenant for life may raise the money so required, on the security of the settled land, or of any part thereof, by a legal mortgage, and the money so raised shall be capital money for that purpose, and may be paid or applied accordingly.

(2) 'Incumbrance' in this section does not include any annual sum payable only during a life or lives or during a term of years absolute or determinable.

(3) The restrictions imposed by this Part of this Act on the leasing powers of a tenant for life do not apply in relation to a mortgage term created under this Act.

72 Completion of transactions by conveyance [343]

(1) On a sale, exchange, lease, mortgage, charge, or other disposition, the tenant for life may, as regards land sold, given in exchange, leased, mortgaged, charged, or otherwise disposed of, or intended so to be, or as regards easements or other rights or privileges sold, given in exchange, leased, mortgaged, or otherwise disposed of, or intended so to be, effect the transaction by deed to the extent of the estate or interest vested or declared to be vested in him by the last or only vesting instrument affecting the settled land or any less estate or interest, in the manner requisite for giving effect to the sale, exchange, lease, mortgage, charge, or other disposition, but so that a mortgage shall be effected by the creation of a term of years absolute in the settled land or by charge by way of legal mortgage, and not otherwise.

145

(2) Such a deed, to the extent and in the manner to and in which it is expressed or intended to operate and can operate under this Act, is effectual to pass the land conveyed, or the easements, rights, privileges or other interests created, discharged from all the limitations, powers, and provisions of the settlement, and from all estates, interests, and charges subsisting or to arise thereunder, but subject to and with the exception of –

(i) all legal estates and charges by way of legal mortgage having priority to the settlement; and

(ii) all legal estates and charges by way of legal mortgage which have been conveyed or created for securing money actually raised at the date of the deed; and

(iii) all leases and grants at fee-farm rents or otherwise, and all grants of easements, rights of common, or other rights or privileges which –

(a) were before the date of the deed granted or made for value in money or money's worth, or agreed so to be, by the tenant for life or statutory owner, or by any of his predecessors in title, or any trustees for them, under the settlement, or under any statutory power, or are at that date otherwise binding on the successors in title of the tenant for life or statutory owner; and

(b) are at the date of the deed protected by registration under the Land Charges Act, 1925, if capable of registration thereunder.

(3) Notwithstanding registration under the Land Charges Act 1925 of –

(a) an annuity within the meaning of Part II of that Act;

(b) a limited owner's charge or a general equitable charge within the meaning of that Act;

a disposition under this Act operates to overreach such annuity or charge which shall, according to its priority, take effect as if limited by the settlement.

(4) Where a lease is by this Act authorised to be made by writing under hand only, such writing shall have the same operation under this section as if it had been a deed.

PART III

INVESTMENT OR OTHER APPLICATION OF CAPITAL MONEY

73 Modes of investment or application   [344]

(1) Capital money arising under this Act, subject to payment of claims properly payable thereout and to the application thereof for any special authorised object for which the capital money was raised, shall, when received, be invested or otherwise applied wholly in one, or partly in one and partly in another or others, of the following modes (namely) –

(i) In investment in Government securities, or in other securities in which the trustees of the settlement are by the settlement or by law authorised to invest trust money of the settlement, with power to vary the investment into or for any other such securities;

(ii) In discharge, purchase, or redemption of incumbrances affecting the whole estate the subject of the settlement, or of rentcharge in lieu of tithe, Crown rent, chief rent, or quit rent, charged on or payable out of the settled land, or of any charge in respect of an improvement created on a holding under the Agricultural Holdings Act 1986 or any similar previous enactment;

(iii) In payment for any improvement authorised by this Act;

(iv) In payment as for an improvement authorised by this Act of any money expended and costs incurred by a landlord under or in pursuance of the Agricultural Holdings Act 1986 or any similar previous enactment, or under custom or agreement or otherwise, in or about the execution of any improvement comprised in Schedule 7 to the said Agricultural Holdings Act;

(v) In payment for equality of exchange of settled land; ...

(ix) In commuting any additional rent made payable on the conversion of a perpetually renewable leasehold interest into a long term, and in satisfying any claim for compensation on such conversion by any officer, solicitor, or other agent of the lessor in respect of fees or remuneration which would have been payable by the lessee or under-lessee on any renewal;

(x) In purchase of the freehold reversion in fee of any part of the settled land, being leasehold land held for years;

(xi) In purchase of land in fee simple, or of leasehold land held for sixty years or more unexpired at the time of purchase, subject or not to any exception or reservation of or in respect of mines or minerals therein, or of or in respect of rights or powers relative to the working of mines or minerals therein, or in other land;

(xii) In purchase either in fee simple, or for a term of sixty years or more, of mines and minerals convenient to be held or worked with the settled land, or of any easement, right, or privilege convenient to be held with the settled land for mining or other purposes;

(xiii) In redemption of an improvement rentcharge, that is to say, a rentcharge (temporary or permanent) created, whether before or after the commencement of this Act, in pursuance of any act of Parliament, with the object of paying off any money advanced for defraying the expenses of an improvement of any kind authorised by Part I of the Third Schedule to this Act;

(xiv) In the purchase, with the leave of the court, of any leasehold interest where the immediate reversion is settled land, so as to merge the leasehold interest (unless the court otherwise directs) in the reversion, and notwithstanding that the leasehold interest may have less than sixty years to run;

(xv) In payment of the costs and expenses of all plans, surveys, and schemes, including schemes under the Town Planning Act 1925 or any similar previous enactment, made with a view to, or in connexion with the improvement or development of the settled land, or any part thereof, or the exercise of any statutory powers, and of all negotiations entered into by the tenant for life with a view to the exercise of any of the said powers, notwithstanding that such negotiations may prove abortive, and in payment of the costs and expenses of opposing any such proposed scheme as aforesaid affecting the settled land, whether or not the scheme is made;

(xvi) In the purchase of an annuity charged under section four of the Tithe Act 1918 on the settled land or any part thereof, or in the discharge of such part of any such annuity as does not represent interest;

(xvii) In payment to a local or other authority of such sum as may be agreed in consideration of such authority taking over and becoming liable to repair a private road on the settled land or a road for the maintenance whereof a tenant for life is liable ratione tenurae;

(xviii) In financing any person who may have agreed to take a lease or grant for building purposes of the settled land, or any part thereof, by making advances to him in the usual manner on the security of an equitable mortgage of his building agreement;

(xix) In payment to any person becoming absolutely entitled or empowered to give an absolute discharge;

(xx) In payment of costs, charges, and expenses of or incidental to the exercise of any of the powers, or the execution of any of the provisions of this Act including the costs and expenses incidental to any of the matters referred to in this section;

(xxi) In any other mode authorised by the settlement with respect to money produced by the sale of the settled land

(2) Notwithstanding anything in this section capital money arising under this Act from settled land in England or Wales shall not be applied in the purchase of land out of England and Wales, unless the settlement expressly authorises the same.

74 Power to acquire land subject to certain incumbrances [345]

(1) Land may be acquired on a purchase or exchange to be made subject to a settlement, notwithstanding that the land is subject to any Crown rent, quit rent, chief rent, or other incident of tenure, or to any easement, right or privilege, or to any restrictive covenant, or to any liability to maintain or repair walls, fences, sea-walls, river banks, dykes, roads, streets, sewers, or drains, or to any improvement rentcharge which is capable under this Act of being redeemed out of capital money ...

75 Regulations respecting investment, devolution and [346] income of securities, etc

(1) Capital money arising under this Act shall, in order to its being invested or applied as aforesaid, be paid either to the trustees of the settlement or into court at the option of the tenant for life, and shall be invested or applied by the trustees, or under the direction of the court, as the case may be, accordingly.

(2) The investment or other application by the trustees shall be made according to the direction of the tenant for life, and in default thereof according to the discretion of the trustees, but in the last-mentioned case subject to any consent required or direction given by the settlement with respect to the investment or other application by the trustees of trust money of the settlement, and any investment shall be in the names or under the control of the trustees.

(3) The investment or other application under the direction of the court shall be made on the application of the tenant for life, or of the trustees.

(4) Any investment or other application shall not during the subsistence of the beneficial interest of the tenant for life be altered without his consent.

(5) Capital money arising under this Act while remaining uninvested or unapplied, and securities on which an investment of any such capital money is made shall for all purposes of disposition, transmission and devolution be treated as land, and shall be held for and go to the same persons successively, in the same manner and for and on the same estates, interests, and trusts, as the land wherefrom the money arises would, if not disposed of, have been held and have gone under the settlement.

(6) The income of those securities shall be paid or applied as the income of that land, if not disposed of, would have been payable or applicable under the settlement.

(7) Those securities may be converted into money, which shall be capital money arising under this Act.

(8) All or any part of any capital money paid into court may, if the court thinks fit, be at any time paid out to the trustees of the settlement.

77 Application of money in hands of trustees under powers of settlement [347]

Where –

(a) under any instrument coming into operation either before or after the commencement of this Act money is in the hands of trustees, and is liable to be laid out in the purchase of land to be made subject to the trusts declared by that instrument; or

(b) under any instrument coming into operation after the commencement of this Act money or securities or the proceeds of sale of any property is or are held by trustees on trusts creating entailed interests therein;

then, in addition to such powers of dealing therewith as the trustees have independently of this Act, they may, at the option of the tenant for life, invest or apply the money securities or proceeds as if they were capital money arising under this Act.

79 Application of money paid for lease or reversion [348]

Where capital money arising under this Act is purchase-money paid in respect of –

(a) a lease for years; or

(b) any other estate or interest in land less than the fee simple; or

(c) a reversion dependent on any such lease, estate, or interest;

the trustees of the settlement or the court, as the case may be, and in the case of the court on the application of any party interested in that money, may, notwithstanding anything in this Act, require and cause the same to be laid out, invested, accumulated, and paid in such manner as, in the judgment of the trustees or of the court, as the case may be, will give to the parties interested in that money the like benefit therefrom as they might lawfully have had from the lease, estate, interest, or reversion in respect whereof the money was paid, or as near thereto as may be.

PART IV

IMPROVEMENTS

83 Description of improvements authorised by Act [349]

Improvements authorised by this Act are the making or execution on, or in connexion with, and for the benefit of settled land, of any of the works mentioned in the Third Schedule to this Act, or of any works for any of the purposes mentioned in that Schedule, and any operation incident to or necessary or proper in the execution of any of those works, or necessary or proper for carrying into effect any of those purposes, or for securing the full benefit of any of those works or purposes.

84 Mode of application of capital money [350]

(1) Capital money arising under this Act may be applied in or towards payment for any improvement authorised by this Act or by the settlement, without any scheme for the execution of the improvement being first submitted for approval to, or approved by, the trustees of the settlement or the court.

(2) Where the capital money to be expended is in the hands of the trustees of the settlement, they may apply that money in or towards payment for the whole or any part of any work or operation comprised in the improvement on –

(i) a certificate to be furnished by a competent engineer or able practical surveyor employed independently of the tenant for life, certifying that the work or operation comprised in the improvement or some specific part thereof, has been properly executed, and what amount is properly payable in respect thereof, which certificate shall be conclusive in favour of the trustees as an authority and discharge for any payment made by them in pursuance thereof; or

(ii) an order of the court directing or authorising the trustees so to apply a specified portion of the capital money:

Provided that –

(a) In the case of improvements not authorised by Part I of the Third Schedule to this Act or by the settlement, the trustees may, if they think fit, and shall if so directed by the court, before they make any such application of capital money require that that money, or any part thereof, shall be repaid to them out of the income of the settled land by not more than fifty half-yearly instalments, the first of such instalments to be paid or to be deemed to have become payable at the expiration of six months from the date when the work or operation, in payment for which the money is to be applied, was completed;

(b) No capital money shall be applied by the trustees in payment for improvements not authorised by Parts I and II of the Third Schedule to this Act, or by the settlement, except subject to provision for the repayment thereof being made in manner mentioned in the preceding paragraph of this proviso.

(3) Where the capital money to be expended is in court, the court may, if it thinks fit, on a report or certificate of the Minister, or of a competent engineer or able practical surveyor approved by the court, or on such other evidence as the court may think sufficient, make such order and give such directions as it thinks fit for the application of the money, or any part thereof, in or towards payment for the whole or any part of any work or operation comprised in the improvement.

(4) Where the court authorises capital money to be applied in payment for any improvement or intended improvement not authorised by Part I of the Third Schedule to this Act or by the settlement, the court, as a condition of making the order, may in any case require that the capital money or any part thereof, and shall as respects an improvement mentioned in Part III of that Schedule (unless the improvement is authorised by the settlement), require that the whole of the capital money shall be repaid to the trustees of the settlement out of the income of the settled land by a fixed number of periodical instalments to be paid at the times appointed by the court, and may require that any incumbrancer of the estate or interest of the tenant for life shall be served with notice of the proceedings.

(5) All money received by the trustees of the settlement in respect of any instalments under this section shall be held by them as capital money arising from freehold land under the settlement, unless the court otherwise directs.

85 Creation of rentcharges to discharge instalments   [351]

(1) When the tenant for life is required by the trustees to repay by instalments the capital money expended, or any part thereof, the tenant for life is by this section authorised to create out of the settled land, or any part thereof, a yearly rentcharge in favour of the trustees of the settlement sufficient in amount to discharge the said half-yearly instalments.

(2) Where an order is made requiring repayment by instalments, the settled land shall stand charged with the payment to the trustees of the settlement of a yearly rentcharge sufficient in amount to discharge the periodical instalments, and the rentcharge shall accrue from day to day, and be payable at the times appointed for

payment of the periodical instalments, and shall have effect as if limited by the settlement prior to the estate of the tenant for life, and the trustees of the settlement shall have all statutory and other powers for recovery thereof.

(3) A rentcharge created by or under this section shall not be redeemed out of capital money, but may be overreached in like manner as if the same were limited by the settlement, and shall cease if and when the land affected by the improvement ceases to be settled or is sold or exchanged, but if part of the land so affected remains subject to the settlement the rentcharge shall remain in force in regard to the settled land.

86 Concurrence in improvements [352]

The tenant for life may join or concur with any other person interested in executing any improvement authorised by this Act, or in contributing to the cost thereof.

87 Court may order payment for improvements executed [353]

The court may, in any case where it appears proper, make an order directing or authorising capital money to be applied in or towards payment for any improvement authorised by the Settled Land Acts 1882 to 1890, or this Act, notwithstanding that a scheme was not, before the execution of the improvement, submitted for approval, as required by the Settled Land Act 1882, to the trustees of the settlement or to the court, and notwithstanding that no capital money is immediately available for the purpose.

88 Obligation on tenant for life and successors to [354]
maintain, insure, etc

(1) The tenant for life, and each of his successors in title having under the trust instrument a limited estate or interest only in the settled land, shall, during such period, if any, as the Minister by certificate in any case prescribes, maintain and repair, at his own expense, every improvement executed under the foregoing provisions of this Act or the enactments replaced thereby, and where a building or work in its nature insurable against damage by fire is comprised in the improvement, shall at his own expense insure and keep insured the improvement in such amount, if any, as the Minister by certificate in any case prescribes.

(2) The tenant for life, or any of his successors as aforesaid, shall not cut down or knowingly permit to be cut down, except in proper thinning, any trees planted as an improvement under the foregoing provisions of this Act, or under the enactments replaced by those provisions.

(3) The tenant for life, and each of his successors as aforesaid, shall from time to time, if required by the Minister on or without the application of any person having under the trust instrument any estate or interest in the settled land in possession, remainder, or otherwise, report to the Minister the state of every improvement executed under this Act, and the fact and particulars of fire insurance, if any.

(4) The Minister may vary any certificate made by him under this section in such manner or to such extent as circumstances appear to him to require, but not so as to increase the liabilities of the tenant for life, or any of his successors as aforesaid.

(5) If the tenant for life, or any of his successors as aforesaid, fails in any respect to comply with the requisitions of this section, or does any act in contravention thereof, any person having, under the trust instrument, any estate or interest in the settled land in possession, remainder, or reversion, shall have a right of action, in

respect of that default or act, against the tenant for life; and the estate of the tenant for life, after his death, shall be liable to make good to the persons entitled under the trust instrument any damages occasioned by that default or act.

(6) Where in connexion with any improvement an improvement rentcharge, as hereinbefore defined, has been created, and that rentcharge has been redeemed out of capital money, this section shall apply to the improvement as if it had been an improvement executed under this Act.

89 Protection as regards waste in execution and   [355]
repair of improvements

The tenant for life, and each of his successors in title having, under the trust instrument, a limited estate or interest only in the settled land, and all persons employed by or under contract with the tenant for life or any such successor, may from time to time enter on the settled land, and, without impeachment of waste by any remainderman or reversioner, thereon execute any improvement authorised by this Act, or inspect, maintain, and repair the same, and for the purposes thereof do, make, and use on the settled land, all acts, works, and conveniences proper for the execution, maintenance, repair, and use thereof, and get and work freestone, limestone, clay, sand, and other substances, and make tramways and other ways, and burn and make bricks, tiles, and other things, and cut down and use timber and other trees not planted or left standing for shelter or ornament.

PART V

MISCELLANEOUS PROVISIONS

90 Power for tenant for life to enter into contracts   [356]

(1) A tenant for life –

(i) may contract to make any sale, exchange, mortgage, charge or other disposition authorised by this Act; and

(ii) may vary or rescind, with or without consideration, the contract in the like cases and manner in which, if he were absolute owner of the settled land, he might lawfully vary or rescind the same, but so that the contract as varied be in conformity with this Act; and

(iii) may contract to make any lease, and in making the lease may vary the terms, with or without consideration, but so that the lease be in conformity with this Act; and

(iv) may accept a surrender of a contract for a lease or a grant in fee simple at a rent, in like manner and on the like terms in and on which he might accept a surrender of a lease or a regrant, and thereupon may make a new or other contract for or relative to a lease or leases, or a grant or grants in fee simple at a rent, in like manner and on the like terms in and on which he might make a new or other lease or grant, or new or other leases or grants, where a lease or a grant in fee simple at a rent had been executed; and

(v) may enter into a contract for or relating to the execution of any improvement authorised by this Act, and may vary or rescind any such contract, and

(vi) may, in any other case, enter into a contract to do any act for carrying into effect any of the purposes of this Act, and may vary or rescind any such contract.

(2) Every contract, including a contract arising by reason of the exercise of an option, shall be binding on and shall enure for the benefit of the settled land, and

shall be enforceable against and by every successor in title for the time being of the tenant for life, or statutory owner, and may be carried into effect by any such successor, but so that it may be varied or rescinded by any such successor, in the like case and manner, if any, as if it had been made by himself.

(3) The court may, on the application of the tenant for life, or statutory owner, or of any such successor as aforesaid, or of any person interested in any contract, give directions respecting the enforcing, carrying into effect, varying, or rescinding thereof.

(4) A preliminary contract under this Act for or relating to a lease, and a contract conferring an option, shall not form part of the title or evidence of the title of any person to the lease, or to the benefit thereof, or to the land the subject of the option.

(5) All money, not being rent, received on the exercise by the tenant for life or statutory owner of the powers conferred by subsection (1) of this section, shall, unless the court on an application made within six months after the receipt of the money, or within such further time as the court may in special circumstances allow, otherwise directs, be capital money arising under this Act.

92 Proceedings for protection or recovery of land settled   [357] or claimed as settled

The court may, if it thinks fit, approve of any action, defence, petition to Parliament, parliamentary opposition, or other proceeding taken or proposed to be taken for the protection of settled land, or of any action or proceeding taken or proposed to be taken for the recovery of land being or alleged to be subject to a settlement, and may direct that any costs, charges, or expenses incurred or to be incurred in relation thereto, or any part thereof, be paid out of property subject to the settlement.

93 Reference of questions to court   [358]

If a question arises or a doubt is entertained –

(a) respecting the exercise or intended exercise of any of the powers conferred by this Act, or any enactment replaced by this Act, or the settlement, or any matter relating thereto; or
(b) as to the person in whose favour a vesting deed or assent ought to be executed, or as to the contents thereof; or
(c) otherwise in relation to property subject to a settlement;

the tenant for life or statutory owner, or the trustees of the settlement, or any other person interested under the settlement, may apply to the court for its decision or directions thereon, or for the sanction of the court to any conditional contract, and the court may make such order or give such directions respecting the matter as the court thinks fit.

PART VI

GENERAL PROVISIONS AS TO TRUSTEES

94 Number of trustees to act   [359]

(1) Notwithstanding anything in this Act, capital money arising under this Act shall not be paid to fewer than two persons as trustees of a settlement, unless the trustee is a trust corporation.

(2) Subject as aforesaid the provisions of this Act referring to the trustees of a settlement apply to the surviving or continuing trustees or trustee of the settlement for the time being.

95 Trustees' receipts   [360]

The receipt or direction in writing of or by the trustees of the settlement, or where a sole trustee is a trust corporation, of or by that trustee, or of or by the personal representatives of the last surviving or continuing trustee, for or relating to any money or securities, paid or transferred to or by the direction of the trustees, trustee, or representatives, as the case may be, effectually discharges the payer or transferor therefrom, and from being bound to see to the application or being answerable for any loss or misapplication thereof, and, in case of a mortgagee or other person advancing money, from being concerned to see that any money advanced by him is wanted for any purpose of this Act, or that no more than is wanted is raised.

96 Protection of each trustee individually   [361]

Each person who is for the time being a trustee of a settlement is answerable for what he actually receives only, notwithstanding his signing any receipt for conformity, and in respect of his own acts, receipts, and defaults only, and is not answerable in respect of those of any other trustee, or of any banker, broker, or other person, or for the insufficiency or deficiency of any securities, or for any loss not happening through his own wilful default.

97 Protection of trustees generally   [362]

The trustees of a settlement, or any of them –

(a) are not liable for giving any consent, or for not making, bringing, taking, or doing any such application, action, proceeding, or thing, as they might make, bring, take, or do; and

(b) in case of a purchase of land with capital money arising under this Act, or of an exchange, lease, or other disposition, are not liable for adopting any contract made by the tenant for life or statutory owner, or bound to inquire as to the propriety of the purchase, exchange, lease, or other disposition, or answerable as regards any price, consideration, or fine; and

(c) are not liable to see to or answerable for the investigation of the title, or answerable for a conveyance of land, if the conveyance purports to convey the land in the proper mode; and

(d) are not liable in respect of purchase-money paid by them by the direction of the tenant for life or statutory owner to any person joining in the conveyance as a conveying party, or as giving a receipt for the purchase-money, or in any other character, or in respect of any other money paid by them by the direction of the tenant for life or statutory owner on the purchase, exchange, lease, or other disposition.

98 Protection of trustees in particular cases   [363]

(1) Where the tenant for life or statutory owner directs capital money to be invested on any authorised security or investment, the trustees of the settlement shall not be liable for the acts of any agent employed by the tenant for life or statutory owner in connexion with the transaction, or for not employing a separate agent in or about the valuation of the subject of the security or the investigation of

the title thereto, or for the form of the security or of any deed conveying the subject thereof to the trustees.

(2) The trustees of the settlement shall not be liable for paying or applying any capital money by the direction of the tenant for life or statutory owner for any authorised purpose.

(3) The trustees of the settlement shall not be liable in any way on account of any vesting instrument or other documents of title relating to the settled land, other than securities for capital money, being placed in the possession of the tenant for life or statutory owner: Provided that where, if the settlement were not disclosed, it would appear that the tenant for life had a general power of appointment over, or was absolutely and beneficially entitled to the settled land, the trustees of the settlement shall, before they deliver the documents to him, require that notice of the last or only principal vesting instrument be written on one of the documents under which the tenant for life acquired his title, and may, if the documents are not in their possession, require such notice to be written as aforesaid, but, in the latter case, they shall not be liable in any way for not requiring the notice to be written.

(4) This section applies to dealings and matters effected before as well as after the commencement of this Act.

99 Indemnities to personal representatives and others   [364]

Personal representatives, trustees, or other persons who have in good faith, pursuant to this Act, executed a vesting deed, assent, or other conveyance of the settled land, or a deed of discharge of trustees, shall be absolutely discharged from all liability in respect of the equitable interests and powers taking effect under the settlement, and shall be entitled to be kept indemnified at the cost of the trust estate from all liabilities affecting the settled land, but the person to whom the settled land is conveyed (not being a purchaser taking free therefrom) shall hold the settled land upon the trusts, if any, affecting the same.

100 Trustees' reimbursements   [365]

The trustees of a settlement may reimburse themselves or pay and discharge out of the trust property all expenses properly incurred by them.

101 Notice to trustees   [366]

(1) Save as otherwise expressly provided by this Act, a tenant for life or statutory owner, when intending to make a sale, exchange, lease, mortgage, or charge or to grant an option –

(a) shall give notice of his intention in that behalf to each of the trustees of the settlement, by posting registered letters, containing the notice, addressed to the trustees severally, each at his usual or last known place of abode in the United Kingdom; and
(b) shall give a like notice to the solicitor for the trustees, if any such solicitor is known to the tenant for life or statutory owner, by posting a registered letter, containing the notice, addressed to the solicitor at his place of business in the United Kingdom;

every letter under this section being posted not less than one month before the making or granting by the tenant for life or statutory owner of the sale, exchange, lease, mortgage, charge, or option, or of a contract for the same: provided that a notice under this section shall not be valid unless at the date thereof the trustee is a trust corporation, or the number of trustees is not less than two.

(2) The notice required by this section of intention to make a sale, exchange, or lease, or to grant an option, may be notice of a general intention in that behalf.

(3) The tenant for life or statutory owner is, upon request by a trustee of the settlement, to furnish to him such particulars and information as may reasonably be required by him from time to time with reference to sales, exchanges, or leases effected, or in progress, or immediately intended.

(4) Any trustee, by writing under his hand, may waive notice either in any particular case, or generally, and may accept less than one month's notice.

(5) A person dealing in good faith with the tenant for life is not concerned to inquire respecting the giving of any such notice as is required by this section.

102 Management of land during minority or   [367]
pending contingency

(1) If and as long as any person who is entitled to a beneficial interest in possession affecting land is an infant, the trustees appointed for this purpose by the settlement, or if there are none so appointed, then the trustees of the settlement, unless the settlement or the order of the court whereby they or their predecessors in office were appointed to be such trustees expressly provides to the contrary, or if there are none, then any persons appointed as trustees for this purpose by the court on the application of a guardian or next friend of the infant, may enter into and continue in possession of the land on behalf of the infant, and in every such case the subsequent provisions of this section shall apply.

(2) The trustees shall manage or superintend the management of the land, with full power –

    (a) to fell timber or cut underwood from time to time in the usual course for sale, or for repairs or otherwise; and

    (b) to erect, pull down, rebuild, and repair houses, and other buildings and erections; and

    (c) to continue the working of mines, minerals, and quarries which have usually been worked; and

    (d) to drain or otherwise improve the land or any part thereof; and

    (e) to insure against loss by fire; and

    (f) to make allowances to and arrangements with tenants and others; and

    (g) to determine tenancies, and to accept surrenders of leases and tenancies; and

    (h) generally to deal with the land in a proper and due course of management;

but so that, where the infant is impeachable for waste, the trustees shall not commit waste, and shall cut timber on the same terms only, and subject to the same restrictions on and subject to which the infant could, if of full age, cut the same.

(3) The trustees may from time to time, out of the income of the land, including the produce of the sale of timber and underwood, pay the expenses incurred in the management, or in the exercise of any power conferred by this section, or otherwise in relation to the land, and all outgoings not payable by any tenant or other person, and shall keep down any annual sum, and the interest of any principal sum, charged on the land.

(4) This section has effect subject to an express appointment by the settlement, or the court, of trustees for the purposes of this section or of any enactment replaced by this section.

(5) Where any person is contingently entitled to land, this section shall, subject to any prior interests or charges affecting that land, apply until his interest vests, or, if

his interest vests during his minority, until he attains the age of eighteen years. This subsection applies only where a person becomes contingently entitled under an instrument coming into operation after the commencement of this Act.

(6) This section applies only if and as far as a contrary intention is not expressed in the instrument, if any, under which the interest of the infant or person contingently entitled as aforesaid arises, and has effect subject to the terms of that instrument and to the provisions therein contained.

PART VII

RESTRICTIONS, SAVINGS, AND PROTECTION OF PURCHASERS

104 Powers not assignable, and contract not to exercise powers void **[368]**

(1) The powers under this Act of a tenant for life are not capable of assignment or release, and do not pass to a person as being, by operation of law or otherwise, an assignee of a tenant for life, and remain exercisable by the tenant for life after and notwithstanding any assignment, by operation of law or otherwise, of his estate or interest under the settlement. This subsection applies notwithstanding that the estate or interest of the tenant for life under the settlement was not in possession when the assignment was made or took effect by operation of law.

(2) A contract by a tenant for life not to exercise his powers under this Act or any of them shall be void.

(3) Where an assignment for value of the estate or interest of the tenant for life was made before the commencement of this Act, this section shall operate without prejudice to the rights of the assignee, and in that case the assignee's rights shall not be affected without his consent, except that –

(a) unless the assignee is actually in possession of the settled land or the part thereof affected, his consent shall not be requisite for the making of leases thereof by the tenant for life or statutory owner, provided the leases are made at the best rent that can reasonably be obtained, without fine, and in other respects are in conformity with this Act; and

(b) the consent of the assignee shall not be required to an investment of capital money for the time being affected by the assignment in securities authorised by statute for the investment of trust money.

(4) Where such an assignment for value is made or comes into operation after the commencement of this Act, the consent of the assignee shall not be requisite for the exercise by the tenant for life of any of the powers conferred by this Act: Provided that –

(a) the assignee shall be entitled to the same or the like estate or interest in or charge on the land, money, or securities for the time being representing the land, money, or securities comprised in the assignment, as he had by virtue of the assignment in the last-mentioned land, money, or securities; and

(b) if the assignment so provides, or if it takes effect by operation of the law of bankruptcy, and after notice thereof to the trustees of the settlement, no investment or application of capital money for the time being affected by the assignment shall be made without the consent of the assignee, except an investment in securities authorised by statute for the investment of trust money; and

(c) notice of the intended transaction shall, unless the assignment otherwise provides, be given to the assignee, but a purchaser shall not be concerned to see or inquire whether such notice has been given.

(5) Where such an assignment for value was made before the commencement of this Act, then on the exercise by the tenant for life after such commencement of any of the powers conferred by this Act –

(a) a purchaser shall not be concerned to see or inquire whether the consent of the assignee has been obtained; and

(b) the provisions of paragraph (a) of the last subsection shall apply for the benefit of the assignee.

(6) A trustee or personal representative who is an assignee for value shall have power to consent to the exercise by the tenant for life of his powers under this Act, or to any such investment or application of capital money as aforesaid, and to bind by such consent all persons interested in the trust estate, or the estate of the testator or intestate.

(7) If by the original assignment, or by any subsequent disposition, the estate or interest assigned or created by the original assignment, or any part thereof, or any derivative interest is settled on persons in succession, whether subject to any prior charge or not, and there is no trustee or personal representative in whom the entirety of the estate or interest so settled is vested, then the person for the time being entitled in possession under the limitations of that settlement, whether as trustee or beneficiary, or who would, if of full age, be so entitled, and notwithstanding any charge or incumbrance subsisting or to arise under such settlement, shall have power to consent to the exercise by the tenant for life of his powers under this Act, or to any such investment or application of capital money as aforesaid, and to bind by such consent all persons interested or to become interested under such settlement.

(8) Where an assignee for value, or any person who has power to consent as aforesaid under this section, is an infant, the consent may be given on his behalf by his parents or parent or testamentary or other guardian in the order named.

(9) The court shall have power to authorise any person interested under any assignment to consent to the exercise by the tenant for life of his powers under this Act, or to any such investment or application of capital money as aforesaid, on behalf of himself and all other persons interested, or who may become interested under such assignment.

(10) An assignment by operation of the law of bankruptcy, where the assignment comes into operation after the commencement of this Act, shall be deemed to be an assignment for value for the purposes of this section.

(11) An instrument whereby a tenant for life, in consideration of marriage or as part or by way of any family arrangement, not being a security for payment of money advanced, makes an assignment of or creates a charge upon his estate or interest under the settlement is to be deemed one of the instruments creating the settlement, and not an assignment for value for the purposes of this section: provided that this subsection shall not have effect with respect to any disposition made before the eighteenth day of August, eighteen hundred and ninety, if inconsistent with the nature or terms of the disposition.

(12) This section extends to assignments made or coming into operation before or after the commencement of this Act, and in this section 'assignment' includes assignment by way of mortgage, and any partial or qualified assignment, and any charge or incumbrance, 'assignee' has a corresponding meaning, and 'assignee for value' includes persons deriving title under the original assignee.

105 Effect of surrender of life estate to the   [369]
next remainderman

(1) Where the estate or interest of a tenant for life under the settlement has been or is absolutely assured with intent to extinguish the same, either before or after

the commencement of this Act, to the person next entitled in remainder or reversion under the settlement, then the statutory powers of the tenant for life under this Act shall, in reference to the property affected by the assurance, and notwithstanding the provisions of the last preceding section, cease to be exercisable by him, and the statutory powers shall thenceforth become exercisable as if he were dead, but without prejudice to any incumbrance affecting the estate or interest assured, and to the rights to which any incumbrancer would have been entitled if those powers had remained exercisable by the tenant for life. This subsection applies whether or not any term of years or charge intervenes, or the estate of the remainder-man or reversioner is liable to be defeated, and whether or not the estate or interest of the tenant for life under the settlement was in possession at the date of the asssurance. This subsection does not prejudice anything done by the tenant for life before the commencement of this Act, in exercise of any power operating under the Settled Land Acts 1882 to 1890 or, unless the assurance provides to the contrary, operate to accelerate any such intervening term of years or charge as aforesaid.

(2) In this section 'assurance' means any surrender, conveyance, assignment or appointment under a power (whether vested in any person solely, or jointly in two or more persons) which operates in equity to extinguish the estate or interest of the tenant for life, and 'assured' has a corresponding meaning.

106 Prohibition or limitation against exercise of powers void, and provision against forfeiture [370]

(1) If in a settlement, will, assurance, or other instrument executed or made before or after, or partly before and partly after, the commencement of this Act a provision is inserted –

(a) purporting or attempting, by way of direction, declaration, or otherwise, to forbid a tenant for life or statutory owner to exercise any power under this Act, or his right to require the settled land to be vested in him; or
(b) attempting, or tending, or intended, by a limitation, gift, or disposition over of settled land, or by a limitation, gift, or disposition of other real or any personal property, or by the imposition of any condition, or by forfeiture, or in any other manner whatever, to prohibit or prevent him from exercising, or to induce him to abstain from exercising, or to put him into a position inconsistent with his exercising, any power under this Act, or his right to require the settled land to be vested in him;

that provision, as far as it purports, or attempts, or tends, or is intended to have, or would or might have, the operation aforesaid, shall be deemed to be void.

(2) For the purposes of this section an estate or interest limited to continue so long only as a person abstains from exercising any such power or right as aforesaid shall be and take effect as an estate or interest to continue for the period for which it would continue if that person were to abstain from exercising the power or right, discharged from liability to determination or cesser by or on his exercising the same.

(3) Notwithstanding anything in a settlement, the exercise by the tenant for life or statutory owner of any power under this Act shall not occasion a forfeiture.

107 Tenant for life trustee for all parties interested [371]

(1) A tenant for life or statutory owner shall, in exercising any power under this Act, have regard to the interests of all parties entitled under the settlement, and shall, in relation to the exercise thereof by him, be deemed to be in the position and to have the duties and liabilities of a trustee for those parties.

(2) The provision by a tenant for life or statutory owner, at his own expense, of dwellings available for the working classes on any settled land shall not be deemed to be an injury to any interest in reversion or remainder in that land, but such provision shall not be made by a tenant for life or statutory owner without the previous approval in writing of the trustees of the settlement.

108 Saving for and exercise of other powers   [372]

(1) Nothing in this Act shall take away, abridge, or prejudicially affect any power for the time being subsisting under a settlement, or by statute or otherwise, exercisable by a tenant for life, or (save as hereinafter provided) by trustees with his consent, or on his request, or by his direction, or otherwise, and the powers given by this Act are cumulative.

(2) In case of conflict between the provisions of a settlement and the provisions of this Act, relative to any matter in respect whereof the tenant for life or statutory owner exercises or contracts or intends to exercise any power under this Act, the provisions of this Act shall prevail; and, notwithstanding anything in the settlement, any power (not being merely a power of revocation or appointment) relating to the settled land thereby conferred on the trustees of the settlement or other persons exercisable for any purpose, whether or not provided for in this Act, shall, after the commencement of this Act, be exercisable by the tenant for life or statutory owner as if it were an additional power conferred on the tenant for life within the next following section of this Act and not otherwise.

(3) If a question arises or a doubt is entertained respecting any matter within this section, the tenant for life or statutory owner, or the trustees of the settlement, or any other person interested, under the settlement may apply to the court for its decision thereon, and the court may make such order respecting the matter as the court thinks fit.

109 Saving for additional or larger powers   [373]
under settlement

(1) Nothing in this Act precludes a settlor from conferring on the tenant for life, or (save as provided by the last preceding section) on the trustees of the settlement, any powers additional to or larger than those conferred by this Act.

(2) Any additional or larger powers so conferred shall, as far as may be, notwithstanding anything in this Act, operate and be exercisable in the like manner, and with all the like incidents, effects, and consequences, as if they were conferred by this Act, and, if relating to the settled land, as if they were conferred by this Act on a tenant for life.

110 Protection of purchasers, etc   [374]

(1) On a sale, exchange, lease, mortgage, charge, or other disposition, a purchaser dealing in good faith with a tenant for life or statutory owner shall, as against all parties entitled under the settlement, be conclusively taken to have given the best price, consideration, or rent, as the case may require, that could reasonably be obtained by the tenant for life or statutory owner, and to have complied with all the requisitions of this Act.

(2) A purchaser of a legal estate in settled land shall not, except as hereby expressly provided, be bound or entitled to call for the production of the trust instrument or any information concerning that instrument or any ad valorem stamp duty thereon, and whether or not he has notice of its contents he shall, save as hereinafter provided, be bound and entitled if the last or only principal vesting

instrument contains the statements and particulars required by this Act to assume that –

(a) the person in whom the land is by the said instrument vested or declared to be vested in the tenant for life or statutory owner and has all the powers of a tenant for life under this Act, including such additional or larger powers, if any, as are therein mentioned;

(b) the persons by the said instrument stated to be the trustees of the settlement, or their successors appearing to be duly appointed, are the properly constituted trustees of the settlement;

(c) the statements and particulars required by this Act and contained (expressly or by reference) in the said instrument were correct at the date thereof;

(d) the statements contained in any deed executed in accordance with this Act declaring who are the trustees of the settlement for the purposes of this Act are correct;

(e) the statements contained in any deed of discharge, executed in accordance with this Act, are correct:

Provided that, as regards the first vesting instrument executed for the purpose of giving effect to –

(a) a settlement subsisting at the commencement of this Act; or

(b) an instrument which by virtue of this Act is deemed to be a settlement; or

(c) a settlement which by virtue of this Act is deemed to have been made by any person after the commencement of this Act; or

(d) an instrument inter vivos intended to create a settlement of a legal estate in land which is executed after the commencement of this Act and does not comply with the requirements of this Act with respect to the method of effecting such a settlement;

a purchaser shall be concerned to see –

(i) that the land disposed of to him is comprised in such settlement or instrument;

(ii) that the person in whom the settled land is by such vesting instrument vested, or declared to be vested, is the person in whom it ought to be vested as tenant for life or statutory owner;

(iii) that the persons thereby stated to be the trustees of the settlement are the properly constituted trustees of the settlement.

(3) A purchaser of a legal estate in settled land from a personal representative shall be entitled to act on the following assumptions –

(i) If the capital money, if any, payable in respect of the transaction is paid to the personal representative, that such representative is acting under his statutory or other powers and requires the money for purposes of administration;

(ii) If such capital money is, by the direction of the personal representative, paid to persons who are stated to be the trustees of a settlement, that such persons are the duly constituted trustees of the settlement for the purposes of this Act, and that the personal representative is acting under his statutory powers during a minority;

(iii) In any other case, that the personal representative is acting under his statutory or other powers.

(4) Where no capital money arises under a transaction, a disposition by a tenant for life or statutory owner shall, in favour of a purchaser of a legal estate, have effect under this Act notwithstanding that at the date of the transaction there are no trustees of the settlement.

(5) If a conveyance of or an assent relating to land formerly subject to a vesting

instrument does not state who are the trustees of the settlement for the purposes of this Act, a purchaser of a legal estate shall be bound and entitled to act on the assumption that the person in whom the land was thereby vested was entitled to the land free from all limitations, powers, and charges taking effect under that settlement, absolutely and beneficially, or, if so expressed in the conveyance or assent, as personal representative, or trustee of land or otherwise, and that every statement of fact in such conveyance or assent is correct.

111 Purchaser of beneficial interest of tenant for life to have remedies of a legal owner [375]

Where –

(a) at the commencement of this Act the legal beneficial interest of a tenant for life under a settlement is vested in a purchaser; or

(b) after the commencement of this Act a tenant for life conveys or deals with his beneficial interest in possession in favour of a purchaser, and the interest so conveyed or created would, but for the restrictions imposed by statute on the creation of legal estates, have been a legal interest;

the purchaser shall (without prejudice to the powers conferred by this Act on the tenant for life) have and may exercise all the same rights and remedies as he would have had or have been entitled to exercise if the interest had remained or been a legal interest and the reversion, if any, on any leases or tenancies derived out of the settled land had been vested in him: provided that, where the conveyance or dealing is effected after the commencement of this Act, the purchaser shall not be entitled to the possession of the documents of title relating to the settled land, but shall have the same rights with respect thereto as if the tenant for life had given to him a statutory acknowledgement of his right to production and delivery of copies thereof, and a statutory undertaking for the safe custody thereof. The tenant for life shall not deliver any such documents to a purchaser of his beneficial interest, who is not also a purchaser of the whole of the settled land to which such documents relate.

112 Exercise of powers; limitation of provisions, etc [376]

(1) Where a power of sale, exchange, leasing, mortgaging, charging, or other power is exercised by a tenant for life, or statutory owner or by the trustees of a settlement, he and they may respectively execute, make, and do all deeds, instruments, and things necessary or proper in that behalf.

(2) Where any provision in this Act refers to sale, purchase, exchange, mortgaging, charging, leasing, or other disposition or dealing, or to any power, consent, payment, receipt, deed, assurance, contract, expenses, act, or transaction, it shall (unless the contrary appears) be construed as extending only to sales, purchases, exchanges, mortgages, charges, leases, dispositions, dealings, powers, consents, payments, receipts, deeds, assurances, contracts, expenses, acts, and transactions under this Act.

PART IX

SUPPLEMENTARY PROVISIONS

117 Definitions [377]

(1) In this Act, unless the context otherwise requires, the following expressions have the meanings hereby assigned to them respectively, that is to say –

(i) 'Building purposes' include the erecting and the improving of, and the adding to, and the repairing of buildings; and a 'building lease' is a lease for any building purposes or purposes connected therewith;

(ii) 'Capital money arising under this Act' means capital money arising under the powers and provisions of this Act or the Acts replaced by this Act, and receivable for the trusts and purposes of the settlement and includes securities representing capital money;

(iii) 'Death duty' means estate duty and every other duty leviable or payable on death;

(iv) 'Determinable fee' means a fee determinable whether by limitation or condition;

(v) 'Disposition' and 'conveyance' include a mortgage, charge by way of legal mortgage, lease, assent, vesting declaration, vesting instrument, disclaimer, release and every other assurance of property or of an interest therein by any instrument, except a will, and 'dispose of' and 'convey' have corresponding meanings;

(vi) 'Dower' includes 'freebench';

(vii) 'Hereditaments' mean real property which on an intestacy might before the commencement of this Act have devolved on an heir;

(viii) 'Instrument' does not include a statute unless the statute creates a settlement;

(ix) 'Land' includes land of any tenure, and mines and minerals whether or not held apart from the surface, buildings or parts of buildings (whether the division is horizontal, vertical or made in any other way) and other corporeal hereditaments; also a manor, an advowson, and a rent and other incorporeal hereditaments, and an easement, right, privilege, or benefit in, over, or derived from land, and any estate or interest in land, but does not (except in the phrase 'trust of land') include an undivided share in land;

(x) 'Lease' includes an agreement for a lease, and 'forestry lease' means a lease to the Forestry Commissioners for any purpose for which they are authorised to acquire land by the Forestry Act, 1919;

(xi) 'Legal mortgage' means a mortgage by demise or sub-demise or a charge by way of legal mortgage, and 'legal mortgagee' has a corresponding meaning; 'legal estate' means an estate interest or charge in or over land (subsisting or created at law) which is by statute authorised to subsist or to be created at law; and 'equitable interests' mean all other interests and charges in or over land or in the proceeds of sale thereof; an equitable interest 'capable of subsisting at law' means such an equitable interest as could validly subsist at law, if clothed with the legal estate; and 'estate owner' means the owner of a legal estate;

(xii) 'Limitation' includes a trust, and 'trust' includes an implied or constructive trust; ...

(xiv) 'Manor' includes lordship, and reputed manor or lordship; and 'manorial incident' has the same meaning as in the Law of Property Act 1922;

(xv) 'Mines and minerals' mean mines and minerals whether already opened or in work or not, and include all minerals and substances in, on, or under the land, obtainable by underground or by surface working; and 'mining purposes' include the sinking and searching for, winning, working, getting, making merchantable, smelting or otherwise converting or working for the purposes of any manufacture, carrying away, and disposing of mines and minerals, in or under the settled land, or any other land, and the erection of buildings, and the execution of engineering and other works suitable for those purposes; and a 'mining lease' is a lease for any mining purposes or purposes connected therewith, and includes a grant or licence for any mining purposes;

(xvi) 'Minister' means the Minister of Agriculture, Fisheries and Food;

(xvii) 'Notice' includes constructive notice;

(xviii) 'Personal representative' means the executor, original or by representation, or administrator, for the time being of a deceased person, and where there are special personal representatives for the purposes of settled land means those personal representatives;

(xix) 'Possession' includes receipt of rents and profits, or the right to receive the same, if any; and 'income' includes rents and profits;

(xx) 'Property' includes any thing in action, and any interest in real or personal property;

(xxi) 'Purchaser' means a purchaser in good faith for value, and includes a lessee, mortgagee or other person who in good faith acquires an interest in settled land for value; and in reference to a legal estate includes a chargee by way of legal mortgage;

(xxii) 'Rent' includes yearly or other rent, and toll, duty, royalty, or other reservation, by the acre, or the ton, or otherwise; and, in relation to rent, 'payment' includes delivery; and 'fine' includes premium or fore-gift, and any payment, consideration, or benefit in the nature of a fine, premium, or fore-gift;

(xxiii) 'Securities' include stocks, funds, and shares;

(xxiv) 'Settled land' includes land which is deemed to be settled land; 'settlement' includes an instrument or instruments which under this Act or the Acts which it replaces is or are deemed to be or which together constitute a settlement, and a settlement which is deemed to have been made by any person or to be subsisting for the purposes of this Act; 'a settlement subsisting at the commencement of this Act' includes a settlement created by virtue of this Act immediately on the commencement thereof; and 'trustees of the settlement' mean the trustees thereof for the purposes of this Act howsoever appointed or constituted;

(xxv) 'Small dwellings 'mean dwelling-houses of a rateable value not exceeding one hundred pounds per annum;

(xxvi) 'Statutory owner' means the trustees of the settlement or other persons who, during a minority, or at any other time when there is no tenant for life, have the powers of a tenant for life under this Act, but does not include the trustees of the settlement, where by virtue of an order of the court or otherwise the trustees have power to convey the settled land in the name of the tenant for life;

(xxvii) 'Steward' includes deputy steward, or other proper officer, of a manor;

(xxviii) 'Tenant for life' includes a person (not being a statutory owner) who has the powers of a tenant for life under this Act, and also (where the context requires) one of two or more persons who together constitute the tenant for life, or have the powers of a tenant for life; and 'tenant in tail' includes a person entitled to an entailed interest in any property; and 'entailed interest' has the same meaning as in the Law of Property Act 1925;

(xxix) A 'term of years absolute' means a term of years, taking effect either in possession or in reversion, with or without impeachment for waste, whether at a rent or not and whether subject or not to another legal estate, and whether certain or liable to determination by notice, re-entry, operation of law, or by a provision for cesser on redemption, or in any other event (other than the dropping of a life, or the determination of a determinable life interest), but does not include any term of years determinable with life or lives or with the cesser of a determinable life interest, nor, if created after the commencement of this Act, a term of years which is not expressed to take effect in possession within twenty-one years after the creation thereof where required by statute to take effect within that period; and in this definition the expression 'term of years' includes a term for less than a year, or for a year or years and a fraction of a year or from year to year;

(xxx) 'Trust corporation' means the Public Trustee or a corporation either appointed by the court in any particular case to be a trustee or entitled by rules made under subsection (3) of section four of the Public Trustee Act 1906 to act as custodian trustee, and 'trust for sale' has the same meaning as in the Law of Property Act 1925;

(xxxi) In relation to settled land 'vesting deed' or 'vesting order' means the instrument whereby settled land is conveyed to or vested or declared to be vested in a tenant for life or statutory owner; 'vesting assent' means the instrument whereby a personal representative, after the death of a tenant for life or statutory owner, or the survivor of two or more tenants for life or statutory owners, vests settled land in a person entitled as tenant for life or statutory owner; 'vesting instrument' means a vesting deed, a vesting assent or, where the land affected remains settled land, a vesting order; 'principal vesting instrument' includes any vesting instrument other than a subsidiary vesting deed; and 'trust instrument' means the instrument whereby the trusts of the settled land are declared, and includes any two or more such instruments and a settlement or instrument which is deemed to be a trust instrument;

(xxxii) 'United Kingdom' means Great Britain and Northern Ireland;

(xxxiii) 'Will' includes codicil.

(1A) Any reference in this Act to money, securities or proceeds of sale being paid or transferred into court shall be construed as referring to the money, securities or proceeds being paid or transferred into the Supreme Court or any other court that has jurisdiction, and any reference in this Act to the court, in a context referring to the investment or application of money, securities or proceeds of sale paid or transferred into court, shall be construed, in the case of money, securities or proceeds paid or transferred into the Supreme Court, as referring to the High Court, and, in the case of money, securities or proceeds paid or transferred into another court, as referring to that other court.

(2) Where an equitable interest in or power over property arises by statute or operation of law, references to the 'creation' of an interest or power include any interest or power so arising.

(3) References to registration under the Land Charges Act 1925 apply to any registration made under any statute which is by the Land Charges Act 1925 to have effect as if the registration had been made under that Act.

THIRD SCHEDULE [378]

PART I

IMPROVEMENTS, THE COSTS OF WHICH ARE NOT LIABLE TO BE REPLACED BY INSTALMENTS

(i) Drainage, including the straightening, widening, or deepening of drains, streams, and watercourses:

(ii) Bridges:

(iii) Irrigation; warping:

(iv) Drains, pipes, and machinery for supply and distribution of sewage as manure:

(v) Embanking or weiring from a river or lake, or from the sea, or a tidal water:

(vi) Groynes; sea walls; defences against water:

(vii) Inclosing; straightening of fences; re-division of fields

(viii) Reclamation; dry warping:

(ix) Farm roads; private roads; roads or streets in villages or towns:

(x) Clearing; trenching; planting:

(xi) Cottages for labourers, farm-servants, and artisans, employed on the settled land or not:

(xii) Farmhouses, offices, and outbuildings, and other buildings for farm purposes:

(xiii) Saw-mills, scutch-mills, and other mills, water-wheels, engine-houses, and kilns, which will increase the value of the settled land for agricultural purposes or as woodland or otherwise:

(xiv) Reservoirs, tanks, conduits, watercourses, pipes, wells, ponds, shafts, dams, weirs, sluices, and other works and machinery for supply and distribution of water for agricultural, manufacturing, or other purposes, or for domestic or other consumption:

(xv) Tramways; railways; canals; docks:

(xvi) Jetties, piers, and landing places on rivers, lakes, the sea, or tidal waters, for facilitating transport of persons and of agricultural stock and produce, and of manure and other things required for agricultural purposes, and of minerals, and of things required for mining purposes:

(xvii) Markets and market-places:

(xviii) Streets, roads, paths, squares, gardens, or other open spaces for the use, gratuitously or on payment, of the public or of individuals, or for dedication to the public, the same being necessary or proper in connexion with the conversion of land into building land:

(xix) Sewers, drains, watercourses, pipe-making, fencing, paving, brick-making, tile-making, and other works necessary or proper in connexion with any of the objects aforesaid:

(xx) Trial pits for mines, and other preliminary works necessary or proper in connection with development of mines:

(xxi) Reconstruction, enlargement, or improvement of any of those works:

(xxii) The provision of small dwellings, either by means of building new buildings or by means of the reconstruction, enlargement, or improvement of existing buildings, if that provision of small dwellings is, in the opinion of the court, not injurious to the settled land or is agreed to by the tenant for life and the trustees of the settlement:

(xxiii) Additions to or alterations in buildings reasonably necessary or proper to enable the same to be let:

(xxiv) Erection of buildings in substitution for buildings within an urban sanitary district taken by a local or other public authority, or for buildings taken under compulsory powers, but so that no more money be expended than the amount received for the buildings taken and the site thereof:

(xxv) The rebuilding of the principal mansion house on the settled land: Provided that the sum to be applied under this head shall not exceed one-half of the annual rental of the settled land.

PART II

IMPROVEMENTS, THE COSTS OF WHICH THE TRUSTEES OF THE SETTLEMENT OR THE COURT MAY REQUIRE TO BE REPLACED BY INSTALMENTS

(i) Residential houses for land or mineral agents, managers, clerks, bailiffs, woodmen, gamekeepers and other persons employed on the settled land, or in connection with the management or development thereof:

(ii) Any offices, workshops and other buildings of a permanent nature required in connection with the management or development of the settled land or any part thereof:

(iii) The erection and building of dwelling houses, shops, buildings for religious, educational, literary, scientific, or public purposes, market places, market houses, places of amusement and entertainment, gasworks, electric light or power works, or any other works necessary or proper in connexion with the development of the settled land, or any part thereof as a building estate:

(iv) Restoration or reconstruction of buildings damaged or destroyed by dry rot:

(v) Structural additions to or alterations in buildings reasonably required, whether the buildings are intended to be let or not, or are already let:

(vi) Boring for water and other preliminary works in connection therewith

PART III

IMPROVEMENTS, THE COSTS OF WHICH THE TRUSTEES OF THE SETTLEMENT AND THE COURT MUST REQUIRE TO BE REPLACED BY INSTALMENTS

(i) Heating, hydraulic or electric power apparatus for buildings, and engines, pumps, lifts, rams, boilers, flues, and other works required or used in connexion therewith:

(ii) Engine houses, engines, gasometers, dynamos, accumulators, cables, pipes, wiring, switchboards, plant and other works required for the installation of electric, gas, or other artificial light, in connexion with any principal mansion house, or other house or buildings; but not electric lamps, gas fittings, or decorative fittings required in any such house or building:

(iii) Steam rollers, traction engines, motor lorries and moveable machinery for farming or other purposes.

[As amended by the Law of Property (Amendment) Act 1926, ss6, 7, Schedule; Law of Property (Entailed Interests) Act 1932, s1(1); Settled Land and Trustee Acts (Court's General Powers) Act 1943, s2; Finance Act 1949, s52, Schedule II, Pt IV; Married Women (Restraint upon Anticipation) Act 1949, s1(4), Schedule 2; Transfer of Functions (Ministry of Food) Order 1955; Highways Act 1959, s312(2), Schedule 25; Mental Health Act 1959, s149, Schedule 7, Pt I, Schedule 8, Pt I; Charities Act 1960, s48(2), Schedule 7, Pts I, II; Finance Act 1963, s73(8)(b),Schedule 11, Pt VI; Administration of Justice Act 1965, s17(1), Schedule 1; Family Law Reform Act 1969, ss1(3), 11(a), Schedule 1; Statute Law (Repeals) Act 1969; Decimal Currency Act 1969, s10(1); Highways Act 1980, s343(2), Schedule 24, para 2; Agricultural Holdings Act 1986, s100, Schedule 14, para 11; Trusts of Land and Appointment of Trustees Act 1996, s25(1), (2), Schedule 3, para 2, Schedule 4.]

TRUSTEE ACT 1925
(15 & 16 Geo 5 c 19)

PART II

GENERAL POWERS OF TRUSTEES AND PERSONAL REPRESENTATIVES

12 Power of trustees for sale to sell by auction, etc [379]

(1) Where a trustee has a duty or power to sell property, he may sell or concur with any other person in selling all or any part of the property, either subject to

prior charges or not, and either together or in lots, by public auction or by private contract, subject to any such conditions respecting title or evidence of title or other matter as the trustee thinks fit, with power to vary any contract for sale, and to buy in at any auction, or to rescind any contract for sale and to re-sell, without being answerable for any loss.

(2) A duty or power to sell or dispose of land includes a duty or power to sell or dispose of part thereof, whether the division is horizontal, vertical or made in any other way.

(3) This section does not enable an express power to sell settled land to be exercised where the power is not vested in the tenant for life or statutory owner.

13 Power to sell subject to depreciatory conditions [380]

(1) No sale made by a trustee shall be impeached by any beneficiary upon the ground that any of the conditions subject to which the sale was made may have been unnecessarily depreciatory, unless it also appears that the consideration for the sale was thereby rendered inadequate.

(2) No sale made by a trustee shall, after the execution of the conveyance, be impeached as against the purchaser upon the ground that any of the conditions subject to which the sale was made may have been unnecessarily depreciatory, unless it appears that the purchaser was acting in collusion with the trustee at the time when the contract for sale was made.

(3) No purchaser, upon any sale made by the trustee, shall be at liberty to make any objection against the title upon any of the grounds aforesaid.

(4) This section applies to sales made before or after the commencement of this Act.

16 Power to raise money by sale, mortgage, etc [381]

(1) Where trustees are authorised by the instrument, if any, creating the trust or by law to pay or apply capital money subject to the trust for any purpose or in any manner, they shall have and shall be deemed always to have had power to raise the money required by sale, conversion, calling in, or mortgage of all or any part of the trust property for the time being in possession.

(2) This section applies notwithstanding anything to the contrary contained in the instrument, if any, creating the trust, but does not apply to trustees of property held for charitable purposes, or to trustees of a settlement for the purposes of the Settled Land Act 1925, not being also the statutory owners.

17 Protection to purchasers and mortgagees [382]
dealing with trustees

No purchaser or mortgagee, paying or advancing money on a sale or mortgage purporting to be made under any trust or power vested in trustees, shall be concerned to see that such money is wanted, or that no more than is wanted is raised, or otherwise as to the application thereof.

PART III

APPOINTMENT AND DISCHARGE OF TRUSTEES

34 Limitation of the number of trustees [383]

(1) Where, at the commencement of this Act, there are more than four trustees of a settlement of land, or more than four trustees holding land on trust for sale, no new trustees shall (except where as a result of the appointment the number is reduced to four or less) be capable of being appointed until the number is reduced to less than four, and thereafter the number shall not be increased beyond four.

(2) In the case of settlements and dispositions creating trusts of land made or coming into operation after the commencement of this Act –

(a) the number of trustees thereof shall not in any case exceed four, and where more than four persons are named as such trustees, the four first named (who are able and willing to act) shall alone be the trustees, and the other persons named shall not be trustees unless appointed on the occurrence of a vacancy;

(b) the number of the trustees shall not be increased beyond four.

(3) This section only applies to settlements and dispositions of land, and the restrictions imposed on the number of trustees do not apply –

(a) in the case of land vested in trustees for charitable, ecclesiastical, or public purposes; or

(b) where the net proceeds of the sale of the land are held for like purposes; or

(c) to the trustees of a term of years absolute limited by a settlement on trusts for raising money, or of a like term created under the statutory remedies relating to annual sums charged on land.

35 Appointments of trustees of settlements and [384] trustees of land

(1) Appointments of new trustees of land and of new trustees of any trust of the proceeds of sale of the land shall, subject to any order of the court, be effected by separate instruments, but in such manner as to secure that the same persons become trustees of land and trustees of the trust of the proceeds of sale.

(2) Where new trustees of a settlement are appointed, a memorandum of the names and addresses of the persons who are for the time being the trustees thereof for the purposes of the Settled Land Act 1925 shall be endorsed on or annexed to the last or only principal vesting instrument by or on behalf of the trustees of the settlement, and such vesting instrument shall, for that purpose, be produced by the person having the possession thereof to the trustees of the settlement when so required.

(3) Where new trustees of land are appointed, a memorandum of the persons who are for the time being the trustees of the land shall be endorsed on or annexed to the conveyance by which the land was vested in trustees of land; and that conveyance shall be produced to the persons who are for the time being the trustees of the land by the person in possession of it in order for that to be done when the trustees require its production.

(4) This section applies only to settlements and dispositions of land.

40 Vesting of trust property in new or continuing trustees   [385]

(1) Where by a deed a new trustee is appointed to perform any trust, then –

(a) if the deed contains a declaration by the appointer to the effect that any estate or interest in any land subject to the trust, or in any chattel so subject, or the right to recover or receive any debt or other thing in action so subject, shall vest in the persons who by virtue of the deed become or are the trustees for performing the trust, the deed shall operate, without any conveyance or assignment, to vest in those persons as joint tenants and for the purposes of the trust the estate interest or right to which the declaration relates; and
(b) if the deed is made after the commencement of this Act and does not contain such a declaration, the deed shall, subject to any express provision to the contrary therein contained, operate as if it had contained such a declaration by the appointer extending to all the estates interests and rights with respect to which a declaration could have been made.

(2) Where by a deed a retiring trustee is discharged under section 39 of this Act or section 19 of the Trusts of Land and Appointment of Trustees Act 1996 without a new trustee being appointed, then –

(a) if the deed contains such a declaration as aforesaid by the retiring and continuing trustees, and by the other persons, if any, empowered to appoint trustees, the deed shall, without any conveyance or assignment, operate to vest in the continuing trustees alone, as joint tenants, and for the purposes of the trust, the estate, interest, or right of which the declaration relates; and
(b) if the deed is made after the commencement of this Act and does not contain such a declaration, the deed shall, subject to any express provision to the contrary therein contained, operate as if it had contained such a declaration by such persons as aforesaid extending to all the estates, interests and rights with respect to which a declaration could have been made.

(3) An express vesting declaration, whether made before or after the commencement of this Act, shall, notwithstanding that the estate, interest or right to be vested is not expressly referred to, and provided that the other statutory requirements were or are complied with, operate and be deemed always to have operated (but without prejudice to any express provision to the contrary contained in the deed of appointment or discharge) to vest in the persons respectively referred to in subsections (1) and (2) of this section, as the case may require, such estates, interests and rights are as capable of being and ought to be vested in those persons.

(4) This section does not extend –

(a) to land conveyed by way of mortgage for securing money subject to the trust, except land conveyed on trust for securing debentures or debenture stock;
(b) to land held under a lease which contains any covenant, condition or agreement against assignment or disposing of the land without licence or consent, unless, prior to the execution of the deed containing expressly or impliedly the vesting declaration, the requisite licence or consent has been obtained, or unless, by virtue of any statute or rule of law, the vesting declaration, express or implied, would not operate as a breach of covenant or give rise to a forfeiture;
(c) to any share, stock, annuity or property which is only transferable in books kept by a company or other body, or in manner directed by or under an Act of Parliament.

In this subsection 'lease' includes an underlease and an agreement for a lease or underlease.

(5) For purposes of registration of the deed in any registry, the person or persons making the declaration expressly or impliedly shall be deemed the conveying party or parties, and the conveyance shall be deemed to be made by him or them under a power conferred by this Act.

(6) This section applies to deeds of appointment and discharge executed on or after the first day of January, eighteen hundred and eighty-two.

44 Vesting orders of land [386]

In any of the following cases, namely –

(i) Where the court appoints or has appointed a trustee, or where a trustee has been appointed out of court under any statutory or express power;
(ii) Where a trustee entitled to or possessed of any land or interest therein, whether by way of mortgage or otherwise, or entitled to a contingent right therein, either solely or jointly with any other person –

(a) is under disability; or
(b) is out of the jurisdiction of the High Court; or
(c) cannot be found, or, being a corporation, has been dissolved;

(iii) Where it is uncertain who was the survivor of two or more trustees jointly entitled to or possessed of any interest in land;
(iv) Where it is uncertain whether the last trustee known to have been entitled to or possessed of any interest in land is living or dead;
(v) Where there is no personal representative of a deceased trustee who was entitled to or possessed of any interest in land, or where it is uncertain who is the personal representative of a deceased trustee who was entitled to or possessed of any interest in land;
(vi) Where a trustee jointly or solely entitled to or possessed of any interest in land, or entitled to a contingent right therein, has been required, by or on behalf of a person entitled to require a conveyance of the land or interest or a release of the right, to convey the land or interest or to release the right, and has wilfully refused or neglected to convey the land or interest or release the right for twenty-eight days after the date of the requirement;
(vii) Where land or any interest therein is vested in a trustee whether by way of mortgage or otherwise, and it appears to the court to be expedient;

the court may make an order (in this Act called a vesting order) vesting the land or interest therein in any such person in any such manner and for any such estate or interest as the court may direct, or releasing or disposing of the contingent right to such person as the court may direct: Provided that –

(a) Where the order is consequential on the appointment of a trustee the land or interest therein shall be vested for such estate as the court may direct in the persons who on the appointment are the trustees; and
(b) Where the order relates to a trustee entitled or formerly entitled jointly with another person, and such trustee is under disability or out of the jurisdiction of the High Court or cannot be found, or being a corporation has been dissolved, the land interest or right shall be vested in such other person who remains entitled, either alone or with any other person the court may appoint.

PART V

GENERAL PROVISIONS

64 Application of Act to Settled Land Act trustees   [387]

(1) All the powers and provisions contained in this Act with reference to the appointment of new trustees, and the discharge and retirement of trustees, apply to and include trustees for the purposes of the Settled Land Act 1925, and trustees for the purpose of the management of land during a minority, whether such trustees are appointed by the court or by the settlement, or under provisions contained in any instrument.

(2) Where, either before or after the commencement of this Act, trustees of a settlement have been appointed by the court for the purposes of the Settled Land Acts 1882 to 1890, or of the Settled Land Act 1925, then, after the commencement of this Act –

(a) the person or persons nominated for the purpose of appointing new trustees by the instrument, if any, creating the settlement, though no trustees for the purposes of the said Acts were thereby appointed; or
(b) if there is no such person, or no such person able and willing to act, the surviving or continuing trustees or trustee for the time being for the purposes of the said Acts or the personal representatives of the last surviving or continuing trustee for those purposes,

shall have the powers conferred by this Act to appoint new or additional trustees of the settlement for the purposes of the said Acts.

(3) Appointments of new trustees for the purposes of the said Acts made or expressed to be made before the commencement of this Act by the trustees or trustee or personal representatives referred to in paragraph (b) of the last preceding subsection or by the persons referred to in paragraph (a) of that subsection are, without prejudice to any order of the court made before such commencement, hereby confirmed.

67 Jurisdiction of the 'court'   [388]

(1) In this Act 'the court' means the High Court or the county court, where those courts respectively have jurisdiction.

(2) The procedure under this Act in county courts shall be in accordance with the Acts and rules regulating the procedure of those courts.

68 Definitions   [389]

(1) In this Act, unless the context otherwise requires, the following expressions have the meanings hereby assigned to them respectively, that is to say – ...

(6) 'Land' includes land of any tenure, and mines and minerals, where or not severed from the surface, buildings or parts of buildings, whether the division is horizontal, vertical or made in any other way, and other corporeal hereditaments; also a manor, an advowson, and a rent and other incorporeal hereditaments, and an easement, right, privilege, or benefit in, over, or derived from land; and in this definition 'mines and minerals' include any strata or seam of minerals or substances in or under any land, and powers of working and getting the same; and 'hereditaments' mean real property which under an intestacy occurring before the commencement of this Act might have devolved on an heir;
(7) 'Mortgage' and 'mortgagee' include a charge or chargee by way of legal

mortgage, and relate to every estate and interest regarded in equity as merely a security for money, and every person deriving title under the original mortgagee; ...

(11) 'Property' includes real and personal property, and any estate share and interest in any property, real or personal, and any debt, and any thing in action, and any other right or interest, whether in possession or not; ...

(15) 'Tenant for life', 'statutory owner', 'settled land', 'settlement', 'trust instrument', 'trustees of the settlement', 'term of years absolute' and 'vesting instrument' have the same meanings as in the Settled Land Act 1925, and 'entailed interest' has the same meaning as in the Law of Property Act 1925; ...

(17) 'Trust' does not include the duties incident to an estate conveyed by way of mortgage, but with this exception the expressions 'trust' and 'trustee' extend to implied and constructive trusts, and to cases where the trustee has a beneficial interest in the trust property, and to the duties incident to the office of a personal representative, and 'trustee', where the context admits, includes a personal representative, and 'new trustee' includes an additional trustee;

(18) 'Trust corporation' means the Public Trustee or a corporation either appointed by the court in any particular case to be a trustee, or entitled by rules made under subsection (3) of section four of the Public Trustee Act 1906, to act as custodian trustee;

(19) 'Trust for sale' in relation to land means an immediate trust for sale, whether or not exercisable at the request or with the consent of any person;

(20) 'United Kingdom' means Great Britain and Northern Ireland.

(2) Any reference in this Act to paying money or securities into court shall be construed as referring to paying the money or transferring or depositing the securities into or in the Supreme Court or into or in any other court that has jurisdiction, and any reference in this Act to payment of money or securities into court shall be construed –

(a) with reference to an order of the High Court, as referring to payment of the money or transfer or deposit of the securities into or in the Supreme Court; and

(b) with reference to an order of any other court, as referring to payment of the money or transfer or deposit of the securities into or in that court.

69 Application of Act [390]

(1) This Act, except where otherwise expressly provided, applies to trusts including, so far as this Act applies thereto, executorship and administrationships constituted or created either before or after the commencement of this Act.

(2) The powers conferred by this Act on trustees are in addition to the powers conferred by the instrument, if any, creating the trust, but those powers, unless otherwise stated, apply if and so far only as a contrary intention is not expressed in the instrument, if any, creating the trust, and have effect subject to the terms of that instrument.

[As amended by the Mental Health Act 1959, s149(2), Schedule 8, Pt I; Courts Act 1971, s56, Schedule 11, Pt II; Trusts of Land and Appointment of Trustees Act 1996, s25(1), (2), Schedule 3, para 3, Schedule 4.]

LAW OF PROPERTY ACT 1925
(15 Geo 5 c 20)

PART I

GENERAL PRINCIPLES AS TO LEGAL ESTATES, EQUITABLE
INTERESTS AND POWERS

1 Legal estates and equitable interests   [391]

(1) The only estates in land which are capable of subsisting or of being conveyed or created at law are –

    (a) An estate in fee simple absolute in possession;
    (b) A term of years absolute.

(2) The only interests or charges in or over land which are capable of subsisting or of being conveyed or created at law are –

    (a) An easement, right, or privilege in or over land for an interest equivalent to an estate in fee simple absolute in possession or a term of years absolute;
    (b) A rentcharge in possession issuing out of or charged on land being either perpetual or for a term of years absolute;
    (c) A charge by way of legal mortgage;
    (d) Any other similar charge on land which is not created by an instrument;
    (e) Rights of entry exercisable over or in respect of a legal term of years absolute, or annexed, for any purpose, to a legal rentcharge.

(3) All other estates, interests, and charges in or over land take effect as equitable interests.

(4) The estates, interests, and charges which under this section are authorised to subsist or to be conveyed or created at law are (when subsisting or conveyed or created at law) in this Act referred to as 'legal estates', and have the same incidents as legal estates subsisting at the commencement of this Act; and the owner of a legal estate is referred to as 'an estate owner' and his legal estate is referred to as his estate.

(5) A legal estate may subsist concurrently with or subject to any other legal estate in the same land in like manner as it could have done before the commencement of this Act.

(6) A legal estate is not capable of subsisting or of being created in an undivided share in land or of being held by an infant.

(7) Every power of appointment over, or power to convey or charge land or any interest therein, whether created by a statute or other instrument or implied by law, and whether created before or after the commencement of this Act (not being a power vested in a legal mortgagee or an estate owner in right of his estate and exercisable by him or by another person in his name and on his behalf), operates only in equity.

(8) Estates, interests, and charges in or over land which are not legal estates are in this Act referred to as 'equitable interests', and powers which by this Act are to operate in equity only are in this Act referred to as 'equitable powers'.

(9) The provisions in any statute or other instrument requiring land to be conveyed to uses shall take effect as directions that the land shall (subject to creating or reserving thereout any legal estate authorised by this Act which may be required) be conveyed to a person of full age upon the requisite trusts.

(10) The repeal of the Statute of Uses (as amended) does not affect the operation thereof in regard to dealings taking effect before the commencement of this Act.

2 Conveyances overreaching certain equitable interests and powers [392]

(1) A conveyance to a purchaser of a legal estate in land shall overreach any equitable interest or power affecting that estate, whether or not he has notice thereof, if –

(i) the conveyance is made under the powers conferred by the Settled Land Act 1925, or any additional powers conferred by a settlement, and the equitable interest or power is capable of being overreached thereby, and the statutory requirements respecting the payment of capital money arising under the settlement are complied with;

(ii) the conveyance is made by trustees of land and the equitable interest or power is at the date of the conveyance capable of being overreached by such trustees under the provisions of subsection (2) of this section or independently of that subsection, and the requirements of section 27 of this Act respecting the payment of capital money arising on such a conveyance are complied with;

(iii) the conveyance is made by a mortgagee or personal representative in the exercise of his paramount powers, and the equitable interest or power is capable of being overreached by such conveyance, and any capital money arising from the transaction is paid to the mortgagee or personal representative;

(iv) the conveyance is made under an order of the court and the equitable interest or power is bound by such order, and any capital money arising from the transaction is paid into, or in accordance with the order of, the court.

(1A) An equitable interest in land subject to a trust of land which remains in, or is to revert to, the settlor shall (subject to any contrary intention) be overreached by the conveyance if it would be so overreached were it an interest under the trust.

(2) Where the legal estate affected is subject to a trust of land, then if at the date of a conveyance made after the commencement of this Act by the trustees, the trustees (whether original or substituted) are either –

(a) two or more individuals approved or appointed by the court or the successors in office of the individuals so approved or appointed; or

(b) a trust corporation,

any equitable interest or power having priority to the trust shall, notwithstanding any stipulation to the contrary, be overreached by the conveyance, and shall, according to its priority, take effect as if created or arising by means of a primary trust affecting the proceeds of sale and the income of the land until sale.

(3) The following equitable interests and powers are excepted from the operation of subsection (2) of this section, namely –

(i) Any equitable interest protected by a deposit of documents relating to the legal estate affected;

(ii) The benefit of any covenant or agreement restrictive of the user of land;

(iii) Any easement, liberty, or privilege over or affecting land and being merely an equitable interest (in this Act referred to as an 'equitable easement');

(iv) The benefit of any contract (in this Act referred to as an 'estate contract') to convey or create a legal estate, including a contract conferring either expressly or by statutory implication a valid option to purchase, a right of pre-emption, or any other like right;

(v) Any equitable interest protected by registration under the Land Charges Act 1925, other than –

(a) an annuity within the meaning of Part II of that Act;

(b) a limited owner's charge or a general equitable charge within the meaning of that Act.

(4) Subject to the protection afforded by this section to the purchaser of a legal estate, nothing contained in this section shall deprive a person entitled to an equitable charge of any of his rights or remedies for enforcing the same.

(5) So far as regards the following interests, created before the commencement of this Act (which accordingly are not within the provisions of the Land Charges Act 1925), namely –

(a) the benefit of any covenant or agreement restrictive of the user of the land;
(b) any equitable easement;
(c) the interest under a puisne mortgage within the meaning of the Land Charges Act 1925, unless and until acquired under a transfer made after the commencement of this Act;
(d) the benefit of an estate contract, unless and until the same is acquired under a conveyance made after the commencement of this Act;

a purchaser of a legal estate shall only take subject thereto if he has notice thereof, and the same are not overreached under the provisions contained or in the manner referred to in this section.

3 Manner of giving effect to equitable interests and powers   [393]

(1) All equitable interests and powers in or over land shall be enforceable against the estate owner of the legal estate affected in manner following (that is to say) –

(a) Where the legal estate affected is settled land, the tenant for life or statutory owner shall be bound to give effect to the equitable interests and powers in manner provided by the Settled Land Act 1925;
(c) In any other case, the estate owner shall be bound to give effect to the equitable interests and powers affecting his estate of which he has notice according to their respective priorities. This provision does not affect the priority or powers of a legal mortgagee, or the powers of personal representatives for purposes of administration.

(3) Where, by reason of an equitable right of entry taking effect, or for any other reason, a person becomes entitled to require a legal estate to be vested in him, then and in any such case the estate owner whose estate is affected shall be bound to convey or create such legal estate as the case may require.

(4) If any question arises whether any and what legal estate ought to be transferred or created as aforesaid, any person interested may apply to the court for directions in the manner provided by this Act.

(5) If the estate owners refuse or neglect for one month after demand to transfer or create any such legal estate, or if by reason of their being out of the United Kingdom or being unable to be found, or by reason of the dissolution of a corporation, or for any other reason, the court is satisfied that the transaction cannot otherwise be effected, or cannot be effected without undue delay or expense, the court may, on the application of any person interested, make a vesting order transferring or creating a legal estate in the manner provided by this Act.

(6) This section does not affect a purchaser of a legal estate taking free from an equitable interest or power ...

4 Creation and disposition of equitable interests   [394]

(1) Interests in land validly created or arising after the commencement of this Act, which are not capable of subsisting as legal estates, shall take effect as equitable interests, and, save as otherwise expressly provided by statute, interests in land

which under the Statute of Uses or otherwise could before the commencement of this Act have been created as legal interests, shall be capable of being created as equitable interests: provided that, after the commencement of this Act (and save as hereinafter expressly enacted), an equitable interest in land shall only be capable of being validly created in any case in which an equivalent equitable interest in property real or personal could have been validly created before such commencement.

(2) All rights and interests in land may be disposed of, including –

(a) a contingent, executory or future equitable interest in any land, or a possibility coupled with an interest in any land, whether or not the object of the gift or limitation of such interest or possibility be ascertained;

(b) a right of entry, into or upon land whether immediate or future, and whether vested or contingent.

(3) All rights of entry affecting a legal estate which are exercisable on condition broken or for any other reason may after the commencement of this Act, be made exercisable by any person and the persons deriving title under him, but, in regard to an estate in fee simple (not being a rentcharge held for a legal estate) only within the period authorised by the rule relating to perpetuities.

5 Satisfied terms, whether created out of freehold [395] or leasehold land to cease

(1) Where the purposes of a term of years created or limited at any time out of freehold land, become satisfied either before or after the commencement of this Act (whether or not that term either by express declaration or by construction of law becomes attendant upon the freehold reversion) it shall merge in the reversion expectant thereon and shall cease accordingly.

(2) Where the purposes of a term of years created or limited, at any time, out of leasehold land, become satisfied after the commencement of this Act, that term shall merge in the reversion expectant thereon and shall cease accordingly.

(3) Where the purposes are satisfied only as respects part of the land comprised in a term, this section shall have effect as if a separate term had been created in regard to that part of the land.

6 Saving of lessors' and lessees' covenants [396]

(1) Nothing in this Part of this Act affects prejudicially the right to enforce any lessor's or lessee's covenants, agreements or conditions (including a valid option to purchase or right of pre-emption over the reversion), contained in any such instrument as is in this section mentioned, the benefit or burden of which runs with the reversion of the term.

(2) This section applies where the covenant, agreement or condition is contained in any instrument –

(a) creating a term of years absolute, or

(b) varying the rights of the lessor or lessee under the instrument creating the term.

7 Saving of certain legal estates and statutory powers [397]

(1) A fee simple which, by virtue of the Lands Clauses Acts or any similar statute, is liable to be divested, is for the purposes of this Act a fee simple absolute, and remains liable to be divested as if this Act had not been passed and a fee simple

subject to a legal or equitable right of entry or re-entry is for the purposes of this Act a fee simple absolute.

(2) A fee simple vested in a corporation which is liable to determine by reason of the dissolution of the corporation is, for the purposes of this Act, a fee simple absolute.

(3) The provisions of –

(b) the Friendly Societies Act 1896, in regard to land to which that Act applies;
(c) any other statutes conferring special facilities or prescribing special modes (whether by way of registered memorial or otherwise) for disposing of or acquiring land, or providing for the vesting (by conveyance or otherwise) of the land in trustees or any person, or the holder for the time being of an office or any corporation sole or aggregate (including the Crown);

shall remain in full force.

(4) Where any such power for disposing of or creating a legal estate is exercisable by a person who is not the estate owner, the power shall, when practicable, be exercised in the name and on behalf of the estate owner.

8 Saving of certain legal powers to lease [398]

(1) All leases or tenancies at a rent for a term of years absolute authorised to be granted by a mortgagor or mortgagee or by the Settled Land Act 1925, or any other statute (whether or not extended by any instrument) may be granted in the name and on behalf of the estate owner by the person empowered to grant the same, whether being an estate owner or not, with the same effect and priority as if this Part of this Act had not been passed; but this section does not (except as respects the usual qualified covenant for quiet enjoyment) authorise any person granting a lease in the name of an estate owner to impose any personal liability on him.

(2) Where a rentcharge is held for a legal estate, the owner thereof may under the statutory power or under any corresponding power, create a legal term of years absolute for securing or compelling payment of the same; but in other cases terms created under any such power shall, unless and until the estate owner of the land charged gives legal effect to the transaction, take effect only as equitable interests.

9 Vesting orders and dispositions of legal estates operating [399] as conveyances by an estate owner

(1) Every such order, declaration, or conveyance as is hereinafter mentioned, namely –

(a) every vesting order made by any court or other competent authority;
(b) every vesting declaration (express or implied) under any statutory power;
(c) every vesting instrument made by the trustees of a settlement or other persons under the provisions of the Settled Land Act 1925;
(d) every conveyance by a person appointed for the purpose under an order of the court or authorised under any statutory power to convey in the name or on behalf of an estate owner;
(e) every conveyance made under any power reserved or conferred by this Act,

which is made or executed for the purpose of vesting, conveying, or creating a legal estate, shall operate to convey or create the legal estate disposed of in like manner as if the same had been a conveyance executed by the estate owner of the legal estate to which the order, declaration, vesting instrument, or conveyance relates.

(2) Where the order, declaration, or conveyance is made in favour of a purchaser,

the provisions of this Act relating to a conveyance of a legal estate to a purchaser shall apply thereto.

(3) The provisions of the Trustee Act 1925 relating to vesting orders and orders appointing a person to convey shall apply to all vesting orders authorised to be made by this Part of this Act.

12 Limitation and Prescription Acts [400]

Nothing in this Part of this Act affects the operation of any statute, or of the general law for the limitation of actions or proceedings relating to land or with reference to the acquisition of easements or rights over or in respect of land.

13 Effect of possession of documents [401]

This Act shall not prejudicially affect the right of interest of any person arising out of or consequent on the possession by him of any documents relating to a legal estate in land, nor affect any question arising out of or consequent upon any omission to obtain or any other absence of possession by any person of any documents relating to a legal estate in land.

14 Interests of persons in possession [402]

This Part of this Act shall not prejudicially affect the interest of any person in possession or in actual occupation of land to which he may be entitled in right of such possession or occupation.

15 Presumption that parties are of full age [403]

The persons expressed to be parties to any conveyance shall, until the contrary is proved, be presumed to be of full age at the date thereof.

20 Infants not to be appointed trustees [404]

The appointment of an infant to be a trustee in relation to any settlement or trust shall be void, but without prejudice to the power to appoint a new trustee to fill the vacancy.

21 Receipts by married infants [405]

A married infant shall have power to give valid receipts for all income (including statutory accumulations of income made during the minority) to which the infant may be entitled in like manner as if the infant were of full age.

22 Conveyances on behalf of persons suffering from mental disorder and as to land held by them in trust [406]

(1) Where a legal estate in land (whether settled or not) is vested in a person suffering from mental disorder, either solely or jointly with any other person or persons, his receiver or (if no receiver is acting for him) any person authorised in that behalf shall, under an order of the authority having jurisdiction under Part VII of the Mental Health Act 1983, or of the court, or under any statutory power, make or concur in making all requisite dispositions for conveying or creating a legal estate in his name and on his behalf.

(2) If land subject to a trust of land is vested, either solely or jointly with any other person or persons, in a person who is incapable, by reason of mental disorder, of

exercising his functions as trustee, a new trustee shall be appointed in the place of that person, or he shall be otherwise discharged from the trust, before the legal estate is dealt with by the trustees.

24 Appointment of trustees of land [407]

(1) The persons having power to appoint new trustees of land shall be bound to appoint the same persons (if any) who are for the time being trustees of any trust of the proceeds of sale of the land.

(2) A purchaser shall not be concerned to see that subsection (1) of this section has been complied with.

(3) This section applies whether the trust of land and the trust of proceeds of sale are created, or arise, before or after the commencement of this Act.

27 Purchaser not to be concerned with the trusts of [408] the proceeds of sale which are to be paid to two or more trustees or to a trust corporation

(1) A purchaser of a legal estate from trustees of land shall not be concerned with the trusts affecting the land, the net income of the land or the proceeds of sale of the land whether or not those trusts are declared by the same instrument as that by which the trust of land is created.

(2) Notwithstanding anything to the contrary in the instrument (if any) creating a trust of land or in any trust affecting the net proceeds of sale of the land if it is sold, the proceeds of sale or other capital money shall not be paid to or applied by the direction of fewer than two persons as trustees, except where the trustee is a trust corporation, but this subsection does not affect the right of a sole personal representative as such to give valid receipts for, or direct the application of, proceeds of sale or other capital money, nor, except where capital money arises on the transaction, render it necessary to have more than one trustee.

31 Trust of mortgaged property where right of [409] redemption is barred

(1) Where any property, vested in trustees by way of security, becomes, by virtue of the statutes of limitation, or of an order for foreclosure or otherwise, discharged from the right of redemption, it shall be held by them in trust.

(a) to apply the income from the property in the same manner as interest paid on the mortgage debt would have been applicable; and
(b) if the property is sold, to apply the net proceeds of sale, after payment of costs and expenses, in the same manner as repayment of the mortgage debt would have been applicable.

(2) Subsection (1) of this section operates without prejudice to any rule of law relating to the apportionment of capital and income between tenant for life and remainderman.

(4) Where –

(a) the mortgage money is capital money for the purposes of the Settled Land Act 1925;
(b) land other than any forming the whole or part of the property mentioned in subsection (1) of this section is, or is deemed to be, subject to the settlement; and
(c) the tenant for life or statutory owner requires the trustees to execute with respect to land forming the whole or part of that property a vesting deed such

as would have been required in relation to the land if it had been acquired on a purchase with capital money,

the trustees shall execute such a vesting deed.

(5) This section applied whether the right of redemption was discharged before or after the first day of January, nineteen hundred and twelve, but has effect without prejudice to any dealings or arrangements made before that date.

33 Application of Part I to personal representatives   **[410]**

The provisions of this Part of this Act relating to trustees of land apply to personal representatives holding land in trust, but without prejudice to their rights and powers for purposes of administration.

34 Effect of future dispositions to tenants in common   **[411]**

(1) An undivided share in land shall not be capable of being created except as provided by the Settled Land Act 1925, or as hereinafter mentioned.

(2) Where, after the commencement of this Act, land is expressed to be conveyed to any persons in undivided shares and those persons are of full age, the conveyance shall (notwithstanding anything to the contrary in this Act) operate as if the land had been expressed to be conveyed to the grantees, or, if there are more than four grantees, to the four first named in the conveyance, as joint tenants in trust for the persons interested in the land: Provided that, where the conveyance is made by way of mortgage the land shall vest in the grantees or such four of them as aforesaid for a term of years absolute (as provided by this Act) as joint tenants subject to cesser on redemption in like manner as if the mortgage money had belonged to them on a joint account, but without prejudice to the beneficial interests in the mortgage money and interest.

(3) A devise bequest or testamentary appointment, coming into operation after the commencement of this Act, of land to two or more persons in undivided shares shall operate as a devise bequest or appointment of the land to the personal representative of the testator, and (but without prejudice to the rights and powers of the personal representatives for purposes of administration) in trust for the persons interested in the land.

(3A) In subsections (2) and (3) of this section references to the persons interested in the land include persons interested as trustees or personal representatives (as well as persons beneficially interested).

36 Joint tenancies   **[412]**

(1) Where a legal estate (not being settled land) is beneficially limited to or held in trust for any persons as joint tenants, the same shall be held in trust, in like manner as if the persons beneficially entitled were tenants in common, but not so as to sever their joint tenancy in equity.

(2) No severance of a joint tenancy of a legal estate, so as to create a tenancy in common in land, shall be permissible, whether by operation of law or otherwise, but this subsection does not affect the right of a joint tenant to release his interest to the other joint tenants, or the right to sever a joint tenancy in an equitable interest whether or not the legal estate is vested in the joint tenants: provided that, where a legal estate (not being settled land) is vested in joint tenants beneficially, and any tenant desires to sever the joint tenancy in equity, he shall give to the other joint tenants a notice in writing of such desire or do such other acts or things as would, in the case of personal estate, have been effectual to sever the tenancy

in equity, and thereupon the land shall be held in trust on terms which would have been requisite for giving effect to the beneficial interests if there had been an actual severance. Nothing in this Act affects the right of a survivor of joint tenants, who is solely and beneficially interested, to deal with his legal estate as if it were not held in trust.

(3) Without prejudice to the right of a joint tenant to release his interest to the other joint tenants no severance of a mortgage term or trust estate, so as to create a tenancy in common, shall be permissible.

37 Rights of husband and wife [413]

A husband and wife shall, for all purposes of acquisition of any interest in property, under a disposition made or coming into operation after the commencement of this Act, be treated as two persons.

38 Party structures [414]

(1) Where under a disposition or other arrangement which, if a holding in undivided shares had been permissible, would have created a tenancy in common, a wall or other structure is or is expressed to be made a party wall or structure, that structure shall be and remains severed vertically as between the respective owners, and the owner of each part shall have such rights to support and user over the rest of the structure as may be requisite for conferring rights corresponding to those which would have subsisted if a valid tenancy in common had been created.

(2) Any person interested may, in case of dispute, apply to the court for an order declaring the rights and interests under this section of the persons interested in any such party structure, and the court may make such order as it thinks fit.

39 Transitional provisions in First Schedule [415]

For the purpose of effecting the transition from the law existing prior to the commencement of the Law of Property Act 1922 to the law enacted by that Act (as amended), the provisions set out in the First Schedule to this Act shall have effect
—

(1) for converting existing legal estates, interests and charges not capable under the said Act of taking effect as legal interests into equitable interests;
(2) for discharging, getting in or vesting outstanding legal estates;
(3) for making provisions with respect to legal estates vested in infants;
(4) for subjecting land held in undivided shares to trusts;
(5) for dealing with party structures and open spaces held in common;
(6) for converting tenancies by entireties into joint tenancies;
(7) for converting existing freehold mortgages into mortgages by demise;
(8) for converting existing leasehold mortgages into mortgages by sub-demise.

PART II

CONTRACTS, CONVEYANCES AND OTHER INSTRUMENTS

51 Lands lie in grant only [416]

(1) All lands and all interests therein lie in grant and are incapable of being conveyed by livery or livery and seisin, or by feoffment, or by bargain and sale; and a conveyance of an interest in land may operate to pass the possession or

right to possession thereof, without actual entry, but subject to all prior rights thereto.

(2) The use of the word grant is not necessary to convey land or to create any interest therein.

52 Conveyances to be by deed [417]

(1) All conveyances of land or of any interest therein are void for the purpose of conveying or creating a legal estate unless made by deed.

(2) This section does not apply to –

(a) assents by a personal representative;
(b) disclaimers made in accordance with sections 178 to 180 or section 315 to 319 of the Insolvency Act 1986 or not required to be evidenced in writing;
(c) surrenders by operation of law, including surrenders which may, by law, be effected without writing;
(d) leases or tenancies or other assurances not required by law to be made in writing;
(e) receipts other than those falling within section 115 below;
(f) vesting orders of the court or other competent authority;
(g) conveyances taking effect by operation of law.

53 Instruments required to be in writing [418]

(1) Subject to the provisions hereinafter contained with respect to the creation of interests in land by parol –

(a) no interest in land can be created or disposed of except by writing signed by the person creating or conveying the same, or by his agent thereunto lawfully authorised in writing, or by will, or by operation of law;
(b) a declaration of trust respecting any land or any interest therein must be manifested and proved by some writing signed by some person who is able to declare such trust or by his will;
(c) a disposition of an equitable interest or trust subsisting at the time of the disposition, must be in writing signed by the person disposing of the same, or by his agent thereunto lawfully authorised in writing or by will.

(2) This section does not affect the creation or operation of resulting, implied or constructive trusts.

54 Creation of interests in land by parol [419]

(1) All interests in land created by parol and not put in writing and signed by the persons so creating the same, or by their agents thereunto lawfully authorised in writing, have, notwithstanding any consideration having been given for the same, the force and effect of interests at will only.

(2) Nothing in the foregoing provisions of this Part of this Act shall affect the creation by parol of leases taking effect in possession for a term not exceeding three years (whether or not the lessee is given power to extend the term) at the best rent which can be reasonably obtained without taking a fine.

55 Savings in regard to last two sections [420]

Nothing in the last two foregoing sections shall –

(a) invalidate dispositions by will; or
(b) affect any interest validly created before the commencement of this Act; or

(c) affect the right to acquire an interest in land by virtue of taking possession; or

(d) affect the operation of the law relating to part performance.

56 Persons taking who are not parties and as to indentures [421]

(1) A person may take an immediate or other interest in land or other property, or the benefit of any condition, right of entry, covenant or agreement over or respecting land or other property, although he may not be named as a party to the conveyance or other instrument.

(2) A deed between parties, to effect its objects, has the effect of an indenture though not indented or expressed to be an indenture.

57 Description of deeds [422]

Any deed, whether or not being an indenture, may be described (at the commencement thereof or otherwise) as a deed simply, or as a conveyance, deed of exchange, vesting deed, trust instrument, settlement, mortgage, charge, transfer of mortgage, appointment, lease or otherwise according to the nature of the transaction intended to be effected.

59 Conditions and certain covenants not implied [423]

(1) An exchange or other conveyance of land made by deed after the first day of October, eighteen hundred and forty-five, does not imply any condition in law.

(2) The word 'give' or 'grant' does not, in a deed made after the date last aforesaid, imply any covenant in law, save where otherwise provided by statute.

60 Abolition of technicalities in regard to conveyances and deeds [424]

(1) A conveyance of freehold land to any person without words of limitation, or any equivalent expression, shall pass to the grantee the fee simple or other the whole interest which the grantor had power to convey in such land, unless a contrary intention appears in the conveyance.

(2) A conveyance of freehold land to a corporation sole by his corporate designation without the word 'successors' shall pass to the corporation the fee simple or other the whole interest which the grantor had power to convey in such land, unless a contrary intention appears in the conveyance.

(3) In a voluntary conveyance a resulting trust for the grantor shall not be implied merely by reason that the property is not expressed to be conveyed for the use or benefit of the grantee.

(4) The foregoing provisions of this section apply only to conveyances and deeds executed after the commencement of this Act: provided that in a deed executed after the thirty-first day of December, eighteen hundred and eighty-one, it is sufficient –

(a) In the limitation of an estate in fee simple, to use the words 'in fee simple', without the word 'heirs'; ...

61 Construction of expressions used in deeds and other instruments [425]

In all deeds, contracts, wills, orders and other instruments executed, made or coming into operation after the commencement of this Act, unless the context otherwise requires –

(a) 'Month' means calendar month;
(b) 'Person' includes a corporation;
(c) The singular includes the plural and vice versa;
(d) The masculine includes the feminine and vice versa.

62 General words implied in conveyances [426]

(1) A conveyance of land shall be deemed to include and shall by virtue of this Act operate to convey, with the land, all buildings, erections, fixtures, commons, hedges, ditches, fences, ways, waters, water-courses, liberties, privileges, easements, rights and advantages whatsoever, appertaining or reputed to appertain to the land, or any part thereof, or, at the time of conveyance, demised, occupied, or enjoyed with, or reputed or known as part or parcel of or appurtenant to the land or any part thereof.

(2) A conveyance of land, having houses or other buildings thereon, shall be deemed to include and shall by virtue of this Act operate to convey, with the land, houses, or other buildings, all outhouses, erections, fixtures, cellars, areas, courts, courtyards, cisterns, sewers, gutters, drains, ways, passages, lights, watercourses, liberties, privileges, easements, rights, and advantages whatsoever, appertaining or reputed to appertain to the land, houses, or other buildings conveyed, or any of them, or any part thereof, or, at the time of conveyance, demised, occupied, or enjoyed with, or reputed or known as part or parcel of or appurtenant to, the land, houses, or other buildings conveyed, or any of them, or any part thereof.

(3) A conveyance of a manor shall be deemed to include and shall by virtue of this Act operate to convey, with the manor, all pastures, feedings, wastes, warrens, commons, mines, minerals, quarries, furzes, trees, woods, underwoods, coppices, and the ground and soil thereof, fishings, fisheries, fowlings, courts leet, courts baron, and other courts, view of frankpledge and all that to view of frankpledge doth belong, mills, mulctures, customs, tolls, duties, reliefs, heriots, fines, sums of money, amerciaments, waifs, estrays, chief-rents, quitrents, rentscharge, rents seck, rents of assize, fee farm rents, services, royalties jurisdictions, franchises, liberties, privileges, easements, profits, advantages, rights, emoluments, and hereditaments whatsoever, to the manor appertaining or reputed to appertain, or, at the time of conveyance, demised, occupied, or enjoyed with the same, or reputed or known as part, parcel or member thereof. For the purpose of this subsection the right to compensation for manorial incidents on the extinguishment thereof shall be deemed to be a right appertaining to the manor.

(4) This section applies only if and as far as a contrary intention is not expressed in the conveyance, and has effect subject to the terms of the conveyance and to the provisions therein contained.

(5) This section shall not be construed as giving to any person a better title to any property, right, or thing in this section mentioned than the title which the conveyance gives to him to the land or manor expressed to be conveyed, or as conveying to him any property, right, or thing in this section mentioned, further or otherwise than as the same could have been conveyed to him by the conveying parties.

(6) This section applies to conveyances made after the thirty-first day of December, eighteen hundred and eighty-one.

63 All estate clause implied [427]

(1) Every conveyance is effectual to pass all the estate, right, title, interest, claim, and demand which the conveying parties respectively have, in, to, or on the

property conveyed, or expressed or intended so to be, or which they respectively have power to convey in, to, or on the same.

(2) This section applies only if and as far as a contrary intention is not expressed in the conveyance, and has effect subject to the terms of the conveyance and to the provisions therein contained.

(3) This section applies to conveyances made after the thirty-first day of December, eighteen hundred and eighty-one.

65 Reservation of legal estates   [428]

(1) A reservation of a legal estate shall operate at law without any execution of the conveyance by the grantee of the legal estate out of which the reservation is made, or any regrant by him, so as to create the legal estate reserved, and so as to vest the same in possession in the person (whether being the grantor or not) for whose benefit the reservation is made.

(2) A conveyance of a legal estate expressed to be made subject to another legal estate not in existence immediately before the date of the conveyance, shall operate as a reservation, unless a contrary intention appears.

(3) This section applies only to reservations made after the commencement of this Act.

67 Receipt in deed sufficient   [429]

(1) A receipt for consideration money or securities in the body of a deed shall be a sufficient discharge for the same to the person paying or delivering the same, without any further receipt for the same being indorsed on the deed ...

68 Receipt in deed or indorsed evidence   [430]

(1) A receipt for consideration money or other consideration in the body of a deed or indorsed thereon shall, in favour of a subsequent purchaser, not having notice that the money or other consideration thereby acknowledged to be received was not in fact paid or given, wholly or in part, be sufficient evidence of the payment or giving of the whole amount thereof ...

72 Conveyances by a person to himself, etc   [431]

(1) In conveyances made after the twelfth day of August, eighteen hundred and fifty-nine, personal property, including chattels real, may be conveyed by a person to himself jointly with another person by the like means by which it might be conveyed by him to another person.

(2) In conveyances made after the thirty-first day of December, eighteen hundred and eighty-one, freehold land, or a thing in action, may be conveyed by a person to himself jointly with another person, by the like means by which it might be conveyed by him to another person; and may, in like manner, be conveyed by a husband to his wife, and by a wife to her husband, alone or jointly with another person.

(3) After the commencement of this Act a person may convey land to or vest land in himself.

(4) Two or more persons (whether or not being trustees or personal representatives) may convey, and shall be deemed always to have been capable of conveying, any property vested in them to any one or more of themselves in like manner as they could have conveyed such property to a third party; provided that

if the persons in whose favour the conveyance is made are, by reason of any fiduciary relationship or otherwise, precluded from validly carrying out the transaction, the conveyance shall be liable to be set aside.

77 Implied covenants in conveyances subject to rents [432]

(1) In addition to the covenants implied under Part I of the Law of Property (Miscellaneous Provisions) Act 1994, there shall in the several cases in this section mentioned, be deemed to be included and implied, a covenant to the effect in this section stated, by and with such persons as are hereinafter mentioned, that is to say –

(A) In a conveyance for valuable consideration, other than a mortgage, of the entirety of the land affected by a rentcharge, a covenant by the grantee or joint and several covenants by the grantees, if more than one, with the conveying parties and with each of them, if more than one, in the terms set out in Part VII of the Second Schedule to this Act. Where a rentcharge has been apportioned in respect of any land, with the consent of the owner of the rentcharge, the covenants in this paragraph shall be implied in the conveyance of that land in like manner as if the apportioned rentcharge were the rentcharge referred to, and the document creating the rentcharge related solely to that land:

(B) In a conveyance for valuable consideration, other than a mortgage, of part of land affected by a rentcharge, subject to a part of that rentcharge which has been or is by that conveyance apportioned (but in either case without the consent of the owner of the rentcharge) in respect of the land conveyed –

(i) A covenant by the grantee of the land or joint and several covenants by the grantees, if more than one, with the conveying parties and with each of them, if more than one, in the terms set out in paragraph (i) of Part VIII of the Second Schedule to this Act;

(ii) A covenant by a person who conveys or is expressed to convey as beneficial owner, or joint and several covenants by the persons who so convey or are expressed to so convey, if at the date of the conveyance any part of the land affected by such rentcharge is retained, with the grantees of the land and with each of them (if more than one) in the terms set out in paragraph (ii) of Part VIII of the Second Schedule to this Act.

(2) Where in a conveyance for valuable consideration, other than a mortgage, part of land affected by a rentcharge is, without the consent of the owner of the rentcharge, expressed to be conveyed subject to or charged with the entire rent, paragraph (B)(i) of subsection (1) of this section shall apply as if, in paragraph (i) of Part VIII of the Second Schedule to this Act –

(a) any reference to the apportioned rent were to the entire rent; and

(b) the words '(other than the covenant to pay the entire rent)' were omitted.

(2A) Where in a conveyance for valuable consideration, other than a mortgage, part of land affected by a rentcharge is, without the consent of the owner of the rentcharge, expressed to be conveyed discharged or exonerated from the entire rent, paragraph (B)(ii) of subsection (1) of this section shall apply as if, in paragraph (ii) of Part VIII of the Second Schedule to this Act –

(a) any reference to the balance of the rent were to the entire rent; and

(b) the words 'other than the covenant to pay the entire rent,' were omitted.

(3) In this section 'conveyance' does not include a demise by way of lease at a rent.

(4) Any covenant which would be implied under this section by reason of a person conveying or being expressed to convey as beneficial owner may, by

express reference to this section, be implied, with or without variation, in a conveyance, whether or not for valuable consideration, by a person who conveys or is expressed to convey as settlor, or as trustee, or as mortgagee, or as personal representative of a deceased person, or under an order of the court.

(5) The benefit of a covenant implied as aforesaid shall be annexed and incident to, and shall go with, the estate or interest of the implied covenantee, and shall be capable of being enforced by every person in whom that estate or interest is, for the whole or any part thereof, from time to time vested.

(6) A covenant implied as aforesaid may be varied or extended by deed, and, as so varied or extended, shall, as far as may be, operate in the like manner, and with all the like incidents, effects and consequences, as if such variations or extensions were directed in this section to be implied.

(7) In particular any covenant implied under this section may be extended by providing that –

(a) the land conveyed; or
(b) the part of the land affected by the rentcharge which remains vested in the covenantor; shall, as the case may require, stand charged with the payment of all money which may become payable under the implied covenant ...

78 Benefit of covenants relating to land   [433]

(1) A covenant relating to any land of the covenantee shall be deemed to be made with the covenantee and his successors in title and the persons deriving title under him or them, and shall have effect as if such successors and other persons were expressed. For the purposes of this subsection in connexion with covenants restrictive of the user of land 'successors in title' shall be deemed to include the owners and occupiers for the time being of the land of the covenantee intended to be benefited ...

79 Burden of covenants relating to land   [434]

(1) A covenant relating to any land of a covenantor or capable of being bound by him, shall, unless a contrary intention is expressed, be deemed to be made by the covenantor on behalf of himself his successors in title and the persons deriving title under him or them, and, subject as aforesaid, shall have effect as if such successors and other persons were expressed. This subsection extends to a covenant to do some act relating to the land, notwithstanding that the subject-matter may not be in existence when the covenant is made.

(2) For the purposes of this section in connexion with covenants restrictive of the user of land 'successors in title' shall be deemed to include the owners and occupiers for the time being of such land ...

80 Covenants binding land   [435]

(1) A covenant and a bond and an obligation or contract made under seal after 31st December 1881 but before the coming into force of section 1 of the Law of Property (Miscellaneous Provisions) Act 1989 or executed as a deed in accordance with that section after its coming into force, binds the real estate as well as the personal estate of the person making the same if and so far as a contrary intention is not expressed in the covenant, bond, obligation, or contract. This subsection extends to a covenant implied by virtue of this Act.

(2) Every covenant running with the land, whether entered into before or after the commencement of this Act, shall take effect in accordance with any statutory

enactment affecting the devolution of the land, and accordingly the benefit or burden of every such covenant shall vest in or bind the persons who by virtue of any such enactment or otherwise succeed to the title of the covenantee or the covenantor, as the case may be.

(3) The benefit of a covenant relating to land entered into after the commencement of this Act may be made to run with the land without the use of any technical expression if the covenant is of such a nature that the benefit could have been made to run with the land before the commencement of this Act.

(4) For the purposes of this section, a covenant runs with the land when the benefit or burden of it, whether at law or in equity, passes to the successors in title of the covenantee or the covenantor, as the case may be.

81 Effect of covenant with two or more jointly [436]

(1) A covenant, and a contract under seal, and a bond or obligation under seal, made with two or more jointly, to pay money or to make a conveyance, or to do any other act, to them or for their benefit, shall be deemed to include, and shall, by virtue of this Act, imply, an obligation to do the act to, or for the benefit of, the survivor or survivors of them, and to, or for the benefit of, any other person to whom the right to sue on the covenant, contract, bond, or obligation devolves, and where made after the commencement of this Act shall be construed as being also made with each of them.

(2) This section extends to a covenant implied by virtue of this Act.

(3) This section applies only if and as far as a contrary intention is not expressed in the covenant, contract, bond, or obligation, and has effect subject to the covenant, contract, bond, or obligation, and to the provisions therein contained.

(4) Except as otherwise expressly provided, this section applies to a covenant, contract, bond, or obligation made or implied after the thirty-first day of December, eighteen hundred and eighty-one.

(5) In its application to instruments made after the coming into force of section 1 of the Law of Property (Miscellaneous Provisions) Act 1989 subsection (1) above shall have effect as if for the words 'under seal, and a bond or obligation under seal,' there were substituted the words 'bond or obligation executed as a deed in accordance with section 1 of the Law of Property (Miscellaneous Provisions) Act 1989'.

82 Covenants and agreements entered into by a person [437] with himself and another or others

(1) Any covenant, whether express or implied, or agreement entered into by a person with himself and one or more other persons shall be construed and be capable of being enforced in like manner as if the covenant or agreement had been entered into with the other person or persons alone.

(2) This section applies to covenants or agreements entered into before or after the commencement of this Act, and to covenants implied by statute in the case of a person who conveys or is expressed to convey to himself and one or more other persons, but without prejudice to any order of the court made before such commencement.

83 Construction of implied covenants [438]

In the construction of a covenant or proviso, or other provision, implied in a deed or assent by virtue of this Act, words importing the singular or plural number, or the masculine gender, shall be read as also importing the plural or singular number, or as extending to females, as the case may require.

84 Power to discharge or modify restrictive [439] covenants affecting land

(1) The Lands Tribunal shall (without prejudice to any concurrent jurisdiction of the court) have power from time to time, on the application of any person interested in any freehold land affected by any restriction arising under covenant or otherwise as to the user thereof or the building thereon, by order wholly or partially to discharge or modify any such restriction on being satisfied –

(a) that by reason of changes in the character of the property or the neighbourhood or other circumstances of the case which the Lands Tribunal may deem material, the restriction ought to be deemed obsolete; or
(aa) that (in a case falling within subsection (1A) below) the continued existence thereof would impede some reasonable user of the land for public or private purposes or, as the case may be, would unless modified so impede such user; or
(b) that the persons of full age and capacity for the time being or from time to time entitled to the benefit of the restriction, whether in respect of estates in fee simple or any lesser estates or interests in the property to which the benefit of the restriction is annexed, have agreed, either expressly or by implication, by their acts or omissions, to the same being discharged or modified; or
(c) that the proposed discharge or modification will not injure the persons entitled to the benefit of the restriction;

and an order discharging or modifying a restriction under this subsection may direct the applicant to pay to any person entitled to the benefit of the restriction such sum by way of consideration as the Tribunal may think it just to award under one, but not both, of the following heads, that is to say, either –

(i) a sum to make up for any loss or disadvantage suffered by that person in consequence of the discharge or modification; or
(ii) a sum to make up for any effect which the restriction had, at the time when it was imposed, in reducing the consideration then received for the land affected by it.

(1A) Subsection (1)(aa) above authorises the discharge or modification of a restriction by reference to its impeding some reasonable user of land in any case in which the Lands Tribunal is satisfied that the restriction, in impeding that user, either –

(a) does not secure to persons entitled to the benefit of it any practical benefits of substantial value or advantage to them; or
(b) is contrary to the public interest;

and that money will be an adequate compensation for the loss or disadvantage (if any) which any such person will suffer from the discharge or modification.

(1B) In determining whether a case is one falling within subsection (1A) above, and in determining whether (in any such case or otherwise) a restriction ought to be discharged or modified, the Lands Tribunal shall take into account the development plan and any declared or ascertainable pattern for the grant or refusal of planning permissions in the relevant areas, as well as the period at which and context in which the restriction was created or imposed and any other material circumstances.

(1C) It is hereby declared that the power conferred by this section to modify a restriction includes power to add such further provisions restricting the user of or the building on the land affected as appear to the Lands Tribunal to be reasonable in view of the relaxation of the existing provisions, and as may be accepted by the applicant; and the Lands Tribunal may accordingly refuse to modify a restriction without some such addition.

(2) The court shall have power on the application of any person interested –

(a) to declare whether or not in any particular case any freehold land is, or would in any given event be, affected by a restriction imposed by any instrument; or

(b) to declare what, upon the true construction of any instrument purporting to impose a restriction, is the nature and extent of the restriction thereby imposed and whether the same is, or would in any given event be, enforceable and if so by whom.

Neither subsections (7) and (11) of this section nor, unless the contrary is expressed, any later enactment providing for this section not to apply to any restrictions shall affect the operation of this subsection or the operation for purposes of this subsection of any other provisions of this section.

(3) The Lands Tribunal shall, before making any order under this section, direct such enquiries, if any, to be made of any government department or local authority, and such notices, if any, whether by way of advertisement or otherwise, to be given to such of the persons who appear to be entitled to the benefit of the restriction intended to be discharged, modified, or dealt with as, having regard to any enquiries, notices or other proceedings previously made, given or taken, the Lands Tribunal may think fit.

(3A) On an application to the Lands Tribunal under this section the Lands Tribunal shall give any necessary directions as to the persons who are or are not to be admitted (as appearing to be entitled to the benefit of the restriction) to oppose the application, and no appeal shall lie against any such direction; but rules under the Lands Tribunal Act 1949 shall make provision whereby, in cases in which there arises on such an application (whether or not in connection with the admission of persons to oppose) any such question as is referred to in subsection (2)(a) or (b) of this section, the proceedings on the application can and, if the rules so provide, shall be suspended to enable the decision of the court to be obtained on that question by an application under that subsection, or by means of a case stated by the Lands Tribunal, or otherwise, as may be provided by those rules or by rules of court.

(5) Any order made under this section shall be binding on all persons, whether ascertained or of full age or capacity or not, then entitled or thereafter capable of becoming entitled to the benefit of any restriction, which is thereby discharged, modified or dealt with, and whether such persons are parties to the proceedings or have been served with notice or not.

(6) An order may be made under this section notwithstanding that any instrument which is alleged to impose the restriction intended to be discharged, modified, or dealt with, may not have been produced to the court or the Lands Tribunal, and the court or the Lands Tribunal may act on such evidence of that instrument as it may think sufficient.

(7) This section applies to restrictions whether subsisting at the commencement of this Act or imposed thereafter, but this section does not apply where the restriction was imposed on the occasion of a disposition made gratuitously or for a nominal consideration for public purposes.

(8) This section applies whether the land affected by the restrictions is registered or not, but, in the case of registered land, the Land Registrar shall give effect on the register to any order under this section in accordance with the Land Registration Act 1925.

(9) Where any proceedings by action or otherwise are taken to enforce a restrictive covenant, any person against whom the proceedings are taken, may in such proceedings apply to the court for an order giving leave to apply to the Lands Tribunal under this section, and staying the proceedings in the meantime.

(11) This section does not apply to restrictions imposed by the Commissioners of Works under any statutory power for the protection of any Royal Park or Garden or to restrictions of a like character imposed upon the occasion of any enfranchisement effected before the commencement of this Act in any manor vested in His Majesty in right of the Crown or the Duchy of Lancaster, nor (subject to subsection (11A) below) to restrictions created or imposed –

(a) for naval, military or air force purposes,
(b) for civil aviation purposes under the powers of the Air Navigation Act 1920, of section 19 or 23 of the Civil Aviation Act 1949 or of section 30 or 41 of the Civil Aviation Act 1982.

(11A) Subsection (11) of this section –

(a) shall exclude the application of this section to a restriction falling within subsection (11)(a), and not created or imposed in connection with the use of any land as an aerodrome, only so long as the restriction is enforceable by or on behalf of the Crown; and
(b) shall exclude the application of this section to a restriction falling within subsection (11)(b), or created or imposed in connection with the use of any land as an aerodrome, only so long as the restriction is enforceable by or on behalf of the Crown or any public or international authority.

(12) Where a term of more than forty years is created in land (whether before or after the commencement of this Act) this section shall, after the expiration of twenty-five years of the term, apply to restrictions, affecting such leasehold land in like manner as it would have applied had the land been freehold: provided that this subsection shall not apply to mining leases.

PART III

MORTGAGES, RENTCHARGES, AND POWERS OF ATTORNEY

85 Mode of mortgaging freeholds [440]

(1) A mortgage of an estate in fee simple shall only be capable of being effected at law either by a demise for a term of years absolute, subject to a provision for cesser on redemption, or by a charge by deed expressed to be by way of legal mortgage: Provided that a first mortgagee shall have the same right to the possession of documents as if his security included the fee simple.

(2) Any purported conveyance of an estate in fee simple by way of mortgage made after the commencement of this Act shall (to the extent of the estate of the mortgagor) operate as a demise of the land to the mortgagee for a term of years absolute, without impeachment for waste, but subject to cesser on redemption, in manner following, namely –

(a) A first or only mortgagee shall take a term of three thousand years from the date of the mortgage:
(b) A second or subsequent mortgagee shall take a term (commencing from the date of the mortgage) one day longer than the term vested in the first or other mortgagee whose security ranks immediately before that of such second or subsequent mortgagee:

and, in this subsection, any such purported conveyance as aforesaid includes an absolute conveyance with a deed of defeasance and any other assurance which, but for this subsection, would operate in effect to vest the fee simple in a mortgagee subject to redemption.

(3) This section applies whether or not the land is registered under the Land Registration Act 1925, or the mortgage is expressed to be made by way of trust for sale or otherwise.

(4) Without prejudice to the provisions of this Act respecting legal and equitable powers, every power to mortgage or to lend money on mortgage of an estate in fee simple shall be construed as a power to mortgage the estate for a term of years absolute, without impeachment for waste, or by a charge by way of legal mortgage or to lend on such security.

86 Mode of mortgaging leaseholds [441]

(1) A mortgage of a term of years absolute shall only be capable of being effected at law either by a subdemise for a term of years absolute, less by one day at least than the term vested in the mortgagor, and subject to a provision for cesser on redemption, or by a charge by deed expressed to be by way of legal mortgage; and where a licence to subdemise by way of mortgage is required, such licence shall not be unreasonably refused: Provided that a first mortgagee shall have the same right to the possession of documents as if his security had been effected by assignment.

(2) Any purported assignment of a term of years absolute by way of mortgage made after the commencement of this Act shall (to the extent of the estate of the mortgagor) operate as a subdemise of the leasehold land to the mortgagee for a term of years absolute, but subject to cesser on redemption, in manner following, namely –

(a) The term to be taken by a first or only mortgagee shall be ten days less than the term expressed to be assigned:
(b) The term to be taken by a second or subsequent mortgagee shall be one day longer than the term vested in the first or other mortgagee whose security ranks immediately before that of the second or subsequent mortgagee, if the length of the last mentioned term permits, and in any case for a term less by one day at least than the term expressed to be assigned:

and, in this subsection, any such purported assignment as aforesaid includes an absolute assignment with a deed of defeasance and any other assurance which, but for this subsection, would operate in effect to vest the term of the mortgagor in a mortgagee subject to redemption.

(3) This section applies whether or not the land is registered under the Land Registration Act 1925, or the mortgage is made by way of sub-mortgage of a term of years absolute, or is expressed to be by way of trust for sale or otherwise.

(4) Without prejudice to the provisions of this Act respecting legal and equitable powers, every power to mortgage for or to lend money on mortgage of a term of years absolute by way of assignment shall be construed as a power to mortgage the term by subdemise for a term of years absolute or by a charge by way of legal mortgage, or to lend on such security.

87 Charges by way of legal mortgage [442]

(1) Where a legal mortgage of land is created by a charge by deed expressed to be by way of legal mortgage, the mortgagee shall have the same protection, powers and remedies (including the right to take proceedings to obtain possession from the occupiers and the persons in receipt of rents and profits, or any of them) as if –

(a) where the mortgage is a mortgage of an estate in fee simple, a mortgage term for three thousand years without impeachment of waste had been thereby created in favour of the mortgagee; and

(b) where the mortgage is a mortgage of a term of years absolute, a sub-term less by one day than the term vested in the mortgagor had been thereby created in favour of the mortgagee.

(2) Where an estate vested in a mortgagee immediately before the commencement of this Act has by virtue of this Act been converted into a term of years absolute or sub-term, the mortgagee may, by a declaration in writing to that effect signed by him, convert the mortgage into a charge by way of legal mortgage, and in that case the mortgage term shall be extinguished in the inheritance or in the head term as the case may be, and the mortgagee shall have the same protection, powers and remedies (including the right to take proceedings to obtain possession from the occupiers and the persons in receipt of rents and profits or any of them) as if the mortgage term or sub-term had remained subsisting. The power conferred by this subsection may be exercised by a mortgagee notwithstanding that he is a trustee or personal representative.

(3) Such declaration shall not affect the priority of the mortgagee or his right to retain possession of documents, nor affect his title to or right over any fixtures or chattels personal comprised in the mortgage.

88 Realisation of freehold mortgages   [443]

(1) Where an estate in fee simple has been mortgaged by the creation of a term of years absolute limited thereout or by a charge by way of legal mortgage and the mortgagee sells under his statutory or express power of sale –

(a) the conveyance by him shall operate to vest in the purchaser the fee simple in the land conveyed subject to any legal mortgage having priority to the mortgage in right of which the sale is made and to any money thereby secured, and thereupon;

(b) the mortgage term or the charge by way of legal mortgage and any subsequent mortgage term or charges shall merge or be extinguished as respects the land conveyed;

and such conveyance may, as respects the fee simple, be made in the name of the estate owner in whom it is vested.

(2) Where any such mortgagee obtains an order for foreclosure absolute, the order shall operate to vest the fee simple in him (subject to any legal mortgage having priority to the mortgage in right of which the foreclosure is obtained and to any money thereby secured), and thereupon the mortgage term, if any, shall thereby be merged in the fee simple, and any subsequent mortgage term or charge by way of legal mortgage bound by the order shall thereupon be extinguished.

(3) Where any such mortgagee acquires a title under the Limitation Acts, he, or the persons deriving title under him, may enlarge the mortgage term into a fee simple under the statutory power for that purpose discharged from any legal mortgage affected by the title so acquired, or in the case of a chargee by way of legal mortgage may by deed declare that the fee simple is vested in him discharged as aforesaid, and the same shall vest accordingly.

(4) Where the mortgage includes fixtures or chattels personal any statutory power of sale and any right to foreclose or take possession shall extend to the absolute or other interest therein affected by the charge.

(5) In the case of a sub-mortgage by subdemise of a long term (less a nominal period) itself limited out of an estate in fee simple, the foregoing provisions of this

section shall operate as if the derivative term, if any, created by the sub-mortgage had been limited out of the fee simple, and so as to enlarge the principal term and extinguish the derivative term created by the sub-mortgage as aforesaid, and to enable the sub-mortgagee to convey the fee simple or acquire it by foreclosure, enlargement, or otherwise as aforesaid.

(6) This section applies to a mortgage whether created before or after the commencement of this Act, and to a mortgage term created by this Act, but does not operate to confer a better title to the fee simple than would have been acquired if the same had been conveyed by the mortgage (being a valid mortgage) and the restrictions imposed by this Act in regard to the effect and creation of mortgages were not in force, and all prior mortgages (if any) not being merely equitable charges had been created by demise or by charge by way of legal mortgage.

89 Realisation of leasehold mortgages [444]

(1) Where a term of years absolute has been mortgaged by the creation of another term of years absolute limited thereout or by a charge by way of legal mortgage and the mortgagee sells under his statutory or express power of sale, –

(a) the conveyance by him shall operate to convey to the purchaser not only the mortgage term, if any, but also (unless expressly excepted with the leave of the court) the leasehold reversion affected by the mortgage, subject to any legal mortgage having priority to the mortgage in right of which the sale is made and to any money thereby secured, and thereupon

(b) the mortgage term, or the charge by way of legal mortgage and any subsequent mortgage term or charge, shall merge in such leasehold reversion or be extinguished unless excepted as aforesaid;

and such conveyance may, as respects the leasehold reversion, be made in the name of the estate owner in whom it is vested. Where a licence to assign is required on a sale by a mortgagee, such licence shall not be unreasonably refused.

(2) Where any such mortgagee obtains an order for foreclosure absolute, the order shall, unless it otherwise provides, ·operate (without giving rise to a forfeiture for want of a licence to assign) to vest the leasehold reversion affected by the mortgage and any subsequent mortgage term in him, subject to any legal mortgage having priority to the mortgage in right of which the foreclosure is obtained and to any money thereby secured, and thereupon the mortgage term and any subsequent mortgage term or charge by way of legal mortgage bound by the order shall, subject to any express provision to the contrary contained in the order, merge in such leasehold reversion or be extinguished.

(3) Where any such mortgagee acquires a title under the Limitation Acts, he, or the persons deriving title under him, may by deed declare that the leasehold reversion affected by the mortgage and any mortgage term affected by the title so acquired shall vest in him, free from any right of redemption which is barred, and the same shall (without giving rise to a forfeiture for want of a licence to assign) vest accordingly, and thereupon the mortgage term, if any, and any other mortgage term or charge by way of legal mortgage affected by the title so acquired shall, subject to any express provision to the contrary contained in the deed, merge in such leasehold reversion or be extinguished.

(4) Where the mortgage includes fixtures or chattels personal, any statutory power of sale and any right to foreclose or take possession shall extend to the absolute or other interest therein affected by the charge.

(5) In the case of a sub-mortgage by subdemise of a term (less a nominal period) itself limited out of a leasehold reversion, the foregoing provisions of this section

shall operate as if the derivative term created by the sub-mortgage had been limited out of the leasehold reversion, and so as (subject as aforesaid) to merge the principal mortgage term therein as well as the derivative term created by the sub-mortgage and to enable the sub-mortgagee to convey the leasehold reversion or acquire it by foreclosure, vesting, or otherwise as aforesaid.

(6) This section takes effect without prejudice to any incumbrance or trust affecting the leasehold reversion which has priority over the mortgage in right of which the sale, foreclosure, or title is made or acquired, and applies to a mortgage whether executed before or after the commencement of this Act, and to a mortgage term created by this Act, but does not apply where the mortgage term does not comprise the whole of the land included in the leasehold reversion unless the rent (if any) payable in respect of that reversion has been apportioned as respects the land affected, or the rent is of no money value or no rent is reserved, and unless the lessee's covenants and conditions (if any) have been apportioned, either expressly or by implication, as respects the land affected. In this subsection references to an apportionment include an equitable apportionment made without the consent of the lessor ...

90 Realisation of equitable charges by the court [445]

(1) Where an order for sale is made by the court in reference to an equitable mortgage on land (not secured by a legal term of years absolute or by a charge by way of legal mortgage) the court may, in favour of a purchaser, make a vesting order conveying the land or may appoint a person to convey the land or create and vest in the mortgagee a legal term of years absolute to enable him to carry out the sale, as the case may require, in like manner as if the mortgage had been created by deed by way of legal mortgage pursuant to this Act, but without prejudice to any incumbrance having priority to the equitable mortgage unless the incumbrancer consents to the sale.

(2) This section applies to equitable mortgages made or arising before or after the commencement of this Act, but not to a mortgage which has been over-reached under the powers conferred by this Act or otherwise ...

91 Sale of mortgaged property in action for redemption [446] or foreclosure

(1) Any person entitled to redeem mortgaged property may have a judgment or order for sale instead of for redemption in an action brought by him either for redemption alone, or for sale alone, or for sale or redemption in the alternative.

(2) In any action, whether for foreclosure, or for redemption, or for sale, or for the raising and payment in any manner of mortgage money, the court, on the request of the mortgagee, or of any person interested either in the mortgage money or in the right of redemption, and, notwithstanding that –

(a) any other person dissents; or
(b) the mortgagee or any person so interested does not appear in the action;

and without allowing any time for redemption or for payment of any mortgage money, may direct a sale of the mortgaged property, on such terms as it thinks fit, including the deposit in court of a reasonable sum fixed by the court to meet the expenses of sale and to secure performance of the terms.

(3) But, in an action brought by a person interested in the right of redemption and seeking a sale, the court may, on the application of any defendant, direct the plaintiff to give such security for costs as the court thinks fit, and may give the conduct of the sale to any defendant, and may give such directions as it thinks fit respecting the costs of the defendants or any of them.

(4) In any case within this section the court may, if it thinks fit, direct a sale without previously determining the priorities of incumbrancers.

(5) This section applies to actions brought either before or after the commencement of this Act.

(6) In this section 'mortgaged property' includes the estate or interest which a mortgagee would have had power to convey if the statutory power of sale were applicable.

(7) For the purposes of this section the court may, in favour of a purchaser, make a vesting order conveying the mortgaged property, or appoint a person to do so, subject or not to any incumbrance, as the court may think fit; or, in the case of an equitable mortgage, may create and vest a mortgage term in the mortgagee to enable him to carry out the sale as if the mortgage had been made by deed by way of legal mortgage ...

92 Power to authorise land and minerals to be [447] dealt with separately

Where a mortgagee's power of sale in regard to land has become exercisable but does not extend to the purposes mentioned in this section, the court may, on his application, authorise him and the persons deriving title under him to dispose –

(a) of the land, with an exception or reservation of all or any mines and minerals, and with or without rights and powers of or incidental to the working, getting or carrying away of minerals; or
(b) of all or any mines and minerals, with or without the said rights or powers separately from the land;

and thenceforth the powers so conferred shall have effect as if the same were contained in the mortgage ...

93 Restriction on consolidation of mortgages [448]

(1) A mortgagor seeking to redeem any one mortgage is entitled to do so without paying any money due under any separate mortgage made by him, or by any person through whom he claims, solely on property other than that comprised in the mortgage which he seeks to redeem. This subsection applies only if and as far as a contrary intention is not expressed in the mortgage deeds or one of them.

(2) This section does not apply where all the mortgages were made before the first day of January, eighteen hundred and eighty-two.

(3) Save as aforesaid, nothing in this Act, in reference to mortgages, affects any right of consolidation or renders inoperative a stipulation in relation to any mortgage made before or after the commencement of this Act reserving a right to consolidate.

94 Tacking and further advances [449]

(1) After the commencement of this Act, a prior mortgagee shall have a right to make further advances to rank in priority to subsequent mortgages (whether legal or equitable) –

(a) if an arrangement has been made to that effect with the subsequent mortgagees; or
(b) if he had no notice of such subsequent mortgages at the time when the further advance was made by him; or
(c) whether or not he had such notice as aforesaid, where the mortgage imposes an obligation on him to make such further advances.

This subsection applies whether or not the prior mortgage was made expressly for securing further advances.

(2) In relation to the making of further advances after the commencement of this Act a mortgagee shall not be deemed to have notice of a mortgage merely by reason that it was registered as a land charge, if it was not so registered at the time when the original mortgage was created or when the last search (if any) by or on behalf of the mortgagee was made, whichever last happened. This subsection only applies where the prior mortgage was made expressly for securing a current account or other further advances.

(3) Save in regard to the making of further advances as aforesaid, the right to tack is hereby abolished: Provided that nothing in this Act shall affect any priority acquired before the commencement of this Act by tacking, or in respect of further advances made without notice of a subsequent incumbrance or by arrangement with the subsequent incumbrancer.

(4) This section applies to mortgages of land made before or after the commencement of this Act, but not to charges registered under the Land Registration Act 1925, or any enactment replaced by that Act.

95 Obligation to transfer instead of reconveying, and as   [450] to right to take possession

(1) Where a mortgagor is entitled to redeem, then subject to compliance with the terms on compliance with which he would be entitled to require a reconveyance or surrender, he shall be entitled to require the mortgagee, instead of reconveying or surrendering, to assign the mortgage debt and convey the mortgaged property to any third person, as the mortgagor directs; and the mortgagee shall be bound to assign and convey accordingly.

(2) The rights conferred by this section belong to and are capable of being enforced by each incumbrancer, or by the mortgagor, notwithstanding any intermediate incumbrance; but a requisition of an incumbrancer prevails over a requisition of the mortgagor, and, as between incumbrancers, a requisition of a prior incumbrancer prevails over a requisition of a subsequent incumbrancer.

(3) The foregoing provisions of this section do not apply in the case of a mortgagee being or having been in possession.

(4) Nothing in this Act affects prejudicially the right of a mortgagee of land whether or not his charge is secured by a legal term of years absolute to take possession of the land, but the taking of possession by the mortgagee does not convert any legal estate of the mortgagor into an equitable interest.

(5) This section applies to mortgages made either before or after the commencement of this Act, and takes effect notwithstanding any stipulation to the contrary.

96 Regulations respecting inspection, production and   [451] delivery of documents, and priorities

(1) A mortgagor, as long as his right to redeem subsists, shall be entitled from time to time, at reasonable times, on his request, and at his own cost, and on payment of the mortgagee's costs and expenses in this behalf, to inspect and make copies or abstracts of or extracts from the documents of title relating to the mortgaged property in the custody or power of the mortgagee. This subsection applies to mortgages made after the thirty-first day of December, eighteen hundred and eighty-one, and takes effect notwithstanding any stipulation to the contrary.

(2) A mortgagee, whose mortgage is surrendered or otherwise extinguished, shall

not be liable on account of delivering documents of title in his possession to the person not having the best right thereto, unless he has notice of the right or claim of a person having a better right, whether by virtue of a right to require a surrender or reconveyance or otherwise. In this subsection notice does not include notice implied by reason of registration under the Land Charges Act 1925.

97 Priorities as between puisne mortgages [452]

Every mortgage affecting a legal estate in land made after the commencement of this Act, whether legal or equitable (not being a mortgage protected by the deposit of documents relating to the legal estate affected) shall rank according to its date of registration as a land charge pursuant to the Land Charges Act 1925. This section does not apply to mortgages or charges to which the Land Charges Act 1972 does not apply by virtue of section 14(3) of that Act (which excludes certain land charges created by instruments necessitating registration under the Land Registration Act 1925), or to mortgages or charges of registered land.

98 Actions for possession by mortgagors [453]

(1) A mortgagor for the time being entitled to the possession or receipt of the rents and profits of any land, as to which the mortgagee has not given notice of his intention to take possession or to enter into the receipt of the rents and profits thereof, may sue for such possession, or for the recovery of such rents or profits, or to prevent or recover damages in respect of any trespass or other wrong relative thereto, in his own name only, unless the cause of action arises upon a lease or other contract made by him jointly with any other person.

(2) This section does not prejudice the power of a mortgagor independently of this section to take proceedings in his own name only, either in right of any legal estate vested in him or otherwise.

(3) This section applies whether the mortgage was made before or after the commencement of this Act.

99 Leasing powers of mortgagor and mortgagee [454]
in possession

(1) A mortgagor of land while in possession shall, as against every incumbrancer, have power to make from time to time any such lease of the mortgaged land, or any part thereof, as is by this section authorised.

(2) A mortgagee of land while in possession shall, as against all prior incumbrancers, if any, and as against the mortgagor, have power to make from time to time any such lease as aforesaid.

(3) The leases which this section authorises are –

(i) agricultural or occupation leases for any term not exceeding twenty-one years, or, in the case of a mortgage made after the commencement of this Act, fifty years; and
(ii) building leases for any term not exceeding ninety-nine years, or, in the case of a mortgage made after the commencement of this Act, nine hundred and ninety-nine years.

(4) Every person making a lease under this section may execute and do all assurances and things necessary or proper in that behalf.

(5) Every such lease shall be made to take effect in possession not later than twelve months after its date.

(6) Every such lease shall reserve the best rent that can reasonably be obtained,

regard being had to the circumstances of the case, but without any fine being taken.

(7) Every such lease shall contain a covenant by the lessee for payment of the rent, and a condition of re-entry on the rent not being paid within a time therein specified not exceeding thirty days.

(8) A counterpart of every such lease shall be executed by the lessee and delivered to the lessor, of which execution and delivery the execution of the lease by the lessor shall, in favour of the lessee and all persons deriving title under him, be sufficient evidence.

(9) Every such building lease shall be made in consideration of the lessee, or some person by whose direction the lease is granted, having erected, or agreeing to erect within not more than five years from the date of the lease, buildings, new or additional, or having improved or repaired buildings, or agreeing to improve or repair buildings within that time, or having executed, or agreeing to execute within that time, on the land leased, an improvement for or in connexion with building purposes.

(10) In any such building lease a peppercorn rent, or a nominal or other rent less than the rent ultimately payable, may be made payable for the first five years, or any less part of the term.

(11) In case of a lease by the mortgagor, he shall, within one month after making the lease, deliver to the mortgagee, or, where there are more than one, to the mortgagee first in priority, a counterpart of the lease duly executed by the lessee, but the lessee shall not be concerned to see that this provision is complied with.

(12) A contract to make or accept a lease under this section may be enforced by or against every person on whom the lease if granted would be binding.

(13) Subject to subsection (13A) below, this section applies only if and as far as contrary intention is not expressed by the mortgagor and mortgagee in the mortgage deed, or otherwise in writing, and has effect subject to the terms of the mortgage deed or of any such writing and to the provisions therein contained.

(13A) Subsection (13) of this section –

(a) shall not enable the application of any provision of this section to be excluded or restricted in relation to any mortgage of agricultural land made after 1st March 1948 but before 1st September 1995, and
(b) shall not enable the power to grant a lease of an agricultural holding to which, by virtue of section 4 of the Agricultural Tenancies Act 1995, the Agricultural Holdings Act 1986 will apply, to be excluded or restricted in relation to any mortgage of agricultural land made on or after 1st September 1995.

(13B) In subsection (13A) of this section –

'agricultural holding' has the same meaning as in the Agricultural Holdings Act 1986; and
'agricultural land' has the same meaning as in the Agriculture Act 1947.

(14) The mortgagor and mortgagee may, by agreement in writing, whether or not contained in the mortgage deed, reserve to or confer on the mortgagor or the mortgagee, or both, any further or other powers of leasing or having reference to leasing; and any further or other powers so reserved or conferred shall be exercisable, as far as may be, as if they were conferred by this Act, and with all the like incidents, effects, and consequences: Provided that the powers so reserved or conferred shall not prejudicially affect the rights of any mortgagee interested under any other mortgage subsisting at the date of the agreement, unless that mortgagee joins in or adopts the agreement.

(15) Nothing in this Act shall be construed to enable a mortgagor or mortgagee to make a lease for any longer term or on any other conditions than such as could have been granted or imposed by the mortgagor, with the concurrence of all the incumbrancers, if this Act and the enactments replaced by this section had not been passed: Provided that, in the case of a mortgage of leasehold land, a lease granted under this section shall reserve a reversion of not less than one day.

(16) Subject as aforesaid, this section applies to any mortgage made after the thirty-first day of December, eighteen hundred and eighty-one, but the provisions thereof, or any of them, may, by agreement in writing made after that date between mortgagor and mortgagee, be applied to a mortgage made before that date, so nevertheless that any such agreement shall not prejudicially affect any right or interest of any mortgagee not joining in or adopting the agreement.

(17) The provisions of this section referring to a lease shall be construed to extend and apply, as far as circumstances admit, to any letting, and to an agreement, whether in writing or not, for leasing or letting.

(18) For the purposes of this section 'mortgagor' does not include any incumbrancer deriving title under the original mortgagor.

(19) The powers of leasing conferred by this section shall, after a receiver of the income of the mortgaged property or any part thereof has been appointed by a mortgagee under his statutory power, and so long as the receiver acts, be exercisable by such mortgagee instead of by the mortgagor, as respects any land affected by the receivership, in like manner as if such mortgagee were in possession of the land, and the mortgagee may, by writing, delegate any of such powers to the receiver.

100 Powers of mortgagor and mortgagee in possession to accept surrenders of leases [455]

(1) For the purpose only of enabling a lease authorised under the last preceding section, or under any agreement made pursuant to that section, or by the mortgage deed (in this section referred to as an authorised lease) to be granted, a mortgagor of land while in possession shall, as against every incumbrancer, have, by virtue of this Act, power to accept from time to time a surrender of any lease of the mortgaged land or any part thereof comprised in the lease, with or without an exception of or in respect of all or any of the mines and minerals therein, and, on a surrender of the lease so far as it comprises part only of the land or mines and minerals leased, the rent may be apportioned.

(2) For the same purpose, a mortgagee of land while in possession shall, as against all prior or other incumbrancers, if any, and as against the mortgagor, have, by virtue of this Act, power to accept from time to time any such surrender as aforesaid.

(3) On a surrender of part only of the land or mines and minerals leased, the original lease may be varied, provided that the lease when varied would have been valid as an authorised lease if granted by the person accepting the surrender; and, on a surrender and the making of a new or other lease, whether for the same or for any extended or other term, and whether subject or not to the same or to any other covenants, provisions, or conditions, the value of the lessee's interest in the lease surrendered may, subject to the provisions of this section, be taken into account in the determination of the amount of the rent to be reserved, and of the nature of the covenants, provisions, and conditions to be inserted in the new or other lease.

(4) Where any consideration for the surrender, other than an agreement to accept an authorised lease, is given by or on behalf of the lessee to or on behalf of the

person accepting the surrender, nothing in this section authorises a surrender to a mortgagor without the consent of the incumbrancers, or authorises a surrender to a second or subsequent incumbrancer without the consent of every prior incumbrancer.

(5) No surrender shall, by virtue of this section, be rendered valid unless –

(a) An authorised lease is granted of the whole of the land or mines and minerals comprised in the surrender to take effect in possession immediately or within one month after the date of the surrender; and

(b) The term certain or other interest granted by the new lease is not less in duration than the unexpired term or interest which would have been subsisting under the original lease if that lease had not been surrendered; and

(c) Where the whole of the land mines and minerals originally leased has been surrendered, the rent reserved by the new lease is not less than the rent which would have been payable under the original lease if it had not been surrendered; or where part only of the land or mines and minerals has been surrendered, the aggregate rents respectively remaining payable or reserved under the original lease and new lease are not less than the rent which would have been payable under the original lease if no partial surrender had been accepted.

(6) A contract to make or accept a surrender under this section may be enforced by or against every person on whom the surrender, if completed, would be binding.

(7) This section applies only if and as far as a contrary intention is not expressed by the mortgagor and mortgagee in the mortgage deed, or otherwise in writing, and shall have effect subject to the terms of the mortgage deed or of any such writing and to the provisions therein contained.

(8) This section applies to a mortgage made after the thirty-first day of December, nineteen hundred and eleven, but the provisions of this section, or any of them, may, by agreement in writing made after that date, between mortgagor and mortgagee, be applied to a mortgage made before that date, so nevertheless that any such agreement shall not prejudicially affect any right or interest of any mortgagee not joining in or adopting the agreement.

(9) The provisions of this section referring to a lease shall be construed to extend and apply, as far as circumstances admit, to any letting, and to any agreement, whether in writing or not, for leasing or letting.

(10) The mortgagor and mortgagee may, by agreement in writing, whether or not contained in the mortgage deed, reserve or confer on the mortgagor or mortgagee, or both, any further or other powers relating to the surrender of leases; and any further or other powers so conferred or reserved shall be exercisable, as far as may be, as if they were conferred by this Act, and with all the like incidents, effects and consequences: Provided that the powers so reserved or conferred shall not prejudicially affect the rights of any mortgagee interested under any other mortgage subsisting at the date of the agreement, unless that mortgagee joins in or adopts the agreement.

(11) Nothing in this section operates to enable a mortgagor or mortgagee to accept a surrender which could not have been accepted by the mortgagor with the concurrence of all the incumbrancers if this Act and the enactments replaced by this section had not been passed.

(12) For the purposes of this section 'mortgagor' does not include an incumbrancer deriving title under the original mortgagor.

(13) The powers of accepting surrenders conferred by this section shall, after a receiver of the income of the mortgaged property or any part thereof has been

appointed by the mortgagee, under the statutory power, and so long as the receiver acts, be exercisable by such mortgagee instead of by the mortgagor, as respects any land affected by the receivership, in like manner as if such mortgagee were in possession of the land; and the mortgagee may, by writing, delegate any of such powers to the receiver.

101 Powers incident to estate or interest of mortgagee [456]

(1) A mortgagee, where the mortgage is made by deed, shall, by virtue of this Act, have the following powers, to the like extent as if they had been in terms conferred by the mortgage deed, but not further (namely) –

(i) A power, when the mortgage money had become due, to sell, or to concur with any other person in selling, the mortgaged property, or any part thereof, either subject to prior charges or not, and either together or in lots, by public auction or by private contract, subject to such conditions respecting title, or evidence of title, or other matter, as the mortgagee thinks fit, with power to vary any contract for sale, and to buy in at an auction, or to rescind any contract for sale, and to re-sell; without being answerable for any loss occasioned thereby; and

(ii) A power, at any time after the date of the mortgage deed, to insure and keep insured against loss or damage by fire any building, or any effects or property of an insurable nature, whether affixed to the freehold or not, being or forming part of the property which or an estate or interest wherein is mortgaged, and the premiums paid for any such insurance shall be a charge on the mortgaged property or estate or interest, in addition to the mortgage money, and with the same priority, and with interest at the same rate, as the mortgage money; and

(iii) A power, when the mortgage money has become due, to appoint a receiver of the income of the mortgaged property, or any part thereof; or, if the mortgaged property consists of an interest in income, or of a rentcharge or an annual or other periodical sum, a receiver of that property or any part thereof; and

(iv) A power, while the mortgagee is in possession, to cut and sell timber and other trees ripe for cutting, and not planted or left standing for shelter or ornament, or to contract for any such cutting and sale, to be completed within any time not exceeding twelve months from the making of the contract.

(2) Where the mortgage deed is executed after the thirty-first day of December, nineteen hundred and eleven, the power of sale aforesaid includes the following powers as incident thereto (namely) –

(i) A power to impose or reserve or make binding, as far as the law permits, by covenant, condition, or otherwise, on the unsold part of the mortgaged property or any part thereof, or on the purchaser and any property sold, any restriction or reservation with respect to building on or other user of land, or with respect to mines and minerals, or for the purpose of the more beneficial working thereof, or with respect to any other thing:

(ii) A power to sell the mortgaged property, or any part thereof, or all or any mines and minerals apart from the surface:

(a) With or without a grant or reservation of rights of way, rights of water, easements, rights, and privileges for or connected with building or other purposes in relation to the property remaining in mortgage or any part thereof, or to any property sold: and

(b) With or without an exception or reservation of all or any of the mines and minerals in or under the mortgaged property, and with or without a grant or reservation of powers of working, wayleaves, or rights of way, rights of water and drainage and other powers, easements, rights and privileges for or connected with mining purposes in relation to the property remaining unsold or any part thereof, or to any property sold: and

(c) With or without covenants by the purchaser to expend money on the land sold.

(3) The provisions of this Act relating to the foregoing powers, comprised either in this section, or in any other section regulating the exercise of those powers, may be varied or extended by the mortgage deed, and, as so varied or extended, shall, as far as may be, operate in the like manner and with all the like incidents, effects, and consequences, as if such variations or extensions were contained in this Act.

(4) This section applies only if and as far as a contrary intention is not expressed in the mortgage deed, and has effect subject to the terms of the mortgage deed and to the provisions therein contained.

(5) Save as otherwise provided, this section applies where the mortgage deed is executed after the thirty-first day of December, eighteen hundred and eighty-one.

(6) The power of sale conferred by this section includes such power of selling the estate in fee simple or any leasehold reversion as is conferred by the provisions of this Act relating to the realisation of mortgages.

102 Provisions as to mortgages of undivided shares in land [457]

(1) A person who was before the commencement of this Act a mortgagee of an undivided share in land shall have the same power to sell his interest under the trust to which the land is subject, as, independently of this Act, he would have had in regard to the share in the land; and shall also have a right to require the trustees in whom the land is vested to account to him for the income attributable to that share or to appoint a receiver to receive the same from such trustees corresponding to the right which, independently of this Act, he would have had to take possession or to appoint a receiver of the rents and profits attributable to the same share.

(2) The powers conferred by this section are exercisable by the persons deriving title under such mortgagee.

103 Regulation of exercise of power of sale [458]

A mortgagee shall not exercise the power of sale conferred by this Act unless and until –

(i) Notice requiring payment of the mortgage money has been served on the mortgagor or one of two or more mortgagors, and default has been made in payment of the mortgage money, or of part thereof, for three months after such service; or

(ii) Some interest under the mortgage is in arrear and unpaid for two months after becoming due; or

(iii) There has been a breach of some provision contained in the mortgage deed or in this Act, or in an enactment replaced by this Act, and on the part of the mortgagor, or of some person concurring in making the mortgage, to be observed or performed, other than and besides a covenant for payment of the mortgage money or interest thereon.

104 Conveyance on sale [459]

(1) A mortgagee exercising the power of sale conferred by this Act shall have power, by deed, to convey the property sold, for such estate and interest therein

as he is by this Act authorised to sell or convey or may be the subject of the mortgage, freed from all estates, interests, and rights to which the mortgage has priority, but subject to all estates, interests, and rights which have priority to the mortgage.

(2) Where a conveyance is made in exercise of the power of sale conferred by this Act, or any enactment replaced by this Act, the title of the purchaser shall not be impeachable on the ground –

(a) that no case had arisen to authorise the sale; or
(b) that due notice was not given; or
(c) where the mortgage is made after the commencement of this Act, that leave of the court, when so required, was not obtained; or
(d) whether the mortgage was made before or after such commencement, that the power was otherwise improperly or irregularly exercised;

and a purchaser is not, either before or on conveyance, concerned to see or inquire whether a case has arisen to authorise the sale, or due notice has been given, or the power is otherwise properly and regularly exercised; but any person damnified by an unauthorised, or improper, or irregular exercise of the power shall have his remedy in damages against the person exercising the power.

(3) A conveyance on sale by a mortgagee, made after the commencement of this Act, shall be deemed to have been made in exercise of the power of sale conferred by this Act unless a contrary intention appears.

105 Application of proceeds of sale [460]

The money which is received by the mortgagee, arising from the sale, after discharge of prior incumbrances to which the sale is not made subject, if any, or after payment into court under this Act of a sum to meet any prior incumbrance, shall be held by him in trust to be applied by him, first, in payment of all costs, charges, and expenses properly incurred by him as incident to the sale or any attempted sale, or otherwise; and secondly, in discharge of the mortgage money, interest, and costs, and other money, if any, due under the mortgage; and the residue of the money so received shall be paid to the person entitled to the mortgaged property, or authorised to give receipts for the proceeds of the sale thereof.

106 Provisions as to exercise of power of sale [461]

(1) The power of sale conferred by this Act may be exercised by any person for the time being entitled to receive and give a discharge for the mortgage money.

(2) The power of sale conferred by this Act does not affect the right of foreclosure.

(3) The mortgagee shall not be answerable for any involuntary loss happening in or about the exercise or execution of the power of sale conferred by this Act, or of any trust connected therewith, or, where the mortgage is executed after the thirty-first day of December, nineteen hundred and eleven, of any power or provision contained in the mortgage deed.

(4) At any time after the power of sale conferred by this Act has become exercisable, the person entitled to exercise the power may demand and recover from any person, other than a person having in the mortgaged property an estate, interest, or right in priority to the mortgage, all the deeds and documents relating to the property, or to the title thereto, which a purchaser under the power of sale would be entitled to demand and recover from him.

107 Mortgagee's receipts, discharges, etc   [462]

(1) The receipt in writing of a mortgagee shall be a sufficient discharge for any money arising under the power of sale conferred by this Act, or for any money or securities comprised in his mortgage, or arising thereunder; and a person paying or transferring the same to the mortgagee shall not be concerned to inquire whether any money remains due under the mortgage.

(2) Money received by a mortgagee under his mortgage or from the proceeds of securities comprised in his mortgage shall be applied in like manner as in this Act directed respecting money received by him arising from a sale under the power of sale conferred by this Act, but with this variation, that the costs, charges, and expenses payable shall include the costs, charges and expenses properly incurred of recovering and receiving the money or securities, and of conversion of securities into money, instead of those incident to sale.

108 Amount and application of insurance money   [463]

(1) The amount of an insurance effected by a mortgagee against loss or damage by fire under the power in that behalf conferred by this Act shall not exceed the amount specified in the mortgage deed, or, if no amount is therein specified, two third parts of the amount that would be required, in case of total destruction, to restore the property insured.

(2) An insurance shall not, under the power conferred by this Act, be effected by a mortgagee in any of the following cases (namely):

(i) Where there is a declaration in the mortgage deed that no insurance is required:

(ii) Where an insurance is kept up by or on behalf of the mortgagor in accordance with the mortgage deed:

(iii) Where the mortgage deed contains no stipulation respecting insurance, and an insurance is kept up by or on behalf of the mortgagor with the consent of the mortgagee to the amount to which the mortgagee is by this Act authorised to insure.

(3) All money received on an insurance of mortgaged property against loss or damage by fire or otherwise effected under this Act, or any enactment replaced by this Act, or on an insurance for the maintenance of which the mortgagor is liable under the mortgage deed, shall, if the mortgagee so requires, be applied by the mortgagor in making good the loss or damage in respect of which the money is received.

(4) Without prejudice to any obligation to the contrary imposed by law, or by special contract, a mortgagee may require that all money received on an insurance of mortgaged property against loss or damage by fire or otherwise effected under this Act, or any enactment replaced by this Act, or on an insurance for the maintenance of which the mortgagor is liable under the mortgage deed, be applied in or towards the discharge of the mortgage money.

109 Appointment, powers, remuneration and   [464]
duties of receiver

(1) A mortgagee entitled to appoint a receiver under the power in that behalf conferred by this Act shall not appoint a receiver until he has become entitled to exercise the power of sale conferred by this Act, but may then, by writing under his hand, appoint such person as he thinks fit to be receiver.

(2) A receiver appointed under the powers conferred by this Act, or any enactment replaced by this Act, shall be deemed to be the agent of the mortgagor; and the

mortgagor shall be solely responsible for the receiver's acts or defaults unless the mortgage deed otherwise provides.

(3) The receiver shall have power to demand and recover all the income of which he is appointed receiver, by action, distress, or otherwise, in the name either of the mortgagor or of the mortgagee, to the full extent of the estate or interest which the mortgagor could dispose of, and to give effectual receipts accordingly for the same, and to exercise any powers which may have been delegated to him by the mortgagee pursuant to this Act.

(4) A person paying money to the receiver shall not be concerned to inquire whether any case has happened to authorise the receiver to act.

(5) The receiver may be removed, and a new receiver may be appointed, from time to time by the mortgagee by writing under his hand.

(6) The receiver shall be entitled to retain out of any money received by him, for his remuneration, and in satisfaction of all costs, charges, and expenses incurred by him as receiver, a commission at such rate, not exceeding five per centum on the gross amount of all money received, as is specified in his appointment, and if no rate is so specified, then at the rate of five per centum on that gross amount, or at such other rate as the court thinks fit to allow, on application made by him for that purpose.

(7) The receiver shall, if so directed in writing by the mortgagee, insure to the extent, if any, to which the mortgagee might have insured and keep insured against loss or damage by fire, out of the money received by him, any building, effects, or property comprised in the mortgage, whether affixed to the freehold or not, being of an insurable nature.

(8) Subject to the provisions of this Act as to the application of insurance money, the receiver shall apply all money received by him as follows, namely:

(i) In discharge of all rents, taxes, rates, and outgoings whatever affecting the mortgaged property; and

(ii) In keeping down all annual sums or other payments, and the interest on all principal sums, having priority to the mortgage in right whereof he is receiver; and

(iii) In payment of his commission, and of the premiums on fire, life, or other insurances, if any, properly payable under the mortgage deed or under this Act, and the cost of executing necessary or proper repairs directed in writing by the mortgagee; and

(iv) In payment of the interest accruing due in respect of any principal money due under the mortgage; and

(v) In or towards discharge of the principal money if so directed in writing by the mortgagee;

and shall pay the residue, if any, of the money received by him to the person who, but for the possession of the receiver, would have been entitled to receive the income of which he is appointed receiver, or who is otherwise entitled to the mortgaged property.

110 Effect of bankruptcy of the mortgagor on the power [465] to sell or appoint a receiver

(1) Where the statutory or express power for a mortgagee either to sell or to appoint a receiver is made exercisable by reason of the mortgagor being adjudged a bankrupt, such power shall not be exercised only on account of the adjudication, without the leave of the court.

(2) This section applies only where the mortgage deed is executed after the commencement of this Act.

111 Effect of advance on joint account   [466]

(1) Where –

(a) in a mortgage, or an obligation for payment of money, or a transfer of a mortgage or of such an obligation, the sum, or any part of the sum, advanced or owing is expressed to be advanced by or owing to more persons than one out of money, or as money, belonging to them on a joint account; or

(b) a mortgage, or such an obligation, or such a transfer is made to more persons than one, jointly;

the mortgage money, or other money or money's worth, for the time being due to those persons on the mortgage or obligation, shall, as between them and the mortgagor or obligor, be deemed to be and remain money or money's worth belonging to those persons on a joint account; and the receipt in writing of the survivors of last survivor of them, or of the personal representative of the last survivor, shall be a complete discharge for all money or money's worth for the time being due, notwithstanding any notice to the payer of a severance of the joint account.

(2) This section applies if and so far as a contrary intention is not expressed in the mortgage, obligation, or transfer, and has effect subject to the terms of the mortgage, obligation, or transfer, and to the provisions therein contained.

(3) This section applies to any mortgage obligation or transfer made after the thirty-first day of December, eighteen hundred and eighty-one.

113 Notice of trusts affecting mortgage debts   [467]

(1) A person dealing in good faith with a mortgagee, or with the mortgagor if the mortgage has been discharged released or postponed as to the whole or any part of the mortgaged property, shall not be concerned with any trust at any time affecting the mortgage money or the income thereof, whether or not he has notice of the trust, and may assume unless the contrary is expressly stated in the instruments relating to the mortgage –

(a) that the mortgagees (if more than one) are or were entitled to the mortgage money on a joint account; and

(b) that the mortgagee has or had power to give valid receipts for the purchase money or mortgage money and the income thereof (including any arrears of interest) and to release or postpone the priority of the mortgage debt or any part thereof or to deal with the same or the mortgaged property or any part thereof;

without investigating the equitable title to the mortgage debt or the appointment or discharge of trustees in reference thereto.

(2) This section applies to mortgages made before or after the commencement of this Act, but only as respects dealings effected after such commencement.

(3) This section does not affect the liability of any person in whom the mortgage debt is vested for the purposes of any trust to give effect to that trust.

114 Transfers of mortgages   [468]

(1) A deed executed by a mortgagee purporting to transfer his mortgage or the benefit thereof shall, unless a contrary intention is therein expressed, and subject to any provisions therein contained, operate to transfer to the transferee –

(a) the right to demand, sue for, recover, and give receipts for, the mortgage money or the unpaid part thereof, and the interest then due, if any, and thenceforth to become due thereon; and

(b) the benefit of all securities for the same, and the benefit of and the right to sue on all covenants with the mortgagee, and the right to exercise all powers of the mortgagee; and

(c) all the estate and interest in the mortgaged property then vested in the mortgagee subject to redemption or cesser, but as to such estate and interest subject to the right of redemption then subsisting.

(2) In this section 'transferee' includes his personal representatives and assigns.

(3) A transfer of mortgage may be made in the form contained in the Third Schedule to this Act with such variations and additions, if any, as the circumstances may require.

(4) This section applies, whether the mortgage transferred was made before or after the commencement of this Act, but applies only to transfers made after the commencement of this Act.

(5) This section does not extend to a transfer of a bill of sale of chattels by way of security.

115 Reconveyances of mortgages by endorsed receipts [469]

(1) A receipt endorsed on, written at the foot of, or annexed to, a mortgage for all money thereby secured, which states the name of the person who pays the money and is executed by the chargee by way of legal mortgage or the person in whom the mortgaged property is vested and who is legally entitled to give a receipt for the mortgage money shall operate, without any reconveyance, surrender, or release –

(a) Where a mortgage takes effect by demise or subdemise, as a surrender of the term, so as to determine the term or merge the same in the reversion immediately expectant thereon;

(b) Where the mortgage does not take effect by demise or subdemise, as a reconveyance thereof to the extent of the interest which is the subject matter of the mortgage, to the person who immediately before the execution of the receipt was entitled to the equity of redemption;

and in either case, as a discharge of the mortgaged property from all principal money and interest secured by, and from all claims under the mortgage, but without prejudice to any term or other interest which is paramount to the estate or interest of the mortgagee or other person in whom the mortgaged property was vested.

(2) Provided that, where by the receipt the money appears to have been paid by a person who is not entitled to the immediate equity of redemption, the receipt shall operate as if the benefit of the mortgage had by deed been transferred to him; unless –

(a) it is otherwise expressly provided; or

(b) the mortgage is paid off out of capital money, or other money in the hands of a personal representative or trustee properly applicable for the discharge of the mortgage, and it is not expressly provided that the receipt is to operate as a transfer.

(3) Nothing in this section confers on a mortgagor a right to keep alive a mortgage paid off by him, so as to affect prejudicially any subsequent incumbrancer; and where there is no right to keep the mortgage alive, the receipt does not operate as a transfer.

(4) This section does not affect the right of any person to require a reassignment, surrender, release, or transfer to be executed in lieu of a receipt.

(5) A receipt may be given in the form contained in the Third Schedule to this Act, with such variations and additions, if any, as may be deemed expedient.

(6) In a receipt given under this section the same covenants shall be implied as if the person who executes the receipt had by deed been expressed to convey the property as mortgagee, subject to any interest which is paramount to the mortgage.

(7) Where the mortgage consists of a mortgage and a further charge or of more than one deed, it shall be sufficient for the purposes of this section, if the receipt refers either to all the deeds whereby the mortgage money is secured or to the aggregate amount of the mortgage money thereby secured and for the time being owing, and is endorsed on, written at the foot of, or annexed to, one of the mortgage deeds.

(8) This section applies to the discharge of a charge by way of legal mortgage, and to the discharge of a mortgage, whether made by way of statutory mortgage or not, executed before or after the commencement of this Act, but only as respects discharges effected after such commencement.

(9) The provisions of this section relating to the operation of a receipt shall (in substitution for the like statutory provisions relating to receipts given by or on behalf of a building society) apply to the discharge of a mortgage made to any such society, provided that the receipts is executed in the manner required by the statute relating to the society.

(10) This section does not apply to the discharge of a charge or incumbrance registered under the Land Registration Act 1925.

(11) In this section 'mortgaged property' means the property remaining subject to the mortgage at the date of the receipt.

116 Cesser of mortgage terms   [470]

Without prejudice to the right of a tenant for life or other person having only a limited interest in the equity of redemption to require a mortgage to be kept alive by transfer or otherwise, a mortgage term shall, when the money secured by the mortgage has been discharged, become a satisfied term and shall cease.

117 Forms of statutory legal charges   [471]

(1) As a special form of charge by way of legal mortgage, a mortgage of freehold or leasehold land may be made by a deed expressed to be made by way of statutory mortgage, being in one of the forms (Nos 1 or 4) set out in the Fourth Schedule to this Act, with such variations and additions, if any, as circumstances may require, and if so made the provisions of this section shall apply thereto.

(2) There shall be deemed to be included, and there shall by virtue of this Act be implied, in such a mortgage deed –

First, a covenant with the mortgagee by the person therein expressed to charge as mortgagor to the effect following, namely:

That the mortgagor will, on the stated day, pay to the mortgagee the stated mortgage money, with interest thereon in the meantime at the stated rate, and will thereafter, if and as long as the mortgage money or any part thereof remains unpaid, pay to the mortgagee (as well after as before any judgment is obtained under the mortgage) interest thereon, or on the unpaid part thereof, at the stated rate, by equal half-yearly payments the first thereof to be made at the end of six months from the day stated for payment of the mortgage money:

Secondly, a provision to the following effect (namely):

That if the mortgagor on the stated day pays to the mortgagee the stated mortgage money, with interest thereon in the meantime at the stated rate, the mortgagee at any time thereafter, at the request and cost of the mortgagor, shall discharge the mortgaged property or transfer the benefit of the mortgage as the mortgagor may direct.

This subsection applies to a mortgage deed made under section twenty-six of the Conveyancing Act 1881, with a substitution of a reference to 'the person therein expressed to convey as mortgagor' for the reference in this subsection to 'the person therein expressed to charge as mortgagor'.

119 Implied covenants, joint and several [472]

In a deed of statutory mortgage, or of statutory transfer of mortgage, where more persons than one are expressed to convey or charge as mortgagors, or to join as covenantors, the implied covenant on their part shall be deemed to be a joint and several covenant by them; and where there are more mortgagees or more transferees than one, the implied covenant with them shall be deemed to be a covenant with them jointly, unless the amount secured is expressed to be secured to them in shares or distinct sums, in which latter case the implied covenant with them shall be deemed to be a covenant with each severally in respect of the share or distinct sum secured to him.

120 Form of discharge of statutory mortgage or charge [473]

A statutory mortgage may be surrendered or discharged by a receipt in the form (No 5) set out in the Fourth Schedule to this Act with such variations and additions, if any, as circumstances may require.

PART IV

EQUITABLE INTERESTS AND THINGS IN ACTION

130 Entailed interests in real and personal property [474]

(4) In default of and subject to the execution of a disentailing assurance or the exercise of the testamentary power conferred by this Act, an entailed interest (to the extent of the property affected) shall devolve as an equitable interest, from time to time, upon the persons who would have been successively entitled thereto as the heirs of the body (either generally or of a particular class) of the tenant in tail or other person, or as tenant by the curtesy, if the entailed interest had, before the commencement of this Act, been limited in respect of freehold land governed by the general law in force immediately before such commencement, and such law had remained unaffected.

(5) Where personal chattels are settled without reference to settled land on trusts creating entailed interests therein, the trustees, with the consent of the usufructuary for the time being if of full age, may sell the chattels or any of them, and the net proceeds of any such sale shall be held in trust for and shall go to the same persons successively, in the same manner and for the same interests, as the chattels sold would have been held and gone if they had not been sold, and the income of investments representing such proceeds of sale shall be applied accordingly.

(7) In this Act where the context so admits 'entailed interest' includes an estate tail

(now made to take effect as an equitable interest) created before the commencement of this Act.

132 As to heirs taking by purchase   [475]

(1) A limitation of real or personal property in favour of the heir, either general or special, of a deceased person which, if limited in respect of freehold land before the commencement of this Act, would have conferred on the heir an estate in the land by purchase, shall operate to confer a corresponding equitable interest in the property on the person who would, if the general law in force immediately before such commencement had remained unaffected, have answered the description of the heir, either general or special, of the deceased in respect of his freehold land, either at the death of the deceased or at the time named in the limitation, as the case may require.

(2) This section applies whether the deceased person dies before or after the commencement of this Act, but only applies to limitations or trusts created by an instrument coming into operation after such commencement.

134 Restriction on executory limitations   [476]

(1) Where there is a person entitled to –

(a) an equitable interest in land for an estate in fee simple or for any less interest not being an entailed interest, or
(b) any interest in other property, not being an entailed interest,

with an executory limitation over on default or failure of all or any of his issue, whether within or at any specified period or time or not, that executory limitation shall be or become void and incapable of taking effect, if and as soon as there is living any issue who has attained the age of eighteen years of the class on default or failure whereof the limitation over was to take effect.

(2) This section applies where the executory limitation is contained in an instrument coming into operation after the thirty-first day of December, eighteen hundred and eighty-two, save that, as regards instruments coming into operation before the commencement of this Act, it only applies to limitations of land for an estate in fee, or for a term of years absolute or determinable on life, or for a term of life.

135 Equitable waste   [477]

An equitable interest for life without impeachment of waste does not confer upon the tenant for life any right to commit waste of the description known as equitable waste, unless an intention to confer such right expressly appears by the instrument creating such equitable interest.

137 Dealings with life interests, reversions and   [478]
other equitable interests

(1) The law applicable to dealings with equitable things in action which regulates the priority of competing interests therein, shall, as respects dealings with equitable interests in land, capital money, and securities representing capital money effected after the commencement of this Act, apply to and regulate the priority of competing interests therein. This subsection applies whether or not the money or securities are in court.

(2) (i) In the case of a dealing with an equitable interest in settled land, capital money or securities representing capital money, the persons to be served with

notice of the dealing shall be the trustees of the settlement; and where the equitable interest is created by a derivative or subsidiary settlement, the persons to be served with notice shall be the trustees of that settlement.

(ii) In the case of a dealing with an equitable interest in land subject to a trust of land, or the proceeds of sale of such land, the persons to be served with notice should be the trustees.

(iii) In any other case the person to be served with notice of a dealing with an equitable interest in land shall be the estate owner of the land affected.

The persons on whom notice is served pursuant to this subsection shall be affected thereby in the same manner as if they had been trustees of personal property out of which the equitable interest was created or arose. This subsection does not apply where the money or securities are in court.

(3) A notice, otherwise than in writing, given to, or received by, a trustee after the commencement of this Act as respects any dealing with an equitable interest in real or personal property, shall not affect the priority of competing claims of purchasers in that equitable interest.

(4) Where, as respects any dealing with an equitable interest in real or personal property –

(a) the trustees are not persons to whom a valid notice of the dealing can be given; or

(b) there are no trustees to whom a notice can be given; or

(c) for any other reason a valid notice cannot be served, or cannot be served without unreasonable cost or delay;

a purchaser may at his own cost require that –

(i) a memorandum of the dealing be endorsed, written on or permanently annexed to the instrument creating the trust;

(ii) the instrument be produced to him by the person having the possession or custody thereof to prove that a sufficient memorandum has been placed thereon or annexed thereto.

Such memorandum shall, as respects priorities, operate in like manner as if notice in writing of the dealing had been given to trustees duly qualified to receive the notice at the time when the memorandum is placed on or annexed to the instrument creating the trust.

(5) Where the property affected is settled land, the memorandum shall be placed on or annexed to the trust instrument and not the vesting instrument. Where the property affected is land subject to a trust of land, the memorandum shall be placed on or annexed to the instrument whereby the equitable interest is created.

(6) Where the trust is created by statute or by operation of law, or in any other case where there is no instrument whereby the trusts are declared, the instrument under which the equitable interest is acquired or which is evidence of the devolution thereof shall, for the purposes of this section, be deemed the instrument creating the trust. In particular, where the trust arises by reason of an intestacy, the letters of administration or probate in force when the dealing was effected shall be deemed such instrument.

(7) Nothing in this section affects any priority acquired before the commencement of this Act.

(8) Where a notice in writing of a dealing with an equitable interest in real or personal property has been served on a trustee under this section, the trustees from time to time of the property affected shall be entitled to the custody of the notice, and the notice shall be delivered to them by any person who for the time being may have the custody thereof; and subject to the payment of costs, any person interested in the equitable interest may require production of the notice.

(9) The liability of the estate owner of the legal estate affected to produce documents and furnish information to persons entitled to equitable interests therein shall correspond to the liability of a trustee for sale to produce documents and furnish information to persons entitled to equitable interests in the proceeds of sale or the land.

(10) This section does not apply until a trust has been created, and in this section 'dealing' includes a disposition by operation of law.

PART V

LEASES AND TENANCIES

139 Effect of extinguishment of reversion   [479]

(1) Where a reversion expectant on a lease of land is surrendered or merged, the estate or interest which as against the lessee for the time being confers the next vested right to the land, shall be deemed the reversion for the purpose of preserving the same incidents and obligations as would have affected the original reversion had there been no surrender or merger thereof ...

140 Apportionment of conditions on severance   [480]

(1) Notwithstanding the severance by conveyance, surrender, or otherwise of the reversionary estate in any land comprised in a lease, and notwithstanding the avoidance or cesser in any other manner of the term granted by a lease as to part only of the land comprised therein, every condition or right of re-entry, and every other condition contained in the lease, shall be apportioned, and shall remain annexed to the severed parts of the reversionary estate as severed, and shall be in force with respect to the term whereon each severed part is reversionary, or the term in the part of the land as to which the term has not been surrendered, or has not be avoided or has not otherwise ceased, in like manner as if the land comprised in each severed part, or the land as to which the term remains subsisting, as the case may be, had alone originally been comprised in the lease.

(2) In this section 'right of re-entry' includes a right to determine the lease by notice to quit or otherwise; but where the notice is served by a person entitled to a severed part of the reversion so that it extends to part only of the land demised, the lessee may within one month determine the lease in regard to the rest of the land by giving to the owner of the reversionary estate therein a counter notice expiring at the same time as the original notice.

(3) This section applies to leases made before or after the commencement of this Act and whether the severance of the reversionary estate or the partial avoidance or cesser of the term was effected before or after such commencement: Provided that, where the lease was made before the first day of January eighteen hundred and eighty-two nothing in this section shall affect the operation of a severance of the reversionary estate or partial avoidance or cesser of the term which was effected before the commencement of this Act.

141 Rent and benefit of lessee's covenants to run   [481]
with the reversion

(1) Rent reserved by a lease, and the benefit of every covenant or provision therein contained, having reference to the subject-matter thereof, and on the lessee's part to be observed or performed, and every condition of re-entry and other condition therein contained, shall be annexed and incident to and shall go

214

with the reversionary estate in the land, or in any part thereof, immediately expectant on the term granted by the lease, notwithstanding severance of that reversionary estate, and without prejudice to any liability affecting a covenantor or his estate.

(2) Any such rent, covenant or provision shall be capable of being recovered, received, enforced, and taken advantage of, by the person from time to time entitled, subject to the term, to the income of the whole or any part, as the case may require, of the land leased.

(3) Where that person becomes entitled by conveyance or otherwise, such rent, covenant or provision may be recovered, received, enforced or taken advantage of by him notwithstanding that he becomes so entitled after the condition of re-entry or forfeiture has become enforceable, but this subsection does not render enforceable any condition of re-entry or other condition waived or released before such person becomes entitled as aforesaid.

(4) This section applies to leases made before or after the commencement of this Act, but does not affect the operation of –

(a) any severance of the reversionary estate; or
(b) any acquisition by conveyance or otherwise of the right to receive or enforce any rent covenant or provision;

effected before the commencement of this Act.

142 Obligation of lessor's covenants to run with reversion   [482]

(1) The obligation under a condition or of a covenant entered into by a lessor with reference to the subject-matter of the lease shall, if and as far as the lessor has power to bind the reversionary estate immediately expectant on the term granted by the lease, be annexed and incident to and shall go with that reversionary estate, or the several parts thereof, notwithstanding severance of that reversionary estate, and may be taken advantage of and enforced by the person in whom the term is from time to time vested by conveyance, devolution in law, or otherwise; and, if and as far as the lessor has power to bind the person from time to time entitled to that reversionary estate, the obligation aforesaid may be taken advantage of and enforced against any person so entitled.

(2) This section applies to leases made before or after the commence-ment of this Act, whether the severance of the reversionary estate was effected before or after such commencement: provided that, where the lease was made before the first day of January eighteen hundred and eighty-two, nothing in this section shall affect the operation of any severance of the reversionary estate effected before such commencement. This section takes effect without prejudice to any liability affecting a covenantor or his estate.

143 Effect of licences granted to lessees   [483]

(1) Where a licence is granted to a lessee to do any act, the licence, unless otherwise expressed, extends only –

(a) to the permission actually given; or
(b) to the specific breach of any provision or covenant referred to; or
(c) to any other matter thereby specifically authorised to be done;

and the licence does not prevent any proceedings for any subsequent breach unless otherwise specified in the licence.

(2) Notwithstanding any such licence –

(a) All rights under covenants and powers of re-entry contained in the lease remain in full force and are available as against any subsequent breach of covenant, condition or other matter not specifically authorised or waived, in the same manner as if no licence had been granted; and

(b) The condition or right of entry remains in force in all respects as if the licence had not been granted, save in respect of the particular matter authorised to be done.

(3) Where in any lease there is a power or condition of re-entry on the lessee assigning, subletting or doing any other specified act without a licence, and a licence is granted –

(a) to any one or two or more lessees to do any act, or to deal with his equitable share or interest; or

(b) to any lessee, or to any one of two or more lessees to assign or underlet part only of the property, or to do any act in respect of part only of the property;

the licence does not operate to extinguish the right of entry in case of any breach of covenant or condition by the co-lessees of the other shares or interests in the property, or by the lessee or lessees of the rest of the property (as the case may be) in respect of such shares or interests or remaining property, but the right of entry remains in force in respect of the shares, interests or property not the subject of the licence. This subsection does not authorise the grant after the commencement of this Act of a licence to create an undivided share in a legal estate ...

144 No fine to be exacted for licence to assign   [484]

In all leases containing a covenant, condition, or agreement against assigning, underletting, or parting with the possession, or disposing of the land or property leased without licence or consent, such covenant, condition, or agreement shall, unless the lease contains an express provision to the contrary, be deemed to be subject to a proviso to the effect that no fine or sum of money in the nature of a fine shall be payable for or in respect of such licence or consent; but this proviso does not preclude the right to require the payment of a reasonable sum in respect of any legal or other expense incurred in relation to such licence or consent.

146 Restrictions on and relief against forfeiture of   [485]
leases and under-leases

(1) A right of re-entry or forfeiture under any proviso or stipulation in a lease for a breach of any covenant or condition in the lease shall not be enforceable, by action or otherwise, unless and until the lessor serves on the lessee a notice –

(a) specifying the particular breach complained of; and

(b) if the breach is capable of remedy, requiring the lessee to remedy the breach; and

(c) in any case, requiring the lessee to make compensation in money for the breach;

and the lessee fails, within a reasonable time thereafter, to remedy the breach, if it is capable of remedy, and to make reasonable compensation in money, to the satisfaction of the lessor, for the breach.

(2) Where a lessor is proceeding, by action or otherwise, to enforce such a right of re-entry or forfeiture, the lessee may, in the lessor's action, if any, or in any action brought by himself, apply to the court for relief; and the court may grant or refuse relief, as the court, having regard to the proceedings and conduct of the parties under the foregoing provisions of this section, and to all the other circumstances,

thinks fit; and in case of relief may grant it on such terms, if any, as to costs, expenses, damages, compensation, penalty, or otherwise, including the granting of an injunction to restrain any like breach in the future, as the court, in the circumstances of each case, thinks fit.

(3) A lessor shall be entitled to recover as a debt due to him from a lessee, and in addition to damages (if any), all reasonable costs and expenses properly incurred by the lessor in the employment of a solicitor and surveyor or valuer, or otherwise, in reference to any breach giving rise to a right of re-entry or forfeiture which, at the request of the lessee, is waived by the lessor, or from which the lessee is relieved, under the provisions of this Act.

(4) Where a lessor is proceeding by action or otherwise to enforce a right of re-entry or forfeiture under any covenant, proviso, or stipulation in a lease, or for non-payment of rent, the court may, on application by any person claiming as under-lessee any estate or interest in the property comprised in the lease or any part thereof, either in the lessor's action (if any) or in any action brought by such person for that purpose, make an order vesting, for the whole term of the lease or any less term, the property comprised in the lease or any part thereof in any person entitled as under-lessee to any estate or interest in such property upon such conditions as to execution of any deed or other document, payment of rent, costs, expenses, damages, compensation, giving security, or otherwise, as the court in the circumstances of each case may think fit, but in no case shall any such under-lessee be entitled to require a lease to be granted to him for any longer term than he had under his original sub-lease.

(5) For the purposes of this section –

(a) 'Lease' includes an original or derivative under-lease; also an agreement for a lease where the lessee has become entitled to have his lease granted; also a grant at a fee farm rent, or securing a rent by condition;

(b) 'Lessee' includes an original or derivative under-lease, and the persons deriving title under a lessee; also a grantee under any such grant as aforesaid and the persons deriving title under him;

(c) 'Lessor' includes an original or derivative under-lessor, and the persons deriving title under a lessor; also a person making such grant as aforesaid and the persons deriving title under him;

(d) 'Under-lease' includes an agreement for an underlease where the under-lessee has become entitled to have his underlease granted;

(e) 'Under-lessee' includes any person deriving title under an under-lessee.

(6) This section applies although the proviso or stipulation under which the right of re-entry or forfeiture accrues is inserted in the lease in pursuance of the directions of any Act of Parliament.

(7) For the purposes of this section a lease limited to continue as long only as the lessee abstains from committing a breach of covenant shall be and take effect as a lease to continue for any longer term for which it could subsist, but determinable by a proviso for re-entry on such a breach.

(8) This section does not extend –

(i) To a covenant or condition against assigning, underletting, parting with the possession, or disposing of the land leased where the breach occurred before the commencement of this Act; or

(ii) In the case of a mining lease, to a covenant or condition for allowing the lessor to have access to or inspect books, accounts, records, weighing machines or other things, or to enter or inspect the mine or the workings thereof.

(9) This section does not apply to a condition for forfeiture on the bankruptcy of

the lessee or on taking in execution of the lessee's interest if contained in a lease of –

(a) Agricultural or pastoral land;

(b) Mines or minerals;

(c) A house used or intended to be used as a public-house or beershop;

(d) A house let as a dwelling-house, with the use of any furniture, books, works of art, or other chattels not being in the nature of fixtures;

(e) Any property with respect to which the personal qualifications of the tenant are of importance for the preservation of the value or character of the property, or on the ground of neighbourhood to the lessor, or to any person holding under him.

(10) Where a condition of forfeiture on the bankruptcy of the lessee or on taking in execution of the lessee's interest is contained in any lease, other than a lease of any of the classes mentioned in the last subsection, then –

(a) if the lessee's interest is sold within one year from the bankruptcy or taking in execution, this section applies to the forfeiture condition aforesaid;

(b) if the lessee's interest is not sold before the expiration of that year, this section only applies to the forfeiture condition aforesaid during the first year from the date of the bankruptcy or taking in execution.

(11) This section does not, save as otherwise mentioned, affect the law relating to re-entry or forfeiture or relief in case of non-payment of rent.

(12) This section has effect notwithstanding any stipulation to the contrary ...

147 Relief against notice to effect decorative repairs　　　[486]

(1) After a notice is served on a lessee relating to the internal decorative repairs to a house or other building, he may apply to the court for relief, and if, having regard to all the circumstances of the case (including in particular the length of the lessee's term or interest remaining unexpired), the court is satisfied that the notice is unreasonable, it may, by order, wholly or partially relieve the lessee from liability for such repairs.

(2) This section does not apply –

(i) where the liability arises under an express covenant or agreement to put the property in a decorative state of repair and the covenant or agreement has never been performed;

(ii) to any matter necessary or proper –

(a) for putting or keeping the property in a sanitary condition, or

(b) for the maintenance or preservation of the structure;

(iii) to any statutory liability to keep a house in all respects reasonably fit for human habitation;

(iv) to any covenant or stipulation to yield up the house or other building in a specified state of repair at the end of the term.

(3) In this section 'lease' includes an underlease and an agreement for a lease, and 'lessee' has a corresponding meaning and includes any person liable to effect the repairs.

(4) This section applies whether the notice is served before or after the commencement of this Act, and has effect notwithstanding any stipulation to the contrary ...

148 Waiver of a covenant in a lease [487]

(1) Where any actual waiver by a lessor or the persons deriving title under him of the benefit of any covenant or condition in any lease is proved to have taken place in any particular instance, such waiver shall not be deemed to extend to any instance, or to any breach of covenant or condition save that to which such waiver specially relates, nor operate as a general waiver of the benefit of any such covenant or condition.

(2) This section applies unless a contrary intention appears ...

149 Abolition of interesse termini, and as to reversionary [488]
leases and leases for lives

(1) The doctrine of interesse termini is hereby abolished.

(2) As from the commencement of this Act all terms of years absolute shall, whether the interest is created before or after such commencement, be capable of taking effect at law or in equity, according to the estate interest or powers of the grantor, from the date fixed for commencement of the term, without actual entry.

(3) A term, at a rent or granted in consideration of a fine, limited after the commencement of this Act to take effect more than twenty-one years from the date of the instrument purporting to create it, shall be void, and any contract made after such commencement to create such a term shall likewise be void; but this subsection does not apply to any term taking effect in equity under a settlement, or created out of an equitable interest under a settlement, or under an equitable power for mortgage, indemnity or other like purposes.

(4) Nothing in subsections (1) and (2) of this section prejudicially affects the right of any person to recover any rent or to enforce or take advantage of any covenants or conditions, or, as respects terms or interests created before the commencement of this Act, operates to vary any statutory or other obligations imposed in respect of such terms or interests.

(5) Nothing in this Act affects the rule of law that a legal term, whether or not being a mortgage term, may be created to take effect in reversion expectant on a longer term, which rule is hereby confirmed.

(6) Any lease or underlease, at a rent, or in consideration of a fine, for life or lives or for any term of years determinable with life or lives, or on the marriage of the lessee, or any contract therefor, made before or after the commencement of this Act, or created by virtue of Part V of the Law of Property Act 1922, shall take effect as a lease, underlease or contract therefor, for a term of ninety years determinable after the death or marriage (as the case may be) of the original lessee, or of the survivor of the original lessees, by at least one month's notice in writing given to determine the same on one of the quarter days applicable to the tenancy, either by the lessor or the persons deriving title under him, to the person entitled to the leasehold interest, or if no such person is in existence by affixing the same to the premises, or by the lessee or other persons in whom the leasehold interest is vested to the lessor or the persons deriving title under him: Provided that –

    (a) this subsection shall not apply to any term taking effect in equity under a settlement or created out of an equitable interest under a settlement for mortgage, indemnity, or other like purposes;

    (b) the person in whom the leasehold interest is vested by virtue of Part V of the Law of Property Act 1922 shall, for the purposes of this subsection, be deemed an original lessee;

    (c) if the lease, underlease, or contract therefor is made determinable on the dropping of the lives of persons other than or besides the lessees, then the notice shall be capable of being served after the death of any person or of the survivor of any persons (whether or not including the lessees) on the cesser of whose life or lives the lease, underlease, or contract is made determinable, instead of after the death of the original lessee or of the survivor of the original lessees;

(d) if there are no quarter days specially applicable to the tenancy, notice may be given to determine the tenancy on one of the usual quarter days.

150 Surrender of a lease, without prejudice to underleases [489] with a view to the grant of a new lease

(1) A lease may be surrendered with a view to the acceptance of a new lease in place thereof, without a surrender of any under-lease derived thereout.

(2) A new lease may be granted and accepted, in place of any lease so surrendered, without any such surrender of an under-lease as aforesaid, and the new lease operates as if all under-leases derived out of the surrendered lease had been surrendered before the surrender of that lease was effected.

(3) The lessee under the new lease and any person deriving title under him is entitled to the same rights and remedies in respect of the rent reserved by and the covenants, agreements and conditions contained in any under-lease as if the original lease had not been surrendered but was or remained vested in him.

(4) Each under-lessee and any person deriving title under him is entitled to hold and enjoy the land comprised in his under-lease (subject to the payment of any rent reserved by and to the observance of the covenants agreements and conditions contained in the under-lease) as if the lease out of which the under-lease was derived had not been surrendered.

(5) The lessor granting the new lease and any person deriving title under him is entitled to the same remedies, by distress or entry in and upon the land comprised in any such under-lease for rent reserved by or for breach of any covenant, agreement or condition contained in the new lease (so far only as the rents reserved by or the covenants, agreements or conditions contained in the new lease do not exceed or impose greater burdens than those reserved by or contained in the original lease out of which the under-lease is derived) as he would have had –

(a) If the original lease had remained on foot; or
(b) If a new under-lease derived out of the new lease had been granted to the under-lessee or a person deriving title under him;

as the case may require.

(6) This section does not affect the powers of the court to give relief against forfeiture.

152 Leases invalidated by reason of non-compliance [490] with terms of powers under which they are granted

(1) Where in the intended exercise of any power of leasing, whether conferred by an Act of Parliament or any other instrument, a lease (in this section referred to as an invalid lease) is granted, which by reason of any failure to comply with the terms of the power is invalid, then –

(a) as against the person entitled after the determination of the interest of the grantor to the reversion; or
(b) as against any other person who, subject to any lease properly granted under the power, would have been entitled to the land comprised in the lease;

the lease, if it was made in good faith, and the lessee has entered thereunder, shall take effect in equity as a contract for the grant, at the request of the lessee, of a valid lease under the power, of like effect as the invalid lease, subject to such variations as may be necessary in order to comply with the terms of the power: Provided that a lessee under an invalid lease shall not, by virtue of any such implied contract, be entitled to obtain a variation of the lease if the other persons who would have been bound by the contract are willing and able to confirm the lease without variation.

(2) Where a lease granted in the intended exercise of such a power is invalid by reason of the grantor not having power to grant the lease at the date thereof, but the grantor's interest in the land comprised therein continues after the time when he might, in the exercise of the power, have properly granted a lease in the like terms, the lease shall take effect as a valid lease in like manner as if it had been granted at that time.

(3) Where during the continuance of the possession taken under an invalid lease the person for the time being entitled, subject to such possession, to the land comprised therein or to the rents and profits thereof, is able to confirm the lease without variation, the lessee, or other person who would have been bound by the lease had it been valid, shall, at the request of the person so able to confirm the lease, be bound to accept a confirmation thereof, and thereupon the lease shall have effect and be deemed to have had effect as a valid lease from the grant thereof. Confirmation under this subsection may be by a memorandum in writing signed by or on behalf of the persons respectively confirming and accepting the confirmation of the lease.

(4) Where a receipt or a memorandum in writing confirming an invalid lease is, upon or before the acceptance of rent thereunder, signed by or on behalf of the person accepting the rent, that acceptance shall, as against that person, be deemed to be a confirmation of the lease.

(5) The foregoing provisions of this section do not affect prejudicially –

(a) any right of action or other right or remedy to which, but for those provisions or any enactment replaced by those provisions, the lessee named in an invalid lease would or might have been entitled under any covenant on the part of the grantor for title or quiet enjoyment contained therein or implied thereby; or

(b) any right of re-entry or other right or remedy to which, but for those provisions or any enactment replaced thereby, the grantor or other person for the time being entitled to the reversion expectant on the termination of the lease, would or might have been entitled by reason of any breach of the covenants, conditions or provisions contained in the lease and binding on the lessee.

(6) Where a valid power of leasing is vested in or may be exercised by a person who grants a lease which, by reason of the determination of the interest of the grantor or otherwise, cannot have effect and continuance according to the terms thereof independently of the power, the lease shall for the purposes of this section be deemed to have been granted in the intended exercise of the power although the power is not referred to in the lease.

(7) This section does not apply to a lease of land held on charitable, ecclesiastical or public trusts.

(8) This section takes effect without prejudice to the provision in this Act for the grant of leases in the name and on behalf of the estate owner of the land affected.

153 Enlargement of residue of long terms into [491] fee simple estates

(1) Where a residue unexpired of not less than two hundred years of a term, which, as originally created, was for not less than three hundred years, is

subsisting in land, whether being the whole land originally comprised in the term, or part only thereof, –

(a) without any trust or right of redemption affecting the term in favour of the freeholder, or other person entitled in reversion expectant on the term; and

(b) without any rent, or with merely a peppercorn rent or other rent having no money value, incident to the reversion, or having had a rent, not being merely a peppercorn rent or other rent having no money value, originally so incident, which subsequently has been released or has become barred by lapse of time, or has in any other way ceased to be payable;

the term may be enlarged into a fee simple in the manner, and subject to the restrictions in this section provided.

(2) This section applies to and includes every such term as aforesaid whenever created, whether or not having the freehold as the immediate reversion thereon; but does not apply to –

(i) Any term liable to be determined by re-entry for condition broken; or

(ii) Any term created by subdemise out of a superior term, itself incapable of being enlarged into fee simple.

(3) This section extends to mortgage terms, where the right of redemption is barred.

(4) A rent not exceeding the yearly sum of one pound which has not been collected or paid for a continuous period of twenty years or upwards shall, for the purposes of this section, be deemed to have ceased to be payable: provided that, of the said period, at least five years must have elapsed after the commencement of this Act.

(5) Where a rent incident to a reversion expectant on a term to which this section applies is deemed to have ceased to be payable for the purposes aforesaid, no claim for such rent or for any arrears thereof shall be capable of being enforced.

(6) Each of the following persons, namely –

(i) Any person beneficially entitled in right of the term, whether subject to any incumbrance or not, to possession of any land comprised in the term, and, in the case of a married woman without the concurrence of her husband, whether or not she is entitled for her separate use or as her separate property;

(ii) Any person being in receipt of income as trustee, in right of the term, or having the term vested in him as a trustee of land, whether subject to any incumbrance or not;

(iii) Any person in whom, as personal representative of any deceased person, the term is vested, whether subject to any incumbrance or not;

shall, so far as regards the land to which he is entitled, or in which he is interested in right of the term, in any such character as aforesaid, have power by deed to declare to the effect that, from and after the execution of the deed, the term shall be enlarged into a fee simple.

(7) Thereupon, by virtue of the deed and of this Act, the term shall become and be enlarged accordingly, and the person in whom the term was previously vested shall acquire and have in the land a fee simple instead of the term.

(8) The estate in fee simple so acquired by enlargement shall be subject to all the same trusts, powers, executory limitations over, rights, and equities, and to all the same covenants and provisions relating to user and enjoyment, and to all the same obligations of every kind, as the term would have been subject to if it had not been so enlarged.

(9) But where –

(a) any land so held for the residue of a term has been settled in trust by reference to other land, being freehold land, so as to go along with that other land, or, in the case of settlements coming into operation before the commencement of this Act, so as to go along with that other land as far as the law permits; and

(b) at the time of enlargement, the ultimate beneficial interest in the term, whether subject to any subsisting particular estate or not, has not become absolutely and indefeasibly vested in any person, free from charges or powers of charging created by a settlement;

the estate in fee simple acquired as aforesaid shall, without prejudice to any conveyance for value previously made by a person having a contingent or defeasible interest in the term, be liable to be, and shall be, conveyed by means of a subsidiary vesting instrument and settled in like manner as the other land, being freehold land, aforesaid, and until so conveyed and settled shall devolve beneficially as if it had been so conveyed and settled.

(10) The estate in fee simple so acquired shall, whether the term was originally created without impeachment of waste or not, include the fee simple in all mines and minerals which at the time of enlargement have not been severed in right or in fact, or have not been severed or reserved by an inclosure Act or award.

154 Application of Part V to existing leases [492]

This part of this Act, except where otherwise expressly provided, applies to leases created before or after the commencement of this Act, and 'lease' includes an under-lease or other tenancy.

PART VI

POWERS

155 Release of powers simply collateral [493]

A person to whom any power, whether coupled with an interest or not, is given may by deed release, or contract not to exercise, the power.

156 Disclaimer of power [494]

(1) A person to whom any power, whether coupled with an interest or not, is given may by deed disclaim the power, and, after disclaimer, shall not be capable of exercising or joining in the exercise of the power.

(2) On such disclaimer, the power may be exercised by the other person or persons or the survivor or survivors of the other persons, to whom the power is given, unless the contrary is expressed in the instrument creating the power.

157 Protection of purchasers claiming under certain [495] void appointments

(1) An instrument purporting to exercise a power of appointment over property, which, in default of and subject to any appointment, is held in trust for the class or number of persons of whom the appointee is one, shall not (save as hereinafter provided) be void on the ground of fraud on the power as against a purchaser in good faith: Provided that, if the interest appointed exceeds, in amount or value, the interest in such property to which immediately before the execution of the instrument the appointee was presumptively entitled under the trust in default of

223

appointment, having regard to any advances made in his favour and to any hotchpot provision, the protection afforded by this section to a purchaser shall not extend to such excess.

(2) In this section 'a purchaser in good faith' means a person dealing with an appointee of the age of not less than twenty-five years for valuable consideration in money or money's worth, and without notice of the fraud, or of any circumstances from which, if reasonable inquiries had been made, the fraud might have been discovered.

(3) Persons deriving title under any purchaser entitled to the benefit of this section shall be entitled to the like benefit ...

158 Validation of appointments where objects are   [496]
excluded or take illusory shares

(1) No appointment made in exercise of any power to appoint any property among two or more objects shall be invalid on the ground that –

(a) an unsubstantial, illusory, or nominal share only is appointed to or left unappointed to devolve upon any one or more of the objects of the power; or

(b) any object of the power is thereby altogether excluded;

but every such appointment shall be valid notwithstanding that any one or more of the objects is not thereby, or in default of appointment, to take any share in the property.

(2) This section does not affect any provision in the instrument creating the power which declares the amount of any share from which any object of the power is not to be excluded ...

159 Execution of powers not testamentary   [497]

(1) A deed executed in the presence of and attested by two or more witnesses (in the manner in which deeds are ordinarily executed and attested) is so far as respects the execution and attestation thereof, a valid execution of a power of appointment by deed or by any instrument in writing, not testamentary, notwithstanding that it is expressly required that a deed or instrument in writing, made in exercise of the power, is to be executed or attested with some additional or other form of execution or attestation or solemnity.

(2) This section does not operate to defeat any direction in the instrument creating the power that –

(a) the consent of any particular person is to be necessary to a valid execution;

(b) in order to give validity to any appointment, any act is to be performed having no relation to the mode of executing and attesting the instrument.

(3) This section does not prevent the donee of a power from executing it in accordance with the power by writing, or otherwise than by an instrument executed and attested as a deed; and where a power is so executed this section does not apply ...

PART VII

PERPETUITIES AND ACCUMULATIONS

161 Abolition of the double possibility rule   [498]

(1) The rule of law prohibiting the limitation, after a life interest to an unborn person, of an interest in land to the unborn child or other issue of an unborn

person is hereby abolished, but without prejudice to any other rule relating to perpetuities.

(2) This section only applies to limitations or trusts created by an instrument coming into operation after the commencement of this Act.

162 Restrictions on the perpetuity rule [499]

(1) For removing doubts, it is hereby declared that the rule of law relating to perpetuities does not apply and shall be deemed never to have applied –

(a) To any power to distrain on or to take possession of land or the income thereof given by way of indemnity against a rent, whether charged upon or payable in respect of any part of that land or not; or

(b) To any rentcharge created only as an indemnity against another rentcharge, although the indemnity rentcharge may only arise or become payable on breach of a condition or stipulation; or

(c) To any power, whether exercisable on breach of a condition or stipulation or not, to retain or withhold payment of any instalment of a rentcharge as an indemnity against another rentcharge; or

(d) To any grant, exception, or reservation of any right of entry on, or user of, the surface of land or of any easements, rights, or privileges over or under land for the purpose of –

(i) winning, working, inspecting, measuring, converting, manufacturing, carrying away, and disposing of mines and minerals;

(ii) inspecting, grubbing up, felling and carrying away timber and other trees, and the tops and lops thereof;

(iii) executing repairs, alterations, or additions to any adjoining land, or the buildings and erections thereon;

(iv) constructing, laying down, altering, repairing, renewing, cleansing, and maintaining sewers, watercourses, cesspools, gutters, drains, water-pipes, gas-pipes, electric wires or cables or other like works.

(2) This section applies to instruments coming into operation before or after the commencement of this Act.

164 General restrictions on accumulation of income [500]

(1) No person may by any instrument or otherwise settle or dispose of any property in such manner that the income thereof shall, save as hereinafter mentioned, be wholly or partially accumulated for any longer period than one of the following, namely –

(a) the life of the grantor or settlor; or

(b) a term of twenty-one years from the death of the grantor, settlor or testator; or

(c) the duration of the minority or respective minorities of any person or persons living or en ventre sa mère at the death of the grantor, settlor or testator; or

(d) the duration of the minority or respective minorities only of any person or persons who under the limitations of the instrument directing the accumulations would, for the time being, if of full age, be entitled to the income directed to be accumulated.

In every case where any accumulation is directed otherwise than as aforesaid, the direction shall (save as hereinafter mentioned) be void; and the income of the property directed to be accumulated shall, so long as the same is directed to be accumulated contrary to this section, go to and be received by the person or persons who would have been entitled thereto if such accumulation had not been directed.

(2) This section does not extend to any provision –

(i) for payment of the debts of any grantor, settlor, testator or other person;

(ii) for raising portions for –

(a) any child, children or remoter issue of any grantor, settlor or testator; or

(b) any child, children or remoter issue of a person taking any interest under any settlement or other disposition directing the accumulations or to whom any interest is thereby limited;

(iii) respecting the accumulation of the produce of timber or wood;

and accordingly such provisions may be made as if no statutory restrictions on accumulation of income had been imposed.

(3) The restrictions imposed by this section apply to instruments made on or after the twenty-eighth day of July, eighteen hundred, but in the case of wills only where the testator was living and of testamentary capacity after the end of one year from that date.

165 Qualification of restrictions on accumulation   [501]

Where accumulations of surplus income are made during a minority under any statutory power or under the general law, the period for which such accumulations are made is not (whether the trust was created or the accumulations were made before or after the commencement of this Act) to be taken into account in determining the periods for which accumulations are permitted to be made by the last preceding section, and accordingly an express trust for accumulation for any other permitted period shall not be deemed to have been invalidated or become invalid, by reason of accumulations also having been made as aforesaid during such minority.

166 Restriction on accumulation for the purchase of land   [502]

(1) No person may settle or dispose of any property in such manner that the income thereof shall be wholly or partially accumulated for the purchase of land only, for any longer period than the duration of the minority or respective minorities of any person or persons who, under the limitations of the instrument directing the accumulation, would for the time being, if of full age, be entitled to the income so directed to be accumulated.

(2) This section does not, nor do the enactments which it replaces, apply to accumulations to be held as capital money for the purposes of the Settled Land Act 1925, or the enactments replaced by that Act, whether or not the accumulations are primarily liable to be laid out in the purchase of land.

(3) This section applies to settlements and dispositions made after the twenty-seventh day of June eighteen hundred and ninety-two.

PART IX

VOIDABLE DISPOSITIONS

173 Voluntary disposition of land how far voidable   [503]
as against purchasers

(1) Every voluntary disposition of land made with intent to defraud a subsequent purchaser is voidable at the instance of that purchaser.

(2) For the purposes of this section, no voluntary disposition, whenever made, shall be deemed to have been made with intent to defraud by reason only that a subsequent conveyance for valuable consideration was made, if such subsequent conveyance was made after the twenty-eighth day of June, eighteen hundred and ninety-three.

174 Acquisitions of reversions at an under value [504]

(1) No acquisition made in good faith, without fraud or unfair dealing, of any reversionary interest in real or personal property, for money or money's worth, shall be liable to be opened or set aside merely on the ground of under value. In this subsection 'reversionary interest' includes an expectancy or possibility.

(2) This section does not affect the jurisdiction of the court to set aside or modify unconscionable bargains.

PART XI

MISCELLANEOUS

184 Presumption of survivorship in regard to claims [505]
to property

In all cases where, after the commencement of this Act, two or more persons have died in circumstances rendering it uncertain which of them survived the other or others, such deaths shall (subject to any order of the court), for all purposes affecting the title to property, be presumed to have occurred in order of seniority, and accordingly the younger shall be deemed to have survived the elder.

185 Merger [506]

There is no merger by operation of law only of any estate the beneficial interest in which would not be deemed to be merged or extinguished in equity.

186 Rights of pre-emption capable of release [507]

All statutory and other rights of pre-emption affecting a legal estate shall be and be deemed always to have been capable of release, and unless released shall remain in force as equitable interests only.

187 Legal easements [508]

(1) Where an easement, right or privilege for a legal estate is created, it shall enure for the benefit of the land to which it is intended to be annexed.

(2) Nothing in this Act affects the right of a person to acquire, hold or exercise an easement, right or privilege over or in relation to land for a legal estate in common with any other person, or the power of creating or conveying such an easement right or privilege.

193 Rights of the public over commons and waste lands [509]

(1) Members of the public shall, subject as hereinafter provided, have rights of access for air and exercise to any land which is a metropolitan common within the meaning of the Metropolitan Commons Acts 1866 to 1898, or manorial waste, or a common, which is wholly or partly situated within an area which immediately

before 1st April 1974 was a borough or urban district, and to any land which at the commencement of this Act is subject to rights of common and to which this section may from time to time be applied in manner hereinafter provided: Provided that –

(a) such rights of access shall be subject to any Act, scheme, or provisional order for the regulation of the land, and to any byelaw, regulation or order made thereunder or under any statutory authority; and

(b) the Minister shall, on the application of any person entitled as lord of the manor or otherwise to the soil of the land, or entitled to any commonable rights affecting the land, impose such limitations on and conditions as to the exercise of the rights of access or as to the extent of the land to be affected as, in the opinion of the Minister, are necessary or desirable for preventing any estate, right or interest of a profitable or beneficial nature in, over, or affecting the land from being injuriously affected, or for protecting any object of historical interest and, where any such limitations or conditions are so imposed, the rights of access shall be subject thereto; and

(c) such rights of access shall not include any right to draw or drive upon the land a carriage, cart, caravan, truck, or other vehicle, or to camp or light any fire thereon; and

(d) the rights of access shall cease to apply –

(i) to any land over which the commonable rights are extinguished under any statutory provision;

(ii) to any land over which the commonable rights are otherwise extinguished if the council of the county, county borough or metropolitan district in which the land is situated by resolution assent to its exclusion from the operation of this section, and the resolution is approved by the Minister.

(2) The lord of the manor or other person entitled to the soil of any land subject to rights of common may by deed, revocable or irrevocable, declare that this section shall apply to the land, and upon such deed being deposited with the Minister the land shall, so long as the deed remains operative, be land to which this section applies.

(3) Where limitations or conditions are imposed by the Minister under this section, they shall be published by such person and in such manner as the Minister may direct.

(4) Any person who, without lawful authority, draws or drives upon any land to which this section applies any carriage, cart, caravan, truck, or other vehicle, or camps or lights any fire thereon, or who fails to observe any limitation or condition imposed by the Minister under this section in respect of any such land, shall be liable on summary conviction to a fine ... for each offence.

(5) Nothing in this section shall prejudice or affect the right of any person to get and remove mines or minerals or to let down the surface of the manorial waste or common.

(6) This section does not apply to any common or manorial waste which is for the time being held for Naval, Military or Air Force purposes and in respect of which rights of common have been extinguished or cannot be exercised.

194 Restrictions on inclosure of commons [510]

(1) The erection of any building or fence, or the construction of any other work, whereby access to land to which this section applies is prevented or impeded, shall not be lawful unless the consent of the Minister thereto is obtained, and in giving or withholding his consent the Minister shall have regard to the same

considerations and shall, if necessary, hold the same inquiries as are directed by the Commons Act 1876 to be taken into consideration and held by the Minister before forming an opinion whether an application under the Inclosure Acts 1845 to 1882 shall be acceded to or not.

(2) Where any building or fence is erected, or any other work constructed without such consent as is required by this section, the county court within whose jurisdiction the land is situated, shall, on an application being made by the council of any county or county borough or district concerned, or by the lord of the manor or any other person interested in the common, have power to make an order for the removal of the work, and the restoration of the land to the condition in which it was before the work was erected or constructed, but any such order shall be subject to the like appeal as an order made under section thirty of the Commons Act 1876.

(3) This section applies to any land which at the commencement of this Act is subject to rights of common: provided that this section shall cease to apply –

(a) to any land over which the rights of common are extinguished under any statutory provision;
(b) to any land over which the rights of common are otherwise extinguished, if the council of the county, county borough or metropolitan district in which the land is situated by resolution assent to its exclusion from the operation of this section and the resolution is approved by the Minister.

(4) This section does not apply to any building or fence erected or work constructed if specially authorised by Act of Parliament, or in pursuance of an Act of Parliament or Order having the force of an Act, or if lawfully erected or constructed in connexion with the taking or working of minerals in or under any land to which the section is otherwise applicable, or to any telecommunication apparatus installed for the purposes of a telecommunications code system.

198 Registration ... to be notice [511]

(1) The registration of any instrument or matter in any register kept under the Land Charges Act 1972 or any local land charges register shall be deemed to constitute actual notice of such instrument or matter, and if the fact of such registration, to all persons and for all purposes connected with the land affected, as from the date of registration or other prescribed date and so long as the registration continues in force.

(2) This section operates without prejudice to the provisions of this Act respecting the making of further advances by a mortgagee, and applies only to instruments and matters required or authorised to be registered in any such register.

199 Restrictions on constructive notice [512]

(1) A purchaser shall not be prejudicially affected by notice of –

(i) any instrument or matter capable of registration under the provisions of the Land Charges Act 1925, or any enactment which it replaces, which is void or not enforceable as against him under that Act or enactment, by reason of the non-registration thereof;
(ii) any other instrument or matter or any fact or thing unless –

(a) it is within his own knowledge, or would have come to his knowledge if such inquiries and inspections had been made as ought reasonably to have been made by him; or
(b) in the same transaction with respect to which a question of notice to the purchaser arises, it has come to the knowledge of his counsel, as such, or of

his solicitor or other agent, as such, or would have come to the knowledge of his solicitor or other agent, as such, if such inquiries and inspections had been made as ought reasonably to have been made by the solicitor or other agent.

(2) Paragraph (ii) of the last subsection shall not exempt a purchaser from any liability under, or any obligation to perform or observe, any covenant, condition, provision, or restriction contained in any instrument under which his title is derived, mediately or immediately; and such liability or obligation may be enforced in the same manner and to the same extent as if that paragraph had not been enacted.

(3) A purchaser shall not by reason of anything in this section be affected by notice in any case where he would not have been so affected if this section had not been enacted.

(4) This section applies to purchases made either before or after the commencement of this Act.

200 Notice of restrictive covenants and easements   [513]

(1) Where land having a common title with other land is disposed of to a purchaser (other than a lessee or a mortgagee) who does not hold or obtain possession of the documents forming the common title, such purchaser, notwithstanding any stipulation to the contrary, may require that a memorandum giving notice of any provision contained in the disposition to him restrictive of user of, or giving rights over, any other land comprised in the common title, shall, where practicable, be written or indorsed on, or, where impracticable, be permanently annexed to some one document selected by the purchaser but retained in the possession or power of the person who makes the disposition, and being or forming part of the common title.

(2) The title of any person omitting to require an indorsement to be made or a memorandum to be annexed shall not, by reason only of this enactment, be prejudiced or affected by the omission.

(3) This section does not apply to dispositions of registered land.

(4) Nothing in this section affects the obligation to register a land charge in respect of –

(a) any restrictive covenant or agreement affecting freehold land; or
(b) any estate contract; or
(c) any equitable easement, liberty or privilege.

PART XII

CONSTRUCTION, JURISDICTION, AND GENERAL PROVISIONS

201 Provisions of Act to apply to incorporeal hereditaments   [514]

(1) The provisions of this Act relating to freehold land apply to manors, reputed manors, lordships, advowsons, perpetual rentcharges, and other incorporeal hereditaments, subject only to the qualifications necessarily arising by reason of the inherent nature of the hereditament affected.

(2) This Act does not affect the special restrictions imposed on dealings with advowsons by the Benefices Act 1898, or any other statute or measure, nor affect the limitation of, or authorise any dispositions to be made of, a title or dignity of honour which in its nature is inalienable.

205 General definitions [515]

(1) In this Act unless the context otherwise requires, the following expressions have the meanings hereby assigned to them respectively, that is to say –

...

(ii) 'Conveyance' includes a mortgage, charge, lease, assent, vesting declaration, vesting instrument, disclaimer, release and every other assurance of property or of an interest therein by any instrument, except a will; 'convey' has a corresponding meaning; and 'disposition' includes a conveyance and also a devise, bequest, or an appointment of property contained in a will; and 'dispose of' has a corresponding meaning;

(iii) 'Building purposes' include the erecting and improving of, and the adding to, and the repairing of buildings; and a 'building lease' is a lease for building purposes or purposes connected therewith;

(iv) 'Death duty' means estate duty and every other duty leviable or payable on a death;

(v) 'Estate owner' means the owner of a legal estate, but an infant is not capable of being an estate owner;

(vi) 'Gazette' means the London Gazette;

(vii) 'Incumbrance' includes a legal or equitable mortgage and a trust for securing money, and a lien, and a charge of a portion, annuity, or other capital or annual sum; and 'incumbrancer' has a meaning corresponding with that of incumbrance, and includes every person entitled to the benefit of an incumbrance, or to require payment or discharge thereof;

(viii) 'Instrument' does not include a statute, unless the statute creates a settlement;

(ix) 'Land' includes land of any tenure, and mines and minerals, whether or not held apart from the surface, buildings or parts of buildings (whether the division is horizontal, vertical or made in any other way) and other corporeal hereditaments; also a manor, an advowson, and a rent and other incorporeal hereditaments, and an easement, right, privilege, or benefit in, over, or derived from land; and 'mines and minerals' include any strata or seam of minerals or substances in or under any land, and powers of working and getting the same; and 'manor' includes a lordship, and reputed manor or lordship; and 'hereditament' means any real property which on an intestacy occurring before the commencement of this Act might have devolved upon an heir;

(x) 'Legal estates' mean the estate, interests and charges, in or over land (subsisting or created at law) which are by this Act authorised to subsist or to be created as legal estates; 'equitable interests' mean all the other interests and charges in or over land; an equitable interest 'capable of subsisting as a legal estate' means such as could validly subsist or be created as a legal estate under this Act;

(xi) 'Legal powers' include the powers vested in a chargee by way of legal mortgage or in an estate owner under which a legal estate can be transferred or created; and 'equitable powers' mean all the powers in or over land under which equitable interests or powers only can be transferred or created;

(xii) 'Limitation Acts' mean the Real Property Limitation Acts 1833, 1837 and 1874, and 'limitation' includes a trust;

(xiii) 'Mental disorder' has the meaning assigned to it by section 1 of the Mental Health Act 1983 and 'receiver' in relation to a person suffering from mental disorder, means a receiver appointed for that person under Part VIII of the Mental Health Act 1959 or Part VII of the said Act of 1983;

(xiv) A 'mining lease' means a lease for mining purposes, that is, the searching for, winning, working, getting, making merchantable, carrying away, or disposing of mines and minerals, or purposes connected therewith, and includes a grant or licence for mining purposes;

(xv) 'Minister' means the Minister of Agriculture, Fisheries and Food;

(xvi) 'Mortgage' includes any charge or lien on any property for securing money or money's worth; 'legal mortgage' means a mortgage by demise or subdemise or a charge by way of legal mortgage and 'legal mortgagee' has a corresponding meaning; 'mortgage money' means money or money's worth secured by a mortgage; 'mortgagor' includes any person from time to time deriving title under the original mortgagor or entitled to redeem a mortgage according to his estate interest or right in the mortgaged property; 'mortgagee' includes a chargee by way of legal mortgage and any person from time to time deriving title under the original mortgagee; and 'mortgagee in possession' is, for the purposes of this Act, a mortgagee who, in right of the mortgage, has entered into and is in possession of the mortgaged property; and 'right of redemption' includes an option to repurchase only if the option in effect creates a right of redemption;

(xvii) 'Notice' includes constructive notice;

(xviii) 'Personal representative' means the executor, original or by representation, or administrator for the time being of a deceased person, and as regards any liability for the payment of death duties includes any person who takes possession of or intermeddles with the property of a deceased person without the authority of the personal representatives or the court;

(xix) 'Possession' includes receipts of rents and profits or the right to receive the same, if any; and 'income' includes rents and profits;

(xx) 'Property' includes any thing in action, and any interest in real or personal property;

(xxi) 'Purchaser' means a purchaser in good faith for valuable consideration and includes a lessee, mortgagee or other person who for valuable consideration acquires an interest in property except that in Part I of this Act and elsewhere where so expressly provided 'purchaser' only means a person who acquires an interest in or charge on property for money or money's worth; and in reference to a legal estate includes a chargee by way of legal mortgage; and where the context so requires 'purchaser' includes an intending purchaser; 'purchase' has a meaning corresponding with that of 'purchaser'; and 'valuable consideration' includes marriage but does not include a nominal consideration in money;

(xxii) 'Registered land' has the same meaning as in the Land Registration Act 1925 and 'Land Registrar' means the Chief Land Registrar under that Act;

(xxiii) 'Rent' includes a rent service or a rentcharge, or other rent, toll, duty, royalty, or annual or periodical payment in money or money's worth, reserved or issuing out of or charged upon land, but does not include mortgage interest; 'rentcharge' includes a fee farm rent; 'fine' includes a premium or foregift and any payment, consideration, or benefit in the nature of a fine, premium or foregift; 'lessor' includes an underlessor and a person deriving title under a lessor or underlessor; and 'lessee' includes an underlessee and a person deriving title under a lessee or underlessee, and 'lease' includes an underlease or other tenancy;

(xxiv) 'Sale' includes an extinguishment of manorial incidents, but in other respects means a sale properly so called;

(xxv) 'Securities' include stocks, funds and shares;

(xxvi) 'Tenant for life', 'statutory owner', 'settled land', 'settlement', 'vesting deed', 'subsidiary vesting deed', 'vesting order', 'vesting instrument', 'trust instrument', 'capital money', and 'trustees of the settlement' have the same meaning as in the Settled Land Act 1925;

(xxvii) 'Term of years absolute' means a term of years (taking effect either in possession or in reversion whether or not at a rent) with or without impeachment for waste, subject or not to another legal estate, and either certain or liable to determination by notice, re-entry, operation of law, or by a provision for cesser on redemption, or in any other event (other than the dropping of a life, or the determination of a determinable life interest); but does not include any term of years determinable with life or lives or with the cesser of a determinable life interest, nor, if created after the commencement of this Act, a term of years which is not expressed to take effect in possession within twenty-one years after the creation thereof where required by this Act to take effect within that period; and in this definition the expression 'term of years' includes a term for less than a year, or for a year or years and a fraction of a year or from year to year;

(xxviii) 'Trust Corporation' means the Public Trustee or a corporation either appointed by the court in any particular case to be a trustee or entitled by rules made under subsection (3) of section four of the Public Trustee Act 1906 to act as custodian trustee;

(xxix) 'Trust for sale', in relation to land, means an immediate trust for sale, whether or not exercisable at the request or with the consent of any person; 'trustees for sale' mean the persons (including a personal representative) holding land on trust for sale;

(xxx) 'United Kingdom' means Great Britain and Northern Ireland;

(xxxi) 'Will' includes codicil.

(1A) Any reference in this Act to money being paid into court shall be construed as referring to the money being paid into the Supreme Court or any other court that has jurisdiction, and any reference in this Act to the court, in a context referring to the investment or application of money paid into court, shall be construed, in the case of money paid into the Supreme Court, as referring to the High Court, and in the case of money paid into another court, as referring to that other court.

(2) Where an equitable interest in or power over property arises by statute or operation of law, references to the creation of an interest or power include references to any interest or power so arising.

(3) References to registration under the Land Charges Act 1925 apply to any registration made under any other statute which is by the Land Charges Act 1925 to have effect as if the registration had been made under that Act.

FIRST SCHEDULE **[516]**

TRANSITIONAL PROVISIONS

PART I

CONVERSION OF CERTAIN EXISTING LEGAL ESTATES INTO
EQUITABLE INTERESTS

All estates, interests and charges in or over land, including fees determinable whether by limitation or condition, which immediately before the commencement of this Act were estates, interests or charges, subsisting at law, or capable of taking effect as such, but which by virtue of Part I of this Act are not capable of taking effect as legal estates, shall as from the commencement of this Act be converted into equitable interests, and shall not fail by reason of being so converted into equitable interests either in the land or in the proceeds of sale thereof, nor shall the priority of any such estate, charge or interest over other equitable interests be affected ...

PART III

PROVISIONS AS TO LEGAL ESTATE VESTED IN INFANT

1. Where immediately before the commencement of this Act a legal estate in land is vested in one or more infants beneficially, or where immediately after the commencement of this Act a legal estate in land would by virtue of this Act have become vested in one or more infants beneficially if he or they had been of full age, the legal estate shall vest in the manner provided by the Settled Land Act 1925 ...

PART V

PROVISIONS AS TO PARTY STRUCTURES AND OPEN SPACES

1. Where, immediately before the commencement of this Act, a party wall or other party structure is held in undivided shares, the ownership thereof shall be deemed to be severed vertically as between the respective owners, and the owner of each part shall have such rights to support and of user over the rest of the structure as may be requisite for conferring rights corresponding to those subsisting at the commencement of this Act ...

SECOND SCHEDULE   [517]

IMPLIED COVENANTS

PART VIII

COVENANT IMPLIED IN A CONVEYANCE FOR VALUABLE CONSIDERATION, OTHER THAN A MORTGAGE, OR PART OF LAND AFFECTED BY A RENTCHARGE, SUBJECT TO A PART (NOT LEGALLY APPORTIONED) OF THAT RENTCHARGE.

(i) That the grantees, or the persons deriving title under them, will at all times, from the date of the conveyance or other date therein stated, pay the apportioned rent and observe and perform all the covenants (other than the covenant to pay the entire rent) and conditions contained in the deed or other document creating the rentcharge, so far as the same relate to the land conveyed:

And also will at all times, from the date aforesaid, save harmless and keep indemnified the conveyancing parties and their respective estates and effects, from and against all proceedings, costs, claims and expenses on account of any omission to pay the said apportioned rent, or any breach of any of the said covenants and conditions, so far as the same relate as aforesaid.

(ii) That the conveyancing parties, or the persons deriving title under them, will at all times, from the date of the conveyance or other date therein stated, pay the balance of the rentcharge (after deducting the apportioned rent aforesaid, and any other rents similarly apportioned in respect of land not retained), and observe and perform all the covenants, other than the covenant to pay the entire rent, and conditions contained in the deed or other document creating the rentcharge, so far as the same relate to the land not included in the conveyance and remaining vested in the covenantors:

And also will at all times, from the date aforesaid, save harmless and keep indemnified the grantees and their estates and effects, from and against all proceedings, costs, claims and expenses on account of any omission to pay the aforesaid balance of the rentcharge, or any breach of any of the said covenants and conditions so far as they relate as aforesaid.

NB Where at the commencement of the Trusts of Land and Appointment of Trustees Act 1996 any land is held on trust for sale, or on the statutory trusts, by virtue of Schedule 1 to the Law of Property Act 1925 (transitional provisions), it is after that commencement held in trust for the persons interested in the land: 1996 Act, s5, Schedule 2, para 7.

[As amended by the Law of Property (Amendment) Act 1926, s7, Schedule; Law of Property (Entailed Interests) Act 1932, s1; Tithe Act 1936, s48(3), Schedule 9; Criminal Justice Act 1948, s83, Schedule 10; Married Women (Restraint upon Anticipation) Act 1949, s1, Schedule 2; Finance Act 1949, s52(9), (10), Schedule 11, Pt IV; Mental Health Act 1959, s149(1), (2), Schedule 7, Pt I, Schedule 8, Pt I; Finance Act 1963, s73(8)(b), Schedule 14, Pt IV; Industrial and Provident Societies Act 1965, s77(1), Schedule 5; Administration of Justice Act 1965, ss17, 18, Schedule 1; Family Law Reform Act 1969, ss1(3), 28(3), Schedule 1; Law of Property Act 1969, s28(1), Schedule 3; Finance Act 1971, s64, Schedule 14, Pt VI; Friendly Societies Act 1971, s14(2), Schedule 3; Land Charges Act 1972, s18, Schedule 3, para 1; Local Government Act 1972, ss189(4), 272(1), Schedule 30; Local Land Charges Act 1975, s17(2), Schedule 1; Civil Aviation Act 1982, s109, Schedule 15, para 1; Mental Health Act 1983, s148, Schedule 4, para 5(a), (b); Telecommunications Act 1984, s109, Schedule 4, para 16; County Courts Act 1984, s148(1), Schedule 2, Pt II, para 2; Local Government Act 1985, s16, Schedule 8, para 10(5); Insolvency Act 1985, s235(3), Schedule 10, Pt III; Insolvency Act 1986, s439(2), Schedule 14; Reverter of Sites Act 1987, s8(2), (3), Schedule; Law of Property (Miscellaneous Provisions) Act 1989, s1(8), Schedule 1, paras 2, 4; High Court and County Courts Jurisdiction Order 1991, art 2(8), Schedule; Local Government (Wales) Act 1994, s66(6), Schedule 16, para 7; Law of Property (Miscellaneous Provisions) Act 1994, s21(1), Schedule 1, para 1; Agricultural Tenancies Act 1995, s31(1)–(3); Landlord and Tenant (Covenants) Act 1995, s14(a), Schedules 1, 2; Trusts of Land and Appointment of Trustees Act 1996, ss5, 25(1), (2), Schedule 2, paras 1–4, Schedule 3, para 4, Schedule 4.]

LAND REGISTRATION ACT 1925
(15 & 16 Geo 5 c 21)

1 Registers to be continued [518]

(1) The Chief Land Registrar shall continue to keep a register of title to freehold land and leasehold land.

(2) The register need not be kept in documentary form.

2 What estates may be registered [519]

(1) After the commencement of this Act, estates capable of subsisting as legal estates shall be the only interests in land in respect of which a proprietor can be registered and all other interests in registered land (except overriding interests and interests entered on the register at or before such commencement) shall take effect in equity, as minor interests, but all interests (except undivided shares in land) entered on the register at such commencement which are not legal estates shall be capable of being dealt with under this Act: Provided that, on the occasion of the first dealing with any such interest, the register shall be rectified in such manner as may be provided by rules made to secure that the entries therein shall be similar to those which would have been made if the title to the land had been registered after the commencement of this Act.

(2) Subject as aforesaid, and save as otherwise expressly provided by this Act, this

Act applies to land registered under any enactment replaced by this Act in like manner as it applies to land registered under this Act.

3 Interpretation [520]

In this Act unless the context otherwise requires, the following expressions have the meanings hereby assigned to them respectively, that is to say –

(i) 'Charge by way of legal mortgage' means a mortgage created by charge under which, by virtue of the Law of Property Act 1925, the mortgagee is to be treated as an estate owner in like manner as if a mortgage term by demise or subdemise were vested in him, and 'legal mortgage' has the same meaning as in that Act;

(ii) 'the court' means the High Court or, where county courts have jurisdiction by virtue of rules made under section 138(1) of this Act, the county court;

(iv) 'Estate owner' means the owner of a legal estate, but an infant is not capable of being an estate owner;

(v) 'Gazette' means the London Gazette;

(vi) 'Income' includes rents and profits;

(vii) 'Instrument' does not include a statute, unless the statute creates a settlement;

(viii) 'Land' includes land of any tenure (including land, subject or not to manorial incidents, enfranchised under Part V of the Law of Property Act 1922), and mines and minerals, whether or not held with the surface, buildings or parts of buildings (whether the division is horizontal, vertical or made in any other way) and other corporeal hereditaments; also a manor, and a rent and other incorporeal hereditaments, and an easement, right, privilege, or benefit in, over, or derived from land; and 'hereditaments' mean real property which on an intestacy might, before the commencement of this Act, have devolved on an heir;

(ix) 'Land Charge' means a land charge of any class described in section 2 of the Land Charges Act 1972 or a local land charge;

(x) 'Lease' includes an under-lease and any tenancy or agreement for a lease, under-lease or tenancy;

(xi) 'Legal estate' means the estate interests and charges in or over land subsisting or created at law which are by the Law of Property Act 1925 authorised to subsist or to be created at law; and 'Equitable interests' mean all the other interests and charges in or over land; an equitable interest 'capable of subsisting at law' means such as could validly subsist at law if clothed with the legal estate;

(xii) 'Limitation Acts' mean the Real Property Limitation Acts 1833, 1837 and 1874, and any Acts amending those Acts;

(xiii) 'Manorial incidents' have the same meaning as in Part V of the Law of Property Act 1922;

(xiv) 'Mines and minerals' include any strata or seam of minerals or substances in or under any land, and powers of working and getting the same;

(xv) 'Minor interest' means the interests not capable of being disposed of or created by registered dispositions and capable of being overridden (whether or not a purchaser has notice thereof) by the proprietors unless protected as provided by this Act, and all rights and interests which are not registered or protected on the register and are not overriding interests, and include –

(a) in the case of land subject to a trust of land, all interests and powers which are under the Law of Property Act 1925 capable of being overridden by the trustees, whether or not such interests and powers are so protected; and

(b) in the case of settled land, all interests and powers which are under the

Settled Land Act 1925, and the Law of Property Act 1925, or either of them, capable of being overridden by the tenant for life or statutory owner, whether or not such interests and powers are so protected as aforesaid;

(xvi) 'Overriding interests' mean all the incumbrances, interests, rights, and powers not entered on the register but subject to which registered dispositions are by this Act to take effect, and in regard to land registered at the commencement of this Act include the matters which are by any enactment repealed by this Act declared not to be incumbrances;

(xvii) 'Personal representative' means the executor, original or by representation or administrator for the time being of a deceased person, and as regards any liability for the payment of death duties includes any person who takes possession of or intermeddles with the property of a deceased person without the authority of the personal representatives or the court; and where there are special personal representatives for the purposes of any settled land, it means, in relation to that land, those representatives;

(xviii) 'Possession' includes receipt of rents and profits or the right to receive the same, if any;

(xix) 'Prescribed' means prescribed by general rules made in pursuance of this Act;

(xx) 'Proprietor' means the registered proprietor for the time being of an estate in land or of a charge;

(xxi) 'Purchaser' means a purchaser in good faith for valuable consideration and includes a lessee, mortgagee, or other person who for valuable consideration acquires any interest in land or in any charge on land;

(xxii) 'Registered dispositions' mean dispositions which take effect under the powers conferred on the proprietor by way of transfer, charge, lease or otherwise and to which (when required to be registered) special effect or priority is given by this Act on registration;

(xxiii) 'Registered estate', in reference to land, means the legal estate, or other registered interest, if any, as respects which a person is for the time being registered as proprietor, but does not include a registered charge and a 'registered charge' includes a mortgage or incumbrance registered as a charge under this Act;

(xxiv) 'Registered land' means land or any estate or interest in land the title to which is registered under this Act or any enactment replaced by this Act, and includes any easement, right, privilege, or benefit which is appurtenant or appendant thereto, and any mines and minerals within or under the same and held therewith;

(xxv) 'Rent' includes a rent service or a rentcharge, or other rent, toll, duty, royalty, or annual or periodical payment, in money or money's worth, issuing out of or charged upon land, but does not include mortgage interest;

(xxvi) 'Settled land', 'settlement', 'tenant for life', 'statutory owner', 'trustees of the settlement', 'capital money', 'trust corporation', 'trust instrument', 'vesting deed', 'vesting order', 'vesting assent' and 'vesting instrument' have the same meanings as in the Settled Land Act 1925;

(xxvii) A 'term of years absolute' means a term of years, whether at a rent or not, taking effect either in possession or in reversion, with or without impeachment for waste, subject or not to another legal estate and either certain or liable to determination by notice, re-entry, operation of law, or by a provision for cesser on redemption, or in any other event (other than the dropping of a life, or the determination of a determinable life interest), but does not include any term of years determinable with life or lives or with the cesser of a determinable life interest, nor, if created after the commencement of this Act, a term of years which is not expressed to take effect in possession within twenty-one years after the creation thereof where required by the Law of Property Act 1925 to take effect within that period; and in this definition the expression 'term of years' includes a term for less than a year, or for a year or years and a fraction of a year or from year to year;

(xxx) 'United Kingdom' means Great Britain and Northern Ireland;

(xxxi) 'Valuable consideration' includes marriage, but does not include a nominal consideration in money;

(xxxii) 'Will' includes codicil.

18 Powers of disposition of registered freeholds   [521]

(1) Where the registered land is a freehold estate the proprietor may, in the prescribed manner, transfer the registered estate in the land or any part thereof, and, subject to any entry in the register to the contrary, may in the prescribed manner –

(a) transfer the fee simple in possession of all or any mines or minerals apart from the surface; or of the surface without all or any of the mines and minerals;

(b) grant an annuity or a rentcharge in possession (either perpetual or for a term of years absolute) in any form which sufficiently refers in the prescribed manner to the registered land charged;

(c) grant in fee simple in possession any easement, right, or privilege in, over, or derived from the registered land or any part thereof, in any form which sufficiently refers, in the prescribed manner, to the registered servient tenement and to the dominant tenement, whether being registered land or not;

(d) transfer the fee simple in possession of the registered land or any part thereof, subject to the creation thereout, by way of reservation, in favour of any person of an annuity or a rentcharge in possession (either perpetual or for a term of years absolute), or of any easement, right, or privilege in possession (either in fee simple or for a term of years absolute);

(e) grant (subject or not to the reservation of an easement, right, or privilege) a lease of the registered land or any part thereof, or of all or any mines and minerals apart from the surface, or of the surface without all or any of the mines and minerals, or of an easement, right or privilege in or over the land, or any part thereof, for any term of years absolute for any purpose (but where by way of mortgage subject to the provisions of this Act and the Law of Property Act 1925 relating thereto), and in any form which sufficiently refers, in the prescribed manner, to the registered land.

(2) A perpetual annuity or rentcharge in possession may be granted or reserved to any person with or without a power of re-entry, exercisable at any time, on default of payment thereof, or on breach of covenant, and shall have incidental thereto all the powers and remedies (as varied if at all by the disposition creating the rentcharge) for recovery thereof conferred by the Law of Property Act 1925; and where an easement, right, or privilege is reserved in a registered disposition for a legal estate, the reservation shall operate to create the same for the benefit of the land for the benefit of which the right is reserved.

(3) A lease for a term, not exceeding twenty-one years, to take effect in possession or within one year from the date thereof may be granted and shall take effect under this section notwithstanding that a caution, notice of deposit of a certificate, restriction, or inhibition (other than a bankruptcy inhibition) may be subsisting, but subject to the interests intended to be protected by any such caution, notice, restriction, or inhibition.

(4) The foregoing powers of disposition shall (subject to the express provisions of this Act and the Law of Property Act 1925 relating to mortgages) apply to dispositions by the registered proprietor by way of charge or mortgage; but no estate, other than a legal estate, shall be capable of being disposed of, or created under, this section.

(5) In this Act 'transfer' or 'disposition' when referring to registered freehold land includes any disposition authorised as aforesaid; and 'transferee' has a corresponding meaning.

19 Registration of disposition of freeholds [522]

(1) The transfer of the registered estate in the land or part thereof shall be completed by the registrar entering on the register the transferee as the proprietor of the estate transferred, but until such entry is made the transferor shall be deemed to remain proprietor of the registered estate; and, where part only of the land is transferred, notice thereof shall also be noted on the register.

(2) All interests transferred or created by dispositions by the proprietor, other than a transfer of the registered estate in the land, or part thereof, shall, subject to the provisions relating to mortgages, be completed by registration in the same manner and with the same effect as provided by this Act with respect to transfers of registered estates and notice thereof shall also be noted on the register: provided that nothing in this subsection –

(a) shall authorise the registration of a lease granted for a term not exceeding twenty-one years, or require the entry of a notice of such a lease; or
(b) shall authorise the registration of a mortgage term where there is a subsisting right of redemption; or
(c) shall render necessary the registration of any easement, right, or privilege except as appurtenant to registered land, or the entry of notice thereof except as against the registered title of the servient land.

Every such disposition shall, when registered, take effect as a registered disposition, and a lease made by the registered proprietor under the last foregoing section which is not required to be registered or noted on the register shall nevertheless take effect as if it were a registered disposition immediately on being granted.

(3) The general words implied in conveyances under the Law of Property Act 1925 shall apply, so far as applicable thereto, to dispositions of a registered estate.

20 Effect of registration and dispositions of freeholds [523]

(1) In the case of a freehold estate registered with an absolute title, a disposition of the registered land or of a legal estate therein, including a lease thereof, for valuable consideration shall, when registered, confer on the transferee or grantee an estate in fee simple or the term of years absolute or other legal estate expressed to be created in the land dealt with, together with all rights, privileges, and appurtenances belonging or appurtenant thereto, including (subject to any entry to the contrary in the register) the appropriate rights and interests which would, under the Law of Property Act 1925, have been transferred if the land had not been registered, subject –

(a) to the incumbrances and other entries, if any, appearing on the register and any charges for capital transfer tax subject to which the disposition takes effect under section 73 of this Act; and
(b) unless the contrary is expressed on the register, to the overriding interests, if any, affecting the estate transferred or created,

but free from all other estates and interests whatsoever, including estates and interests of His Majesty, and the disposition shall operate in like manner as if the registered transferor or grantor were (subject to any entry to the contrary in the register) entitled to the registered land in fee simple in possession for his own benefit.

(2) In the case of a freehold estate registered with a qualified title a disposition of the registered land or of a legal estate therein, including a lease thereof, for valuable consideration shall, when registered, have the same effect as it would have had if the land had been registered with an absolute title, save that such disposition shall not affect or prejudice the enforcement of any right or interest appearing by the register to be excepted.

(3) In the case of a freehold estate registered with a possessory title, a disposition of the registered land or of a legal estate therein, including a lease thereof, for valuable consideration shall not affect or prejudice the enforcement of any right or interest adverse to or in derogation of the title of the first registered proprietor, and subsisting or capable of arising at the time of the registration of such proprietor; but, save as aforesaid, shall when registered have the same effect as it would have had if the land had been registered with an absolute title.

(4) Where any such disposition is made without valuable consideration, it shall, so far as the transferee or grantee is concerned, be subject to any minor interests subject to which the transferor or grantor held the same, but, save as aforesaid, shall, when registered, in all respects, and in particular as respects any registered dealings on the part of the transferee or grantee, have the same effect as if the disposition had been made for valuable consideration.

21 Powers of disposition of registered leaseholds   [524]

(1) Where the registered land is a leasehold interest the proprietor may, in the prescribed manner, transfer the registered estate in the land or any part thereof, and, subject to any entry in the register to the contrary may in the prescribed manner –

(a) transfer all or any of the leasehold mines and minerals apart from the surface; or the surface without all or any of the leasehold mines and minerals;

(b) grant (to the extent of the registered estate) any annuity or rentcharge in possession, easement, right or privilege in, over, or derived from the registered land or any part thereof, in any form which sufficiently refers, in the prescribed manner, to the registered lease, and to the dominant tenement, whether being registered land or not;

(c) transfer the registered land or any part thereof subject to a reservation to any person of any such annuity, rentcharge, easement, right, or privilege;

(d) grant (subject or not to the reservation of an easement, right or privilege) an underlease of the registered land, or any part thereof, or of all or any mines and minerals apart from the surface, or of the surface without all or any of the mines and minerals, or of an easement, right or privilege, in or over the registered land or any part thereof, for any term of years absolute of less duration than the registered estate and for any purpose (but where by way of mortgage, subject to the provisions of this Act and of the Law of Property Act 1925 relating thereto), and in any form which sufficiently refers in the prescribed manner to the registered land, and in the case of an easement, right, or privilege, to the dominant tenement, whether being registered land or not.

(2) A disposition of registered leasehold land may be made subject to a rent legally apportioned in the prescribed manner, or to a rent not so apportioned.

(3) An underlease for a term, not exceeding twenty-one years, to take effect in possession or within one year from the date thereof, may be granted and shall take effect under this section, notwithstanding that a caution, notice of deposit of a certificate, restriction, or inhibition (other than a bankruptcy inhibition) may be subsisting, but subject to the interests intended to be protected by any such caution, notice, restriction or inhibition.

240

(4) The foregoing powers of disposition shall (subject to the express provisions of this Act and of the Law of Property Act 1925 relating to mortgages) apply to dispositions by the registered proprietor by way of charge or mortgage, but no estate, other than a legal estate, shall be capable of being disposed of or created under this section.

(5) In this Act 'transfer' or 'disposition' when referring to registered leasehold land includes any disposition authorised as aforesaid and 'transferee' has a corresponding meaning.

22 Registration of dispositions of leaseholds [525]

(1) A transfer of the registered estate in the land or part thereof shall be completed by the registrar entering on the register the transferee as proprietor of the estate transferred, but until such entry is made the transferor shall be deemed to remain the proprietor of the registered estate; and where part only of the land is transferred, notice thereof shall also be noted on the register.

(2) All interests transferred or created by dispositions by the registered proprietor other than the transfer of his registered estate in the land or in part thereof shall (subject to the provisions relating to mortgages) be completed by registration in the same manner and with the same effect as provided by this Act with respect to transfers of the registered estate, and notice thereof shall also be noted on the register in accordance with this Act: Provided that nothing in this subsection –

(a) shall authorise the registration of an underlease originally granted for a term not exceeding twenty-one years, or require the entry of a notice of such an underlease; or
(b) shall authorise the registration of a mortgage term where there is a subsisting right of redemption, or
(c) shall render necessary the registration of any easement, right, or privilege except as appurtenant to registered land, or the entry of notice thereof except as against the registered title of the servient land.

Every such disposition shall, when registered, take effect as a registered disposition, and an underlease made by the registered proprietor which is not required to be registered or noted on the register shall nevertheless take effect as if it were a registered disposition immediately on being granted.

(3) The general words implied in conveyances under the Law of Property Act 1925 shall apply, so far as applicable thereto, to transfers of a registered leasehold estate.

23 Effect of registration of dispositions of leaseholds [526]

(1) In the case of a leasehold estate registered with an absolute title, a disposition (including a subdemise thereof) for valuable consideration shall, when registered, be deemed to vest in the transferee or underlessee the estate transferred or created to the extent of the registered estate, or for the term created by the subdemise, as the case may require, with all implied or expressed rights, privileges, and appurtenances attached to the estate transferred or created, including (subject to any entry to the contrary on the register) the appropriate rights and interests which would under the Law of Property Act 1925 have been transferred if the land had not been registered, but subject as follows –

(a) To all implied and express covenants, obligations, and liabilities incident to the estate transferred or created; and
(b) To the incumbrances and other entries (if any) appearing on the register and any charge for capital transfer tax subject to which the disposition takes effect under section 73 of this Act; and

(c) Unless the contrary is expressed on the register, to the overriding interests, if any, affecting the estate transferred or created,

but free from all other estates and interests whatsoever, including estates and interests of His Majesty; and the transfer or subdemise shall operate in like manner as if the registered transferor or sublessor were (subject to any entry to the contrary on the register) absolutely entitled to the registered lease for his own benefit.

(2) In the case of a leasehold estate registered with a good leasehold title, a disposition (including a subdemise thereof) for valuable consideration shall, when registered, have the same effect as it would have had if the land had been registered with an absolute title, save that it shall not affect or prejudice the enforcement of any right or interest affecting or in derogation of the lessor to grant the lease.

(3) In the case of a leasehold estate registered with a qualified title, a disposition (including a subdemise thereof) for valuable consideration shall, when registered, have the same effect as it would have had if the land had been registered with an absolute title, save that such disposition shall not affect or prejudice the enforcement of any right or interest (whether in respect of the lessor's title or otherwise) appearing by the register to be excepted.

(4) In the case of a leasehold estate registered with a possessory title, a disposition (including a subdemise thereof) for valuable consideration shall not affect or prejudice the enforcement of any right or interest (whether in respect of the lessor's title or otherwise) adverse to or in derogation of the title of the first registered proprietor, and subsisting or capable of arising at the time of the registration of such proprietor, but save as aforesaid shall, when registered, have the same effect as it would have had if the land had been registered with an absolute title.

(5) Where any such disposition is made without valuable consideration it shall, so far as the transferee or underlessee is concerned, be subject to any minor interests subject to which the transferor or sublessor held the same; but, save as aforesaid, shall, when registered, in all respects, and in particular as respects any registered dealings on the part of the transferee or underlessee, have the same effect as if the disposition had been made for valuable consideration.

25 Proprietor's power to create charges   [527]

(1) The proprietor of any registered land may by deed –

(a) charge the registered land with the payment at an appointed time of any principal sum of money either with or without interest;
(b) charge the registered land in favour of a building society (within the meaning of the Building Societies Act 1986), in accordance with the rules of that society.

(2) A charge may be in any form provided that –

(a) the registered land comprised in the charge is described by reference to the register or in any other manner sufficient to enable the registrar to identify the same without reference to any other document;
(b) the charge does not refer to any other interest or charge affecting the land which –

(i) would have priority over the said and is not registered or protected on the register.
(ii) is not an overriding interest.

(3) Any provision contained in a charge which purports to –

(i) take away from the proprietor thereof the power of transferring it by registered disposition or of requiring the cessation thereof to be noted on the register; or

(ii) affect any registered land or charge other than that in respect of which the charge is to be expressly registered,

shall be void.

26 Registration of charges [528]

(1) The charge shall be completed by the registrar entering on the register the person in whose favour the charge is made as the proprietor of such charge, and the particulars of the charge.

(2) A charge may be registered notwithstanding that it contains any trust, power to appoint new trustees, or other provisions for giving effect to the security.

(3) Where the land, in respect of which a charge is registered, is registered with a good leasehold, qualified or possessory title, the charge shall take effect subject to the provisions of this Act with respect to land registered with such a title.

27 Terms of years implied in or granted by charges [529]

(1) A registered charge shall, unless made or taking effect by demise or subdemise, and subject to any provision to the contrary contained in the charge, take effect as a charge by way of legal mortgage.

(2) Subject to the provisions of the Law of Property Act 1925, a registered charge may contain in the case of freehold land, an express demise, and in the case of leasehold land an express subdemise of the land to the creditor for a term of years absolute, subject to a proviso for cesser on redemption.

(3) Any such demise or subdemise or charge by way of legal mortgage shall take effect from the date of the delivery of the deed containing the same, but subject to the estate or interest of any person (other than the proprietor of the land) whose estate or interest (whenever created) is registered or noted on the register before the date of registration of the charge.

(4) Any charge registered before the commencement of this Act shall take effect as a demise or subdemise of the land in accordance with the provisions of the Law of Property Act 1925, and the registered estate shall (without prejudice to any registered charge or any term or subterm created by a charge or by this Act) vest in the person appearing by the register to be entitled to the ultimate equity of redemption.

28 Implied covenants in charges [530]

(1) Where a registered charge is created on any land there shall be implied on the part of the person being proprietor of such land at the time of the creation of the charge, unless there be an entry on the register negativing such implication –

(a) a covenant with the proprietor for the time being of the charge to pay the principal sum charged, and interest, if any, thereon, at the appointed time and rate; and

(b) a covenant, if the principal sum of any part thereof is unpaid at the appointed time, to pay interest half-yearly at the appointed rate as well after as before any judgment is obtained in respect of the charge on so much of the principal sum as for the time being remains unpaid.

(2) Where a registered charge is created on any leasehold land there shall (in

addition to the covenants aforesaid) be implied on the part of the person being proprietor of such land at the time of the creation of the charge, unless there be an entry on the register negativing such implication, a covenant with the proprietor for the time being of the charge, that the person being proprietor of such land at the time of the creation of the charge, or the persons deriving title under him, will pay, perform, and observe the rent, covenants, and conditions, by and in the registered lease reserved and contained, and on the part of the lessee to be paid, performed, and observed, and will keep the proprietor of the charge, and the persons deriving title under him, indemnified against all proceedings, expenses, and claims, on account of the non-payment of the said rent, or any part thereof, or the breach of the said covenants or conditions, or any of them.

29 Priorities of registered charges [531]

Subject to any entry to the contrary on the register, registered charges on the same land shall as between themselves rank according to the order in which they are entered on the register, and not according to the order in which they are created.

35 Discharge of charges [532]

(1) The registrar shall, on the requisition of the proprietor of any charge, or on due proof of the satisfaction (whole or partial) thereof, notify on the register in the prescribed manner, by cancelling or varying the original entry or otherwise, the cessation (whole or partial) of the charge, and thereupon the charge shall be deemed to have ceased (in whole or in part) accordingly.

(2) On the notification on the register of the entire cessation of a registered charge, whether as to the whole or part only of the land affected thereby, the term or sub-term implied in or granted by the charge or by any deed or alteration, so far as it affects the land to which the discharge extends, shall merge and be extinguished in the registered estate in reversion without any surrender.

37 Powers of persons entitled to be registered [533]

(1) Where a person on whom the right to be registered as proprietor of registered land or of a registered charge has devolved by reason of the death of the proprietor, or has been conferred by a disposition or charge, in accordance with this Act, desires to dispose of or charge the land or to deal with the charge before he is himself registered as proprietor, he may do so in the prescribed manner, and subject to the prescribed conditions.

(2) Subject to the provisions of this Act with regard to registered dealings for valuable consideration, a disposition or charge so made shall have the same effect as if the person making it were registered as proprietor.

(3) Rules may be made for extending the provisions of this section to the case of any person entitled to be registered as first proprietor, and to any other case for which it may be deemed expedient to prescribe.

38 Certain provisions of the Law of Property Act to apply [534]

(1) The provisions as to the execution of a conveyance on sale contained in the Law of Property Act 1925 shall apply, so far as applicable thereto, to transfers on sale of registered land.

(2) Rules may be made for prescribing the effect of covenants implied by virtue of the Law of Property Act 1925 or Part I of the Law of Property (Miscellaneous Provisions) Act 1994 in dispositions of registered land.

39 Deeds off register, how far to be void [535]

(1) Where any transaction relating exclusively to registered land or to a registered charge is capable of being effected and is effected by a registered disposition, then, subject to any prescribed exceptions, any deed or instrument, other than the registered disposition, which is executed by the proprietor for the purpose of giving effect to the transaction shall be void, but only so far as the transaction is carried out by the registered disposition.

(2) Rules may be made for providing for cases in which any additional deed or instrument may be properly executed and for enabling the registrar to certify that in any special cases an additional deed or instrument will be proper and valid.

48 Registration of notice of lease [536]

(1) Any lessee or other person entitled to or interested in a lease of registered land, where the term grantee is not an overriding interest, may apply to the registrar to register notice of such lease in the prescribed manner, and when so registered, every proprietor and the persons deriving title under him shall be deemed to be affected with notice of such lease, as being an incumbrance on the registered land in respect of which the notice is entered: Provided that a proprietor of a charge or incumbrance registered or protected on the register prior to the registration of such notice shall not be deemed to be so affected by the notice unless such proprietor is, by reason of the lease having been made under a statutory or other power or by reason of his concurrence or otherwise, bound by the terms of the lease.

(2) In order to register notice of a lease, if the proprietor of the registered land affected does not concur in the registration thereof, the applicant shall obtain an order of the court authorising the registration of notice of the lease, and shall deliver the order to the registrar, accompanied with the original lease or a copy thereof, and thereupon the registrar shall make a notice in the register identifying the lease or copy so deposited, and the lease or copy so deposited shall be deemed to be the instrument of which notice is given; but if the proprietor concurs in the notice being registered, notice may be entered in such manner as may be agreed upon: Provided that, where the lease is binding on the proprietor of the land, neither the concurrence of such proprietor nor an order of the court shall be required.

49 Rules to provide for notices of other rights, [537]
interests and claims

(1) The provisions of the last foregoing section shall be extended by the rules so as to apply to the registration of notices of or of claims in respect of –

(a) The grant or reservation of any annuity or rentcharge in possession, either perpetual or for a term of years absolute.

(b) The severance of any mines or minerals from the surface, except where the mines and minerals severed are expressly included in the registration.

(c) Land charges until the land charge is registered as a registered charge.

(d) The right of any person interested in land subject to a trust of land or in land subject to a settlement to require that (unless a trust corporation is acting as trustee) there shall be at least two trustees of the trust or settlement.

(e) The rights of any widow in respect of dower or under the Intestates' Estates Act 1890, and any right to free bench or other like right saved by any statute coming into force concurrently with this Act (which rights shall take effect in equity as minor interests).

(f) Creditors' notices and any other right, interest, or claim which it may be deemed expedient to protect by notice instead of by caution, inhibition, or restriction.

(g) Charging orders (within the meaning of the Charging Orders Act 1979, the Criminal Justice Act 1988 or the Drug Trafficking Act 1994, or regulations under paragraph 11 of Schedule 4 to the Local Government Finance Act 1988, or regulations under paragraph 11 of Schedule 4 to the Local Government Finance Act 1992) which in the case of unregistered land may be protected by registration under the Land Charges Act 1972 and which, notwithstanding section 59 of this Act, it may be deemed expedient to protect by notice instead of by caution.

(h) Acquisition orders (within the meaning of Part III of the Landlord and Tenant Act 1987) which in the case of unregistered land may be protected by registration under the Land Charges Act 1972 and which, notwithstanding section 59 of this Act, it may be deemed expedient to protect by notice instead of by caution.

(j) Access orders under the Access to Neighbouring Land Act 1992 which, notwithstanding section 59 of this Act, it may be deemed expedient to protect by notice instead of by caution.

(k) Orders made under section 26(1) or 50(1) of the Leasehold Reform, Housing and Urban Development Act 1993 which in the case of unregistered land may be protected by registration under the Land Charges Act 1972 and which, notwithstanding section 59 of this Act, it may be deemed expedient to protect by notice instead of by caution.

(2) A notice shall not be registered in respect of any estate, right, or interest which (independently of this Act) is capable of being overridden by the proprietor under a trust of land or the powers of the Settled Land Act 1925, or any other statute, or of a settlement, and of being protected by a restriction in the prescribed manner: provided that notice of such an estate right or interest may be lodged pending the appointment of trustees of land, or trustees of a settlement, and if so lodged, shall be cancelled if and when the appointment is made and the proper restriction (if any) is entered.

(3) A notice when registered in respect of a right, interest, or claim shall not affect prejudicially –

(a) The powers of disposition of the personal representative of the deceased under whose will or by the operation of whose intestacy the right, interest, or claim arose; or

(b) The powers of disposition (independently of this Act) of a proprietor holding the registered land subject to a trust of land.

52 Effect of notices   [538]

(1) A disposition by the proprietor shall take effect subject to all estates, rights, and claims which are protected by way of notice on the register at the date of the registration or entry of notice of the disposition, but only if and so far as such estates, rights, and claims may be valid and are not (independently of this Act) overridden by the disposition.

(2) Where notice of a claim is entered on the register, such entry shall operate by way of notice only, and shall not operate to render the claim valid whether made adversely to or for the benefit of the registered land or charge.

53 Cautions against first registration   [539]

(1) Any person having or claiming such an interest in land not already registered as entitles him to object to any disposition thereof being made without his

consent, may lodge a caution with the registrar to the effect that the cautioner is entitled to notice in the prescribed form, and to be served in the prescribed manner, of any application that may be made for the registration of an interest in the land affecting the right of the cautioner.

(2) The caution shall be supported by an affidavit or declaration in the prescribed form, stating the nature of the interest of the cautioner, the land and estate therein to be affected by such caution, and such other matters as may be prescribed.

(3) After a caution has been lodged in respect of any estate, which has not already been registered, registration shall not be made of such estate until notice has been served on the cautioner to appear and oppose, if he thinks fit, such registration, and the prescribed time has elapsed since the date of the service of such notice, or the cautioner has entered an appearance, whichever may first happen.

54 Cautions against dealings [540]

(1) Any person interested under any unregistered instrument, or interested as a judgment creditor, or otherwise howsoever, in any land or charge registered in the name of any other person, may lodge a caution with the registrar to the effect that no dealing with such land or charge on the part of the proprietor is to be registered until notice has been served upon the cautioner: Provided that a person whose estate, right, interest, or claim has been registered or protected by a notice or restriction shall not be entitled (except with the consent of the registrar) to lodge a caution in respect of such estate, right, interest, or claim.

(2) A caution lodged under this section shall be supported by such evidence as may be prescribed.

55 Effect of cautions against dealings [541]

(1) After any such caution against dealings has been lodged in respect of any registered land or charge, the registrar shall not, without the consent of the cautioner, register any dealing or make any entry on the register for protecting the rights acquired under a deposit of a land or charge certificate or other dealing by the proprietor with such land or charge until he has served notice on the cautioner, warning him that his caution will cease to have any effect after the expiration of the prescribed number of days next following the date at which such notice is served; and after the expiration of such time as aforesaid the caution shall cease unless an order to the contrary is made by the registrar, and upon the caution so ceasing the registered land or charge may be dealt with in the same manner as if no caution had been lodged.

(2) If before the expiration of the said period the cautioner, or some person on his behalf, appears before the registrar, and where so required by the registrar gives sufficient security to indemnify every party against any damage that may be sustained by reason of any dealing with the registered land or charge, or the making of any such entry as aforesaid, being delayed, the registrar may thereupon, if he thinks fit to do so, delay registering any dealing with the land or charge or making any such entry for such period as he thinks just.

56 General provisions as to cautions [542]

(1) Any person aggrieved by an act done by the registrar in relation to a caution under this Act may appeal to the court in the prescribed manner.

(2) A caution lodged in pursuance of this Act shall not prejudice the claim or title of any person and shall have no effect whatever except as in this Act mentioned.

(3) If any person lodges a caution with the registrar without reasonable cause, he shall be liable to make to any person who may have sustained damage by the lodging of the caution such compensation as may be just, and such compensation shall be recoverable as a debt by the person who has sustained damage from the person who lodged the caution.

(4) The personal representative of a deceased cautioner may consent or object to registration or a dealing in the same manner as the cautioner.

57 Power for court or registrar to inhibit   [543]
registered dealings

(1) The court, or, subject to an appeal to the court, the registrar, upon the application of any person interested, made in the prescribed manner, in relation to any registered land or charge, may, after directing such inquiries (if any) to be made and notices to be given and hearing such persons as the court or registrar thinks expedient, issue an order or make an entry inhibiting for a time, or until the occurrence of an event to be named in such order or entry, or generally until further order or entry, the registration or entry of any dealing with any registered land or registered charge.

(2) The court or registrar may make or refuse to make any such order or entry, and annex thereto any terms or conditions the court or registrar may think fit, and discharge such order or cancel such entry when granted, with or without costs, and generally act in the premises in such manner as the justice of the case requires.

(3) Any person aggrieved by any act done by the registrar in pursuance of this section may appeal to the court in the prescribed manner.

(4) The court or the registrar may, in lieu of an inhibition, order a notice or restriction to be placed on the register.

58 Power to place restrictions on register   [544]

(1) Where the proprietor of any registered land or charge desires to place restrictions on transferring or charging the land or on disposing of or dealing with the land or charge in any manner in which he is by this Act authorised to dispose of or deal with it, or on the deposit by way of security of any certificate, the proprietor may apply to the registrar to make an entry in the register that no transaction to which the application relates shall be effected, unless the following things, or such of them as the proprietor may determine, are done –

    (a) unless notice of an application for the transaction is transmitted by post to such address as he may specify to the registrar;
    (b) unless the consent of some person or persons, to be named by the proprietor, is given to the transaction;
    (c) unless some such other matter or thing is done as may be required by the applicant and approved by the registrar:

Provided that no restriction under this section shall extend or apply to dispositions of or dealings with minor interests.

(2) The registrar shall thereupon, if satisfied of the right of the applicant to give the directions, enter the requisite restrictions on the register, and no transaction to which the restriction relates shall be effected except in conformity therewith; but it shall not be the duty of the registrar to enter any such restriction, except upon such terms as to payment of fees and otherwise as may be prescribed, or to enter any restriction that the registrar may deem unreasonable or calculated to cause inconvenience.

(3) In the case of joint proprietors the restriction may be to the effect that when the number of proprietors is reduced below a certain specified number no disposition shall be registered except under an order of the court, or of the registrar after inquiry into title, subject to appeal to the court, and, subject to general rules, such an entry under this subsection as may be prescribed, shall be obligatory unless it is shown to the registrar's satisfaction that the joint proprietors are entitled for their own benefit, or can give valid receipts for capital money, or that one of them is a trust corporation.

(4) Any such restrictions, except such as are in this section declared to be obligatory, may at any time be withdrawn or modified at the instance of all the persons for the time being appeared by the register to be interested in such directions, and shall also be liable to be set aside by an order of the court.

(5) Rules may be made to enable applications to be made for the entry of restrictions by persons other than the proprietor.

59 Writs, orders, deeds of arrangement, pending [545] actions, etc

(1) A writ, order, deed of arrangement, pending action, or other interest which in the case of unregistered land may be protected by registration under the Land Charges Act 1925, shall, where the land affected or the charge securing the debt affected is registered, be protected only by lodging a creditor's notice, a bankruptcy inhibition or a caution against dealings with the land or the charge.

(2) Registration of a land charge (other than a local land charge) shall, where the land affected is registered, be effected only by registering under this Act a notice caution or other prescribed entry: Provided that before a land charge including a local land charge affecting registered land (being a charge to secure money) is realised, it shall be registered and take effect as a registered charge under this Act in the prescribed manner, without prejudice to the priority conferred by the land charge.

(4) When a land charge protected by notice has been discharged as to all or any part of the land comprised therein, the notices relating thereto and to all devolutions of and dealings therewith shall be vacated as to the registered land affected by the discharge.

(5) The foregoing provisions of this section shall apply only to writs and orders, deeds of arrangement, pending actions and land charges which if the land were unregistered would for purposes of protection be required to be registered or re-registered after the commencement of this Act under the Land Charges Act 1925; and for the purposes of this section a land charge does not include a puisne mortgage.

(6) Subject to the provisions of this Act relating to fraud and to the title of a trustee in bankruptcy, a purchaser acquiring title under a registered disposition, shall not be concerned with any pending action, writ, order, deed of arrangement, or other document, matter, or claim (not being an overriding interest or a charge for capital transfer tax subject to which the disposition takes effect under section 73 of this Act) which is not protected by a caution or other entry on the register, whether he has or has not notice thereof, express, implied, or constructive.

(7) In this section references to registration under the Land Charges Act 1925 apply to any registration made under any other statute which, in the case of unregistered land, is by the Land Charges Act 1925 to have effect as if the registration had been made under that Act.

63 Issue of land and charge certificates   [546]

(1) On the first registration of a freehold or leasehold interest in land, and on the registration of a charge, a land certificate, or charge certificate, as the case may be, shall be prepared in the prescribed form; it shall state whether the title is absolute, good leasehold, qualified or possessory, and it shall be either delivered to the proprietor or deposited in the registry as the proprietor may prefer.

(2) If so deposited in the registry it shall be officially endorsed from time to time, as in this Act provided, with notes of all subsequent entries in the register affecting the registered land or charge to which it relates.

(3) The proprietor may at any time apply for the delivery of the certificate to himself or to such person as he may direct, and may at any time again deposit it in the land registry.

(4) The preparation, issue, endorsement, and deposit in the registry of the certificate shall be effected without cost to the proprietor.

66 Creation of liens by deposit of certificates   [547]

The proprietor of any registered land or charge may, subject to the overriding interests, if any, to any entry to the contrary on the register, and to any estates, interests, charges, or rights registered or protected on the register at the date of the deposit, create a lien on the registered land or charge by deposit of the land certificate or charge certificate; and such lien shall, subject as aforesaid, be equivalent to a lien created in the case of unregistered land by the deposit of documents of title or of the mortgage deed by an owner entitled for his own benefit to the registered estate, or a mortgage beneficially entitled to the mortgage, as the case may be.

69 Effect of registration on the legal estate   [548]

(1) The proprietor of land (whether he was registered before or after the commencement of this Act) shall be deemed to have vested in him without any conveyance, where the registered land is freehold, the legal estate in fee simple in possession, and where the registered land is leasehold the legal term created by the registered lease, but subject to the overriding interests, if any, including any mortgage term or charge by way of legal mortgage created by or under the Law of Property Act 1925, or this Act or otherwise which has priority to the registered estate.

(2) Where any legal estate or term left outstanding at the date of first registration (whether before or after the commencement of this Act), or disposed of or created under section forty-nine of the Land Transfer Act 1875, before the commencement of this Act, becomes satisfied, or the proprietor of the land becomes entitled to require the same to be vested in or surrendered to him, and the entry, if any, for protecting the same on the register has been cancelled, the same shall thereupon, without any conveyance, vest in the proprietor of the land, as if the same had been conveyed or surrendered to him as the case may be.

(3) If and when any person is registered as first proprietor of land in a compulsory area after the commencement of this Act, the provisions of the Law of Property Act 1925 for getting in legal estates shall apply to any legal estate in the land which was expressed to be conveyed or created in favour of a purchaser or lessee before the commencement of this Act but which failed to pass or to be created by reason of the omission of such purchaser or lessee to be registered as proprietor of the land under the Land Transfer Acts 1875 and 1897, and shall operate to vest that legal estate in the person so registered as proprietor on his registration, but subject to any mortgage term or charge by way of legal mortgage having priority thereto.

(4) The estate for the time being vested in the proprietor shall only be capable of being disposed of or dealt with by him in manner authorised by this Act.

(5) Nothing in this section operates to render valid a lease registered with possessory or good leasehold title.

70 Liability of registered land to overriding interests [549]

(1) All registered land shall, unless under the provisions of this Act the contrary is expressed on the register, be deemed to be subject to such of the following overriding interests as may be for the time being subsisting in reference thereto, and such interests shall not be treated as incumbrances within the meaning of this Act, (that is to say) –

(a) Rights of common, drainage rights, customary rights (until extinguished), public rights, profits à prendre, rights of sheepwalk, rights of way, watercourses, rights of water, and other easements not being equitable easements required to be protected by notice on the register;

(b) Liability to repair highways by reason of tenure, quit-rents, crown rents, heriots, and other rents and charges (until extinguished) having their origin in tenure;

(c) Liability to repair the chancel of any church;

(d) Liability in respect of embankments, and sea and river walls;

(e) Payments in lieu of tithe, and charges or annuities payable for the redemption of tithe rentcharges;

(f) Subject to the provisions of this Act, rights acquired or in course of being acquired under the Limitation Acts;

(g) The rights of every person in actual occupation of the land or in receipt of the rents and profits thereof, save where enquiry is made of such person and the rights are not disclosed;

(h) In the case of a possessory, qualified, or good leasehold title, all estates, rights, interests, and powers excepted from the effect of registration;

(i) Rights under local land charges unless and until registered or protected on the register in the prescribed manner;

(j) Rights of fishing and sporting, seignorial and manorial rights of all descriptions (until extinguished), and franchises;

(k) Leases granted for a term not exceeding twenty-one years;

(l) In respect of land registered before the commencement of this Act, rights to mines and minerals, and rights of entry, search, and user, and other rights and reservations incidental to or required for the purpose of giving full effect to the enjoyment of rights to mines and minerals or of property in mines or minerals, being rights which, where the title was first registered before the first day of January, eighteen hundred and ninety-eight, were created before that date, and where the title was first registered after the thirty-first day of December, eighteen hundred and ninety-seven, were created before the date of first registration;

(m) Any interest or right which is an overriding interest by virtue of paragraph 1(1) of Schedule 9 to the Coal Industry Act 1994:

Provided that, where it is proved to the satisfaction of the registrar that any land registered or about to be registered is exempt from land tax, or tithe rentcharge or payments in lieu of tithe, or from charges or annuities payable for the redemption of tithe rentcharge, the registrar may notify the fact on the register in the prescribed manner.

(2) Where at the time of first registration any easement, right, privilege, or benefit created by an instrument and appearing on the title adversely affects the land, the registrar shall enter a note thereof on the register.

(3) Where the existence of any overriding interest mentioned in this section is proved to the satisfaction of the registrar or admitted, he may (subject to any prescribed exceptions) enter notice of the same or of a claim thereto on the register, but no claim to an easement, right, or privilege not created by an instrument shall be noted against the title to the servient land if the proprietor of such land (after the prescribed notice is given to him) shows sufficient cause to the contrary.

(4) Neither subsection (2) nor subsection (3) of this section shall apply in the case of any such interest or right as is mentioned in subsection (1)(m) of this section.

71 Dispositions by virtue of overriding interests   [550]

Where by virtue of any interest or power which is an overriding interest a mortgagee or other person disposes of any estate, charge, or right in or upon a registered estate, and the disposition is capable of being registered, the registrar shall, if so required, give effect to the disposition on the register.

74 Notice of trust not to affect registered dealing   [551]

Subject to the provisions of this Act as to settled land, neither the registrar nor any person dealing with a registered estate or charge shall be affected with notice of a trust express implied or constructive, and references to trusts shall, so far as possible, be excluded from the register.

75 Acquisition of title by possession   [552]

(1) The Limitation Acts shall apply to registered land in the same manner and to the same extent as those Acts apply to land not registered, except that where, if the land were not registered, the estate of the person registered as proprietor would be extinguished, such estate shall not be extinguished but shall be deemed to be held by the proprietor for the time being in trust for the person who, by virtue of the said Acts, has acquired title against any proprietor, but without prejudice to the estates and interests of any other person interested in the land whose estate or interest is not extinguished by those Acts.

(2) Any person claiming to have acquired a title under the Limitation Acts to a registered estate in the land may apply to be registered as proprietor thereof.

(3) The registrar shall, on being satisfied as to the applicant's title, enter the applicant as proprietor either with absolute, good leasehold, qualified, or possessory title, as the case may require, but without prejudice to any estate or interest protected by any entry on the register which may not have been extinguished under the Limitation Acts, and such registration shall, subject as aforesaid, have the same effect as the registration of a first proprietor; but the proprietor or the applicant or any other person interested may apply to the court for the determination of any question arising under this section.

(5) Rules may be made for applying (subject to any necessary modifications) the provisions of this section to cases where an easement, right or privilege has been acquired by prescription.

76 Description of registered land   [553]

Registered land may be described –

(a) by means of a verbal description and a filed plan or general map, based on the ordnance map; or
(b) by reference to a deed or other document, a copy or extract whereof is

filed at the registry, containing a sufficient description, and a plan or map thereof; or

(c) otherwise as the applicant for registration may desire, and the registrar, or, if the applicant prefers, the court, may approve,

regard being had to ready identification of parcels, correct descriptions of boundaries, and, so far as may be, uniformity of practice; but the boundaries of all freehold land and all requisite details in relation to the same shall, whenever practicable, be entered on the register or filed plan, or general map, and the filed plan, if any, or general map shall be used for assisting the identification of the land.

77 Conversion of title [554]

(1) Where land is registered with a good leasehold title, or satisfies the conditions for such registration under this section, the registrar may, and on application by the proprietor shall, if he is satisfied as to the title to the freehold and the title to any intermediate leasehold, enter the title as absolute.

(2) Where land is registered with a possessory title, the registrar may, and on application by the proprietor shall –

(a) if he is satisfied as to the title, or

(b) if the land has been so registered for at least twelve years and he is satisfied that the proprietor is in possession,

enter the title in the case of freehold land as absolute and in the case of leasehold land as good leasehold.

(3) Where land is registered with a qualified title, the registrar may, and on application by the proprietor shall, if he is satisfied as to title, enter it in the case of freehold land as absolute and in the case of leasehold land as good leasehold.

(4) If any claim adverse to the title of the proprietor has been made, an entry shall not be made in the register under this section unless and until the claim has been disposed of.

(5) No fee shall be charged for the making of an entry in the register under this section at the instance of the registrar or on an application by the proprietor made in connection with a transfer for valuable consideration of the land to which the application relates.

(6) Any person, other than the proprietor, who suffers loss by reason of any entry on the register made by virtue of this section shall be entitled to be indemnified under this Act as if a mistake had been made in the register.

80 Bona vacantia and forfeiture [555]

Subject to the express provisions of this Act relating to the effect of first registration of title and the effect of registration of a disposition for valuable consideration, nothing in this Act affects any right of His Majesty to any bona vacantia or forfeiture.

82 Rectification of the register [556]

(1) The register may be rectified pursuant to an order of the court or by the registrar, subject to an appeal to the court, in any of the following cases, but subject to the provisions of this section –

(a) Subject to any express provision of this Act to the contrary, where a court of competent jurisdiction has decided that any person is entitled to any estate right or interest in or to any registered land or charge, and as a consequence of such decision such court is of opinion that a rectification of the register is required, and makes an order to that effect;

(b) Subject to any express provisions of this Act to the contrary, where the court, on the application in the prescribed manner of any person who is aggrieved by any entry made in, or by the omission of any entry from, the register, or by any default being made, or unnecessary delay taking place, in the making of any entry in the register, makes an order for the rectification of the register;

(c) In any case and at any time with the consent of all persons interested;

(d) Where the court or the registrar is satisfied that any entry in the register has been obtained by fraud;

(e) Where two or more persons are, by mistake, registered as proprietors of the same registered estate or of the same charge;

(f) Where a mortgagee has been registered as proprietor of the land instead of as proprietor of a charge and a right of redemption is subsisting;

(g) Where a legal estate has been registered in the name of a person who if the land had not been registered would not have been the estate owner; and

(h) In any other case where, by reason of any error or omission in the register, or by reason of any entry made under a mistake, it may be deemed just to rectify the register.

(2) The register may be rectified under this section, notwithstanding that the rectification may affect any estates, rights, charges, or interests acquired or protected by registration, or by any entry on the register, or otherwise.

(3) The register shall not be rectified, except for the purpose of giving effect to an overriding interest or an order of the court, so as to affect the title of the proprietor who is in possession –

(a) unless the proprietor has caused or substantially contributed to the error or omission by fraud or lack of proper care; or

(c) unless for any other reason, in any particular case, it is considered that it would be unjust not to rectify the register against him.

(4) Where a person is in possession of registered land in right of a minor interest, he shall, for the purposes of this section, be deemed to be in possession as agent for the proprietor.

(5) The registrar shall obey the order of any competent court in relation to any registered land on being served with the order or an official copy thereof.

(6) On every rectification of the register the land certificate and any charge certificate which may be affected shall be produced to the registrar unless an order to the contrary is made by him.

83 Right to indemnity in certain cases   [557]

(1) Subject to the provisions of this Act to the contrary, any person suffering loss by reason of any rectification of the register under this Act shall be entitled to be indemnified.

(2) Where an error or omission has occurred in the register, but the register is not rectified, any person suffering loss by reason of such error or omission shall, subject to the provisions of this Act, be entitled to be indemnified.

(3) Where any person suffers loss by reason of the loss or destruction of any document lodged at the registry for inspection or safe custody or by reason of an error in any official search, he shall be entitled to be indemnified under this Act.

(4) Subject as hereinafter provided, a proprietor of any registered land or charge claiming in good faith under a forged disposition shall, where the register is

rectified, be deemed to have suffered loss by reason of such rectification and shall be entitled to be indemnified under this Act.

(5) No indemnity shall be payable under this Act in any of the following cases –

(a) Where the applicant or a person from whom he derives title (otherwise than under a disposition for valuable consideration which is registered or protected on the register) has caused or substantially contributed to the loss by fraud or lack of proper care;

(b) On account of any mines or minerals or of the existence of any rights to work or get mines or minerals, unless a note is entered on the register that the mines or minerals are included in the registered title;

(c) On account of costs incurred in taking or defending any legal proceedings without the consent of the registrar.

(6) Where an indemnity is paid in respect of the loss of an estate or interest in or charge on land the amount so paid shall not exceed –

(a) Where the register is not rectified, the value of the estate, interest or charge at the time when the error or omission which caused the loss was made;

(b) Where the register is rectified, the value (if there had been no rectification) of the estate, interest or charge, immediately before the time of rectification.

(8) Subject to subsection (5)(c) of this section, as amended by section 2(2) of the Land Registration and Land Charges Act 1971 [costs of application for determination of amount of any indemnity] –

(a) an indemnity under any provision of this Act shall include such amount, if any, as may be reasonable in respect of any costs or expenses properly incurred by the applicant in relation to the matter; and

(b) an applicant for an indemnity under any such provision shall be entitled to an indemnity thereunder of such amount, if any, as may be reasonable in respect of any such costs or expenses, notwithstanding that no other indemnity money is payable thereunder.

(9) Where indemnity is paid for a loss, the registrar, on behalf of the Crown, shall be entitled to recover the amount paid for any person who has caused or substantially contributed to the loss by his fraud.

(10) The registrar shall be entitled to enforce, on behalf of the Crown, any express or implied covenant or other right which the person who is indemnified would have been entitled to enforce in relation to the matter in respect of which indemnity has been paid.

(11) A liability to pay indemnity under this Act shall be deemed a simple contract debt; and for the purposes of the Limitation Act 1980, the cause of action shall be deemed to arise at the time when the claimant knows, or but for his own default might have known, of the existence of his claim: Provided that, when a claim to indemnity arises in consequence of the registration of an estate in land with an absolute or good leasehold title, the claim shall be enforceable only if made within six years from the date of such registration, except in the following cases –

(a) Where at the date of registration the person interested is an infant, the claim by him may be made within six years from the time he attains full age;

(b) In the case of settled land, or land subject to a trust of land, a claim by a person interested in remainder or reversion, may be made within six years from the time when his interest falls into possession;

(c) Where a claim arises in respect of a restrictive covenant or agreement affecting freehold land which by reason of notice or the registration of a land charge or otherwise was binding on the first proprietor at the time of first registration, the claim shall only be enforceable within six years from the breach of the covenant or agreement;

(d) Where any person interested is entitled as a proprietor of a charge or as a mortgagee protected by a caution in the specially prescribed form, the claim by him may be made within six years from the last payment in respect of principal or interest.

(12) This section applies to the Crown in like manner as it applies to a private person.

84 Application of indemnity in case of settled land [558]

Where any indemnity is paid in respect of settled land, and not in respect of any particular estate, remainder, or reversion therein, the money shall be paid to the trustees of the settlement and held by them as capital money for the purpose of the Settled Land Act 1925 arising from the settled land.

86 Registration of settled land [559]

(1) Settled land shall be registered in the name of the tenant for life or statutory owner.

(2) The successive or other interests created by or arising under a settlement shall (save as regards any legal estate which cannot be overridden under the powers of the Settled Land Act 1925, or any other statute) take effect as minor interests and not otherwise; and effect shall be given thereto by the proprietor of the settled land as provided by statute with respect to the estate owner, with such adaptations, if any, as may be prescribed in the case of registered land by rules made under this Act.

(3) There shall also be entered on the register such restrictions as may be prescribed, or may be expedient, for the protection of the rights of the persons beneficially interested in the land, and such restrictions shall (subject to the provisions of this Act relating to releases by the trustees of a settlement and to transfers by a tenant for life whose estate has ceased in his lifetime) be binding on the proprietor during his life, but shall not restrain or otherwise affect a disposition by his personal representative.

(4) Where land already registered is acquired with capital money, the same shall be transferred by a transfer in a specially prescribed form to the tenant for life or statutory owner, and such transfer shall state the names of the persons who are trustees of the settlement for the purposes of the Settled Land Act 1925, and contain an application to register the prescribed restrictions applicable to the case; a transfer made in the specially prescribed form shall be deemed to comply with the requirements of that Act, respecting vesting deeds; and where no capital money is paid but land already registered is to be made subject to a settlement, it shall not be necessary for the trustees of the settlement to concur in the transfer.

References in this Act to the 'tenant for life' shall, where the context admits, be read as referring to the tenant for life, statutory owner, or personal representative who is entitled to be registered.

93 As to persons in a fiduciary position [560]

A person in a fiduciary position may apply for, or concur in, or assent to, any registration authorised by the provisions of this Act, and, if he is a proprietor, may execute a charge or other disposition in favour of any person whose registration is so authorised.

94 Land held in trust   [561]

(1) Where registered land is subject to a trust of land, the land shall be registered in the names of the trustees.

(2) Where an order obtained under section seven of the Settled Land Act 1884 is in force at the commencement of this Act, the person authorised by the order to exercise any of the powers conferred by the Settled Land Act 1925 may, in the names and on behalf of the proprietors, do all such acts and things under this Act as may be requisite for giving effect on the register to the powers authorised to be exercised in like manner as if such person were registered as proprietor of the land, and a copy of the order shall be filed at the registry.

(3) Where, by virtue of any statute, registered land is made subject to a trust of land, the trustees (unless already registered) shall be registered as proprietors thereof, and shall in the prescribed manner apply for registration accordingly, and no fee shall be charged in respect of such registration or consequential alteration of the register, but this subsection has effect subject to the provisions of this Act relating to the registration of the Public Trustee and the removal of an undivided share from the register before the title to the entirety of the land is registered.

(4) There shall also be entered on the register such restrictions as may be prescribed, or may be expedient, for the protection of the rights of the persons beneficially interested in the land.

(5) Where a deed has been executed under section 16(4) of the Trusts of Land and Appointment of Trustees Act 1996 by trustees of land the registrar is entitled to assume that, as from the date of the deed, the land to which the deed relates is not subject to the trust unless he has actual notice that the trustees were mistaken in their belief that the land was conveyed to beneficiaries absolutely entitled to the land under the trust and of full age and capacity.

95 Restriction on number of trustees   [562]

The statutory restrictions affecting the number of persons entitled to hold land in trust and the number of trustees of a settlement apply to registered land.

98 Land subject to charitable trusts   [563]

Where an application is made to register a legal estate in land subject to charitable trusts and that estate is vested in the official custodian for charities, he shall, notwithstanding that the powers of disposition are vested in the managing trustees or committee, be registered as proprietor thereof.

101 Dispositions off register creating 'minor interests'   [564]

(1) Any person, whether being the proprietor or not, having a sufficient interest or power in or over registered land, may dispose of or deal with the same, and create any interests or rights therein which are permissible in like manner and by the like modes of assurance in all respects as if the land were not registered, but subject as provided by this section.

(2) All interests and rights disposed of or created under subsection (1) of this section (whether by the proprietor or any other person) shall, subject to the provisions of this section, take effect as minor interests, and be capable of being overridden by registered dispositions for valuable consideration.

(3) Minor interests shall, subject to the express exceptions contained in this section, take effect only in equity, but may be protected by entry on the register of

such notices, cautions, inhibitions and restrictions as are provided for by this Act or rules.

(4) A minor interest in registered land subsisting or capable of taking effect at the commencement of this Act, shall not fail or become invalid by reason of the same being converted into an equitable interest; but after such commencement a minor interest in registered land shall only be capable of being validly created in any case in which an equivalent equitable interest could have been validly created if the land had not been registered.

(5) Where after the commencement of this Act, the proprietor of the registered estate which is settled, disposes of or deals with his beneficial interest in possession in favour of a purchaser, and accordingly the minor interest disposed of or created would, but for the restrictions imposed by the Law of Property Act 1925 and this section, on the creation of legal estates, have been a legal estate, the purchaser (subject as provided by the next following section in regard to priorities) may exercise all such rights and remedies as he might have exercised had the minor interest been a legal estate, and the reversion (if any) on any leases or tenancies derived out of the registered estate had been vested in him.

(6) A minor interest created under this section does not operate to prevent a registered estate passing to the personal representative of a deceased proprietor, or to the survivor or survivors of two or more joint proprietors, nor does this section affect the right of any person entitled to an overriding interest, or having any power to dispose of or create an overriding interest, to dispose of or create the same.

102 Priorities as between minor interests [565]

(1) If a minor interest subsisting or capable of taking effect at the commencement of this Act would, if the Law of Property Acts 1922 and 1925 and this Act had not been passed have taken effect as a legal estate, then (subject and without prejudice to the estate and powers of the proprietor whose estate is affected) the conversion thereof into an equitable interest shall not affect its priority over other minor interests.

103 Obligation to give effect on the register to certain [566] minor interests

(1) Where by the operation of any statute or statutory or other power, or by virtue of any vesting order of any court or other competent authority, or an order appointing a person to convey, or of a vesting declaration (express or implied) or of an appointment or other assurance, a minor interest in the registered land is disposed of or created which would, if registered, be capable of taking effect as a legal estate or charge by way of legal mortgage, then –

(i) if the estate owner would, had the land not been registered, have been bound to give effect thereto by conveying or creating a legal estate or charge by way of legal mortgage, the proprietor shall, subject to proper provision being made for payment of costs, be bound to give legal effect to the transaction by a registered disposition:

(ii) if the proprietor is unable or refuses to make the requisite disposition or cannot be found, or if for any other reason a disposition by him cannot be obtained within a reasonable time, or if, had the land not been registered, no conveyance by the estate owner would have been required to give legal effect to the transaction, the registrar shall give effect thereto in the prescribed manner in like manner and with the like consequences as if the transaction had been carried out by a registered disposition:

Provided that –

(a) So long as the proprietor has power under the Settled Land Act 1925, or any other statute conferring special powers on a tenant for life or statutory owner, or under the settlement, to override the minor interest so disposed of or created, no estate or charge shall be registered which would prejudicially affect any such powers:

(b) So long as the proprietor holds the land subject to a trust of land, no estate or charge shall be registered in respect of an interest which, under the Law of Property Act 1925, or otherwise, ought to remain liable to be overridden on sale of land by the trustees:

(c) Nothing in this subsection shall impose on a proprietor an obligation to make a disposition unless the person requiring the disposition to be made has a right in equity to call for the same:

(d) Nothing in this subsection shall prejudicially affect the rights of a personal representative in relation to the administration of the estate of the deceased.

(2) On every alteration in the register made pursuant to this section the land certificate and any charge certificate which may be affected shall be produced to the registrar unless an order to the contrary is made by him.

106 Creation and protection of mortgages of registered land   [567]

(1) The proprietor of any registered land may, subject to any entry to the contrary on the register, mortgage, by deed or otherwise, the land or any part of it in any manner which would have been permissible if the land had not been registered and, subject to this section, with the like effect.

(2) Unless and until the mortgage becomes a registered charge –

(a) it shall take effect only in equity, and

(b) it shall be capable of being overriden as a minor interest unless it is protected as provided by subsection (3) below.

(3) A mortgage which is not a registered charge may be protected on the register by –

(a) a notice under section 49 of this Act,

(b) any such other notice as may be prescribed, or

(c) a caution under section 54 of this Act.

(4) A mortgage which is not a registered charge shall devolve and may be transferred, discharged, surrendered or otherwise dealt with by the same instruments and in the same manner as if the land had not been registered.

107 Power for proprietors to bind successors and   [568]
to enforce contracts

(1) Subject to any entry to the contrary on the register, the proprietor of any registered land or charge may enter into any contract in reference thereto in like manner as if the land or charge had not been registered, and, subject to any disposition for valuable consideration which may be registered or protected on the register before the contract is completed or protected on the register, the contract may be enforced as a minor interest against any succeeding proprietor in like manner and to the same extent as if the land or charge had not been registered.

(2) A contract entered into for the benefit of any registered land or charge may (if the same would have been enforceable by the owner for the time being of the land or charge, if not registered, or by a person deriving title under the party contracting for the benefit) be enforced by the proprietor for the time being of the land or charge.

112 Open register   [569]

(1) Any person may, subject to such conditions as may be prescribed and on payment of any fee payable, inspect and make copies of and extracts from –

(a) entries on the register, and

(b) documents referred to in the register which are in the custody of the registrar (other than leases or charges or copies of leases or charges).

(2) Documents in the custody of the registrar relating to any land or charge but not falling within subsection (1)(b) of this section may be inspected, and copies of and extracts from them may be made –

(a) as of right, in such cases as may be prescribed, and

(b) at the discretion of the registrar, in any other case,

but subject in all cases to such conditions as may be prescribed and on payment of any fee payable.

(3) References in this section to documents include references to things kept otherwise than in documentary form.

113 Office copies to be evidence   [570]

Office copies of and extracts from the register and of and from documents filed in the registry shall be admissible in evidence in all actions and matters, and between all persons or parties, to the same extent as the originals would be admissible, but any person suffering loss by reason of the inaccuracy of any such copy or extract shall be entitled to be indemnified under this Act, and no solicitor, trustee, personal representative, or other person in a fiduciary position shall be answerable in respect of any loss occasioned by relying on any such copy or extract.

123 Effect of Act in areas where registration is compulsory   [571]

(1) In any area in which an Order in Council declaring that registration of title to land within that area is to be compulsory on sale is for the time being in force, every conveyance on sale of freehold land and every grant of a term of years absolute of more than twenty-one years from the date of delivery of the grant and every assignment on sale of leasehold land held for a term of years absolute having more than twenty-one years to run from the date of delivery of the assignment shall (save as hereinafter provided), on the expiration of two months from the date thereof or of any authorised extension of that period, become void so far as regards the grant or conveyance of the legal estate in the freehold or leasehold land comprised in the conveyance, grant, or assignment, or so much of such land as is situated within the area affected, unless the grantee (that is to say, the person who is entitled to be registered as proprietor of the freehold or leasehold land) or his successor in title or assign has in the meantime applied to be registered as proprietor of such land: Provided that the registrar, or the court on appeal from the registrar, may, on the application of any persons interested in any particular case in which the registrar or the court is satisfied that the application for first registration cannot be made within the said period, or can only be made within that period by incurring unreasonable expense, or that the application has not been made within the said period by reason of some accident or other sufficient cause, make an order extending the said period; and if such order be made, then, upon the registration of the grantee or his successor or assign, a note of the order shall be endorsed on the conveyance, grant or assignment:

In the case of land in an area where, at the date of the commencement of this Act, registration of title is already compulsory on sale, this subsection shall apply to every such conveyance, grant, or assignment, executed on or after that date.

(2) Rules under this Act may provide for applying the provisions thereof to dealings with the land which may take place between the date of such conveyance, grant, or assignment and the date of application to register as if such dealings had taken place after the date of first registration, and for registration to be effected as of the date of the application to register.

(3) In this section the expressions 'conveyance on sale' and 'assignment on sale' mean an instrument made on sale by virtue whereof there is conferred or completed a title under which an application for registration as first proprietor of land may be made under this Act, and include a conveyance or assignment by way of exchange where money is paid for equality of exchange, but do not include an enfranchisement or extinguishment of manorial incidents, whether under the Law of Property Act 1922, or otherwise, or an assignment or surrender of a lease to the owner of the immediate reversion containing a declaration that the term is to merge in such reversion.

[As amended by the Tithe Act 1936, s48(3), Schedule 9; Mental Health Act 1959, s149(2), Schedule 8, Pt I; Charities Act 1960, s48(1), Schedule 6; Finance Act 1963, s73(8)(b), Schedule 14, Pt IV; Land Registration and Land Charges Act 1971, ss2(4), 3, 14(1)(b), (2)(b), Schedule 2, Pts I, II; Finance Act 1975, ss52(1), (2), 59(5), Schedule 12, paras 2, 5(1), (2), (3), Schedule 13, Pt I; Local Land Charges Act 1975, s17(2), Schedule 1; Administration of Justice Act 1977, ss24(a), (b), (c), 26(1), 32, Schedule 5, Pt IV; Charging Orders Act 1979, s3(3); Limitation Act 1980, s40(2), Schedule 3, para 1; Administration of Justice Act 1982, ss6(1), 67, Schedule 5, para (a); Patronage (Benefices) Measure 1986, s6(2); Building Societies Act 1986, s120(1), Schedule 18, Pt I, para 2; Land Registration Act 1986, ss1(1), 4(2), (3), (5), 5(1), (5)(a), (b); Landlord and Tenant Act 1987, s61(1), Schedule 4, para 1; Criminal Justice Act 1988, s 170(1), Schedule 15, para 6; Land Registration Act 1988, ss1(1), (2), 2, Schedule; Community Charges (Administration and Enforcement) Regulations 1989; Council Tax (Administration and Enforcement) Regulations 1992; Access to Neighbouring Land Act 1992, s5(2); Leasehold Reform, Housing and Urban Development Act 1993, s187(1), Schedule 21, para 1; Drug Trafficking Act 1994, ss65(1), 67(1), Schedule 1, para 1, Schedule 3; Coal Industry Act 1994, s67(1), Schedule 9, para 1(2); Law of Property (Miscellaneous Provisions) Act 1994, s21(1), (2), Schedule 1, para 2, Schedule 2; Trusts of Land and Appointment of Trustees Act 1996, s25(1), Schedule 3, para 5, Schedule 4.]

ADMINISTRATION OF ESTATES ACT 1925
(15 & 16 Geo 5 c 23)

PART I

DEVOLUTION OF REAL ESTATE

1 Devolution of real estate on personal representative [572]

(1) Real estate to which a deceased person was entitled for an interest not ceasing on his death shall on his death, and notwithstanding any testamentary disposition thereof, devolve from time to time on the personal representative of the deceased, in like manner as before the commencement of this Act chattels real devolved on the personal representative from time to time of a deceased person.

(2) The personal representatives for the time being of a deceased person are deemed in law his heirs and assigns within the meaning of all trusts and powers.

(3) The personal representatives shall be the representatives of the deceased in regard to his real estate to which he was entitled for an interest not ceasing on his death as well as in regard to his personal estate.

2 Application to real estate of law affecting chattels real [573]

(1) Subject to the provisions of this Act, all enactments and rules of law, and all jurisdiction of any court with respect to the appointment of administrators or to probate or letters of administration, or to dealings before probate in the case of chattels real, and with respect to costs and other matters in the administration of personal estate, in force before the commencement of this Act, and all powers, duties, rights, equities, obligations, and liabilities of a personal representative in force at the commencement of this Act with respect to chattels real, shall apply and attach to the personal representative and shall have effect with respect to real estate vested in him, and in particular all such powers of disposition and dealing as were before the commencement of this Act exercisable as respects chattels real by the survivor or survivors of two or more personal representatives, as well as by a single personal representative, or as by all the personal representatives together, shall be exercisable by the personal representatives or representative of the deceased with respect to his real estate.

(2) Where as respects real estate there are two or more personal representatives, a conveyance of real estate devolving under this Part of this Act or a contract for such a conveyance shall not be made without the concurrence therein of all such representatives or an order of the court, but where probate is granted to one or some of two or more persons named as executors, whether or not power is reserved to the other or others to prove, any conveyance of the real estate or contract for such a conveyance may be made by the proving executor or executors for the time being, without an order of the court, and shall be as effectual as if all the persons named as executors had concurred therein.

(3) Without prejudice to the rights and powers of a personal representative, the appointment of a personal representative in regard to real estate shall not, save as hereinafter provide, affect –

(a) any rule as to marshalling or as to administration of assets;
(b) the beneficial interest in real estate under any testamentary disposition;
(c) any mode of dealing with any beneficial interest in real estate, or the proceeds of sale thereof;
(d) the right of any person claiming to be interested in the real estate to take proceedings for the protection or recovery thereof against any person other than the personal representative.

3 Interpretation of Part I [574]

(1) In this Part of this Act 'real estate' includes –

(i) chattels real, and land in possession, remainder, or reversion, and every interest in or over land to which a deceased person was entitled at the time of his death; and
(ii) real estate held on trust (including settled land) or by way of mortgage or security, but not money secured or charged on land.

(2) A testator shall be deemed to have been entitled at his death to any interest in real estate passing under any gift contained in his will which operates as an appointment under a general power to appoint by will, or operates under the testamentary power conferred by statute to dispose of an entailed interest.

(3) An entailed interest of a deceased person shall (unless disposed of under the testamentary power conferred by statute) be deemed an interest ceasing on his death, but any further or other interest of the deceased in the same property in remainder or reversion which is capable of being disposed of by his will shall not be deemed to be an interest so ceasing.

(4) The interest of a deceased person under a joint tenancy where another tenant survives the deceased is an interest ceasing on his death.

9 Vesting of estate in Public Trustee where intestacy   [575] of lack of executors

(1) Where a person dies intestate, his real and personal estate shall vest in the Public Trustee until the grant of administration.

(2) Where a testator dies and –

(a) at the time of his death there is no executor with power to obtain probate of the will, or

(b) at any time before probate of the will is granted there ceases to be any executor with power to obtain probate,

the real and personal estate of which he disposes by the will shall vest in the Public Trustee until the grant of representation.

(3) The vesting of real or personal estate in the Public Trustee by virtue of this section does not confer on him any beneficial interest in, or impose on him any duty, obligation or liability in respect of, the property.

33 Trust for sale   [576]

(1) On the death of a person intestate as to any real or personal estate, that estate shall be held in trust by his personal representatives with the power to sell it.

(2) The personal representatives shall pay out of –

(a) the ready money of the deceased (so far as not disposed of by his will, if any); and

(b) any net money arising from disposing of any other part of his estate (after payment of costs),

all such funeral, testamentary and administration expenses, debts and other liabilities as are properly payable thereout having regard to the rules of administration contained in this Part of this Act, and out of the residue of the said money the personal representative shall set aside a fund sufficient to provide for any pecuniary legacies bequeathed by the will (if any) of the deceased.

(3) During the minority of any beneficiary or the subsistence of any life interest and pending the distribution of the whole or any part of the estate of the deceased, the personal representatives may invest the residue of the said money, or so much thereof as may not have been distributed, in any investments for the time being authorised by statute for the investment of trust money, with power, at the discretion of the personal representatives, to change such investments for others of a like nature.

(4) The residue of the said money and any investments for the time being representing the same, and any part of the estate of the deceased which remains unsold and is not required for the administration purposes aforesaid, is in this Act referred to as 'the residuary estate of the intestate'.

(5) The income (including net rents and profits of real estate and chattels real after payment of rates, taxes, rent, costs of insurance, repairs and other outgoings properly attributable to income) of so much of the real and personal estate of the deceased as may not be disposed of by his will, if any, or may not be required for the administration purposes aforesaid, may, however such estate is invested, as from the death of the deceased, be treated and applied as income, and for that purpose any necessary apportionment may be made between tenant for life and remainderman.

(6) Nothing in this section affects the rights of any creditor of the deceased or the rights of the Crown in respect of death duties.

(7) Where the deceased leaves a will, this section has effect subject to the provisions contained in the will.

35 Charges on property of deceased to be paid primarily out of the property charged   [577]

(1) Where a person dies possessed of, or entitled to, or, under a general power of appointment (including the statutory power to dispose of entailed interest) by his will disposes of, an interest in property, which at the time of his death is charged with the payment of money, whether by way of legal mortgage, equitable charge or otherwise (including a lien for unpaid purchase money), and the deceased has not by will deed or other document signified a contrary or other intention, the interest so charged shall, as between the different persons claiming through the deceased, be primarily liable for the payment of the charge; and every part of the said interest, according to its value, shall bear a proportionate part of the charge on the whole thereof.

(2) Such contrary or other intention shall not be deemed to be signified –

(a) by a general direction for the payment of debts or of all the debts of the testator out of his personal estate, or his residuary real and personal estate, or his residuary real estate; or
(b) by a charge of debts upon any such estate;

unless such intention is further signified by words expressly or by necessary implication referring to all or some part of the charge.

(3) Nothing in this section affects the right of a person entitled to the charge to obtain payment or satisfaction thereof either out of the other assets of the deceased or otherwise.

36 Effect of assent or conveyance by personal representative   [578]

(1) A personal representative may assent to the vesting, in any person who (whether by devise, bequest, devolution, appropriation or otherwise) may be entitled thereto, either beneficially or as a trustee or personal representative, of any estate or interest in real estate to which the testator or intestate was entitled or over which he exercised a general power of appointment by his will, including the statutory power to dispose of entailed interests, and which devolved upon the personal representative.

(2) The assent shall operate to vest in that person the estate or interest to which the assent relates, and, unless a contrary intention appears, the assent shall relate back to the death of the deceased.

(4) An assent to the vesting of a legal estate shall be in writing, signed by the personal representative, and shall name the person in whose favour it is given and shall operate to vest in that person the legal estate to which it relates; and an assent not in writing or not in favour of a named person shall not be effectual to pass a legal estate.

(5) Any person in whose favour an assent or conveyance of a legal estate is made by a personal representative may require that notice of the assent or conveyance be written or endorsed on or permanently annexed to the probate or letters of administration, at the cost of the estate of the deceased, and that the probate or letters of administration be produced, at the like cost, to prove that the notice has been placed thereon or annexed thereto.

(6) A statement in writing by a personal representative that he has not given or made an assent or conveyance in respect of a legal estate, shall, in favour of a purchaser, but without prejudice to any previous disposition made in favour of another purchaser deriving title mediately or immediately under the personal representative, be sufficient evidence that an assent or conveyance has not been given or made in respect of the legal estate to which the statement relates, unless notice of a previous assent or conveyance affecting that estate has been placed on or annexed to the probate or administration.

A conveyance by a personal representative of a legal estate to a purchaser accepted in the faith of such a statement shall (without prejudice as aforesaid and unless notice of a previous assent or conveyance affecting that estate has been placed on or annexed to the probate or administration) operate to transfer or create the legal estate expressed to be conveyed in like manner as if no previous assent or conveyance had been made by the personal representative.

A personal representative making a false statement, in regard to any such matter, shall be liable in like manner as if the statement had been contained in a statutory declaration.

(7) An assent or conveyance by a personal representative in respect of a legal estate shall, in favour of a purchaser, unless notice of a previous assent or conveyance affecting that legal estate has been placed on or annexed to the probate or administration, be taken as sufficient evidence that the person in whose favour the assent or conveyance is given or made is the person entitled to have the legal estate conveyed to him, and upon the proper trusts, if any, but shall not otherwise prejudicially affect the claim of any person rightfully entitled to the estate vested or conveyed or any charge thereon.

(8) A conveyance of a legal estate by a personal representative to a purchaser shall not be invalidated by reason only that the purchaser may have notice that all the debts, liabilities, funeral, and testamentary or administration expenses, duties and legacies of the deceased have been discharged or provided for.

(9) An assent or conveyance given or made by a personal representative shall not, except in favour of a purchaser of a legal estate, prejudice the right of the personal representative or any other person to recover the estate or interest to which the assent or conveyance relates, or to be indemnified out of such estate or interest against any duties, debt or liability to which such estate or interest would have been subject if there had not been any assent or conveyance.

(10) A personal representative may, as a condition of giving an assent or making a conveyance, require security for the discharge of any such duties, debt, or liability, but shall not be entitled to postpone the giving of an assent merely by reason of the subsistence of any such duties, debt or liability if reasonable arrangements have been made for discharging the same; and an assent may be given subject to any legal estate or charge by way of legal mortgage.

(11) This section shall not operate to impose any stamp duty in respect of an assent, and in this section 'purchaser' means a purchaser for money or money's worth.

(12) This section applies to assents and conveyances made after the commencement of this Act, whether the testator or intestate died before or after such commencement.

PART V

SUPPLEMENTAL

55 Definitions   [579]

In this Act, unless the context otherwise requires, the following expressions have the meanings hereby assigned to them respectively, that is to say –

(1) (i) 'Administration' means, with reference to the real and personal estate of a deceased person, letters of administration, whether general or limited, or with the will annexed or otherwise;

(ii) 'Administrator' means a person to whom administration is granted; ...

(v) 'Income' includes rents and profits;

(vi) 'Intestate' includes a person who leaves a will but dies intestate as to some beneficial interest in his real or personal estate;

(via) 'Land' has the same meaning as in the Law of Property Act 1925;

(vii) 'Legal estates' mean the estates' charges and interests in or over land (subsisting or created at law) which are by statute authorised to subsist or to be created at law; and 'equitable interests' mean all other interests and charges in or over land; ...

(ix) 'Pecuniary legacy' includes an annuity, a general legacy, a demonstrative legacy so far as it is not discharged out of the designated property, and any other general direction by a testator for the payment of money, including all death duties free from which any devise, bequest, or payment is made to take effect;

(x) 'Personal chattels' mean carriages, horses, stable furniture and effects (not used for business purposes), motor cars and accessories (not used for business purposes), garden effects, domestic animals, plate, plated articles, linen, china, glass, books, pictures, prints, furniture, jewellery, articles of household or personal use or ornament, musical and scientific instruments and apparatus, wines, liquors and consumable stores, but do not include any chattels used at the death of the intestate for business purposes nor money or securities for money.

(xi) 'Personal representative' means the executor, original or by representation, or administrator for the time being of a deceased person, and as regards any liability for the payment of death duties includes any person who takes possession of or intermeddles with the property of a deceased person without the authority of the personal representatives or the court, and 'executor' includes a person deemed to be appointed executor as respects settled land; ...

(xviii) 'Purchaser' means a lessee, mortgagee or other person who in good faith acquires an interest in property for valuable consideration, also an intending purchaser and 'valuable consideration' includes marriage, but does not include a nominal consideration in money;

(xix) 'Real estate' save as provided in Part IV of this Act means real estate, including chattels real, which by virtue of Part I of this Act devolves on the personal representative of a deceased person; ...

(xxiv) 'Tenants for life', 'statutory owner', 'settled land', 'settlement', 'trustees of the settlement', 'term of years absolute', 'death duties', and 'legal mortgage', have the same meanings as in the Settled Land Act 1925, and 'entailed interest' and 'charge by way of legal mortgage' have the same meanings as in the Law of Property Act 1925; ...

(xxviii) 'Will' includes codicil.

(2) References to a child or issue living at the death of any person include a child or issue en ventre sa mère at the death.

(3) References to the estate of a deceased person include property over which the

deceased exercises a general power of appointment (including the statutory power to dispose of entailed interests) by his will.

[As amended by the Law of Property (Miscellaneous Provisions) Act 1994, ss14(1), 16(1), 21(2), Schedule 2; Trusts of Land and Appointment of Trustees Act 1996, ss5, 25(1), Schedule 2, para 5, Schedule 3, para 6, Schedule 4.]

LAW OF PROPERTY (AMENDMENT) ACT 1926
(16 & 17 Geo 5 c 11)

1 Conveyance of legal estates subject to certain interests [580]

(1) Nothing in the Settled Land Act 1925 shall prevent a person on whom the powers of a tenant for life are conferred by paragraph (ix) of subsection (1) of section twenty of that Act from conveying or creating a legal estate subject to a prior interest as if the land had not been settled land.

(2) In any of the following cases, namely –

(a) where a legal estate has been conveyed or created under subsection one of this section, or under section sixteen of the Settled Land Act 1925, subject to any prior interest, or
(b) where before the first day of January, nineteen hundred and twenty-six, land has been conveyed to a purchaser for money or money's worth subject to any prior interest whether or not on the purchase the land was expressed to be exonerated from, or the grantor agreed to indemnify the purchaser against, such prior interest,

the estate owner for the time being of the land subject to such prior interest may, notwithstanding any provision contained in the Settled Land Act 1925, but without prejudice to any power whereby such prior interest is capable of being overreached, convey or create a legal estate subject to such prior interest as if the instrument creating the prior interest was not an instrument or one of the instruments constituting a settlement of the land.

(3) In this section 'interest' means an estate, interest, charge or power of charging subsisting, or capable of arising or of being exercised, under a settlement, and, where a prior interest arises under the exercise of a power, 'instrument' includes both the instrument conferring the power and the instrument exercising it.

LANDLORD AND TENANT ACT 1927
(17 & 18 Geo 5 c 36)

18 Provisions as to covenants to repair [581]

(1) Damages for a breach of a covenant or agreement to keep or put premises in repair during the currency of a lease, or to leave or put premises in repair at the termination of a lease, whether such covenant or agreement is expressed or implied, and whether general or specific, shall in no case exceed the amount (if any) by which the value of the reversion (whether immediate or not) in the premises is diminished owing to the breach of such covenant or agreement as aforesaid; and in particular no damage shall be recovered for a breach of any such covenant or agreement to leave or put premises in repair at the termination of a lease, if it is shown that the premises, in whatever state of repair they might be, would at or shortly after the termination of the tenancy have been or be pulled down, or such structural alterations made therein as would render valueless the repairs covered by the covenant or agreement.

(2) A right of re-entry or forfeiture for a breach of any such covenant or agreement as aforesaid shall not be enforceable, by action or otherwise, unless the lessor proves that the fact that such a notice as is required by section one hundred and forty-six of the Law of Property Act 1925 has been served on the lessee was known either –

(a) to the lessee; or

(b) to an under-lessee holding under an under-lease which reserved a nominal reversion only to the lessee; or

(c) to the person who last paid the rent due under the lease either on his own behalf or as agent for the lessee or under-lessee;

and that a time reasonably sufficient to enable the repairs to be executed had elapsed since the time when the fact of the service of the notice came to the knowledge of any such person.

Where a notice has been sent by registered post addressed to a person at his last known place of abode in the United Kingdom, then, for the purposes of this subsection, that person shall be deemed, unless the contrary is proved, to have had knowledge of the fact that the notice had been served as from the time at which the letter would have been delivered in the ordinary course of post.

This subsection shall be construed as one with section one hundred and forty-six of the Law of Property Act 1925.

(3) This section applies whether the lease was created before or after the commencement of this Act.

19 Provisions as to covenants not to assign, etc   [582]
without licence or consent

(1) In all leases whether made before or after the commencement of this Act containing a covenant condition or agreement against assigning, underletting, charging or parting with the possession of demised premises or any part thereof without licence or consent, such covenant condition or agreement shall, notwithstanding any express provision to the contrary, be deemed to be subject –

(a) to a proviso to the effect that such licence or consent is not to be unreasonably withheld, but this proviso does not preclude the right of the landlord to require payment of a reasonable sum in respect of any legal or other expenses incurred in connection with such licence or consent; and

(b) (if the lease is for more than forty years, and is made in consideration wholly or partially of the erection, or the substantial improvement, addition or alteration of buildings, and the lessor is not a Government department or local or public authority, or a statutory or public utility company) to a proviso to the effect that in the case of any assignment, under-letting, charging or parting with the possession (whether by the holders of the lease or any under-tenant whether immediate or not) effected more than seven years before the end of the term no consent or licence shall be required, if notice in writing of the transaction is given to the lessor within six months after the transaction is effected.

(1A) Where the landlord and the tenant under a qualifying lease have entered into an agreement specifying for the purposes of this subsection –

(a) any circumstances in which the landlord may withhold his licence or consent to an assignment of the demised premises or any part of them, or

(b) any conditions subject to which any such licnece or consent may be granted,

then the landlord –

(i) shall not be regarded as unreasonably withholding his licence or consent to any such assignment if he withholds it on the ground (and it is the case) that any such circumstances exist, and

(ii) if he gives any such licence or consent subject to any such conditions, shall not be regarded as giving it subject to unreasonable conditions;

and section 1 of the Landlord and Tenant Act 1988 (qualified duty to consent to assignment etc) shall have effect subject to the provisions of this subsection.

(1B) Subsection (1A) of this section applies to such an agreement as is mentioned in that subsection –

(a) whether it is contained in the lease or not, and

(b) whether it is made at the time when the lease is granted or at any other time falling before the application for the landlord's licence or consent is made.

(1C) Subsection (1A) shall not, however, apply to any such agreement to the extent that the circumstances or conditions specified in it are framed by reference to any matter falling to be determined by the landlord or by any other person for the purposes of the agreement, unless under the terms of the agreement –

(a) that person's power to determine that matter is required to be exercised reasonably, or

(b) the tenant is given an unrestricted right to have any such determination reviewed by a person independent of both landlord and tenant whose identity is ascertainable by reference to the agreement,

and in the latter case the agreement provides for the determination made by any such independent person on the review to be conclusive as to the matter in question.

(1D) In its application to a qualifying lease, subsection (1)(b) of this section shall not have effect in relation to any assignment of the lease.

(1E) In subsections (1A) and (1D) of this section –

(a) 'qualifying lease' means any lease which is a new tenancy for the purposes of section 1 of the Landlord and Tenant (Covenants) Act 1995 other than a residential lease, namely a lease by which a building or part of a building is let wholly or mainly as a single private residence; and

(b) references to assignment include parting with possession on assignment.

(2) In all leases whether made before or after the commencement of this Act containing a covenant condition or agreement against the making of improvements without licence or consent, such covenant condition or agreement shall be deemed, notwithstanding any express provision to the contrary, to the subject to a proviso that such licence or consent is not to be unreasonably withheld; but this proviso does not preclude the right to require as a condition of such licence or consent the payment of a reasonable sum in respect of any damage to or diminution in the value of the premises or any neighbouring premises belonging to the landlord, and of any legal or other expenses properly incurred in connection with such licence or consent nor, in the case of an improvement which does not add to the letting value of the holding, does it preclude the right to require as a condition of such licence or consent, where such a requirement would be reasonable, an undertaking on the part of the tenant to reinstate the premises in the condition in which they were before the improvement was executed.

(3) In all leases whether made before or after the commencement of this Act containing a covenant condition or agreement against the alteration of the user of the demised premises, without licence or consent, such covenant condition or agreement shall, if the alteration does not involve any structural alteration of the

premises, be deemed, notwithstanding any express provision to the contrary, to be subject to a proviso that no fine or sum of money in the nature of a fine, whether by way of increase of rent or otherwise, shall be payable for or in respect of such licence or consent; but this proviso does not preclude the right of the landlord to require payment of a reasonable sum in respect of any damage to or diminution in the value of the premises or any neighbouring premises belonging to him and of any legal or other expenses incurred in connection with such licence or consent.

Where a dispute as to the reasonableness of any such sum has been determined by a court of competent jurisdiction, the landlord shall be bound to grant the licence or consent on payment of the sum so determined to be reasonable.

(4) This section shall not apply to leases of agricultural holdings within the meaning of the Agricultural Holdings Act 1986 which are leases in relation to which that Act applies, or to farm business tenancies within the meaning of the Agricultural Tenancies Act 1995, and paragraph (b) of subsection (1), subsection (2) and subsection (3) of this section shall not apply to mining leases.

[As amended by the Agricultural Holdings Act 1986, s100, Schedule 14, para 15; Agricultural Tenancies Act 1995, s40, Schedule, para 5; Landlord and Tenant (Covenants) Act 1995, s22.]

LAW OF PROPERTY (AMENDMENT) ACT 1929
(19 & 20 Geo 5 c 9)

1 Relief of under-lessees against breach of covenant   [583]

Nothing in subsection (8), subsection (9) or subsection (10) of section one hundred and forty-six of the Law of Property Act 1925 (which relates to restrictions on and relief against forfeiture of leases and under-leases) shall affect the provisions of subsection (4) of the said section.

LAW OF PROPERTY (ENTAILED INTERESTS) ACT 1932
(22 & 23 Geo 5 c 27)

2 Definition of rentcharge   [584]

For removing doubt it is hereby declared that a rentcharge (not being a rentcharge limited to take effect in remainder after or expectant on the failure or determination of some other interest) is a rentcharge in possession within the meaning of paragraph (b) of subsection (2) of section one of the Law of Property Act 1925, notwithstanding that the payments in respect thereof are limited to commence or accrue at some time subsequent to its creation.

LEASEHOLD PROPERTY (REPAIRS) ACT 1938
(1 & 2 Geo 6 c 34)

1 Restriction on enforcement of repairing covenants   [585]
in long leases of small houses

(1) Where a lessor serves on a lessee under subsection (1) of section one hundred and forty-six of the Law of Property Act 1925, a notice that relates to a breach of a covenant or agreement to keep or put in repair during the currency of the lease all or any of the property comprised in the lease, and at the date of the service of the notice three years or more of the term of the lease remain unexpired, the lessee

may within twenty-eight days from that date serve on the lessor a counter-notice to the effect that he claims the benefit of this Act.

(2) A right to damages for a breach of such a covenant as aforesaid shall not be enforceable by action commenced at any time at which three years or more of the term of the lease remain unexpired unless the lessor has served on the lessee not less than one month before the commencement of the action such a notice as is specified in subsection (1) of section one hundred and forty-six of the Law of Property Act 1925, and where a notice is served under this subsection, the lessee may, within twenty-eight days from the date of the service thereof, serve on the lessor a counter-notice to the effect that he claims the benefit of this Act.

(3) Where a counter-notice is served by a lessee under this section, then, notwithstanding anything in any enactment or rule of law, no proceedings, by action or otherwise, shall be taken by the lessor for the enforcement of any right of re-entry or forfeiture under any proviso or stipulation in the lease for breach of the covenant or agreement in question, or for damages for breach thereof, otherwise than with the leave of the court.

(4) A notice served under subsection (1) of section one hundred and forty-six of the Law of Property Act 1925, in the circumstances specified in subsection (1) of this section, and a notice served under subsection (2) of this section shall not be valid unless it contains a statement, in characters not less conspicuous than those used in any other part of the notice, to the effect that the lessee is entitled under this Act to serve on the lessor a counter-notice claiming the benefit of this Act, and a statement in the like characters specifying the time within which, and the manner in which, under this Act a counter-notice may be served and specifying the name and address for service of the lessor.

(5) Leave for the purposes of this section shall not be given unless the lessor proves –

(a) that the immediate remedying of the breach in question is requisite for preventing substantial diminution in the value of his reversion, or that the value thereof has been substantially diminished by the breach;
(b) that the immediate remedying of the breach is required for giving effect in relation to the premises to the purposes of any enactment, or of any byelaw or other provision having effect under an enactment, or for giving effect to any order of a court or requirement of any authority under any enactment or any such byelaw or other provision as aforesaid;
(c) in a case in which the lessee is not in occupation of the whole of the premises as respects which the covenant or agreement is proposed to be enforced, that the immediate remedying of the breach is required in the interests of the occupier of those premises or of part thereof;
(d) that the breach can be immediately remedied at an expense that is relatively small in comparison with the much greater expense that would probably be occasioned by postponement of the necessary work; or
(e) special circumstances which in the opinion of the court, render it just and equitable that leave should be given.

(6) The court may, in granting or in refusing leave for the purposes of this section, impose such terms and conditions on the lessor or on the lessee as it may think fit.

2 Restriction on right to recover expenses of survey, etc   [586]

A lessor on whom a counter-notice is served under the preceding section shall not be entitled to the benefit of subsection (3) of section one hundred and forty-six of the Law of Property Act 1925, (which relates to costs and expenses incurred by a lessor in reference to breaches of covenant), so far as regards any costs or expenses incurred in reference to the breach in question, unless he makes an application for leave for the purposes of the preceding section, and on such an application the court shall have power to direct whether and to what extent the lessor is to be entitled to the benefit thereof.

3 Saving for obligation to repair on taking possession [587]

This Act shall not apply to a breach of a covenant or agreement in so far as it imposes on the lessee an obligation to put premises in repair that is to be performed upon the lessee taking possession of the premises or within a reasonable time thereafter.

6 Court having jurisdiction under this Act [588]

(1) In this Act the expression 'the court' means the county court, except in a case in which any proceedings by action for which leave may be given would have to be taken in a court other than the county court, and means in the said excepted case that other court.

7 Application of certain provisions of Law of [589] Property Act 1925

(1) In this Act the expressions 'lessor', 'lessee' and 'lease' have the meanings assigned to them respectively by sections one hundred and forty-six and one hundred and fifty-four of the Law of Property Act 1925, except that they do not include any reference to such a grant as is mentioned in the said section one hundred and forty-six, or to the person making, or to the grantee under such a grant, or to persons deriving title under such a person; and 'lease' means a lease for a term of seven years or more, not being a lease of an agricultural holding within the meaning of the Agricultural Holdings Act 1986 which is a lease in relation to which that Act applies and not being a farm business tenancy within the meaning of the Agricultural Tenancies Act 1995.

(2) The provisions of section one hundred and ninety-six of the said Act (which relate to the service of notices) shall extend to notices and counter-notices required or authorised by this Act.

[As amended by the Landlord and Tenant Act 1954, s51(1), (2), (5); Agricultural Holdings Act 1986, s100, Schedule 14, para 17; Agricultural Tenancies Act 1995, s40, Schedule, para 8.]

SETTLED LAND AND TRUSTEE ACTS (COURT'S GENERAL POWERS) ACT 1943
(6 & 7 Geo 6 c 25)

1 Extension of powers under 15 Geo 5 c 18, s64 and c 19, s57 [590]

(1) The jurisdiction of the court under section 64 of the Settled Land Act 1925 (which confers power on a tenant for life to effect under an order of the court any transaction, including an application of capital money), and, so far as regards trustees of land, the jurisdiction of the court under section 57 of the Trustee Act 1925 (under which the court may make an order conferring on trustees power to effect any transaction, including an expenditure of money, and may direct in what manner money to be expended is to be paid as between capital and income) shall include power, in the circumstances specified in subsection (2) of this section, to make an order authorising any expense of action taken or proposed in or for the

management of settled land or of land subject to a trust of land, as the case may be, to be treated as a capital outgoing, notwithstanding that in other circumstances that expense could not properly have been so treated.

(2) The said circumstances are that the court is satisfied –

(a) that the action taken or proposed was or would be for the benefit of the persons entitled under the settlement, or under the trust of land, as the case may be, generally; and either

(b) that the available income from all sources of a person who, as being beneficially entitled to possession or receipt of rents and profits of the land or to reside in a house comprised therein, might otherwise have been expected to bear the expense of the action taken or proposed has been so reduced as to render him unable to bear the expense thereof, or unable to bear it without undue hardship; or

(c) in a case in which there is no such person as aforesaid, that the income available for meeting that expense has become insufficient.

(3) In determining whether to make such an order as aforesaid the court shall have regard to all the circumstances of the case, including the extent of the obligations, whether legally enforceable or not and whether or not relating to the land, of the person referred to in paragraph (b) of the last preceding subsection, the extent to which other persons entitled under the settlement or trust of land are likely to benefit from the action taken or proposed or from the relief which would accrue to that person from the making of the order, and the extent to which the making of the order would be likely to involve a loss to any other person so entitled without his receiving any corresponding benefit.

(4) Such an order as aforesaid may be made notwithstanding that the action in question was taken, or the expense thereof discharged, before the passing of this Act or before the application for the order, and the court may direct such adjustments of accounts and such repayments to be made as may appear to the court to be requisite for giving full effect to the purposes of any such order.

(5) In this section –

the expression 'management' includes all the acts referred to in subsection (2) of section 102 of the Settled Land Act 1925, and references in this section to expense of management include references to the expense of the employment of a solicitor, accountant, surveyor, or other person in an advisory or supervisory capacity.

[As amended by the Emergency Laws (Miscellaneous Provisions) Act 1953, ss9, 14, Schedule 3; Trusts of Land and Appointment of Trustees Act 1996, s25(1), Schedule 3, para 8.]

LANDLORD AND TENANT ACT 1954
(2 & 3 Eliz 2 c 56)

PART II

SECURITY OF TENURE FOR BUSINESS, PROFESSIONAL

AND OTHER TENANTS

23 Tenancies to which Part II applies   [591]

(1) Subject to the provisions of this Act, this Part of this Act applies to any tenancy where the property comprised in the tenancy is or includes premises which are

occupied by the tenant and are so occupied for the purposes of a business carried on by him or for those and other purposes.

(2) In this Part of this Act the expression 'business' includes a trade, profession or employment and includes any activity carried on by a body of persons, whether corporate or unincorporate.

(3) In the following provisions of this Part of this Act the expression 'the holding', in relation to a tenancy to which this Part of this Act applies, means the property comprised in the tenancy, there being excluded any part thereof which is occupied neither by the tenant nor by a person employed by the tenant and so employed for the purposes of a business by reason of which the tenancy is one to which this Part of this Act applies.

(4) Where the tenant is carrying on a business, in all or any part of the property comprised in a tenancy, in breach of a prohibition (however expressed) of use for business purposes which subsists under the terms of the tenancy and extends to the whole of that property, this Part of this Act shall not apply to the tenancy unless the immediate landlord or his predecessor in title has consented to the breach or the immediate landlord has acquiesced therein.

In this subsection the reference to a prohibition of use for business purposes does not include a prohibition of use for the purposes of a specified business, or of use for purposes of any but a specified business, but save as aforesaid includes a prohibition of use for the purposes of some one or more only of the classes of business specified in the definition of that expression in subsection (2) of this section.

24 Continuation of tenancies to which Part II applies and grant of new tenancies   [592]

(1) A tenancy to which this Part of this Act applies shall not come to an end unless terminated in accordance with the provisions of this Part of this Act; and, subject to the provisions of section twenty-nine of this Act, the tenant under such a tenancy may apply to the court for a new tenancy –

(a) if the landlord has given notice under section 25 of this Act to terminate the tenancy, or
(b) if the tenant has made a request for a new tenancy in accordance with section twenty-six of this Act.

(2) The last foregoing subsection shall not prevent the coming to an end of a tenancy by notice to quit given by the tenant, by surrender or forfeiture, or by the forfeiture of a superior tenancy unless –

(a) in the case of a notice to quit, the notice was given before the tenant had been in occupation in right of the tenancy for one month; or
(b) in the case of an instrument of surrender, the instrument was executed before, or was executed in pursuance of an agreement made before, the tenant had been in occupation in right of the tenancy for one month.

(3) Notwithstanding anything in subsection (1) of this section –

(a) where a tenancy to which this Part of this Act applies ceases to be such a tenancy, it shall not come to an end by reason only of the cesser, but if it was granted for a term of years certain and has been continued by subsection (1) of this section then (without prejudice to the termination thereof in accordance with any terms of the tenancy) it may be terminated by not less than three nor more than six months' notice in writing given by the landlord to the tenant;
(b) where, at a time when a tenancy is not one to which this Part of this Act applies, the landlord gives notice to quit, the operation of the notice shall not

be affected by reason that the tenancy becomes one to which this Part of this Act applies after the giving of the notice.

24A Rent while tenancy continues by virtue of s24 [593]

(1) The landlord of a tenancy to which this Part of this Act applies may –

(a) if he has given notice under section 25 of this Act to terminate the tenancy; or

(b) if the tenant has made a request for a new tenancy in accordance with section 26 of this Act;

apply to the court to determine a rent which it would be reasonable for the tenant to pay while the tenancy continues by virtue of section 24 of this Act, and the court may determine a rent accordingly.

(2) A rent determined in proceedings under this section shall be deemed to be the rent payable under the tenancy from the date on which the proceedings were commenced or the date specified in the landlord's notice or the tenant's request, whichever is the later.

(3) In determining a rent under this section the court shall have regard to the rent payable under the terms of the tenancy, but otherwise subsections (1) and (2) of section 34 of this Act shall apply to the determination as they would apply to the determination of a rent under that section if a new tenancy for year to year of the whole of the property comprised in the tenancy were granted to the tenant by order of the court.

25 Termination of tenancy by the landlord [594]

(1) The landlord may terminate a tenancy to which this Part of this Act applies by a notice given to the tenant in the prescribed form specifying the date at which the tenancy is to come to an end (hereinafter referred to as 'the date of termination'): Provided that this subsection has effect subject to the provisions of Part IV of this Act as to the interim continuation of tenancies pending the disposal of applications to the court.

(2) Subject to the provisions of the next following subsection, a notice under this section shall not have effect unless it is given not more than twelve nor less than six months before the date of termination specified therein.

(3) In the case of a tenancy which apart from this Act could have been brought to an end by notice to quit given by the landlord –

(a) the date of termination specified in a notice under this section shall not be earlier than the earliest date on which apart from this Part of this Act the tenancy could have been brought to an end by notice to quit given by the landlord on the date of the giving of the notice under this section; and

(b) where apart from this Part of this Act more than six months' notice to quit would have been required to bring the tenancy to and end, the last foregoing subsection shall have effect with the substitution for twelve months of a period six months longer than the length of notice to quit which would have been required as aforesaid.

(4) In the case of any other tenancy, a notice under this section shall not specify a date of termination earlier than the date on which apart from this Part of this Act the tenancy would have come to an end by effluxion of time.

(5) A notice under this section shall not have effect unless it requires the tenant, within two months after the giving of the notice, to notify the landlord in writing whether or not, at the date of termination, the tenant will be willing to give up possession of the property comprised in the tenancy.

(6) A notice under this section shall not have effect unless it states whether the landlord would oppose an application to the court under this Part of this Act for the grant of a new tenancy and, if so, also states on which of the grounds mentioned in section thirty of this Act he would do so.

28 Renewal of tenancies by agreement   [595]

Where the landlord and tenant agree for the grant to the tenant of a future tenancy of the holding, or of the holding with other land, on terms and from a date specified in the agreement, the current tenancy shall continue until that date but no longer, and shall not be a tenancy to which this Part of this Act applies.

33 Duration of new tenancy   [596]

Where on an application under this Part of this Act the court makes an order for the grant of a new tenancy, the new tenancy shall be such tenancy as may be agreed between the landlord and the tenant, or, in default of such an agreement, shall be such a tenancy as may be determined by the court to be reasonable in all the circumstances, being, if it is a tenancy for a term of years certain, a tenancy for a term not exceeding fourteen years, and shall begin on the coming to an end of the current tenancy.

34 Rent under new tenancy   [597]

(1) The rent payable under a tenancy granted by order of the court under this Part of this Act shall be such as may be agreed between the landlord and the tenant or as, in default of such agreement, may be determined by the court to be that at which, having regard to the terms of the tenancy (other than those relating to rent), the holding might reasonably be expected to be let in the open market by a willing lessor, there being disregarded –

(a) any effect on rent of the fact that the tenant has or his predecessors in title have been in occupation of the holding,

(b) any goodwill attached to the holding by reason of the carrying on thereat of the business of the tenant (whether by him or by a predecessor of his in that business),

(c) any effect on rent of an improvement to which this paragraph applies;

(d) in the case of a holding comprising licensed premises, any addition to its value attributable to the licence, if it appears to the court that having regard to the terms of the current tenancy and any other relevant circumstances the benefit of the licence belongs to the tenant.

(2) Paragraph (c) of the foregoing subsection applies to any improvement carried out by a person who at the time it was carried out was the tenant, but only if it was carried out otherwise than in pursuance of an obligation to his immediate landlord, and either it was carried out during the current tenancy or the following conditions are satisfied, that is to say, –

(a) that it was completed not more than twenty-one years before the application for the new tenancy was made; and

(b) that the holding or any part of it affected by the improvement has at all times since the completion of the improvement been comprised in tenancies of the description specified in section 23(1) of this Act; and

(c) that at the termination of each of those tenancies the tenant did not quit.

(3) Where the rent is determined by the court the court may, if it thinks fit, further determine that the terms of the tenancy shall include such provision for varying the rent as may be specified in the determination.

(4) It is hereby declared that the matters which are to be taken into account by the court in determining the rent include any effect on rent of the operation of the provisions of the Landlord and Tenant (Covenants) Act 1995.

35 Other terms of new tenancy [598]

(1) The terms of a tenancy granted by order of the court under this Part of this Act (other than terms as to the duration thereof and as to the rent payable thereunder) shall be such as may be agreed between the landlord and the tenant or as, in default of such agreement, may be determined by the court; and in determining those terms the court shall have regard to the terms of the current tenancy and to all relevant circumstances.

(2) In subsection (1) of this section the reference to all relevant circumstances includes (without prejudice to the gnerality of that reference) a reference to the operation of the provisions of the Landlord and Tenant (Covenants) Act 1995.

43 Tenancies excluded from Part II [599]

(1) This Part of this Act does not apply –

(a) to a tenancy of an agricultural holding which is a tenancy in relation to which the Agricultural Holdings Act 1986 applies or a tenancy which would be a tenancy of an agricultural holding in relation to which that Act applied if subsection (3) of section 2 of that Act did not have effect or, in a case where approval was given under subsection (1) of that section, if that approval had not been given;
(aa) to a farm business tenancy;
(b) to a tenancy created by a mining lease.

(2) This Part of this Act does not apply to a tenancy granted by reason that the tenant was the holder of an office, appointment or employment from the grantor thereof and continuing only so long as the tenant holds the office, appointment or employment, or terminable by the grantor on the tenant's ceasing to hold it, or coming to an end at a time fixed by reference to the time at which the tenant ceases to hold it: Provided that this subsection shall not have effect in relation to a tenancy granted after the commencement of this Act unless the tenancy was granted by an instrument in writing which expressed the purpose for which the tenancy was granted.

(3) This Part of this Act does not apply to a tenancy granted for a term certain not exceeding six months unless –

(a) the tenancy contains provision for renewing the term or for extending it beyond six months from its beginning; or
(b) the tenant has been in occupation for a period which, together with any period during which any predecessor in the carrying on of the business carried on by the tenant was in occupation, exceeds twelve months.

PART IV

MISCELLANEOUS AND SUPPLEMENTARY

51 Extension of Leasehold Property (Repairs) Act 1938 [600]

(1) The Leasehold Property (Repairs) Act 1938 (which restricts the enforcement of repairing covenants in long leases of small houses) shall extend to every tenancy (whether of a house or of other property, and without regard to rateable value) where the following conditions are fulfilled, that is to say –

(a) that the tenancy was granted for a term of years certain of not less than seven years;

(b) that three years or more of the term remain unexpired at the date of the service of the notice of dilapidations or, as the case may be, at the date of commencement of the action for damages; and

(c) that the tenancy is neither a tenancy of an agricultural holding in relation to which the Agricultural Holdings Act 1986 applies nor a farm business tenancy [as defined in section 1 of the 1995 Act].

(6) In this section the expression 'notice of dilapidations' means a notice under subsection (1) of section one hundred and forty-six of the Law of Property Act 1925.

53 Jurisdiction of county court where lessor refuses licence or consent   [601]

(1) Where a landlord withholds his licence or consent –

(a) to an assignment of the tenancy or a subletting, charging or parting with the possession of the demised property or any part thereof, or

(b) to the making of an improvement on the demised property or any part thereof, or

(c) to a change in the use of the demised property or any part thereof, or to the making of a specified use of that property,

and the High Court has jurisdiction to make a declaration that the licence or consent was unreasonably withheld, then without prejudice to the jurisdiction of the High Court the county court shall have the like jurisdiction whatever the net annual value for rating of the demised property is taken to be for the purposes of the County Courts Act 1984 and notwithstanding that the tenant does not seek any relief other than the declaration.

(2) Where on the making of an application to the county court for such a declaration the court is satisfied that the licence or consent was unreasonably withheld, the court shall make a declaration accordingly.

(3) The foregoing provisions of this section shall have effect whether the tenancy in question was created before or after the commencement of this Act and whether the refusal of the licence or consent occurred before or after the commencement of this Act.

(4) Nothing in this section shall be construed as conferring jurisdiction on the county court to grant any relief other than such a declaration as aforesaid.

[As amended by the Agricultural Act 1958, s8(1), Schedule 1, Pt I, para 29; Law of Property Act 1969, ss1(1), 3(1), (2), 2, 4(1), 12; County Courts Act 1984, s148(1), Schedule, Pt V, para 23; Agricultural Holdings Act 1986, s100, Schedule 14, para 21; Landlord and Tenant (Licensed Premises) Act 1990, ss1, 2(a); Agricultural Tenancies Act 1995, s40, Schedule, paras 10–12; Landlord and Tenant (Covenants) Act 1995, s30(1), Schedule 1, paras 3, 4.]

RIGHTS OF LIGHT ACT 1959
(7 & 8 Eliz 2 c 56)

2 Registration of notice in lieu of obstruction of access of light   [602]

(1) For the purpose of preventing the access and use of light from being taken to be enjoyed without interruption, any person who is an owner of land (in this and

the next following section referred to as 'the servient land') over which light passes to a dwelling-house, workshop or other building (in this and then next following section referred to as 'the dominant building') may apply to the local authority in whose area the dominant building is situated for the registration of a notice under this section.

(2) An application for the registration of a notice under this section shall be in the prescribed form and shall –

(a) identify the servient land and the dominant building in the prescribed manner, and

(b) state that the registration of a notice in pursuance of the application is intended to be equivalent to the obstruction of the access of light to the dominant building across the servient land which would be caused by the erection, in such position on the servient land as may be specified in the application, of an opaque structure of such dimensions specified.

(3) Any such application shall be accompanied by one or other of the following certificates issued by the Lands Tribunal, that is to say –

(a) a certificate certifying that adequate notice of the proposed application has been given to all persons who, in the circumstances existing at the time when the certificate is issued, appear to the Lands Tribunal to be persons likely to be affected by the registration of a notice in pursuance of the application;

(b) a certificate certifying that, in the opinion of the Lands Tribunal, the case is one of exceptional urgency, and that accordingly a notice should be registered forthwith as a temporary notice for such period as may be specified in the certificate.

(4) Where application is duly made to a local authority for the registration of a notice under this section, it shall be the duty of that authority to register the notice in the appropriate local land charges register, and –

(a) any notice so registered under this section shall be a local land charge; but

(b) section 5(1) and (2) and section 10 of the Local Land Charges Act 1975 shall not apply in relation thereto.

(5) Provision shall be made by rules under section three of the Lands Tribunal Act 1949, for regulating proceedings before the Lands Tribunal with respect to the issue of certificates for the purposes of this section, and, subject to the approval of the Treasury, the fees chargeable in respect of those proceedings; and, without prejudice to the generality of subsection (6) of that section, any such rules made for the purposes of this section shall include provision –

(a) for requiring applicants for certificates under paragraph (a) of subsection (3) of this section to give such notices, whether by way of advertisement or otherwise, and to produce such documents and provide such information, as may be determined by or under the rules;

(b) for determining the period to be specified in a certificate issued under paragraph (b) of subsection (3) of this section; and

(c) in connection with any certificate issued under the said paragraph (b), for enabling a further certificate to be issued in accordance (subject to the necessary modifications) with paragraph (a) of subsection (3) of this section.

3 Effect of registered notice and proceedings relating thereto [603]

(1) Where, in pursuance of an application made in accordance with the last preceding section, a notice is registered thereunder, then, for the purpose of determining whether any person is entitled (by virtue of the Prescription Act 1832,

or otherwise) to a right to the access of light to the dominant building across the servient land, the access of light to that building across that land shall be treated as obstructed to the same extent, and with the like consequences, as if an opaque structure, of the dimensions specified in the application –

(a) had, on the date of registration of the notice, been erected in the position on the servient land specified in the application, and had been so erected by the person who made the application, and

(b) had remained in that position during the period for which the notice has effect and had been removed at the end of that period.

(2) For the purposes of this section a notice registered under the last preceding section shall be taken to have effect until either –

(a) the registration is cancelled, or

(b) the period of one year beginning with the date of registration of the notice expires, or

(c) in the case of a notice registered in pursuance of an application accompanied by a certificate issued under paragraph (b) of subsection (3) of the last preceding section, the period specified in the certificate expires without such a further certificate as is mentioned in paragraph (c) of subsection (5) of that section having before the end of that period been lodged with the local authority,

and shall cease to have effect on the occurrence of any one of those events.

(3) Subject to the following provisions of this section, any person who, if such a structure as is mentioned in subsection (1) of this section had been erected as therein mentioned, would have had a right of action in any court in respect of that structure, on the grounds that he was entitled to a right to the access of light to the dominant building across the servient land, and that the said right was infringed by that structure, shall have the like right of action in that court in respect of the registration of a notice under the last preceding section: Provided that an action shall not be begun by virtue of this subsection after the notice in question has ceased to have effect.

(4) Where, at any time during the period for which a notice registered under the last preceding section has effect, the circumstances are such that, if the access of light to the dominant building had been enjoyed continuously from a date one year earlier than the date on which the enjoyment thereof in fact began, a person would have had a right of action in any court by virtue of the last preceding subsection in respect of the registration of the notice, that person shall have the like right of action in that court by virtue of this subsection in respect of the registration of the notice.

(5) The remedies available to the plaintiff in an action brought by virtue of subsection (3) or subsection (4) of this section (apart from any order as to costs) shall be such declaration as the court may consider appropriate in the circumstances, and an order directing the registration of the notice to be cancelled or varied, as the court may determine.

(6) For the purposes of section four of the Prescription Act 1832 (under which a period of enjoyment of any of the rights to which that Act applies is not to be treated as interrupted except by a matter submitted to or acquiesced in for one year after notice thereof) –

(a) as from the date of registration of a notice under the last preceding section, all persons interested in the dominant building or any part thereof shall be deemed to have notice of the registration thereof and of the person on whose application it was registered;

(b) until such time as an action is brought by virtue of subsection (3) or subsection (4) of this section in respect of the registration of a notice under the last preceding section, all persons interested in the dominant building or any part thereof shall be deemed to acquiesce in the obstruction which, in accordance with subsection (1) of this section, is to be treated as resulting from the registration of the notice;

(c) as from the date on which such an action is brought, no person shall be treated as submitting to or acquiescing in that obstruction;

Provided that if, in any such action, the court decides against the claim of the plaintiff, the court may direct that the preceding provisions of this subsection shall apply in relation to the notice as if that action had not been brought.

7 Interpretation   [604]

(1) In this Act, except in so far as the context otherwise requires, the following expressions have the meanings hereby assigned to them respectively, that is to say:

'action' includes a counterclaim, and any reference to the plaintiff in an action shall be construed accordingly;

'local authority', in relation to land in a district or a London borough, means the council of the district or borough, and, in relation to land in the City of London, means the Common Council of the City;

'owner', in relation to any land, means a person who is the estate owner in respect of the fee simple thereof, or is entitled to a tenancy thereof (within the meaning of the Landlord and Tenant Act 1954) for a term of years certain of which, at the time in question, not less than seven years remain unexpired, or is a mortgagee in possession (within the meaning of the Law of Property Act 1925) where the interest mortgaged is either the fee simple of the land or such a tenancy thereof; ...

(2) References in this Act to any enactment shall, except where the context otherwise requires, be construed as references to that enactment as amended by or under any other enactment.

[As amended by the Local London Charges Act 1975, s17(2), Schedule 1.]

MARRIED WOMEN'S PROPERTY ACT 1964
(1964 c 19)

1 Money and property derived from   [605]
housekeeping allowance

If any question arises as to the right of a husband or wife to money derived from any allowance made by the husband for the expenses of the matrimonial home or for similar purposes, or to any property acquired out of such money, the money or property shall, in the absence of any agreement between them to the contrary, be treated as belonging to the husband and the wife in equal shares.

PERPETUITIES AND ACCUMULATIONS ACT 1964
(1964 c 55)

1 Power to specify perpetuity period   [606]

(1) Subject to section 9(2) of this Act and subsection (2) below, where the instrument by which any disposition is made so provides, the perpetuity period

applicable to the disposition under the rule against perpetuities, instead of being of any other duration, shall be of a duration equal to such number of years not exceeding eighty as is specified in that behalf in the instrument.

(2) Subsection (1) above shall not have effect where the disposition is made in exercise of a special power of appointment, but where a period is specified under that subsection in the instrument creating such a power the period shall apply in relation to any disposition under the power as it applies in relation to the power itself.

2 Presumptions and evidence as to future parenthood   [607]

(1) Where in any proceedings there arises on the rule against perpetuities a question which turns on the ability of a person to have a child at some future time, then –

(a) subject to paragraph (b) below, it shall be presumed that a male can have a child at the age of fourteen years or over, but not under that age, and that a female can have a child at the age of twelve years or over, but not under that age or over the age of fifty-five years; but

(b) in the case of a living person evidence may be given to show that he or she will or will not be able to have a child at the time in question.

(2) Where any such question is decided by treating a person as unable to have a child at a particular time, and he or she does so, the High Court may make such order as it thinks fit for placing the persons interested in the property comprised in the disposition, so far as may be just, in the position they would have held if the question had not been so decided.

(3) Subject to subsection (2) above, where any such question is decided in relation to a disposition by treating a person as able or unable to have a child at a particular time, then he or she shall be so treated for the purpose of any question which may arise on the rule against perpetuities in relation to the same disposition in any subsequent proceedings.

(4) In the foregoing provisions of this section references to having a child are references to begetting or giving birth to a child, but those provisions (except subsection (1)(b)) shall apply in relation to the possibility that a person will at any time have a child by adoption, legitimation or other means as they apply to his or her ability at that time to beget or give birth to a child.

3 Uncertainty as to remoteness   [608]

(1) Where, apart from the provisions of this section and sections 4 and 5 of this Act, a disposition would be void on the ground that the interest disposed of might not become vested until too remote a time, the disposition shall be treated, until such time (if any) as it becomes established that the vesting must occur, if at all, after the end of the perpetuity period, as if the disposition were not subject to the rule against perpetuities; and its becoming so established shall not affect the validity of anything previously done in relation to the interest disposed of by way of advancement, application of intermediate income or otherwise.

(2) Where, apart from the said provisions, a disposition consisting of the conferring of a general power of appointment would be void on the ground that the power might not become exercisable until too remote a time, the disposition shall be treated, until such time (if any) as it becomes established that the power will not be exercisable within the perpetuity period, as if the disposition were not subject to the rule against perpetuities.

(3) Where, apart from the said provisions, a disposition consisting of the

conferring of any power, option or other right would be void on the ground that the right might be exercised at too remote a time, the disposition shall be treated as regards any exercise of the right within the perpetuity period as if it were not subject to the rule against perpetuities and, subject to the said provisions, shall be treated as void for remoteness only if, and so far as, the right is not fully exercised within that period.

(4) Where this section applies to a disposition and the duration of the perpetuity period is not determined by virtue of section 1 or 9(2) of this Act, it shall be determined as follows:

(a) where any persons falling within subsection (5) below are individuals in being and ascertainable at the commencement of the perpetuity period the duration of the period shall be determined by reference to their lives and no others, but so that the lives of any description of persons falling within paragraph (b) or (c) of that subsection shall be disregarded if the number of persons of that description is such as to render it impracticable to ascertain the date of birth of the survivor;

(b) where there are no lives under paragraph (a) above the period shall be twenty-one years.

(5) The said persons are as follows:

(a) the person by whom the disposition was made;

(b) a person to whom or in whose favour the disposition was made, that is to say –

(i) in the case of a disposition to a class of persons, any member or potential member of that class;

(ii) in the case of an individual disposition to a person taking only on certain conditions being satisfied, any person as to whom some of the conditions are satisfied and the remainder may in time be satisfied;

(iii) in the case of a special power of appointment exercisable in favour of members of a class, any member or potential member of the class;

(iv) in the case of a special power of appointment exercisable in favour of one person only, that person or, where the object of the power is ascertainable only on certain conditions being satisfied, any person as to whom some of the conditions are satisfied and the remainder may in time be satisfied;

(v) in the case of any power, option or other right, the person on whom the right is conferred;

(c) a person having a child or grandchild within sub-paragraphs (i) to (iv) of paragraph (b) above, or any of whose children or grandchildren, if subsequently born, would by virtue of his or her descent fall within those sub-paragraphs;

(d) any person on the failure or determination of whose prior interest the disposition is limited to take effect.

4 Reduction of age and exclusion of class members   **[609]**
to avoid remoteness

(1) Where a disposition is limited by reference to the attainment by any person or persons of a specified age exceeding twenty-one years, and it is apparent at the time the disposition is made or becomes apparent at a subsequent time –

(a) that the disposition would, apart from this section, be void for remoteness, but

(b) that it would not be so void if the specified age had been twenty-one years, the disposition shall be treated for all purposes as if, instead of being limited by reference to the age in fact specified, it had been limited by reference to the age nearest to that age which would, if specified instead, have prevented the disposition from being so void.

(2) Where in the case of any disposition different ages exceeding twenty-one years are specified in relation to different persons –

(a) the reference in paragraph (b) of subsection (1) above to the specified age shall be construed as a reference to all the specified ages, and
(b) that subsection shall operate to reduce each such age so far as is necessary to save the disposition from being void for remoteness.

(3) Where the inclusion of any persons, being potential members of a class or unborn persons who at birth would become members or potential members of the class, prevents the foregoing provisions of this section from operating to save a disposition from being void for remoteness, those persons shall thenceforth be deemed for all the purposes of the disposition to be excluded from the class, and the said provisions shall thereupon have effect accordingly.

(4) Where, in the case of a disposition to which subsection (3) above does not apply, it is apparent at the time the disposition is made or becomes apparent at a subsequent time that, apart from this subsection, the inclusion of any persons, being potential members of a class or unborn persons who at birth would become members or potential members of the class, would cause the disposition to be treated as void for remoteness, those persons shall, unless their exclusion would exhaust the class, thenceforth be deemed for all the purposes of the disposition to be excluded from the class.

(5) Where this section has effect in relation to a disposition to which section 3 above applies, the operation of this section shall not effect the validity of anything previously done in relation to the interest disposed of by way of advancement, application of intermediate income or otherwise ...

(7) For the avoidance of doubt it is hereby declared that a question arising under section 3 of this Act or subsection (1)(a) above of whether a disposition would be void apart from this section is to be determined as if subsection (6) above [repealed s163 of the Law of Property Act 1925] had been a separate section of this Act.

5 Condition relating to death of surviving spouse [610]

Where a disposition is limited by reference to the time of death of the survivor of a person in being at the commencement of the perpetuity period and any spouse of that person, and that time has not arrived at the end of the perpetuity period, the disposition shall be treated for all purposes, where to do so would save it from being void for remoteness, as if it had instead been limited by reference to the time immediately before the end of that period.

6 Saving and acceleration of expectant interests [611]

A disposition shall not be treated as void for remoteness by reason only that the interest disposed of is ulterior to and dependent upon an interest under a disposition which is so void, and the vesting of an interest shall not be prevented from being accelerated on the failure of a prior interest by reason only that the failure arises because of remoteness.

7 Powers of appointment [612]

For the purposes of the rule against perpetuities, a power of appointment shall be treated as a special power unless –

(a) in the instrument creating the power it is expressed to be exercisable by one person only, and

(b) it could, at all times during its currency when that person is of full age and capacity, be exercised by him so as immediately to transfer to himself the whole of the interest governed by the power without the consent of any other person or compliance with any other condition, not being a formal condition relating only to the mode of exercise of the power:

Provided that for the purpose of determining whether a disposition made under a power of appointment exercisable by will only is void for remoteness, the power shall be treated as a general power where it would have fallen to be so treated if exercisable by deed.

8 Administrative powers of trustees [613]

(1) The rule against perpetuities shall not operate to invalidate a power conferred on trustees or other persons to sell, lease, exchange or otherwise dispose of any property for full consideration, or to do any other act in the administration (as opposed to the distribution) of any property, and shall not prevent the payment to trustees or other persons of reasonable remuneration for their services.

(2) Subsection (1) above shall apply for the purposes of enabling a power to be exercised at any time after the commencement of this Act notwithstanding that the power is conferred by an instrument which took effect before that commencement.

9 Options relating to land [614]

(1) The rule against perpetuities shall not apply to a disposition consisting of the conferring of an option to acquire for valuable consideration an interest reversionary (whether directly or indirectly) on the term of a lease if –

(a) the option is exercisable only by the lessee or his successors in title, and

(b) it ceases to be exercisable at or before the expiration of one year following the determination of the lease.

This subsection shall apply in relation to an agreement for a lease as it applies in relation to a lease, and 'lessee' shall be construed accordingly.

(2) In the case of a disposition consisting of the conferring of an option to acquire for valuable consideration any interest in land, the perpetuity period under the rule against perpetuities shall be twenty-one years, and section 1 of this Act shall not apply: provided that this subsection shall not apply to a right of pre-emption conferred on a public or local authority in respect of land used or to be used for religious purposes where the right becomes exercisable only if the land ceases to be used for such purposes.

10 Avoidance of contractual and other rights in cases [615]
of remoteness

Where a disposition inter vivos would fall to be treated as void for remoteness if the rights and duties thereunder were capable of transmission to persons other than the original parties and had been so transmitted, it shall be treated as void as between the person by whom it was made and the person to whom or in whose favour it was made or any successor of his, and no remedy shall lie in contract or otherwise for giving effect to it or making restitution for its lack of effect.

11 Rights for enforcement of rentcharges   [616]

(1) The rule against perpetuities shall not apply to any powers or remedies for recovering or compelling the payment of an annual sum to which section 121 or 122 of the Law of Property Act 1925 applies, or otherwise becoming exercisable or enforceable on the breach of any condition or other requirement relating to that sum ...

12 Possibilities of reverter, conditions subsequent,   [617]
exceptions and reservations

(1) In the case of –

(a) a possibility of reverter on the determination of a determinable fee simple, or

(b) a possibility of a resulting trust on the determination of any other determinable interest in property,

the rule against perpetuities shall apply in relation to the provision causing the interest to be determinable as it would apply if that provision were expressed in the form of a condition subsequent giving rise, on breach thereof, to a right of re-entry or an equivalent right in the case of property other than land, and where the provision falls to be treated as void for remoteness the determinable interest shall become an absolute interest.

(2) Where a disposition is subject to any such provision, or to any such condition subsequent, or to any exception or reservation, the disposition shall be treated for the purposes of this Act as including a separate disposition of any rights arising by virtue of the provision, condition subsequent, exception or reservation.

13 Amendment of s164 of Law of Property Act 1925   [618]

(1) The periods for which accumulations of income under a settlement or other disposition are permitted by section 164 of the Law of Property Act 1925 shall include –

(a) a term of twenty-one years from the date of the making of the disposition, and

(b) the duration of the minority or respective minorities of any person or persons in being at that date.

(2) It is hereby declared that the restrictions imposed by the said section 164 apply in relation to a power to accumulate income whether or not there is a duty to exercise that power, and that they apply whether or not the power to accumulate extends to income produced by the investment of income previously accumulated.

14 Right to stop accumulations   [619]

Section 2 above shall apply to any question as to the right of beneficiaries to put an end to accumulations of income under any disposition as it applies to questions arising on the rule against perpetuities.

15 Short title, interpretation and extent   [620]

(1) This Act may be cited as the Perpetuities and Accumulations Act 1964.

(2) In this Act –

> 'disposition' includes the conferring of a power of appointment and any other disposition of an interest in or right over property, and references to the interest disposed of shall be construed accordingly;
> 'in being' means living or en ventre sa mère;
> 'power of appointment' includes any discretionary power to transfer a beneficial interest in property without the furnishing of valuable consideration;
> 'will' includes a codicil;

and for the purposes of this Act a disposition contained in a will shall be deemed to be made at the death of the testator.

(3) For the purposes of this Act a person shall be treated as a member of a class if in his case all the conditions identifying a member of the class are satisfied, and shall be treated as a potential member if in his case some only of those conditions are satisfied but there is a possibility that the remainder will in time be satisfied.

(4) Nothing in this Act shall affect the operation of the rule of law rendering void for remoteness certain dispositions under which property is limited to be applied for purposes other than the benefit of any person or class of persons in cases where the property may be so applied after the end of the perpetuity period.

(5) The foregoing sections of this Act shall apply (except as provided in section 8(2) above) only in relation to instruments taking effect after the commencement of this Act, and in the case of an instrument made in the exercise of a special power of appointment shall apply only where the instrument creating the power takes effect after that commencement: provided that section 7 above shall apply in all cases for construing the foregoing reference to a special power of appointment.

(6) This Act shall apply in relation to a disposition made otherwise than by an instrument as if the disposition had been contained in an instrument taking effect when the disposition was made.

(7) This Act binds the Crown ...

[As amended by the Children Act 1975, s108(1)(a), Schedule 3, para 43.]

LAW OF PROPERTY (JOINT TENANTS) ACT 1964
(1964 c 63)

1 Assumptions on sale of land by survivor of joint tenants   [621]

(1) For the purposes of section 36(2) of the Law of Property Act 1925, as amended by section 7 of and the Schedule to the Law of Property (Amendment) Act 1926, the survivor of two or more joint tenants shall in favour of a purchaser of the legal estate, be deemed to be solely and beneficially interested if the conveyance includes a statement that he is so interested.

Provided that the foregoing provisions of this subsection shall not apply if, at any time before the date of the conveyance by the survivor –

> (a) a memorandum of severance (that is to say a note or memorandum signed by the joint tenants or one of them and recording that the joint tenancy was severed in equity on a date therein specified) had been endorsed on or annexed to the conveyance by virtue of which the legal estate was vested in the joint tenants; or
> (b) a bankruptcy order made against any of the joint tenants, or a petition for such an order, had been registered under the Land Charges Act 1925, being an order or petition of which the purchaser has notice, by virtue of the registration, on the date of the conveyance by the survivor.

(2) The foregoing provisions of this section shall apply with the necessary modifications in relation to a conveyance by the personal representatives of the survivor of joint tenants as they apply in relation to a conveyance by such a survivor.

3 Exclusion of registered land   [622]

This Act shall not apply to any land the title of which has been registered under the provisions of the Land Registration Acts 1925 and 1936.

[As amended by the Insolvency Act 1985, s235(1), Schedule 8, para 13; Law of Property (Miscellaneous Provisions) Act 1994, s21(1), Schedule 1, para 3.]

COMMONS REGISTRATION ACT 1965
(1965 c 64)

1 Registration of commons and towns or village greens and   [623] ownership of and rights over them

(1) There shall be registered, in accordance with the provisions of this Act and subject to the exceptions mentioned therein –

    (a) land in England or Wales which is common land or a town or village green;
    (b) rights of common over such land; and
    (c) persons claiming to be or found to be owners of such land or becoming the owners thereof by virtue of this Act;

and no rights of common over land which is capable of being registered under this Act shall be registered under the Land Registration Acts 1925 and 1936.

(2) After the end of such period, not being less than three years from the commencement of this Act, as the Minister may by order determine –

    (a) no land capable of being registered under this Act shall be deemed to be common land or a town or village green unless it is so registered; and
    (b) no rights of common shall be exercisable over any such land unless they are registered either under this Act or under the Land Registration Acts 1925 and 1936.

(3) Where any land is registered under this Act but no person is registered as the owner thereof under this Act or under the Land Registration Acts 1925 and 1936, it shall –

    (a) if it is a town or village green, be vested in accordance with the following provisions of this Act; and
    (b) if it is common land, be vested as Parliament may hereafter determine.

8 Vesting of unclaimed land   [624]

(1) Where the registration under section 4 of this Act [provisional registration] of any land as common land or as a town or village green has become final but no person is registered under that section as the owner of the land, then unless the land is registered under the Land Registration Acts 1925 and 1936, the registration authority shall refer the question of the ownership of the land to a Commons Commissioner.

(2) After the registration authority has given such notices as may be prescribed, the Commons Commissioner shall inquire into the matter and shall, if satisfied that any person is the owner of the land, direct the registration authority to register that person accordingly; and the registration authority shall comply with the direction.

(3) If the Commons Commissioner is not so satisfied and the land is a town or village green he shall direct the registration authority to register as the owner of the land the local authority specified in subsection (5) of this section [as substituted]; and the registration authority shall comply with the direction ...

9 Protection of unclaimed common land [625]

Where the registration under section 4 of this Act of any land as common land has become final but no person is registered under this Act or the Land Registration Acts 1925 and 1936 as the owner of the land, then, until the land is vested under any provision hereafter made by Parliament, any local authority in whose area the land or part of the land is situated may take such steps for the protection of the land against unlawful interference as could be taken by an owner in possession of the land, and may (without prejudice to any power exercisable apart from this section) institute proceedings for any offence committed in respect of that land.

10 Effect of registration [626]

The registration under this Act of any land as common land or as a town or village green, or of any rights of common over any such land, shall be conclusive evidence of the matters registered, as at the date of registration, except where the registration is provisional only.

12 Subsequent registration under Land Registration [627]
Acts 1925 and 1936

The following provisions shall have effect with respect to the registration under the Land Registration Acts 1925 and 1936 of any land after the ownership of the land has been registered under this Act, that is to say –

(a) section 123 of the Land Registration Act 1925 (compulsory registration of title on sale) shall have effect in relation to the land whether or not the land is situated in an area in which an Order in Council under section 120 of that Act is for the time being in force, unless the registration under this Act is provisional only; and
(b) if the registration authority is notified by the Chief Land Registrar that the land has been registered under the Land Registration Acts 1925 and 1936 the authority shall delete the registration of the ownership under this Act and indicate in the register in the prescribed manner that it has been registered under those Acts.

16 Disregard of certain interruptions in prescriptive [628]
claims to rights of common

(1) Where during any period a right of common claimed over any land was not exercised, but during the whole or part of that period either –

(a) the land was requisitioned; or
(b) where the right claimed is a right to graze animals, the right could not be or was not exercised for reasons of animal health;

that period or part shall be left out of account, both –

(i) in determining for the purposes of the Prescription Act 1832 whether there was an interruption within the meaning of that Act of the actual enjoyment of the right; and
(ii) in computing the period of thirty or sixty years mentioned in section 1 of that Act.

(2) For the purposes of the said Act any objection under this Act to the registration of a right of common shall be deemed to be such a suit or action as is referred to in section 4 of that Act.

(3) In this section 'requisitioned' means in the possession of a Government department in the exercise or purported exercise of powers conferred by regulations made under the Emergency Powers (Defence) Act 1939 or by Part VI of the Requisitioned Land and War Works Act 1945; and in determining in any proceedings any question arising under this section whether any land was requisitioned during any period a document purporting to be a certificate to that effect issued by a Government department shall be admissible in evidence.

(4) Where it is necessary for the purposes of this section to establish that a right to graze animals on any land could not be or was not exercised for reasons of animal health it shall be sufficient to prove either –

(a) that the movement of the animals to that land was prohibited or restricted by or under the Diseases of Animals Act 1950 or any enactment repealed by that Act; or
(b) that the land was not, but some other land was, approved for grazing under any scheme in force under that Act or any such enactment and the animals were registered, or were undergoing tests with a view to registration, under the scheme.

21 Savings   [629]

(1) Section 1(2) of this Act shall not affect the application to any land registered under this Act of section 193 or section 194 of the Law of Property Act 1925 (rights of access to, and restriction on inclosure of, land over which rights of common are exercisable).

(2) Section 10 of this Act shall not apply for the purpose of deciding whether any land forms part of a highway.

22 Interpretation   [630]

(1) In this Act, unless the context otherwise requires –

'common land' means –

(a) land subject to rights of common (as defined in this Act) whether those rights are exercisable at all times or only during limited periods;
(b) waste land of a manor not subject to rights of common;

but does not include a town or village green or any land which forms part of a highway;
'land' includes land covered with water;
'local authority' means the council of a county, London borough or county district, the council of a parish;
'the Minister' means the Minister of Housing and Local Government;
'prescribed' means prescribed by regulations under this Act;
'registration' includes an entry in the register made in pursuance of section 13 of this Act [amendment of registers];
'rights of common' includes cattlegates or beastgates (by whatever name known) and rights of sole or several vesture or herbage or of sole or several pasture, but does not include rights held for a term of years or from year to year;
'town or village green' means land which has been allotted by or under any Act for the exercise or recreation of the inhabitants of any locality or on which the inhabitants of any locality have a customary right to indulge in lawful

sports and pastimes or on which the inhabitants of any locality have indulged in such sports and pastimes as of right for not less than twenty years.

(2) References in this Act to the ownership and the owner of any land are references to the ownership of a legal estate in fee simple in any land and to the person holding that estate, and references to land registered under the Land Registration Acts 1925 and 1936 are references to land the fee simple of which is so registered.

[As amended by the Local Government Act 1972, s272(1), Schedule 30; Local Government Act 1985, s102(2), Schedule 17.]

MISREPRESENTATION ACT 1967
(1967 c 7)

1 Removal of certain bars to rescission for innocent misrepresentation [631]

Where a person has entered into a contract after a misrepresentation has been made to him, and –

(a) the misrepresentation has become a term of the contract; or
(b) the contract has been performed;

or both, then, if otherwise he would be entitled to rescind the contract without alleging fraud, he shall be so entitled, subject to the provisions of this Act, notwithstanding the matters mentioned in paragraphs (a) and (b) of this section.

2 Damages for misrepresentation [632]

(1) Where a person has entered into a contract after a misrepresentation has been made to him by another party thereto and as a result thereof he has suffered loss, then, if the person making the misrepresentation would be liable to damages in respect thereof had the misrepresentation been made fraudulently, that person shall be so liable notwithstanding that the misrepresentation was not made fraudulently, unless he proves that he had reasonable ground to believe and did believe up to the time the contract was made that the facts represented were true.

(2) Where a person has entered into a contract after a misrepresentation has been made to him otherwise than fraudulently, and he would be entitled, by reason of the misrepresentation, to rescind the contract, then, if it is claimed, in any proceedings arising out of the contract, that the contract ought to be or has been rescinded the court or arbitrator may declare the contract subsisting and award damages in lieu of rescission, if of opinion that it would be equitable to do so, having regard to the nature of the misrepresentation and the loss that would be caused by it if the contract were upheld, as well as to the loss that rescission would cause to the other party.

(3) Damages may be awarded against a person under subsection (2) of this section whether or not he is liable to damages under subsection (1) thereof, but where he is so liable any award under the said subsection (2) shall be taken into account in assessing his liability under the said subsection (1).

3 Avoidance of provision excluding liability for misrepresentation [633]

If a contract contains a term which would exclude or restrict –

(a) any liability to which a party to a contract may be subject by reason of any misrepresentation made by him before the contract was made; or

(b) any remedy available to another party to the contract by reason of such misrepresentation,

that term shall be of no effect except in so far as it satisfies the requirement of reasonableness stated in section 11(l) of the Unfair Contract Terms Act 1977; and it is for those claiming that the term satisfies that requirement to show that it does.

[As amended by the Unfair Contract Terms Act 1977, s8(1).]

LEASEHOLD REFORM ACT 1967
(1967 c 88)

PART I

ENFRANCHISEMENT AND EXTENSION OF LONG LEASEHOLDS

1 Tenants entitled to enfranchisement or extension   [634]

(1) This Part of this Act shall have effect to confer on a tenant of a leasehold house, occupying the house as his residence, a right to acquire on fair terms the freehold or an extended lease of the house and premises where –

(a) his tenancy is a long tenancy at a low rent and –

(i) if the tenancy was entered into before 1st April 1990, or on or after 1st April 1990 in pursuance of a contract made before that date, and the house and premises had a rateable value at the date of commencement of the tenancy or else at any time before 1st April 1990, subject to subsections (5) and (6) below, the rateable value of the house and premises on the appropriate day was not more than £200 or, if it is in Greater London, than £400; and

(ii) if the tenancy does not fall within sub-paragraph (i) above, on the date the contract for the grant of the tenancy was made or, if there was no such contract, on the date the tenancy was entered into R did not exceed £25,000 under the formula –

$$R = \frac{P \times I}{1 - (1 + I)^{-t}}$$

where –

P is the premium payable as a condition of the grant of the tenancy (and includes a payment of money's worth) or, where no premium is so payable, zero,

I is 0.06, and

T is the term, expressed in years, granted by the tenancy (disregarding any right to terminate the tenancy before the end of the term or to extend the tenancy); and

(b) at the relevant time (that is to say, at the time when he gives notice in accordance with this Act of his desire to have the freehold or to have an extended lease, as the case may be) he has been tenant of the house under a long tenancy at a low rent, and occupying it as his residence, for the last three years or for periods amounting to three years in the last ten years;

and to confer the like right in the other cases for which provision is made in this Part of this Act.

(1A) The references in subsection (1)(a) and (b) to a long tenancy at a low rent do not include a tenancy excluded from the operation of this Part by section 33A of and Schedule 4A to this Act.

(2) In this Part of this Act references, in relation to any tenancy, to the tenant occupying a house as his residence shall be construed as applying where, but only where, the tenant is, in right of the tenancy, occupying it as his only or main residence (whether or not he uses it also for other purposes); but –

(a) references to a person occupying a house shall apply where he occupies it in part only; and

(b) in determining in what right the tenant occupies, there shall be disregarded any mortgage term and any interest arising in favour of any person by his attorning tenant to a mortgagee or chargee.

(3) This Part of this Act shall not confer on the tenant of a house any right by reference to his occupation of it as his residence (but shall apply as if he were not so occupying it) at any time when –

(a) it is let to and occupied by him with other land or premises to which it is ancillary; or

(b) it is comprised in –

(i) an agricultural holding within the meaning of the Agricultural Holdings Act 1986 held under a tenancy in relation to which that Act applies, or

(ii) the holding held under a farm business tenancy within the meaning of the Agricultural Tenancies Act 1995;

or, in the case of any right to which subsection (3A) below applies, at any time when the tenant's immediate landlord is a charitable housing trust and the house forms part of the housing accommodation provided by the trust in the pursuit of its charitable purposes.

(3A) For the purposes of subsection (3) above this subsection applies as follows –

(a) where the tenancy was created after the commencement of Chapter III of Part I of the Leasehold Reform, Housing and Urban Development Act 1993, this subsection applies to any right to acquire the freehold of the house and premises; but

(b) where the tenancy was created before that commencement, this subsection applies only to any such right exercisable by virtue of any one or more of the provisions of sections 1A, 1AA and 1B below;

and in that subsection 'charitable housing trust' means a housing trust within the meaning of the Housing Act 1985 which is a charity within the meaning of the Charities Act 1993.

(4) In subsection (1)(a) above, 'the appropriate day', in relation to any house and premises, means the 23rd March 1965 or such later day as by virtue of section 25(3) of the Rent Act 1977 would be the appropriate day for purposes of that Act in relation to a dwelling house consisting of that house.

(4A) Schedule 8 to the Housing Act 1974 shall have effect to enable a tenant to have the rateable value of the house and premises reduced for purposes of this section in consequence of tenant's improvements.

(5) If, in relation to any house and premises, the appropriate day for the purposes of subsection (1)(a) above falls on or after 1st April 1973 that subsection shall have effect in relation to the house and premises –

(a) in a case where the tenancy was created on or before 18th February 1966, as if for the sums of £200 and £400 specified in that subsection there were substituted respectively the sums of £750 and £1,500; and

(b) in a case where the tenancy was created after 18th February 1966, as if for those sums of £200 and £400 there were substituted respectively the sums of £500 and £1,000.

(6) If, in relation to any house and premises –

(a) the appropriate day for the purposes of subsection (1)(a) above falls before 1st April 1973, and

(b) the rateable value of the house and premises on the appropriate day was more than £200 or, if it was then in Greater London, £400, and

(c) the tenancy was created on or before 18th February 1966,

subsection (1)(a) above shall have effect in relation to the house and premises as if for the reference to the appropriate day there were substituted a reference to 1st April 1973 and as if for the sums of £200 and £400 specified in that subsection there were substituted respectively the sums of £750 and £1,500.

(7) The Secretary of State may by order replace any amount referred to in subsection (1)(a)(ii) above and the number in the definition of 'I' in that subsection by such amount or number as is specified in the order ...

1A Right to enfranchisement only in case of houses whose   [635] value or rent exceeds applicable limit under s1 or 4

(1) Where subsection (1) of section 1 above would apply in the case of the tenant of a house but for the fact that the applicable financial limit specified in subsection (1)(a)(i) or (ii) or (as the case may be) subsection (5) or (6) of that section is exceeded, this Part of this Act shall have effect to confer on the tenant the same right to acquire the freehold of the house and premises as would be conferred by subsection (1) of that section if that limit were not exceeded.

(2) Where a tenancy of any property is not a tenancy at a low rent in accordance with section 4(1) below but is a tenancy falling within section 4A(1) below, the tenancy shall nevertheless be treated as a tenancy at a low rent for the purposes of this Part of this Act so far as it has effect for conferring on any person a right to acquire the freehold of a house and premises.

1AA Additional right to enfranchisement only in case   [636] of houses whose rent exceeds applicable limit under section 4

(1) Where –

(a) section 1(1) above would apply in the case of the tenant of a house but for the fact that the tenancy is not a tenancy at a low rent, and

(b) the tenancy falls within subsection (2) below and is not an excluded tenancy,

this Part of this Act shall have effect to confer on the tenant the same right to acquire the freehold of the house and premises as would be conferred by section 1(1) above if it were a tenancy at a low rent.

(2) A tenancy falls within this subsection if –

(a) it is granted for a term of years certain exceeding thirty-five years, whether or not it is (or may become) terminable before the end of that term by notice given by or to the tenant or by re-entry, forfeiture or otherwise,

(b) it is for a term fixed by law under a grant with a covenant or obligation for perpetual renewal, unless it is a tenancy by sub-demise from one which is not a tenancy which falls within this subsection,

(c) it is a tenancy taking effect under section 149(6) of the Law of Property Act 1925 (leases terminable after a death or marriage), or

(d) it is a tenancy which –

(i) is or has been granted for a term of years certain not exceeding thirty-five years, but with a covenant or obligation for renewal without payment of a premium (but not for perpetual renewal), and

(ii) is or has been once or more renewed so as to bring to more than thirty-five years the total of the terms granted (including any interval between the end of a tenancy and the grant of a renewal).

(3) A tenancy is an excluded tenancy for the purposes of subsection (1) above if –

(a) the house which the tenant occupies under the tenancy is in an area designated for the purposes of this provision as a rural area by order made by the Secretary of State,

(b) the freehold of that house is owned together with adjoining land which is not occupied for residential purposes and has been owned together with such land since the coming into force of section 106 of the Housing Act 1996, and

(c) the tenancy was granted on or before the day on which that section came into force.

(4) Where this Part of this Act applies as if there were a single tenancy of property comprised in two or more separate tenancies, then, if each of the separate tenancies falls within subsection (2) above, this section shall apply as if the single tenancy did so. ...

1B Right of enfranchisement only in case of certain [637] tenancies terminable after death or marriage

Where a tenancy granted so as to become terminable by notice after a death or marriage –

(a) is (apart from this section) a long tenancy in accordance with section 3(1) below, but

(b) was granted before 18th April 1980 or in pursuance of a contract entered into before that date,

then (notwithstanding section 3(1)) the tenancy shall be a long tenancy for the purposes of this Part of this Act only so far as this Part has effect for conferring on any person a right to acquire the freehold of a house and premises.

2 Meaning of 'house' and 'house and premises', and [638] adjustment of boundary

(1) For purposes of this Part of this Act, 'house' includes any building designed or adapted for living in and reasonably so called, notwithstanding that the building is not structurally detached, or was or is not solely designed or adapted for living in, or is divided horizontally into flats or maisonettes; and –

(a) where a building is divided horizontally, the flats or other units into which it is so divided are not separate 'houses', though the building as a whole may be; and

(b) where a building is divided vertically the building as a whole is not a 'house' though any of the units into which it is divided may be.

(2) References in this Part of this Act to a house do not apply to a house which is not structurally detached and of which a material part lies above or below a part of the structure not comprised in the house ...

3 Meaning of 'long tenancy' [639]

(1) In this Part of this Act 'long tenancy' means, subject to the provisions of this section, a tenancy granted for a term of years certain exceeding twenty-one years, whether or not the tenancy is (or may become) terminable before the end of that term by notice given by or to the tenant or by re-entry, forfeiture or otherwise, and

includes both a tenancy taking effect under section 149(6) of the Law of Property Act 1925 (leases terminable after a death or marriage) and a tenancy for a term fixed by law under a grant with a covenant or obligation for perpetual renewal unless it is a tenancy by sub-demise from one which is not a long tenancy: provided that a tenancy granted so as to become terminable by notice after a death or marriage is not to be treated as a long tenancy if –

(a) the notice is capable of being given at any time after the death or marriage of the tenant;

(b) the length of the notice is not more than three months; and

(c) the terms of the tenancy preclude both –

(i) its assignment otherwise than by virtue of section 92 of the Housing Act 1985 (assignments by way of exchange), and

(ii) the sub-letting of the whole of the premises comprised in it …

4 Meaning of 'low rent'   [640]

(1) For purposes of this Part of this Act a tenancy of any property is a tenancy at a low rent at any time when rent is not payable under the tenancy in respect of the property at a yearly rate –

(i) if the tenancy was entered into before 1st April 1990, or on or after 1st April 1990 in pursuance of a contract made before that date, and the property had a rateable value other than nil at the date of the commencement of the tenancy or else at any time before 1st April 1990, equal to or more than two-thirds of the rateable value of the property on the appropriate day or, if later, the first day of the term;

(ii) if the tenancy does not fall within paragraph (i) above …

4A Alternative rent limits for purposes of section 1A(2)   [641]

(1) For the purposes of section 1A(2) above a tenancy of any property falls within this subsection if either no rent was payable under it in respect of the property during the initial year or the aggregate amount of rent so payable during the year did not exceed the following amount, namely –

(a) where the tenancy was entered into before 1st April 1963, two-thirds of the letting value of the property (on the same terms) on the date of the commencement of the tenancy;

(b) where –

(i) the tenancy was entered into either on or after 1st April 1963 but before 1st April 1990, or on or after 1st April 1990 in pursuance of a contract made before that date, and

(ii) the property had a rateable value other than nil at the date of commencement of the tenancy or else at any time before 1st April 1990,

two-thirds of the rateable value of the property on the relevant date; or

(c) in any other case, £1,000 if the property is in Greater London or £250 if elsewhere.

(2) For the purposes of subsection (1) above –

(a) 'the initial year', in relation to any tenancy, means the period of one year beginning with the date of the commencement of the tenancy;

(b) 'the relevant date' means the date of the commencement of the tenancy or, if the property did not have a rateable value or had a rateable value of nil, on that date, the date on which it first had a rateable value other than nil; and

(c) paragraphs (b) and (c) of section 4(1) above shall apply as they apply for the purposes of section 4(1);

and it is hereby declared that in subsection (1) above the reference to the letting value of any property is to be construed in like manner as the reference in similar terms which appears in the proviso to section 4(1) above.

(3) Section 1(7) above applies to any amount referred to in subsection (1)(c) above as it applies to the amount referred to in subsection (1)(a)(ii) of that section.

[As amended by the Housing Act 1974, s118(1); Housing and Planning Act 1968, s18, Schedule 4, paras 3, 11(1); Rent Act 1977, s155, Schedule 23, para 42; Housing Act 1980, s141, Schedule 21, paras 1, 2; Agricultural Holdings Act 1986, s100, Schedule 14, para 13; References to Rating (Housing) Regulations 1990, as amended; Leasehold Reform, Housing and Urban Development Act 1993, ss63, 64(1), (2), 65, 67; Agricultural Tenancies Act 1995, s40, Schedule, para 22; Housing Act 1996, ss105(1), (2), 106, 114, Schedule 9, paras 1, 2(2).]

LAW OF PROPERTY ACT 1969
(1969 c 59)

23 Reduction of statutory period of title [642]

Section 44(1) of the Law of Property Act 1925 (under which the period of commencement of title which may be required under a contract expressing no contrary intention is thirty years except in certain cases) shall have effect, in its application to contracts made after the commencement of this Act, as if it specified fifteen years instead of thirty years as the period of commencement of title which may be so required.

24 Contracts for purchase of land affected by [643]
land charge, etc

(1) Where under a contract for the sale or other disposition of any estate or interest in land the title to which is not registered under the Land Registration Act 1925 or any enactment replaced by it any question arises whether the purchaser had knowledge, at the time of entering into the contract, of a registered land charge, that question shall be determined by reference to his actual knowledge and without regard to the provisions of section 198 of the Law of Property Act 1925 (under which registration under the Land Charges Act 1925 or any enactment replaced by it is deemed to constitute actual notice).

(2) Where any estate or interest with which such a contract is concerned is affected by a registered land charge and the purchaser, at the time of entering into the contract, had not received notice and did not otherwise actually know that the estate or interest was affected by the charge, any provision of the contract shall be void so far as it purports to exclude the operation of subsection (1) above or to exclude or restrict any right or remedy that might otherwise be exercisable by the purchaser on the ground that the estate or interest is affected by the charge.

(3) In this section –

'purchaser' includes a lessee, mortgagee or other person acquiring or intending to acquire an estate or interest in land; and
'registered land charge' means any instrument or matter registered, otherwise than in a register of local land charges, under the Land Charges Act 1925 or any Act replaced by it.

(4) For the purposes of this section any knowledge acquired in the course of a transaction by a person who is acting therein as counsel, or as solicitor or other agent, for another shall be treated as the knowledge of that other ...

25 Compensation in certain cases for loss due to undisclosed land charges [644]

(1) Where a purchaser of any estate or interest in land under a disposition to which this section applies has suffered loss by reason that the estate or interest is affected by a registered land charge, then if –

(a) the date of completion was after the commencement of this Act; and

(b) on that date the purchaser had no actual knowledge of the charge; and

(c) the charge was registered against the name of an owner of an estate in the land who was not as owner of any such estate a party to any transaction, or concerned in any event, comprised in the relevant title;

the purchaser shall be entitled to compensation for the loss.

(2) For the purposes of subsection (1)(b) above, the question whether any person had actual knowledge of a charge shall be determined without regard to the provisions of section 198 of the Law of Property Act 1925 (under which registration under the Land Charges Act 1925 or any enactment replaced by it is deemed to constitute actual notice).

(3) Where a transaction comprised in the relevant title was effected or evidenced by a document which expressly provided that it should take effect subject to an interest or obligation capable of registration in any of the relevant registers, the transaction which created that interest or obligation shall be treated for the purposes of subsection (1)(c) above as comprised in the relevant title.

(4) Any compensation for loss under this section shall be paid by the Chief Land Registrar, and where the purchaser of the estate or interest in question has incurred expenditure for the purpose –

(a) of securing that the estate or interest is no longer affected by the registered land charge or is so affected to a less extent; or

(b) of obtaining compensation under this section;

the amount of the compensation shall include the amount of the expenditure (so far as it would not otherwise fall to be treated as compensation for loss) reasonably incurred by the purchaser for that purpose.

(5) In the case of an action to recover compensation under this section, the cause of action shall be deemed for the purposes of the Limitation Act 1980 to accrue at the time when the registered land charge affecting the estate or interest in question comes to the notice of the purchaser ...

(8) Where compensation under this section has been paid in a case where the purchaser would have had knowledge of the registered land charge but for the fraud of any person, the Chief Land Registrar, on behalf of the Crown, may recover the amount paid from that person.

(9) This section applies to the following dispositions, that is to say –

(a) any sale or exchange and, subject to the following provisions of this subsection, any mortgage of an estate or interest in land;

(b) any grant of a lease for a term of years derived out of a leasehold interest;

(c) any compulsory purchase, by whatever procedure, of land; and

(d) any conveyance of a fee simple in land under Part I of the Leasehold Reform Act 1967;

but does not apply to the grant of a term of years derived out of the freehold or the mortgage of such a term by the lessee; and references in this section to a purchaser shall be construed accordingly.

(10) In this section –

'date of completion', in relation to land which vests in the Land Commission or another acquiring authority by virtue of a general vesting declaration under the

Land Commission Act 1967 or the Town and Country Planning Act 1968, means the date on which it so vests;

'mortgage' includes any charge;

'registered land charge' means any instrument or matter registered, otherwise than in a register of local land charges, under the Land Charges Act 1925 or any Act replaced by it, except that –

(a) in relation to an assignment of a lease or underlease or a mortgage by an assignee under such an assignment, it does not include any instrument or matter affecting the title to the freehold or to any relevant leasehold reversion; and

(b) in relation to the grant of an underlease or the mortgage by the underlessee of the term of years created by an underlease, it does not include any instrument or matter affecting the title to the freehold or to any leasehold reversion superior to the leasehold interest out of which the term of years is derived;

'relevant registers' means the registers kept under section 1 of the Land Charges Act [1972];

'relevant title' means –

(a) in relation to a disposition made under a contract, the title which the purchaser was, apart from any acceptance by him (by agreement or otherwise) of a shorter or an imperfect title, entitled to require; or

(b) in relation to any other disposition, the title which he would have been entitled to require if the disposition had been made under a contract to which section 44(1) of the Law of Property Act 1925 applied and that contract had been made on the date of completion.

(11) For the purposes of this section any knowledge acquired in the course of a transaction by a person who is acting therein as counsel, or as solicitor or other agent, for another shall be treated as the knowledge of that other.

[As amended by the Limitation Act 1980, s40(2), Schedule 3, para 9.]

ADMINISTRATION OF JUSTICE ACT 1970
(1970 c 31)

36 Additional powers of court in action by mortgagee for possession of dwelling-house   **[645]**

(1) Where the mortgagee under a mortgage of land which consists of or includes a dwelling-house brings an action in which he claims possession of the mortgaged property, not being an action for foreclosure in which a claim for possession of the mortgaged property is also made, the court may exercise any of the powers conferred on it by subsection (2) below if it appears to the court that in the event of its exercising the power the mortgagor is likely to be able within a reasonable period to pay any sums due under the mortgage or to remedy a default consisting of a breach of any other obligation arising under or by virtue of the mortgage.

(2) The court –

(a) may adjourn the proceedings, or

(b) on giving judgment, or making an order, for delivery of possession of the mortgaged property, or at any time before the execution of such judgment or order, may –

(i) stay or suspend execution of the judgment or order, or

(ii) postpone the date for delivery of possession,

for such period or periods as the court thinks reasonable.

(3) Any such adjournment, stay, suspension or postponement as is referred to in subsection (2) above may be made subject to such conditions with regard to payment by the mortgagor of any sum secured by the mortgage or the remedying of any default as the court thinks fit.

(4) The court may from time to time vary or revoke any condition imposed by virtue of this section.

(5) This section shall have effect in relation to such an action as is referred to in subsection (1) above begun before the date on which this section comes into force unless in that action judgment has been given, or an order made, for delivery of possession of the mortgaged property and that judgment or order was executed before that date ...

39 Interpretation of Part IV [646]

(1) In this Part of this Act –

'dwelling-house' includes any building or part thereof which is used as a dwelling;
'mortgage' includes a charge and 'mortgagor' and 'mortgagee' shall be construed accordingly;
'mortgagor' and 'mortgagee' includes any person deriving title under the original mortgagor or mortgagee.

(2) The fact that part of the premises comprised in a dwelling-house is used as a shop or office or for business, trade or professional purposes shall not prevent the dwelling-house from being a dwelling-house for the purposes of this Part of this Act.

LAND REGISTRATION AND LAND CHARGES ACT 1971
(1971 c 54)

2 Determination of questions as to right to or [647] amount of indemnity

(1) If any question arises as to whether a person is entitled to an indemnity under any provision of the Land Registration Act 1925 or as to the amount of any such indemnity, he may apply to the court to have that question determined ...

(5) Nothing in this section shall be taken to preclude the registrar from settling by agreement claims for indemnity under the Land Registration Act 1925 ...

DEFECTIVE PREMISES ACT 1972
(1972 c 35)

4 Landlord's duty of care in virtue of obligation or right [648] to repair premises demised

(1) Where premises are let under a tenancy which puts on the landlord an obligation to the tenant for the maintenance or repair of the premises, the landlord owes to all persons who might reasonably be expected to be affected by defects in the state of the premises a duty to take such care as is reasonable in all the circumstances to see that they are reasonably safe from personal injury or from damage to their property caused by a relevant defect.

(2) The said duty is owed if the landlord knows (whether as the result of being

notified by the tenant or otherwise) or if he ought in all the circumstances to have known of the relevant defect.

(3) In this section 'relevant defect' means a defect in the state of the premises existing at or after the material time and arising from, or continuing because of, an act or omission by the landlord which constitutes or would if he had had notice of the defect have constituted a failure by him to carry out his obligation to the tenant for the maintenance or repair of the premises; and for the purposes of the foregoing provision 'the material time' means –

(a) where the tenancy commenced before this Act, the commencement of this Act; and

(b) in all other cases, the earliest of the following times, that is to say –

(i) the time when the tenancy commences;

(ii) the time when the tenancy agreement is entered into;

(iii) the time when possession is taken of the premises in contemplation of the letting.

(4) Where premises are let under a tenancy which expressly or impliedly gives the landlord the right to enter the premises to carry out any description of maintenance or repair of the premises, then, as from the time when he first is, or by notice or otherwise can put himself, in a position to exercise the right and so long as he is or can put himself in that position, he shall be treated for the purposes of subsections (1) to (3) above (but for no other purpose) as if he were under an obligation to the tenant for that description of maintenance or repair of the premises; but the landlord shall not owe the tenant any duty by virtue of this subsection in respect of any defect in the state of the premises arising from, or continuing because of, a failure to carry out an obligation expressly imposed on the tenant by the tenancy.

(5) For the purposes of this section obligations imposed or rights given by any enactment in virtue of a tenancy shall be treated as imposed or given by the tenancy.

(6) This section applies to a right of occupation given by contract or any enactment and not amounting to a tenancy as if the right were a tenancy, and 'tenancy' and cognate expressions shall be construed accordingly.

6 Supplemental [649]

(1) In this Act –

...

'personal injury' includes any disease and any impairment of a person's physical or mental condition;

'tenancy' means –

(a) a tenancy created either immediately or derivatively out of the freehold, whether by a lease or underlease, by an agreement for a lease or underlease or by a tenancy agreement, but not including a mortgage term or any interest arising in favour of a mortgagor by his attorning tenant to his mortgagee; or

(b) a tenancy at will or a tenancy on sufferance; or

(c) a tenancy, whether or not constituting a tenancy at common law, created by or in pursuance of any enactment; and cognate expressions shall be construed accordingly.

(2) Any duty imposed by or enforceable by virtue of any provision of this Act is in addition to any duty a person may owe apart from that provision.

(3) Any term of an agreement which purports to exclude or restrict, or has the

effect of excluding or restricting, the operation of any of the provisions of this Act, or any liability arising by virtue of any such provision, shall be void.

LAND CHARGES ACT 1972
(1972 c 61)

1 The registers and the index [650]

(1) The registrar shall continue to keep at the registry in the prescribed manner the following registers, namely –

    (a) a register of land charges;
    (b) a register of pending actions;
    (c) a register of writs and orders affecting land;
    (d) a register of deeds of arrangement affecting land;
    (e) a register of annuities,

and shall also continue to keep there an index whereby all entries made in any of those registers can readily be traced.

(2) Every application to register shall be in the prescribed form and shall contain the prescribed particulars.

(3) Where any charge or other matter is registrable in more than one of the registers kept under this Act, it shall be sufficient if it is registered in one such register, and if it is so registered the person entitled to the benefit of it shall not be prejudicially affected by any provision of this Act as to the effect of non-registration in any other such register.

(3A) Where any charge or other matter is registrable in a register kept under this Act and was also, before the commencement of the Local Land Charges Act 1975, registrable in a local land charges register, then, if before the commencement of the said Act it was registered in the appropriate local land charges register, it shall be treated for the purposes of the provisions of this Act as to the effect of non-registration as if it had been registered in the appropriate register under this Act; and any certificate setting out the result of an official search of the appropriate local land charges register shall, in relation to it, have effect as if it were a certificate setting out the result of an official search under this Act.

(4) Schedule 1 to this Act shall have effect in relation to the register of annuities.

(5) An office copy of an entry in any register kept under this section shall be admissible in evidence in all proceedings and between all parties to the same extent as the original would be admissible.

(6) Subject to the provisions of this Act, registration may be vacated pursuant to an order of the court.

(6A) The county courts have jurisdiction under subsection (6) above –

    (a) in the case of a land charge of Class C(i), C(ii) or D(i), if the amount does not exceed £30,000;
    (b) in the case of a land charge of Class C(iii), if it is for a specified capital sum of money not exceeding £30,000 or, where it is not for a specified capital sum, if the capital value of the land affected does not exceed £30,000;
    (c) in the case of a land charge of Class A, Class B, Class C(iv), Class D(ii), Class D(iii) or Class E if the capital value of the land affected does not exceed £30,000;
    (d) in the case of a land charge of Class F, if the land affected by it is the subject of an order made by the court under section 1 of the Matrimonial Homes Act 1983 or an application for an order under that section relating to that land has been made to the court;

(e) in a case where an application under section 23 of the Deeds of Arrangement Act 1914 could be entertained by the court.

(7) In this section 'index' includes any device or combination of devices serving the purpose of an index.

2 The register of land charges [651]

(1) If a charge on or obligation affecting land falls into one of the classes described in this section, it may be registered in the register of land charges as a land charge of that class.

(2) A Class A land charge is –

(a) a rent or annuity or principal money payable by instalments or otherwise, with or without interest, which is not a charge created by deed but is a charge upon land (other than a rate) created pursuant to the application of some person under the provisions of any Act of Parliament, for securing to any person either the money spent by him or the costs, charges and expenses incurred by him under such Act, or the money advanced by him for repaying the money spent or the costs, charges and expenses incurred by another person under the authority of an Act of Parliament; or

(b) a rent or annuity or principal money payable as mentioned in paragraph (a) above which is not a charge created by deed but is a charge upon land (other than a rate) created pursuant to the application of some person under any of the enactments mentioned in Schedule 2 to this Act.

(3) A Class B land charge is a charge on land (not being a local land charge) of any of the kinds described in paragraph (a) of subsection (2) above, created otherwise than pursuant to the application of any person.

(4) A Class C land charge is any of the following (not being a local land charge), namely –

(i) a puisne mortgage;
(ii) a limited owner's charge;
(iii) a general equitable charge;
(iv) an estate contract;

and for this purpose –

(i) a puisne mortgage is a legal mortgage which is not protected by a deposit of documents relating to the legal estate affected;

(ii) a limited owner's charge is an equitable charge acquired by a tenant for life or statutory owner under the Capital Transfer Tax Act 1984 or under any other statute by reason of the discharge by him of any capital transfer tax or other liabilities and to which special priority is given by the statute;

(iii) a general equitable charge is any equitable charge which –

(a) is not secured by a deposit of documents relating to the legal estate affected; and

(b) does not arise or affect an interest arising under a trust of land or a settlement; and

(c) is not a charge given by way of indemnity against rents equitably apportioned or charged exclusively on land in exoneration of other land and against the breach or non-observance of covenants or conditions; and

(d) is not included in any other class of land charge;

(iv) an estate contract is a contract by an estate owner or by a person entitled at the date of the contract to have a legal estate conveyed to him to convey or create a legal estate, including a contract conferring either expressly or by statutory implication a valid option to purchase, a right of pre-emption or any other like right.

(5) A Class D land charge is any of the following (not being a local land charge), namely –

(i) an Inland Revenue charge;
(ii) a restrictive covenant;
(iii) an equitable easement;

and for this purpose –

(i) an Inland Revenue charge is a charge on land, being a charge acquired by the Board under the Capital Transfer Tax Act 1984;
(ii) a restrictive covenant is a covenant or agreement (other than a covenant or agreement between a lessor and a lessee) restrictive of the user of land and entered into on or after 1st January 1926;
(iii) an equitable easement is an easement, right or privilege over or affecting land created or arising on or after 1st January 1926, and being merely an equitable interest.

(6) A Class E land charge is an annuity created before 1st January 1926 and not registered in the register of annuities.

(7) A Class F land charge is a charge affecting any land by virtue of the Matrimonial Homes Act 1983.

(8) A charge or obligation created before 1st January 1926 can only be registered as a Class B land charge or a Class C land charge if it is acquired under a conveyance made on or after that date.

3 Registration of land charges [652]

(1) A land charge shall be registered in the name of the estate owner whose estate is intended to be affected.

(1A) Where a person has died and a land charge created before his death would apart from his death have been registered in his name, it shall be so registered notwithstanding his death.

(4) The expenses incurred by the person entitled to the charge in registering a land charge of Class A, Class B or Class C (other than an estate contract) or by the Board in registering an Inland Revenue charge shall be deemed to form part of the land charge, and shall be recoverable accordingly on the day for payment of any part of the land charge next after such expenses are incurred.

(5) Where a land charge is not created by an instrument, short particulars of the effect of the charge shall be furnished with the application to register the charge.

(6) An application to register an Inland Revenue charge shall state the tax in respect of which the charge is claimed and, so far as possible, shall define the land affected, and such particulars shall be entered or referred to in the register.

(7) In the case of a land charge for securing money created by a company before 1st January 1970 or so created at any time as a floating charge, registration under any of the enactments mentioned in subsection (8) below shall be sufficient in place of registration under this Act, and shall have effect as if the land charge had been registered under this Act.

(8) The enactments referred to in subsection (7) above are section 93 of the Companies (Consolidation) Act 1908, section 79 of the Companies Act 1929, section 95 of the Companies Act 1948 and sections 395 to 398 of the Companies Act 1985.

4 Effect of land charges and protection of purchasers [653]

(1) A land charge of Class A (other than a land improvement charge registered after 31st December 1969) or of Class B shall, when registered, take effect as if it had been created by a deed of charge by way of legal mortgage, but without prejudice to the priority of the charge.

(2) A land charge of Class A created after 31st December 1888 shall be void as against a purchaser of the land charged with it or of any interest in such land, unless the land charge is registered in the register of land charges before the completion of the purchase.

(3) After the expiration of one year from the first conveyance occurring on or after 1st January 1889 of a land charge of Class A created before that date the person entitled to the land charge shall not be able to recover the land charge or any part of it as against a purchaser of the land charged with it or of any interest in the land, unless the land charge is registered in the register of land charges before the completion of the purchase.

(4) If a land improvement charge was registered as a land charge of Class A before 1st January 1970, any body corporate which, but for the charge, would have power to advance money on the security of the estate or interest affected by it shall have that power notwithstanding the charge.

(5) A land charge of Class B and a land charge of Class C (other than an estate contract) created or arising on or after 1st January 1926 shall be void as against a purchaser of the land charged with it, or of any interest in such land, unless the land charge is registered in the appropriate register before the completion of the purchase.

(6) An estate contract and a large charge of Class D created or entered into on or after 1st January 1926 shall be void as against a purchaser for money or money's worth (or, in the case of an Inland Revenue charge, a purchaser within the meaning of the Capital Transfer Tax Act 1984) of a legal estate in the land charged with it, unless the land charge is registered in the appropriate register before the completion of the purchase.

(7) After the expiration of one year from the first conveyance occurring on or after 1st January 1926 of a land charge of Class B or Class C created before that date the person entitled to the land charge shall not be able to enforce or recover the land charge or any part of it as against a purchaser of the land charged with it, or of any interest in the land, unless the land charge is registered in the appropriate register before the completion of the purchase.

(8) A land charge of Class F shall be void as against a purchaser of the land charged with it, or of any interest in such land, unless the land charge is registered in the appropriate register before the completion of the purchase.

5 The register of pending actions [654]

(1) There may be registered in the register of pending actions –

    (a) a pending land action;
    (b) a petition in bankruptcy filed on or after 1st January 1926.

(2) Subject to general rules under section 16 of this Act, every application for registration under this section shall contain particulars of the title of the proceedings and the name, address and description of the estate owner or other person whose estate or interest is intended to be affected.

(3) An application for registration shall also state –

    (a) if it relates to a pending land action, the court in which and the day on which the action was commenced; and

(b) if it relates to a petition in bankruptcy, the court in which and the day on which the petition was filed.

(4) The registrar shall forthwith enter the particulars in the register, in the name of the estate owner or other person whose estate or interest is intended to be affected ...

(4A) Where a person has died and a pending land action would apart from his death have been registered in his name, it shall be so registered notwithstanding his death.

(7) A pending land action shall not bind a purchaser without express notice of it unless it is for the time being registered under this section.

(8) A petition in bankruptcy shall not bind a purchaser of a legal estate in good faith, for money or money's worth, unless it is for the time being registered under this section.

(10) The court, if it thinks fit, may upon the determination of the proceedings, or during the pendency of the proceedings if satisfied that they are not prosecuted in good faith, make an order vacating a registration under this section, and direct the party on whose behalf it was made to pay all or any of the costs and expenses occasioned by the registration and by its vacation ...

6 The register of writs and orders affecting land [655]

(1) There may be registered in the register of writs and orders affecting land –

(a) any writ or order affecting land issued or made by any court for the purpose of enforcing a judgment or recognisance;
(b) any order appointing a receiver or sequestrator of land;
(c) any bankruptcy order, whether or not the bankrupt's estate is known to include land;
(d) any access order under the Access to Neighbouring Land Act 1992.

(1A) No writ or order affecting an interest under a trust of land may be registered under subsection (1) above.

(2) Every entry made pursuant to this section shall be made in the name of the estate owner or other person whose land, if any, is affected by the writ or order registered.

(2A) Where a person has died and any such writ or order as is mentioned in subsection (1)(a) or (b) above would apart from his death have been registered in his name, it shall be so registered notwithstanding his death ...

(4) Except as provided by subsection (5) below and by section 37(5) of the Supreme Court Act 1981 and section 107(3) of the County Courts Act 1984 (which make special provision as to receiving orders in respect of land of judgment debtors) every such writ and order as is mentioned in subsection (1) above, and every delivery in execution or other proceeding taken pursuant to any such writ or order, or in obedience to any such writ or order, shall be void as against a purchaser of the land unless the writ or order is for the time being registered under this section ...

7 The register of deeds of arrangement affecting land [656]

(1) The deed of arrangement affecting land may be registered in the register of deeds of arrangement affecting land, in the name of the debtor, on the application of a trustee of the deed or a creditor assenting to or taking the benefit of the deed.

(2) Every deed of arrangement shall be void as against a purchaser of land comprised in it or affected by it unless it is for the time being registered under this section.

8 Expiry and renewal of registrations [657]

A registration under section 5, section 6 or section 7 of this Act shall cease to have effect at the end of the period of five years from the date on which it is made, but may be renewed from time to time and, if so renewed, shall have effect for five years from the date of renewal.

9 Searches [658]

(1) Any person may search in any register kept under this Act on paying the prescribed fee.

(2) Without prejudice to subsection (1) above, the registrar may provide facilities for enabling persons entitled to search in any such register to see photographic or other images or copies of any portion of the register which they may wish to examine.

10 Official searches [659]

(1) Where any person requires search to be made at the registry for entries of any matters or documents, entries of which are required or allowed to be made in the registry by this Act, he may make a requisition in that behalf to the registrar, which may be either –

(a) a written requisition delivered at or sent by post to the registry; or
(b) a requisition communicated by teleprinter, telephone or other means in such manner as may be prescribed in relation to the means in question, in which case it shall be treated as made to the registrar if, but only if, he accepts it;

and the registrar shall not accept a requisition made in accordance with paragraph (b) above unless it is made by a person maintaining a credit account at the registry, and may at his discretion refuse to accept it notwithstanding that it is made by such a person ...

(3) Where a requisition is made under subsection (1) above and the fee payable in respect of it is paid or debited in accordance with subsection (2) above, the registrar shall thereupon make the search required and –

(a) shall issue a certificate setting out the result of the search; and
(b) without prejudice to paragraph (a) above, may take such other steps as he considers appropriate to communicate that result to the person by whom the requisition was made.

(4) In favour of a purchaser or an intending purchaser, as against persons interested under or in respect of matters or documents entries of which are required or allowed as aforesaid, the certificate, according to its tenor, shall be conclusive, affirmatively or negatively, as the case may be ...

11 Date of effective registration and priority notices [660]

(1) Any person intending to make an application for the registration of any contemplated charge, instrument or other matter in pursuance of this Act or any rule made under this Act may give a priority notice in the prescribed form at least the relevant number of days before the registration is to take effect.

(2) Where a notice is given under subsection (1) above, it shall be entered in the register to which the intended application when made will relate.

(3) If the application is presented within the relevant number of days thereafter and refers in the prescribed manner to the notice, the registration shall take effect

as if the registration had been made at the time when the charge, instrument or matter was created, entered into, made or arose, and the date at which the registration so takes effect shall be deemed to be the date of registration ...

(5) Where a purchaser has obtained a certificate under section 10 above, any entry which is made in the register after the date of the certificate and before the completion of the purchase, and is not made pursuant to a priority notice entered in the register on or before the date of the certificate, shall not affect the purchaser if the purchase is completed before the expiration of the relevant number of days after the date of the certificate.

(6) The relevant number of days is –

(a) for the purposes of subsections (1) and (5) above, fifteen;
(b) for the purposes of subsection (3) above, thirty;

or such other number as may be prescribed; but in reckoning the relevant number of days for any of the purposes of this section any days when the registry is not open to the public shall be excluded.

12 Protection of solicitors, trustees, etc   [661]

A solicitor, or a trustee, personal representative, agent or other person in a fiduciary position, shall not be answerable –

(a) in respect of any loss occasioned by reliance on an office copy of an entry in any register kept under this Act;
(b) for any loss that may arise from error in a certificate under section 10 above obtained by him.

13 Saving for overreaching powers   [662]

(1) The registration of any charge, annuity or other interest under this Act shall not prevent the charge, annuity or interest being overreached under any other Act, except where otherwise provided by that other Act.

(2) The registration as a land charge of a puisne mortgage or charge shall not operate to prevent that mortgage or charge being overreached in favour of a prior mortgagee or a person deriving title under him where, by reason of a sale or foreclosure, or otherwise, the right of the puisne mortgagee or subsequent chargee to redeem is barred.

14 Exclusion of matters affecting registered land or created   [663]
by instruments necessitating registration of land

(1) This Act shall not apply to instruments or matters required to be registered or re-registered on or after 1st January 1926, if and so far as they affect registered land, and can be protected under the Land Registration Act 1925 by lodging or registering a creditor's notice, restriction, caution, inhibition or other notice.

(2) Nothing in this Act imposes on the registrar any obligation to ascertain whether or not an instrument or matter affects registered land.

(3) Where an instrument executed on or after 27th July 1971 conveys, grants or assigns an estate in land and creates a land charge affecting that estate, this Act shall not apply to the land charge, so far as it affects that estate, if under section 123 of the Land Registration Act 1925 (effect of that Act in areas where registration is compulsory) the instrument will, unless the necessary application for registration under that Act is made within the time allowed by or under that section, become void so far as respects the conveyance, grant or assignment of that estate.

17 Interpretation [664]

(1) In this Act, unless the context otherwise requires –

'annuity' means a rentcharge or an annuity for a life or lives or for any term of years or greater estate determinable on a life or on lives and created after 25th April 1855 and before 1st January 1926, but does not include an annuity created by a marriage settlement or will;

'the Board' means the Commissioners of Inland Revenue;

'conveyance' includes a mortgage, charge, lease, assent, vesting declaration, vesting instrument, release and every other assurance of property, or of an interest in property, by an instrument except a will, and 'convey' has a corresponding meaning;

'court' means the High Court, or the county court in a case where that court has jurisdiction;

'deed of arrangement' has the same meaning as in the Deeds of Arrangement Act 1914;

'estate owner', 'legal estate', 'equitable interest', 'charge by way of legal mortgage' and 'will' have the same meanings as in the Law of Property Act 1925;

'judgment' includes any order or decree having the effect of a judgment;

'land' includes land of any tenure and mines and minerals, whether or not severed from the surface, buildings or parts of buildings (whether the division is horizontal, vertical or made in any other way) and other corporeal hereditaments, also a manor, an advowson and a rent and other incorporeal hereditaments, and an easement, right, privilege or benefit in, over or derived from land, but not an undivided share in land, and 'hereditament' means real property which, on an intestacy occurring before 1st January 1926, might have devolved on an heir;

'land improvement charge' means any charge under the Improvement of Land Act 1864 or under any special improvement Act within the meaning of the Improvement of Land Act 1899;

'pending land action' means any action or proceedings pending in court relating to land or any interest in or charge on land;

'prescribed' means prescribed by rules made pursuant to this Act;

'purchaser' means any person (including a mortgagee or lessee) who, for valuable consideration, takes any interest in land or in a charge on land, and 'purchase' has a corresponding meaning;

'registrar' means the Chief Land Registrar, 'registry' means Her Majesty's Land Registry, and 'registered land' has the same meaning as in the Land Registration Act 1925;

'tenant for life', 'statutory owner', 'vesting instrument' and 'settlement' have the same meanings as in the Settled Land Act 1925 ...

SCHEDULE 1 [665]

ANNUITIES

1. No further entries shall be made in the register of annuities ...

SCHEDULE 2 [666]

CLASS A LAND CHARGES

1. Charges created pursuant to applications under the enactments mentioned in this Schedule may be registered as land charges of Class A by virtue of paragraph (b) of section 2(2) of this Act –

(i) The Agricultural Holdings Act 1986

Section 85 (charges in respect of sums due to tenant of agricultural holding).

Section 86 (charges in favour of landlord of agricultural holdings in respect of compensation for or cost of certain improvements) ...

[As amended by the Local Land Charges Act 1975, ss17(1)(a), (b), 19, Schedule 2; Finance Act 1975, s52(1), Schedule 12, paras 2, 18(1), (2), (4), (5), (6); Supreme Court Act 1981, s152(1), Schedule 5; Matrimonial Homes Act 1983, s12, Schedule 2; Capital Transfer Act 1984, s276, Schedule 8, para 3(1)(a), (b), (2); County Courts Act 1984, s148(1), Schedule 2, Pt IV, para 18; Companies Consolidation (Consequential Provisions) Act 1985, s30, Schedule 2; Insolvency Act 1985, s235(1), (3), Schedule 8, para 21(2), (3), Schedule 10, Pt III; Agricultural Holdings Act 1986, ss100, 101, Schedule 14, para 51, Schedule 15, Pt I; High Court and County Courts Jurisdiction Order 1991, art 2(8), Schedule; Access to Neighbouring Land Act 1992, s5(1); Law of Property (Miscellaneous Provisions) Act 1994, s15(2)–(4); Trusts of Land and Appointment of Trustees Act 1996, s25(1), Schedule 3, para 12.]

ADMINISTRATION OF JUSTICE ACT 1973
(1973 c 15)

8 Extension of powers of court in action by mortgagee [667]
of dwelling-house

(1) Where by a mortgage of land which consists of or includes a dwelling-house, or by any agreement between the mortgagee under such a mortgage and the mortgagor, the mortgagor is entitled or is to be permitted to pay the principal sum secured by instalments or otherwise to defer payment of it in whole or in part, but provision is also made for earlier payment in the event of any default by the mortgagor or of a demand by the mortgagee or otherwise, then for purposes of section 36 of the Administration of Justice Act 1970 (under which a court has power to delay giving a mortgagee possession of the mortgaged property so as to allow the mortgagor a reasonable time to pay any sums due under the mortgage) a court may treat as due under the mortgage on account of the principal sum secured and of interest on it only such amounts as the mortgagor would have expected to be required to pay if there had been no such provision for earlier payment.

(2) A court shall not exercise by virtue of subsection (1) above the powers conferred by section 36 of the Administration of Justice Act 1970 unless it appears to the court not only that the mortgagor is likely to be able within a reasonable period to pay any amounts regarded (in accordance with subsection (1) above) as due on account of the principal sum secured, together with the interest on those amounts, but also that he is likely to be able by the end of that period to pay any further amounts that he would have expected to be required to pay by then on account of that sum and of interest on it if there had been no such provision as is referred to in subsection (1) above for earlier payment.

(3) Where subsection (1) above would apply to an action in which a mortgagee only claimed possession of the mortgaged property, and the mortgagee brings an action for foreclosure (with or without also claiming possession of the property), then section 36 of the Administration of Justice Act 1970 together with subsections (1) and (2) above shall apply as they would apply if it were an action in which the mortgagee only claimed possession of the mortgaged property, except that –

(a) section 36(2)(b) shall apply only in relation to any claim for possession; and
(b) section 36(5) shall not apply.

(4) For purposes of this section the expressions 'dwelling-house', 'mortgage', 'mortgagee' and 'mortgagor' shall be construed in the same way as for the purposes of Part IV of the Administration of Justice Act 1970.

(5) This section shall have effect in relation to an action begun before the date on which this section comes into force if before that date judgment has not been given, nor an order made, in that action for delivery of possession of the mortgaged property and, where it is a question of subsection (3) above, an order nisi for foreclosure has not been made in that action ...

MATRIMONIAL CAUSES ACT 1973
(1973 c 18)

24 Property adjustment orders in connection with divorce proceedings, etc [668]

(1) On granting a decree of divorce, a decree of nullity of marriage or a decree of judicial separation or at any time thereafter (whether, in the case of a decree of divorce, or of nullity of marriage, before or after the decree is made absolute), the court may make any one or more of the following orders, that is to say –

(a) an order that a party to the marriage shall transfer to the other party, to any child of the family or to such person as may be specified in the order for the benefit of such a child such property as may be so specified, being property to which the first-mentioned party is entitled, either in possession or reversion;
(b) an order that a settlement of such property as may be so specified, being property to which a party to the marriage is so entitled, be made to the satisfaction of the court for the benefit of the other party to the marriage and of the children of the family or either or any of them;
(c) an order varying for the benefit of the parties to the marriage and of the children of the family or either or any of them any ante-nuptial or post-nuptial settlement (including such a settlement made by will or codicil) made on the parties to the marriage;
(d) an order extinguishing or reducing the interest of either of the parties to the marriage under any such settlement;

subject, however, in the case of an order under paragraph (a) above, to the restrictions imposed by section 29(1) and (3) below on the making of orders for a transfer of property in favour of children who have attained the age of eighteen.

(2) The court may make an order under subsection (1)(c) above notwithstanding that there are no children of the family.

(3) Without prejudice to the power to give a direction under section 30 below for the settlement of an instrument by conveyancing counsel, where an order is made under this section on or after granting a decree of divorce or nullity of marriage, neither the order nor any settlement made in pursuance of the order shall take effect unless the decree has been made absolute.

24A Orders for sale of property [669]

(1) Where the court makes under section 23 or 24 of this Act a secured periodical payments order, an order for the payment of a lump sum or a property adjustment order, then, on making that order or at any time thereafter, the court may make a further order for the sale of such property as may be specified in the order, being property in which or in the proceeds of sale of which either or both of the parties to the marriage has or have a beneficial interest, either in possession or reversion.

(2) Any order made under subsection (1) above may contain such consequential or supplementary provisions as the court thinks fit and, without prejudice to the generality of the foregoing provision, may include –

(a) provision requiring the making of a payment out of the proceeds of sale of the property to which the order relates, and
(b) provision requiring any such property to be offered for sale to a person, or class of persons, specified in the order.

(3) Where an order is made under subsection (1) above on or after the grant of a decree of divorce or nullity of marriage, the order shall not take effect unless the decree has been made absolute.

(4) Where an order is made under subsection (1) above, the court may direct that the order, or such provision thereof as the court may specify, shall not take effect until the occurrence of an event specified by the court or the expiration of a period so specified.

(5) Where an order under subsection (1) above contains a provision requiring the proceeds of sale of the property to which the order relates to be used to secure periodical payments to a party to the marriage, the order shall cease to have effect on the death or re-marriage of that person.

(6) Where a party to a marriage has a beneficial interest in any property, or in the proceeds of sale thereof, and some other person who is not a party to the marriage also has a beneficial interest in that property or in the proceeds of sale thereof, then, before deciding whether to make an order under this section in relation to that property, it shall be the duty of the court to give that other person an opportunity to make representations with respect to the order; and any representations made by that other person shall be included among the circumstances to which the court is required to have regard under section 25(1) below.

[As amended by the Matrimonial Homes and Property Act 1981, s7; Matrimonial and Family Proceedings Act 1984, s46(1), Schedule 1, para 11.]

CONSUMER CREDIT ACT 1974
(1974 c 39)

8 Consumer credit agreements [670]

(1) A personal credit agreement is an agreement between an individual ('the debtor') and any other person ('the creditor') by which the creditor provides the debtor with credit of any amount.

(2) A consumer credit agreement is a personal credit agreement by which the creditor provides the debtor with credit not exceeding £15,000.

(3) A consumer credit agreement is a regulated agreement within the meaning of this Act if it is not an agreement (an 'exempt agreement') specified in or under section 16.

9 Meaning of credit [671]

(1) In this Act 'credit' includes a cash loan, and any other form of financial accommodation ...

94 Right to complete payments ahead of time [672]

(1) The debtor under a regulated consumer credit agreement is entitled at any

time, by notice to the creditor and the payment to the creditor of all amounts payable by the debtor to him under the agreement (less any rebate allowable under section 95), to discharge the debtor's indebtedness under the agreement.

(2) A notice under subsection (1) may embody the exercise by the debtor of any option to purchase goods conferred on him by the agreement, and deal with any other matter arising on, or in relation to, the termination of the agreement.

137 Extortionate credit bargains [673]

(1) If the court finds a credit bargain extortionate it may reopen the credit agreement so as to do justice between the parties.

(2) In this section and sections 138 to 140 –

(a) 'credit agreement' means any agreement between an individual (the 'debtor') and any other person (the 'creditor') by which the creditor provides the debtor with credit of any amount, and
(b) 'credit bargain' –

(i) where no transaction other than the credit agreement is to be taken into account in computing the total charge for credit, means the credit agreement, or
(ii) where one or more other transactions are to be so taken into account, means the credit agreement and those other transactions, taken together.

138 When bargains are extortionate [674]

(1) A credit bargain is extortionate if it –

(a) requires the debtor or a relative of his to make payments (whether unconditionally, or on certain contingencies) which are grossly exorbitant, or
(b) otherwise grossly contravenes ordinary principles of fair dealing.

(2) In determining whether a credit bargain is extortionate, regard shall be had to such evidence as is adduced concerning –

(a) interest rates prevailing at the time it was made,
(b) the factors mentioned in subsections (3) to (5), and
(c) any other relevant considerations.

(3) Factors applicable under subsection (2) in relation to the debtor include –

(a) his age, experience, business capacity and state of health; and
(b) the degree to which, at the time of making the credit bargain, he was under financial pressure, and the nature of that pressure.

(4) Factors applicable under subsection (2) in relation to the creditor include –

(a) the degree of risk accepted by him, having regard to the value of any security provided;
(b) his relationship to the debtor; and
(c) whether or not a colourable cash price was quoted for any goods or services included in the credit bargain.

(5) Factors applicable under subsection (2) in relation to a linked transaction include the question how far the transaction was reasonably required for the protection of debtor or creditor, or was in the interest of the debtor.

139 Reopening of extortionate agreements [675]

(1) A credit agreement may, if the court thinks just, be reopened on the ground that the credit bargain is extortionate –

(a) on an application for the purpose made by the debtor or any surety to the High Court, county court ...; or

(b) at the instance of the debtor or a surety in any proceedings to which the debtor and creditor are parties, being proceedings to enforce the agreement, any security relating to it, or any linked transaction; or

(c) at the instance of the debtor or a surety in other proceedings in any court where the amount paid or payable under the credit agreement is relevant.

(2) In reopening the agreement, the court may, for the purpose of relieving the debtor or a surety from payment of any sum in excess of that fairly due and reasonable, by order –

(a) direct accounts to be taken ... between any persons,

(b) set aside the whole or part of any obligation imposed on the debtor or a surety by the credit bargain or any related agreement,

(c) require the creditor to repay the whole or part of any sum paid under the credit bargain or any related agreement by the debtor or a surety, whether paid to the creditor or any other person,

(d) direct the return to the surety of any property provided for the purposes of the security, or

(e) alter the terms of the credit agreement or any security instrument.

(3) An order may be made under subsection (2) notwithstanding that its effect is to place a burden on the creditor in respect of an advantage unfairly enjoyed by another person who is a party to a linked transaction ...

140 Interpretation of sections 137 to 139 [676]

Where the credit agreement is not a regulated agreement, expressions used in sections 137 to 139 which, apart from this section, apply only to regulated agreements, shall be construed as nearly as may be as if the credit agreement were a regulated agreement.

NB Section 16 of the 1974 Act exempts consumer credit agreements where the creditor is a local authority or is specified in the Consumer Credit (Exempt Agreements) Order 1989, as amended. Section 16 does not affect the application of ss137 to 140: s16(7).

[As amended by the Consumer Credit (Increase of Monetary Limits) Order 1983.]

LOCAL LAND CHARGES ACT 1975
(1975 c 76)

1 Local land charges [677]

(1) A charge or other matter affecting land is a local land charge if it falls within any of the following descriptions and is not one of the matters set out in section 2 below –

(a) any charge acquired either before or after the commencement of this Act by a local authority or National Park authority, water authority, sewerage undertaker or new town development corporation under the Public Health Acts 1936 and 1937, the Public Health Act 1961 or the Highways Act 1980 (or any Act repealed by that Act) or the Building Act 1984 or any similar charge acquired by a local authority or National Park authority under any other Act, whether passed before or after this Act, being a charge that is binding on successive owners of the land affected;

(b) any prohibition of or restriction on the use of land –

(i) imposed by a local authority or National Park authority on or after 1st January 1926 (including any prohibition or restriction embodied in any condition attached to a consent, approval or licence granted by a local authority or National Park authority on or after that date), or

(ii) enforceable by a local authority or National Park authority under any covenant or agreement made with them on or after that date,

being a prohibition or restriction binding on successive owners of the land affected;

(c) any prohibition of or restriction on the use of land –

(i) imposed by a Minister of the Crown or government department on or after the date of the commencement of this Act (including any prohibition or restriction embodied in any condition attached to a consent, approval or licence granted by such a Minister or department on or after that date), or

(ii) enforceable by such a Minister or department under any covenant or agreement made with him or them on or after that date, being a prohibition or restriction binding on successive owners of the land affected;

(d) any positive obligation affecting land enforceable by a Minister of the Crown, government department or local authority or National Park authority under any covenant or agreement made with him or them on or after the date of the commencement of this Act and binding on successive owners of the land affected;

(e) any charge or other matter which is expressly made a local land charge by any statutory provision not contained in this section.

(2) For the purposes of subsection (1)(a) above, any sum which is recoverable from successive owners or occupiers of the land in respect of which the sum is recoverable shall be treated as a charge, whether the sum is expressed to be a charge on the land or not.

(3) For the purposes of this section and section 2 of this Act, the Broads Authority shall be treated as a local authority or National Park authority.

2 Matters which are not local land charges [678]

The following matters are not local land charges –

(a) a prohibition or restriction enforceable under a covenant or agreement made between a lessor and a lessee;

(b) a positive obligation enforceable under a covenant or agreement made between a lessor and a lessee;

(c) a prohibition or restriction enforceable by a Minister of the Crown, government department or local authority or National Park authority under any covenant or agreement, being a prohibition or restriction binding on successive owners of the land affected by reason of the fact that the covenant or agreement is made for the benefit of land of the Minister, government department or local authority or National Park authority;

(d) a prohibition or restriction embodied in any bye-laws;

(e) a condition or limitation subject to which planning permission was granted at any time before the commencement of this Act or was or is (at any time) deemed to be granted under any statutory provision relating to town and country planning, whether by a Minister of the Crown, government department or local authority or National Park authority;

(f) a prohibition or restriction embodied in a scheme under the Town and Country Planning Act 1932 or any enactment repealed by that Act;

(g) a prohibition or restriction enforceable under a forestry dedication covenant entered into pursuant to section 5 of the Forestry Act 1967;

(h) a prohibition or restriction affecting the whole or any of the following areas –

(i) England, Wales or England and Wales;
(ii) England, or England and Wales, with the exception of, or of any part of, Greater London;
(iii) Greater London.

3 Registering authorities, local land charges registers, and indexes [679]

(1) Each of the following local authorities –

(a) the council of any district;
(aa) a Welsh county council;
(ab) a county borough council;
(b) the council of any London borough; and
(c) the Common Council of the City of London,

shall be a registering authority for the purposes of this Act.

(2) There shall continue to be kept for the area of each registering authority –

(a) a local land charges register, and
(b) an index whereby all entries made in that register can readily be traced,

and as from the commencement of this Act the register and index kept for the area of a registering authority shall be kept by that authority.

(3) Neither a local land charges register nor an index such as is mentioned in subsection (2(b)) above need be kept in documentary form.

(4) For the purposes of this Act the area of the Common Council of the City of London includes the Inner Temple and the Middle Temple.

4 The appropriate local land charges register [680]

In this Act, unless the context otherwise requires, 'the appropriate local land charges register', in relation to any land or to a local land charge, means the local land charges register for the area in which the land or, as the case may be, the land affected by the charge is situated or, if the land in question is situated in two or more areas for which local land charges registers are kept, each of the local land charges registers kept for those areas respectively.

6 Local authority's right to register a general charge against land in certain circumstances [681]

(1) Where a local authority have incurred any expenditure in respect of which, when any relevant work is completed and any requisite resolution is passed or order is made, there will arise in their favour a local land charge (in this section referred to as 'the specific charge'), the following provisions of this section shall apply.

(2) At any time before the specific charge comes into existence, a general charge against the land, without any amount being specified, may be registered in the appropriate local land charges register by the registering authority if they are the originating authority and, if they are not, shall be registered therein by them if the originating authority make an application for that purpose.

(3) A general charge registered under this section shall be a local land charge ...

(5) Where a general charge is registered under this section its registration shall be cancelled within such period starting with the day on which the specific charge

comes into existence, and not being less than one year, as may be prescribed, and the specific charge shall not be registered before the general charge is cancelled ...

7 Effect of registering certain financial charges [682]

A local land charge falling within section 1(1)(a) above shall, when registered, take effect as if it had been created by a deed of charge by way of legal mortgage within the meaning of the Law of Property Act 1925, but without prejudice to the priority of the charge.

10 Compensation for non-registration or defective [683] official search certificate

(1) Failure to register a local land charge in the appropriate local land charges register shall not affect the enforceability of the charge but where a person has purchased any land affected by a local land charge, then –

(a) in a case where a material personal search of the appropriate local land charges register was made in respect of the land in question before the relevant time, if at the time of the search the charge was in existence but not registered in that register; or

(aa) in a case where the appropriate local land charges register is kept otherwise than in documentary form and a material personal search of that register was made in respect of the land in question before the relevant time, if the entitlement to search in that register conferred by section 8 above was not satisfied as mentioned in subsection (1A) [availability in visible and legible form] of that section; or

(b) in a case where a material official search of the appropriate local land charges register was made in respect of the land in question before the relevant time, if the charge was in existence at the time of the search but (whether registered or not) was not shown by the official search certificate as registered in that register,

the purchaser shall (subject to section 11(1) below) be entitled to compensation for any loss suffered by him in consequence ...

(3) For the purposes of this section –

(a) a person purchases land where, for valuable consideration, he acquires any interest in land or the proceeds of sale of land, and this includes cases where he acquires as lessee or mortgagee and shall be treated as including cases where an interest is conveyed or assigned at his direction to another person;

(b) the relevant time –

(i) where the acquisition of the interest in question was preceded by a contract for its acquisition, other than a qualified liability contract, is the time when that contract was made;

(ii) in any other case, is the time when the purchaser acquired the interest in question or, if he acquired it under a disposition which took effect only when registered under the Land Registration Act 1925, the time when that disposition was made; and for the purposes of sub-paragraph (i) above, a qualified liability contract is a contract containing a term the effect of which is to make the liability of the purchaser dependent upon, or avoidable by reference to, the outcome of a search for local land charges affecting the land to be purchased.

(c) a personal search is material if, but only if –

(i) it is made after the commencement of this Act, and

(ii) it is made by or on behalf of the purchaser or, before the relevant time, the purchaser or his agent has knowledge of the result of it;

(d) an official search is material if, but only if –

(i) it is made after the commencement of this Act, and

(ii) it is requisitioned by or on behalf of the purchaser or, before the relevant time, the purchaser or his agent has knowledge of the contents of the official search certificate.

(4) Any compensation for loss under this section shall be paid by the registering authority in whose area the land affected is situated; and where the purchaser has incurred expenditure for the purpose of obtaining compensation under this section, the amount of the compensation shall include the amount of the expenditure reasonably incurred by him for that purpose (so far as that expenditure would not otherwise fall to be treated as loss for which he is entitled to compensation under this section).

(5) Where any compensation for loss under this section is paid by a registering authority in respect of a local land charge as respects which they are not the originating authority, then, unless an application for registration of the charge was made to the registering authority in time for it to be practicable for the registering authority to avoid incurring liability to pay that compensation, an amount equal thereto shall be recoverable from the originating authority by the registering authority.

(6) Where any compensation for loss under this section is paid by a registering authority, no part of the amount paid, or of any corresponding amount paid to that authority by the originating authority under subsection (5) above, shall be recoverable by the registering authority or the originating authority from any other person except as provided by subsection (5) above or under a policy of insurance or on grounds of fraud.

(7) In the case of an action to recover compensation under this section the cause of action shall be deemed for the purposes of the Limitation Act [1980] to accrue at the time when the local land charge comes to the notice of the purchaser; and for the purposes of this subsection the question when the charge came to his notice shall be determined without regard to the provisions of section 198 of the Law of Property Act 1925 (under which registration under certain enactments is deemed to constitute actual notice).

(8) Where the amount claimed by way of compensation under this section does not exceed £5,000, proceedings for the recovery of such compensation may be begun in the county court.

(9) If in any proceedings for the recovery of compensation under this section the court dismisses a claim to compensation, it shall not order the purchaser to pay the registering authority's costs unless it considers that it was unreasonable for the purchaser to commence the proceedings.

11 Mortgages, trusts for sale and settled land   [684]

(1) Where there appear to be grounds for a claim under section 10 above in respect of an interest that is subject to a mortgage –

(a) the claim may be made by any mortgagee of the interest as if he were the person entitled to that interest but without prejudice to the making of a claim by that person;

(b) no compensation shall be payable under that section in respect of the interest of the mortgagee (as distinct from the interest which is subject to the mortgage);

(c) any compensation payable under that section in respect of the interest that is subject to the mortgage shall be paid to the mortgagee or, if there is more than one mortgagee, to the first mortgagee and shall in either case be applied by him as if it were proceeds of sale.

(2) Where an interest is subject to a trust of land any compensation payable in respect of it under section 10 above shall be dealt with as if it were proceeds of sale arising under the trust.

(3) Where an interest is settled land for the purposes of the Settled Land Act 1925 any compensation payable in respect of it under section 10 above shall be treated as capital money arising under that Act.

12 Office copies as evidence [685]

An office copy of an entry in any local land charges register shall be admissible in evidence in all proceedings and between all parties to the same extent as the original would be admissible.

13 Protection of solicitors, trustees, etc [686]

A solicitor or a trustee, personal representative, agent or other person in a fiduciary position, shall not be answerable in respect of any loss occasioned by reliance on an erroneous official search certificate or an erroneous office copy of an entry in a local land charges register.

[As amended by the Interpretation Act 1978, s25(1), Schedule 3; Highways Act 1980, s343(2), Schedule 24, para 26; Local Government (Miscellaneous Provisions) Act 1982, s34(a), (d)(i), (ii); Building Act 1984, s133(1), Schedule 6, para 16; Norfolk and Suffolk Broads Act 1988, s21, Schedule 6, para 14; Water Act 1989, s190(1), Schedule 25, para 52; High Court and County Courts Jurisdiction Order 1991, art 2(8), Schedule; Local Government (Wales) Act 1994, s66(6), Schedule 16, para 49; Environment Act 1995, s78, Schedule 10, para 14; Trusts of Land and Appointment of Trustees Act 1996, s25(1), Schedule 3, para 14.]

RACE RELATIONS ACT 1976
(1976 c 74)

21 Discrimination in disposal or management of premises [687]

(1) It is unlawful for a person, in relation to premises in Great Britain of which he has power to dispose, to discriminate against another –

(a) in the terms on which he offers him those premises; or
(b) by refusing his application for those premises; or
(c) in his treatment of him in relation to any list of persons in need of premises of that description.

(2) It is unlawful for a person, in relation to premises managed by him, to discriminate against a person occupying the premises –

(a) in the way he affords him access to any benefits or facilities, or by refusing or deliberately omitting to afford him access to them; or
(b) by evicting him, or subjecting him to any other detriment.

(3) Subsection (1) does not apply to a person who owns an estate or interest in the premises and wholly occupies them unless he uses the services of an estate agent for the purposes of the disposal of the premises, or publishes or causes to be published an advertisement in connection with the disposal.

22 Exception from ss20(1) and 21: small dwellings   [688]

(1) Sections 20(1) [discrimination in provision of goods, facilities or services] and 21 do not apply to the provision by a person of accommodation in any premises, or the disposal of premises by him, if –

(a) that person or a near relative of his ('the relevant occupier') resides, and intends to continue to reside, on the premises; and
(b) there is on the premises, in addition to the accommodation occupied by the relevant occupier, accommodation (not being storage accommodation or means of access) shared by the relevant occupier with other persons residing on the premises who are not members of his household; and
(c) the premises are small premises.

(2) Premises shall be treated for the purposes of this section as small premises if –

(a) in the case of premises comprising residential accommodation for one or more households (under separate letting or similar agreements) in addition to the accommodation occupied by the relevant occupier, there is not normally residential accommodation for more than two such households and only the relevant occupier and any member of his household reside in the accommodation occupied by him;
(b) in the case of premises not falling within paragraph (a), there is not normally residential accommodation on the premises for more than six persons in addition to the relevant occupier and any members of his household.

23 Further exceptions from ss10(1) and 21   [689]

...

(2) Section 20(1) does not apply to anything done by a person as a participant in arrangements under which he (for reward or not) takes into his home, and treats as if they were members of his family, children, elderly persons, or persons requiring a special degree of care and attention.

24 Discrimination: consent for assignment or sub-letting   [690]

(1) Where the licence or consent of the landlord or of any other person is required for the disposal to any person of premises in Great Britain comprised in a tenancy, it is unlawful for the landlord or other person to discriminate against a person by withholding the licence or consent for disposal of the premises to him.

(2) Subsection (1) does not apply if –

(a) the person withholding a licence or consent, or a near relative of his ('the relevant occupier') resides, and intends to continue to reside, on the premises; and
(b) there is on the premises, in addition to the accommodation occupied by the relevant occupier, accommodation (not being storage accommodation or means of access) shared by the relevant occupier with other persons residing on the premises who are not members of his household; and
(c) the premises are small premises.

(3) Section 22(2) (meaning of 'small premises') shall apply for the purposes of this as well as of that section.

(4) In this section 'tenancy' means a tenancy created by a lease or sub-lease, by an agreement for a lease or sub-lease or by a tenancy agreement or in pursuance of any enactment; and 'disposal', in relation to premises comprised in a tenancy, includes assignment or assignation of the tenancy and sub-letting or parting with possession of the premises or any part of the premises.

(5) This section applies to tenancies created before the passing of this Act, as well as to others.

78 General interpretation provisions [691]

(1) In this Act, unless the context otherwise requires –

'advertisement' includes every form of advertisement or notice, whether to the public or not, and whether in a newspaper or other publication, by television or radio, by display of notices, signs, labels, showcards or goods, by distribution of samples, circulars, catalogues, price lists or other material, by exhibition of pictures, models or films, or in any other way, and references to the publishing of advertisements shall be construed accordingly; ...

'dispose', in relation to premises, includes granting a right to occupy the premises, and any reference to acquiring premises shall be construed accordingly; ...

'estate agent' means a person who, by way of profession or trade, provides services for the purpose of finding premises for persons seeking to acquire them or assisting in the disposal of premises; ...

(2) It is hereby declared that in this Act 'premises', unless the context otherwise requires, includes land of any description ...

(5) For the purposes of this Act a person is a near relative of another if that person is the wife or husband, a parent or child, a grandparent or grandchild, or a brother or sister of the other (whether of full blood or half-blood or by affinity), and 'child' includes an illegitimate child and the wife or husband of an illegitimate child ...

NB For provisions equivalent to ss21, 22 and 24 above against discrimination on grounds of sex, see ss30, 31 and 32 of the Sex Discrimination Act 1975.

RENT ACT 1977
(1977 c 42)

PART I

PRELIMINARY

1 Protected tenants and tenancies [692]

Subject to this Part of the Act, a tenancy under which a dwelling-house (which may be a house or part of a house) is let as a separate dwelling is a protected tenancy for the purposes of this Act.

Any reference in this Act to a protected tenant shall be construed accordingly.

2 Statutory tenants and tenancies [693]

(1) Subject to this Part of this Act –

(a) after the termination of a protected tenancy of a dwelling-house the person who, immediately before that termination, was the protected tenant of the dwelling-house shall, if and so long as he occupies the dwelling-house as his residence, be the statutory tenant of it; and

(b) Part I of Schedule 1 to this Act shall have effect for determining what person (if any) is the statutory tenant of a dwelling-house or, as the case may be, is entitled to an assured tenancy of a dwelling-house by succession at any time after the death of a person who, immediately before his death, was either a protected tenant of the dwelling-house or the statutory tenant of it by virtue of paragraph (a) above.

(2) In this Act a dwelling-house is referred to as subject to a statutory tenancy when there is a statutory tenant of it.

(3) In subsection (1)(a) above and in Part I of Schedule 1, the phrase 'if and so long as he occupies the dwelling-house as his residence' shall be construed as it was immediately before the commencement of this Act (that is to say, in accordance with section 3(2) of the Rent Act 1968).

(4) A person who becomes a statutory tenant of a dwelling-house as mentioned in subsection (1)(a) above is, in this Act, referred to as a statutory tenant by virtue of his previous protected tenancy.

(5) A person who becomes a statutory tenant as mentioned in subsection (1)(b) above is, in this Act, referred to as a statutory tenant by succession.

3 Terms and conditions of statutory tenancies   [694]

(1) So long as he retains possession, a statutory tenant shall observe and be entitled to the benefit of all the terms and conditions of the original contract of tenancy, so far as they are consistent with the provisions of this Act.

(2) It shall be a condition of a statutory tenancy of a dwelling-house that the statutory tenant shall afford to the landlord access to the dwelling-house and all reasonable facilities for executing therein any repairs which the landlord is entitled to execute.

(3) Subject to section 5 of the Protection from Eviction Act 1977 (under which at least four weeks' notice to quit is required), a statutory tenant of a dwelling-house shall be entitled to give up possession of the dwelling-house if, and only if, he gives such notice as would have been required under the provisions of the original contract of tenancy, or, if no notice would have been so required, on giving not less than three months' notice.

(4) Notwithstanding anything in the contract of tenancy, a landlord who obtains an order for possession of a dwelling-house as against a statutory tenant shall not be required to give to the statutory tenant any notice to quit.

(5) Part II of Schedule 1 of this Act shall have effect in relation to the giving up of possession of statutory tenancies and the changing of statutory tenants by agreement.

4 Dwelling-houses above certain rateable values   [695]

(1) A tenancy which is entered into before 1st April 1990 or (where the dwelling-house had a rateable value on 31st March 1990) is entered into on or after 1st April 1990 in pursuance of a contract made before that date is not a protected tenancy if the dwelling-house falls within one of the Classes set out in subsection (2) below.

(2) Where alternative rateable values are mentioned in this subsection, the higher applies if the dwelling-house is in Greater London and the lower applies if it is elsewhere.

Class A

The appropriate day in relation to the dwelling-house falls or fell on or after 1st April 1973 and the dwelling-house on the appropriate day has or had a rateable value exceeding £1,500 or £750.

Class B

The appropriate day in relation to the dwelling-house fell on or after 22nd March 1973, but before 1st April 1973, and the dwelling-house –

(a) on the appropriate day had a rateable value exceeding £600 or £300, and
(b) on 1st April 1973 had a rateable value exceeding £1,500 or £750.

Class C

The appropriate day in relation to the dwelling-house fell before 22nd March 1973 and the dwelling-house –

(a) on the appropriate day had a rateable value exceeding £400 or £200, and
(b) on 22nd March 1973 had a rateable value exceeding £600 or £300, and
(c) on 1st April 1973 had a rateable value exceeding £1,500 or £750.

(3) If any question arises in any proceedings whether a dwelling-house falls within a Class in subsection (2) above, by virtue of its rateable value at any time, it shall be deemed not to fall within that Class unless the contrary is shown.

(4) A tenancy is not a protected tenancy if –

(a) it is entered into on or after 1st April 1990 (otherwise than, where the dwelling-house had a rateable value on 31st March 1990, in pursuance of a contract made before 1st April 1990), and
(b) under it the rent payable for the time being is payable at a rate exceeding £25,000 a year.

(5) In subsection (4) above 'rent' does not include any sum payable by the tenant as is expressed (in whatever terms) to be payable in respect of rates, council tax, services, repairs, maintenance or insurance, unless it could not have been regarded by the parties as a sum so payable.

(6) If any question arises in any proceedings whether a tenancy is precluded from being a protected tenancy by subsection (4) above, the tenancy shall be deemed to be a protected tenancy unless the contrary is shown.

(7) The Secretary of State may by order replace the amount referred to in subsection (4) above by an amount specified in the order ...

5 Tenancies at low rents [696]

(1) A tenancy which was entered into before 1st April 1990 or (where the dwelling-house had a rateable value on 31st March 1990) is entered into on or after 1st April 1990 in pursuance of a contract made before that date is not a protected tenancy if under the tenancy either no rent is payable or the rent payable is less than two-thirds of the rateable value which is or was the rateable value of the dwelling-house on the appropriate day.

(2) Where –

(a) the appropriate day in relation to a dwelling-house fell before 22nd March 1973, and
(b) the dwelling-house had on the appropriate day a rateable value exceeding, if it is in Greater London, £400 or, if it is elsewhere, £200,

subsection (1) above shall apply in relation to the dwelling-house as if the reference to the appropriate day were a reference to 22nd March 1973.

(2A) A tenancy is not a protected tenancy if –

(a) it is entered into on or after 1st April 1990 (otherwise than, where the dwelling-house had a rateable value on 31st March 1990, in pursuance of a contract made before 1st April 1990), and

(b) under the tenancy for the time being either no rent is payable or the rent is payable at a rate of, if the dwelling-house is in Greater London, £1,000 or less a year, and, if the dwelling-house is elsewhere, £250 or less a year.

(2B) Subsection (7) of section 4 above shall apply to any amount referred to in subsection (2A) above as it applies to the amount referred to in subsection (4) of that section.

(3) In this Act a tenancy falling within subsection (1) above, is referred to as a 'tenancy at a low rent'.

(4) In determining whether a long tenancy is a tenancy at a low rent, there shall be disregard such part (if any) of the sums payable by the tenant as is expressed (in whatever terms) to be payable in respect of rates, council tax, services, repairs, maintenance, or insurance, unless it could not have been regarded by the parties as a part so payable.

(5) In subsection (4) above 'long tenancy' means a tenancy granted for a term certain exceeding 21 years, other than a tenancy which is, or may become, terminable before the end of that term by notice given to the tenant.

5A Certain shared ownership leases [697]

(1) A tenancy is not a protected tenancy if it is a qualifying shared ownership lease, that is –

(a) a lease granted [after 11th December 1987] in pursuance of the right to be granted a shared ownership lease under Part V of the Housing Act 1985, or
(b) a lease granted [after 11th December 1987] by a housing association and which complies with the conditions set out in subsection (2) below.

(2) The conditions referred to in subsection (1)(b) above are that the lease –

(a) was granted for a term of 99 years or more and is not (and cannot become) terminable except in pursuance of a provision for re-entry or forfeiture;
(b) was granted at a premium, calculated by reference to the value of the dwelling-house or the cost of providing it, of not less than 25 per cent, or such other percentage as may be prescribed, of the figure by reference to which it was calculated;
(c) provides for the tenant to acquire additional shares in the dwelling-house on terms specified in the lease and complying with such requirements as may be prescribed;
(d) does not restrict the tenant's powers to assign, mortgage or charge his interest in the dwelling-house;
(e) if it enables the landlord to require payment for outstanding shares in the dwelling-house, does so only in such circumstances as may be prescribed;
(f) provides, in the case of a house, for the tenant to acquire the landlord's interest on terms specified in the lease and complying with such requirements as may be prescribed; and
(g) states the landlord's opinion that by virtue of this section the lease is excluded from the operation of this Act ...

(5) In any proceedings the court may, if of opinion that it is just and equitable to do so, treat a lease as a qualifying shared ownership lease notwithstanding that the condition specified in subsection (2)(g) above is not satisfied.

(6) In this section –

'house' has the same meaning as in Part I of the Leasehold Reform Act 1967;
'housing association' has the same meaning as in the Housing Associations Act 1985; and
'lease' includes an agreement for a lease, and references to the grant of a lease shall be construed accordingly.

6 Dwelling-houses let with other land [698]

Subject to section 26 of this Act, a tenancy is not a protected tenancy if the dwelling-house which is subject to the tenancy is let together with land other than the site of the dwelling-house.

7 Payments for board or attendance [699]

(1) A tenancy is not a protected tenancy if under the tenancy the dwelling-house is bona fide let at a rent which includes payments in respect of board or attendance.

(2) For the purposes of subsection (1) above, a dwelling-house shall not be taken to be bona fide let at a rent which includes payments in respect of attendance unless the amount of rent which is fairly attributable to attendance, having regard to the value of the attendance to the tenant, forms a substantial part of the whole rent.

8 Lettings to students [700]

(1) A tenancy is not a protected tenancy if it is granted to a person who is pursuing, or intends to pursue, a curse of study provided by a specified educational institution and is so granted either by that institution or by another specified institution or body of persons.

(2) In subsection (1) above 'specified' means specified, or of a class specified, for the purposes of this section by regulations made by the Secretary of State by statutory instrument ...

9 Holiday lettings [701]

A tenancy is not a protected tenancy if the purpose of the tenancy is to confer on the tenant the right to occupy the dwelling-house for a holiday.

10 Agricultural holdings, etc [702]

(1) A tenancy is not a protected tenancy if –

(a) the dwelling-house is comprised in an agricultural holding and is occupied by the person responsible for the control (whether as tenant or as servant or agent of the tenant) of the farming of the holding, or
(b) the dwelling-house is comprised in the holding held under a farm business tenancy and is occupied by the person responsible for the control (whether as tenant or as servant or agent of the tenant) of the management of the holding.

(2) In subsection (1) above –

'agricultural holding' means any agricultural holding within the meaning of the Agricultural Holdings Act 1986 held under a tenancy in relation to which that Act applies, and
'farm business tenancy', and 'holding' in relation to such a tenancy, have the same meaning as in the Agricultural Tenancies Act 1995.

11 Licensed premises [703]

A tenancy of a dwelling-house which consists of or comprises premises licensed for the sale of intoxicating liquors for consumption on the premises shall not be a protected tenancy, nor shall such a dwelling-house be the subject of a statutory tenancy.

12 Resident landlords [704]

(1) Subject to subsection (2) below, a tenancy of a dwelling-house granted on or after 14th August 1974 shall not be a protected tenancy at any time if –

(a) the dwelling-house forms part only of a building and, except in a case where the dwelling-house also forms part of a flat, the building is not a purpose-built block of flats; and

(b) the tenancy was granted by a person who, at the time when he granted it, occupied as his residence another dwelling-house which –

(i) in the case mentioned in paragraph (a) above, also forms part of the flat; or

(ii) in any other case, also forms part of the building; and

(c) subject to paragraph 1 of Schedule 2 of this Act, at all times since the tenancy was granted the interest of the landlord under the tenancy has belonged to a person who, at the time he owed that interest, occupied as his residence another dwelling-house which –

(i) in the case mentioned in paragraph (a) above, also formed part of the flat; or

(ii) in any other case, also formed part of the building.

(2) This section does not apply to a tenancy of a dwelling-house which forms part of a building if the tenancy is granted to a person who, immediately before it was granted, was a protected or statutory tenant of that dwelling-house or of any other dwelling-house in that building.

(4) Schedule 2 to this Act shall have effect for the purpose of supplementing this section.

14 Landlord's interest belonging to local authority, etc [705]

A tenancy shall not be a protected tenancy at any time when the interest of the landlord under that tenancy belongs to –

(a) the council of a county or county borough;

(b) the council of a district or, in the application of this Act to the Isles of Scilly, the Council of the Isles of Scilly;

(bb) the Broads Authority;

(bc) a National Park Authority;

(c) the council of a London borough or the Common Council of the City of London;

(caa) a police authority established under section 3 of the Police Act 1964;

(cb) a joint authority established by Part IV of the Local Government Act 1985;

(d) the Commission for the New Towns;

(e) a development corporation established by an order made, or having effect as if made, under the New Towns Act 1981; or

(f) the Development Board for Rural Wales; or

(g) an urban development corporation within the meaning of Part XVI of the Local Government, Planning and Land Act 1980;

(h) a housing action trust established under Part III of the Housing Act 1988;

(i) the Residuary Body for Wales (Corff Gweddilliol Cymru);

nor shall a person at any time be a statutory tenant of a dwelling-house if the interest of his immediate landlord would belong at that time to any of those bodies.

15 Landlord's interest belonging to housing association, etc   **[706]**

(1) A tenancy shall not be a protected tenancy at any time when the interest of the landlord under that tenancy belongs to a housing association falling within subsection (3) below; nor shall a person at any time be a statutory tenant of a dwelling-house if the interest of his immediate landlord would belong at that time to such a housing association.

(2) A tenancy shall not be a protected tenancy at any time when the interest of the landlord under that tenancy belongs to –

(a) the Housing Corporation;
(aa) Housing for Wales; or
(b) a housing trust which is a charity within the meaning of the Charities Act 1993;

nor shall a person at any time be a statutory tenant of a dwelling-house if the interest of his immediate landlord would belong at that time to any of those bodies ...

16 Landlord's interest belonging to housing co-operative   **[707]**

A tenancy shall not be a protected tenancy at any time when the interest of the landlord under that tenancy belongs to a housing co-operative, within the meaning of section 27B of the Housing Act 1985 (agreements with housing co-operatives under certain superseded provisions) and the dwelling-house is comprised in a housing co-operative agreement within the meaning of that section.

18 Regulated tenancies   **[708]**

(1) Subject to sections 24(3) and 143 [release by order from rent regulation of dwelling-houses within particular areas] of this Act, a 'regulated tenancy' is, for the purposes of this Act, a protected or statutory tenancy.

(2) Where a regulated tenancy is followed by a statutory tenancy of the same dwelling-house, the two shall be treated for the purposes of this Act as together constituting one regulated tenancy.

24 Premises with a business use   **[709]**

(3) A tenancy shall not be a regulated tenancy if it is a tenancy to which Part II of the Landlord and Tenant Act 1954 applies (but this provision is without prejudice to the application of any other provisions of this Act to a sub-tenancy of any part of the premises comprised in such a tenancy).

26 Land and premises let with dwelling-house   **[710]**

(1) For the purposes of this Act, any land or premises let together with a dwelling-house shall, unless it consists of agricultural land exceeding two acres in extent, be treated as part of the dwelling-house.

(2) For the purposes of subsection (1) above 'agricultural land' has the meaning set out in section 26(3)(a) of the General Rate Act 1967 (exclusion of agricultural land and premises from liability for rating).

PART VII

SECURITY OF TENURE

98 Grounds for possession of certain dwelling-houses [711]

(1) Subject to this Part of this Act, a court shall not make an order for possession of a dwelling-house which is for the time being let on a protected tenancy or subject to a statutory tenancy unless the court considers it reasonable to make such an order and either –

(a) the court is satisfied that suitable alternative accommodation is available for the tenant or will be available for him when the order in question takes effect, or

(b) the circumstances are as specified in any of the Cases in Part I of Schedule 15 to this Act.

(2) If, apart from subsection (1) above, the landlord would be entitled to recover possession of a dwelling-house which is for the time being let on or subject to a regulated tenancy, the court shall make an order for possession if the circumstances of the case are as specified in any of the Cases in Part II of Schedule 15.

(3) Part III of Schedule 15 shall have effect in relation to Case 9 in that Schedule and for determining the relevant date for the purposes of the Cases in Part II of that Schedule.

(4) Part IV of Schedule 15 shall have effect for determining whether, for the purposes of subsection (1)(a) above, suitable alternative accommodation is or will be available for a tenant.

(5) Part V of Schedule 15 shall have effect for the purpose of setting out conditions which are relevant to Cases 11 and 12 of that Schedule.

PART IX

PREMIUMS, ETC

119 Prohibition of premiums and loans on grant [712]
of protected tenancies

(1) Any person who, as a condition of the grant, renewal or continuance of a protected tenancy, requires, in addition to the rent, the payment of any premium or the making of any loan (whether secured or unsecured) shall be guilty of an offence.

(2) Any person who, in connection with the grant, renewal or continuance of a protected tenancy, receives any premium in addition to the rent shall be guilty of an offence ...

(4) The court by which a person is convicted of an offence under this section relating to requiring or receiving any premium may order the amount of the premium to be repaid to the person by whom it was paid.

123 Excessive price for furniture to be treated as premium [713]

Where the purchase of any furniture has been required as a condition of the grant, renewal, continuance or assignment –

(a) of a protected tenancy, or

(b) of rights under a restricted contract which relates to premises falling within section 122(1) of this Act,

then, if the price exceeds the reasonable price of the furniture, the excess shall be treated, for the purposes of this Part of this Act, as if it were a premium required to be paid as a condition of the grant, renewal, continuance or assignment of the protected tenancy or, as the case may be, the rights under the restricted contract.

128 Interpretation of Part IX   [714]

(1) In this Part of this Act, unless the context otherwise requires –

'furniture' includes fittings and other articles; and
'premium' includes –

(a) any fine or other like sum;
(b) any other pecuniary consideration in addition to rent; and
(c) any sum paid by way of a deposit, other than one which does not exceed one-sixth of the annual rent and is reasonable in relation to the potential liability in respect of which it is paid.

(2) For the avoidance of doubt it is hereby declared that nothing in this Part of this Act shall render any amounts recoverable more than once.

SCHEDULE 15   **[715]**

GROUNDS FOR POSSESSION OF DWELLING-HOUSES
LET ON OR SUBJECT TO PROTECTED OR
STATUTORY TENANCIES

PART I

CASES IN WHICH COURT MAY ORDER POSSESSION

Case 1

Where any rent lawfully due from the tenant has not been paid, or any obligation of the protected or statutory tenancy which arises under this Act, or –

(a) in the case of a protected tenancy, or other obligation of the tenancy, in so far as is consistent with the provisions of Part VII of that Act, or
(b) in the case of a statutory tenancy, any other obligation of the previous protected tenancy which is applicable to the statutory tenancy,

has been broken or not performed.

Case 2

Where the tenant or any person residing or lodging with him or any sub-tenant of his has been guilty of conduct which is a nuisance or annoyance to adjoining occupiers, or has been convicted of using the dwelling-house or allowing the dwelling-house to be used for immoral or illegal purposes.

Case 3

Where the condition of the dwelling-house has, in the opinion of the court, deteriorated owing to acts of waste by, or the neglect or default of, the tenant or any person residing or lodging with him or any sub-tenant of his and, in the case of any act of waste by, or the neglect or default of, a person lodging with the tenant or a sub-tenant of his, where the court is satisfied that the tenant has not, before the making of the order in question, taken such steps as he ought reasonably to have taken for the removal of the lodger or sub-tenant, as the case may be.

Case 4

Where the condition of any furniture provided for use under the tenancy has, in the opinion of the court, deteriorated owing to ill-treatment by the tenant or any person residing or lodging with him or any sub-tenant of his and, in the case of any ill-treatment by a person lodging with the tenant or a sub-tenant of his, where the court is satisfied that the tenant has not, before the making of the order in question, taken such steps as he ought reasonably to have taken for the removal of the lodger or sub-tenant, as the case may be.

Case 5

Where the tenant has given notice to quit and, in consequence of that notice, the landlord has contracted to sell or let the dwelling-house or has taken any other steps as the result of which he would, in the opinion of the court, be seriously prejudiced if he could not obtain possession.

Case 6

Where, without the consent of the landlord, the tenant has, at any time after –

(b) 22nd March 1973, in the case of a tenancy which became a regulated tenancy by virtue of section 14 of the Counter-Inflation Act 1973;
(bb) the commencement of section 73 of the Housing Act 1980, in the case of a tenancy which became a regulated tenancy by virtue of that section;
(c) 14th August 1974, in the case of a regulated furnished tenancy; or
(d) 8th December 1965, in the case of any other tenancy,

assigned or sublet the whole of the dwelling-house or sublet part of the dwelling-house, the remainder being already sublet.

Case 8

Where the dwelling-house is reasonably required by the landlord for occupation as a residence for some person engaged in his whole-time employment, or in the whole-time employment of some tenant from him or with whom, conditional on housing being provided, a contract for such employment has been entered into, and the tenant was in the employment of the landlord or a former landlord, and the dwelling-house was let to him in consequence of that employment and he has ceased to be in that employment.

Case 9

Where the dwelling-house is reasonably required by the landlord for occupation as a residence for –

(a) himself, or
(b) any son or daughter of his over 18 years of age, or
(c) his father or mother, or
(d) if the dwelling-house is let on or subject to a regulated tenancy, the father or mother of his wife or husband,

and the landlord did not become landlord by purchasing the dwelling-house or any interest therein after –

(i) 7th November 1956, in the case of a tenancy which was then a controlled tenancy;
(ii) 8th March 1973, in the case of a tenancy which became a regulated tenancy by virtue of section 14 of the Counter-Inflation Act 1973;

(iii) 24th May 1974, in the case of a regulated furnished tenancy; or
23rd March 1965, in the case of any other tenancy.

PART II

CASES IN WHICH COURT MUST ORDER POSSESSION WHERE DWELLING-HOUSE SUBJECT TO REGULATED TENANCY

Case 11

Where a person (in this Case referred to as 'the owner-occupier') who let the dwelling-house on a regulated tenancy had, at any time before the letting, occupied it as his residence and –

(a) not later than the relevant date the landlord gave notice in writing to the tenant that possession might be recovered under this Case, and
(b) the dwelling-house has not, since –

(i) 22nd March 1973, in the case of a tenancy which became a regulated tenancy by virtue of section 14 of the Counter-Inflation Act 1973;
(ii) 14th August 1974, in the case of a regulated furnished tenancy; or
(iii) 8th December 1965, in the case of any other tenancy,

been let by the owner-occupier on a protected tenancy with respect to which the condition mentioned in paragraph (a) above was not satisfied, and
(c) the court is of the opinion that of the conditions set out in Part V of this Schedule one of those in paragraphs (a) and (c) to (f) is satisfied.

If the court is of the opinion that, notwithstanding that the condition in paragraph (a) or (b) above is not complied with, it is just and equitable to make an order for possession of the dwelling-house, the court may dispense with the requirements of either or both of those paragraphs, as the case may require ...

Where the dwelling-house has been let by the owner-occupier on a protected tenancy (in this paragraph referred to as 'the earlier tenancy') granted on or after 16th November 1984 but not later than the end of the period of two months beginning with the commencement of the Rent (Amendment) Act 1985 and either –

(i) the earlier tenancy was granted for a term certain (whether or not to be followed by a further term or to continue thereafter from year to year or some other period) and was during that term a protected shorthold tenancy as defined in section 52 of the Housing Act 1980, or
(ii) the conditions mentioned in paragraphs (a) to (c) of Case 20 were satisfied with respect to the dwelling-house and the earlier tenancy,

then for the purposes of paragraph (b) above the condition in paragraph (a) above is to be treated as having been satisfied with respect to the earlier tenancy.

Case 12

Where the landlord (in this Case referred to as 'the owner') intends to occupy the dwelling-house as his residence at such time as he might retire from regular employment and has let it on a regulated tenancy before he has so retired and –

(a) not later than the relevant date the landlord gave notice in writing to the tenant that possession might be recovered under this Case; and
(b) the dwelling-house has not, since 14th August 1974, been let by the owner on a protected tenancy with respect to which the condition mentioned in paragraph (a) above was not satisfied; and
(c) the court is of the opinion that of the conditions set out in Part V of this Schedule one of those paragraphs (b) to (e) is satisfied.

If the court is of the opinion that, notwithstanding that the condition in paragraph (a) or (b) above is not complied with, it is just and equitable to make an order for possession of the dwelling-house, the court may dispense with the requirements of either or both of those paragraphs, as the case may require.

Case 13

Where the dwelling-house is let under a tenancy for a term of years certain not exceeding 8 months and –

(a) not later than the relevant date the landlord gave notice in writing to the tenant that possession might be recovered under this Case; and
(b) the dwelling-house was, at some time within the period of 12 months ending on the relevant date, occupied under a right to occupy it for a holiday.

For the purposes of this Case a tenancy shall be treated as being for a term of years certain notwithstanding that it is liable to determination by re-entry or on the happening of any event other than the giving of notice by the landlord to determine the term.

Case 14

Where the dwelling-house is let under a tenancy for a term of years certain not exceeding 12 months and –

(a) not later than the relevant date the landlord gave notice in writing to the tenant that possession might be recovered under this Case; and
(b) at some time within the period of 12 months ending on the relevant date, the dwelling-house was subject to such a tenancy as is referred to in section 8(1) of this Act.

For the purposes of this Case a tenancy shall be treated as being for a term of years certain notwithstanding that it is liable to determination by re-entry or on the happening of any event other than the giving of notice by the landlord to determine the term.

Case 15

Where the dwelling-house is held for the purpose of being available for occupation by a minister of religion as a residence from which to perform the duties of his office and –

(a) not later than the relevant date the tenant was given notice in writing that possession might be recovered under this Case, and
(b) the court is satisfied that the dwelling-house is required for occupation by a minister of religion as such a residence.

Case 16

Where the dwelling-house was at any time occupied by a person under the terms of his employment as a person employed in agriculture, and

(a) the tenant neither is nor at any time was so employed by the landlord and is not the widow of a person who was so employed, and
(b) not later than the relevant date, the tenant was given notice in writing that possession might be recovered under this Case, and
(c) the court is satisfied that the dwelling-house is required for occupation by a person employed, or to be employed, by the landlord in agriculture.

For the purposes of this Case 'employed', 'employment' and 'agriculture' have the same meanings as in the Agricultural Wages Act 1948 ...

Case 19

Where the dwelling-house was let under a protected shorthold tenancy (or is treated under section 55 of the Housing Act 1980 as having been so let) and –

(a) there either has been no grant of a further tenancy of the dwelling-house since the end of the protected shorthold tenancy or, if there was such a grant, it was to a person who immediately before the grant was in possession of the dwelling-house as a protected or statutory tenant; and

(b) the proceedings for possession were commenced after appropriate notice by the landlord to the tenant and not later than three months after the expiry of the notice.

A notice is appropriate for this Case if –

(i) it is in writing and states that proceedings for possession under this Case may be brought after its expiry; and

(ii) it expires not earlier than three months after it is served nor, if, when it is served, the tenancy is a periodic tenancy, before that periodic tenancy could be brought to an end by a notice to quit served by the landlord on the same day;

(iii) it is served –

(a) in the period of three months immediately preceding the date on which the protected shorthold tenancy comes to an end; or

(b) if that date has passed, in the period of three months immediately preceding any anniversary of that date; and

(iv) in a case where a previous notice has been served by the landlord on the tenant n respect of the dwelling-house, and that notice was an appropriate notice, it is served not earlier than three months after the expiry of the previous notice.

PART III

PROVISION APPLICABLE TO CASE 9 AND PART II OF THIS SCHEDULE

Provision for Case 9

1. A court shall not make an order for possession of a dwelling-house by reason only that the circumstances of the case fall within Case 9 in Part I of this Schedule if the court is satisfied that, having regard to all the circumstances of the case, including the question whether other accommodation is available for the landlord or the tenant, greater hardship would be caused by granting the order than by refusing to grant it.

Provision for Part II

2. Any reference in Part II of this Schedule to the relevant date shall be construed as follows –

(a) except in a case falling within paragraph (b) or (c) below, if the protected tenancy, or, in the case of a statutory tenancy, the previous contractual tenancy, was created before 8th December 1965, the relevant date means 7th June 1966; and

(b) except in a case falling within paragraph (c) below, if the tenancy became a regulated tenancy by virtue of section 14 of the Counter-Inflation Act 1973 and the tenancy or, in the case of a statutory tenancy, the previous contractual tenancy, was created before 22nd March 1973, the relevant date means 22nd September 1973; and

(c) in the case of a regulated furnished tenancy, if the tenancy or, in the case of a statutory furnished tenancy, the previous contractual tenancy was created before 14th August 1974, the relevant date means 13th February 1975; and

(d) in any other case, the relevant date means the date of the commencement of the regulated tenancy in question.

PART IV

SUITABLE ALTERNATIVE ACCOMMODATION

3. For the purposes of section 98(1)(a) of this Act, a certificate of the local housing authority for the district in which the dwelling-house in question is situated, certifying that the authority will provide suitable alternative accommodation for the tenant by a date specified in the certificate, shall be conclusive evidence that suitable alternative accommodation will be available for him by that date.

4.–(1) Where no such certificate as is mentioned in paragraph 3 above is produced to the court, accommodation shall be deemed to be suitable for the purposes of section 98(1)(a) of this Act if it consists of either –

(a) premises which are to be let as a separate dwelling such that they will then be let on a protected tenancy (other than one under which the landlord might recover possession of the dwelling-house under one of the Cases in Part II of this Schedule), or

(b) premises to be let as a separate dwelling on terms which will, in the opinion of the court, afford to the tenant security of tenure reasonably equivalent to the security afforded by Part VII of this Act in the case of a protected tenancy of a kind mentioned in paragraph (a) above,

and, in the opinion of the court, the accommodation fulfils the relevant condition as defined in paragraph 5 below.

5.–(1) For the purposes of paragraph 4 above, the relevant conditions are that the accommodation is reasonably suitable to the needs of the tenant and his family as regards proximity to place of work, and either –

(a) similar as regards rental and extent to the accommodation afforded by dwelling-houses provided in the neighbourhood by any local housing authority for persons whose needs as regards extent are, in the opinion of the court, similar to those of the tenant and of his family; or

(b) reasonably suitable to the means of the tenant and to the needs of the tenant and his family as regards extent and character; and

that if any furniture was provided for use under the protected or statutory tenancy in question, furniture is provided for use in the accommodation which is either similar to that so provided or is reasonably suitable to the needs of the tenant and his family.

(2) For the purposes of sub-paragraph (1)(a) above, a certificate of a local housing authority stating –

(a) the extent of the accommodation afforded by dwelling-houses provided by the authority to meet the needs of tenants with families of such number as may be specified in the certificate, and

(b) the amount of the rent charged by the authority for dwelling-houses affording accommodation of that extent,

shall be conclusive evidence of the facts so stated.

6. Accommodation shall not be deemed to be suitable to the needs of the tenant and his family if the result of their occupation of the accommodation would be that it would be an overcrowded dwelling-house for the purposes of Part X of the Housing Act 1985.

7. Any document purporting to be a certificate of a local housing authority named therein issued for the purposes of this Schedule and to be signed by the proper officer of that authority shall be received in evidence and, unless the contrary is shown, shall be deemed to be such a certificate without further proof.

8. In this Part 'local housing authority' and 'district' in relation to such an authority have the same meaning as in the Housing Act 1985.

PART V

PROVISIONS APPLYING TO CASES 11, 12 AND 20

1. In this Part of this Schedule –

'mortgage' includes a charge and 'mortgagee' shall be construed accordingly;
'owner' means, in relation to Case 11, the owner-occupier; and
'successor in title' means any person deriving title from the owner, other than a purchaser for value or a person deriving title from a purchaser for value.

2. The condition referred to in paragraph (c) in each of Cases 11 and 12 and in paragraph (e)(ii) of Case 20 are that –

(a) the dwelling-house is required as a residence for the owner or any member of his family who resided with the owner when he last occupied the dwelling-house as a residence;

(b) the owner has retired from regular employment and requires the dwelling-house as a residence;

(c) the owner has died and the dwelling-house is required as a residence for a member of his family who was residing with him at the time of his death;

(d) the owner has died and the dwelling-house is required by a successor in title as his residence or for the purpose of disposing of it with vacant possession;

(e) the dwelling-house is subject to a mortgage, made by deed and granted before the tenancy, and the mortgagee –

(i) is entitled to exercise a power of sale conferred on him by the mortgage or by section 101 of the Law of Property Act 1925; and

(ii) requires the dwelling-house for the purpose of disposing of it with vacant possession in exercise of that power; and

(f) the dwelling-house is not reasonably suitable to the needs of the owner, having regard to his place of work, and he requires it for the purpose of disposing of it with vacant possession and of using the proceeds of that disposal in acquiring, as his residence, a dwelling-house which is more suitable to those needs.

NB For the phasing out of the Rent Acts, see Housing Act 1988, chapter V, below.

[As amended by the Local Government, Planning and Land Act 1980, s155(1); Housing Act 1980, ss55(1), 65(1), 66(1–6), 69(4), 73, 79, 152, Schedule 7, Schedule 8, para 2, Schedule 25, paras 28, 35, 57, 75, Schedule 26; New Towns Act 1981, s81, Schedule 12, para 24; Local Government Act 1985, ss84, 102(2), Schedule 14, para 56, Schedule 17; Rent (Amendment) Act 1985, s1(1), (2), (4); Housing (Consequential Provisions) Act 1985, s4, Schedule 2, para 35(1), (12); Agricultural Holdings Act 1986, s100, Schedule 14, para 59; Housing and Planning Act 1986, s24(2), Schedule 5, Pt II, para 15; Housing Act 1988, ss39(1), 62(7), 140(1), Schedule 17, Pt II, para 99; Norfolk and Suffolk Broads Act 1988, s21, Schedule 6, para 18; References to Rating (Housing) Regulations 1990, reg 2, Schedule, paras 15, 16, 17, 18; Local Government Finance (Housing) (Consequential Amendments) Order 1993, art 2(1), Schedule 1, paras 3, 4; Charities Act 1993, s98(1), Schedule 6, para 30; Local Government (Wales) Act 1994, ss22(2), 39(2), Schedule 8, para 3(1),

Schedule 13, para 28; Police and Magistrates' Courts Act 1994, s43, Schedule 4, Pt II, para 53; Agricultural Tenancies Act 1995, s40, Schedule, para 27; Environment Act 1995, s78, Schedule 10, para 18.]

PROTECTION FROM EVICTION ACT 1977
(1977 c 43)

1 Unlawful eviction and harassment of occupier   [716]

(1) In this section 'residential occupier', in relation to any premises, means a person occupying the premises as a residence, whether under a contract or by virtue of any enactment or rule of law giving him the right to remain in occupation or restricting the right of any other person to recover possession of the premises.

(2) If any person unlawfully deprives the residential occupier of any premises of his occupation of the premises or any part thereof, or attempts to do so, he shall be guilty of an offence unless he proves that he believed, and had reasonable cause to believe, that the residential occupier had ceased to reside in the premises.

(3) If any person with intent to cause the residential occupier of any premises –

(a) to give up the occupation of the premises or any part thereof; or
(b) to refrain from exercising any right or pursuing any remedy in respect of the premises or part thereof;

does acts likely to interfere with the peace or comfort of the residential occupier or members of his household, or persistently withdraws or withholds services reasonably required for the occupation of the premises as a residence, he shall be guilty of an offence.

(3A) Subject to subsection (3B) below, the landlord of a residential occupier or an agent of the landlord shall be guilty of an offence if –

(a) he does acts likely to interfere with the peace or comfort of the residential occupier or members of his household, or
(b) he persistently withdraws or withholds services reasonably required for the occupation of the premises in question as a residence,

and (in either case) he knows, or has reasonable cause to believe, that that conduct is likely to cause the residential occupier to give up the occupation of the whole or part of the premises or to refrain from exercising any right or pursuing any remedy in respect of the whole or part of the premises.

(3B) A person shall not be guilty of an offence under subsection (3A) above if he proves that he had reasonable grounds for doing the acts or withdrawing or withholding the services in question.

(3C) In subsection (3A) above 'landlord', in relation to a residential occupier of any premises, means the person who, but for –

(a) the residential occupier's right to remain in occupation of the premises, or
(b) a restriction on the person's rights to recover possession of the premises,

would be entitled to occupation of the premises and any superior landlord under whom that person derives title ...

(5) Nothing in this section shall be taken to prejudice any liability or remedy to which a person guilty of an offence thereunder may be subject in civil proceedings ...

2 Restriction on re-entry without due process of law [717]

Where any premises are let as a dwelling on a lease which is subject to a right of re-entry or forfeiture it shall not be lawful to enforce that right otherwise than by proceedings in the court while any person is lawfully residing in the premises or part of them.

3 Prohibition of eviction without due process of law [718]

(1) Where any premises have been let as a dwelling under a tenancy which is neither a statutorily protected tenancy nor an excluded tenancy and –

(a) the tenancy (in this section referred to as the former tenancy) has come to an end, but

(b) the occupier continues to reside in the premises or part of them,

it shall not be lawful for the owner to enforce against the occupier, otherwise than by proceedings in the court, his right to recover possession of the premises.

(2) In this section 'the occupier', in relation to any premises, means any person lawfully residing in the premises or part of them at the termination of the former tenancy.

(2A) Subsections (1) and (2) above apply in relation to any restricted contract (within the meaning of the Rent Act 1977) which –

(a) creates a licence; and

(b) is entered into after the commencement of section 69 of the Housing Act 1980;

as they apply in relation to a restricted contract which creates a tenancy.

(2B) Subsections (1) and (2) above apply in relation to any premises occupied as a dwelling under a licence, other than an excluded licence, as they apply in relation to premises let as a dwelling under a tenancy, and in those subsections the expression 'let' and 'tenancy' shall be construed accordingly.

(2C) References in the preceding provisions of this section and section 4(2A) below to an excluded tenancy do not apply to –

(a) a tenancy entered into before the date on which the Housing Act 1988 came into force, or

(b) a tenancy entered into on or after that date but pursuant to a contract made before that date,

but, subject to that, 'excluded tenancy' and 'excluded licence' shall be construed in accordance with section 3A below.

(3) This section shall, with the necessary modifications, apply where the owner's right to recover possession arises on the death of the tenant under a statutory tenancy within the meaning of the Rent Act 1977 or the Rent (Agriculture) Act 1976.

3A Excluded tenancies and licences [719]

(1) Any reference in this Act to an excluded tenancy or an excluded licence is a reference to a tenancy or licence which is excluded by virtue of any of the following provisions of this section.

(2) A tenancy or licence is excluded if –

(a) under its terms the occupier shares any accommodation with the landlord or licensor; and

(b) immediately before the tenancy or licence was granted and also at the time it comes to an end, the landlord or licensor occupied as his only or principal home premises of which the whole or part of the shared accommodation formed part.

(3) A tenancy or licence is also excluded if –

(a) under its terms the occupier shares any accommodation with a member of the family of the landlord or licensor;

(b) immediately before the tenancy or licence was granted and also at the time it comes to a end, the member of the family of the landlord or licensor occupied as his only or principal home premises of which the whole or part of the shared accommodation formed part; and

(c) immediately before the tenancy or licence was granted and also at the time it comes to an end, the landlord or licensor occupied as his only or principal home premises in the same building as the shared accommodation and that building is not a purpose-built block of flats.

(4) For the purposes of subsections (2) and (3) above, an occupier shares accommodation with another person if he has the use of it in common with that person (whether or not also in common with others) and any reference in those subsections to shared accommodation shall be construed accordingly, and if, in relation to any tenancy or licence, there is at any time more than one person who is the landlord or licensor, any reference in those subsections to the landlord or licensor shall be construed as a reference to any one of those persons.

(5) In subsections (2) to (4) above –

(a) 'accommodation' includes neither an area used for storage nor a staircase, passage, corridor or other means of access;

(b) 'occupier' means, in relation to a tenancy, the tenant and, in relation to a licence, the licensee; and

(c) 'purpose-built block of flats' has the same meaning as in Part III of Schedule 1 to the Housing Act 1988;

and section 113 of the Housing Act 1985 shall apply to determine whether a person is for the purposes of subsection (3) above a member of another's family as it applies for the purposes of Part IV of that Act.

(6) A tenancy or licence is excluded if it was granted as a temporary expedient to a person who entered the premises in question or any other premises as a trespasser (whether or not, before the beginning of that tenancy or licence, another tenancy or licence to occupy the premises or any other premises had been granted to him).

(7) A tenancy or licence is excluded if –

(a) it confers on the tenant or licensee the right to occupy the premises for a holiday only, or

(b) it is granted otherwise than for money or money's worth.

(8) A licence is excluded if it confers rights of occupation in a hostel, within the meaning of the Housing Act 1985, which is provided by –

(a) the council of a county, county borough, district or London Borough, the Common Council of the City of London, the Council of the Isles of Scilly, a joint authority within the meaning of the Local Government Act 1985 or a residuary body within the meaning of that Act;

(b) a development corporation within the meaning of the New Towns Act 1981;

(c) the Commission for the New Towns;

(d) an urban development corporation established by an order under section 135 of the Local Government, Planning and Land Act 1980;

(e) a housing action trust established under Part III of the Housing Act 1988;
(f) the Development Board for Rural Wales;
(g) the Housing Corporation or Housing for Wales;
(h) a housing trust which is a charity or a registered housing association, within the meaning of the Housing Associations Act 1985; or
(i) any other person who is, or who belongs to a class of person which is, specified in an order made by the Secretary of State ...

5 Validity of notices to quit [720]

(1) Subject to subsection (1B) below no notice by a landlord or a tenant to quit any premises let (whether before or after the commencement of this Act) as a dwelling shall be valid unless –

(a) it is in writing and contains such information as may be prescribed, and
(b) it is given not less than four weeks before the date on which it is to take effect.

(1A) Subject to subsection (1B) below, no notice by a licensor or a licensee to determine a periodic licence to occupy premises as a dwelling (whether the licence was granted before or after the passing of this Act) shall be valid unless –

(a) it is in writing and contains such information as may be prescribed, and
(b) it is given not less than four weeks before the date on which it is to take effect.

(1B) Nothing in subsection (1) or subsection (1A) above applies to –

(a) premises let on an excluded tenancy which is entered into on or after the date on which the Housing Act 1988 came into force unless it is entered into pursuant to a contract made before that date; or
(b) premises occupied under an excluded licence.

(2) In this section 'prescribed' means prescribed by regulations made by the Secretary of State by statutory instrument ...

8 Interpretation [721]

(1) In this Act 'statutorily protected tenancy' means –

(a) a protected tenancy within the meaning of the Rent Act 1977 or a tenancy to which Part I of the Landlord and Tenant Act 1954 applies:
(b) a protected occupancy or statutory tenancy as defined in the Rent (Agriculture) Act 1976;
(c) a tenancy to which Part II of the Landlord and Tenant Act 1954 applies;
(d) a tenancy of an agricultural holding within the meaning of the Agricultural Holdings Act 1986 which is a tenancy in relation to which that Act applies;
(e) an assured tenancy or assured agricultural occupancy under Part I of the Housing Act 1988;
(f) a tenancy to which Schedule 10 to the Local Government and Housing Act 1989 applies;
(g) a farm business tenancy within the meaning of the Agricultural Tenancies Act 1995.

(2) For the purposes of Part I of this Act [sections 1–4] a person who, under the terms of his employment, had exclusive possession of any premises other than as a tenant shall be deemed to have been a tenant and the expression 'let' and 'tenancy' shall be construed accordingly.

(3) In Part I of this Act 'the owner', in relation to any premises, means the person who, as against the occupier, is entitled to possession thereof.

(4) In this Act 'excluded tenancy' and 'excluded licence' have the meaning assigned by section 3A of this Act.

(5) If, on or after the date on which the Housing Act 1988 came into force, the terms of an excluded tenancy or excluded licence entered into before that date are varied, then –

(a) if the variation affects the amount of the rent which is payable under the tenancy or licence, the tenancy or licence shall be treated for the purposes of sections 3(2C) and 5(1B) above as a new tenancy or licence entered into at the time of the variation; and

(b) if the variation does not affect the amount of the rent which is so payable nothing in this Act shall affect the determination of the question whether the variation is such as to give rise to a new tenancy or licence.

(6) Any reference in subsection (5) above to a variation affecting the amount of the rent which is payable under a tenancy or licence does not include a reference to –

(a) a reduction or increase effected under Part III or Part VI of the Rent Act 1977 (rents under regulated tenancies and housing association tenancies), section 78 of that Act (power of rent tribunal in relation to restricted contracts) or sections 11 to 14 of the Rent (Agriculture) Act 1976; or

(b) a variation which is made by the parties and has the effect of making the rent expressed to be payable under the tenancy or licence the same as a rent for the dwelling which is entered in the register under Part IV or section 79 of the Rent Act 1977.

[As amended by the Agricultural Holdings Act 1986, s100, Schedule 14, para 61; Housing Act 1988, ss29, 30(1), (2), 31, 32, 33; Local Government and Housing Act 1989, s194(1), Schedule 11, para 54; Local Government (Wales) Act 1994, s22(2), Schedule 8, para 4(1); Agricultural Tenancies Act 1995, s40, Schedule, para 29.]

CRIMINAL LAW ACT 1977
(1977 c 45)

6 Violence for securing entry   [722]

(1) Subject to the following provisions of this section, any person who, without lawful authority, uses or threatens violence for the purpose of securing entry into any premises for himself or for any other person is guilty of an offence, provided that –

(a) there is someone present on those premises at the time who is opposed to the entry which the violence is intended to secure; and

(b) the person using or threatening the violence knows that this is the case.

(1A) Subsection (1) above does not apply to a person who is a displaced residential occupier or a protected intending occupier of the premises in question or who is acting on behalf of such an occupier; and if the accused adduces sufficient evidence that he was, or was acting on behalf of, such an occupier he shall be presumed to be, or to be acting on behalf of, such an occupier unless the contrary is proved by the prosecution.

(2) Subject to subsection (1A) above, the fact that a person has any interest in or right to possession or occupation of any premises shall not for the purposes of subsection (1) above constitute lawful authority for the use or threat of violence by him or anyone else for the purpose of securing his entry into those premises.

(4) It is immaterial for the purposes of this section –

(a) whether the violence in question is directed against the person or against property; and

(b) whether the entry which the violence is intended to secure is for the purpose of acquiring possession of the premises in question or for any other purpose.

(5) A person guilty of an offence under this section shall be liable on summary conviction to imprisonment for a term not exceeding six months or to a fine not exceeding level 5 on the standard scale or to both.

(6) A constable in uniform may arrest without warrant anyone who is, or whom he, with reasonable cause, suspects to be, guilty of an offence under this section.

(7) Section 12 below contains provisions which apply for determining when any person is to be regarded for the purposes of this Part of this Act as a displaced residential occupier of any premises or of any access to any premises and section 12A below contains provisions which apply for determining when any person is to be regarded for the purposes of this Part of this Act as a protected intending occupier of any premises or of any access to any premises.

7 Adverse occupation of residential premises [723]

(1) Subject to the following provisions of this section and to section 12A(9) below, any person who is on any premises as a trespasser after having entered as such is guilty of an offence if he fails to leave those premises on being required to do so by or on behalf of –

(a) a displaced residential occupier of the premises; or

(b) an individual who is a protected intending occupier of the premises.

(2) In any proceedings for an offence under this section it shall be a defence for the accused to prove that he believed that the person requiring him to leave the premises was not a displaced residential occupier or protected intending occupier of the premises or a person acting on behalf of a displaced residential occupier or protected intending occupier.

(3) In any proceedings for an offence under this section it shall be a defence for the accused to prove –

(a) that the premises in question are or form part of premises used mainly for non-residential purposes; and

(b) that he was not on any part of the premises used wholly or mainly for residential purposes.

(4) Any reference in the preceding provisions of this section to any premises includes a reference to any access to them, whether or not any such access itself constitutes premises, within the meaning of this Part of this Act.

(5) A person guilty of an offence under this section shall be liable on summary conviction to imprisonment for a term not exceeding six months or to a fine not exceeding level 5 on the standard scale or to both.

(6) A constable in uniform may arrest without warrant anyone who is, or whom he, with reasonable cause, suspects to be, guilty of an offence under this section.

(7) Section 12 below contains provisions which apply for determining when any person is to be regarded for the purposes of this Part of this Act as a displaced residential occupier of any premises or of any access to any premises and section 12A below contains provisions which apply for determining when any person is to be regarded for the purposes of this Part of this Act as a protected intending occupier of any premises or of any access to any premises.

12 Supplementary provisions   [724]

(3) Subject to subsection (4) below, any person who was occupying any premises as a residence immediately before being excluded from occupation by anyone who entered those premises, or any access to those premises, as a trespasser is a displaced residential occupier of the premises for the purposes of this Part of this Act so long as he continues to be excluded from occupation of the premises by the original trespasser or by any subsequent trespasser.

(4) A person who was himself occupying the premises in question as a trespasser immediately before being excluded from occupation shall not by virtue of subsection (3) above be a displaced residential occupier of the premises for the purposes of this Part of this Act.

(5) A person who by virtue of subsection (3) above is a displaced residential occupier of any premises shall be regarded for the purposes of this Part of this Act as a displaced residential occupier also of any access to those premises.

(6) Anyone who entered or is on or in occupation of any premises by virtue of –

(a) any title derived from a trespasser; or
(b) any licence or consent given by a trespasser or by a person deriving title from a trespasser,

shall himself be treated as a trespasser for the purposes of this Part of this Act (without prejudice to whether or not he would be a trespasser apart from this provision); and references in this Part of this Act to a person's entering or being on or occupying any premises as a trespasser shall be construed accordingly.

(7) Anyone who is on any premises as a trespasser shall not cease to be a trespasser for the purposes of this Part of this Act by virtue of being allowed time to leave the premises, nor shall anyone cease to be a displaced residential occupier of any premises by virtue of any such allowance of time to a trespasser.

12A Protected intending occupiers: [725]
supplementary provisions

(1) For the purposes of this Part of this Act an individual is a protected intending occupier of any premises at any time if at that time he falls within subsection (2), (4) or (6) below.

(2) An individual is a protected intending occupier of any premises if –

(a) he has in those premises a freehold interest or a leasehold interest with not less than two years still to run;
(b) he requires the premises for his own occupation as a resident;
(c) he is excluded from occupation of the premises by a person who entered them, or any access to them, as a trespasser; and
(d) he or a person acting on his behalf holds a written statement –

(i) which specifies his interest in the premises;
(ii) which states that he requires the premises for occupation as a residence for himself; and
(iii) with respect to which the requirements in subsection (3) below are fulfilled.

(3) The requirements referred to in subsection (2)(d)(iii) above are –

(a) that the statement is signed by the person whose interest is specified in it in the presence of a justice of the peace or commissioner for oaths; and
(b) that the justice of the peace or commissioner for oaths has subscribed his name as a witness to the signature.

(4) An individual is also a protected intending occupier of any premises if –

(a) he has a tenancy of those premises (other than a tenancy falling within subsection (2)(a) above or (6)(a) below) or a licence to occupy those premises granted by a person with a freehold interest or a leasehold interest with not less than two years still to run in the premises;
(b) he requires the premises for his own occupation as a residence;
(c) he is excluded from occupation of the premises by a person who entered them, or any access to them, as a trespasser; and
(d) he or a person acting on his behalf holds a written statement –

(i) which states that he has been granted a tenancy of those premises or a licence to occupy those premises;
(ii) which specifies the interest in the premises of the person who granted that tenancy or licence to occupy ('the landlord');
(iii) which states that he requires the premises for occupation as a residence for himself; and
(iv) with respect to which the requirements in subsection (5) below are fulfilled.

(5) The requirements referred to in subsection (4)(d)(iv) above are –

(a) that the statement is signed by the landlord and by the tenant or licensee in the presence of a justice of the peace or commissioner for oaths;
(b) that the justice of the peace or commissioner for oaths has subscribed his name as a witness to the signatures.

(6) An individual is also a protected intending occupier of any premises if –

(a) he has a tenancy of those premises (other than a tenancy falling within subsection (2)(a) or (4)(a) above) or a licence to occupy those premises granted by an authority to which this subsection applies;
(b) he requires the premises for his own occupation as a residence;
(c) he is excluded from occupation of the premises by a person who entered the premises, or any access to them, as a trespasser; and
(d) there has been issued to him by or on behalf of the authority referred to in paragraph (a) above a certificate stating that –

(i) he has been granted a tenancy of those premises or a licence to occupy those premises as a residence by the authority; and
(ii) the authority which granted that tenancy or licence to occupy is one to which this subsection applies, being of a description specified in the certificate.

(7) Subsection (6) above applies to the following authorities –

(a) any body mentioned in section 14 of the Rent Act 1977 (landlord's interest belonging to local authority etc.);
(b) the Housing Corporation;
(c) Housing for Wales; and
(d) a registered housing association within the meaning of the Housing Association Act 1985.

(8) A person is guilty of an offence if he makes a statement for the purposes of subsection (2)(d) or (4)(d) above which he knows to be false in a material particular or if he recklessly makes such a statement which is false in a material particular.

(9) In any proceedings for an offence under section 7 of this Act where the accused was requested to leave the premises by a person claiming to be or to act on behalf of a protected intending occupier of the premises –

(a) it shall be a defence for the accused to prove that, although asked to do so by the accused at the time the accused was requested to leave, that person failed at that time to produce to the accused such a statement as is referred to in subsection (2)(d) or (4)(d) above or such a certificate as is referred to in subsection (6)(d) above; and

(b) any document purporting to be a certificate under subsection (6)(d) above shall be received in evidence and, unless the contrary is proved, shall be deemed to have been issued by or on behalf of the authority stated in the certificate.

(10) A person guilty of an offence under subsection (8) above shall be liable on summary conviction to imprisonment for a term not exceeding six months or to a fine not exceeding level 5 on the standard scale or to both.

(11) A person who is a protected intending occupier of any premises shall be regarded for the purposes of this Part of this Act as a protected intending occupier also of any access to those premises.

[As amended by the Criminal Justice and Public Order Act 1994, ss72, 73, 74, 168(3), Schedule 11.]

CHARGING ORDERS ACT 1979
(1979 c 53)

1 Charging orders   [726]

(1) Where, under a judgment or order of the High Court or a county court, a person (the 'debtor') is required to pay a sum of money to another person (the 'creditor') then, for the purpose of enforcing that judgment or order, the appropriate court may make an order in accordance with the provisions of this Act imposing on any such property of the debtor as may be specified in the order a charge for securing the payment of any money due or to become due under the judgment or order ...

(3) An order under subsection (1) above is referred to in this Act as a 'charging order' ...

(5) In deciding whether to make a charging order the court shall consider all the circumstances of the case and, in particular, any evidence before it as to –

(a) the personal circumstances of the debtor, and
(b) whether any other creditor of the debtor would be likely to be unduly prejudiced by the making of the order.

2 Property which may be charged   [727]

(1) Subject to subsection (3) below, a charge may be imposed by a charging order only on –

(a) any interest held by the debtor beneficially –

(i) in any asset of a kind mentioned in subsection (2) below, or
(ii) under any trust; or

(b) any interest held by a person as trustee of a trust ('the trust'), if the interest is in such an asset or is an interest under another trust and –

(i) the judgment or order in respect of which a charge is to be imposed was made against that person as trustee of the trust, or
(ii) the whole beneficial interest under the trust is held by the debtor unencumbered and for his own benefit, or
(iii) in a case where there are two or more debtors all of whom are liable to

the creditor for the same debt, they together hold the whole beneficial interest under the trust unencumbered and for their own benefit.

(2) The assets referred to in subsection (1) above are –

(a) land ...

3 Provisions supplementing sections 1 and 2 [728]

(1) A charging order may be made either absolutely or subject to conditions as to notifying the debtor or as to the time when the charge is to become enforceable, or as to other matters.

(2) The Land Charges Act 1972 and the Land Registration Act 1925 shall apply in relation to charging orders as they apply in relation to other orders or writs issued or made for the purposes of enforcing judgments ...

(4) Subject to the provisions of this Act, a charge imposed by a charging order shall have the like effect and shall be enforceable in the same courts and in the same manner as an equitable charge created by the debtor by writing under his hand.

(5) The court by which a charging order was made may at any time, on the application of the debtor or of any person interested in any property to which the order relates, make an order discharging or varying the charging order.

(6) Where a charging order has been protected by an entry registered under the Land Charges Act 1972 or the Land Registration Act 1925, an order under subsection (5) above discharging the charging order may direct that the entry be cancelled ...

6 Interpretation [729]

(2) For the purposes of section 1 of this Act references to a judgment or order of the High Court or a county court shall be taken to include references to a judgment, order, decree or award (however called) of any court or arbitrator (including any foreign court or arbitrator) which is or has become enforceable (whether wholly or to a limited extent) as if it were a judgment or order of the High Court or a county court ...

LIMITATION ACT 1980

(1980 c 58)

PART I

ORDINARY TIME LIMITS FOR DIFFERENT CLASSES OF ACTION

1 Time limits under Part I subject to extension [730] or exclusion under Part II

(1) This Part of this Act gives the ordinary time limits for bringing actions of the various classes mentioned in the following provisions of this Part.

(2) The ordinary time limits given in this Part of this Act are subject to extension or exclusion in accordance with the provisions of Part II of this Act.

5 Time limit for actions founded on simple contract [731]

An action founded on simple contract shall not be brought after the expiration of six years from the date on which the cause of action accrued.

15 Time limit for actions to recover land   [732]

(1) No action shall be brought by any person to recover any land after the expiration of twelve years form the date on which the right of action accrued to him or, if it first accrued to some person through whom he claims, to that person.

(2) Subject to the following provisions of this section, where –

  (a) the estate or interest claimed was an estate or interest in reversion or remainder or any other future estate or interest and the right of action to recover the land accrued on the date on which the estate or interest fell into possession by the determination of the preceding estate or interest; and
  (b) the person entitled to the preceding estate or interest (not being a term of years absolute) was not in possession of the land on that date;

no action shall be brought by the person entitled to the succeeding estate or interest after the expiration of twelve years from the date on which the right of action accrued to the person entitled to the preceding estate or interest or six years from the date on which the right of action accrued to the person entitled to the succeeding estate or interest, which ever period last expires.

(3) Subsection (2) above shall not apply to any estate or interest which falls into possession on the determination of an entailed interest and which might have been barred by the person entitled to the entailed interest.

(4) No person shall bring an action to recover any estate or interest in land under an assurance taking effect after the right of action to recover the land had accrued to the person by whom the assurance was made or some person through whom he claimed or some person entitled to a preceding estate or interest, unless the action is brought within the period during which the person by whom the assurance was made could have brought such an action.

(5) Where any person is entitled to any estate or interest in land in possession and, while so entitled, is also entitled to any future estate or interest in that land, and his right to recover the estate or interest in possession is barred under this Act, no action shall be brought by that person, or by any person claiming through him, in respect of the future estate or interest, unless in the meantime possession of the land has been recovered by a person entitled to an intermediate estate or interest.

(6) Part I of Schedule 1 to this Act contains provisions for determining the date of accrual of rights of action to recover land in the cases there mentioned.

(7) Part II of that Schedule contains provisions modifying the provisions of this section in their application to actions brought by, or by a person claiming through, the Crown or any spiritual or eleemosynary corporation sole.

16 Time limit for redemption actions   [733]

When a mortgagee of land has been in possession of any of the mortgaged land for a period of twelve years, no action to redeem the land of which the mortgagee has been so in possession shall be brought after the end of that period by the mortgagor or any person claiming through him.

17 Extinction of title to land after expiration of time limit   [734]

Subject to –

  (a) section 18 of this Act; and
  (b) section 75 of the Land Registration Act 1925;

at the expiration of the period prescribed by this Act for any person to bring an action to recover land (including a redemption action) the title of that person to the land shall be extinguished.

18 Settled land and land held on trust [735]

(1) Subject to section 21(1) and (2) of this Act, the provisions of this Act shall apply to equitable interests in land as they apply to legal estates. Accordingly a right to action to recover the land shall, for the purposes of this Act but not otherwise, be treated as accruing to a person entitled in possession to such an equitable interest in the like manner and circumstances, and on the same date, as it would accrue if his interest were a legal estate in the land (and any relevant provision of Part I of Schedule 1 to this Act shall apply in any such case accordingly).

(2) Where the period prescribed by this Act has expired for the bringing of an action to recover land by a tenant for life or a statutory owner of settled land –

(a) his legal estate shall not be extinguished if and so long as the right of action to recover the land of any person entitled to a beneficial interest in the land either has not accrued or has not been barred by this Act; and

(b) the legal estate shall accordingly remain vested in the tenant for life or statutory owner and shall devolve in accordance with the Settled Land Act 1925;

but if and when every such right of action has been barred by this Act, his legal estate shall be extinguished.

(3) Where any land is held upon trust and the period prescribed by this Act has expired for the bringing of an action to recover the land by the trustees, the estate of the trustees shall not be extinguished if and so long as the right of action to recover the land of any person entitled to a beneficial interest in the land either has not accrued or has not been barred by this Act; but if and when every such right of action has been so barred the estate of the trustees shall be extinguished.

(4) Where –

(a) any settled land is vested in a statutory owner; or

(b) any land is held upon trust;

an action to recover the land may be brought by the statutory owner or trustees on behalf of any person entitled to a beneficial interest in possession in the land whose right of action has not been barred by this Act, notwithstanding that the right of action of the statutory owner or trustees would apart from this provision have been barred by this Act.

19 Time limit for actions to recover rent [736]

No action shall be brought, or distress made, to recover arrears of rent, or damages in respect of arrears of rent, after the expiration of six years from the date on which the arrears became due.

20 Time limit for actions to recover money secured [737] by a mortgage or charge or to recover proceeds of the sale of land

(1) No action shall be brought to recover –

(a) any principal sum of money secured by a mortgage or other charge on property (whether real or personal); or

(b) proceeds of the sale of land;

after the expiration of twelve years from the date on which the right to receive the money accrued.

(2) No foreclosure action in respect of mortgaged personal property shall be

brought after the expiration of twelve years from the date on which the right to foreclose accrued.

But if the mortgagee was in possession of the mortgaged property after that date, the right to foreclose on the property which was in his possession shall not be treated as having accrued for the purposes of this subsection until the date on which his possession discontinued.

(3) The right to receive any principal sum of money secured by a mortgage or other charge and the right to foreclose on the property subject to the mortgage or charge shall not be treated as accruing so long as that property comprises any future interest or any life insurance policy which has not matured or been determined.

(4) Nothing in this section shall apply to a foreclosure action in respect of mortgaged land, but the provisions of this Act relating to actions to recover land shall apply to such an action.

(5) Subject to subsections (6) and (7) below, no action to recover arrears of interest payable in respect of any sum of money secured by a mortgage or other charge or payable in respect of proceeds of the sale of land, or to recover damages in respect of such arrears [,] shall be brought after the expiration of six years from the date on which the interest became due.

(6) Where –

(a) a prior mortgagee or other incumbrancer has been in possession of the property charged; and
(b) an action is brought within one year of the discontinuance of that possession by the subsequent incumbrancer;

the subsequent incumbrancer may recover by that action all the arrears of interest which fell due during the period of possession by the prior incumbrancer or damages in respect of those arrears, notwithstanding that the period exceeded six years.

(7) Where –

(a) the property subject to the mortgage or charge comprises any future interest or life insurance policy; and
(b) it is a term of the mortgage or charge that arrears of interest shall be treated as part of the principal sum of money secured by the mortgage or charge;

interest shall not be treated as becoming due before the right to recover the principal sum of money has accrued or is treated as having accrued.

28 Extension of limitation period in case of disability   [738]

(1) Subject to the following provisions of this section, if on the date when any right of action accrued for which a period of limitation is prescribed by this Act, the person to whom it accrued was under a disability, the action may be brought at any time before the expiration of six years from the date when he ceased to be under a disability or died (whichever first occurred) notwithstanding that the period of limitation has expired.

(2) This section shall not affect any case where the right of action first accrued to some person (not under a disability) through whom the person under a disability claims.

(3) When a right of action which has accrued to a person under a disability accrues, on the death of that person while still under a disability, to another person under a disability, no further extension of time shall be allowed by reason of the disability of the second person.

(6) If the action is one to which sections 11 or 12(2) of this Act applies, subsection (1) above shall have effect as if for the words 'six years' there were substituted the words 'three years'.

(7) If the action is one to which section 11A of this Act applies or one by virtue of section 6(1)(a) of the Consumer Protection Act 1987 (death caused by defective product), subsection (1) above –

(a) shall not apply to the time limit prescribed by subsection (3) of the said section 11A or to that time limit as applied by virtue of section 12(1) of this Act; and

(b) in relation to any other time limit prescribed by this Act shall have effect as if for the words 'six years' there were substituted the words 'three years'.

29 Fresh accrual of action on acknowledgment or part payment [739]

(5) Subject to subsection (6) below, where any right of action has accrued to recover –

(a) any debt or other liquidated pecuniary claim; or

(b) any claim to the personal estate of a deceased person or to any share or interest in any such estate;

and the person liable or accountable for the claim acknowledges the claim or makes any payment in respect of it the right shall be treated as having accrued on and not before the date of the acknowledgment or payment.

(6) A payment of a part of the rent or interest due at any time shall not extend the period for claiming the remainder then due, but any payment of interest shall be treated as a payment in respect of the principal debt.

(7) Subject to subsection (6) above, a current period of limitation may be repeatedly extended under this section by further acknowledgments or payments, but a right of action, once barred by this Act, shall not be revived by any subsequent acknowledgment or payment.

30 Formal provisions as to acknowledgments and part payments [740]

(1) To be effective for the purposes of section 29 of this Act, an acknowledgment must be in writing and signed by the person making it.

(2) For the purposes of section 29, any acknowledgment or payment –

(a) may be made by the agent of the person by whom it is required to be made under that section; and

(b) shall be made to the person, or to an agent of the person, whose title or claim is being acknowledged or, as the case may be, in respect of whose claim the payment is being made.

31 Effect of acknowledgment or part payment on persons other than the maker or recipient [741]

(6) An acknowledgment of any debt or other liquidated pecuniary claim shall bind the acknowledgor and his successors but not any other person.

(7) A payment made in respect of any debt or other liquidated pecuniary claim shall bind all persons liable in respect of the debt or claim.

(8) An acknowledgment by one of several personal representatives of any claim to the personal estate of a deceased person or to any share or interest in any such

estate, or a payment by one of several personal representatives in respect of any such claim, shall bind the estate of the deceased person.

(9) In this section 'successor', in relation to any mortgagee or person liable in respect of any debt or claim, means his personal representatives and any other person on whom the rights under the mortgage or, as the case may be, the liability in respect of the debt or claim devolve (whether on death or bankruptcy or the disposition of property or the determination of a limited estate or interest in settled property or otherwise).

32 Postponement of limitation period in case of fraud,   [742] concealment or mistake

(1) Subject to subsections (3) and (4A) below, where in the case of any action for which a period of limitation is prescribed by this Act, either –

(a) the action is based upon the fraud of the defendant; or
(b) any fact relevant to the plaintiff's right of action has been deliberately concealed from him by the defendant; or
(c) the action is for relief from the consequences of a mistake;

the period of limitation shall not begin to run until the plaintiff has discovered the fraud, concealment or mistake (as the case may be) or could with reasonable diligence have discovered it.

References in this subsection to the defendant include references to the defendant's agent and to any person through whom the defendant claims and his agent.

(2) For the purposes of subsection (1) above, deliberate commission of a breach of duty in circumstances in which it is unlikely to be discovered for some time amounts to deliberate concealment of the facts involved in that breach of duty.

(3) Nothing in this section shall enable any action –

(a) to recover, or recover the value of, any property; or
(b) to enforce any charge against, or set aside any transaction affecting, any property;

to be brought against the purchaser of the property or any person claiming through him in any case where the property has been purchased for valuable consideration by an innocent third party since the fraud or concealment or (as the case may be) the transaction in which the mistake was made took place.

(4) A purchase is an innocent third party for the purposes of this section –

(a) in the case of fraud or concealment of any fact relevant to the plaintiff's right of action, if he was not a party to the fraud or (as the case may be) to the concealment of that fact and did not at the time of the purchase know or have reason to believe that the fraud or concealment had taken place; and
(b) in the case of mistake, if he did not at the time of the purchase know or have reason to believe that the mistake had been made.

(4A) Subsection (1) above shall not apply in relation to the time limit prescribed by section 11A(3) of this Act or in relation to that time limit as applied by virtue of section 12(1) of this Act.

PART III

MISCELLANEOUS AND GENERAL

36 Equitable jurisdiction and remedies [743]

(1) The following time limits under this Act, that is to say –

(b) the time limit under section 5 for actions founded on simple contract;
(c) the time limit under section 7 for actions to enforce awards where the submission is not by an instrument under seal;
(d) the time limit under section 8 for actions on a specialty;

shall not apply to any claim for specific performance of a contract or for an injunction or for other equitable relief, except in so far as any such time limit may be applied by the court by analogy in like manner as the corresponding time limit under any enactment repealed by the Limitation Act 1939 was applied before 1st July 1940.

(2) Nothing in this Act shall affect any equitable jurisdiction to refuse relief on the ground of acquiescence or otherwise.

38 Interpretation [744]

(1) In this Act, unless the context otherwise requires –

'action' includes any proceeding in a court of law, including an ecclesiastical court;
'land' includes corporeal hereditaments, tithes and rent charges and any legal or equitable estate or interest therein, but except as provided above in this definition does not include any incorporeal hereditament;
'personal estate' and 'personal property' do not include chattels real;
'personal injuries' includes any disease and any impairment of a person's physical or mental condition, and 'injury' and cognate expressions shall be construed accordingly;
'rent' includes a rentcharge and a rent service;
'rentcharge' means any annuity or periodical sum of money charged upon or payable out of land, except a rent service or interest on a mortgage on land;
'settled land', 'statutory owner' and 'tenant for life' have the same meanings respectively as in the Settled Land Act 1925;
'trust' and 'trustee' have the same meanings respectively as in the Trustee Act 1925.

(2) For the purposes of this Act a person shall be treated as under a disability while he is an infant, or of unsound mind.

(3) For the purposes of subsection (2) above a person is of unsound mind if he is a person who, by reason of mental disorder within the meaning of the Mental Health Act 1983, is incapable of managing and administering his property and affairs.

(4) Without prejudice to the generality of subsection (3) above, a person shall be conclusively presumed for the purposes of subsection (2) above to be of unsound mind:

(a) while he is liable to be detained or subject to guardianship under the Mental Health Act 1983 (otherwise than by virtue of section 35 or 89); and
(b) while he is receiving treatment as an in-patient in any hospital within the meaning of the Mental Health Act 1983 or mental nursing home within the meaning of the Nursing Homes Act 1975 without being liable to be detained under the said Act of 1983 (otherwise than by virtue of section 35 or 89), being

treatment which follows without any interval a period during which he was liable to be detained or subject to guardianship under the Mental Health Act 1959, or the said Act of 1983 (otherwise than by virtue of section 35 or 89) or by virtue of any enactment repealed or excluded by the Mental Health Act 1959.

(5) Subject to subsection (6) below, a person shall be treated as claiming through another person if he became entitled by, through, under, or by the act of that other person to the right claimed, and any person whose estate or interest might have been barred by a person entitled to an entailed interest in possession shall be treated as claiming through the person so entitled.

(6) A person becoming entitled to any estate or interest by virtue of a special power of appointment shall not be treated as claiming through the appointor.

(7) References in this Act to a right of action to recover land shall include references to a right to enter into possession of the land or, in the case of rentcharges and tithes, to distrain for arrears of rent or tithe, and references to the bringing of such an action shall include references to the making of such an entry or distress.

(8) References in this Act to the possession of land shall, in the case of tithes and rentcharges, be construed as references to the receipt of the tithe or rent, and references to the date of dispossession or discontinuance of possession of land shall, in the case of rentcharges, be construed as references to the date of the last receipt of rent.

(9) References in Part II of this Act to a right of action shall include references to –

(a) a cause of action;
(b) a right to receive money secured by a mortgage or charge on any property;
(c) a right to recover proceeds of the sale of land; and
(d) a right to receive a share or interest in the personal estate of a deceased person.

(10) References in Part II to the date of the accrual of a right of action shall be construed –

(a) in the case of an action upon a judgment, as references to the date on which the judgment became enforceable; and

(b) in the case of an action to recover arrears of rent or interest, or damages in respect of arrears of rent or interest, as references to the date on which the rent or interest became due.

SCHEDULE 1   **[745]**

PROVISIONS WITH RESPECT TO
ACTIONS TO RECOVER LAND

PART I

ACCRUAL OF RIGHTS OF ACTION TO RECOVER LAND

1. Where the person bringing an action to recover land, or some person through whom he claims, has been in possession of the land, and has while entitled to the land been dispossessed or discontinued his possession, the right of action shall be treated as having accrued on the date of the dispossession or discontinuance.

2. Where any person brings an action to recover any land of a deceased person (whether under a will or on intestacy) and the deceased person –

(a) was on the date of his death in possession of the land or, in the case of a rentcharge created by will or taking effect upon his death, in possession of the land charged; and

(b) was the last person entitled to the land to be in possession of it;

the right of action shall be treated as having accrued on the date of his death.

3. Where any person brings an action to recover land, being an estate or interest in possession assured otherwise than by will to him, or to some person through whom he claims, and –

(a) the person making the assurance was on the date when the assurance took effect in possession of the land or, in the case of a rentcharge created by the assurance, in possession of the land charged; and

(b) no person has been in possession of the land by virtue of the assurance;

the right of action shall be treated as having accrued on the date when the assurance took effect.

4. The right of action to recover any land shall, in a case where –

(a) the estate or interest claimed was an estate or interest in reversion or remainder or any other future estate or interest; and

(b) no person has taken possession of the land by virtue of the estate or interest claimed;

be treated as having accrued on the date on which the estate or interest fell into possession by the determination of the preceding estate or interest.

5.–(1) Subject to sub-paragraph (2) below, a tenancy from year to year or other period, without a lease in writing, shall for the purposes of this Act be treated as being determined at the expiration of the first year or other period; and accordingly the right of action of the person entitled to the land subject to the tenancy shall be treated as having accrued at the date on which in accordance with this sub-paragraph the tenancy is determined.

(2) Where any rent has subsequently been received in respect of the tenancy, the right of action shall be treated as having accrued on the date of the last receipt of rent.

6.–(1) Where –

(a) any person is in possession of land by virtue of a lease in writing by which a rent of not less than ten pounds a year is reserved; and

(b) the rent is received by some person wrongfully claiming to be entitled to the land in reversion immediately expectant on the determination of the lease; and

(c) no rent is subsequently received by the person rightfully so entitled;

the right of action to recover the land of the person rightfully so entitled shall be treated as having accrued on the date when the rent was first received by the person wrongfully claiming to be so entitled and not on the date of the determination of the lease ...

7.–(1) Subject to sub-paragraph (2) below, a right of action to recover land by virtue of a forfeiture or breach of condition shall be treated as having accrued on the date on which the forfeiture was incurred or the condition broken.

(2) If any such right has accrued to a person entitled to an estate or interest in reversion or remainder and the land was not recovered by virtue of that right, the right of action to recover the land shall not be treated as having accrued to that person until his estate or interest fell into possession, as if no such forfeiture or breach of condition had occurred.

8.–(1) No right of action to recover land shall be treated as accruing unless the land is in the possession of some person in whose favour the period of limitation can run (referred to below in this paragraph as 'adverse possession'); and where under the preceding provisions of this Schedule any such right of action is treated as accruing on a certain date and no person is in adverse possession on that date, the right of action shall not be treated as accruing unless and until adverse possession is taken on the land.

(2) Where a right of action to recover land has accrued and after its accrual, before the right is barred, the land ceases to be in adverse possession, the right of action shall no longer be treated as having accrued and no fresh right of action shall be treated as accruing unless and until the land is again taken into adverse possession.

(3) For the purposes of this paragraph –

(a) possession of any land subject to a rentcharge by a person (other than the person entitled to the rentcharge) who does not pay the rent shall be treated as adverse possession of the rentcharge; and

(b) receipt of rent under a lease by a person wrongfully claiming to be entitled to the land in reversion immediately expectant on the determination of the lease shall be treated as adverse possession of the land.

(4) For the purpose of determining whether a person occupying any land is in adverse possession of the land it shall not be assumed by implication of law that his occupation is by permission of the person entitled to the land merely by virtue of the fact that his occupation is not inconsistent with the latter's present or future enjoyment of the land. This provision shall not be taken as prejudicing a finding to the effect that a person's occupation of any land is by implied permission of the person entitled to the land in any case where such a finding is justified on the actual facts of the case.

9. Where any settled land or any land subject to a trust of land is in the possession of a person entitled to a beneficial interest in the land (not being a person solely or absolutely entitled to the land), no right of action to recover the land shall be treated for the purposes of this Act as accruing during that possession to any person in whom the land is vested as tenant for life, statutory owner or trustee, or to any other person entitled to a beneficial interest in the land.

[As amended by the Mental Health Act 1983, s148, Schedule 4, para 55; Consumer Protection Act 1987, s6(6), Schedule 1, paras 4, 6; Trusts of Land and Appointment of Trustees Act 1996, s25(1), (2), Schedule 3, para 18, Schedule 4.]

SUPREME COURT ACT 1981
(1981 c 54)

37 Powers of High Court with respect to injunctions   [746]
and receivers

(1) The High Court may by order (whether interlocutory or final) grant an injunction or appoint a receiver in all cases in which it appears to the court to be just and convenient to do so.

(2) Any such order may be made either unconditionally or on such terms and conditions as the court thinks just.

(3) The power of the High Court under subsection (1) to grant an interlocutory injunction restraining a party to any proceedings from removing from the jurisdiction of the High Court, or otherwise dealing with, assets located within that jurisdiction shall be exercisable in cases where that party is, as well as in cases where he is not, domiciled, resident or present within that jurisdiction.

(4) The power of the High Court to appoint a receiver by way of equitable execution shall operate in relation to all legal estates and interests in land; and that power –

(a) may be exercised in relation to an estate or interest in land whether or not a charge has been imposed on that land under section 1 of the Charging Orders Act 1979 for the purpose of enforcing the judgment, order or award in question; and

(b) shall be in addition to, and not in derogation of, any power of any court to appoint a receiver in proceedings for enforcing such a charge.

(5) Where an order under the said section 1 imposing a charge for the purpose of enforcing a judgment, order or award has been, or has effect as if, registered under section 6 of the Land Charges Act 1972, subsection (4) of the said section 6 (effect of non-registration of writs and orders registrable under that section) shall not apply to an order appointing a receiver made either –

(a) in proceedings for enforcing the charge; or

(b) by way of equitable execution of the judgment, order or award or, as the case may be, of so much of it as requires payment of moneys secured by the charge.

38 Relief against forfeiture for non-payment of rent [747]

(1) In any action in the High Court for the forfeiture of a lease for non-payment of rent, the court shall have power to grant relief against forfeiture in a summary manner, and may do so subject to the same terms and conditions as to the payment of rent, costs or otherwise as could have been imposed by it in such an action immediately before the commencement of this Act.

(2) Where the lessee or a person deriving title under him is granted relief under this section, he shall hold the demised premises in accordance with the terms of the lease without the necessity for a new lease.

39 Execution of instrument by person nominated by [748] High Court

(1) Where the High Court has given or made a judgment or order directing a person to execute any conveyance, contract or other document, or to indorse any negotiable instrument, then, if that person –

(a) neglects or refuses to comply with the judgment or order; or

(b) cannot after reasonable inquiry be found, the High Court may, on such terms and conditions, if any, as may be just, order that the conveyance, contract or other document shall be executed, or that the negotiable instrument shall be indorsed, by such person as the court may nominate for that purpose.

(2) A conveyance, contract, document or instrument executed or indorsed in pursuance of an order under this section shall operate, and be for all purposes available, as if it had been executed or indorsed by the person originally directed to execute or indorse it.

CIVIL AVIATION ACT 1982
(1982 c 16)

76 Liability of aircraft in respect of trespass, nuisance and surface damage [749]

(1) No action shall lie in respect of trespass or in respect of nuisance, by reason only of the flight of an aircraft over any property at a height above the ground which, having regard to wind, weather and all the circumstances of the case is reasonable, or the ordinary incidents of such flight, so long as the provisions of any Air Navigation Order and of any orders under section 62 [orders in time of war or great national emergency] above have been duly complied with and there has been no breach of section 81 [dangerous flying] below.

(2) Subject to subsection (3) below, where material loss or damage is caused to any person or property on land or water by, or by a person in, or an article, animal or person falling from, an aircraft while in flight, taking off or landing, then unless the loss or damage was caused or contributed to by the negligence of the person by whom it was suffered, damages in respect of the loss or damage shall be recoverable without proof of negligence or intention or other cause of action, as if the loss or damage had been caused by the wilful act, neglect, or default of the owner of the aircraft.

(3) Where material loss or damage is caused as aforesaid in circumstances in which –

(a) damages are recoverable in respect of the said loss or damage by virtue only of subsection (2) above, and
(b) a legal liability is created in some person other than the owner to pay damages in respect of the said loss or damage,

the owner shall be entitled to be indemnified by that other person against any claim in respect of the said loss or damage.

(4) Where the aircraft concerned has been bona fide demised, let or hired out for any period exceeding fourteen days to any other person by the owner thereof, and no pilot, commander, navigator or operative member of the crew of the aircraft is in the employment of the owner, this section shall have effect as if for references to the owner there were substituted references to the person to whom the aircraft has been so demised, let or hired out.

105 General interpretation [750]

(1) In this Act, except where the context otherwise requires –

'Air Navigation Order' means an Order in Council under section 60 above; ...
'flight' means a journey by air beginning when the aircraft in question takes off and ending when it next lands; ...
'loss or damage' includes, in relation to persons, loss of life and personal injury; ...

NB In the Air Navigation Order 1995, 'aircraft' includes, inter alia, balloons, airships, gliders and helicopters.

MATRIMONIAL HOMES ACT 1983
(1983 c 19)

1 Rights concerning matrimonial home where one spouse has no estate, etc [751]

(1) Where one spouse is entitled to occupy a dwelling-house by virtue of a beneficial estate or interest or contract or by virtue of any enactment giving him or her the right to remain in occupation, and the other spouse is not so entitled, then, subject to the provisions of this Act, the spouse not so entitled shall have the following rights (in this Act referred to as 'rights of occupation') –

(a) if in occupation, a right not to be evicted or excluded from the dwelling-house or any part thereof by the other spouse except with the leave of the court given by an order under this section;

(b) if not in occupation, a right with the leave of the court so given to enter into and occupy the dwelling-house.

(2) So long as one spouse has rights of occupation, either of the spouses may apply to the court for an order –

(a) declaring, enforcing, restricting or terminating those rights, or

(b) prohibiting, suspending or restricting the exercise of either spouse of the right to occupy the dwelling-house, or

(c) requiring either spouse to permit the exercise by the other of that right.

(3) On an application for an order under this section, the court may make such order as it thinks just and reasonable having regard to the conduct of the spouses in relation to each other and otherwise, to their respective needs and financial resources, to the needs of any children and to all the circumstances of the case, and, without prejudice to the generality of the foregoing provision –

(a) may except part of the dwelling-house from a spouse's rights of occupation (and in particular a part used wholly or mainly for or in connection with the trade, business or profession of the other spouse),

(b) may order a spouse occupying the dwelling-house or any part thereof by virtue of this section to make periodical payments to the other in respect of the occupation,

(c) may impose on either spouse obligations as to the repair and maintenance of the dwelling-house or the discharge of any liabilities in respect of the dwelling-house.

(4) Orders under this section may, in so far as they have a continuing effect, be limited so as to have effect for a period specified in the order or until further order.

(5) Where a spouse is entitled under this section to occupy a dwelling-house or any part thereof, any payment or tender made or other thing done by that spouse in or towards satisfaction of any liability of the other spouse in respect of rent, rates, mortgage payments or other outgoings affecting the dwelling-house shall, whether or not it is made or done in pursuance of an order under this section, be as good as if made or done by the other spouse.

(6) A spouse's occupation by virtue of this section shall, for the purposes of the Rent (Agriculture) Act 1976, and of the Rent Act 1977 (other than Part V and sections 103 to 106), be treated as possession by the other spouse and for the purposes of Part IV of the Housing Act 1985 and Part I of the Housing Act 1988 (secure tenancies) be treated as occupation by the other spouse.

(7) Where a spouse is entitled under this section to occupy a dwelling-house or any part thereof and makes any payment in or towards satisfaction of any liability

of the other spouse in respect of mortgage payments affecting the dwelling-house, the person to whom the payment is made may treat it as having been made by that other spouse, but the fact that that person has treated any such payment as having been so made shall not affect any claim of the first-mentioned spouse against the other to an interest in the dwelling-house by virtue of the payment.

(8) Where a spouse is entitled under this section to occupy a dwelling-house or part thereof by reason of an interest of the other spouse under a trust, all the provisions of subsections (5) to (7) above shall apply in relation to the trustees as they apply in relation to the other spouse.

(9) The jurisdiction conferred on the court by this section shall be exercisable by the High Court or by a county court, and shall be exercisable by a county court notwithstanding that by reason of the amount of the net annual value for rating of the dwelling-house or otherwise the jurisdiction would not but for this subsection be exercisable by a county court.

(10) This Act shall not apply to a dwelling-house which has at no time been a matrimonial home of the spouses in question; and a spouse's right of occupation shall continue only so long as the marriage subsists and the other spouse is entitled as mentioned in subsection (1) above to occupy the dwelling-house, except where provision is made by section 2 of this Act for those rights to be a charge on an estate or interest in the dwelling-house.

(11) It is hereby declared that a spouse who has an equitable interest in a dwelling-house or in the proceeds of sale thereof, not being a spouse in whom is vested (whether solely or as a joint tenant) a legal estate in fee simple or a legal term of years absolute in the dwelling-house, is to be treated for the purpose only of determining whether he or she has rights of occupation under this section as not being entitled to occupy the dwelling-house by virtue of that interest.

2 Effect of rights of occupation as charge on dwelling-house   [752]

(1) Where, at any time during the subsistence of a marriage, one spouse is entitled to occupy a dwelling-house by virtue of a beneficial estate or interest, then the other spouse's rights of occupation shall be a charge on that estate or interest, having the like priority as if it were an equitable interest created at whichever is the latest of the following dates, that is to say –

   (a) the date when the spouse so entitled acquires the estate or interest,
   (b) the date of the marriage, and
   (c) 1st January 1968 (which is the date of commencement of the Act of 1967).

(2) If, at any time when a spouse's rights of occupation are a charge on an interest of the other spouse under a trust, there are, apart from either of the spouses, no persons, living or unborn, who are or could become beneficiaries under the trust, then those rights shall be a charge also on the estate or interest of the trustees for the other spouse, having the like priority as if it were an equitable interest created (under powers overriding the trusts) on the date when it arises.

(3) In determining for purposes of subsection (2) above whether there are any persons who are not, but could become, beneficiaries under the trust, there shall be disregarded any potential exercise of a general power of appointment exercisable by either or both of the spouses alone (whether or not the exercise of it requires the consent of another person).

(4) Notwithstanding that a spouse's rights of occupation are a charge on an estate or interest in the dwelling-house, those rights shall be brought to an end by –

   (a) the death of the other spouse, or
   (b) the termination (otherwise than by death) of the marriage,

unless in the event of a matrimonial dispute or estrangement the court sees fit to direct otherwise by an order made under section 1 above during the subsistence of the marriage.

(5) Where a spouse's rights of occupation are a charge on the estate or interest of the other spouse or of trustees for the other spouse –

(a) any order under section 1 above against the other spouse shall, except in so far as the contrary intention appears, have the like effect against persons deriving title under the other spouse or under the trustees and affected by the charge, and

(b) subsections (2) to (8) of section 1 above shall apply in relation to any person deriving title under the other spouse or under the trustees and affected by the charge as they apply in relation to the other spouse.

(6) Where –

(a) a spouse's rights of occupation are a charge on an estate or interest in the dwelling-house, and

(b) that estate or interest is surrendered so as to merge in some other estate or interest expectant thereon in such circumstances that, but for the merger, the person taking the estate or interest surrendered would be bound by the charge,

the surrender shall have effect subject to the charge and the persons thereafter entitled to the other estate or interest shall, for so long as the estate or interest surrendered would have endured if not so surrendered, be treated for all purposes of this Act as deriving title to the other estate or interest under the other spouse or, as the case may be, under the trustees for the other spouse, by virtue of the surrender.

(8) Where the title to the legal estate by virtue of which a spouse is entitled to occupy a dwelling-house (including any legal estate held by trustees for that spouse) is registered under the Land Registration Act 1925 or any enactment replaced by that Act –

(a) registration of a land charge affecting the dwelling-house by virtue of this Act shall be effected by registering a notice under that Act, and

(b) a spouse's rights of occupation shall not be an overriding interest within the meaning of that Act affecting the dwelling-house notwithstanding that the spouse is in actual occupation of the dwelling-house.

(9) A spouse's rights of occupation (whether or not constituting a charge) shall not entitle that spouse to lodge a caution under section 54 of the Land Registration Act 1925.

(10) Where –

(a) a spouse's rights of occupation are a charge on the estate of the other spouse or of trustees for the other spouse, and

(b) that estate is the subject of a mortgage within the meaning of the Law of Property Act 1925,

then, if, after the date of creation of the mortgage, the charge is registered under section 2 of the Land Charges Act 1972, the charge shall, for the purposes of section 94 of that Act of 1925 (which regulates the rights of mortgagees to make further advances ranking in priority to subsequent mortgages), be deemed to be a mortgage subsequent in date to the first-mentioned mortgage.

(11) It is hereby declared that a charge under subsection (1) or (2) above is not registrable under section 2 of the Land Charges Act 1972 or subsection (8) above unless it is a charge on a legal estate.

10 Interpretation   [753]

(1) In this Act –

'Act of 1967' means the Matrimonial Homes Act 1967; ...

'dwelling-house' includes any building or part thereof which is occupied as a dwelling, and any yard, garden, garage or outhouse belonging to the dwelling-house and occupied therewith;

'mortgage' includes a charge and 'mortgagor' and 'mortgagee' shall be construed accordingly;

'mortgagor' and 'mortgagee' includes any person deriving title under the original mortgagor or mortgagee;

'rights of occupation' has the meaning assigned to it in section 1(1) above.

(2) It is hereby declared that this Act applies as between the parties to a marriage notwithstanding that either of them is, or has at any time during the marriage's subsistence been, married to more than one person.

(3) Reference in this Act to registration under section 2(8) above includes (as well as references to registration by notice under section 2(7) of the Act of 1967) references to registration by caution duly lodged under the said section 2(7) before the 14th February 1983 (the date of commencement of section 4(2) of the Act of 1981).

[As amended by the Housing (Consequential Provisions) Act 1985, s4, Schedule 2, para 56; Insolvency Act 1985, s235(3), Schedule 10, Pt III; Housing Act 1988, s140(1), Schedule 17, Pt I, para 33; Private International Law (Miscellaneous Provisions) Act 1995, s8(1), Schedule, para 3.]

COUNTY COURTS ACT 1984
(1984 c 28)

138 Provisions as to forfeiture for non-payment of rent   [754]

(1) This section has effect where a lessor is proceeding by action in a county court (being an action in which the county court has jurisdiction) to enforce against a lessee a right of re-entry or forfeiture in respect of any land for non-payment of rent.

(2) If the lessee pays into court or to the lessor not less than five clear days before the return day all the rent in arrear and the costs of the action, the action shall cease, and the lessee shall hold the land according to the lease without any new lease.

(3) If –

(a) the action does not cease under subsection (2); and

(b) the court at the trial is satisfied that the lessor is entitled to enforce the right of re-entry or forfeiture,

the court shall order possession of the land to be given to the lessor at the expiration of such period, not being less than four weeks from the date of the order, as the court thinks fit, unless within that period the lessee pays into court or to the lessor all the rent in arrear and the costs of the action.

(4) The court may extend the period specified under subsection (3) at any time before possession of the land is recovered in pursuance of the order under that subsection.

(5) If –

(a) within the period specified in the order; or

(b) within that period as extended under subsection (4),

the lessee pays into court or to the lessor –

(i) all the rent in arrear; and
(ii) the costs of the action,

he shall hold the land according to the lease without any new lease.

(6) Subsection (2) shall not apply where the lessor is proceeding in the same action to enforce a right of re-entry or forfeiture on any other ground as well as for non-payment of rent, or to enforce any other claim as well as the right of re-entry or forfeiture and the claim for arrears of rent.

(7) If the lessee does not –

(a) within the period specified in the order; or
(b) within that period as extended under subsection (4), pay into court or to the lessor –

(i) all the rent in arrear; and
(ii) the costs of the action,

the order shall be enforceable in the prescribed manner and so long as the order remains unreversed the lessee shall, subject to subsections (8) and (9A), be barred from all relief.

(8) The extension under subsection (4) of a period fixed by a court shall not be treated as relief from which the lessee is barred by subsection (7) if he fails to pay into court or to the lessor all the rent in arrear and the costs of the action within that period.

(9) Where the court extends a period under subsection (4) at a time when –

(a) that period has expired; and
(b) a warrant has been issued for the possession of the land, the court shall suspend the warrant for the extended period; and, if, before the expiration period, the lessee pays into court or to the lessor all the rent in arrear and all the costs of the action, the court shall cancel the warrant.

(9A) Where the lessor recovers possession of the land at any time after the making of the order under subsection (3) (whether as a result of the enforcement of the order or otherwise) the lessee may, at any time within six months from the date on which the lessor recovers possession, apply to the courts for relief; and on any such application the court may, if it thinks fit, grant to the lessee such relief, subject to such terms and conditions, as it thinks fit.

(9B) Where the lessee is granted relief on an application under subsection (9A) he shall hold the land according to the lease without any new lease.

(9C) An application under subsection (9A) may be made by a person with an interest under a lease of the land derived (whether immediately or otherwise) from the lessee's interest therein in like manner as if he were the lessee; and on any such application the court may make an order which (subject to such terms and conditions as the court thinks fit) vests the land in such a person, as lessee of the lessor, for the remainder of the term of the lease under which he has any such interest as aforesaid, or for any lesser term.

In this subsection any reference to the land includes a reference to a part of the land.

(10) Nothing in this section or section 139 shall be taken to affect –

(a) the power of the court to make any order which it would otherwise have power to make as respects a right of re-entry or forfeiture on any ground other than non-payment of rent; or
(b) section 146(4) of the Law of Property Act 1925 (relief against forfeiture).

139 Service of summons and re-entry   [755]

(1) In a case where section 138 has effect if –

(a) one-half year's rent is in arrear at the time of the commencement of the action; and
(b) the lessor has a right to re-enter for non-payment of that rent; and
(c) no sufficient distress is to be found on the premises countervailing the arrears then due,

the service of the summons in the action in the prescribed manner shall stand in lieu of a demand and re-entry.

(2) Where a lessor has enforced against a lessee, by re-entry without action, a right of re-entry or forfeiture as respects any land for non-payment of rent, the lessee may at any time within six months from the date on which the lessor re-entered apply to the county court for relief, and on any such application the court may, if it thinks fit, grant to the lessee such relief as the High Court could have granted.

(3) Subsections (9B) and (9C) of section 138 shall have effect in relation to an application under subsection (2) of this section as they have effect in relation to an application under subsection (9A) of that section.

140 Interpretation of sections 138 and 139   [756]

For the purposes of sections 138 and 139 –

'lease' includes –

(a) an original or derivative under-lease;
(b) an agreement for a lease where the lessee has become entitled to have his lease granted; and
(c) a grant at a fee farm rent, or under a grant securing a rent by condition;

'lessee' includes –

(a) an original or derivative under-lessee;
(b) the persons deriving title under a lessee;
(c) a grantee under a grant at a fee farm rent, or under a grant securing a rent by condition; and
(d) the persons deriving title under such a grantee;

'lessor' includes –

(a) an original or derivative under-lessor;
(b) the persons deriving title under a lessor;
(c) a person making a grant at a fee farm rent, or a grant securing a rent by condition; and
(d) the persons deriving title under such a grantor;

'under-lease' includes an agreement for an under-lease where the under-lessee has become entitled to have his underlease granted; and

'under-lessee' includes any person deriving title under an under-lessee.

[As amended by the Administration of Justice Act 1985, ss55(1)–(5), 67(2), Schedule 8, Pt III; Courts and Legal Services Act 1990, s125(2), Schedule 17, para 17; High Court and County Courts Jurisdiction Order 1991, art 2(8), Schedule.]

HOUSING ACT 1985
(1985 c 68)

118 The right to buy [757]

(1) A secure tenant has the right to buy, that is to say, the right, in the circumstances and subject to the conditions and exceptions stated in the following provisions of this Part –

(a) if the dwelling-house is a house and the landlord owns the freehold, to acquire the freehold of the dwelling-house;
(b) if the landlord does not own the freehold or if the dwelling-house is a flat (whether or not the landlord owns the freehold), to be granted a lease of the dwelling-house.

(2) Where a secure tenancy is a joint tenancy then, whether or not each of the joint tenants occupies the dwelling-house as his only or principal home, the right to buy belongs jointly to all of them or to such one or more of them as may be agreed between them; but such an agreement is not valid unless the person or at least one of the persons to whom the right to buy is to belong occupies the dwelling-house as his only or principal home.

119 Qualifying period for right to buy [758]

(1) The right to buy does not arise unless the period which, in accordance with Schedule 4, is to be taken into account for the purposes of this section is at least two years.

(2) Where the secure tenancy is a joint tenancy the condition in subsection (1) need be satisfied with respect to one only of the joint tenants.

120 Exceptions to the right to buy [759]

The right to buy does not arise in the cases specified in Schedule 5 (exceptions to the right to buy).

121 Circumstances in which the right to buy cannot [760]
be exercised

(1) The right to buy cannot be exercised if the tenant is obliged to give up possession of the dwelling-house in pursuance of an order of the court or will be so obliged at a date specified in the order.

(2) The right to buy cannot be exercised if the person, or one of the persons, to whom the right to buy belongs –

(a) has a bankruptcy petition pending against him,
(c) is an undischarged bankrupt, or
(d) has made a composition or arrangement with his creditors the terms of which remain to be fulfilled.

183 Meaning of 'house', 'flat' and 'dwelling-house' [761]

(1) The following provisions apply to the interpretation of 'house', 'flat' and 'dwelling-house' when used in this Part.

(2) A dwelling-house is a house if, and only if, it (or so much of it as does not consist of land included by virtue of section 184) is a structure reasonably so called; so that –

(a) where a building is divided horizontally, the flats or other units into which it is divided are not houses;

(b) where a building is divided vertically, the units into which it is divided may be houses;

(c) where a building is not structurally detached, it is not a house if a material part of it lies above or below the remainder of the structure.

(3) A dwelling-house which is not a house is a flat.

610 Power of court to authorise conversion of premises into flats   [762]

(1) The local housing authority or a person interested in any premises may apply to the county court where –

(a) owing to changes in the character of the neighbourhood in which the premises are situated, they cannot readily be let as a single dwelling-house but could readily be let for occupation if converted into two or more dwelling-houses, or

(b) planning permission has been granted under Part III of the Town and Country Planning Act 1990 (general planning control) for the use of the premises as converted into two or more separate dwelling-houses instead of as a single dwelling-house,

and the conversion is prohibited or restricted by the provisions of the lease of the premises, or by a restrictive covenant affecting the premises, or otherwise.

(2) The court may, after giving any person interested an opportunity of being heard, vary the terms of the lease or other instrument imposing the prohibition or restriction, subject to such conditions and upon such terms as the court may think just.

SCHEDULE 5   [763]

EXCEPTIONS TO THE RIGHT TO BUY

1. The right to buy does not arise if the landlord is a housing trust or a housing association and is a charity.

2. The right to buy does not arise if the landlord is a co-operative housing association ...

10.–(1) The right to buy does not arise if the dwelling-house is one of a group of dwelling-houses –

(a) which are particularly suitable, having regard to their location, size, design, heating systems and other features, for occupation by elderly persons, and

(b) which it is the practice of the landlord to let for occupation by persons aged 60 or more, or for occupation by such persons and physically disabled persons,

and special facilities such as are mentioned in sub-paragraph (2) are provided wholly or mainly for the purposes of assisting those persons.

(2) The facilities referred to above are facilities which consist of or include –

(a) the services of a resident warden, or

(b) the services of a non-resident warden, a system for calling him and the use of a common room in close proximity to the group of dwelling-houses ...

[As amended by the Insolvency Act 1985, s235(3), Schedule 10, Pt III; Local Government and Housing Act 1989, s165(1), Schedule 9, Pt V, para 89; Planning

(Consequential Provisions) Act 1990, s4, Schedule 2, para 71(5); Leasehold Reform, Housing and Urban Development Act 1993, s106(1).]

LANDLORD AND TENANT ACT 1985
(1985 c 70)

8 Implied terms as to fitness for human habitation   [764]

(1) In a contract to which this section applies for the letting of a house for human habitation there is implied, notwithstanding any stipulation to the contrary –

(a) a condition that the house is fit for human habitation at the commencement of the tenancy, and
(b) an undertaking that the house will be kept by the landlord fit for human habitation during the tenancy.

(2) The landlord, or a person authorised by him in writing, may at reasonable times of the day, on giving 24 hours' notice in writing to the tenant or occupier, enter premises to which this section applies for the purpose of viewing their state and condition.

(3) This section applies to a contract if –

(a) the rent does not exceed the figure applicable in accordance with subsection (4), and
(b) the letting is not on such terms as to the tenant's responsibility as are mentioned in subsection (5).

(4) The rent limit for the application of this section is shown by the following Table, by reference to the date of making of the contract and the situation of the premises:

TABLE

Date of making of contract	Rent limit
Before 31st July 1923.	In London: £40. Elsewhere: £26 or £16 …
On or after 31st July 1923 and before 6th July 1957.	In London: £40. Elsewhere: £26.
On or after 6th July 1957.	In London: £80. Elsewhere: £52 …

(5) This section does not apply where a house is let for a term of three years or more (the lease not being determinable at the option of either party before the expiration of three years) upon terms that the tenant puts the premises into a condition reasonably fit for human habitation.

(6) In this section 'house' includes –

(a) a part of a house, and
(b) any yard, garden, outhouses and appurtenances belonging to the house or usually enjoyed with it.

9 Application of s8 to certain houses occupied   [765]
by agricultural workers

(1) Where under the contract of employment of a worker employed in agriculture the provision of a house for his occupation forms part of his remuneration and the

provisions of section 8 (implied terms as to fitness for human habitation) are inapplicable by reason only of the house not being let to him –

(a) there are implied as part of the contract of employment, notwithstanding any stipulation to the contrary, the like condition and undertaking as would be implied under that section if the house were so let, and

(b) the provisions of that section apply accordingly, with the substitution of 'employer' for 'landlord' and such other modifications as may be necessary.

(2) This section does not affect any obligation of a person other than the employer to repair a house to which this section applies, or any remedy for enforcing such an obligation.

(3) In this section 'house' includes –

(a) a part of a house, and

(b) any yard, garden, outhouses and appurtenances belonging to the house or usually enjoyed with it.

10 Fitness for human habitation [766]

In determining for the purposes of this Act whether a house is unfit for human habitation, regard shall be had to its condition in respect of the following matters –

repair,
stability,
freedom from damp,
internal arrangement,
natural lighting,
ventilation,
water supply,
drainage and sanitary conveniences,
facilities for preparation and cooking of food and for the disposal of waste water;

and the house shall be regarded as unfit for human habitation if, and only if, it is so far defective in one or more of those matters that it is not reasonably suitable for occupation in that condition.

11 Repairing obligations in short leases [767]

(1) In a lease to which this section applies (as to which, see sections 13 and 14) there is implied a covenant by the lessor –

(a) to keep in repair the structure and exterior of the dwelling-house (including drains, gutters and external pipes),

(b) to keep in repair and proper working order the installations in the dwelling-house for the supply of water, gas and electricity and for sanitation (including basins, sinks, baths and sanitary conveniences, but not other fixtures, fittings and appliances for making use of the supply of water, gas or electricity), and

(c) to keep in repair and proper working order the installations in the dwelling-house for space heating and heating water.

(1A) If a lease to which this section applies is a lease of a dwelling-house which forms part only of a building, then, subject to subsection (1B), the covenant implied by subsection (1) shall have effect as if –

(a) the reference in paragraph (a) of that subsection to the dwelling-house included a reference to any part of the building in which the lessor has an estate or interest; and

(b) any reference in paragraphs (b) and (c) of that subsection to an installation in the dwelling-house included a reference to an installation which, directly or indirectly, serves the dwelling-house and which either –

(i) forms part of any part of a building in which the lessor has an estate or interest; or
(ii) is owned by the lessor or under his control.

(1B) Nothing in subsection (1A) shall be construed as requiring the lessor to carry out any works or repairs unless the disrepair (or failure to maintain in working order) is such as to affect the lessee's enjoyment of the dwelling-house or of any common parts, as defined in section 60(1) of the Landlord and Tenant Act 1987, which the lessee, as such, is entitled to use.

(2) The covenant implied by subsection (1) ('the lessor's repairing covenant') shall not be construed as requiring the lessor –

(a) to carry out works or repairs for which the lessee is liable by virtue of his duty to use the premises in a tenant-like manner, or would be so liable but for an express covenant on his part,
(b) to rebuild or reinstate the premises in the case of destruction or damage by fire, or by tempest, flood or other inevitable accident, or
(c) to keep in repair or maintain anything which the lessee is entitled to remove from the dwelling-house.

(3) In determining the standard of repair required by the lessor's repairing covenant, regard shall be had to the age, character and prospective life of the dwelling-house and the locality in which it is situated.

(3A) In any case where –

(a) the lessor's repairing covenant has effect as mentioned in subsection (1A), and
(b) in order to comply with the covenant the lessor needs to carry out works or repairs otherwise than in, or to an installation in, the dwelling-house, and
(c) the lessor does not have a sufficient right in the part of the building or the installation concerned to enable him to carry out the required works or repairs,

then, in any proceedings relating to a failure to comply with the lessor's repairing covenant, so far as it requires the lessor to carry out the works or repairs in question, it shall be a defence for the lessor to prove that he used all reasonable endeavours to obtain, but was unable to obtain, such rights as would be adequate to enable him to carry out the works or repairs.

(4) A covenant by the lessee for the repair of the premises is of no effect so far as it relates to the matters mentioned in subsection (1)(a) to (c), except so far as it imposes on the lessee any of the requirements mentioned in subsection (2)(a) or (c).

(5) The reference in subsection (4) to a covenant by the lessee for the repair of the premises includes a covenant –

(a) to put in repair or deliver up in repair,
(b) to paint, point or render,
(c) to pay money in lieu of repairs by the lessee, or
(d) to pay money on account of repairs by the lessor.

(6) In a lease in which the lessor's repairing covenant is implied there is also implied a covenant by the lessee that the lessor, or any person authorised by him in writing, may at reasonable times of the day and on giving 24 hours' notice in writing to the occupier, enter the premises comprised in the lease for the purpose of viewing their condition and state of repair.

367

12 Restriction on contracting out of s11   [768]

(1) A covenant or agreement, whether contained in a lease to which section 11 applies or in an agreement collateral to such a a lease, is void in so far as it purports –

> (a) to exclude or limit the obligations of the lessor or the immunities of the lessee under that section, or
> (b) to authorise any forfeiture or impose on the lessee any penalty, disability or obligation in the event of his enforcing or relying upon those obligations or immunities,

unless the inclusion of the provision was authorised by the county court.

(2) The county court may, by order made with the consent of the parties, authorise the inclusion in a lease, or in an agreement collateral to a lease, of provisions excluding or modifying in relation to the lease, the provisions of section 11 with respect to the repairing obligations of the parties if it appears to the court that it is reasonable to do so, having regard to all the circumstances of the case, including the other terms and conditions of the lease.

13 Leases to which s11 applies: general rule   [769]

(1) Section 11 (repairing obligations) applies to a lease of a dwelling-house granted on or after 24th October 1961 for a term of less than seven years.

(2) In determining whether a lease is one to which section 11 applies –

> (a) any part of the term which falls before the grant shall be left out of account and the lease shall be treated as a lease for a term commencing with the grant,
> (b) a lease which is determinable at the option of the lessor before the expiration of seven years from the commencement of the term shall be treated as a lease for a term of less than seven years, and
> (c) a lease (other than a lease to which paragraph (b) applies) shall not be treated as a lease for a term of less than seven years if it confers on the lessee an option for renewal for a term which, together with the original term, amounts to seven years or more.

(3) This section has effect subject to –

> section 14 (leases to which section 11 applies: exceptions), and
> section 32(2) (provisions not applying to tenancies with Part II of the Landlord and Tenant Act 1954).

14 Leases to which s11 applies: exceptions   [770]

(1) Section 11 (repairing obligations) does not apply to a new lease granted to an existing tenant, or to a former tenant still in possession, if the previous lease was not a lease to which section 11 applied (and, in the case of a lease granted before 24th October 1961, would not have been if it had been granted on or after that date).

(2) In subsection (1) –

> 'existing tenant' means a person who is when, or immediately before, the new lease is granted, the lessee under another lease of the dwelling-house;
> 'former tenant still in possession' means a person who –

> > (a) was the lessee under another lease of the dwelling-house which terminated at some time before the new lease was granted, and
> > (b) between the termination of that other lease and the grant of the new lease was continuously in possession of the dwelling-house or of the rents and profits of the dwelling-house; and

'the previous lease' means the other lease referred to in the above definitions.

(3) Section 11 does not apply to a lease of a dwelling-house which is a tenancy of an agricultural holding within the meaning of the Agricultural Holdings Act 1986 and in relation to which that Act applies or to a farm business tenancy within the meaning of the Agricultural Tenancies Act 1995.

(4) Section 11 does not apply to a lease granted on or after 3rd October 1980 to –

a local authority,
a National Park authority,
a new town corporation,
an urban development corporation,
the Development Board for Rural Wales,
a registered housing association,
a co-operative housing association,
an educational institution or other body specified, or of a class specified, by regulations under section 8 of the Rent Act 1977 or paragraph 8 of Schedule 1 to the Housing Act 1988 (bodies making student lettings), or
a housing action trust established under Part III of the Housing Act 1988.

(5) Section 11 does not apply to a lease granted on or after 3rd October 1980 to –

(a) Her Majesty in right of the Crown (unless the lease is under the management of the Crown Estate Commissioners), or
(b) a government department or a person holding in trust for Her Majesty for the purposes of a government department.

15 Jurisdiction of county court [771]

The county court has jurisdiction to make a declaration that section 11 (repairing obligations) applies, or does not apply, to a lease –

(a) whatever the net annual value of the property in question, and
(b) notwithstanding that no other relief is sought than a declaration.

16 Meaning of 'lease' and related expressions [772]

In sections 11 to 15 (repairing obligations in short leases) –

(a) 'lease' does not include a mortgage term;
(b) 'lease of a dwelling-house' means a lease by which a building or part of a building is let wholly or mainly as a private residence, and 'dwelling-house' means that building or part of a building;
(c) 'lessee' and 'lessor' mean, respectively, the person for the time being entitled to the term of a lease and to the reversion expectant on it.

17 Specific performance of landlord's repairing obligations [773]

(1) In proceedings in which a tenant of a dwelling alleges a breach on the part of his landlord of a repairing covenant relating to any part of the premises in which the dwelling is comprised, the court may order specific performance of the covenant whether or not the breach relates to a part of the premises let to the tenant and notwithstanding any equitable rule restricting the scope of the remedy, whether on the basis of a lack of mutuality or otherwise.

(2) In this section –

(a) 'tenant' includes a statutory tenant,
(b) in relation to a statutory tenant the reference to the premises let to him is to the premises of which he is a statutory tenant,

(c) 'landlord', in relation to a tenant, includes any person against whom the tenant has a right to enforce a repairing covenant, and

(d) 'repairing covenant' means a covenant to repair, maintain, renew, construct or replace any property.

18 Meaning of 'service charge' and 'relevant costs'   [774]

(1) In the following provisions of this Act 'service charge' means an amount payable by a tenant of a dwelling as part of or in addition to the rent –

(a) which is payable, directly or indirectly, for services, repairs, maintenance or insurance or the landlord's costs of management, and

(b) the whole or part of which varies or may vary according to the relevant costs.

(2) The relevant costs are the costs or estimated costs incurred or to be incurred by or on behalf of the landlord, or a superior landlord, in connection with the matters for which the service charge is payable.

(3) For this purpose –

(a) 'costs' includes overheads, and

(b) costs are relevant costs in relation to a service charge whether they are incurred, or to be incurred, in the period for which the service charge is payable or in an earlier or later period.

32 Provisions not applying to tenancies within Part II   [775]
of the Landlord and Tenant Act 1954

(1) The following provisions do not apply to a tenancy to which Part II of the Landlord and Tenant Act 1954 (business tenancies) applies –

sections 1 to 3 (information to be given to tenant),
section 17 (specific performance of landlord's repairing obligations).

(2) Section 11 (repairing obligations) does not apply to a new lease granted to an existing tenant, or to a former tenant still in possession, if the new lease is a tenancy to which Part II of the Landlord and Tenant Act 1954 applies and the previous lease either is such a tenancy or would be but for section 28 of that Act (tenancy not within Part II if renewal agreed between the parties).

In this subsection 'existing tenant', 'former tenant still in possession' and 'previous lease' have the same meaning as in section 14(2).

(3) Section 31 (reserve power to limit rents) does not apply to a dwelling forming part of a property subject to a tenancy to which Part II of the Landlord and Tenant Act 1954 applies; but without prejudice to the application of that section in relation to a sub-tenancy of a part of the premises comprised in such a tenancy.

36 Meaning of 'lease' and 'tenancy' and related expressions   [776]

(1) In this Act 'lease' and 'tenancy' have the same meaning.

(2) Both expressions include –

(a) a sub-lease or sub-tenancy, and

(b) an agreement for a lease or tenancy (or sub-lease or sub-tenancy).

(3) The expressions 'lessor' and 'lessee' and 'landlord' and 'tenant', and references to letting, to the grant of a lease or to covenants or terms, shall be construed accordingly.

37 Meaning of 'statutory tenant' and related expressions   [777]

In this Act –

(a) 'statutory tenancy' and 'statutory tenant' mean a statutory tenancy or statutory tenant within the meaning of the Rent Act 1977 or the Rent (Agriculture) Act 1976; and

(b) 'landlord', in relation to a statutory tenant, means the person who, apart from the statutory tenancy, would be entitled to possession of the premises.

38 Minor definitions   [778]

In this Act –

...

'co-operative housing association' has the same meaning as in the Housing Associations Act 1985;

'dwelling' means a building or part of a building occupied or intended to be occupied as a separate dwelling, together with any yard, garden, outhouses and appurtenances belonging to it or usually enjoyed with it;

'housing association' has the same meaning as in the Housing Associations Act 1985;

'local authority' means a district, county, county borough or London borough council, the Common Council of the City of London or the Council of the Isles of Scilly and in sections 14(4), 26(1) and 28(6) includes the Broads Authority, a police authority established under section 3 of the Police Act 1964 and a joint authority established by Part IV of the Local Government Act 1985; ...

'new town corporation' means –

(a) a development corporation established by an order made, or treated as made, under the New Towns Act 1981, or

(b) the Commission for the New Towns; ...

'registered', in relation to a housing association, means registered under the Housing Associations Act 1985; ...

'urban development corporation' has the same meaning as in Part XVI of the Local Government, Planning and Land Act 1980.

NB Section 11(1A), (1B) and (3A) above do not apply to leases (or contracts for leases) made before 15 January 1989.

[As amended by the Agricultural Holdings Act 1986, s100, Schedule 14, para 64; Landlord and Tenant Act 1987, s41(1), Schedule 2, para 1; Housing Act 1988, s116(1)–(3), (4); Norfolk and Suffolk Broads Act 1988, s21, Schedule 6, para 26; Education Reform Act 1988, s237(2), Schedule 13, Pt I; Local Government and Housing Act 1989, s194(1), Schedule 11, para 89; Local Government (Wales) Act 1994, s22(2), Schedule 8, para 7; Police and Magistrates' Courts Act 1994, s43, Schedule 4, Pt II, para 60; Agricultural Tenancies Act 1995, s40, Schedule, para 31; Environment Act 1995, s78, Schedule 10, para 25(1).]

AGRICULTURAL HOLDINGS ACT 1986
(1986 c 5)

1 Principal definitions   [779]

(1) In this Act 'agricultural holding' means the aggregate of the land (whether agricultural land or not) comprised in a contract of tenancy which is a contract for an agricultural tenancy, not being a contract under which the land is let to the

tenant during his continuance in any office, appointment or employment held under the landlord.

(2) For the purposes of this section, a contract of tenancy relating to any land is a contract for an agricultural tenancy if, having regard to –

(a) the terms of the tenancy,
(b) the actual or contemplated use of the land at the time for the conclusion of the contract and subsequently, and
(c) any other relevant circumstances,

the whole of the land comprised in the contract, subject to such exceptions only as do not substantially affect the character of the tenancy, is let for use as agricultural land.

(3) A change in user of the land concerned subsequent to the conclusion of a contract of tenancy which involves any breach of the terms of the tenancy shall be disregarded for the purpose of determining whether a contract which was not originally a contract for an agricultural tenancy has subsequently become one unless it is effected with the landlord's permission, consent or acquiescence.

(4) In this Act 'agricultural land' means –

(a) land used for agriculture which is so used for the purposes of a trade or business, and
(b) any other land which, by virtue of a designation under section 109(1) of the Agriculture Act 1947, is agricultural land within the meaning of that Act.

(5) In this Act 'contract of tenancy' means a letting of land, or agreement for letting land, for a term of years or from year to year; and for the purposes of this definition a letting of land, or an agreement for letting land, which, by virtue of subsection (6) of section 149 of the Law of Property Act 1925, takes effect as such a letting of land or agreement for letting land as is mentioned in that subsection shall be deemed to be a letting of land or, as the case may be, an agreement for letting land, for a term of years.

2 Restriction on letting agricultural land for less than from year to year   [780]

(1) An agreement to which this section applies shall take effect, with the necessary modifications, as if it were an agreement for the letting of land for a tenancy from year to year unless the agreement was approved by the Minister before it was entered into.

(2) Subject to subsection (3) below, this section applies to an agreement under which –

(a) any land is let to a person for use as agricultural land for an interest less than a tenancy from year to year, or
(b) a person is granted a licence to occupy land for use as agricultural land,

if the circumstances are such that if his interest were a tenancy from year to year he would in respect of that land be the tenant of an agricultural holding.

(3) This section does not apply to an agreement for the letting of land, or the granting of a licence to occupy land –

(a) made (whether or not it expressly so provides) in contemplation of the use of the land only for grazing or mowing (or both) during some specified period of the year, or
(b) by a person whose interest in the land is less than a tenancy from year to year and has not taken effect as such a tenancy by virtue of this section.

(4) Any dispute arising as to the operation of this section in relation to any agreement shall be determined by arbitration under this Act.

3 Tenancies for two years or more to continue from [781] year to year unless terminated by notice

(1) Subject to section 5 below, a tenancy of an agricultural holding for a term of two years or more shall, instead of terminating on the term date, continue (as from that date) as a tenancy from year to year, but otherwise on the terms of the original tenancy so far as applicable, unless –

(a) not less than one year nor more than two years before the term date a written notice has been given by either party to the other of his intention to terminate the tenancy, or
(b) section 4 below applies.

(2) A notice given under subsection (1) above shall be deemed, for the purposes of this Act, to be a notice to quit.

(3) This section does not apply to a tenancy which, by virtue of subsection (6) of section 149 of the Law of Property Act 1925, takes effect as such a term of years as is mentioned in that subsection.

(4) In this section 'term date', in relation to a tenancy granted for a term of years, means the date fixed for the expiry of that term.

4 Death of tenant before term date [782]

(1) This section applies where –

(a) a tenancy such as is mentioned in subsection (1) of section 3 above is granted on or after 12th September 1984 to any person or persons,
(b) the person, or the survivor of the persons, dies before the term date, and
(c) no notice effective to terminate the tenancy on the term date has been given under that subsection.

(2) Where this section applies, the tenancy, instead of continuing as mentioned in section 3(1) above –

(a) shall, if the death is one year or more before the term date, terminate on that date, or
(b) shall, if the death is at any other time, continue (as from the term date) for a further period of twelve months, but otherwise on the terms of the tenancy so far as applicable, and shall accordingly terminate on the first anniversary of the term date.

(3) For the purposes of the provisions of this Act with respect to compensation any tenancy terminating in accordance with this section shall be deemed to terminate by reason of a notice to quit given by the landlord of the holding.

(4) In this section 'term date' has the same meaning as in section 3 above.

5 Restriction on agreements excluding effect of section 3 [783]

(1) Except as provided in this section, section 3 above shall have effect notwithstanding any agreement to the contrary.

(2) Where before the grant of a tenancy of an agricultural holding for a term of not less than two, and not more than five, years –

(a) the persons who will be the landlord and the tenant in relation to the tenancy agree that section 3 above shall not apply to the tenancy, and

(b) those persons make a joint application in writing to the Minister for his approval of that agreement, and
(c) the Minister notifies them of his approval,

section 3 shall not apply to the tenancy if it satisfies the requirements of subsection (3) below.

(3) A tenancy satisfies the requirements of this subsection if the contract of tenancy is in writing and it, or a statement endorsed upon it, indicates (in whatever terms) that section 3 does not apply to the tenancy.

10 Tenant's right to remove fixtures and buildings   [784]

(1) Subject to the provisions of this section –

(a) any engine, machinery, fencing or other fixture (of whatever description) affixed, whether for the purposes of agriculture or not, to an agricultural holding by the tenant, and
(b) any building erected by him on holding,

shall be removable by the tenant at any time during the continuance of the tenancy or before the expiry of two months from its termination, and shall remain his property so long as he may remove it by virtue of this subsection.

(2) Subsection (1) above shall not apply –

(a) to a fixture affixed or a building erected in pursuance of some obligation,
(b) to a fixture affixed or a building erected instead of some fixture or building belonging to the landlord,
(c) to a building in respect of which the tenant is entitled to compensation under this Act or otherwise, or
(d) to a fixture affixed or a building erected before 1st January 1884.

(3) The right conferred by subsection (1) above shall not be exercisable in relation to a fixture or building unless the tenant –

(a) has paid all rent owing by him and has performed or satisfied all his other obligations to the landlord in respect of the holding, and
(b) has, at least one month before both the exercise of the right and the termination of the tenancy, given to the landlord notice in writing of his intention to remove the fixture or building.

(4) If, before the expiry of the notice mentioned in subsection (3) above, the landlord gives to the tenant a counter-notice in writing electing to purchase a fixture or building comprised in the notice, subsection (1) above shall cease to apply to that fixture or building, but the landlord shall be liable to pay to the tenant the fair value of the fixture or building to an incoming tenant of the holding.

(5) In the removal of a fixture or building by virtue of subsection (1) above, the tenant shall not do any avoidable damage to any other building or other part of the holding, and immediately after the removal shall make good all damage so done that is occasioned by the removal.

(6) Any dispute between the landlord and the tenant with respect to the amount payable by the landlord under subsection (4) above in respect of any fixture or building shall be determined by arbitration under this Act.

(7) This section shall apply to a fixture or building acquired by a tenant as it applies to a fixture or building affixed or erected by him.

(8) This section shall not be taken as prejudicing any right to remove a fixture that subsists otherwise than by virtue of this section.

16 No distress for rent due more than a year previously [785]

(1) Subject to subsection (2) below, the landlord of an agricultural holding shall not be entitled to distrain for rent which became due in respect of that holding more than one year before the making of the distress.

(2) Where it appears that, according to the ordinary course of dealing between the landlord and the tenant of the holding, the payment of rent has been deferred until the expiry of a quarter or half-year after the date at which the rent legally became due, the rent shall, for the purposes of subsection (1) above, be deemed to have become due at the expiry of that quarter or half-year and not at the date at which it became legally due.

17 Compensation to be set off against rent for purposes [786] of distress

Where the amount of any compensation due to the tenant of an agricultural holding, whether under this Act or under custom or agreement, has been ascertained before the landlord distrains for rent, that amount may be set off against the rent and the landlord shall not be entitled to distrain for more than the balance.

18 Restrictions on distraining on property of third party [787]

(1) Property belonging to a person other than the tenant of an agricultural holding shall not be distrained for rent if –

(a) the property is agricultural or other machinery and is on the holding under an agreement with the tenant for its hire or use in the conduct of his business, or

(b) the property is livestock and is on the holding solely for breeding purposes.

(2) Agisted livestock shall not be distrained by the landlord of an agricultural holding for rent where there is other sufficient distress to be found; and if such livestock is distrained by him by reason of other sufficient distress not being found, there shall not be recovered by that distress a sum exceeding the amount of the price agreed to be paid for the feeding, or any part of the price which remains unpaid.

(3) The owner of the agisted livestock may, at any time before it is sold, redeem it by paying to the distrainer a sum equal to the amount mentioned in subsection (2) above, and payment of that sum to the distrainer shall be in full discharge as against the tenant of any sum of that amount which would otherwise be due from the owner of the livestock to the tenant in respect of the price of feeding.

(4) Any portion of the agisted livestock shall, so long as it remains on the holding, continue liable to be distrained for the amount for which the whole of the livestock is distrainable.

(5) In this section 'livestock' includes any animal capable of being distrained; and 'agisted livestock' means livestock belonging to another person which has been taken by the tenant of an agricultural holding to be fed at a fair price.

23 Landlord's power of entry [788]

The landlord of an agricultural holding or any person authorised by him may at all reasonable times enter on the holding for any of the following purposes, namely –

(a) viewing the state of the holding,

(b) fulfilling the landlord's responsibilities to manage the holding in accordance with the rules of good estate management,

(c) providing or improving fixed equipment on the holding otherwise than in fulfilment of those responsibilities.

24 Restriction of landlord's remedies for breach of   [789] contract of tenancy

Notwithstanding any provision in a contract of tenancy of an agricultural holding making the tenant liable to pay a higher rent or other liquidated damages in the event of a breach or non-fulfilment of a term or condition of the contract, the landlord shall not be entitled to recover in consequence of any such breach or non-fulfilment, by distress or otherwise, any sum in excess of the damage actually suffered by him in consequence of the breach or non-fulfilment.

96 Interpretation   [790]

(1) In this Act, unless the context otherwise requires –

'agreement' includes an agreement arrived at by means of valuation or otherwise, and 'agreed' has a corresponding meaning;
'agricultural holding' has the meaning given by section 1 above;
'agricultural land' has the meaning given by section 1 above; ...
'agriculture' includes horticulture, fruit growing, seed growing, dairy farming and livestock breeding and keeping, the use of land as grazing land, meadow land, osier land, market gardens and nursery grounds, and the use of land for woodlands where that use is ancillary to the farming of land for other agricultural purposes and 'agricultural' shall be construed accordingly;
'building' includes any part of a building; ...
'contract of tenancy' has the meaning given by section 1 above; ...
'landlord' means any person for the time being entitled to receive the rents and profits of any land;
'livestock' includes any creature kept for the production of food, wool, skins, or fur or for the purpose of its use in the farming of land or the carrying on in relation to land of any agricultural activity; ...
'the Minister' means –

(a) in relation to England, the Minister of Agriculture, Fisheries and Food, and
(b) in relation to Wales, the Secretary of State; ...

'tenant' means the holder of land under a contract of tenancy, and includes the executors, administrators, assigns, or trustee in bankruptcy of a tenant, or other person deriving title from a tenant;
'termination', in relation to a tenancy, means the cesser of the contract of tenancy by reason of effluxion of time or from any other cause; ...

(3) Sections 10 and 11 of the Agriculture Act 1947 (which specify the circumstances in which an owner of agricultural land is deemed for the purposes of that Act to fulfil his responsibilities to manage the land in accordance with the rules of good estate management and an occupier of such land is deemed for those purposes to fulfil his responsibilities to farm it in accordance with the rules of good husbandry) shall apply for the purposes of this Act.

(4) References in this Act to the farming of land include references to the carrying on in relation to the land of any agricultural activity.

(5) References in this Act to the use of land for agriculture include, in relation to land forming part of an agricultural unit, references to any use of the land in connection with the farming of the unit.

(6) The designations of landlord and tenant shall continue to apply to the parties

until the conclusion of any proceedings taken under or in pursuance of this Act in respect of compensation.

LAND REGISTRATION ACT 1986
(1986 c 26)

1 Conversion of title [791]

(2) In the case of land registered with a possessory title before the commencement of this Act –

(a) subsection (2)(b) of section 77 of the [Land Registration Act 1925] as substituted by [subsection (1) above] applies only where the land has been so registered for a period of at least 12 years after that commencement, but
(b) nothing in this section affects the operation of subsection (3)(b) of section 77 of the 1925 Act as originally enacted (which provides for conversion of a possessory title after 15 years' registration in the case of freehold land and 10 years' registration in the case of leasehold land) in relation to a period of registration beginning before that commencement.

4 Gratuitous leases and leases granted at a premium [792]

(4) Where a lease granted before the commencement of this Act was not an overriding interest because it was not granted at a rent or without taking a fine, the amendment made by subsection (1) above [to section 70(1)(k) of the 1925 Act] applies in relation to it only if the land was subject to it immediately before that commencement.

(5) The amendments made by subsections (2) [to sections 18(3) and 21(3) of the 1925 Act] and (3) [to sections 19(2) and 22(2) of the 1925 Act] above apply only in relation to dispositions after the commencement of this Act.

5 Abolition of Minor Interests Index [793]

(1) In section 102 of the 1925 Act, subsection (2) (under which priorities between certain dealings with equitable interests are regulated by the order of lodging of priority cautions and inhibitions) is repealed, and accordingly –

(a) the index maintained for the purposes of that subsection and known as the Minor Interests Index shall cease to be kept, and
(b) any question of priority which would have fallen to be determined in accordance with that subsection shall be determined in accordance with the rule of law referred to in section 137(1) of the Law of Property Act 1925 (which applies to dealings with equitable interests in land the rule commonly known as the rule in *Dearle* v *Hall*) ...

BUILDING SOCIETIES ACT 1986
(1986 c 53)

13 Security for advances: valuation and supplementary and related provisions [794]

(1) It shall be the duty of every director of a building society to satisfy himself that the arrangements made for assessing the adequacy of the security for any advance to be fully secured on land which is to be made by the society are such as may reasonably be expected to ensure that –

(a) an assessment will be made on the occasion of each advance whether or not any previous assessment was made with a view to further advances or re-advances;

(b) each assessment will be made by a person holding office in or employed by the society who is competent to make the assessment and is not disqualified under this section from making it;

(c) each person making the assessment will have furnished to him a written report on the value of the land and any factors likely materially to affect its value made by a person who is competent to value, and is not disqualified under this section from making a report on, the land in question;

but the arrangements need not require each report to be made with a view to a particular assessment so long as it is adequate for the purpose of making the assessment ...

(7) Schedule 4 to this Act, which contains supplementary provisions as to mortgages, shall have effect.

SCHEDULE 4 [795]

ADVANCES: SUPPLEMENTARY PROVISIONS

Provisions as to sale of mortgaged property

1.– (1) Where any land has been mortgaged to a building society as security for an advance and a person sells the land in the exercise of a power (whether statutory or express) exercisable by virtue of the mortgage, it shall be his duty –

(a) in exercising that power, to take reasonable care to ensure that the price at which the land is sold is the best price that can reasonably be obtained, and

(b) within 28 days from the completion of the sale, to send to the mortgagor at his last-known address by the recorded delivery service a notice containing the prescribed particulars of the sale.

(1A) Subparagraph (1)(b) above shall not apply where the person selling the land has reasonable cause to believe that communications sent to the mortgagor at his last-known address are unlikely to be received by him.

(2) In so far as any agreement relieves, or may have the effect of relieving, a building society or any other person from the obligation imposed by sub-paragraph (1)(a) above, the agreement shall be void.

(3) Breach by a building society or any other person of the duty imposed by sub-paragraph (1)(b) above, if without reasonable excuse, shall be an offence ...

(5) Nothing in this section shall affect the operation of any rule of law relating to the duty of a mortgagee to account to his mortgagor.

(6) In sub-paragraph (1) above 'mortgagor', in relation to a mortgage in favour of a building society, includes any person to whom, to the knowledge of the person selling the land, any of the rights or liabilities of the mortgagor under the mortgage have passed, whether by operation of law or otherwise.

2.– (1) When all money intended to be secured by a mortgage given to a building society has been fully paid or discharged, the society may endorse on or annex to the mortgage one or other of the following –

(a) a receipt in the prescribed form under the society's seal, countersigned by any person acting under the authority of the board of directors;

(b) a reconveyance of the mortgaged property to the mortgagor;

(c) a reconveyance of the mortgaged property to such person of full age, and on such trusts (if any), as the mortgagor may direct.

(2) Where in pursuance of sub-paragraph (1) above a receipt is endorsed on or annexed to a mortgage, not being a charge or encumbrance registered under the Land Registration Act 1925, the receipt shall operate in accordance with section 115(1), (3), (6) and (8) of the Law of Property Act 1925 (discharge of mortgages by receipt) in the like manner as a receipt which fulfils all the requirements of subsection (1) of that section.

(3) Section 115(9) of the Law of Property Act 1925 shall not apply to a receipt in the prescribed form endorsed or annexed by a building society in pursuance of sub-paragraph (1) above; and in the application of that subsection to a receipt so endorsed or annexed which is not in that form, the receipt shall be taken to be executed in the manner required by the statute relating to the society if it is under the society's seal and countersigned as mentioned in sub-paragraph (1)(a) above.

(4) The foregoing sub-paragraphs shall, in the case of a mortgage of registered land, have effect without prejudice to the operation of the Land Registration Act 1925 or any rules in force under it.

(5) In this paragraph –

'mortgage' includes a further charge;
'the mortgagor', in relation to a mortgage, means the person for the time being entitled to the equity of redemption; and
'registered land' has the same meaning as in the Land Registration Act 1925.

[As amended by the Deregulation (Building Societies) Order 1995, art 7.]

REVERTER OF SITES ACT 1987
(1987 c 15)

1 Right of reverter replaced by trust [796]

(1) Where any relevant enactment provides for land to revert to the ownership of any person at any time, being a time when the land ceases, or has ceased for a specified period, to be used for particular purposes, that enactment shall have effect, and (subject to subsection (4) below) shall be deemed always to have had effect, as if it provided (instead of for the reverter) for the land to be vested after that time, on the trust arising under this section, in the persons in whom it was vested immediately before that time.

(2) Subject to the following provisions of this Act, the trust arising under this section in relation to any land is a trust for the persons who (but for this Act) would from time to time be entitled to the ownership of the land by virtue of its reverter with a power, without consulting them, to sell the land and to stand possessed of the net proceeds of sale (after payment of costs and expenses) and of the net rents and profits until sale (after payment of rates, taxes, costs of insurance, repairs and other outgoings) in trust for those persons; but they shall not be entitled by reason of their interest to occupy the land.

(3) Where –

(a) a trust in relation to any land has arisen or is treated as having arisen under this section at such a time as is mentioned in subsection (1) above; and
(b) immediately before that time the land was vested in any persons in their capacity as the minister and churchwardens of any parish,

those persons shall be treated as having become trustees under this section in that capacity and, accordingly, their interest in the land shall pass and, if the case so requires, be treated as having passed to their successors from time to time.

(4) This section shall not confer any right on any person as a beneficiary –

(a) in relation to any property in respect of which that person's claim was statute-barred before the commencement of this Act, or in relation to any property derived from any such property; or

(b) in relation to any rents or profits received, or breach of trust committed, before the commencement of this Act;

and anything validly done before the commencement of this Act in relation to any land which by virtue of this section is deemed to have been held at the time in trust shall, if done by the beneficiaries, be deemed, so far as necessary for preserving its validity, to have been done by the trustees.

(5) Where any property is held by any persons as trustees of a trust which has arisen under this section and, in consequence of subsection (4) above, there are no beneficiaries of that trust, the trustees shall have no power to act in relation to that property except –

(a) for the purpose for which they could have acted in relation to that property if this Act had not been passed; or

(b) for the purpose of securing the establishment of a scheme under section 2 below or the making of an order under section 2 of the Education Act 1973 (special powers as to trusts for religious education).

(6) In this section –

'churchwardens' includes chapel wardens;
'minister' includes a rector, vicar or perpetual curate; and
'parish' includes a parish of the Church in Wales;

and the reference to a person's claim being statute-barred is a reference to the Limitation Act 1980 providing that no proceedings shall be brought by that person to recover the property in respect of which the claim subsists.

2 Charity Commissioners' schemes   [797]

(1) Subject to the following provisions of this section and to sections 3 and 4 [provisions supplemental to sections 2 and 3] below, where any persons hold any property as trustees of a trust which has arisen under section 1 above, the Charity Commissioners may, on the application of the trustees, by order establish a scheme which –

(a) extinguishes the rights of beneficiaries under the trust; and

(b) requires the trustees to hold the property on trust for such charitable purposes as may be specified in the order.

(2) Subject to subsections (3) and (4) below, an order made under this section –

(a) may contain any such provision as may be contained in an order made by the High Court for establishing a scheme for the administration of a charity; and

(b) shall have the same effect as an order so made.

(3) The charitable purposes specified in an order made under this section on an application with respect to any trust shall be as similar in character as the Charity Commissioners think is practicable in all the circumstances to the purposes (whether charitable or not) for which the trustees held the relevant land before the cesser of use in consequence of which the trust arose; but in determining the character of the last-mentioned purposes the Commissioners, if they think it appropriate to do so, may give greater weight to the persons or locality benefited by the purposes than to the nature of the benefit.

(4) An order made under this section on an application with respect to any trust shall be so framed as to secure that if a person who –

(a) but for the making of the order would have been a beneficiary under the trust; and

(b) has not consented to the establishment of a scheme under this section,

notifies a claim to the trustees within the period of five years after the date of the making of the order, that person shall be paid an amount equal to the value of his rights at the time of their extinguishment.

(5) The Charity Commissioners shall not make any order under this section establishing a scheme unless –

(a) the requirements of section 3 below with respect to the making of the application for the order are satisfied or, by virtue of subsection (4) of that section, do not apply;

(b) one of the conditions specified in subsection (6) below is fulfilled;

(c) public notice of the Commissioners' proposals has been given inviting representations to be made to them within a period specified in the notice, being a period ending not less than one month after the date of the giving of the notice; and

(d) that period has ended and the Commissioners have taken into consideration any representations which have been made within that period and not withdrawn.

(6) The conditions mentioned in subsection (5)(b) above are –

(a) that there is no claim by any person to be a beneficiary in respect of rights proposed to be extinguished –

(i) which is outstanding; or

(ii) which has at any time been accepted as valid by the trustees or by persons whose acceptance binds the trustees; or

(iii) which has been upheld in proceedings that have been concluded;

(b) that consent to the establishment of a scheme under this section has been given by every person whose claim to be a beneficiary in respect of those rights is outstanding or has been so accepted or upheld.

(7) The Charity Commissioners shall refuse to consider an application under this section unless it is accompanied by a statutory declaration by the applicants –

(a) that the requirements of section 3 below are satisfied with respect to the making of the application or, if the declaration so declares, do not apply; and

(b) that a condition specified in subsection (6) above and identified in the declaration is fulfilled;

and the declaration shall be conclusive for the purposes of this section of the matters declared therein.

(8) A notice given for the purposes of subsection (5)(c) above shall contain such particulars of the Commissioners' proposals, or such directions for obtaining information about them, and shall be given in such manner, as they think sufficient and appropriate; and a further such notice shall not be required where the Commissioners decide, before proceeding with any proposals of which notice has been given, to modify them.

3 Applications for schemes [798]

(1) Where an application is made under section 2 above by the trustees of any trust that has arisen under section 1 above, the requirements of this section are satisfied with respect to the making of that application if, before the application is made –

(a) notices under subsection (2) below have been published in two national newspapers and in a local newspaper circulating in the locality where the relevant land is situated;

(b) each of those notices specified a period for the notification to the trustees of claims by beneficiaries, being a period ending not less than three months after the date of publication of the last of those notices to be published;

(c) that period has ended;

(d) for a period of not less than twenty-one days during the first month of that period, a copy of one of those notices was affixed to some object on the relevant land in such a position and manner as, so far as practicable, to make the notice easy for members of the public to see and read without going to the land; and

(e) the trustees have considered what other steps could be taken to trace the persons who are or may be beneficiaries and to inform those persons of the application to be made under section 2 above and have taken such of the steps considered by them as it was reasonably practicable for them to take.

(2) A notice under this subsection shall –

(a) set out the circumstances that have resulted in a trust having arisen under section 1 above;

(b) state that an application is to be made for the establishment of a scheme with respect to the property subject to the trust; and

(c) contain a warning to every beneficiary that, if he wishes to oppose the extinguishment of his rights, he should notify his claim to the trustees in the manner, and within the period, specified in the notice.

(3) Where at the time when the trustees publish a notice for the purposes of subsection (2) above –

(a) the relevant land is not under their control; and

(b) it is not reasonably practicable for them to arrange for a copy of the notice to be affixed as required by paragraph (d) of subsection (1) above to some object on the land,

that paragraph shall be disregarded for the purposes of this section.

(4) The requirements of this section shall not apply in the case of an application made in respect of any trust if –

(a) the time when that trust is treated as having arisen was before the commencement of this Act; and

(b) more than twelve years have elapsed since that time.

6 Clarification of status, etc of land before reverter   [799]

(1) Nothing in this Act shall require any land which is or has been the subject of any grant, conveyance or other assurance under any relevant enactment to be treated as or as having been settled land.

(2) It is hereby declared –

(a) that the power conferred by section 14 of the School Sites Act 1841 (power of sale etc) is exercisable at any time in relation to land in relation to which (but for the exercise of the power) a trust might subsequently arise under section 1 above; and

(b) that the exercise of that power in respect of any land prevents any trust from arising under section 1 above in relation to that land or any land representing the proceeds of sale of that land.

7 Construction [800]

(1) In this Act –

'relevant enactment' means any enactment contained in –

(a) the School Sites Acts;
(b) the Literary and Scientific Institutions Act 1854; or
(c) the Places of Worship Sites Act 1873;

'relevant land', in relation to a trust which has arisen under section 1 above, means the land which but for this Act would have reverted to the persons who are the first beneficiaries under the trust.

(2) In this Act references to land include references to –

(a) any part of any land which has been the subject of a grant, conveyance or other assurance under any relevant enactment;
(b) any land an interest in which (including any future or contingent interest arising under any such enactment) belongs to the Crown, the Duchy of Lancaster or the Duchy of Cornwall.

(3) For the purposes of this Act a claim by any person to be a beneficiary under trust is outstanding if –

(a) it has been notified to the trustees;
(b) it has not been withdrawn; and
(c) proceedings for determining whether it should be upheld have not been commenced or (if commenced) have not been concluded.

(4) For the purposes of this Act proceedings shall not, in relation to any person's claim, be treated as concluded where the time for appealing is unexpired or an appeal is pending unless that person has indicated his intention not to appeal or, as the case may be, not to continue with the appeal.

[As Amended by the Trusts of Land and Appointment of Trustees Act 1996, s5, Schedule 2, para 6.]

LANDLORD AND TENANT ACT 1988
(1988 c 26)

1 Qualified duty to consent to assigning, [801]
underletting, etc of premises

(1) This section applies in any case where –

(a) a tenancy includes a covenant on the part of the tenant not to enter into one or more of the following transactions, that is –

(i) assigning,
(ii) underletting,
(iii) charging, or
(iv) parting with the possession of,

the premises comprised in the tenancy or any part of the premises without the consent of the landlord or some other person, but
(b) the covenant is subject to the qualification that the consent is not to be unreasonably withheld (whether or not it is also subject to any other qualification).

(2) In this section and section 2 [duty to pass on applications] of this Act –

(a) references to a proposed transaction are to any assignment, underletting, charging or parting with possession to which the covenant relates, and

(b) references to the person who may consent to such a transaction are to the person who under the covenant may consent to the tenant entering into the proposed transaction.

(3) Where there is served on the person who may consent to a proposed transaction a written application by the tenant for consent to the transaction, he owes a duty to the tenant within a reasonable time –

(a) to give consent, except in a case where it is reasonable not to give consent,
(b) to serve on the tenant written notice of his decision whether or not to give consent specifying in addition –

(i) if the consent is given subject to conditions, the conditions,
(ii) if the consent is withheld, the reasons for withholding it.

(4) Giving consent subject to any condition that is not a reasonable condition does not satisfy the duty under subsection (3)(a) above.

(5) For the purposes of this Act it is reasonable for a person not to give consent to a proposed transaction only in a case where, if he withheld consent and the tenant completed the transaction, the tenant would be in breach of a covenant.

(6) It is for the person who owed any duty under subsection (3) above –

(a) if he gave consent and the question arises whether he gave it within a reasonable time, to show that he did,
(b) if he gave consent subject to any condition and the question arises whether the condition was a reasonable condition, to show that it was,
(c) if he did not give consent and the question arises whether it was reasonable for him not to do so, to show that it was reasonable,

and, if the question arises whether he served notice under that subsection within a reasonable time, to show that he did.

3 Qualified duty to approve consent by another [802]

(1) This section applies in any case where –

(a) a tenancy includes a covenant on the part of the tenant not without the approval of the landlord to consent to the sub-tenant –

(i) assigning,
(ii) underletting,
(iii) charging, or
(iv) parting with the possession of,

the premises comprised in the sub-tenancy or any part of the premises, but
(b) the covenant is subject to the qualification that the approval is not to be unreasonably withheld (whether or not it is also subject to any other qualification).

(2) Where there is served on the landlord a written application by the tenant for approval or a copy of a written application to the tenant by the sub-tenant for consent to a transaction to which the covenant relates the landlord owes a duty to the sub-tenant within a reasonable time –

(a) to give approval, except in a case where it is reasonable not to give approval,
(b) to serve on the tenant and the sub-tenant written notice of his decision whether or not to give approval specifying in addition –

(i) if approval is given subject to conditions, the conditions,
(ii) if approval is withheld, the reasons for withholding.

(3) Giving approval subject to any condition that is not a reasonable condition does not satisfy the duty under subsection (2)(a) above.

(4) For the purposes of this section it is reasonable for the landlord not to give approval only in a case where, if he withheld approval and the tenant gave his consent, the tenant would be in breach of covenant.

(5) It is for a landlord who owed any duty under subsection (2) above –

(a) if he gave approval and the question arises whether he gave it within a reasonable time, to show that he did,
(b) if he gave approval subject to any condition and the question arises whether the condition was a reasonable condition, to show that it was,
(c) if he did not give approval and the question arises whether it was reasonable for him not to do so, to show that it was reasonable,

and, if the question arises whether he served notice under that subsection within a reasonable time, to show that he did.

4 Breach of duty [803]

A claim that a person has broken any duty under this Act may be made the subject of civil proceedings in like manner as any other claim in tort for breach of statutory duty.

5 Interpretation [804]

(1) In this Act –

'covenant' includes condition and agreement,
'consent' includes licence,
'landlord' includes any superior landlord from whom the tenant's immediate landlord directly or indirectly holds,
'tenancy', subject to subsection (3) below, means any lease or other tenancy (whether made before or after the coming into force of this Act) and includes –

(a) a sub-tenancy, and
(b) an agreement for a tenancy

and references in this Act to the landlord and to the tenant are to be interpreted accordingly, and
'tenant', where the tenancy is affected by a mortgage (within the meaning of the Law of Property Act 1925) and the mortgagee proposes to exercise his statutory or express power of sale, includes the mortgagee.

(2) An application or notice is to be treated as served for the purposes of this Act if –

(a) served in any manner provided in the tenancy, and
(b) in respect of any matter for which the tenancy makes no provision, served in any manner provided by section 23 of the Landlord and Tenant Act 1927.

(3) This Act does not apply to a secure tenancy (defined in section 79 of the Housing Act 1985) ...

HOUSING ACT 1988
(1988 c 50)

PART I

RENTED ACCOMMODATION

CHAPTER I

ASSURED TENANCIES

1 Assured tenancies   [805]

(1) A tenancy under which a dwelling-house is let as a separate dwelling is for the purposes of this Act an assured tenancy if and so long as –

(a) the tenant or, as the case may be, each of the joint tenants is an individual; and

(b) the tenant or, as the case may be, at least one of the joint tenants occupies the dwelling-house as his only or principal home; and

(c) the tenancy is not one which, by virtue of subsection (2) or subsection (6) below, cannot be an assured tenancy.

(2) Subject to subsection (3) below, if and so long as a tenancy falls within any paragraph in Part I of Schedule 1 to this Act, it cannot be an assured tenancy; and in that Schedule –

(a) 'tenancy' means a tenancy under which a dwelling-house is let as a separate dwelling;

(b) Part II has effect for determining the rateable value of a dwelling-house for the purposes of Part I; and

(c) Part III has effect for supplementing paragraph 10 in Part I.

(2A) The Secretary of State may by order replace any amount referred to in paragraphs 2 and 3A of Schedule 1 to this Act by such amount as is specified in the order ...

(3) Except as provided in Chapter V below, at the commencement of this Act, a tenancy –

(a) under which a dwelling-house was then let as a separate dwelling, and

(b) which immediately before that commencement was an assured tenancy for the purposes of sections 56 to 58 of the Housing Act 1980 (tenancies granted by approved bodies),

shall become an assured tenancy for the purposes of this Act.

(4) In relation to an assured tenancy falling within subsection (3) above –

(a) Part I of Schedule 1 to this Act shall have effect, subject to subsection (5) below, as if it consisted only of paragraphs 11 and 12; and

(b) sections 56 to 58 of the Housing Act 1980 (and Schedule 5 to that Act) shall not apply after the commencement of this Act.

(5) In any case where –

(a) immediately before the commencement of this Act the landlord under a tenancy is a fully mutual housing association, and

(b) at the commencement of this Act the tenancy becomes an assured tenancy by virtue of subsection (3) above,

then, so long as that association remains the landlord under that tenancy (and under any statutory periodic tenancy which arises on the coming to an end of that tenancy), paragraph 12 of Schedule 1 to this Act shall have effect in relation to that tenancy with the omission of sub-paragraph (1)(h).

(6) If, in pursuance of its duty under –

(a) section 63 of the Housing Act 1985 (duty to house pending inquiries in case of apparent priority need)

(b) section 65(3) of that Act (duty to house temporarily person found to have priority need but to have become homeless intentionally), or

(c) section 68(1) of that Act (duty to house pending determination whether conditions for referral of application are satisfied),

a local housing authority have made arrangements with another person to provide accommodation, a tenancy granted by that other person in pursuance of the arrangements to a person specified by the authority cannot be an assured tenancy before the expiry of the period of twelve months beginning with the date specified in subsection (7) below unless, before the expiry of that period, the tenant is notified by the landlord (or, in the case of joint landlords, as least one of them) that the tenancy is to be regarded as an assured tenancy.

(7) The date referred to in subsection (6) above is the date on which the tenant received the notification required by section 64(1) of the Housing Act 1985 (notification of decision on question of homelessness or threatened homelessness) or, if he received a notification under section 68(3) of that Act (notification of which authority has duty to house), the date on which he received that notification.

2 Letting of a dwelling-house together with other land   [806]

(1) If, under a tenancy, a dwelling-house is let together with other land, then, for the purpose of this Part of this Act, –

(a) if and so long as the main purpose of the letting is the provision of a home for the tenant or, where there are joint tenants, at least one of them, the other land shall be treated as part of the dwelling-house; and

(b) if and so long as the main purpose of the letting is not as mentioned in paragraph (a) above, the tenancy shall be treated as not being one under which a dwelling-house is let as a separate dwelling.

(2) Nothing in subsection (1) above affects any question whether a tenancy is precluded from being an assured tenancy by virtue of any provision of Schedule 1 to this Act.

3 Tenant sharing accommodation with persons   [807]
other than landlord

(1) Where a tenant has the exclusive occupation of any accommodation (in this section referred to as 'the separate accommodation') and –

(a) the terms as between the tenant and his landlord on which he holds the separate accommodation include the use of other accommodation (in this section referred to as 'the shared accommodation') in common with another person or other persons, not being or including the landlord, and

(b) by reason only of the circumstances mentioned in paragraph (a) above, the separate accommodation would not, apart form this section, be a dwelling house let on an assured tenancy,

the separate accommodation shall be deemed to be a dwelling-house let on an assured tenancy and the following provisions of this section shall have effect.

(2) For the avoidance of doubt it is hereby declared that where, for the purpose of determining the rateable value of the separate accommodation, it is necessary to make an apportionment under Part II of Schedule 1 to this Act, regard is to be had to the circumstances mentioned in subsection (1)(a) above.

(3) While the tenant is in possession of the separate accommodation, any term of the tenancy terminating or modifying, or providing for the termination or modification of, his right to the use of any of the shared accommodation which is living accommodation shall be of no effect.

(4) Where the terms of the tenancy are such that, at any time during the tenancy, the persons in common with whom the tenant is entitled to the use of the shared accommodation could be varied or their number could be increased, nothing in subsection (3) above shall prevent those terms from having effect so far as they relate to any such variation or increase.

(5) In this section 'living accommodation' means accommodation of such a nature that the fact that it constitutes or is included in the shared accommodation is sufficient, apart from this section, to prevent the tenancy from constituting an assured tenancy of a dwelling-house.

4 Certain sublettings not to exclude any part of sub-lessor's premises from assured tenancy [808]

(1) Where the tenant of a dwelling-house has sub-let a part but not the whole of the dwelling-house, then, as against his landlord or any superior landlord, no part of the dwelling-house shall be treated as excluded from being a dwelling-house let on an assured tenancy by reason only that the terms on which any person claiming under the tenant holds any part of the dwelling-house include the use of accommodation in common with other persons.

(2) Nothing in this section affects the rights against, and liabilities to, each other of the tenant and any person claiming under him, or of any two such persons.

5 Security of tenure [809]

(1) An assured tenancy cannot be brought to an end by the landlord except by obtaining an order of the court in accordance with the following provisions of this Chapter or Chapter II below or, in the case of a fixed term tenancy which contains power for the landlord to determine the tenancy in certain circumstances, by the exercise of that power and, accordingly, the service by the landlord of a notice to quit shall be of no effect in relation to a periodic assured tenancy.

(2) If an assured tenancy which is a fixed term tenancy comes to an end otherwise than by virtue of –

(a) an order of the court, or
(b) a surrender or other action on the part of the tenant,

then, subject to section 7 and Chapter II below, the tenant shall be entitled to remain in possession of the dwelling-house let under that tenancy and, subject to subsection (4) below, his right to possession shall depend upon a periodic tenancy arising by virtue of this section.

(3) The periodic tenancy referred to in subsection (2) above is one –

(a) taking effect in possession immediately on the coming to an end of the fixed term tenancy;
(b) deemed to have been granted by the person who was the landlord under the fixed term tenancy immediately before it came to an end to the person who was then the tenant under that tenancy;
(c) under which the premises which are let are the same dwelling-house as was let under the fixed term tenancy;
(d) under which the periods of the tenancy are the same as those for which rent was last payable under the fixed term tenancy; and
(e) under which, subject to the following provisions of this Part of this Act, the

other terms are the same as those of the fixed term tenancy immediately before it came to an end, except that any term which makes provision for determination by the landlord or the tenant shall not have effect while the tenancy remains an assured tenancy.

(4) The periodic tenancy referred to in subsection (2) above shall not arise if, on the coming to an end of the fixed term tenancy, the tenant is entitled, by virtue of the grant of another tenancy, to possession of the same or substantially the same dwelling-house as was let to him under the fixed term tenancy.

(5) If, on or before the date on which a tenancy is entered into or is deemed to have been granted as mentioned in subsection (3)(b) above, the person who is to be the tenant under that tenancy –

(a) enters into an obligation to do any act which (apart from this subsection) will cause the tenancy to come to an end at a time when it is an assured tenancy, or
(b) executes, signs or gives any surrender, notice to quit or other document which (apart from this subsection) has the effect of bringing the tenancy to an end at a time when it is an assured tenancy,

the obligation referred to in paragraph (a) above shall not be enforceable or, as the case may be, the surrender, notice to quit or other document referred to in paragraph (b) above shall be of no effect.

(6) If, by virtue of any provision of this Part of this Act, Part I of Schedule 1 to this Act has effect in relation to a fixed term tenancy as if it consisted only of paragraphs 11 and 12, that Part shall have the like effect in relation to any periodic tenancy which arises by virtue of this section on the coming to an end of the fixed term tenancy.

(7) Any reference in this Part of this Act to a statutory periodic tenancy is a reference to a periodic tenancy arising by virtue of this section.

6 Fixing of terms of statutory periodic tenancy [810]

(1) In this section, in relation to a statutory periodic tenancy, –

(a) 'the former tenancy' means the fixed term tenancy on the coming to an end of which the statutory periodic tenancy arises; and
(b) 'the implied terms' means the terms of the tenancy which have effect by virtue of section 5(3)(e) above, other than terms as to the amount of the rent;

but nothing in the following provisions of this section applies to a statutory periodic tenancy at a time when, by virtue of paragraph 11 or paragraph 12 in Part 1 of Schedule 1 to this Act, it cannot be an assured tenancy.

(2) Not later than the first anniversary of the day on which the former tenancy came to an end, the landlord may serve on the tenant, or the tenant may serve on the landlord, a notice in the prescribed form proposing terms of the statutory periodic tenancy different from the implied terms and, if the landlord or the tenant considers it appropriate, proposing an adjustment of the amount of the rent to take account of the proposed terms.

(3) Where a notice has been served under subsection (2) above, –

(a) within the period of three months beginning on the date on which the notice was served on him, the landlord or the tenant, as the case may be, may, by an application in the prescribed form, refer the notice to a rent assessment committee under subsection (4) below; and
(b) if the notice is not so referred, then, with effect from such date, not falling within the period referred to in paragraph (a) above, as may be specified in the

notice, the terms proposed in the notice shall become terms of the tenancy in substitution for any of the implied terms dealing with the same subject matter and the amount of the rent shall be varied in accordance with any adjustment so proposed.

(4) Where a notice under subsection (2) above is referred to a rent assessment committee, the committee shall consider the terms proposed in the notice and shall determine whether those terms, or some other terms (dealing with the same subject matter as the proposed terms), are such as, in the committee's opinion, might reasonably be expected to be found in an assured periodic tenancy of the dwelling-house concerned, being a tenancy –

(a) which begins on the coming to an end of the former tenancy; and
(b) which is granted by a willing landlord on terms which, except in so far as they relate to the subject matter of the proposed terms, are those of the statutory periodic tenancy at the time of the committee's consideration.

(5) Whether or not a notice under subsection (2) above proposes an adjustment of the amount of the rent under the statutory periodic tenancy, where a rent assessment committee determine any terms under subsection (4) above, they shall, if they consider it appropriate, specify such an adjustment to take account of the terms so determined.

(6) In making a determination under subsection (4) above, or specifying an adjustment of an amount of rent under subsection (5) above, there shall be disregarded any effect on the terms or the amount of the rent attributable to the granting of a tenancy to a sitting tenant.

(7) Where a notice under subsection (2) above is referred to a rent assessment committee, then, unless the landlord and the tenant otherwise agree, with effect from such date as the committee may direct –

(a) the terms determined by the committee shall become terms of the statutory periodic tenancy in substitution for any of the implied terms dealing with the same subject matter; and
(b) the amount of the rent under the statutory periodic tenancy shall be altered to accord with any adjustment specified by the committee;

but for the purposes of paragraph (b) above the committee shall not direct a date earlier than the date specified, in accordance with subsection (3)(b) above, in the notice referred to them.

(8) Nothing in this section requires a rent assessment committee to continue with a determination under subsection (4) above if the landlord and tenant give notice writing that they no longer require such a determination or if the tenancy has come to an end.

7 Orders for possession   [811]

(1) The court shall not make an order for possession of a dwelling-house let on an assured tenancy except on one or more of the grounds set out in Schedule 2 to this Act; but nothing in this Part of this Act relates to proceedings for possession of such a dwelling-house which are brought by a mortgagee, within the meaning of the Law of Property Act 1925, who has lent money on the security of the assured tenancy.

(2) The following provisions of this section have effect, subject to section 8 [notice of proceedings for possession] below, in relation to proceedings for the recovery of possession of a dwelling-house let on an assured tenancy.

(3) If the court is satisfied that any of the grounds in Part 1 of Schedule 2 to this Act is established then, subject to subsections (5A) and (6) below, the court shall make an order for possession.

(4) If the court is satisfied that any of the grounds in Part II of Schedule 2 to this Act is established, then, subject to subsections (5A) and (6) below, the court may make an order for possession if it considers it reasonable to do so.

(5) Part III of Schedule 2 to this Act shall have effect for supplementing Ground 9 in that Schedule and Part IV of that Schedule shall have effect in relation to notices given as mentioned in Grounds 1 to 5 of that Schedule.

(5A) The court shall not make an order for possession of a dwelling-house let on an assured periodic tenancy arising under Schedule 10 to the Local Government and Housing Act 1989 on any of the following grounds, that is to say, –

(a) Grounds 1, 2 and 5 in Part I of Schedule 2 to this Act;

(b) Ground 16 in Part II of that Schedule; and

(c) if the assured periodic tenancy arose on the termination of a former 1954 Act tenancy, within the meaning of the said Schedule 10, Ground 6 in Part I of Schedule 2 to this Act.

(6) The court shall not make an order for possession of a dwelling-house to take effect at a time when it is let on an assured fixed term tenancy unless –

(a) the ground for possession is Ground 2 or Ground 8 in Part I of Schedule 2 to this Act or any of the grounds in Part II of that Schedule, other than Ground 9 or Ground 16; and

(b) the terms of the tenancy make provision for it to be brought to an end on the ground in question (whether that provision takes the form of a provision for re-entry, for forfeiture, for determination by notice or otherwise).

(7) Subject to the proceeding provisions of this section, the court may make an order for possession of a dwelling-house on grounds relating to a fixed term tenancy which has come to an end; and where an order is made in such circumstances, any statutory periodic tenancy which has arisen on the ending of the fixed term tenancy shall end (without any notice and regardless of the period) on the day on which the order takes effect.

15 Limited prohibition on assignment, etc without consent   [812]

(1) Subject to subsection (3) below, it shall be an implied term of every assured tenancy which is a periodic tenancy that, except with the consent of the landlord, the tenant shall not –

(a) assign the tenancy (in whole or in part); or

(b) sub-let or part with possession of the whole or any part of the dwelling-house let on the tenancy.

(2) Section 19 of the Landlord and Tenant Act 1927 (consents to assign not to be unreasonably withheld etc) shall not apply to a term which is implied into an assured tenancy by subsection (1) above.

(3) In the case of a periodic tenancy which is not a statutory periodic tenancy subsection (1) above does not apply if –

(a) there is a provision (whether contained in the tenancy or not) under which the tenant is prohibited (whether absolutely or conditionally) from assigning or sub-letting or parting with possession or is permitted (whether absolutely or conditionally) to assign, sub-let or part with possession; or

(b) a premium is required to be paid on the grant or renewal of the tenancy.

(4) In subsection (3)(b) above 'premium' includes –

(a) any fine or other like sum;

(b) any other pecuniary consideration in addition to rent; and

(c) any sum paid by way of deposit, other than one which does not exceed one-sixth of the annual rent payable under the tenancy immediately after the grant or renewal in question.

16 Access for repairs   [813]

It shall be an implied term of every assured tenancy that the tenant shall afford to the landlord access to the dwelling-house let on the tenancy and all reasonable facilities for executing therein any repairs which the landlord is entitled to execute.

CHAPTER II

ASSURED SHORTHOLD TENANCIES

20 Assured shorthold tenancies   [814]

(1) Subject to subsection (3) below, an assured shorthold tenancy is an assured tenancy –

(a) which is a fixed term tenancy granted for a term certain of not less than six months; and
(b) in respect of which there is no power for the landlord to determine the tenancy at any time earlier than six months from the beginning of the tenancy; and
(c) in respect of which a notice is served as mentioned in subsection (2) below.

(2) The notice referred to in subsection (1)(c) above is one which –

(a) is in such form as may be prescribed;
(b) is served before the assured tenancy is entered into;
(c) is served by the person who is to be the landlord under the assured tenancy on the person who is to be the tenant under that tenancy; and
(d) states that the assured tenancy to which it relates is to be a shorthold tenancy.

(3) Notwithstanding anything in subsection (1) above, where –

(a) immediately before a tenancy (in this subsection referred to as 'the new tenancy') is granted, the person to whom it is granted or, as the case may be, at least one of the persons to whom it is granted was a tenant under an assured tenancy which was not a shorthold tenancy, and
(b) the new tenancy is granted by the person who, immediately before the beginning of the tenancy, was the landlord under the assured tenancy referred to in paragraph (a) above,

the new tenancy cannot be an assured shorthold tenancy.

(4) Subject to subsection (5) below, if, on the coming to an end of an assured shorthold tenancy (including a tenancy which was an assured shorthold but ceased to be assured before it came to an end), a new tenancy of the same or substantially the same premises comes into being under which the landlord and the tenant are the same as at the coming to an end of the earlier tenancy, then, if and so long as the new tenancy is an assured tenancy, it shall be an assured shorthold tenancy, whether or not it fulfils the conditions in paragraphs (a) to (c) of subsection (1) above.

(5) Subsection (4) above does not apply if, before the new tenancy is entered into (or, in the case of a statutory periodic tenancy, take effect in possession), the landlord serves notice on the tenant that the new tenancy is not to be a shorthold tenancy.

(6) In the case of joint landlords –

(a) the reference in subsection (2)(c) above to the person who is to be the landlord is a reference to at least one of the persons who are to be joint landlords; and

(b) the reference in subsection (5) above to the landlord is a reference to at least one of the joint landlords.

(7) Section 14 [determination of rent by rent assessment committee] above shall apply in relation to an assured shorthold tenancy as if in subsection (1) of that section the reference to an assured tenancy were a reference to an assured shorthold tenancy.

21 Recovery of possession on expiry or termination **[815]** of assured shorthold tenancy

(1) Without prejudice to any right of the landlord under an assured shorthold tenancy to recover possession of the dwelling-house let on the tenancy in accordance with Chapter I above, on or after the coming to an end of an assured shorthold tenancy which was a fixed term tenancy, a court shall make an order for possession of the dwelling-house if it is satisfied –

(a) that the assured shorthold tenancy has come to an end and no further assured tenancy (whether shorthold or not) is for the time being in existence, other than an assured shorthold periodic tenancy (whether statutory or not); and

(b) the landlord or, in the case of joint landlords, at least one of them has given to the tenant not less than two months' notice stating that he requires possession of the dwelling-house.

(2) A notice under paragraph (b) of subsection (1) above may be given before or on the day on which the tenancy comes to an end; and that subsection shall have effect notwithstanding that on the coming to an end of the fixed term tenancy a statutory periodic tenancy arises.

(3) Where a court makes an order for possession of a dwelling-house by virtue of subsection (1) above, any statutory periodic tenancy which has arisen on the coming to an end of the assured shorthold tenancy shall end (without further notice and regardless of the period) on the day on which the order takes effect.

(4) Without prejudice to any such right as is referred to in subsection (1) above, a court shall make an order for possession of a dwelling-house let on an assured shorthold tenancy which is a periodic tenancy if the court is satisfied –

(a) that the landlord or, in the case of joint landlords, at least one of them has given to the tenant a notice stating that, after a date specified in the notice, being the last day of a period of the tenancy and not earlier than two months after the date the notice was given, possession of the dwelling-house is required by virtue of this section; and

(b) that the date specified in the notice under paragraph (a) above is not earlier than the earliest day on which, apart from section 5(1) above, the tenancy could be brought to an end by a notice to quit given by the landlord on the same date as the notice under paragraph (a) above.

CHAPTER IV

PROTECTION FROM EVICTION

27 Damages for unlawful eviction   [816]

(1) This section applies if, at any time after 9th June 1988, a landlord (in this section referred to as 'the landlord in default') or any person acting on behalf of the landlord in default unlawfully deprives the residential occupier of any premises of his occupation of the whole or part of the premises.

(2) This section also applies if, at any time after 9th June 1988, a landlord (in this section referred to as 'the landlord in default') or any person acting on behalf of the landlord in default –

(a) attempts unlawfully to deprive the residential occupier of any premises of his occupation of the whole or part of the premises, or
(b) knowing or having reasonable cause to believe that the conduct is likely to cause the residential occupier of any premises –

(i) to give up his occupation of the premises or any part thereof, or
(ii) to refrain from exercising any right or pursuing any remedy in respect of the premises or any part thereof,

does acts likely to interfere with the peace or comfort of the residential occupier or members of his household, or persistently withdraws or withholds services reasonably required for the occupation of the premises as a residence,

and, as a result, the residential occupier gives up his occupation of the premises as a residence.

(3) Subject to the following provisions of this section, where this section applies, the landlord in default shall, by virtue of this section, be liable to pay to the former residential occupier, in respect of his loss of the right to occupy the premises in question as his residence, damages assessed on the basis set out in section 28 below.

(4) Any liability arising by virtue of subsection (3) above –

(a) shall be in the nature of a liability in tort; and
(b) subject to subsection (5) below, shall be in addition to any liability arising apart from this section (whether in tort, contract or otherwise).

(5) Nothing in this section affects the right of a residential occupier to enforce any liability which arises apart from this section in respect of his loss of the right to occupy premises as his residence; but damages shall not be awarded both in respect of such a liability and in respect of a liability arising by virtue of this section on account of the same loss.

(6) No liability shall arise by virtue of subsection (3) above if –

(a) before the date on which proceedings to enforce the liability are finally disposed of, the former residential occupier is reinstated in the premises in question in such circumstances that he becomes again the residential occupier of them; or
(b) at the request of the former residential occupier, a court makes an order (whether in the nature of an injunction or otherwise) as a result of which he is reinstated as mentioned in paragraph (a) above;

and, for the purposes of paragraph (a) above, proceedings to enforce a liability are finally disposed of on the earliest date by which the proceedings (including any proceedings on or in consequence of an appeal) have been determined and any time for appealing or further appealing has expired, except that if any appeal is abandoned, the proceedings shall be taken to be disposed of on the date of the abandonment.

(7) If, in proceedings to enforce a liability arising by virtue of subsection (3) above, it appears to the court –

(a) that, prior to the event which gave rise to the liability, the conduct of the former residential occupier or any person living with him in the premises concerned was such that it is reasonable to mitigate the damages for which the landlord in default would otherwise be liable, or

(b) that, before the proceedings were begun, the landlord in default offered to reinstate the former residential occupier in the premises in question and either it was unreasonable of the former residential occupier to refuse that offer or, if he had obtained alternative accommodation before the offer was made, it would have been unreasonable of him to refuse that offer if he had not obtained that accommodation,

the court may reduce the amount of damages which would otherwise be payable to such amount as it thinks appropriate.

(8) In proceedings to enforce a liability arising by virtue of subsection (3) above, it shall be a defence for the defendant to prove that he believed, and had reasonable cause to believe –

(a) that the residential occupier had ceased to reside in the premises in question at the time when he was deprived of occupation as mentioned in subsection (1) above or, as the case may be, when the attempt was made or the acts were done as a result of which he gave up his occupation of those premises; or

(b) that, where the liability would otherwise arise by virtue only of the doing of acts or the withdrawal or withholding of services, he had reasonable grounds for doing the acts or withdrawing or withholding the services in question.

(9) In this section –

(a) 'residential occupier', in relation to any premises, has the same meaning as in section 1 of the [Protection from Eviction Act 1977];

(b) 'the right to occupy', in relation to a residential occupier, includes any restriction on the right of another person to recover possession of the premises in question;

(c) 'landlord', in relation to a residential occupier, means the person who, but for the occupier's right to occupy, would be entitled to occupation of the premises and any superior landlord under whom that person derives title;

(d) 'former residential occupier', in relation to any premises, means the person who was the residential occupier until he was deprived of or gave up his occupation as mentioned in subsection (1) or subsection (2) above (and, in relation to a former residential occupier, 'the right to occupy' and 'landlord' shall be construed accordingly).

CHAPTER V

PHASING OUT OF RENT ACTS AND OTHER TRANSITIONAL PROVISIONS

34 New protected tenancies and agricultural occupancies restricted to special cases [817]

(1) A tenancy which is entered into on or after the commencement of this Act cannot be a protected tenancy, unless –

(a) it is entered into in pursuance of a contract made before the commencement of this Act; or

(b) it is granted to a person (alone or jointly with others) who, immediately before the tenancy was granted, was a protected or statutory tenant and is so granted by the person who at that time was the landlord (or one of the joint landlords) under the protected or statutory tenancy; or

(c) it is granted to a person (alone or jointly with others) in the following circumstances –

(i) prior to the grant of the tenancy, an order for possession of a dwelling-house was made against him (alone or jointly with others) on the court being satisfied as mentioned in section 98(1)(a) of, or Case 1 in Schedule 16 to, the Rent Act 1977 or Case 1 of Schedule 4 to the Rent (Agriculture) Act 1976 (suitable alternative accommodation available); and

(ii) the tenancy is of the premises which constitute the suitable alternative accommodation as to which the court was so satisfied; and

(iii) in the proceedings for possession the court considered that, in the circumstances, the grant of an assured tenancy would not afford the required security and, accordingly, directed that the tenancy would be a protected tenancy; or

(d) it is a tenancy under which the interest of the landlord was at the time the tenancy was granted held by a new town corporation, within the meaning of section 80 of the Housing Act 1985, and, before the date which has effect by virtue of paragraph (a) or paragraph (b) of subsection (4) of section 38 below, ceased to be so held by virtue of a disposal by the Commission for the New Towns made pursuant to a direction under section 37 of the New Towns Act 1981.

(2) In subsection (1)(b) above 'protected tenant' and 'statutory tenant' do not include –

(a) a tenant under a protected shorthold tenancy;

(b) a protected or statutory tenant of a dwelling-house which was let under a protected shorthold tenancy which ended before the commencement of this Act and in respect of which at that commencement either there has been no grant of a further tenancy or any grant of a further tenancy has been to the person who, immediately before the grant, was in possession of the dwelling-house as a protected or statutory tenant;

and in this subsection 'protected shorthold tenancy' includes a tenancy which, in proceedings for possession under Case 19 in Schedule 15 to the Rent Act 1977, is treated as a protected shorthold tenancy.

(3) In any case where –

(a) by virtue of subsections (1) and (2) above, a tenancy entered into on or after the commencement of this Act is an assured tenancy, but

(b) apart from subsection (2) above, the effect of subsection (1)(b) above would be that the tenancy would be a protected tenancy, and

(c) the landlord and the tenant under the tenancy are the same as at the coming to an end of the protected or statutory tenancy which, apart from subsection (2) above, would fall within subsection (1)(b) above,

the tenancy shall be an assured shorthold tenancy (whether or not it fulfils the conditions in section 20(1) above) unless, before the tenancy is entered into, the landlord serves notice on the tenant that it is not to be a shorthold tenancy.

(4) A licence or tenancy which is entered into on or after the commencement of this Act cannot be a relevant licence or relevant tenancy for the purposes of the Rent (Agriculture) Act 1976 (in this subsection referred to as 'the 1976 Act') unless –

(a) it is entered into in pursuance of a contract made before the commencement of this Act; or

(b) it is granted to a person (alone or jointly with others) who, immediately before the licence or tenancy was granted, was a protected occupier or statutory tenant, within the meaning of the 1976 Act, and is so granted by the person who at that time was the landlord or licensor (or one of the joint landlords or licensors) under the protected occupancy or statutory tenancy in question.

(5) Except as provided in subsection (4) above, expressions used in this section have the same meaning as in the Rent Act 1977.

35 Removal of special regimes for tenancies of housing associations, etc [818]

(1) In this section 'housing association tenancy' has the same meaning as in Part VI of the Rent Act 1977.

(2) A tenancy which is entered into on or after the commencement of this Act cannot be a housing association tenancy unless –

(a) it is entered into in pursuance of a contract made before the commencement of this Act; or

(b) it is granted to a person (alone or jointly with others) who, immediately before the tenancy was granted, was a tenant under a housing association tenancy and is so granted by the person who at that time was the landlord under that housing association tenancy; or

(c) it is granted to a person (alone or jointly with others) in the following circumstances –

(i) prior to the grant of the tenancy, an order for possession of a dwelling-house was made against him (alone or jointly with others) on the court being satisfied as mentioned in paragraph (b) or paragraph (c) of subsection (2) of section 94 of the Housing Act 1985; and

(ii) the tenancy is of the premises which constitute the suitable accommodation as to which the court was so satisfied; and

(iii) in the proceedings for possession the court directed that the tenancy would be a housing association tenancy; or

(d) it is a tenancy under which the interest of the landlord was at the time the tenancy was granted held by a new town corporation, within the meaning of section 80 of the Housing Act 1985, and, before the date which has effect by virtue of paragraph (a) or paragraph (b) of subsection (4) of section 38 below, ceased to be so held by virtue of a disposal by the Commission for the New Towns made pursuant to a direction under section 37 of the New Towns Act 1981.

(3) Where, on or after the commencement of this Act, a registered housing association, within the meaning of the Housing Associations Act 1985, grants a secure tenancy pursuant to an obligation under section 554(2A) of the Housing Act 1985 (as set out in Schedule 17 to this Act) then, in determining whether that tenancy is a housing association tenancy, it shall be assumed for the purposes only of section 86(2)(b) of the Rent Act 1977 (tenancy would be a protected tenancy but for section 15 or 16 of that Act) that the tenancy was granted before the commencement of this Act.

(4) Subject to section 38(4A) below, a tenancy or licence which is entered into on or after the commencement of this Act cannot be a secure tenancy unless –

(a) the interest of the landlord belongs to a local authority, a new town corporation or an urban development corporation, all within the meaning of section 80 of the Housing Act 1985, a housing action trust established under Part III of this Act or the Development Board for Rural Wales; or

(b) the interest of the landlord belongs to a housing co-operative within the meaning of section 27B of the Housing Act 1985 (agreements between local housing authorities and housing co-operatives) and the tenancy or licence is of a dwelling-house comprised in a housing co-operative agreement falling within that section; or

(c) it is entered into in pursuance of a contract made before the commencement of this Act; or

(d) it is granted to a person (alone or jointly with others) who, immediately before it was entered into, was a secure tenant and is so granted by the body which at that time was the landlord or licensor under the secure tenancy; or

(e) it is granted to a person (alone or jointly with others) in the following circumstances –

(i) prior to the grant of the tenancy or licence, an order for possession of a dwelling-house was made against him (alone or jointly with others) on the court being satisfied as mentioned in paragraph (b) or paragraph (c) of subsection (2) of section 84 of the Housing Act 1985; and

(ii) the tenancy or licence is of the premises which constitute the suitable accommodation as to which the court was so satisfied; and

(iii) in the proceedings for possession the court considered that, in the circumstances, the grant of an assured tenancy would not afford the required security and, accordingly, directed that the tenancy or licence would be a secure tenancy; or

(f) it is granted pursuant to an obligation under section 554(2A) of the Housing Act 1985 (as set out in Schedule 17 to this Act).

(5) If, on or after the commencement of this Act, the interest of the landlord under a protected or statutory tenancy becomes held by a housing association, a housing trust, the Housing Corporation or Housing for Wales, nothing in the preceding provisions of this section shall prevent the tenancy from being a housing association tenancy or a secure tenancy and, accordingly, in such a case section 80 of the Housing Act 1985 (and any enactment which refers to that section) shall have effect without regard to the repeal of provisions of that section effected by this Act.

(6) In subsection (5) above 'housing association' and 'housing trust' have the same meaning as in the Housing Act 1985.

36 New restricted contracts limited to transitional cases [819]

(1) A tenancy or other contract entered into after the commencement of this Act cannot be a restricted contract for the purposes of the Rent Act 1977 unless it is entered into in pursuance of a contract made before the commencement of this Act.

(2) If the terms of a restricted contract are varied after this Act comes into force then, subject to subsection (3) below, –

(a) if the variation affects the amount of the rent which, under the contract, is payable for the dwelling in question, the contract shall be treated as a new contract entered into at the time of the variation (and subsection (1) above shall have effect accordingly); and

(b) if the variation does not affect the amount of the rent which, under the contract, is so payable, nothing in this section shall affect the determination of the question whether the variation is such as to give rise to a new contract.

(3) Any reference in subsection (2) above to a variation affecting the amount of the rent which, under a contract, is payable for a dwelling does not include a reference to –

(a) a reduction or increase effected under section 78 of the Rent Act 1977 (power of rent tribunal); or

(b) a variation which is made by the parties and has the effect of making the rent expressed to be payable under the contract the same as the rent for the dwelling which is entered in the register under section 79 of the Rent Act 1977.

(4) In subsection (1) of section 81A of the Rent Act 1977 (cancellation of registration of rent relating to a restricted contract) paragraph (a) (no cancellation until two years have elapsed since the date of the entry) shall cease to have effect.

(5) In this section 'rent' has the same meaning as in Part V of the Rent Act 1977.

37 No further assured tenancies under Housing Act 1980   [820]

(1) A tenancy which is entered into on or after the commencement of this Act cannot be an assured tenancy for the purposes of section 56 to 58 of the Housing Act 1980 (in this section referred to as a '1980 Act tenancy').

(2) In any case where –

(a) before the commencement of this Act, a tenant under a 1980 Act tenancy made an application to the court under section 24 of the Landlord and Tenant Act 1954 (for the grant of a new tenancy), and

(b) at the commencement of this Act the 1980 Act tenancy is continuing by virtue of that section or of any provision of Part IV of the said Act of 1954,

section 1(3) of this Act shall not apply to the 1980 Act tenancy.

(3) If, in a case falling within subsection (2) above, the court makes an order for the grant of a new tenancy under section 29 of the Landlord and Tenant Act 1954, that tenancy shall be an assured tenancy for the purposes of this Act.

(4) In any case where –

(a) before the commencement of this Act a contract was entered into for the grant of a 1980 Act tenancy, but

(b) at the commencement of this Act the tenancy had not been granted,

the contract shall have effect as a contract for the grant of an assured tenancy (within the meaning of this Act).

(5) In relation to an assured tenancy falling within subsection (3) above or granted pursuant to a contract falling within subsection (4) above, Part I of Schedule 1 to this Act shall have effect as if it consisted only of paragraphs 11 and 12; and, if the landlord granting the tenancy is a fully mutual housing association, then, so long as that association remains the landlord under that tenancy (and under any statutory periodic tenancy which arises on the coming to an end of that tenancy), the said paragraph 12 shall have effect in relation to that tenancy with the omission of sub-paragraph (1)(h).

(6) Any reference in this section to a provision of the Landlord and Tenant Act 1954 is a reference only to that provision as applied by section 58 of the Housing Act 1980.

38 Transfer of existing tenancies from public to private sector   [821]

(1) The provisions of subsection (3) below apply in relation to a tenancy which was entered into before, or pursuant to a contract made before, the commencement of this Act if, –

(a) at that commencement or, if it is later, at the time it is entered into, the interest of the landlord is held by a public body (within the meaning of subsection (5) below); and

(b) at some time after that commencement, the interest of the landlord ceases to be so held.

(2) The provisions of subsection (3) below also apply in relation to a tenancy which was entered into before, or pursuant to a contract made before, the commencement of this Act if, –

(a) at the commencement of this Act or, if it is later, at the time it is entered into, it is a housing association tenancy; and

(b) at some time after that commencement, it ceases to be such a tenancy.

(3) Subject to subsections (4) and (4A) below, on and after the time referred to in subsection (1)(b) or, as the case may be, subsection (2)(b) above –

(a) the tenancy shall not be capable of being a protected tenancy, a protected occupancy or a housing association tenancy;

(b) the tenancy shall not be capable of being a secure tenancy unless (and only at a time when) the interest of the landlord under the tenancy is (or is again) held by a public body; and

(c) paragraph 1 of Schedule 1 to this Act shall not apply in relation to it, and the question whether at any time thereafter it becomes (or remains) an assured tenancy shall be determined accordingly.

(4) In relation to a tenancy under which, at the commencement of this Act or, if it is later, at the time the tenancy is entered into, the interest of the landlord is held by a new town corporation, within the meaning of section 80 of the Housing Act 1985 and which subsequently ceases to be so held by virtue of a disposal by the Commission for the New Towns made pursuant to a direction under section 37 of the New Towns Act 1981, subsections (1) and (3) above shall have effect as if any reference in subsection (1) above to the commencement of this Act were a reference to –

(a) the date on which expires the period of two years beginning on the day this Act is passed; or

(b) if the Secretary of State by order made by statutory instrument within that period so provides, such other date (whether earlier or later) as may be specified by the order for the purposes of this subsection.

(4A) Where, by virtue of a disposal falling within subsection (4) above and made before the date which has effect by virtue of paragraph (a) or paragraph (b) of that subsection, the interest of the landlord under a tenancy passes to a registered housing association, then, notwithstanding anything in subsection (3) above, so long as the tenancy continues to be held by a body which would have been specified in subsection (1) of section 80 of the Housing Act 1985 if the repeal of provisions of that section effected by this Act had not been made, the tenancy shall continue to be a secure tenancy and to be capable of being a housing association tenancy.

(5) For the purposes of this section, the interest of a landlord under a tenancy is held by a public body at a time when –

(a) it belongs to a local authority, a new town corporation or an urban development corporation, all within the meaning of section 80 of the Housing Act 1985; or

(b) it belongs to a housing action trust established under Part III of this Act; or

(c) it belongs to the Development Board for Rural Wales; or

(d) it belongs to Her Majesty in right of the Crown or to a government department or is held in trust for Her Majesty for the purposes of a government department.

(6) In this section –

(a) 'housing association tenancy' means a tenancy to which Part VI of the Rent Act 1977 applies;

(b) 'protected tenancy' has the same meaning as in that Act; and

(c) 'protected occupancy' has the same meaning as in the Rent (Agriculture) Act 1976.

SCHEDULE 1 [822]

TENANCIES WHICH CANNOT BE ASSURED TENANCIES

PART I

THE TENANCIES

Tenancies entered into before commencement

1. A tenancy which is entered into before, or pursuant to a contract made before, the commencement of this Act.

Tenancies of dwelling-houses with high rateable values

2.–(1) A tenancy –

(a) which is entered into on or after 1st April 1990 (otherwise than, where the dwelling-house had a rateable value on 31st March 1990, in pursuance of a contract made before 1st April 1990), and

(b) under which the rent payable for the time being is payable at a rate exceeding £25,000 a year.

(2) In sub-paragraph (1) 'rent' does not include any sum payable by the tenant as is expressed (in whatever terms) to be payable in respect of rates, council tax, services, management, repairs, maintenance or insurance, unless it could not have been regarded by the parties to the tenancy as a sum so payable.

2A. A tenancy –

(a) which was entered into before 1st April 1990 or on or after that date in pursuance of a contract made before that date, and

(b) under which the dwelling-house had a rateable value on the 31st March 1990 which, if it is in Greater London, exceeded £1,500 and, if it is elsewhere, exceeded £750.

Tenancies at a low rent

3. A tenancy under which for the time being no rent is payable.

3A. A tenancy –

(a) which is entered into on or after 1st April 1990 (otherwise than, where the dwelling-house had a rateable value on 31st March 1990, in pursuance of a contract made before 1st April 1990), and

(b) under which the rent payable for the time being is payable at a rate of, if the dwelling-house is in Greater London, £1,000 or less a year and, if it is elsewhere, £250 or less a year.

3B. A tenancy –

(a) which was entered into before 1st April 1990 or, where the dwelling-house had a rateable value on 31st March 1990, on or after 1st April 1990 in pursuance of a contract made before that date, and

(b) under which the rent for the time being payable is less than two-thirds of the rateable value of the dwelling-house on 31st March 1990.

3C. Paragraph 2(2) above applies for the purposes of paragraphs 3, 3A and 3B as it applies for the purposes of paragraph 2(1).

Business tenancies

4. A tenancy to which Part II of the Landlord and Tenant Act 1954 applies (business tenancies).

Licensed premises

5. A tenancy under which the dwelling-house consists of or comprises premises licensed for the sale of intoxicating liquors for consumption on the premises.

Tenancies of agricultural land

6.– (1) A tenancy under which agricultural land, exceeding two acres, is let together with the dwelling-house.

(2) In this paragraph 'agricultural land' has the meaning set out in section 26(3)(a) of the General Rate Act 1967 (exclusion of agricultural land and premises from liability for rating).

Tenancies of agricultural holdings, etc

7. A tenancy under which the dwelling-house –

(a) is comprised in an agricultural holding, and
(b) is occupied by the person responsible for the control (whether as tenant or as servant or agent of the tenant) of the farming of the holding.

(2) A tenancy under which the dwelling-house –

(a) is comprised in the holding held under a farm business tenancy, and
(b) is occupied by the person responsible for the control (whether as tenant or as servant or agent of the tenant) of the management of the holding.

(3) In this paragraph –

'agricultural holding' means any agricultural holding within the meaning of the Agricultural Holdings Act 1986 held under a tenancy in relation to which that Act applies, and
'farm business tenancy' and 'holding', in relation to such a tenancy, have the same meaning as in the Agricultural Tenancies Act 1995.

Lettings to students

8.– (1) A tenancy which is granted to a person who is pursuing, or intends to pursue, a course of study provided by a specified educational institution and is so granted either by that institution or by another specified institution or body of persons.

(2) In sub-paragraph (1) above 'specified' means specified, or of a class specified, for the purposes of this paragraph by regulations made by the Secretary of State by statutory instrument.

(3) A statutory instrument made in the exercise of the power conferred by sub-paragraph (2) above shall be subject to annulment in pursuance of a resolution of either House of Parliament.

Holiday lettings

9. A tenancy the purpose of which is to confer on the tenant the right to occupy the dwelling-house for a holiday.

Resident landlords

10.–(1) A tenancy in respect of which the following conditions are fulfilled –

(a) that the dwelling-house forms part only of a building and, except in a case where the dwelling-house also forms part of a flat, the building is not a purpose-built block of flats; and
(b) that, subject to Part III of this Schedule, the tenancy was granted by an individual who, at the time when the tenancy was granted, occupied as his only or principal home another dwelling-house which, –

(i) in the case mentioned in paragraph (a) above, also forms part of the flat; or
(ii) in any other case, also forms part of the building; and

(c) that, subject to Part III of this Schedule, at all times since the tenancy was granted the interest of the landlord under the tenancy has belonged to an individual who, at the time he owned that interest, occupied as his only or principal home another dwelling-house which, –

(i) in the case mentioned in paragraph (a) above, also forms part of the flat; or
(ii) in any other case, also formed part of the building; and

(d) that the tenancy is not one which is excluded from this sub-paragraph by sub-paragraph (3) below.

(2) If a tenancy was granted by two or more persons jointly, the reference in sub-paragraph (1)(b) above to an individual is a reference to any one of those persons and if the interest of the landlord is for the time being held by two or more persons jointly, the reference in sub-paragraph (1)(c) above to an individual is a reference to any one of those persons.

(3) A tenancy (in this sub-paragraph referred to as 'the new tenancy') is excluded from sub-paragraph (1) above if –

(a) it is granted to a person (alone, or jointly with others) who, immediately before it was granted, was a tenant under an assured tenancy (in this sub-paragraph referred to as 'the former tenancy') of the same dwelling-house or of another dwelling-house which forms part of the building in question; and
(b) the landlord under the new tenancy and under the former tenancy is the same person or, if either of those tenancies is or was granted by two or more persons jointly, the same person is the landlord or one of the landlords under each tenancy.

Crown tenancies

11.– (1) A tenancy under which the interest of the landlord belongs to Her Majesty in right of the Crown or to a government department or is held in trust for Her Majesty for the purposes of a government department.

(2) The reference in sub-paragraph (1) above to the case where the interest of the landlord belongs to Her Majesty in right of the Crown does not include the case where that interest is under the management of the Crown Estate Commissioners.

Local authority tenancies, etc

12.– (1) A tenancy under which the interest of the landlord belongs to –

(a) a local authority, as defined in sub-paragraph (2) below;
(b) the Commission for the New Towns;
(c) the Development Board for Rural Wales;
(d) an urban development corporation established by an order under section 135 of the Local Government, Planning and Land Act 1980;

(e) a development corporation, within the meaning of the New Towns Act 1981;

(f) an authority established under section 10 of the Local Government Act 1985 (waste disposal authorities);

(g) a residuary body, within the meaning of the Local Government Act 1985;

(h) a fully mutual housing association; or

(i) a housing action trust established under Part III of this Act.

(2) The following are local authorities for the purposes of sub-paragraph (1)(a) above –

(a) the council of a county, district or London borough;

(b) the Common Council of the City of London;

(c) the Council of the Isles of Scilly;

(d) the Broads Authority; and

(f) a joint authority, within the meaning of the Local Government Act 1985.

Transitional cases

13.– (1) A protected tenancy, within the meaning of the Rent Act 1977.

(2) A housing association tenancy, within the meaning of Part VI of that Act.

(3) A secure tenancy.

(4) Where a person is a protected occupier of a dwelling-house, within the meaning of the Rent (Agriculture) Act 1976, the relevant tenancy, within the meaning of that Act, by virtue of which he occupies the dwelling-house.

SCHEDULE 2   **[823]**

GROUNDS FOR POSSESSION OF DWELLING-HOUSES LET ON ASSURED TENANCIES

PART I

GROUNDS ON WHICH COURT MUST ORDER POSSESSION

Ground 1

Not later than the beginning of the tenancy the landlord gave notice in writing to the tenant that possession might be recovered on this ground or the court is of the opinion that it is just and equitable to dispense with the requirement of notice and (in either case) –

(a) at some time before the beginning of the tenancy, the landlord who is seeking possession or, in the case of joint landlords seeking possession, at least one of them occupied the dwelling-house as his only or principal home; or

(b) the landlord who is seeking possession or, in the case of joint landlords seeking possession, at least one of them requires the dwelling-house as his or his spouse's only or principal home and neither the landlord (or, in the case of joint landlords, any one of them) nor any other person who, as landlord, derived title under the landlord who gave notice mentioned above acquired the reversion on the tenancy for money or money's worth.

Ground 2

The dwelling-house is subject to a mortgage granted before the beginning of the tenancy and –

(a) the mortgagee is entitled to exercise a power of sale conferred on him by the mortgage or by section 101 of the Law of Property Act 1925; and

(b) the mortgagee requires possession of the dwelling-house for the purpose of disposing of it with vacant possession in exercise of that power; and
(c) either notice was given as mentioned in Ground 1 above or the court is satisfied that it is just and equitable to dispense with the requirement of notice;

and for the purposes of this ground 'mortgage' includes a charge and 'mortgagee' shall be construed accordingly.

Ground 3

The tenancy is a fixed term tenancy for a term not exceeding eight months and –

(a) not later than the beginning of the tenancy the landlord gave notice in writing to the tenant that possession might be recovered on this ground; and
(b) at some time within the period of twelve months ending with the beginning of the tenancy, the dwelling-house was occupied under a right to occupy it for a holiday.

Ground 4

The tenancy is a fixed term tenancy for a term not exceeding twelve months and –

(a) not later than the beginning of the tenancy the landlord gave notice in writing to the tenant that possession might be recovered on this ground; and
(b) at some time within the period of twelve months ending with the beginning of the tenancy, the dwelling-house was let on a tenancy falling within paragraph 8 of Schedule 1 to this Act.

Ground 5

The dwelling-house is held for the purpose of being available for occupation by a minister of religion as a residence from which to perform the duties of his office and –

(a) not later than the beginning of the tenancy the landlord gave notice in writing to the tenant that possession might be recovered on this ground; and
(b) the court is satisfied that the dwelling-house is required for occupation by a minister of religion as such a residence.

Ground 6

[Landlord intends to demolish or reconstruct.]

Ground 7

The tenancy is a periodic tenancy (including a statutory periodic tenancy) which has devolved under the will or intestacy of the former tenant and the proceedings for the recovery of possession are begun not later than twelve months after the death of the former tenant or, if the court so directs, after the date on which, in the opinion of the court, the landlord or, in the case of joint landlords, any one of them became aware of the former tenant's death.

For the purposes of this ground, the acceptance by the landlord of rent from a new tenant after the death of the former tenant shall not be regarded as creating a new periodic tenancy, unless the landlord agrees in writing to a change (as compared with the tenancy before the death) in the amount of the rent, the period of the tenancy, the premises which are let or any other term of the tenancy.

Ground 8

Both at the date of the service of the notice under section 8 of this Act relating to the proceedings for possession and at the date of the hearing –

(a) if rent is payable weekly or fortnightly, at least thirteen weeks' rent is unpaid;

(b) if rent is payable monthly, at least three months' rent is unpaid;

(c) if rent is payable quarterly, at least one quarter's rent is more than three months in arrears; and

(d) if rent is payable yearly, at least three months' rent is more than three months in arrears;

and for the purpose of this ground 'rent' means rent lawfully due from the tenant.

PART II

GROUNDS ON WHICH COURT MAY ORDER POSSESSION

Ground 9

Suitable alternative accommodation is available for the tenant or will be available for him when the order for possession takes effect.

Ground 10

Some rent lawfully due from the tenant –

(a) is unpaid on the date on which the proceedings for possession are begun; and

(b) except where subsection (1)(b) of section 8 of this Act applies, was in arrears at the date of the service of the notice under that section relating to those proceedings.

Ground 11

Whether or not any rent is in arrears on the date on which proceedings for possession are begun, the tenant has persistently delayed paying rent which has become lawfully due.

Ground 12

Any obligation of the tenancy (other than one related to the payment of rent) has been broken or not performed.

Ground 13

The condition of the dwelling-house or any of the common parts has deteriorated owing to acts of waste by, or the neglect or default of, the tenant or any other person residing in the dwelling-house and, in the case of an act of waste by, or the neglect or default of, a person lodging with the tenant or a sub-tenant of his, the tenant has not taken such steps as he ought reasonably to have taken for the removal of the lodger or sub-tenant.

For the purposes of this ground, 'common parts' means any part of a building comprising the dwelling-house and any other premises which the tenant is entitled under the terms of the tenancy to use in common with the occupiers of other dwelling-houses in which the landlord has an estate or interest.

Ground 14

The tenant or any other person residing in the dwelling-house has been guilty of conduct which is a nuisance or annoyance to adjoining occupiers, or has been convicted of using the dwelling-house or allowing the dwelling-house to be used for immoral or illegal purposes.

Ground 15

The condition of any furniture provided for use under the tenancy has, in the opinion of the court, deteriorated owing to ill-treatment by the tenant or any other person residing in the dwelling-house and, in the case of ill-treatment by a person lodging with the tenant or by a sub-tenant of his, the tenant has not taken such steps as he ought reasonably to have taken for the removal of the lodger or sub-tenant.

Ground 16

The dwelling-house was let to the tenant in consequence of his employment by the landlord seeking possession or a previous landlord under the tenancy and the tenant has ceased to be in that employment.

For the purposes of this ground, at a time when the landlord is or was the Secretary of State, employment by a health service body, as defined in section 60(7) of the National Health Service and Community Care Act 1990, shall be regarded as employment by the Secretary of State.

PART III

SUITABLE ALTERNATIVE ACCOMMODATION

1. For the purposes of Ground 9 above, a certificate of the local housing authority for the district in which the dwelling-house in question is situated, certifying that the authority will provide suitable alternative accommodation for the tenant by a date specified in the certificate, shall be conclusive evidence that suitable alternative accommodation will be available for him by that date.

2. Where no such certificate as is mentioned in paragraph 1 above is produced to the court, accommodation shall be deemed to be suitable for the purposes of Ground 9 above if it consists of either –

(a) premises which are to be let as a separate dwelling such that they will then be let on an assured tenancy, other than –

(i) a tenancy in respect of which notice is given not later than the beginning of the tenancy that possession might be recovered on any of Grounds 1 to 5 above, or
(ii) an assured shorthold tenancy, within the meaning of Chapter II of Part I of this Act, or

(b) premises to be let as a separate dwelling on terms which will, in the opinion of the court, afford to the tenant security of tenure reasonably equivalent to the security afforded by Chapter I of Part I of this Act in the case of an assured tenancy of a kind mentioned in sub-paragraph (a) above,

and, in the opinion of the court, the accommodation fulfils the relevant conditions as defined in paragraph 3 below.

3.–(1) For the purposes of paragraph 2 above, the relevant conditions are that the accommodation is reasonably suitable to the needs of the tenant and his family as regards proximity to place of work, and either –

(a) similar as regards rental and extent to the accommodation afforded by dwelling-houses provided in the neighbourhood by any local housing authority for persons whose needs as regards extent are, in the opinion of the court, similar to those of the tenant and of family; or
(b) reasonably suitable to the means of the tenant and to the needs of the tenant and his family as regards extent and character; and

that if any furniture was provided for use under the assured tenancy in question, furniture is provided for use in the accommodation which is either similar to that so provided or is reasonable to the needs of the tenant and his family ...

[As amended by the Local Government and Housing Act 1989, s194(1), Schedule 11, paras 101, 103, 104, 105, 106; National Health Service and Community Care Act 1990, s60, Schedule 8, Pt II, para 10; References to Rating (Housing) Regulations 1990, reg 2, Schedule, paras 27, 29, 30; Local Government Finance (Housing) (Consequential Amendments) Order 1993, art 2(1), Schedule 1, para 19; Agricultural Tenancies Act 1995, s40, Schedule, para 34.]

LAW OF PROPERTY (MISCELLANEOUS PROVISIONS) ACT 1989
(1989 c 34)

1 Deeds and their execution   **[824]**

(1) Any rule of law which –

(a) restricts the substances on which a deed may be written;
(b) requires a seal for the valid execution of an instrument as a deed by an individual; or
(c) requires authority by one person to another to deliver an instrument as a deed on his behalf to be given by deed,

is abolished.

(2) An instrument shall not be a deed unless –

(a) it makes it clear on its face that it is intended to be a deed by the person making it or, as the case may be, by the parties to it (whether by describing itself as a deed or expressing itself to be executed or signed as a deed or otherwise); and
(b) it is validly executed as a deed by that person or, as the case may be, one or more of those parties.

(3) An instrument is validly executed as a deed by an individual if, and only if –

(a) it is signed –

(i) by him in the presence of a witness who attests the signature; or
(ii) at his direction and in his presence and the presence of two witnesses who each attest the signature; and

(b) it is delivered as a deed by him or a person authorised to do so on his behalf.

(4) In subsections (2) and (3) above 'sign', in relation to an instrument, includes making one's mark on the instrument and 'signature' is to be construed accordingly.

(5) Where a solicitor, duly certificated notary public or licensed conveyancer, or an agent or employee of a solicitor, duly certificated notary public or licensed conveyancer, in the course of or in connection with a transaction involving the disposition or creation of an interest in land, purports to deliver an instrument as a deed on behalf of a party to the instrument, it shall be conclusively presumed in favour of a purchaser that he is authorised so to deliver the instrument.

(6) In subsection (5) above –

'disposition' and 'purchaser' have the same meanings as in the Law of Property Act 1925;
'duly certificated notary public' has the same meaning as it has in the Solicitors Act 1974 by virtue of section 87 of that Act; and
'interest in land' means any estate, interest or charge in or over land.

(7) Where an instrument under seal that constitutes a deed is required for the purposes of an Act passed before this section comes into force, this section shall have effect as to signing, sealing or delivery of an instrument by an individual in place of any provision of that Act as to signing, sealing or delivery.

(9) Nothing in subsection (1)(b), (2), (3), (7) or (8) above applies in relation to deeds required or authorised to be made under –

(a) the seal of the County Palatine of Lancaster;
(b) the seal of the Duchy of Lancaster; or
(c) the seal of the Duchy of Cornwall.

(10) The references in this section to the execution of a deed by an individual do not include execution by a corporation sole and the reference in subsection (7) above to signing, sealing or delivery by an individual does not include signing, sealing or delivery by such a corporation.

(11) Nothing in this section applies in relation to instruments delivered as deeds before this section comes into force.

2 Contracts for sale, etc of land to be made by signed writing [825]

(1) A contract for the sale or other disposition of an interest in land can only be made in writing and only by incorporating all the terms which the parties have expressly agreed in one document or, where contracts are exchanged, in each.

(2) The terms may be incorporated in a document either by being set out in it or by reference to some other document.

(3) The document incorporating the terms or, where contracts are exchanged, one of the documents incorporating them (but not necessarily the same one) must be signed by or on behalf of each party to the contract.

(4) Where a contract for the sale or other disposition of an interest in land satisfies the conditions of this section by reason only of the rectification of one or more documents in pursuance of an order of a court, the contract shall come into being, or be deemed to have come into being, at such time as may be specified in the order.

(5) This section does not apply in relation to –

(a) a contract to grant such a lease as is mentioned in section 54(2) of the Law of Property Act 1925 (short leases);
(b) a contract made in the course of a public auction; or
(c) a contract regulated under the Financial Services Act 1986;

and nothing in this section affects the creation or operation of resulting, implied or constructive trusts.

(6) In this section –

'disposition' has the same meaning as in the Law of Property Act 1925;
'interest in land' means any estate, interest or charge in or over land.

(7) Nothing in this section shall apply in relation to contracts made before this section comes into force.

(8) Section 40 of the Law of Property Act 1925 (which is superseded by this section) shall cease to have effect.

NB The repeal of s40 of the Law of Property Act 1925 took effect on 27 September 1989.

[As amended by the Courts and Legal Services Act 1990, s125(2), Schedule 17, para 20(1), (2); Trusts of Land and Appointment of Trustees Act 1996, s25(2), Schedule 4.]

LOCAL GOVERNMENT AND HOUSING ACT 1989
(1989 c 42)

186 Security of tenure on ending of long   [826]
residential tenancies

(1) Schedule 10 to this Act shall have effect (in place of Part I of the Landlord and Tenant Act 1954) to confer security of tenure on certain tenants under long tenancies and, in particular, to establish assured periodic tenancies when such long tenancies come to an end.

(2) Schedule 10 to this Act applies, and section 1 of the Landlord and Tenant Act 1954 does not apply, to a tenancy of a dwelling-house –

(a) which is a long tenancy at a low rent, as defined in Schedule 10 to this Act; and

(b) which is entered into on or after the day appointed for the coming into force of this section, otherwise than in pursuance of a contract made before that day.

(3) If a tenancy –

(a) is in existence on 15th January 1999, and

(b) does not fall within subsection (2) above, and

(c) immediately before that date was, or was deemed to be, a long tenancy at a low rent for the purposes of Part I of the Landlord and Tenant Act 1954,

then, on and after that date (and so far as concerns any notice specifying a date of termination on or after that date and any steps taken in consequence thereof), section 1 of that Act shall cease to apply to it and Schedule 10 to this Act shall apply to it unless, before that date, the landlord has served a notice under section 4 of that Act specifying a date of termination which is earlier than that date.

(4) The provisions of Schedule 10 to this Act have effect notwithstanding any agreement to the contrary, but nothing in this subsection or that Schedule shall be construed as preventing the surrender of a tenancy ...

(6) Where, by virtue of subsection (3) above, Schedule 10 to this Act applies to a tenancy which is not a long tenancy at a low rent as defined in that Schedule, it shall be deemed to be such a tenancy for the purposes of that Schedule.

SCHEDULE 10   [827]

SECURITY OF TENURE ON ENDING OF
LONG RESIDENTIAL TENANCIES

1– (1) This Schedule applies to a long tenancy of a dwelling-house at a low rent as respects which for the time being the following condition (in this Schedule referred to as 'the qualifying condition') is fulfilled, that is to say, that the circumstances (as respects the property let under the tenancy, the use of that property and all other relevant matters) are such that, if the tenancy were not at a low rent, it would at that time be an assured tenancy within the meaning of Part I of the Housing Act 1988.

(2) For the purpose only of determining whether the qualifying condition is fulfilled with respect to a tenancy, Schedule 1 to the Housing Act 1988 (tenancies which cannot be assured tenancies) shall have effect with the omission of paragraph 1 (which excludes tenancies entered into before, or pursuant to contracts made before, the coming into force of Part I of that Act) ...

NB Section 186 above came into force on 1st April 1990.

TOWN AND COUNTRY PLANNING ACT 1990
(1990 c 8)

55 Meaning of 'development' and 'new development'   **[828]**

(1) Subject to the following provisions of this section, in this Act, except where the context otherwise requires, 'development' means the carrying out of building, engineering, mining or other operations in, on, over or under land, or the making of any material change in the use of any buildings or other land.

(1A) For the purposes of this Act 'building operations' includes –

(a) demolition of buildings;
(b) rebuilding;
(c) structural alterations of or additions to buildings; and
(d) other operations normally undertaken by a person carrying on business as a builder.

(2) The following operations or uses of land shall not be taken for the purposes of this Act to involve development of the land –

(a) the carrying out for the maintenance, improvement or other alteration of any building of works which –

(i) affect only the interior of the building, or
(ii) do not materially affect the external appearance of the building,

and are not works for making good war damage or works begun after 5th December 1968 for the alteration of a building by providing additional space in it underground;

(b) the carrying out on land within the boundaries of a road by a local highway authority of any works required for the maintenance or improvement of the road;

(c) the carrying out by a local authority or statutory undertakers of any works for the purpose of inspecting, repairing or renewing any sewers, mains, pipes, cables or other apparatus, including the breaking open of any street or other land for that purpose;

(d) the use of any building or other land within the curtilage of a dwelling-house for any purpose incidental to the enjoyment of the dwelling-house as such;

(e) the use of any land for the purposes of agriculture or forestry (including afforestation) and the use for any of those purposes of any building occupied together with land so used;

(f) in the case of buildings or other land which are used for a purpose of any class specified in an order made by the Secretary of State under this section, the use of the buildings or other land or, subject to the provisions of the order, of any part of the buildings or the other land, for any other purpose of the same class.

(g) the demolition of any description of building specified in a direction given by the Secretary of State to local planning authorities generally or to a particular local planning authority.

(3) For the avoidance of doubt it is hereby declared that for the purposes of this section –

(a) the use as two or more separate dwelling-houses of any building previously used as a single dwelling-house involves a material change in the use of the building and of each part of it which is so used;

(b) the deposit of refuse or waste materials on land involves a material change in its use, notwithstanding that the land is comprised in a site already used for that purpose, if –

(i) the superficial area of the deposit is extended, or
(ii) the height of the deposit is extended and exceeds the level of the land adjoining the site.

(4) For the purposes of this Act mining operations include –

(a) the removal of material of any description –

(i) from a mineral-working deposit;
(ii) from a deposit of pulverised fuel ash or other furnace ash or clinker; or
(iii) from a deposit of iron, steel or other metallic slags; and

(b) the extraction of minerals from a disused railway embankment.

(4A) Where the placing or assembly of any tank in any part of any inland waters for the purpose of fish farming there would not, apart from this subsection, involve development of the land below, this Act shall have effect as if the tank resulted from carrying out engineering operations over that land; and in this subsection –

'fish farming' means the breeding, rearing or keeping of fish or shellfish (which includes any kind of crustacean and mollusc));
'inland waters' means waters which do not form part of the sea or of any creek, bay or estuary or of any river as far as the tide flows; and
'tank' includes any cage and any other structure for use in fish farming.

(5) Without prejudice to any regulations made under the provisions of this Act relating to the control of advertisements, the use for the display of advertisements of any external part of a building which is not normally used for that purpose shall be treated for the purposes of this section as involving a material change in the use of that part of the building.

57 Planning permission required for development [829]

(1) Subject to the following provisions of this section, planning permission is required for the carrying out of any development of land.

(2) Where planning permission to develop land has been granted for a limited period, planning permission is not required for the resumption, at the end of that period, of its use for the purpose for which it was normally used before the permission was granted.

(3) Where by a development order planning permission to develop land has been granted subject to limitations, planning permission is not required for the use of that land which (apart from its use in accordance with that permission) is its normal use.

(4) Where an enforcement notice has been issued in respect of any development of land, planning permission is not required for its use for the purpose for which (in accordance with the provisions of this Part of this Act) it could lawfully have been used if that development had not been carried out.

(5) In determining for the purposes of subsections (2) and (3) what is or was the normal use of land, no account shall be taken of any use begun in contravention of this Part or of previous planning control.

(6) For the purposes of this section a use of land shall be taken to have begun in contravention of previous planning control if it was begun in contravention of Part III of the [Town and Country Planning Act 1947], Part III of the [Town and Country Planning Act 1962] or Part III of the [Town and Country Planning Act 1971].

(7) Subsection (1) has effect subject to Schedule 4 (which makes special provision about use of land on 1st July 1948).

58 Granting of planning permission: general [830]

(1) Planning permission may be granted –

(a) by a development order;
(b) by the local planning authority (or, in the cases provided in this Part, by the Secretary of State) on application to the authority in accordance with a development order;
(c) on the adoption or approval of a simplified planning zone scheme or alterations to such a scheme in accordance with section 82 or, as the case may be, section 86; or
(d) on the designation of an enterprise zone or the approval of a modified scheme under Schedule 32 to the Local Government, Planning and Land Act 1980 in accordance with section 88 of this Act.

(2) Planning permission may also be deemed to be granted under section 90 (development with government authorisation).

(3) This section is without prejudice to any other provisions of this Act providing for the granting of permission.

59 Development orders: general [831]

(1) The Secretary of State shall by order (in this Act referred to as a 'development order') provide for the granting of planning permission.

(2) A development order may either –

(a) itself grant planning permission for development specified in the order or for development of any class specified; or
(b) in respect of development for which planning permission is not granted by the order itself, provide for the granting of planning permission by the local planning authority (or, in the cases provided in the following provisions, by the Secretary of State) on application to the authority in accordance with the provisions of the order.

(3) A development order may be made either –

(a) as a general order applicable, except so far as the order otherwise provides, to all land, or
(b) as a special order applicable only to such land or descriptions of land as may be specified in the order.

62 Form and content of applications for [832]
planning permission

Any application to a local planning authority for planning permission –

(a) shall be made in such manner as may be prescribed by regulations under this Act; and
(b) shall include such particulars and be verified by such evidence as may be required by the regulations or by directions given by the local planning authority under them.

70 Determination of applications: general considerations [833]

(1) Where an application is made to a local planning authority for planning permission –

(a) subject to sections 91 and 92, they may grant planning permission, either unconditionally or subject to such conditions as they think fit; or

(b) they may refuse planning permission.

(2) In dealing with such an application the authority shall have regard to the provisions of the development plan, so far as material to the application, and to any other material considerations.

(3) Subsection (1) has effect subject to section 65 and to the following provisions of this Act, to sections 66, 67, 72 and 73 of the Planning (Listed Buildings and Conservation Areas) Act 1990 and to section 15 of the Health Services Act 1976.

70A Power of local planning authority to decline to determine applications   [834]

(1) A local planning authority may decline to determine an application for planning permission for the development of any land if –

(a) within the period of two years ending with the date on which the application is received, the Secretary of State has refused a similar application referred to him under section 77 or has dismissed an appeal against the refusal of a similar application; and

(b) in the opinion of the authority there has been no significant change since the refusal or, as the case may be, dismissal mentioned in paragraph (a) in the development plan, so far as material to the application, or in any other material considerations.

(2) For the purposes of this section an application for planning permission for the development of any land shall only be taken to be similar to a later application if the development and the land to which the applications relate are in the opinion of the local planning authority the same or substantially the same.

(3) The reference in subsection (1)(a) to an appeal against the refusal of an application includes an appeal under section 78(2) in respect of an application.

106 Planning obligations   [835]

(1) Any person interested in land in the area of a local planning authority may, by agreement or otherwise, enter into an obligation (referred to in this section and sections 106A and 106B as 'a planning obligation'), enforceable to the extent mentioned in subsection (3) –

(a) restricting the development or use of the land in any specified way;

(b) requiring specified operations or activities to be carried out in, on, under or over the land;

(c) requiring the land to be used in any specified way; or

(d) requiring a sum or sums to be paid to the authority on a specified date or dates or periodically.

(2) A planning obligation may –

(a) be unconditional or subject to conditions;

(b) impose any restriction or requirement mentioned in subsection (1)(a) to (c) either indefinitely or for such period or periods as may be specified; and

(c) if it requires a sum or sums to be paid, require the payment of a specified amount or an amount determined in accordance with the instrument by which the obligation is entered into and, if it requires the payment of periodical sums, require them to be paid indefinitely or for a specified period.

(3) Subject to subsection (4) a planning obligation is enforceable by the authority identified in accordance with subsection (9)(d) –

(a) against the person entering into the obligation; and

(b) against any person deriving title from that person.

(4) The instrument by which a planning obligation is entered into may provide that a person shall not be bound by the obligation in respect of any period during which he no longer has an interest in the land ...

(11) A planning obligation shall be a local land charge and for the purposes of the Local Land Charges Act 1975 the authority by whom the obligation is enforceable shall be treated as the originating authority as respects such a charge ...

(13) In this section 'specified' means specified in the instrument by which the planning obligation is entered into and in this section and section 106A [modification and discharge of planning obligations] 'land' has the same meaning as in the Local Land Charges Act 1975.

242 Overriding of rights of possession   [836]

If the Secretary of State certifies that possession of a house which –

(a) has been acquired or appropriated by a local authority for planning purposes, and

(b) is for the time being held by the authority for the purposes for which it was acquired or appropriated,

is immediately required for those purposes, nothing in the Rent Act 1977 or Part I of the Housing Act 1988 shall prevent the acquiring or appropriating authority from obtaining possession of the house.

328 Settled land ...   [837]

(1) The purposes authorised for the application of capital money –

(a) by section 73 of the Settled Land Act 1925 ...

shall include the payment of any sum recoverable under section 111 or 112 [compensation on subsequent development].

(2) The purposes authorised as purposes for which money may be raised by mortgage –

(a) by section 71 of the Settled Land Act 1925 ...

shall include the payment of any sum so recoverable.

[As amended by the Planning and Compensation Act 1991, ss12(1), 13(1), (2), 14(1), 17(1), 31(4), 84(6), Schedule 6, paras 8, 9, 37, Schedule 19, Pts I, II; Trusts of Land and Appointment of Trustees Act 1996, s25(2), Schedule 4.]

**PLANNING (LISTED BUILDINGS AND
CONSERVATION AREAS) ACT 1990**

(1990 c 9)

1 Listing of buildings of special architectural or   [838]
historic interest

(1) For the purposes of this Act and with a view to the guidance of local planning authorities in the performance of their functions under this Act and the [Town and Country Planning Act 1990] in relation to buildings of special architectural or historic interest, the Secretary of State shall compile lists of such buildings, or approve, with or without modifications, such lists compiled by the Historic

Buildings and Monuments Commission for England (in this Act referred to as 'the Commission') or by other persons or bodies of persons, and may amend any list so compiled or approved ...

(5) In this Act 'listed building' means a building which is for the time being included in a list compiled or approved by the Secretary of State under this section; and for the purposes of this Act –

(a) any object or structure fixed to the building;
(b) any object or structure within the curtilage of the building which, although not fixed to the building, forms part of the land and has done so since before 1st July 1948,

shall be treated as part of the building ...

72 General duty as respects conservation areas in exercise of planning functions [839]

(1) In the exercise, with respect to any buildings or other land in a conservation area, of any functions under or by virtue of any of the provisions mentioned in subsection (2), special attention shall be paid to the desirability of preserving or enhancing the character or appearance of that area.

(2) The provisions referred to in subsection (1) are the planning Acts and Part I of the Historic Buildings and Ancient Monuments Act 1953 and sections 70 and 73 of the Leasehold Reform, Housing and Urban Development Act 1993.

87 Settled land [840]

The classes of works specified in Part II of Schedule 3 to the Settled Land Act 1925 (which specifies improvements which may be paid for out of capital money, subject to provisions under which repayment out of income may be required to be made) shall include works specified by the Secretary of State as being required for properly maintaining a listed building which is settled land within the meaning of that Act.

[As amended by the Leasehold Reform, Housing and Urban Development Act 1993, s187(1), Schedule 21, para 30.]

WATER RESOURCES ACT 1991
(1991 c 57)

24 Restrictions on abstraction [841]

(1) Subject to the following provisions of this Chapter [Chapter II] and to any drought order under Chapter III of this Part, no person shall –

(a) abstract water from any source of supply; or
(b) cause or permit any other person so to abstract any water,

except in pursuance of a licence under this Chapter granted by the Agency and in accordance with the provision of that licence.

(2) Where by virtue of subsection (1) above the abstraction of water contained in any underground strata is prohibited except in pursuance of a licence under this Chapter, no person shall begin, or cause or permit any other person to begin –

(a) to construct any well, borehole or other work by which water may be abstracted from those strata;
(b) to extend any such well, borehole or other work; or

(c) to install or modify any machinery or apparatus by which additional quantities of water may be abstracted from those strata by means of a well, borehole or other work,

unless the conditions specified in subsection (3) below are satisfied.

(3) The conditions mentioned in subsection (2) above are –

(a) that the abstraction of the water or, as the case may be, of the additional quantities of water is authorised by a licence under this Chapter; and
(b) that –

(i) the well, borehole or work, as constructed or extended; or
(ii) the machinery or apparatus, as installed or modified,

fulfils the requirements of that licence as to the means by which water is authorised to be abstracted ...

(6) The restrictions imposed by this section shall have effect notwithstanding anything in any enactment contained in any Act passed before the passing of the Water Resources Act 1963 on 31st July 1963 or in any statutory provision made or issued, whether before or after the passing of that Act, by virtue of such an enactment.

27 Rights to abstract small quantities [842]

(1) The restriction on abstraction shall not apply to any abstraction of a quantity of water not exceeding five cubic metres if it does not form part of a continuous operation, or of a series of operations, by which a quantity of water which, in aggregate, is more than five cubic metres is abstracted.

(2) The restriction on abstraction shall not apply to any abstraction of a quantity of water not exceeding twenty cubic metres if the abstraction –

(a) does not form part of a continuous operation, or of a series of operations, by which a quantity of water which, in aggregate, is more than twenty cubic metres is abstracted; and
(b) is with the consent of the Agency.

(3) The restriction on abstraction shall not apply to so much of any abstraction from any inland waters by or on behalf of an occupier of contiguous land as falls within subsection (4) below, unless the abstraction is such that the quantity of water abstracted from the inland waters by or on behalf of the occupier by virtue of this subsection exceeds twenty cubic metres, in aggregate, in any period of twenty-four hours.

(4) Subject to section 28 below, an abstraction of water falls within this subsection in so far as the water –

(a) is abstracted for use on a holding consisting of the contiguous land with or without other land held with that land; and
(b) is abstracted for use on that holding for either or both of the following purposes, that is to say –

(i) the domestic purposes of the occupier's household;
(ii) agricultural purposes other than spray irrigation.

(5) The restriction on abstraction shall not apply to the abstraction of water from underground strata, in so far as the water is abstracted by or on behalf of an individual as a supply of water for the domestic purposes of his household, unless the abstraction is such that the quantity of water abstracted from the strata by or on behalf of that individual by virtue of this subsection exceeds twenty cubic metres, in aggregate, in any period of twenty-four hours.

(6) For the purposes of this Chapter a person who is in a position to abstract water in such circumstances that, by virtue of subsection (3) or (5) above, the restriction on abstraction does not apply shall be taken to have a right to abstract water to the extent specified in that subsection.

(7) In the case of any abstraction of water from underground strata which falls within subsection (5) above, the restriction imposed by section 24(2) above shall not apply –

(a) to the construction or extension of any well, borehole or other work; or
(b) to the installation or modification of machinery or other apparatus,

if the well, borehole or other work is constructed or extended, or the machinery or apparatus is installed or modified, for the purpose of abstracting the water.

(8) In this section 'contiguous land', in relation to the abstraction of any water from inland waters, means land contiguous to those at the place where the abstraction is effected.

72 Interpretation of Chapter II   [843]

(1) In this Chapter –

...

'the restriction on abstraction' means the restriction imposed by section 24(1) above; ...
'spray irrigation' means (subject to subsection (5) below) the irrigation of land or plants (including seeds) by means of water or other liquid emerging (in whatever form) from apparatus designed or adapted to eject liquid into the air in the form of jets or spray; and
'statutory provision' means a provision (whether of a general or special nature) which is contained in, or in any document made or issued under, any Act (whether of a general or special nature) ...

(4) For the purposes of this Chapter land shall be taken to be contiguous to any inland waters notwithstanding that it is separated from those waters by a towpath or by any other land used, or acquired for use, in connection with the navigation of the inland waters, unless that other land comprises any building or works other than a lock, pier, wharf, landing-stage or similar works.

(5) The Ministers may by order direct that references to spray irrigation in this Chapter, and in any other enactments in which 'spray irrigation' is given the same meaning as in this Chapter, or such of those references as may be specified in the order –

(a) shall be construed as not including spray irrigation if carried out by such methods or in such circumstances or for such purposes as may be specified in the order; and
(b) without prejudice to the exercise of the power conferred by virtue of paragraph (a) above, shall be construed as including references to the carrying out, by such methods or in such circumstances or for such purposes as may be specified in the order, of irrigation of any such description, other than spray irrigation, as may be so specified.

221 General interpretation   [844]

(1) In this Act, except in so far as the context otherwise requires – ...

'abstraction', in relation to water contained in any source of supply, means the doing of anything whereby any of that water is removed from that source of supply, whether temporarily or permanently, including anything whereby the

water is so removed for the purpose of being transferred to another source of supply; and 'abstract' shall be construed accordingly; ...
'the Agency' means the Environment Agency;
'agriculture' has the same meaning as in the Agriculture Act 1947 and 'agricultural' shall be construed accordingly; ...
'inland waters' means the whole or any part of –

(a) any river, stream or other watercourse (within the meaning of Chapter II of Part II of this Act), whether natural or artificial and whether tidal or not;
(b) any lake or pond, whether natural or artificial, or any reservoir or dock, in so far as the lake, pond, reservoir or dock does not fall within paragraph (a) of this definition; and
(c) so much of any channel, creek, bay, estuary or arm of the sea as does not fall within paragraph (a) or (b) of this definition; ...

'source of supply' means –

(a) any inland waters except, without prejudice to subsection (3) below in its application to paragraph (b) of this definition, any which are discrete waters; or
(b) any underground strata in which water is or at any time may be contained; ...

'underground strata' means strata subjacent to the surface of any land; ...

[As amended by the Environment Act 1995, s120, Schedule 22, paras 128, 177, Schedule 24.]

ACCESS TO NEIGHBOURING LAND ACT 1992
(1992 c 23)

1 Access orders   [845]

(1) A person –

(a) who, for the purpose of carrying out works to any land (the 'dominant land'), desires to enter upon any adjoining or adjacent land (the 'servient land'), and
(b) who needs, but does not have, the consent of some other person to that entry,

may make an application to the court for an order under this section ('an access order') against that person.

(2) On an application under this section, the court shall make an access order if, and only if, it is satisfied –

(a) that the works are reasonably necessary for the preservation of the whole or any part of the dominant land; and
(b) that they cannot be carried out, or would be substantially more difficult to carry out, without entry upon the servient land;

but this subsection is subject to subsection (3) below.

(3) The court shall not make an access order in any case where it is satisfied that, were it to make such an order –

(a) the respondent or any other person would suffer interference with, or disturbance of, his use or enjoyment of the servient land, or
(b) the respondent, or any other person (whether of full age or capacity or not) in occupation of the whole or any part of the servient land, would suffer hardship,

to such a degree by reason of the entry (notwithstanding any requirement of this Act or any term or condition that may be imposed under it) that it would be unreasonable to make the order.

(4) Where the court is satisfied on an application under this section that it is reasonably necessary to carry out any basic preservation works to the dominant land, those works shall be taken for the purposes of this Act to be reasonably necessary for the preservation of the land; and in this subsection 'basic preservation works' means any of the following, that is to say –

(a) the maintenance, repair or renewal of any part of a building or other structure comprised in, or situate on, the dominant land;
(b) the clearance, repair or renewal of any drain, sewer, pipe or cable so comprised or situate;
(c) the treatment, cutting back, felling, removal or replacement of any hedge, tree, shrub or other growing thing which is so comprised and which is, or is in danger of becoming, damaged, diseased, dangerous, insecurely rooted or dead;
(d) the filling in, or clearance, of any ditch so comprised;

but this subsection is without prejudice to the generality of the works which may, apart from it, be regarded by the court as reasonably necessary for the preservation of any land.

(5) If the court considers it fair and reasonable in all the circumstances of the case, works may be regarded for the purposes of this Act as being reasonably necessary for the preservation of any land (or, for the purposes of subsection (4) above, as being basic preservation works which it is reasonably necessary to carry out to any land) notwithstanding that the works incidentally involve –

(a) the making of some alteration, adjustment or improvement to the land, or
(b) the demolition of the whole or any part of a building or structure comprised in or situate upon the land.

(6) Where any works are reasonably necessary for the preservation of the whole or any part of the dominant land, the doing to the dominant land of anything which is requisite for, incidental to, or consequential on, the carrying out of those works shall be treated for the purposes of this Act as the carrying out of works which are reasonably necessary for the preservation of that land; and references in this Act to works, or to the carrying out of works, shall be construed accordingly.

(7) Without prejudice to the generality of subsection (6) above, if it is reasonably necessary for a person to inspect the dominant land –

(a) for the purpose of ascertaining whether any works may be reasonably necessary for the preservation of the whole or any part of that land,
(b) for the purpose of making any map or plan, or ascertaining the course of any drain, sewer, pipe or cable, in preparation for, or otherwise in connection with, the carrying out of works which are so reasonably necessary, or
(c) otherwise in connection with the carrying out of any such works,

the making of such an inspection shall be taken for the purposes of this Act to be the carrying out to the dominant land of works which are reasonably necessary for the preservation of that land; and references in this Act to works, or to the carrying out of works, shall be construed accordingly.

3 Effect of access orders [846]

(1) An access order requires the respondent, so far as he has power to do so, to permit the applicant or any of his associates to do anything which the applicant or associate is authorised or required to do under or by virtue of the order or this section.

(2) Except as otherwise provided by or under this Act, an access order authorises the applicant or any of his associates, without the consent of the respondent, –

(a) to enter upon the servient land for the purpose of carrying out the specified works;

(b) to bring on to that land, leave there during the period permitted by the order and, before the end of that period, remove, such materials, plant and equipment as are reasonably necessary for the carrying out of those works; and

(c) to bring on to that land any waste arising from the carrying out of those works, if it is reasonably necessary to do so in the course of removing it from the dominant land;

but nothing in this Act or in any access order shall authorise the applicant or any of his associates to leave anything in, on or over the servient land (otherwise than in discharge of their duty to make good that land) after their entry for the purpose of carrying out works to the dominant land ceases to be authorised under or by virtue of the order.

(3) An access order requires the applicant –

(a) to secure that any waste arising from the carrying out of the specified works is removed from the servient land forthwith;

(b) to secure that, before the entry ceases to be authorised under or by virtue of the order, the servient land is, so far as reasonably practicable, made good; and

(c) to indemnify the respondent against any damage which may be caused to the servient land or any goods by the applicant or any of his associates which would not have been so caused had the order not been made;

but this subsection is subject to subsections (4) and (5) below.

(4) In making an access order, the court may vary or exclude, in whole or in part, –

(a) any authorisation that would otherwise be conferred by subsection (2)(b) or (c) above; or

(b) any requirement that would otherwise be imposed by subsection (3) above.

(5) Without prejudice to the generality of subsection (4) above, if the court is satisfied that it is reasonably necessary for any such waste as may arise from the carrying out of the specified works to be left on the servient land for some period before removal, the access order may, in place of subsection (3)(a) above, include provision –

(a) authorising the waste to be left on that land for such period as may be permitted by the order; and

(b) requiring the applicant to secure that the waste is removed before the end of that period.

(6) Where the applicant or any of his associates is authorised or required under or by virtue of an access order or this section to enter, or do any other thing, upon the servient land, he shall not (as respects that access order) be taken to be a trespasser from the beginning on account of his, or any other person's, subsequent conduct.

(7) For the purposes of this section, the applicant's 'associates' are such number of persons (whether or not servants or agents of his) whom he may reasonably authorise under this subsection to exercise the power of entry conferred by the access order as may be reasonably necessary for the carrying out the specified works.

4 Persons bound by access order, unidentified persons   [847]
and bar on contracting out

(1) In addition to the respondent, an access order shall, subject to the provisions of the Land Charges Act 1972 and the Land Registration Act 1925, be binding on –

(a) any of his successors in title to the servient land; and

(b) any person who has an estate or interest in, or right over, the whole or any part of the servient land which was created after the making of the order and who derives his title to that estate, interest or right under the respondent;

and references to the respondent shall be construed accordingly.

(2) If and to the extent that the court considers it just and equitable to allow him to do so, a person on whom an access order becomes binding by virtue of subsection (1)(a) or (b) above shall be entitled, as respects anything falling to be done after the order becomes binding on him, to enforce the order or any of its terms or conditions as if he were the respondent, and references to the respondent shall be construed accordingly ...

(4) Any agreement, whenever made, shall be void if and to the extent that it would, apart from this subsection, prevent a person from applying for an access order or restrict his right to do so.

5 Registration of access orders and of applications   [848]
for such orders ...

(4) In any case where –

(a) an access order is discharged [by the court] under s6(1)(a) below, and

(b) the order has been protected by an entry registered under the Land Charges Act 1972 or by a notice or caution under the Land Registration Act 1925,

the court may by order direct that the entry, notice or caution shall be cancelled.

(5) The rights conferred on a person by or under an access order are not capable of constituting an overriding interest within the meaning of the Land Registration Act 1925, notwithstanding that he or any other person is in actual occupation of the whole or any part of the servient land in question.

(6) An application for an access order shall be regarded as a pending land action for the purposes of the Land Charges Act 1972 and the Land Registration Act 1925.

8 Interpretation and application   [849]

(1) Any reference in this Act to an 'entry' upon any servient land includes a reference to the doing on that land of anything necessary for carrying out the works to the dominant land which are reasonably necessary for its preservation; and 'enter' shall be construed accordingly.

(2) This Act applies in relation to any obstruction of, or other interference with, a right over, or interest in, any land as it applies in relation to an entry upon that land; and 'enter' and 'entry' shall be construed accordingly.

(3) In this Act –

'access order' has the meaning given by section 1(1) above;

'applicant' means a person making an application for an access order and, subject to section 4 above, 'the respondent' means the respondent, or any of the respondents, to such an application;

'the court' means the High Court or a county court;

'the dominant land' and 'the servient land' respectively have the meanings given by section 1(1) above, but subject, in the case of servient land, to section 2(1) above;

'land' does not include a highway;

'the specified works' means the works specified in the access order in pursuance of section 2(1)(a) above.

CHARITIES ACT 1993

(1993 c 10)

35 Application of provisions to trust corporations   [850] appointed under s16 or 18

(1) In the definition of 'trust corporation' contained in the following provisions –

    (a) section 117(xxx) of the Settled Land Act 1925,
    (b) section 68(18) of the Trustee Act 1925,
    (c) section 205(xxviii) of the Law of Property Act 1925,
    (d) section 55(xxvi) of the Administration of Estates Act 1925 ...

the reference to a corporation appointed by the court in any particular case to be a trustee includes a reference to a corporation appointed by the Commissioners under this Act to be a trustee ...

36 Restrictions on dispositions   [851]

(1) Subject to the following provisions of this section and section 40 below, no land held by or in trust for a charity shall be sold, leased or otherwise disposed of without an order of the court or of the Commissioners.

(2) Subsection (1) above shall not apply to a disposition of such land if –

    (a) the disposition is made to a person who is not –

        (i) a connected person (as defined in Schedule 5 to this Act), or
        (ii) a trustee for, or nominee of, a connected person; and

    (b) the requirements of subsection (3) or (5) below have been complied with in relation to it.

(3) Except where the proposed disposition is the granting of such a lease as is mentioned in subsection (5) below, the charity trustees must, before entering into an agreement for the sale, or (as the case may be) for a lease or other disposition, of the land –

    (a) obtain and consider a written report on the proposed disposition from a qualified surveyor instructed by the trustees and acting exclusively for the charity;
    (b) advertise the proposed disposition for such period and in such manner as the surveyor has advised in his report (unless he has there advised that it would not be in the best interests of the charity to advertise the proposed disposition); and
    (c) decide that they are satisfied, having considered the surveyor's report, that the terms on which the disposition is proposed to be made are the best that can reasonably be obtained for the charity ...

(5) Where the proposed disposition is the granting of a lease for a term ending not more than seven years after it is granted (other than one granted wholly or partly in consideration of a fine), the charity trustees must, before entering into an agreement for the lease –

    (a) obtain and consider the advice on the proposed disposition of a person who is reasonably believed by the trustees to have the requisite ability and practical experience to provide them with competent advice on the proposed disposition; and

(b) decide that they are satisfied, having considered that person's advice, that the terms on which the disposition is proposed to be made are the best that can reasonably be obtained for the charity ...

LEASEHOLD REFORM, HOUSING AND URBAN DEVELOPMENT ACT 1993

(1993 c 28)

PART I

LANDLORD AND TENANT

CHAPTER I

COLLECTIVE ENFRANCHISEMENT IN CASE OF TENANTS OF FLATS

1 The right to collective enfranchisement   [852]

(1) This Chapter has effect for the purpose of conferring on qualifying tenants of flats contained in premises to which this Chapter applies on the relevant date the right, exercisable subject to and in accordance with this Chapter, to have the freehold of those premises acquired on their behalf –

(a) by a person or persons appointed by them for the purpose, and
(b) at a price determined in accordance with this Chapter;

and that right is referred to in this Chapter as 'the right to collective enfranchisement'.

(2) Where the right to collective enfranchisement is exercised in relation to any such premises ('the relevant premises') –

(a) the qualifying tenants by whom the right is exercised shall be entitled, subject to and in accordance with this Chapter, to have acquired, in like manner, the freehold of any property which is not comprised in the relevant premises but to which this paragraph applies by virtue of subsection (3); and
(b) section 2 has effect with respect to the acquisition of leasehold interests to which paragraph (a) or (b) of subsection (1) of that section applies.

(3) Subsection (2)(a) applies to any property at the relevant date either –

(a) it is appurtenant property which is demised by the lease held by a qualifying tenant of a flat contained in the relevant premises; or
(b) it is property which any such tenant is entitled under the terms of the lease of his flat to use in common with the occupiers of other premises (whether those premises are contained in the relevant premises or not).

(4) The right of acquisition in respect of the freehold of any such property as is mentioned in subsection (3)(b) shall, however, be taken to be satisfied with respect to that property if, on the acquisition of the relevant premises in pursuance of this Chapter, either –

(a) there are granted by the freeholder –

(i) over that property, or
(ii) over any other property,

such permanent rights as will ensure that thereafter the occupier of the flat referred to in that provision has as nearly as may be the same rights as those enjoyed in relation to that property on the relevant date by the qualifying tenant under the terms of his lease; or

(b) there is acquired from the freeholder the freehold of any other property over which any such permanent rights may be granted.

(5) A claim by qualifying tenants to exercise the right to collective enfranchisement may be made in relation to any premises to which this Chapter applies despite the fact that those premises are less extensive than the entirety of the premises in relation to which those tenants are entitled to exercise that right.

(6) Any right or obligation under this Chapter to acquire any interest in property shall not extend to underlying minerals in which that interest subsists if –

(a) the owner of the interest requires the minerals to be excepted, and

(b) proper provision is made for the support of the property as it is enjoyed on the relevant date.

(7) In this section –

'appurtenant property', in relation to a flat, means any garage, outhouse, garden, yard or appurtenances belonging to, or usually enjoyed with, the flat;
'the freeholder' means the person who owns the freehold of the relevant premises;
'the relevant premises' means any such premises as are referred to in subsection (2).

(8) In this Chapter 'the relevant date', in relation to any claim to exercise the right to collective enfranchisement, means the date on which notice of the claim is given under section 13.

2 Acquisition of leasehold interests   **[853]**

(1) Where the right to collective enfranchisement is exercised in relation to any premises to which this Chapter applies ('the relevant premises') then, subject to and in accordance with this Chapter –

(a) there shall be acquired on behalf of the qualifying tenants by whom the right is exercised every interest to which this paragraph applies by virtue of subsection (2); and

(b) those tenants shall be entitled to have acquired on their behalf any interest to which this paragraph applies by virtue of subsection (3);

and any interest so acquired on behalf of those tenants shall be acquired in the manner mentioned in paragraphs (a) and (b) of section 1(1).

(2) Paragraph (a) of subsection (1) above applies to the interest of the tenant under any lease which is superior to the lease held by a qualifying tenant of a flat contained in the relevant premises.

(3) Paragraph (b) of subsection (1) above applies to the interest of the tenant under any lease (not falling within subsection (2) above) under which the demised premises consist of or include –

(a) any common parts of the relevant premises, or

(b) any property falling within section 1(2)(a) which is to be acquired by virtue of that provision,

where the acquisition of that interest is reasonably necessary for the proper management or maintenance of those common parts, or (as the case may be) that property, on behalf of the tenants by whom the right to collective enfranchisement is exercised ...

(7) In this section 'the relevant premises' means any such premises as are referred to in subsection (1).

3 Premises to which this Chapter applies [854]

(1) Subject to section 4, this Chapter applies to any premises if –

(a) they consist of a self-contained building or part of a building;
(b) they contain two or more flats held by qualifying tenants; and
(c) the total number of flats held by such tenants is not less than two thirds of the total number of flats contained in the premises.

4 Premises excluded from right [855]

(1) This Chapter does not apply to premises falling within section 3(1) if –

(a) any part or parts of the premises is or are neither –

(i) occupied, or intended to be occupied, for residential purposes, nor
(ii) comprised in any common parts of the premises; and

(b) the internal floor area of that part or of those parts (taken together) exceeds 10 per cent of the internal floor area of the premises (taken as a whole).

(2) Where in the case of any such premises any part of the premises (such as, for example, a garage, parking space or storage area) is used, or intended for use, in conjunction with a particular dwelling contained in the premises (and accordingly is not comprised in any common parts of the premises), it shall be taken to be occupied, or intended to be occupied, for residential purposes.

(3) For the purpose of determining the internal floor area of a building or of any part of a building, the floor or floors of the building or part shall be taken to extend (without interruption) throughout the whole of the interior of the building or part, except that the area of any common parts of the building or part shall be disregarded.

(3A) Where different persons own the freehold of different parts of premises within subsection (1) of section 3, this Chapter does not apply to the premises if any of those parts is a self-contained part of a building for the purposes of that section.

(4) This Chapter does not apply to premises falling within section 3(1) if the premises are premises with a resident landlord and do not contain more than four units.

5 Qualifying tenants [856]

(1) Subject to the following provisions of this section, a person is a qualifying tenant of a flat for the purpose of this Chapter if he is tenant of the flat under a long lease at a low rent.

(2) Subsection (1) does not apply where –

(a) the lease is a business lease; or
(b) the immediate landlord under the lease is a charitable housing trust and the flat forms part of the housing accommodation provided by it in the pursuit of its charitable purposes; or
(c) the lease was granted by sub-demise out of a superior lease other than a long lease at a low rent, the grant was made in breach of the terms of the superior lease, and there has been no waiver of the breach by the superior landlord;

and in paragraph (b) 'charitable housing trust' means a housing trust within the meaning of the Housing Act 1985 which is a charity within the meaning of the Charities Act 1993.

(3) No flat shall have more than one qualifying tenant at any one time ...

6 Qualifying tenants satisfying residence condition   [857]

(1) For the purposes of this Chapter a qualifying tenant of a flat satisfies the residence condition at any time when the condition specified in subsection (2) is satisfied with respect to him.

(2) That condition is that the tenant has occupied the flat as his only or principal home –

(a) for the last twelve months, or
(b) for periods amounting to three years in the last ten years,

whether or not he has used it also for other purposes.

(3) For the purposes of subsection (2) –

(a) any reference to the tenant's flat includes a reference to part of it; and
(b) it is immaterial whether at any particular time the tenant's occupation was in right of the lease by virtue of which he is a qualifying tenant or in right of some other lease or otherwise;

but any occupation by a company or other artificial person, or (where the tenant is a corporation sole) by the corporator, shall not be regarded as occupation for the purposes of that subsection.

(4) Subsection (1) shall not apply where a lease is vested in trustees (other than a sole tenant for life within the meaning of the Settled Land Act 1925), and, in that case, a qualifying tenant of a flat shall, for the purposes of this Chapter, be treated as satisfying the residence condition at any time when the condition in subsection (5) is satisfied with respect to an individual having an interest under the trust (whether or not also a trustee).

(5) That condition is that the individual has occupied the flat as his only or principal home –

(a) for the last twelve months, or
(b) for periods amounting to three years in the last ten years, whether or not he has used the flat also for other purposes.

(6) For the purposes of subsection (5) –

(a) any reference to the flat includes a reference to part of it; and
(b) it is immaterial whether at any particular time the individual's occupation was in right of the lease by virtue of which the trustees are a qualifying tenant or in right of some other lease or otherwise.

7 Meaning of 'long lease'   [858]

(1) In this Chapter 'long lease' means (subject to the following provisions of this section) –

(a) a lease granted for a term of years certain exceeding 21 years, whether or not it is (or may become) terminable before the end of that term by notice given by or to the tenant or by re-entry, forfeiture or otherwise;
(b) a lease for a term fixed by law under a grant with a covenant or obligation for perpetual renewal (other than a lease by sub-demise from one which is not a long lease) or a lease taking effect under section 149(6) of the Law of Property Act 1925 (leases terminable after death or marriage);
(c) a lease granted in pursuance of the right to buy conferred by Part V of the Housing Act 1985 or in pursuance of the right to acquire on rent to mortgage terms conferred by that Part of that Act; or
(d) a shared ownership lease, whether granted in pursuance of that Part of that Act or otherwise, where the tenant's total share is 100 per cent ...

8 Leases at a low rent [859]

(1) For the purposes of this Chapter a lease of a flat is a lease at a low rent if either no rent was payable under it in respect of the flat during the initial year or the aggregate amount of rent so payable during that year did not exceed the following amount, namely –

(a) where the lease was entered into before 1st April 1963, two-thirds of the letting value of the flat (on the same terms) on the date of the commencement of the lease;

(b) where –

(i) the lease was entered into either on or after 1st April 1963 but before 1st April 1990, or on or after 1st April 1990 in pursuance of a contract made before that date, and

(ii) the flat had a rateable value at the date of the commencement of the lease or else at any time before 1st April 1990,

two-thirds of the rateable value of the flat on the appropriate date; or

(c) in any other case, £1,000 if the flat is in Greater London or £250 if elsewhere ...

CHAPTER II

INDIVIDUAL RIGHT OF TENANT OF FLAT TO ACQUIRE NEW LEASE

39 Right of qualifying tenant of flat to acquire new lease [860]

(1) This Chapter has effect for the purpose of conferring on a tenant of a flat, in the circumstances mentioned in subsection (2), the right, exercisable subject to and in accordance with this Chapter, to acquire a new lease of the flat on payment of a premium determined in accordance with this Chapter.

(2) Those circumstances are that on the relevant date for the purposes of this Chapter –

(a) the tenant is a qualifying tenant of the flat; and

(b) the condition specified in subsection (2A) or, as the case may be, (2B) is satisfied.

(2A) Where the lease by virtue of which the tenant is a qualifying tenant vested in trustees (other than a sole tenant for life within the meaning of the Settled Land Act 1925), the condition is that an individual having an interest under the trust (whether or not also a trustee) has occupied the flat as his only or principal home –

(a) for the last three years, or

(b) for periods amounting to three years in the last ten years, whether or not he has used it also for other purposes.

(2B) Where the lease by virtue of which the tenant is a qualifying tenant is not vested as mentioned in subsection (2A), the condition is that the tenant has occupied the flat as his only or principal home –

(a) for the last three years, or

(b) for periods amounting to three years in the last ten years, whether or not he has used it also for other purposes.

(3) The following provisions, namely –

(a) section 5 (with the omission of subsections (5) and (6)),

(b) section 7, and

(c) section 8,

shall apply for the purposes of this Chapter as they apply for the purposes of Chapter I; and references in this Chapter to a qualifying tenant of a flat shall accordingly be construed by reference to those provisions.

(4) For the purposes of this Chapter a person can be (or be among those constituting) the qualifying tenant of each of two or more flats at the same time, whether he is tenant of those flats under one lease or under two or more separate leases.

(4A) For the purposes of subsection (2A) –

(a) any reference to the flat includes a reference to part of it; and

(b) it is immaterial whether at any particular time the individual's occupation was in right of the lease by virtue of which the trustees are a qualifying tenant or in right of some other lease or otherwise.

(5) For the purposes of subsection (2B) above –

(a) any reference to the tenant's flat includes a reference to part of it; and

(b) it is immaterial whether at any particular time the tenant's occupation was in right of the lease by virtue of which he is a qualifying tenant or in right of some other lease or otherwise;

but any occupation by a company or other artificial person, or (where the tenant is a corporation sole) by the corporator, shall not be regarded as occupation for the purposes of that provision.

(6) In the case of a lease held by joint tenants –

(a) the condition in subsection (2)(b) need only be satisfied with respect to one of the joint tenants; and

(b) subsection (5) shall apply accordingly (the reference to the lease by virtue of which the tenant is a qualifying tenant being read for this purpose as a reference to the lease by virtue of which the joint tenants are a qualifying tenant).

(7) The right conferred by this Chapter on a tenant to acquire a new lease shall not extend to underlying minerals comprised in his existing lease if –

(a) the landlord requires the minerals to be excepted, and

(b) proper provision is made for the support of the premises demised by that existing lease as they are enjoyed on the relevant date.

(8) In this Chapter 'the relevant date', in relation to a claim by a tenant under this Chapter, means the date on which notice of the claim is given to the landlord under section 42.

[As amended by the Housing Act 1966, ss107, 111(1), 112.]

LAW OF PROPERTY (MISCELLANEOUS PROVISIONS) ACT 1994

(1994 c 36)

PART I

IMPLIED COVENANTS FOR TITLE

1 Covenants to be implied on a disposition of property   [861]

(1) In an instrument effecting or purporting to effect a disposition of property there shall be implied on the part of the person making the disposition, whether

or not the disposition is for valuable consideration, such of the covenants specified in sections 2 to 5 as are applicable to the disposition.

(2) Of those sections –

(a) sections 2, 3(1) and (2), 4 and 5 apply where dispositions are expressed to be made with full title guarantee; and
(b) sections 2, 3(3), 4 and 5 apply where dispositions are expressed to be made with limited title guarantee.

(3) Sections 2 to 4 have effect subject to section 6 (no liability under covenants in certain cases); and sections 2 to 5 have effect subject to section 8(1) (limitation or extension of covenants by instrument effecting the disposition).

(4) In this Part –

'disposition' includes the creation of a term of years;
'instrument' includes an instrument which is not a deed; and
'property' includes a thing in action, and any interest in real or personal property.

2 Right to dispose and further assurance   [862]

(1) If the disposition is expressed to be made with full title guarantee or with limited title guarantee there shall be implied the following covenants –

(a) that the person making the disposition has the right (with the concurrence of any other person conveying the property) to dispose of the property as he purports to, and
(b) that that person will at his own cost do all that he reasonably can to give the person to whom he disposes of the property the title he purports to give.

(2) The latter obligation includes –

(a) in relation to a disposition of an interest in land the title to which is registered, doing all that he reasonably can to ensure that the person to whom the disposition is made is entitled to be registered as proprietor with at least the class of title registered immediately before the disposition; and
(b) in relation to a disposition of an interest in land the title to which is required to be registered by virtue of the disposition, giving all reasonable assistance fully to establish to the satisfaction of the Chief Land Registrar the right of the person to whom the disposition is made to registration as proprietor.

(3) In the case of a disposition of an existing legal interest in land, the following presumptions apply, subject to the terms of the instrument, in ascertaining for the purposes of the covenants implied by this section what the person making the disposition purports to dispose of –

(a) where the title to the interest is registered, it shall be presumed that the disposition is of the whole of that interest;
(b) where the title to the interest is not registered, then –

(i) if it appears from the instrument that the interest is a leasehold interest, it shall be presumed that the disposition is of the property for the unexpired portion of the term of years created by the lease; and
(ii) in any other case, it shall be presumed that what is disposed of is the fee simple.

3 Charges incumbrances and third party rights   [863]

(1) If the disposition is expressed to be made with full title guarantee there shall

be implied a covenant that the person making the disposition is disposing of the property free –

(a) from all charges and incumbrances (whether monetary or not), and

(b) from all other rights exercisable by third parties,

other than any charges, incumbrances or rights which that person does not and could not reasonably be expected to know about.

(2) In its application to charges, incumbrances and other third party rights subsection (1) extends to liabilities imposed and rights conferred by or under any enactment, except to the extent that such liabilities and rights are, by reason of –

(a) being, at the time of the disposition, only potential liabilities
and rights in relation to the property, or

(b) being liabilities and rights imposed or conferred in relation to property generally,

not such as to constitute defects in title.

(3) If the disposition is expressed to be made with limited title guarantee there shall be implied a covenant that the person making the disposition has not since the last disposition for value –

(a) charged or incumbered the property by means of any charge or incumbrance which subsists at the time when the disposition is made, or granted third party rights in relation to the property which so subsists, or

(b) suffered the property to be so charged or incumbered or subjected to any such rights,

and that he is not aware that anyone else has done so since the last disposition for value.

4 Validity of lease [864]

(1) Where the disposition is of leasehold land and is expressed to be made with full title guarantee or with limited title guarantee, the following covenants shall also be implied –

(a) that the lease is subsisting at the time of the disposition, and

(b) that there is no subsisting breach of a condition or tenant's obligation, and nothing which at that time would render the lease liable to forfeiture.

(2) If the disposition is the grant of an underlease, the references to 'the lease' in subsection (1) are references to the lease out of which the underlease is created.

5 Discharge of obligations where property subject [865] to rentcharge or leasehold land

(1) Where the disposition is a mortgage of property subject to a rentcharge, or of leasehold land, and is expressed to be made with full title guarantee or with limited title guarantee, the following covenants shall also be implied.

(2) If the property is subject to a rentcharge, there shall be implied a covenant that the mortgagor will fully and promptly observe and perform all the obligations under the instrument creating the rentcharge that are for the time being enforceable with respect to the property by the owner of the rentcharge in his capacity as such.

(3) If the property is leasehold land, there shall be implied a covenant that the mortgagor will fully and promptly observe and perform all the obligations under the lease subject to the mortgage that are for the time being imposed on him in his capacity as tenant under the lease.

(4) In this section 'mortgage' includes charge, and 'mortgagor' shall be construed accordingly.

6 No liability under covenants in certain cases   [866]

(1) The person making the disposition is not liable under the covenants implied by virtue of –

    (a) section 2(1)(a) (right to dispose),
    (b) section 3 (charges, incumbrances and third party rights), or
    (c) section 4 (validity of lease),

in respect of any particular matter to which the disposition is expressly made subject.

(2) Furthermore that person is not liable under any of those covenants for anything (not falling within subsection (1)) –

    (a) which at the time of the disposition is within the actual knowledge, or
    (b) which is a necessary consequence of facts that are then within the actual knowledge,

of the person to whom the disposition is made.

(3) For this purpose section 198 of the Law of Property Act 1925 (deemed notice by virtue of registration) shall be disregarded.

7 Annexation of benefit of covenants   [867]

The benefit of a covenant implied by virtue of this Part shall be annexed and incident to, and shall go with, the estate or interest of the person to whom the disposition is made, and shall be capable of being enforced by every person in whom that estate or interest is (in whole or in part) for the time being vested.

8 Supplementary provisions   [868]

(1) The operation of any covenant implied in an instrument by virtue of this Part may be limited or extended by a term of that instrument.

(2) Sections 81 and 83 of the Law of Property Act 1925 (effect of covenant with two or more jointly; construction of implied covenants) apply to a covenant implied by virtue of this Part as they apply to a covenant implied by virtue of that Act.

(3) Where in an instrument effecting or purporting to effect a disposition of property a person is expressed to direct the disposition, this Part applies to him as if he were the person making the disposition.

(4) This Part has effect –

    (a) where 'gyda gwarant teitl llawn' is used instead of 'with full title guarantee', and
    (b) where 'gyda gwarant teitl cyfyngedig' is used instead of 'with limited title guarantee',

as it has effect where the English words are used.

9 Modifications of statutory forms   [869]

(1) Where a form set out in an enactment, or in an instrument made under an enactment, includes words which (in an appropriate case) would have resulted in the implication of a covenant by virtue of section 76 of the Law of Property Act

1925, the form shall be taken to authorise instead the use of the words 'with full title guarantee' or 'with limited title guarantee' or their Welsh equivalent given in section 8(4).

(2) This applies in particular to the forms set out in Schedule 1 to the Settled Land Act 1925 and Schedules 4 and 5 to the Law of Property Act 1925.

10 General saving for covenants in old form [870]

(1) Except as provided by section 11 below (cases in which covenants in old form implied on disposition after commencement), the following provisions, namely –

    (a) section 76 of the Law of Property Act 1925, and
    (b) section 24(1)(a) of the Land Registration Act 1925,

are repealed as regards dispositions of property made after the commencement of this Part.

(2) The repeal of those provisions by this Act accordingly does not affect the enforcement of a covenant implied by virtue of either of them on a disposition before the commencement of this Part

11 Covenants in old form implied in certain cases [871]

(1) Section 76 of the Law of Property Act 1925 applies in relation to a disposition of property made after the commencement of this Part in pursuance of a contract entered into before commencement where –

    (a) the contract contains a term providing for a disposition to which that section would have applied if the disposition had been made before commencement, and
    (b) the existence of the contract and of that term is apparent on the face of the instrument effecting the disposition,

unless there has been an intervening disposition of the property expressed, in accordance with this Part, to be made with full title guarantee.

(2) Section 24(1)(a) of the Land Registration Act 1925 applies in relation to a disposition of a leasehold interest in land made after the commencement of this Part in pursuance of a contract entered into before commencement where –

    (a) the covenant specified in that provision would have been implied on the disposition if it had been made before commencement, and
    (b) the existence of the contract is apparent on the face of the instrument effecting the disposition,

unless there has been an intervening disposition of the leasehold interest expressed, in accordance with this Part, to be made with full title guarantee.

(3) In subsections (1) and (2) an 'intervening disposition' means a disposition after the commencement of this Part to, or to a predecessor in title of, the person by whom the disposition in question is made.

(4) Where in order for subsection (1) or (2) to apply it is necessary for certain matters to be apparent on the face of the instrument effecting the disposition, the contract shall be deemed to contain an implied term that they should so appear.

12 Covenants in new form to be implied in other cases [872]

(1) This section applies to a contract for the disposition of property entered into before the commencement of this Part where the disposition is made after commencement and section 11 (cases in which covenants in old form to be

433

implied) does not apply because there has been an intervening disposition expressed, in accordance with this Part, to be with full title guarantee.

(2) A contract which contains a term that the person making the disposition shall do so as beneficial owner shall be construed as requiring that person to do so by an instrument expressed to be made with full title guarantee.

(3) A contract which contains a term that the person making the disposition shall do so –

   (a) as settlor, or

   (b) as trustee or mortgagee or personal representative,

shall be construed as requiring that person to do so by an instrument expressed to be made with limited title guarantee.

(4) A contract for the disposition of a leasehold interest in land entered into at a date when the title to the leasehold interest was registered shall be construed as requiring the person making the disposition for which it provides to do so by an instrument expressed to be made with full title guarantee.

(5) Where this section applies and the contract provides that any of the covenants to be implied by virtue of section 76 of the Law of Property Act 1925 or section 24(1)(a) of the Land Registration Act 1925 shall be implied in a modified form, the contract shall be construed as requiring a corresponding modification of the covenants implied by virtue of this Part.

13 Application of transitional provisions in relation   [873]
to options

For the purposes of sections 11 and 12 (transitional provisions implication of covenants in old form in certain cases and new form in others) as they apply in relation to a disposition of property in accordance with an option granted before the commencement of this Part and exercised after commencement, the contract for the disposition shall be deemed to have been entered into on the grant of the option.

PART II

MATTERS ARISING IN CONNECTION WITH DEATH

14 Vesting of estate in case of intestacy or lack of executors ... [874]

(2) Any real or personal estate of a person dying before the commencement of this section shall, if it is property to which this subsection applies, vest in the Public Trustee on the commencement of this section.

(3) Subsection (2) above applies to any property –

   (a) if it was vested in the Probate Judge under section 9 of the Administration of Estates Act 1925 immediately before the commencement of this section, or

   (b) if it was not so vested but as at commencement there has been no grant of representation in respect of it and there is no executor with power to obtain such a grant.

(4) Any property vesting in the Public Trustee by virtue of subsection (2) above shall –

   (a) if the deceased died intestate, be treated as vesting in the Public Trustee under section 9(1) of the Administration of Estates Act 1925 (as substituted by subsection (1) above); and

(b) otherwise be treated as vesting in the Public Trustee under section 9(2) of that Act (as so substituted).

(5) Anything done by or in relation to the Probate Judge with respect to property vested in him as mentioned in subsection (3)(a) above shall be treated as having been done by or in relation to the Public Trustee.

(6) So far as may be necessary in consequence of the transfer to the Public Trustee of the functions of the Probate Judge under section 9 of the Administration of Estates Act 1925, any reference in an enactment or instrument to the Probate Judge shall be construed as a reference to the Public Trustee.

15 Registration of land charges after death ... [875]

(5) The amendments made by this section [to sections 3, 5 and 6 of the Land Charges Act 1972] do not apply where the application for registration was made before the commencement of this section, but without prejudice to a person's right to make a new application after commencement.

16 Concurrence of personal representatives in [876] dealings with interests in land ...

(3) The amendments made by subsection (1) apply to contracts made after the commencement of this section.

17 Notices affecting land: absence of knowledge [877] of intended recipient's death

(1) Service of a notice affecting land which would be effective but for the death of the intended recipient is effective despite his death if the person service the notice has no reason to believe that he has died.

(2) Where the person serving a notice affecting land has no reason to believe that the intended recipient has died, the proper address for the purposes of section 7 of the Interpretation Act 1978 (service of documents by post) shall be what would be the proper address apart from his death.

(3) The above provisions do not apply to a notice authorised or required to be served for the purposes of proceedings before –

(a) any court,
(b) any tribunal specified in Schedule 1 to the Tribunals and Inquiries Act 1992 (tribunals within general supervision of Council on Tribunals), or
(c) the Chief Land Registrar or any district registrar or assistant district registrar;

but this is without prejudice to the power to make provision in relation to such proceedings by rules of court, procedural rules within the meaning of section 8 of the Tribunals and Inquiries Act 1992 or rules under section 144 of the Land Registration Act 1925.

18 Notices affecting land: service on personal [878] representatives before filing of grant

(1) A notice affecting land which would have been authorised or required to be served on a person but for his death shall be sufficiently served before a grant of representation has been filed if –

(a) it is addressed to 'The Personal Representatives of' the deceased (naming him) and left at or sent by post to his last known place of residence or business in the United Kingdom, and
(b) a copy of it, similarly addressed, is served on the Public Trustee.

(2) The reference in subsection (1) to the filing of a grant of representation is to the filing at the Principal Registry of the Family Division of the High Court of a copy of a grant of representation in respect of the deceased's estate or, as the case may be, the part of his estate which includes the land in question.

(3) The method of service provided for by this section is not available where provision is made –

(a) by or under any enactment, or
(b) by an agreement in writing,

requiring a different method of service, or expressly prohibiting the method of service provided for by this section, in the circumstances.

PART III

GENERAL PROVISIONS

20 Crown application   [879]

This Act binds the Crown.

21 Consequential amendments and repeals ...   [880]

(3) In the case of section 76 of the Law of Property Act 1925 and section 24(1)(a) of the Land Registration Act 1925, those provisions are repealed in accordance with section 10(1) above (general saving for covenants in old form).

(4) The amendments consequential on Part I of this Act (namely those in paragraphs 1, 2, 3, 5, 7, 9 and 12 of Schedule 1) shall not have effect in relation to any disposition of property to which, by virtue of section 10(1) or 11 above (transitional provisions), section 76 of the Law of Property Act 1925 or section 24(1)(a) of the Land Registration Act 1925 continues to apply.

23 Commencement   [881]

(1) The provisions of this Act come into force on such day as the Lord Chancellor may appoint by order made by statutory instrument.

(2) Different days may be appointed for different provisions and for different purposes.

NB All of the above provisions came into force on 1 July1995 and the Act was fully in force on that date.

[As amended by the Trusts of Land and Appointment of Trustees Act 1996, s25(2), Schedule 4.]

AGRICULTURAL TENANCIES ACT 1995
(1995 c 8)

PART I

GENERAL PROVISIONS

1 Meaning of 'farm business tenancy'   [882]

(1) A tenancy is a 'farm business tenancy' for the purposes of this Act if –

(a) it meets the business conditions together with either the agriculture condition or the notice conditions, and

(b) it is not a tenancy which, by virtue of section 2 of this Act, cannot be a farm business tenancy.

(2) The business conditions are –

(a) that all or part of the land comprised in the tenancy is farmed for the purposes of a trade or business, and
(b) that, since the beginning of the tenancy, all or part of the land so comprised has been so farmed.

(3) The agriculture condition is that, having regard to –

(a) the terms of the tenancy,
(b) the use of the land comprised in the tenancy,
(c) the nature of any commercial activities carried on on that land, and
(d) any other relevant circumstances,

the character of the tenancy is primarily or wholly agricultural.

(4) The notice conditions are –

(a) that, on or before the relevant day, the landlord and the tenant each gave the other a written notice –

(i) identifying (by name or otherwise) the land to be comprised in the tenancy or proposed tenancy, and
(ii) containing a statement to the effect that the person giving the notice intends that the tenancy or proposed tenancy is to be, and remain, a farm business tenancy, and

(b) that, at the beginning of the tenancy, having regard to the terms of the tenancy and any other relevant circumstances, the character of the tenancy was primarily or wholly agricultural.

(5) In subsection (4) above 'the relevant day' means whichever is the earlier of the following –

(a) the day on which the parties enter into any instrument creating the tenancy, other than an agreement to enter into a tenancy on a future date, or
(b) the beginning of the tenancy.

(6) The written notice referred to in subsection (4) above must not be included in any instrument creating the tenancy.

(7) If in any proceedings –

(a) any question arises as to whether a tenancy was a farm business tenancy at any time, and
(b) it is proved that all or part of the land comprised in the tenancy was farmed for the purposes of a trade or business at that time,

it shall be presumed, unless the contrary is proved, that all or part of the land so comprised has been so farmed since the beginning of the tenancy.

(8) Any use of land in breach of the terms of the tenancy, any commercial activities carried on in breach of those terms, and any cessation of such activities in breach of those terms, shall be disregarded in determining whether at any time the tenancy meets the business conditions or the agriculture condition, unless the landlord or his predecessor in title has consented to the breach or the landlord has acquiesced in the breach.

2 Tenancies which cannot be farm business tenancies [883]

(1) A tenancy cannot be a farm business tenancy for the purposes of this Act if –

(a) the tenancy begins before 1st September 1995, or

(b) it is a tenancy of an agricultural holding beginning on or after that date with respect to which, by virtue of section 4 of this Act, the Agricultural Holdings Act 1986 applies.

(2) In this section 'agricultural holding' has the same meaning as in the Agricultural Holdings Act 1986.

5 Tenancies for more than two years to continue from year to year unless terminated by notice [884]

(1) A farm business tenancy for a term of more than two years shall, instead of terminating on the term date, continue (as from that date) as a tenancy from year to year, but otherwise on the terms of the original tenancy so far as applicable, unless at least twelve months but less than twenty-four months before the term date a written notice has been given by either party to the other of his intention to terminate the tenancy.

(2) In subsection (1) above 'the term date', in relation to a fixed term tenancy, means the date fixed for the expiry of the term.

(3) For the purposes of section 140 of the Law of Property Act 1925 (apportionment of conditions on severance of reversion), a notice under subsection 1) above shall be taken to be a notice to quit.

(4) This section has effect notwithstanding any agreement to the contrary.

8 Tenant's right to remove fixtures and buildings [885]

(1) Subject to the provision of this section –

(a) any fixture (of whatever description) affixed, whether for the purposes of agriculture or not, to the holding by the tenant under a farm business tenancy, and
(b) any building erected by him on the holding,

may be removed by the tenant at any time during the continuance of the tenancy or at any time after the termination of the tenancy when he remains in possession as tenant (whether or not under a new tenancy), and shall remain his property so long as he may remove it by virtue of this subsection.

(2) Subsection (1) above shall not apply –

(a) to a fixture affixed or a building erected in pursuance of some obligation,
(b) to a fixture affixed or a building erected instead of some fixture or building belonging to the landlord,
(c) to a fixture or building in respect of which the tenant has obtained compensation under section 16 of this Act or otherwise, or
(d) to a fixture or building in respect of which the landlord has given his consent under section 17 of this Act on condition that the tenant agrees not to remove it and which the tenant has agreed not to remove.

(3) In the removal of a fixture or building by virtue of subsection (1) above, the tenant shall not do any avoidable damage to the holding,

(4) Immediately after removing a fixture or building by virtue of subsection (1) above, the tenant shall make good all damage to the holding that is occasioned by the removal.

(5) This section applies to a fixture or building acquired by a tenant as it applies to a fixture or building affixed or erected by him.

(6) Except as provided by subsection (2)(d) above, this section has effect notwithstanding any agreement or custom to the contrary.

(7) No right to remove fixtures that subsists otherwise than by virtue of this section shall be exercisable by the tenant under a farm business tenancy.

PART II

RENT REVIEW UNDER FARM BUSINESS TENANCY

9 Application of Part II [886]

This part of this Act applies in relation to a farm business tenancy (notwithstanding any agreement to the contrary) unless the tenancy is created by an instrument which –

(a) expressly states that the rent is not to be reviewed during the tenancy, or
(b) provides that the rent is to be varied, at a specified time or times during the tenancy –

(i) by or to a specified amount, or
(ii) in accordance with a specified formula which does not preclude a reduction and which does not require or permit the exercise by any person of any judgment or discretion in relation to the determination of the rent of the holding,

but otherwise is to remain fixed.

10 Notice requiring statutory rent review [887]

(1) The landlord or tenant under a farm business tenancy in relation to which this Part of this Act applies may by notice in writing given to the other (in this Part of this Act referred to as a 'statutory review notice') require that the rent to be payable in respect of the holding as from the review date shall be referred to arbitration in accordance with this Act.

(2) In this Part of this Act 'the review date', in relation to a statutory review notice, means a date which –

(a) is specified in the notice, and
(b) complies with subsections (3) to (6) below.

(3) The review date must be at least twelve months but less than twenty-four months after the day on which the statutory review notice is given ...

12 Appointment of arbitrator [888]

Where a statutory review notice has been given in relation to a farm business tenancy, but –

(a) no arbitrator has been appointed under an agreement made since the notice was given, and
(b) no person has been appointed under such an agreement to determine the question of the rent (otherwise than as arbitrator) on a basis agreed by the parties,

either party may, at any time during the period of six months ending with the review date, apply to the President of the Royal Institution of Chartered Surveyors (in this Act referred to as 'the RICS') for the appointment of an arbitrator by him.

13 Amount of rent [889]

(1) On any reference made in pursuance of a statutory review notice, the arbitrator shall determine the rent properly payable in respect of the holding at the review

date and accordingly shall, with effect from that date, increase or reduce the rent previously payable or direct that it shall continue unchanged. ...

14 Interpretation of Part II   [890]

In this Part of this Act, unless the context otherwise requires –

'the review date', in relation to a statutory review notice, has the meaning given by section 10(2) of this Act;

'statutory review notice' has the meaning given by section 10(1) of this Act.

PART III

COMPENSATION ON TERMINATION
OF FARM BUSINESS TENANCY

15 Meaning of 'tenant's improvement'   [891]

For the purposes of this Part of this Act a 'tenant's improvement', in relation to any farm business tenancy, means –

(a) any physical improvement which is made on the holding by the tenant by his own effort or wholly or partly at his own expense, or

(b) any intangible advantage which –

(i) is obtained for the holding by the tenant by his own effort or wholly or partly at his own expense, and

(ii) becomes attached to the holding,

and references to the provision of a tenant's improvement are references to the making by the tenant of any physical improvement falling within paragraph (a) above or the obtaining by the tenant of any intangible advantage falling within paragraph (b) above.

16 Tenant's right to compensation for   [892]
tenant's improvement

(1) The tenant under a farm business tenancy shall, subject to the provisions of this Part of this Act, be entitled on the termination of the tenancy, on quitting the holding, to obtain from his landlord compensation in respect of any tenant's improvement.

(2) A tenant shall not be entitled to compensation under this section in respect of –

(a) any physical improvement which is removed from the holding, or

(b) any intangible advantage which does not remain attached to the holding.
...

17 Consent of landlord as condition of compensation   [893]
for tenant's improvement

(1) A tenant shall not be entitled to compensation under section 16 of this Act in respect of any tenant's improvement unless the landlord has given his consent in writing to the provision of the tenant's improvement.

(2) Any such consent may be given in the instrument creating the tenancy or elsewhere. ...

18 Conditions in relation to compensation for planning permission **[894]**

(1) A tenant shall not be entitled to compensation under section 16 of this Act in respect of a tenant's improvement which consists of planning permission unless –

(a) the landlord has given his consent in writing to the making of the application for planning permission,

(b) that consent is expressed to be given for the purpose –

(i) of enabling a specified physical improvement falling within paragraph (a) of section 15 of this Act lawfully to be provided by the tenant, or

(ii) of enabling the tenant lawfully to effect a specified change of use, and

(c) on the termination of the tenancy, the specified physical improvement has not been completed or the specified change of use has not been effected. ...

19 Reference to arbitration of refusal or failure to give consent or of condition attached to consent **[895]**

(1) Where, in relation to any tenant's improvement, the tenant under a farm business tenancy is aggrieved by –

(a) the refusal of his landlord to give his consent under section 17(1) of this Act,

(b) the failure of his landlord to give such consent within two months of a written request by the tenant for such consent, or

(c) any variation in the terms of the tenancy required by the landlord as a condition of giving such consent,

the tenant may by notice in writing given to the landlord demand that the question shall be referred to arbitration under this section; ...

(7) If the arbitrator gives his approval, that approval shall have effect for the purposes of this Part of this Act and for the purposes of the terms of the farm business tenancy as if it were the consent of the landlord. ...

20 Amount of compensation for tenant's improvement not consisting of planning permission **[896]**

(1) The amount of compensation payable to the tenant under section 16 of this Act in respect of any tenant's improvement shall be an amount equal to the increase attributable to the improvement in the value of the holding at the termination of the tenancy as land comprised in a tenancy.

(2) Where a landlord and the tenant have entered into an agreement in writing whereby any benefit is given or allowed to the tenant in consideration of the provision of a tenant's improvement, the amount of compensation otherwise payable in respect of that improvement shall be reduced by the proportion which the value of the benefit bears to the amount of the total cost of providing the improvement. ...

(5) This section does not apply where the tenant's improvement consists of planning permission.

21 Amount of compensation for planning permission **[897]**

(1) The amount of compensation payable to the tenant under section 16 of this Act in respect of a tenant's improvement which consists of planning permission shall be an amount equal to the increase attributable to the fact that the relevant development is authorised by the planning permission in the value of the holding at the termination of the tenancy as land comprised in a tenancy.

(2) In subsection (1) above, 'the relevant development' means the physical improvement or change of use specified in the landlord's consent under section 18 of this Act in accordance with subsection (1)(b) of that section.

(3) Where the landlord and the tenant have entered into an agreement in writing whereby any benefit is given or allowed to the tenant in consideration of the obtaining of planning permission by the tenant, the amount of compensation otherwise payable in respect of that permission shall be reduced by the proportion which the value of the benefit bears to the amount of the total cost of obtaining the permission.

22 Settlement of claims for compensation   [898]

(1) Any claim by the tenant under a farm business tenancy for compensation under section 16 of this Act shall, subject to the provisions of this section, be determined by arbitration under this section.

(2) No such claim for compensation shall be enforceable unless before the end of the period of two months beginning with the date of the termination of the tenancy the tenant has given notice in writing to his landlord of his intention to make the claim and of the nature of the claim. ...

27 Interpretation of Part III   [899]

In this Part of this Act, unless the context otherwise requires –

'planning permission' has the meaning given by section 336(1) of the Town and Country Planning Act 1990;

'tenant's improvement', and references to the provision of such an improvement, have the meaning given by section 15 of this Act.

30 General provisions applying to arbitrations under Act   [900]

(1) Any matter which is required to be determined by arbitration under this Act shall be determined by the arbitration of a sole arbitrator. ...

32 Power of limited owners to give consents, etc   [901]

The landlord under a farm business tenancy, whatever his estate or interest in the holding, may, for the purposes of this Act, give any consent, make any agreement or do or have done to him any other act which he might give, make, do or have done to him if he were owner in fee simple or, if his interest is an interest in a leasehold, were absolutely entitled to that leasehold.

33 Power to apply and raise capital money   [902]

(1) The purposes authorised by section 73 of the Settled Land Act 1925 or section 26 of the Universities and College Estates Act 1925 for the application of capital money shall include –

(a) the payment of expenses incurred by a landlord under a farm business tenancy in, or in connection with, the making of any physical improvement on the holding,
(b) the payment of compensation under section 16 of this Act, and
(c) the payment of the costs, charges and expenses incurred by him on a reference to arbitration under section 19 or 22 of this Act.

(2) The purposes authorised by section 71 of the Settled Land Act 1925 as

purposes for which money may be raised by mortgage shall include the payment of compensation under section 16 of this Act.

(3) Where the landlord under a farm business tenancy –

(a) is a tenant for life or in a fiduciary position, and

(b) is liable to pay compensation under section 16 of this Act,

he may require the sum payable as compensation and any costs, charges and expenses incurred by him in connection with the tenant's claim under that section to be paid out of any capital money held on the same trusts as the settled land.

(4) In subsection (3) above –

'capital money' includes any personal estate held on the same trusts as the land.

34 Estimation of best rent for purposes of Acts and [903] other instruments

(1) In estimating the best rent or reservation in the nature of rent of land comprised in a farm business tenancy for the purposes of a relevant instrument, it shall not be necessary to take into account against the tenant any increase in the value of that land arising from any tenant's improvements.

(2) In subsection (1) above –

'a relevant instrument' means any Act of Parliament, deed or other instrument which authorises a lease to be made on the condition that the best rent or reservation in the nature of rent is reserved;

'tenant's improvement' has the meaning given by section 15 of this Act.

37 Crown land [904]

(1) This Act shall apply in relation to land in which there subsists, or has at any material time subsisted, a Crown interest as it applies in relation to land in which no such interest subsists or has ever subsisted. ...

(3) If any question arises as to who is to be treated as the owner of a Crown interest, that question shall be referred to the Treasury, whose decision shall be final.

(4) In subsections (1) and (3) above 'Crown interest' means an interest which belongs to Her Majesty in right of the Crown or of the Duchy of Lancaster or to the Duchy of Cornwall, or to a government department, or which is held in trust for Her Majesty for the purposes of a government department. ...

38 Interpretation [905]

(1) In this Act, unless the context otherwise requires –

'agriculture' includes horticulture, fruit growing, seed growing, dairy farming and livestock breeding and keeping, the use of land as grazing land, meadow land, osier land, market gardens and nursery grounds, and the use of land for woodlands where that use is ancillary to the farming of land for other agricultural purposes, and 'agricultural' shall be construed accordingly;

'building' includes any part of a building;

'fixed term tenancy' means any tenancy other than a periodic tenancy;

'holding', in relation to a farm business tenancy, means the aggregate of the land comprised in the tenancy;

'landlord' includes any person from time to time deriving title from the original landlord;

'livestock' includes any creature kept for the production of food, wool, skins or fur or for the purpose of its use in the farming of land; ...

'tenancy' means any tenancy other than a tenancy at will, and includes a sub-tenancy and an agreement for a tenancy or sub-tenancy;

'tenant' includes a sub-tenant and any person deriving title from the original tenant or sub-tenant;

'termination', in relation to a tenancy, means the cesser of the tenancy by reason of effluxion of time or from any other cause.

(2) References in this Act to the farming of land include references to the carrying on in relation to land of any agricultural activity.

(3) A tenancy granted pursuant to a contract shall be taken for the purposes of this Act to have been granted when the contract was entered into.

(4) For the purposes of this Act a tenancy begins on the day on which, under the terms of the tenancy, the tenant is entitled to possession under that tenancy; and references in this Act to the beginning of the tenancy are references to that day.

(5) The designations of landlord and tenant shall continue to apply until the conclusion of any proceedings taken under this Act in respect of compensation.

41 Short title, commencement and extent ... [906]

(2) This Act shall come into force on 1st September 1995. ...

[As amended by the Trusts of Land and Appointment of Trustees Act 1996, s25(2), Schedule 4.]

LANDLORD AND TENANT (COVENANTS) ACT 1995
(1995 c 30)

1 Tenancies to which the Act applies [907]

(1) Sections 3 to 16 and 21 apply only to new tenancies.

(2) Sections 17 to 20 apply to both new and other tenancies.

(3) For the purposes of this section a tenancy is a new tenancy if it is granted on or after the date on which this Act comes into force otherwise than in pursuance of—

    (a) an agreement entered into before that date, or
    (b) an order of a court made before that date.

(4) Subsection (3) has effect subject to section 20(1) in the case of overriding leases granted under section 19.

(5) Without prejudice to the generality of subsection (3), that subsection applies to the grant of a tenancy where by virtue of any variation of a tenancy there is a deemed surrender and regrant as it applies to any other grant of a tenancy.

(6) Where a tenancy granted on or after the date on which this Act comes into force is so granted in pursuance of an option granted before that date, the tenancy shall be regarded for the purposes of subsection (3) as granted in pursuance of an agreement entered into before that date (and accordingly is not a new tenancy), whether or not the option was exercised before that date.

(7) In subsection (6) 'option' includes right of first refusal.

2 Covenants to which the Act applies [908]

(1) This Act applies to a landlord covenant or a tenant covenant of a tenancy –

(a) whether or not the covenant has reference to the subject matter of the tenancy, and
(b) whether the covenant is express, implied or imposed by law,

but does not apply to a covenant falling within subsection (2).

(2) Nothing in this Act affects any covenant imposed in pursuance of –

(a) section 35 or 155 of the Housing Act 1985 (covenants for repayment of discount on early disposals);
(b) paragraph 1 of Schedule 6A to that Act (covenants requiring redemption of landlord's share); or
(c) paragraph 1 or 3 of Schedule 2 to the Housing Associations Act 1985 (covenants for repayment of discount on early disposals or for restricting disposals).

3 Transmission of benefit and burden of covenants [909]

(1) The benefit and burden of all landlord and tenant covenants of a tenancy –

(a) shall be annexed and incident to the whole, and to each and every part, of the premises demised by the tenancy and of the reversion in them, and
(b) shall in accordance with this section pass on an assignment of the whole or any part of those premises or of the reversion in them.

(2) Where the assignment is by the tenant under the tenancy, then as from the assignment the assignee –

(a) becomes bound by the tenant covenants of the tenancy except to the extent that –

(i) immediately before the assignment they did not bind the assignor, or
(ii) they fall to be complied with in relation to any demised premises not comprised in the assignment; and

(b) becomes entitled to the benefit of the landlord covenants of the tenancy except to the extent that they fall to be complied with in relation to any such premises.

(3) Where the assignment is by the landlord under the tenancy, then as from the assignment the assignee –

(a) becomes bound by the landlord covenants of the tenancy except to the extent that –

(i) immediately before the assignment they did not bind the assignor, or
(ii) they fall to be complied with in relation to any demised premises not comprised in the assignment; and

(b) becomes entitled to the benefit of the tenant covenants of the tenancy except to the extent that they fall to be complied with in relation to any such premises.

(4) In determining for the purposes of subsection (2) or (3) whether any covenant bound the assignor immediately before the assignment, any waiver or release of the covenant which (in whatever terms) is expressed to be personal to the assignor shall be disregarded.

(5) Any landlord or tenant covenant of a tenancy which is restrictive of the user of land shall, as well as being capable of enforcement against an assignee, be capable of being enforced against any other person who is the owner or occupier

of any demised premises to which the covenant relates, even though there is no express provision in the tenancy to that effect.

(6) Nothing in this section shall operate –

(a) in the case of a covenant which (in whatever terms) is expressed to be personal to any person, to make the covenant enforceable by or (as the case may be) against any other person; or

(b) to make a covenant enforceable against any person if, apart from this section, it would not be enforceable against him by reason of its not having been registered under the Land Registration Act 1925 or the Land Charges Act 1972.

(7) To the extent that there remains in force any rule of law by virtue of which the burden of a covenant whose subject matter is not in existence at the time when it is made does not run with the land affected unless the covenantor covenants on behalf of himself and his assigns, that rule of law is hereby abolished in relation to tenancies.

4 Transmission of rights of re-entry   [910]

The benefit of a landlord's right of re-entry under a tenancy –

(a) shall be annexed and incident to the whole, and to each and every part, of the reversion in the premises demised by the tenancy,

and

(b) shall pass on an assignment of the whole or any part of the reversion in those premises.

5 Tenant released from covenants on assignment   [911]
of tenancy

(1) This section applies where a tenant assigns premises demised to him under a tenancy.

(2) If the tenant assigns the whole of the premises demised to him, he –

(a) is released from the tenant covenants of the tenancy, and

(b) ceases to be entitled to the benefit of the landlord covenants of the tenancy,

as from the assignment.

(3) If the tenant assigns part only of the premises demised to him, then as from the assignment he –

(a) is released from the tenant covenants of the tenancy, and

(b) ceases to be entitled to the benefit of the landlord covenants of the tenancy,

only to the extent that those covenants fall to be complied with in relation to that part of the demised premises.

(4) This section applies as mentioned in subsection (1) whether or not the tenant is tenant of the whole of the premises comprised in the tenancy.

6 Landlord may be released from covenants on   [912]
assignment of reversion

(1) This section applies where a landlord assigns the reversion in premises of which he is the landlord under a tenancy.

(2) If the landlord assigns the reversion in the whole of the premises of which he is the landlord –

(a) he may apply to be released from the landlord covenants of the tenancy in accordance with section 8; and

(b) if he is so released from all of those covenants, he ceases to be entitled to the benefit of the tenant covenants of the tenancy as from the assignment.

(3) If the landlord assigns the reversion in part only of the premises of which he is the landlord –

(a) he may apply to be so released from the landlord covenants of the tenancy to the extent that they fall to be complied with in relation to that part of those premises; and

(b) if he is, to that extent, so released from all of those covenants, then as from the assignment he ceases to be entitled to the benefit of the tenant covenants only to the extent that they fall to be complied with in relation to that part of those premises.

(4) This section applies as mentioned in subsection (1) whether or not the landlord is landlord of the whole of the premises comprised in the tenancy.

7 Former landlord may be released from covenants [913] on assignment of reversion

(1) This section applies where –

(a) a landlord assigns the reversion in premises of which he is the landlord under a tenancy, and

(b) immediately before the assignment a former landlord of the premises remains bound by a landlord covenant of the tenancy ('the relevant covenant').

(2) If immediately before the assignment the former landlord does not remain the landlord of any other premises demised by the tenancy, he may apply to be released from the relevant covenant in accordance with section 8.

(3) In any other case the former landlord may apply to be so released from the relevant covenant to the extent that it falls to be complied with in relation to any premises comprised in the assignment.

(4) If the former landlord is so released from every landlord covenant by which he remained bound immediately before the assignment, he ceases to be entitled to the benefit of the tenant covenants of the tenancy.

(5) If the former landlord is so released from every such landlord covenant to the extent that it falls to be complied with in relation to any premises comprised in the assignment, he ceases to be entitled to the benefit of the tenant covenants of the tenancy to the extent that they fall to be so complied with.

(6) This section applies as mentioned in subsection (1) –

(a) whether or not the landlord making the assignment is landlord of the whole of the premises comprised in the tenancy; and

(b) whether or not the former landlord has previously applied (whether under section 6 or this section) to be released from the relevant covenant.

8 Procedure for seeking release from a covenant [914] under section 6 or 7

(1) For the purposes of section 6 or 7 an application for the release of a covenant to any extent is made by serving on the tenant, either before or within the period of four weeks beginning with the date of the assignment in question, a notice informing him of –

(a) the proposed assignment or (as the case may be) the fact that the assignment has taken place, and
(b) the request for the covenant to be released to that extent.

(2) Where an application for the release of a covenant is made in accordance with subsection (1), the covenant is released to the extent mentioned in the notice if –

(a) the tenant does not, within the period of four weeks beginning with the day on which the notice is served, serve on the landlord or former landlord a notice in writing objecting to the release, or
(b) the tenant does so serve such a notice but the court, on the application of the landlord or former landlord, makes a declaration that it is reasonable for the covenant to be so released, or
(c) the tenant serves on the landlord or former landlord a notice in writing consenting to the release and, if he has previously served a notice objecting to it, stating that that notice is withdrawn.

(3) Any release from a covenant in accordance with this section shall be regarded as occurring at the time when the assignment in question takes place.

(4) In this section –

(a) 'the tenant' means the tenant of the premises comprised in the assignment in question (or, if different parts of those premises are held under the tenancy by different tenants, each of those tenants);
(b) any reference to the landlord or the former landlord is a reference to the landlord referred to in section 6 or the former landlord referred to in section 7, as the case may be; and
(c) 'the court' means a county court.

9 Apportionment of liability under covenants binding both assignor and assignee of tenancy or reversion [915]

(1) This section applies where –

(a) a tenant assigns part only of the premises demised to him by a tenancy;
(b) after the assignment both the tenant and his assignee are to be bound by a non-attributable tenant covenant of the tenancy; and
(c) the tenant and his assignee agree that as from the assignment liability under the covenant is to be apportioned between them in such manner as is specified in the agreement.

(2) This section also applies where –

(a) a landlord assigns the reversion in part only of the premises of which he is the landlord under a tenancy;
(b) after the assignment both the landlord and his assignee are to be bound by a non-attributable landlord covenant of the tenancy; and
(c) the landlord and his assignee agree that as from the assignment liability under the covenant is to be apportioned between them in such manner as is specified in the agreement.

(3) Any such agreement as is mentioned in subsection (1) or (2) may apportion liability in such a way that a party to the agreement is exonerated from all liability under a covenant.

(4) In any case falling within subsection (1) or (2) the parties to the agreement may apply for the apportionment to become binding on the appropriate person in accordance with section 10.

(5) In any such case the parties to the agreement may also apply for the apportionment to become binding on any person (other than the appropriate

person) who is for the time being entitled to enforce the covenant in question; and section 10 shall apply in relation to such an application as it applies in relation to an application made with respect to the appropriate person.

(6) For the purposes of this section a covenant is, in relation to an assignment, a 'non-attributable' covenant if it does not fall to be complied with in relation to any premises comprised in the assignment.

(7) In this section 'the appropriate person' means either –

(a) the landlord of the entire premises referred to in subsection (1)(a) (or, if different parts of those premises are held under the tenancy by different landlords, each of those landlords), or

(b) the tenant of the entire premises referred to in subsection (2)(a) (or, if different parts of those premises are held under the tenancy by different tenants, each of those tenants),

depending on whether the agreement in question falls within subsection (1) or subsection (2).

10 Procedure for making apportionment bind [916]
other party to lease

(1) For the purposes of section 9 the parties to an agreement falling within subsection (1) or (2) of that section apply for an apportionment to become binding on the appropriate person if, either before or within the period of four weeks beginning with the date of the assignment in question, they serve on that person a notice informing him of –

(a) the proposed assignment or (as the case may be) the fact that the assignment has taken place;

(b) the prescribed particulars of the agreement; and

(c) their request that the apportionment should become binding on him.

(2) Where an application for an apportionment to become binding has been made in accordance with subsection (1), the apportionment becomes binding on the appropriate person if –

(a) he does not, within the period of four weeks beginning with the day on which the notice is served under subsection (1), serve on the parties to the agreement a notice in writing objecting to the apportionment becoming binding on him, or

(b) he does so serve such a notice but the court, on the application of the parties to the agreement, makes a declaration that it is reasonable for the apportionment to become binding on him, or

(c) he serves on the parties to the agreement a notice in writing consenting to the apportionment becoming binding on him and, if he has previously served a notice objecting thereto, stating that that notice is withdrawn.

(3) Where any apportionment becomes binding in accordance with this section, this shall be regarded as occurring at the time when the assignment in question takes place.

(4) In this section –

'the appropriate person' has the same meaning as in section 9;

'the court' means a county court;

'prescribed' means prescribed by virtue of section 27.

11 Assignments in breach of covenant or by operation   [917]
of law

(1) This section provides for the operation of sections 5 to 10 in relation to assignments in breach of a covenant of a tenancy or assignments by operation of law ('excluded assignments').

(2) In the case of an excluded assignment subsection (2) or (3) of section 5 –

(a) shall not have the effect mentioned in that subsection in relation to the tenant as from that assignment, but
(b) shall have that effect as from the next assignment (if any) of the premises assigned by him which is not an excluded assignment.

(3) In the case of an excluded assignment subsection (2) or (3) of section 6 or 7 –

(a) shall not enable the landlord or former landlord to apply for such a release as is mentioned in that subsection as from that assignment, but
(b) shall apply on the next assignment (if any) of the reversion assigned by the landlord which is not an excluded assignment so as to enable the landlord or former landlord to apply for any such release as from that subsequent assignment.

(4) Where subsection (2) or (3) of section 6 or 7 does so apply –

(a) any reference in that section to the assignment (except where it relates to the time as from which the release takes effect) is a reference to the excluded assignment; but
(b) in that excepted case and in section 8 as it applies in relation to any application under that section made by virtue of subsection (3) above, any reference to the assignment or proposed assignment is a reference to any such subsequent assignment as is mentioned in that subsection.

(5) In the case of an excluded assignment section 9 –

(a) shall not enable the tenant or landlord and his assignee to apply for an agreed apportionment to become binding in accordance with section 10 as from that assignment, but
(b) shall apply on the next assignment (if any) of the premises or reversion assigned by the tenant or landlord which is not an excluded assignment so as to enable him and his assignee to apply for such an apportionment to become binding in accordance with section 10 as from that subsequent assignment.

(6) Where section 9 does so apply –

(a) any reference in that section to the assignment or the assignee under it is a reference to the excluded assignment and the assignee under that assignment; but
(b) in section 10 as it applies in relation to any application under section 9 made by virtue of subsection (5) above, any reference to the assignment or proposed assignment is a reference to any such subsequent assignment as is mentioned in that subsection.

(7) If any such subsequent assignment as is mentioned in subsection (2), (3) or (5) above comprises only part of the premises assigned by the tenant or (as the case may be) only part of the premises the reversion in which was assigned by the landlord on the excluded assignment –

(a) the relevant provision or provisions of section 5, 6, 7 or 9 shall only have the effect mentioned in that subsection to the extent that the covenants or covenant in question fall or falls to be complied with in relation to that part of those premises; and
(b) that subsection may accordingly apply on different occasions in relation to different parts of those premises.

12 Covenants with management companies, etc   [918]

(1) This section applies where –

(a) a person other than the landlord or tenant ('the third party') is under a covenant of a tenancy liable (as principal) to discharge any function with respect to all or any of the demised premises ('the relevant function'); and

(b) that liability is not the liability of a guarantor or any other financial liability referable to the performance or otherwise of a covenant of the tenancy by another party to it.

(2) To the extent that any covenant of the tenancy confers any rights against the third party with respect to the relevant function, then for the purposes of the transmission of the benefit of the covenant in accordance with this Act it shall be treated as if it were –

(a) a tenant covenant of the tenancy to the extent that those rights are exercisable by the landlord; and

(b) a landlord covenant of the tenancy to the extent that those rights are exercisable by the tenant.

(3) To the extent that any covenant of the tenancy confers any rights exercisable by the third party with respect to the relevant function, then for the purposes mentioned in subsection (4), it shall be treated as if it were –

(a) a tenant covenant of the tenancy to the extent that those rights are exercisable against the tenant; and

(b) a landlord covenant of the tenancy to the extent that those rights are exercisable against the landlord.

(4) The purposes mentioned in subsection (3) are –

(a) the transmission of the burden of the covenant in accordance with this Act; and

(b) any release from, or apportionment of liability in respect of, the covenant in accordance with this Act.

(5) In relation to the release of the landlord from any covenant which is to be treated as a landlord covenant by virtue of subsection (3), section 8 shall apply as if any reference to the tenant were a reference to the third party.

13 Covenants binding two or more persons   [919]

(1) Where in consequence of this Act two or more persons are bound by the same covenant, they are so bound both jointly and severally.

(2) Subject to section 24(2), where by virtue of this Act –

(a) two or more persons are bound jointly and severally by the same covenant, and

(b) any of the persons so bound is released from the covenant,

the release does not extend to any other of those persons.

(3) For the purpose of providing for contribution between persons who, by virtue of this Act, are bound jointly and severally by a covenant, the Civil Liability (Contribution) Act 1978 shall have effect as if –

(a) liability to a person under a covenant were liability in respect of damage suffered by that person;

(b) references to damage accordingly included a breach of a covenant of a tenancy; and

(c) section 7(2) of that Act were omitted.

15 Enforcement of covenants [920]

(1) Where any tenant covenant of a tenancy, or any right of re-entry contained in a tenancy, is enforceable by the reversioner in respect of any premises demised by the tenancy, it shall also be so enforceable by –

(a) any person (other than the reversioner) who, as the holder of the immediate reversion in those premises, is for the time being entitled to the rents and profits under the tenancy in respect of those premises, or
(b) any mortgagee in possession of the reversion in those premises who is so entitled.

(2) Where any landlord covenant of a tenancy is enforceable against the reversioner in respect of any premises demised by the tenancy, it shall also be so enforceable against any person falling within subsection (1)(a) or (b).

(3) Where any landlord covenant of a tenancy is enforceable by the tenant in respect of any premises demised by the tenancy, it shall also be so enforceable by any mortgagee in possession of those premises under a mortgage granted by the tenant.

(4) Where any tenant covenant of a tenancy, or any right of re-entry contained in a tenancy, is enforceable against the tenant in respect of any premises demised by the tenancy, it shall also be so enforceable against any such mortgagee.

(5) Nothing in this section shall operate –

(a) in the case of a covenant which (in whatever terms) is expressed to be personal to any person, to make the covenant enforceable by or (as the case may be) against any other person; or
(b) to make a covenant enforceable against any person if, apart from this section, it would not be enforceable against him by reason of its not having been registered under the Land Registration Act 1925 or the Land Charges Act 1972.

(6) In this section –

'mortgagee' and 'mortgage' include 'chargee' and 'charge' respectively;

'the reversioner', in relation to a tenancy, means the holder for the time being of the interest of the landlord under the tenancy.

16 Tenant guaranteeing performance of covenant [921] by assignee

(1) Where on an assignment a tenant is to any extent released from a tenant covenant of a tenancy by virtue of this Act ('the relevant covenant'), nothing in this Act (and in particular section 25) shall preclude him from entering into an authorised guarantee agreement with respect to the performance of that covenant by the assignee.

(2) For the purposes of this section an agreement is an authorised guarantee agreement if –

(a) under it the tenant guarantees the performance of the relevant covenant to any extent by the assignee; and
(b) it is entered into in the circumstances set out in subsection (3); and
(c) its provisions conform with subsections (4) and (5).

(3) Those circumstances are as follows –

(a) by virtue of a covenant against assignment (whether absolute or qualified) the assignment cannot be effected without the consent of the landlord under the tenancy or some other person;

(b) any such consent is given subject to a condition (lawfully imposed) that the tenant is to enter into an agreement guaranteeing the performance of the covenant by the assignee; and

(c) the agreement is entered into by the tenant in pursuance of that condition.

(4) An agreement is not an authorised guarantee agreement to the extent that it purports –

(a) to impose on the tenant any requirement to guarantee in any way the performance of the relevant covenant by any person other than the assignee; or

(b) to impose on the tenant any liability, restriction or other requirement (of whatever nature) in relation to any time after the assignee is released from that covenant by virtue of this Act.

(5) Subject to subsection (4), an authorised guarantee agreement may –

(a) impose on the tenant any liability as sole or principal debtor in respect of any obligation owed by the assignee under the relevant covenant;

(b) impose on the tenant liabilities as guarantor in respect of the assignee's performance of that covenant which are no more onerous than those to which he would be subject in the event of his being liable as sole or principal debtor in respect of any obligation owed by the assignee under that covenant;

(c) require the tenant, in the event of the tenancy assigned by him being disclaimed, to enter into a new tenancy of the premises comprised in the assignment –

(i) whose term expires not later than the term of the tenancy assigned by the tenant, and

(ii) whose tenant covenants are no more onerous than those of that tenancy;

(d) make provision incidental or supplementary to any provision made by virtue of any of paragraphs (a) to (c).

(6) Where a person ('the former tenant') is to any extent released from a covenant of a tenancy by virtue of section 11(2) as from an assignment and the assignor under the assignment enters into an authorised guarantee agreement with the landlord with respect to the performance of that covenant by the assignee under the assignment –

(a) the landlord may require the former tenant to enter into an agreement under which he guarantees, on terms corresponding to those of that authorised guarantee agreement, the performance of that covenant by the assignee under the assignment; and

(b) if its provisions conform with subsections (4) and (5), any such agreement shall be an authorised guarantee agreement for the purposes of this section; and

(c) in the application of this section in relation to any such agreement –

(i) subsections (2)(b) and (c) and (3) shall be omitted, and

(ii) any reference to the tenant or to the assignee shall be read as a reference to the former tenant or to the assignee under the assignment.

(7) For the purposes of subsection (1) it is immaterial that –

(a) the tenant has already made an authorised guarantee agreement in respect of a previous assignment by him of the tenancy referred to in that subsection, it having been subsequently revested in him following a disclaimer on behalf of the previous assignee, or

(b) the tenancy referred to in that subsection is a new tenancy entered into by the tenant in pursuance of an authorised guarantee agreement;

and in any such case subsections (2) to (5) shall apply accordingly.

(8) It is hereby declared that the rules of law relating to guarantees (and in particular those relating to the release of sureties) are, subject to its terms, applicable in relation to any authorised guarantee agreement as in relation to any other guarantee agreement.

17 Restriction on liability of former tenant or his guarantor for rent or service charge, etc [922]

(1) This section applies where a person ('the former tenant') is as a result of an assignment no longer a tenant under a tenancy but –

(a) (in the case of a tenancy which is a new tenancy) he has under an authorised guarantee agreement guaranteed the performance by his assignee of a tenant covenant of the tenancy under which any fixed charge is payable; or
(b) (in the case of any tenancy) he remains bound by such a covenant.

(2) The former tenant shall not be liable under that agreement or (as the case may be) the covenant to pay any amount in respect of any fixed charge payable under the covenant unless, within the period of six months beginning with the date when the charge becomes due, the landlord serves on the former tenant a notice informing him –

(a) that the charge is now due; and
(b) that in respect of the charge the landlord intends to recover from the former tenant such amount as is specified in the notice and (where payable) interest calculated on such basis as is so specified.

(3) Where a person ('the guarantor') has agreed to guarantee the performance by the former tenant of such a covenant as is mentioned in subsection (1), the guarantor shall not be liable under the agreement to pay any amount in respect of any fixed charge payable under the covenant unless, within the period of six months beginning with the date when the charge becomes due, the landlord serves on the guarantor a notice informing him –

(a) that the charge is now due; and
(b) that in respect of the charge the landlord intends to recover from the guarantor such amount as is specified in the notice and (where payable) interest calculated on such basis as is so specified.

(4) Where the landlord has duly served a notice under subsection (2) or (3), the amount (exclusive of interest) which the former tenant or (as the case may be) the guarantor is liable to pay in respect of the fixed charge in question shall not exceed the amount specified in the notice unless –

(a) his liability in respect of the charge is subsequently determined to be for a greater amount,
(b) the notice informed him of the possibility that that liability would be so determined, and
(c) within the period of three months beginning with the date of the determination, the landlord serves on him a further notice informing him that the landlord intends to recover that greater amount from him (plus interest, where payable).

(5) For the purposes of subsection (2) or (3) any fixed charge which has become due before the date on which this Act comes into force shall be treated as becoming due on that date; but neither of those subsections applies to any such charge if before that date proceedings have been instituted by the landlord for the recovery from the former tenant of any amount in respect of it.

(6) In this section –

'fixed charge', in relation to a tenancy, means –

(a) rent,

(b) any service charge as defined by section 18 of the Landlord and Tenant Act 1985 (the words 'of a dwelling' being disregarded for this purpose), and

(c) any amount payable under a tenant covenant of the tenancy providing for the payment of a liquidated sum in the event of a failure to comply with any such covenant;

'landlord', in relation to a fixed charge, includes any person who has a right to enforce payment of the charge.

18 Restriction of a liability of former tenant or his   **[923]**
guarantor where tenancy subsequently varied

(1) This section applies where a person ('the former tenant') is as a result of an assignment no longer a tenant under a tenancy but –

(a) (in the case of a new tenancy) he has under an authorised guarantee agreement guaranteed the performance by his assignee of any tenant covenant of the tenancy; or

(b) (in the case of any tenancy) he remains bound by such a covenant.

(2) The former tenant shall not be liable under the agreement or (as the case may be) the covenant to pay any amount in respect of the covenant to the extent that the amount is referable to any relevant variation of the tenant covenants of the tenancy effected after the assignment.

(3) Where a person ('the guarantor') has agreed to guarantee the performance by the former tenant of a tenant covenant of the tenancy, the guarantor (where his liability to do so is not wholly discharged by any such variation of the tenant covenants of the tenancy) shall not be liable under the agreement to pay any amount in respect of the covenant to the extent that the amount is referable to any such variation.

(4) For the purposes of this section a variation of the tenant covenants of a tenancy is a 'relevant variation' if either –

(a) the landlord has, at the time of the variation, an absolute right to refuse to allow it; or

(b) the landlord would have had such a right if the variation had been sought by the former tenant immediately before the assignment by him but, between the time of that assignment and the time of the variation, the tenant covenants of the tenancy have been so varied as to deprive the landlord of such a right.

(5) In determining whether the landlord has or would have had such a right at any particular time regard shall be had to all the circumstances (including the effect of any provision made by or under any enactment).

(6) Nothing in this section applies to any variation of the tenant covenants of a tenancy effected before the date on which this Act comes into force.

(7) In this section 'variation' means a variation whether effected by deed or otherwise.

19 Right of former tenant or his guarantor to   **[924]**
overriding lease

(1) Where in respect of any tenancy ('the relevant tenancy') any person ('the claimant') makes full payment of an amount which he has been duly required to pay in accordance with section 17, together with any interest payable, he shall be entitled (subject to and in accordance with this section) to have the landlord under that tenancy grant him an overriding lease of the premises demised by the tenancy.

(2) For the purposes of this section 'overriding lease' means a tenancy of the reversion expectant on the relevant tenancy which –

(a) is granted for a term equal to the remainder of the term of the relevant tenancy plus three days or the longest period (less than three days) that will not wholly displace the landlord's reversionary interest expectant on the relevant tenancy, as the case may require; and

(b) (subject to subsections (3) and (4) and to any modifications agreed to by the claimant and the landlord) otherwise contains the same covenants as the relevant tenancy, as they have effect immediately before the grant of the lease.

(3) An overriding lease shall not be required to reproduce any covenant of the relevant tenancy to the extent that the covenant is (in whatever terms) expressed to be a personal covenant between the landlord and the tenant under that tenancy.

(4) If any right, liability or other matter arising under a covenant of the relevant tenancy falls to be determined or otherwise operates (whether expressly or otherwise) by reference to the commencement of that tenancy –

(a) the corresponding covenant of the overriding lease shall be so framed that that right, liability or matter falls to be determined or otherwise operates by reference to the commencement of that tenancy; but

(b) the overriding lease shall not be required to reproduce any covenant of that tenancy to the extent that it has become spent by the time that that lease is granted.

(5) A claim to exercise the right to an overriding lease under this section is made by the claimant making a request for such a lease to the landlord; and any such request –

(a) must be made to the landlord in writing and specify the payment by virtue of which the claimant claims to be entitled to the lease ('the qualifying payment'); and

(b) must be so made at the time of making the qualifying payment or within the period of 12 months beginning with the date of that payment.

(6) Where the claimant duly makes such a request –

(a) the landlord shall (subject to subsection (7)) grant and deliver to the claimant an overriding lease of the demised premises within a reasonable time of the request being received by the landlord; and

(b) the claimant –

(i) shall thereupon deliver to the landlord a counterpart of the lease duly executed by the claimant, and

(ii) shall be liable for the landlord's reasonable costs of and incidental to the grant of the lease.

(7) The landlord shall not be under any obligation to grant an overriding lease of the demised premises under this section at a time when the relevant tenancy has been determined; and a claimant shall not be entitled to the grant of such a lease if at the time when he makes his request –

(a) the landlord has already granted such a lease and that lease remains in force; or

(b) another person has already duly made a request for such a lease to the landlord and that request has been neither withdrawn nor abandoned by that person.

(8) Where two or more requests are duly made on the same day, then for the purposes of subsection (7) –

(a) a request made by a person who was liable for the qualifying payment as a former tenant shall be treated as made before a request made by a person who was so liable as a guarantor; and

(b) a request made by a person whose liability in respect of the covenant in question commenced earlier than any such liability of another person shall be treated as made before a request made by that other person.

(9) Where a claimant who has duly made a request for an overriding lease under this section subsequently withdraws or abandons the request before he is granted such a lease by the landlord, the claimant shall be liable for the landlord's reasonable costs incurred in pursuance of the request down to the time of its withdrawal or abandonment; and for the purposes of this section –

(a) a claimant's request is withdrawn by the claimant notifying the landlord in writing that he is withdrawing his request; and

(b) a claimant is to be regarded as having abandoned his request if –

(i) the landlord has requested the claimant in writing to take, within such reasonable period as is specified in the landlord's request, all or any of the remaining steps required to be taken by the claimant before the lease can be granted, and

(ii) the claimant fails to comply with the landlord's request,

and is accordingly to be regarded as having abandoned it at the time when that period expires.

(10) Any request or notification under this section may be sent by post.

(11) The preceding provisions of this section shall apply where the landlord is the tenant under an overriding lease granted under this section as they apply where no such lease has been granted; and accordingly there may be two or more such leases interposed between the first such lease and the relevant tenancy.

20 Overriding leases: supplementary provisions [925]

(1) For the purposes of section 1 an overriding lease shall be a new tenancy only if the relevant tenancy is a new tenancy.

(2) Every overriding lease shall state –

(a) that it is a lease granted under section 19, and

(b) whether it is or is not a new tenancy for the purposes of section 1;

and any such statement shall comply with such requirements as may be prescribed by rules made in pursuance of section 144 of the Land Registration Act 1925 (power to make general rules).

(3) A claim that the landlord has failed to comply with subsection (6)(a) of section 19 may be made the subject of civil proceedings in like manner as any other claim in tort for breach of statutory duty; and if the claimant under that section fails to comply with subsection (6)(b)(i) of that section he shall not be entitled to exercise any of the rights otherwise exercisable by him under the overriding lease.

(4) An overriding lease –

(a) shall be deemed to be authorised as against the persons interested in any mortgage of the landlord's interest (however created or arising); and

(b) shall be binding on any such persons;

and if any such person is by virtue of such a mortgage entitled to possession of the documents of title relating to the landlord's interest –

(i) the landlord shall within one month of the execution of the lease deliver to that person the counterpart executed in pursuance of section 19(6)(b)(i); and

(ii) if he fails to do so, the instrument creating or evidencing the mortgage shall apply as if the obligation to deliver a counterpart were included in the terms of the mortgage as set out in that instrument.

(5) It is hereby declared –

(a) that the fact that an overriding lease takes effect subject to the relevant tenancy shall not constitute a breach of any covenant of the lease against subletting or parting with possession of the premises demised by the lease or any part of them; and

(b) that each of sections 16, 17 and 18 applies where the tenancy referred to in subsection (1) of that section is an overriding lease as it applies in other cases falling within that subsection.

(6) No tenancy shall be registrable under the Land Charges Act 1972 or be taken to be an estate contract within the meaning of that Act by reason of any right or obligation that may arise under section 19, and any right arising from a request made under that section shall not be an overriding interest within the meaning of the Land Registration Act 1925; but any such request shall be registrable under the Land Charges Act 1972, or may be the subject of a notice or caution under the Land Registration Act 1925, as if it were an estate contract.

(7) In this section –

(a) 'mortgage' includes 'charge'; and

(b) any expression which is also used in section 19 has the same meaning as in that section.

21 Forfeiture or disclaimer limited to part only of   [926] demised premises

(1) Where –

(a) as a result of one or more assignments a person is the tenant of part only of the premises demised by a tenancy, and

(b) under a proviso or stipulation in the tenancy there is a right of re-entry or forfeiture for a breach of a tenant covenant of the tenancy, and

(c) the right is (apart from this subsection) exercisable in relation to that part and other land demised by the tenancy,

the right shall nevertheless, in connection with a breach of any such covenant by that person, be taken to be a right exercisable only in relation to that part.

(2) Where –

(a) a company which is being wound up, or a trustee in bankruptcy, is as a result of one or more assignments the tenant of part only of the premises demised by a tenancy, and

(b) the liquidator of the company exercises his power under section 178 of the Insolvency Act 1986, or the trustee in bankruptcy exercises his power under section 315 of that Act, to disclaim property demised by the tenancy,

the power is exercisable only in relation to the part of the premises referred to in paragraph (a).

23 Effects of becoming subject to liability under, or   [927] entitled to benefit of, covenant, etc

(1) Where as a result of an assignment a person becomes, by virtue of this Act, bound by or entitled to the benefit of a covenant, he shall not by virtue of this Act have any liability or rights under the covenant in relation to any time falling before the assignment.

(2) Subsection (1) does not preclude any such rights being expressly assigned to the person in question.

(3) Where as a result of an assignment a person becomes, by virtue of this Act, entitled to a right of re-entry contained in a tenancy, that right shall be exercisable in relation to any breach of a covenant of the tenancy occurring before the assignment as in relation to one occurring thereafter, unless by reason of any waiver or release it was not so exercisable immediately before the assignment.

24 Effects of release from liability under, or loss of benefit of, covenant [928]

(1) Any release of a person from a covenant by virtue of this Act does not affect any liability of his arising from a breach of the covenant occurring before the release.

(2) Where –

(a) by virtue of this Act a tenant is released from a tenant covenant of a tenancy, and

(b) immediately before the release another person is bound by a covenant of the tenancy imposing any liability or penalty in the event of a failure to comply with that tenant covenant,

then, as from the release of the tenant, that other person is released from the covenant mentioned in paragraph (b) to the same extent as the tenant is released from that tenant covenant.

(3) Where a person bound by a landlord or tenant covenant of a tenancy –

(a) assigns the whole or part of his interest in the premises demised by the tenancy, but

(b) is not released by virtue of this Act from the covenant (with the result that subsection (1) does not apply),

the assignment does not affect any liability of his arising from a breach of the covenant occurring before the assignment.

(4) Where by virtue of this Act a person ceases to be entitled to the benefit of a covenant, this does not affect any rights of his arising from a breach of the covenant occurring before he ceases to be so entitled.

25 Agreement void if it restricts operation of the Act [929]

(1) Any agreement relating to a tenancy is void to the extent that –

(a) it would apart from this section have effect to exclude, modify or otherwise frustrate the operation of any provision of this Act, or

(b) it provides for –

(i) the termination or surrender of the tenancy, or

(ii) the imposition on the tenant of any penalty, disability or liability,

in the event of the operation of any provision of this Act, or

(c) it provides for any of the matters referred to in paragraph (b)(i) or (ii) and does so (whether expressly or otherwise) in connection with, or in consequence of, the operation of any provision of this Act.

(2) To the extent that an agreement relating to a tenancy constitutes a covenant (whether absolute or qualified) against the assignment, or parting with the possession, of the premises demised by the tenancy or any part of them –

(a) the agreement is not void by virtue of subsection (1) by reason only of the fact that as such the covenant prohibits or restricts any such assignment or parting with possession; but

(b) paragraph (a) above does not otherwise affect the operation of that subsection in relation to the agreement (and in particular does not preclude its application to the agreement to the extent that it purports to regulate the giving of, or the making of any application for, consent to any such assignment or parting with possession).

(3) In accordance with section 16(1) nothing in this section applies to any agreement to the extent that it is an authorised guarantee agreement; but (without prejudice to the generality of subsection (1) above) an agreement is void to the extent that it is one falling within section 16(4)(a) or (b).

(4) This section applies to an agreement relating to a tenancy whether or not the agreement is –

(a) contained in the instrument creating the tenancy; or
(b) made before the creation of the tenancy.

26 Miscellaneous savings, etc   [930]

(1) Nothing in this Act is to be read as preventing –

(a) a party to a tenancy from releasing a person from a landlord covenant or a tenant covenant of the tenancy; or
(b) the parties to a tenancy from agreeing to an apportionment of liability under such a covenant.

(2) Nothing in this Act affects the operation of section 3(3A) of the Landlord and Tenant Act 1985 (preservation of former landlord's liability until tenant notified of new landlord).

(3) No apportionment which has become binding in accordance with section 10 shall be affected by any order or decision made under or by virtue of any enactment not contained in this Act which relates to apportionment.

28 Interpretation   [931]

(1) In this Act (unless the context otherwise requires) –

'assignment' includes equitable assignment and in addition (subject to section 11) assignment in breach of a covenant of a tenancy or by operation of law;

'authorised guarantee agreement' means an agreement which is an authorised guarantee agreement for the purposes of section 16;

'collateral agreement', in relation to a tenancy, means any agreement collateral to the tenancy, whether made before or after its creation;

'consent' includes licence;

'covenant' includes term, condition and obligation, and references to a covenant (or any description of covenant) of a tenancy include a covenant (or a covenant of that description) contained in a collateral agreement;

'landlord' and 'tenant', in relation to a tenancy, mean the person for the time being entitled to the reversion expectant on the term of the tenancy and the person so entitled to that term respectively;

'landlord covenant', in relation to a tenancy, means a covenant falling to be complied with by the landlord of premises demised by the tenancy;

'new tenancy' means a tenancy which is a new tenancy for the purposes of section 1;

'reversion' means the interest expectant on the termination of a tenancy;

'tenancy' means any lease or other tenancy and includes –

(a) a sub-tenancy, and

(b) an agreement for a tenancy,

but does not include a mortgage term;

'tenant covenant', in relation to a tenancy, means a covenant falling to be complied with by the tenant of premises demised by the tenancy.

(2) For the purposes of any reference in this Act to a covenant falling to be complied with in relation to a particular part of the premises demised by a tenancy, a covenant falls to be so complied with if –

(a) it in terms applies to that part of the premises, or
(b) in its practical application it can be attributed to that part of the premises (whether or not it can also be so attributed to other individual parts of those premises).

(3) Subsection (2) does not apply in relation to covenants to pay money; and, for the purposes of any reference in this Act to a covenant falling to be complied with in relation to a particular part of the premises demised by a tenancy, a covenant of a tenancy which is a covenant to pay money falls to be so complied with if –

(a) the covenant in terms applies to that part; or
(b) the amount of the payment is determinable specifically by reference –

(i) to that part, or
(ii) to anything falling to be done by or for a person as tenant or occupier of that part (if it is a tenant covenant), or
(iii) to anything falling to be done by or for a person as landlord of that part (if it is a landlord covenant).

(4) Where two or more persons jointly constitute either the landlord or the tenant in relation to a tenancy, any reference in this Act to the landlord or the tenant is a reference to both or all of the persons who jointly constitute the landlord or the tenant, as the case may be (and accordingly nothing in section 13 applies in relation to the rights and liabilities of such persons between themselves).

(5) References in this Act to the assignment by a landlord of the reversion in the whole or part of the premises demised by a tenancy are to the assignment by him of the whole of his interest (as owner of the reversion) in the whole or part of those premises.

(6) For the purposes of this Act –

(a) any assignment (however effected) consisting in the transfer of the whole of the landlord's interest (as owner of the reversion) in any premises demised by a tenancy shall be treated as an assignment by the landlord of the reversion in those premises even if it is not effected by him; and
(b) any assignment (however effected) consisting in the transfer of the whole of the tenant's interest in any premises demised by a tenancy shall be treated as an assignment by the tenant of those premises even if it is not effected by him.

29 Crown application [932]

This Act binds the Crown.

30 Consequential amendments and repeals [933]

(1) The enactments specified in Schedule 1 are amended in accordance with that Schedule, the amendments being consequential on the provisions of this Act.

(2) The enactments specified in Schedule 2 are repealed to the extent specified.

(3) Subsections (1) and (2) do not affect the operation of –

(a) section 77 of, or Part IX or X of Schedule 2 to, the Law of Property Act 1925, or

(b) section 24(1)(b) or (2) of the Land Registration Act 1925,

in relation to tenancies which are not new tenancies.

(4) In consequence of this Act nothing in the following provisions, namely –

(a) sections 78 and 79 of the Law of Property Act 1925 (benefit and burden of covenants relating to land), and

(b) sections 141 and 142 of that Act (running of benefit and burden of covenants with reversion),

shall apply in relation to new tenancies ...

31 Commencement [934]

(1) The provisions of this Act come into force on such a day as the Lord Chancellor may appoint by order made by statutory instrument. ...

NB This Act came into force on 1 January 1996.

DISABILITY DISCRIMINATION ACT 1995
(1995 c 50)
PART II
EMPLOYMENT

16 Alterations to premises occupied under leases [935]

(1) This section applies where –

(a) an employer or trade organisation ('the occupier') occupies premises under a lease;

(b) but for this section, the occupier would not be entitled to make a particular alteration to the premises; and

(c) the alteration is one which the occupier proposes to make in order to comply with a section 6 duty [to make adjustments, eg to premises] or section 15 duty [duty of trade organisation to make adjustments].

(2) Except to the extent to which it expressly so provides, the lease shall have effect by virtue of this subsection as if it provided –

(a) for the occupier to be entitled to make the alteration with the written consent of the lessor;

(b) for the occupier to have to make a written application to the lessor for consent if he wishes to make the alteration;

(c) if such an application is made, for the lessor not to withhold his consent unreasonably; and

(d) for the lessor to be entitled to make his consent subject to reasonable conditions.

(3) In this section –

'lease' includes a tenancy, sub-lease or sub-tenancy and an agreement for a lease, tenancy, sub-lease or sub-tenancy; and

'sub-lease' and 'sub-tenancy' have such meaning as may be prescribed.

(4) If the terms and conditions of a lease –

(a) impose conditions which are to apply if the occupier alters the premises, or

(b) entitle the lessor to impose conditions when consenting to the occupier's altering the premises,

the occupier is to be treated for the purposes of subsection (1) as not being entitled to make the alteration ...

PART III

DISCRIMINATION IN OTHER AREAS

22 Discrimination in relation to premises [936]

(1) It is unlawful for a person with power to dispose of any premises to discriminate against a disabled person –

(a) in the terms on which he offers to dispose of those premises to the disabled person;
(b) by refusing to dispose of those premises to the disabled person; or
(c) in his treatment of the disabled person in relation to any list of persons in need of premises of that description.

(2) Subsection (1) does not apply to a person who owns an estate or interest in the premises and wholly occupies them unless, for the purpose of disposing of the premises, he –

(a) uses the services of an estate agent, or
(b) publishes an advertisement or causes an advertisement to be published.

(3) It is unlawful for a person managing any premises to discriminate against a disabled person occupying those premises –

(a) in the way he permits the disabled person to make use of any benefits or facilities;
(b) by refusing or deliberately omitting to permit the disabled person to make use of any benefits or facilities; or
(c) by evicting the disabled person, or subjecting him to any other detriment.

(4) It is unlawful for any person whose licence or consent is required for the disposal of any premises comprised in ... a tenancy to discriminate against a disabled person by withholding his licence or consent for the disposal of the premises to the disabled person.

(5) Subsection (4) applies to tenancies created before as well as after the passing of this Act.

(6) In this section –

'advertisement' includes every form of advertisement or notice, whether to the public or not;
'dispose', in relation to premises, includes granting a right to occupy the premises, and, in relation to premises comprised in, or (in Scotland) the subject of, a tenancy, includes –

(a) assigning the tenancy, and
(b) sub-letting or parting with possession of the premises or any part of the premises;

and 'disposal' shall be construed accordingly;
'estate agent' means a person who, by way of profession or trade, provides services for the purpose of finding premises for persons seeking to acquire them or assisting in the disposal of premises; and
'tenancy' means a tenancy created –

(a) by a lease or sub-lease,
(b) by an agreement for a lease or sub-lease,
(c) by a tenancy agreement, or
(d) in pursuance of any enactment ...

23 Exemption for small dwellings [937]

(1) Where the conditions mentioned in subsection (2) are satisfied, subsection (1), (3) or (as the case may be) (4) of section 22 does not apply.

(2) The conditions are that –

(a) the relevant occupier resides, and intends to continue to reside, on the premises;
(b) the relevant occupier shares accommodation on the premises with persons who reside on the premises and are not members of his household;
(c) the shared accommodation is not storage accommodation or a means of access; and
(d) the premises are small premises.

(3) For the purposes of this section, premises are 'small premises' if they fall within subsection (4) or (5).

(4) Premises fall within this subsection if –

(a) only the relevant occupier and members of his household reside in the accommodation occupied by him;
(b) the premises comprise, in addition to the accommodation occupied by the relevant occupier, residential accommodation for at least one other household;
(c) the residential accommodation for each other household is let, or available for letting, on a separate tenancy or similar agreement; and
(d) there are not normally more than two such other households.

(5) Premises fall within this subsection if there is not normally residential accommodation on the premises for more than six persons in addition to the relevant occupier and any members of his household.

(6) For the purposes of this section 'the relevant occupier' means –

(a) in a case falling within section 22(1), the person with power to dispose of the premises, or a near relative of his;
(b) in a case falling within section 22(4), the person whose licence or consent is required for the disposal of the premises, or a near relative of his.

(7) For the purposes of this section –

'near relative' means a person's spouse, partner, parent, child, grandparent, grandchild, or brother or sister (whether of full or half blood or by affinity); and
'partner' means the other member of a couple consisting of a man and a woman who are not married to each other but are living together as husband and wife.

24 Meaning of 'discrimination' [938]

(1) For the purposes of section 22, a person ('A') discriminates against a disabled person if –

(a) for a reason which relates to the disabled person's disability, he treats him less favourably than he treats or would treat others to whom that reason does not or would not apply; and
(b) he cannot show that the treatment in question is justified.

(2) For the purposes of this section, treatment is justified only if –

(a) in A's opinion, one or more of the conditions mentioned in subsection (3) are satisfied; and
(b) it is reasonable, in all the circumstances of the case, for him to hold that opinion.

(3) The conditions are that –

(a) in any case, the treatment is necessary in order not to endanger the health or safety of any person (which may include that of the disabled person);
(b) in any case, the disabled person is incapable of entering into an enforceable agreement, or of giving an informed consent, and for that reason the treatment is reasonable in that case;
(c) in a case falling within section 22(3)(a), the treatment is necessary in order for the disabled person or the occupiers of other premises forming part of the building to make use of the benefit or facility;
(d) in a case falling within section 22(3)(b), the treatment is necessary in order for the occupiers of other premises forming part of the building to make use of the benefit or facility. ...

25 Enforcement, remedies and procedure   [939]

(1) A claim by any person that another person –

(a) has discriminated against him in a way which is unlawful under this Part; ...

may be made the subject of civil proceedings in the same way as another claim in tort ... for breach of statutory duty.

(2) For the avoidance of doubt it is hereby declared that damages in respect of discrimination in a way which is unlawful under this Part may include compensation for injury to feelings whether or not they include compensation under any other head.

(3) Proceedings in England and Wales shall be brought only in a county court ...

TRUSTS OF LAND AND APPOINTMENT OF TRUSTEES ACT 1996
(1996 c 47)

PART I

TRUSTS OF LAND

1 Meaning of 'trust of land'   [940]

(1) In this Act –

(a) 'trust of land' means (subject to subsection (3)) any trust of property which consists of or includes land, and
(b) 'trustees of land' means trustees of a trust of land.

(2) The reference in subsection (1)(a) to a trust –

(a) is to any description of a trust (whether express, implied, resulting or constructive), including a trust for sale and a bare trust, and
(b) includes a trust created, or arising, before the commencement of this Act,

(3) The reference to land in subsection (1)(a) does not include land which (despite section 2) is settled land or which is land to which the Universities and College Estates Act 1925 applies.

2 Trusts in place of settlements   [941]

(1) No settlement created after the commencement of this Act is a settlement for the purposes of the Settled Land Act 1925; and no settlement shall be deemed to be made under that Act after that commencement.

(2) Subsection (1) does not apply to a settlement created on the occasion of an alteration in any interest in, or of a person becoming entitled under, a settlement which –

  (a) is in existence at the commencement of this Act, or
  (b) derives from a settlement within paragraph (a) or this paragraph.

(3) But a settlement created as mentioned in subsection (2) is not a settlement for the purposes of the Settled land Act 1925 if provision to the effect that it is not is made in the instrument, or any of the instruments, by which it is created.

(4) Where at any time after the commencement of this Act there is in the case of any settlement which is a settlement for the purposes of the Settled land Act 1925 no relevant property which is, or is deemed to be, subject to the settlement, the settlement permanently ceases at that time to be a settlement for the purposes of that Act. In this subsection 'relevant property' means land and personal chattels to which section 67(1) of the Settled Land Act 1925 (heirlooms) applies.

(5) No land held on charitable, ecclesiastical or public trusts shall be or be deemed to be settled land after the commencement of this Act, even if it was or was deemed to be settled land before that commencement.

(6) Schedule 1 has effect to make provision consequential on this section (including provision to impose a trust in circumstances in which, apart from this section, there would be a settlement for the purposes of the Settled Land Act 1925 (and there would not otherwise be a trust)).

3 Abolition of doctrine of conversion   [942]

(1) Where land is held by trustees subject to a trust for sale, the land is not to be regarded as personal property; and where personal property is subject to a trust for sale in order that the trustees may acquire land, the personal property is not to be regarded as land.

(2) Subsection (1) does not apply to a trust created by a will if the testator died before the commencement of this Act.

(3) Subject to that, subsection (1) applies to a trust whether it is created, or arises, before or after that commencement.

4 Express trusts for sale as trusts of land   [943]

(1) In the case of every trust for sale of land created by a disposition there is to be implied, despite any provision to the contrary made by the disposition, a power for the trustees to postpone sale of the land; and the trustees are not liable in any way for postponing sale of the land, in the exercise of their discretion, for an indefinite period.

(2) Subsection (1) applies to a trust whether it is created, or arises, before or after the commencement of this Act

(3) Subsection (1) does not affect any liability incurred by trustees before that commencement.

5 Implied trusts for sale as trusts of land   [944]

(1) Schedule 2 has effect in relation to statutory provisions which impose a trust for sale of land in certain circumstances so that in those circumstances there is instead a trust of the land (without a duty to sell).

(2) Section 1 of the Settled Land Act 1925 does not apply to land held on any trust arising by virtue of that Schedule (so that any such land is subject to a trust of land).

6 General powers of trustees   [945]

(1) For the purpose of exercising their functions as trustees, the trustees of land have in relation to the land subject to the trust all the powers of an absolute owner.

(2) Where in the case of any land subject to a trust of land each of the beneficiaries interested in the land is a person of full age and capacity who is absolutely entitled to the land, the powers conferred on the trustees by subsection (1) include the power to convey the land to the beneficiaries even though they have not required the trustees to do so; and where land is conveyed by virtue of this subsection –

    (a) the beneficiaries shall do whatever is necessary to secure that it vests in them, and
    (b) if they fail to do so, the court may make an order requiring them to do so.

(3) The trustees of land have power to purchase a legal estate in any land in England or Wales.

(4) The power conferred by subsection (3) may be exercised by trustees to purchase land –

    (a) by way of investment,
    (b) for occupation by any beneficiary, or
    (c) for any other reason.

(5) In exercising the powers conferred by this section trustees shall have regard to the rights of the beneficiaries.

(6) The powers conferred by this section shall not be exercised in contravention of, or of any order made in pursuance of, any other enactment or any rule of law or equity.

(7) The reference in subsection (6) to an order includes an order of any court or of the Charity Commissioners.

(8) Where any enactment other than this section confers on trustees authority to act subject to any restriction, limitation or condition, trustees of land may not exercise the powers conferred by this section to do any act which they are prevented from doing under the other enactment by reason of the restriction, limitation or condition.

7 Partition by trustees   [946]

(1) The trustees of land may, where beneficiaries of full age are absolutely entitled in undivided shares to land subject to the trust, partition the land, or any part of it, and provide (by way of mortgage or otherwise) for the payment of any equality money.

(2) The trustees shall give effect to any such partition by conveying the partitioned land in severalty (whether or not subject to any legal mortgage created for raising

equality money), either absolutely or in trust, in accordance with the rights of those beneficiaries.

(3) Before exercising their powers under subsection (2) the trustees shall obtain the consent of each of those beneficiaries.

(4) Where a share in the land is affected by an incumbrance, the trustees may either give effect to it or provide for its discharge from the property allotted to that share as they think fit.

(5) If a share in the land is absolutely vested in a minor, subsections (1) to (4) apply as if he were of full age, except that the trustees may act on his behalf and retain land or other property representing his share in trust for him.

8 Exclusion and restriction of powers   [947]

(1) Sections 6 and 7 do not apply in the case of a trust of land created by a disposition in so far as provision to the effect that they do not apply is made by the disposition.

(2) If the disposition creating such a trust makes provision requiring any consent to be obtained to the exercise of any power conferred by section 6 or 7, the power may not be exercised without that consent.

(3) Subsection (1) does not apply in the case of charitable, ecclesiastical or public trusts.

(4) Subsections (1) and (2) have effect subject to any enactment which prohibits or restricts the effect of provision of the description mentioned in them.

9 Delegation by trustees   [948]

(1) The trustees of land may, by power of attorney, delegate to any beneficiary or beneficiaries of full age and beneficially entitled to an interest in possession in land subject to the trust any of their functions as trustees which relate to the land.

(2) Where trustees purport to delegate to a person by a power of attorney under subsection (1) functions relating to any land and another person in good faith deals with him in relation to the land, he shall be presumed in favour of that other person to have been a person to whom the functions could be delegated unless that other person has knowledge at the time of the transaction that he was not such a person. And it shall be conclusively presumed in favour of any purchaser whose interest depends on the validity of that transaction that that other person dealt in good faith and did not have such knowledge if that other person makes a statutory declaration to that effect before or within three months after the completion of the purchase.

(3) A power of attorney under subsection (1) shall be given by all the trustees jointly and (unless expressed to be irrevocable and to be given by way of security) may be revoked by any one or more of them; and such a power is revoked by the appointment as a trustee of a person other than those by whom it is given (though not by any of those persons dying or otherwise ceasing to be a trustee).

(4) Where a beneficiary to whom functions are delegated by a power of attorney under subsection (1) ceases to be a person beneficially entitled to an interest in possession in land subject to the trust –

(a) if the functions are delegated to him alone, the power is revoked,
(b) if the functions are delegated to him and to other beneficiaries to be exercised by them jointly (but not separately), the power is revoked if each of the other beneficiaries ceases to be so entitled (but otherwise functions exercisable in accordance with the power are so exercisable by the remaining beneficiary or beneficiaries), and

(c) if the functions are delegated to him and to other beneficiaries to be exercised by them separately (or either separately or jointly), the power is revoked in so far as it relates to him.

(5) A delegation under subsection (1) may be for any period or indefinite.

(6) A power of attorney under subsection (1) cannot be an enduring power within the meaning of the Enduring Powers of Attorney Act 1985.

(7) Beneficiaries to whom functions have been delegated under subsection (1) are, in relation to the exercise of the functions, in the same position as trustees (with the same duties and liabilities); but such beneficiaries shall not be regarded as trustees for any other purposes (including, in particular, the purposes of any enactment permitting the delegation of functions by trustees or imposing requirements relating to the payment of capital money).

(8) Where any function has been delegated to a beneficiary or beneficiaries under subsection (1), the trustees are jointly and severally liable for any act or default of the beneficiary, or any of the beneficiaries, in the exercise of the function if, and only if, the trustees did not exercise reasonable care in deciding to delegate the function to the beneficiary or beneficiaries.

(9) Neither this section nor the repeal by this Act of section 29 of the Law of Property Act 1925 (which is superseded by this section) affects the operation after the commencement of this Act of any delegation effected before that commencement.

10 Consents [949]

(1) If a disposition creating a trust of land requires the consent of more than two persons to the exercise by the trustees of any function relating to the land, the consent of any two of them to the exercise of the function is sufficient in favour of a purchaser.

(2) Subsection (1) does not apply to the exercise of a function by trustees of land held on charitable, ecclesiastical or public trusts.

(3) Where at any time a person whose consent is expressed by a disposition creating a trust of land to be required to the exercise by the trustees of any function relating to the land is not of full age –

(a) his consent is not, in favour of a purchaser, required to the exercise of the function, but
(b) the trustees shall obtain the consent of a parent who has parental responsibility for him (within the meaning of the Children Act 1989) or of a guardian of his.

11 Consultation with beneficiaries [950]

(1) The trustees of land shall in the exercise of any function relating to land subject to the trust –

(a) so far as is practicable, consult the beneficiaries of full age and beneficially entitled to an interest in possession in the land, and
(b) so far as consistent with the general interest of the trust, give effect to the wishes of those beneficiaries, or (in case of dispute) of the majority (according to the value of their combined interests).

(2) Subsection (1) does not apply –

(a) in relation to a trust created by a disposition in so far as provision that it does not apply is made by the disposition,
(b) in relation to a trust created or arising under a will made before the commencement of this Act, or

(c) in relation to the exercise of the power mentioned in section 6(2).

(3) Subsection (1) does not apply to a trust created before the commencement of this Act by a disposition, or a trust created after that commencement by reference to such a trust, unless provision to the effect that it is to apply is made by a deed executed –

(a) in a case in which the trust was created by one person and he is of full capacity, by that person, or
(b) in a case in which the trust was created by more than one person, by such of the persons who created the trust as are alive and of full capacity.

(4) A deed executed for the purposes of subsection (3) is irrevocable.

12 The right to occupy   [951]

(1) A beneficiary who is beneficially entitled to an interest in possession in land subject to a trust of land is entitled by reason of his interest to occupy the land at any time if at that time –

(a) the purposes of the trust include making the land available for his occupation (or for the occupation of beneficiaries of a class of which he is a member or of beneficiaries in general), or
(b) the land is held by the trustees so as to be so available.

(2) Subsection (1) does not confer on a beneficiary a right to occupy land if it is either unavailable or unsuitable for occupation by him.

(3) This section is subject to section 13.

13 Exclusion and restriction of right to occupy   [952]

(1) Where two or more beneficiaries are (or apart from this subsection would be) entitled under section 12 to occupy land, the trustees of land may exclude or restrict the entitlement of any one or more (but not all) of them.

(2) Trustees may not under subsection (1) –

(a) unreasonably exclude any beneficiary's entitlement to occupy land, or
(b) restrict any such entitlement to an unreasonable extent.

(3) The trustees of land may from time to time impose reasonable conditions on any beneficiary in relation to his occupation of land by reason of his entitlement under section 12.

(4) The matters to which trustees are to have regard in exercising the powers conferred by this section include –

(a) the intentions of the person or persons (if any) who created the trust,
(b) the purposes for which the land is held, and
(c) the circumstances and wishes of each of the beneficiaries who is (or apart from any previous exercise by the trustees of those powers would be) entitled to occupy the land under section 12.

(5) The conditions which may be imposed on a beneficiary under subsection (3) include, in particular, conditions requiring him –

(a) to pay any outgoings or expenses in respect of the land, or
(b) to assume any other obligation in relation to the land or to any activity which is or is proposed to be conducted there.

(6) Where the entitlement of any beneficiary to occupy land under section 12 has been excluded or restricted, the conditions which may be imposed on any other beneficiary under subsection (3) include, in particular, conditions requiring him to –

(a) make payments by way of compensation to the beneficiary whose entitlement has been excluded or restricted, or

(b) forgo any payment or other benefit to which he would otherwise be entitled under the trust so as to benefit that beneficiary.

(7) The powers conferred on trustees by this section may not be exercised –

(a) so as to prevent any person who is in occupation of land (whether or not by reason of an entitlement under section 12) from continuing to occupy the land, or

(b) in a manner likely to result in any such person ceasing to occupy the land,

unless he consents or the court has given approval.

(8) The matters to which the court is to have regard in determining whether to give approval under subsection (7) include the matters mentioned in subsection (4)(a) to (c).

14 Applications for order   [953]

(1) Any person who is a trustee of land or has an interest in property subject to a trust of land may make an application to the court for an order under this section.

(2) On application for an order under this section the court may make any such order –

(a) relating to the exercise by the trustees of any of their functions (including an order relieving them of any obligation to obtain the consent of, or to consult, any person in connection with the exercise of any of their functions), or

(b) declaring the nature or extent of a person's interest in property subject to the trust,

as the court thinks fit.

(3) The court may not under this section make any order as to the appointment or removal of trustees.

(4) The powers conferred on the court by this section are exercisable on an application whether it is made before or after the commencement of this Act.

15 Matters relevant in determining applications   [954]

(1) The matters to which the court is to have regard in determining an application for an order under section 14 include –

(a) the intentions of the person or persons (if any) who created the trust,

(b) the purposes for which the property subject to the trust is held,

(c) the welfare of any minor who occupies or might reasonably be expected to occupy any land subject to the trust as his home, and

(d) the interests of any secured creditor of any beneficiary.

(2) In the case of an application relating to the exercise in relation to any land of the powers conferred on the trustees by section 13, the matters to which the court is to have regard also include the circumstances and wishes of each of the beneficiaries who is (or apart from any previous exercise by the trustees of those powers would be) entitled to occupy the land under section 12.

(3) In the case of any other application, other than one relating to the exercise of the power mentioned in section 6(2), the matters to which the court is to have regard also include the circumstances and wishes of any beneficiaries of full age and entitled to an interest in possession in property subject to the trust or (in case of dispute) of the majority (according to the value of their combined interests).

(4) This section does not apply to an application if section 335A of the Insolvency Act 1986 (which is inserted by Schedule 3 and relates to applications by a trustee of a bankrupt) applies to it.

16 Protection of purchasers   [955]

(1) A purchaser of land which is or has been subject to a trust need not be concerned to see that any requirement imposed on the trustees by section 6(5), 7(3) or 11(1) has been complied with.

(2) Where –

(a) trustees of land who convey land which (immediately before it is conveyed) is subject to the trust contravene section 6(6) or (8), but

(b) the purchaser of the land from the trustees has no actual notice of the contravention,

the contravention does not invalidate the conveyance.

(3) Where the powers of trustees of land are limited by virtue of section 8 –

(a) the trustees shall take all reasonable steps to bring the limitation to the notice of any purchaser of the land from them, but

(b) the limitation does not invalidate any conveyance by the trustees to a purchaser who has no actual notice of the limitation.

(4) Where trustees of land convey land which (immediately before it is conveyed) is subject to the trust to persons believed by them to be beneficiaries absolutely entitled to the land under the trust and of full age and capacity –

(a) the trustees shall execute a deed declaring that they are discharged from the trust in relation to that land, and

(b) if they fail to do so, the court may make an order requiring them to do so.

(5) A purchaser of land to which a deed under subsection (4) relates is entitled to assume that, as from the date of the deed, the land is not subject to the trust unless he has actual notice that the trustees were mistaken in their belief that the land was conveyed to beneficiaries absolutely entitled to the land under the trust and of full age and capacity.

(6) Subsections (2) and (3) do not apply to land held on charitable, ecclesiastical or public trusts.

(7) This section does not apply to registered land.

17 Application of provisions to trusts of proceeds of sale   [956]

(1) Section 6(3) applies in relation to trustees of a trust of proceeds of sale of land as in relation to trustees of land.

(2) Section 14 applies in relation to a trust of proceeds of sale of land and trustees of such a trust as in relation to a trust of land and trustees of land.

(3) In this section 'trust of proceeds of sale of land' means (subject to subsection (5)) any trust of property (other than a trust of land) which consists of or includes –

(a) any proceeds of a disposition of land held in trust (including settled land), or

(b) any property representing any such proceeds.

(4) The references in subsection (3) to a trust –

(a) are to any description of trust (whether express, implied, resulting or constructive), including a trust for sale and a bare trust, and

(b) include a trust created, or arising, before the commencement of this Act.

(5) A trust which (despite section 2) is a settlement for the purposes of the Settled Land Act 1925 cannot be a trust of proceeds of sale of land.

(6) In subsection (3) –

(a) 'disposition' includes any disposition made, or coming into operation, before the commencement of this Act, and

(b) the reference to settled land includes personal chattels to which section 67(1) of the Settled Land Act 1925 (heirlooms) applies.

18 Application of Part to personal representatives   **[957]**

(1) The provisions of this Part relating to trustees, other than sections 10, 11 and 14, apply to personal representatives, but with appropriate modifications and without prejudice to the functions of personal representatives for the purposes of administration.

(2) The appropriate modifications include –

(a) the substitution of references to persons interested in the due administration of the estate for references to beneficiaries, and

(b) the substitution of references to the will for references to the disposition creating the trust.

(3) Section 3(1) does not apply to personal representatives if the death occurs before the commencement of this Act.

PART II

APPOINTMENT AND RETIREMENT OF TRUSTEES

19 Appointment and retirement of trustee at instance   **[958]**
of beneficiaries

(1) This section applies in the case of a trust where –

(a) there is no person nominated for the purpose of appointing new trustees by the instrument, if any, creating the trust, and

(b) the beneficiaries under the trust are of full age and capacity and (taken together) are absolutely entitled to the property subject to the trust.

(2) The beneficiaries may give a direction or directions of either or both of the following descriptions –

(a) a written direction to a trustee or trustees to retire from the trust, and

(b) a written direction to the trustees or trustee for the time being (or, if there are none, to the personal representative of the last person who was a trustee) to appoint by writing to be a trustee or trustees the person or persons specified in the direction.

(3) Where –

(a) a trustee has been given a direction under subsection (2)(a),

(b) reasonable arrangements have been made for the protection of any rights of his in connection with the trust,

(c) after he has retired there will be either a trust corporation or at least two persons to act as trustees to perform the trust, and

(d) either another person is to be appointed to be a new trustee on his retirement (whether in compliance with a direction under subsection (2)(b) or otherwise) or the continuing trustees by deed consent to his retirement,

he shall make a deed declaring his retirement and shall be deemed to have retired and be discharged from the trust.

(4) Where a trustee retires under subsection (3) he and the continuing trustees (together with any new trustee) shall (subject to any arrangements for the protection of his rights) do anything necessary to vest the trust property in the continuing trustees (or the continuing and new trustees).

(5) This section has effect subject to the restrictions imposed by the Trustee Act 1925 on the number of trustees.

20 Appointment of substitute for incapable trustee   [959]

(1) This section applies where –

(a) a trustee is incapable by reason of mental disorder of exercising his functions as trustee,

(b) there is no person who is both entitled and willing and able to appoint a trustee in place of him under section 36(1) of the Trustee Act 1925, and

(c) the beneficiaries under the trust are of full age and capacity and (taken together) are absolutely entitled to the property subject to the trust.

(2) The beneficiaries may give to –

(a) a receiver of the trustee,

(b) an attorney acting for him under the authority of a power of attorney created by an instrument which is registered under section 6 of the Enduring Powers of Attorney Act 1985, or

(c) a person authorised for the purpose by the authority having jurisdiction under Part VII of the Mental Health Act 1983,

a written declaration to appoint by writing the person or persons specified in the direction to be a trustee or trustees in place of the incapable trustee.

21 Supplementary   [960]

(1) For the purposes of section 19 or 20 a direction is given by beneficiaries if –

(a) a single direction is jointly given by all of them, or

(b) (subject to subsection (2)) a direction is given by each of them (whether solely or jointly with one or more, but not all, of the others),

and none of them by writing withdraws the direction given by him before it has been complied with.

(2) Where more than one direction is given each must specify for appointment or retirement the same person or persons.

(3) Subsection (7) of section 36 of the Trustee Act 1925 (powers of trustees appointed under that section) applies to a trustee appointed under section 19 or 20 as if he were appointed under that section.

(4) A direction under section 19 or 20 must not specify a person or persons for appointment if the appointment of that person or those persons would be in contravention of section 35(1) of the Trustee Act 1925 or section 24(1) of the Law of Property Act 1925 (requirements as to identity of trustees).

(5) Sections 19 and 20 do not apply in relation to a trust created by a disposition in so far as provision that they do not apply is made by the disposition.

(6) Sections 19 and 20 do not apply in relation to a trust created before the commencement of this Act by a disposition in so far as provision to the effect that they do not apply is made by a deed executed –

(a) in a case in which the trust was created by one person and he is of full capacity, by that person, or

(b) in a case in which the trust was created by more than one person, by such of the persons who created the trust as are alive and of full capacity.

(7) A deed executed for the purposes of subsection (6) is irrevocable.

(8) Where a deed is executed for the purposes of subsection (6) –

(a) it does not affect anything done before its execution to comply with a direction under section 19 or 20, but
(b) a direction under section 19 or 20 which has been given but not complied with before its execution shall cease to have effect.

PART III

SUPPLEMENTARY

22 Meaning of 'beneficiary'   **[961]**

(1) In this Act 'beneficiary', in relation to a trust, means any person who under the trust has an interest in property subject to the trust (including a person who has such an interest as a trustee or a personal representative).

(2) In this Act references to a beneficiary who is beneficially entitled do not include a beneficiary who has an interest in property subject to the trust only by reason of being a trustee or personal representative.

(3) For the purposes of this Act a person who is a beneficiary only by reason of being an annuitant is not to be regarded as entitled to an interest in possession in land subject to the trust.

23 Other interpretation provisions   **[962]**

(1) In this Act 'purchaser' has the same meaning as in Part I of the Law of Property Act 1925.

(2) Subject to that, where an expression used in this Act is given a meaning by the Law of Property Act 1925 it has the same meaning as in that Act unless the context otherwise requires.

(3) In this Act 'the court' means –

(a) the High Court, or
(b) a county court.

24 Application to Crown   **[963]**

(1) Subject to subsection (2), this Act binds the Crown.

(2) This Act (except so far as it relates to undivided shares and joint ownership) does not affect or alter the descent, devolution or nature of the estates and interests of or in –

(a) land for the time being vested in Her Majesty in right of the Crown or of the Duchy of Lancaster, or
(b) land for the time being belonging to the Duchy of Cornwall and held in right or respect of the Duchy.

25 Amendments, repeals, etc ...   **[964]**

(4) The amendments and repeals made by this Act do not affect any entailed interest created before the commencement of this Act.

(5) The amendments and repeals made by this Act in consequence of section 3 –

(a) do not affect a trust created by a will if the testator died before the commencement of this Act, and

(b) do not affect personal representatives of a person who died before that commencement;

and the repeal of section 22 of the Partnership Act 1890 does not apply in any circumstances involving the personal representatives of a partner who died before that commencement.

26 Power to make consequential provision   [965]

(1) The Lord Chancellor may by order made by statutory instrument make any such supplementary, transitional or incidental provision as appears to him to be appropriate for any of the purposes of this Act or in consequence of any of the provisions of this Act. ...

27 Short title, commencement and extent ...   [966]

(2) This Act comes into force on such day as the Lord Chancellor appoints by order made by statutory instrument. ...

SCHEDULE 1   [967]

Minors

1. (1) Where after commencement of this Act a person purports to convey a legal estate in land to a minor, or two or more minors, alone, the conveyance –

(a) is not effective to pass the legal estate, but
(b) operates as a declaration that the land is held in trust for the minor or minors (or if he purports to convey it to the minor or minors in trust for any persons, for those persons).

(2) Where after the commencement of this Act a person purports to convey a legal estate in land to –

(a) a minor or two or more minors, and
(b) another person who is, or other persons who are, of full age,

the conveyance operates to vest the land in the other person or persons in trust for the minor or minors and the other person or persons (or if he purports to convey it to them in trust for any persons, for those persons).

(3) Where immediately before the commencement of this Act a conveyance is operating (by virtue of section 27 of the Settled Land Act 1925) as an agreement to execute a settlement in favour of a minor or minors –

(a) the agreement ceases to have effect on the commencement of this Act, and
(b) the conveyance subsequently operates instead as a declaration that the land is held in trust for the minor or minors.

2. Where after the commencement of this Act a legal estate in land would, by reason of intestacy or in any other circumstances not dealt with in paragraph 1, vest in a person who is a minor if he were a person of full age, the land is held in trust for the minor.

Family charges

3. Where by virtue of an instrument coming into operation after the commencement of this Act, land becomes charged voluntarily (or in consideration of marriage) or by way of family arrangement, whether immediately or after an interval, with the payment of –

(a) a rent charge for the life of a person or a shorter period, or

476

(b) capital, annual or periodical sums for the benefit of a person,

the instrument operates as a declaration that the land is held in trust for giving effect to the charge.

Charitable, ecclesiastical and public trusts

4. (1) This paragraphs applies in the case of land held on charitable, ecclesiastical or public trusts (other than land to which the Universities and College Estates Act 1925 applies).

(2) Where there is a conveyance of such land –

(a) if neither section 37(1) nor section 39(1) of the Charities Act 1993 applies to the conveyance, it shall state that the land is held on such trusts, and
(b) if neither section 37(2) nor section 39(2) of that Act has been complied with in relation to the conveyance and a purchaser has notice that the land is held on such trusts, he must see that any consents or orders necessary to authorise the transaction have been obtained.

(3) Where any trustees or the majority of any set of trustees have power to transfer or create any legal estate in the land, the estate shall be transferred or created by them in the names and on behalf of the persons in whom it is vested.

Entailed interests

5. (1) Where a person purports by an instrument coming into operation after the commencement of this Act to grant to another person an entailed interest in real or personal property, the instrument –

(a) is not effective to grant an entailed interest, but
(b) operates instead as a declaration that the property is held in trust absolutely for the person to whom an entailed interest in the property was purportedly granted.

(2) Where a person purports by an instrument coming into operation after the commencement of this Act to declare himself a tenant in tail of real or personal property, the instrument is not effective to create an entailed interest.

Property held on settlement ceasing to exist

6. Where a settlement ceases to be a settlement for the purposes of the Settled land Act 1925 because no relevant property (within the meaning of section 2(4)) is, or is deemed to be, subject to the settlement, any property which is or later becomes subject to the settlement is held in trust for the persons interested under the settlement.

SCHEDULE 2   **[968]**

AMENDMENTS OF STATUTORY PROVISIONS
IMPOSING TRUST FOR SALE

1. (1)–(6) [Amends s31 of the Law of Property Act 1925]

(7) The amendments made by this paragraph –

(a) apply whether the right of redemption is discharged before or after the commencement of this Act, but
(b) are without prejudice to any dealings or arrangements made before the commencement of this Act.

2. (1) [Repeals s32 of the Law of Property Act 1925]

(2) The repeal made by this paragraph applies in relation to land purchased after

the commencement of this Act whether the trust or will in pursuance of which it is purchased comes into operation before or after the commencement of this Act.

3. (1)–(5) [Amends s34 of the Law of Property Act 1925]

(6) The amendments made by this paragraph apply whether the disposition is made, or comes into operation, before or after the commencement of this Act.

4. (1)–(3) [Amends s36 of the Law of Property Act 1925]

(4) The amendments made by this paragraph apply whether the legal estate is limited, or becomes held in trust, before or after the commencement of this Act.

5. (1)–(4) [Amends s33 of the Administration of Estates Act 1925]

(5) The amendments made by this paragraph apply whether the death occurs before or after the commencement of this Act.

6. (1)–(5) [Amends s1 of the Reverter of Sites Act 1987]

(6) The amendments made by this paragraph apply whether the trust arises before or after the commencement of this Act.

NB It is expected that this Act will come into force on 1 January 1997.

Glossary
of Latin and other words and phrases

Ab extra. From outside.

Ab inconvenienti. *See* ARGUMENTUM

Ab initio. From the beginning.

Accessio. Addition; appendage. The combination of two chattels belonging to different persons into a single article.

Acta exteriora indicant interiora secreta. A man's outward actions are evidence of his innermost thoughts and intentions.

Acta jure imperii. Acts performed in the exercise of sovereign authority.

Actio personalis moritur cum persona. A personal right of action dies on the death of the person by or against whom it could be enforced.

Actio quanti minoris. Action for how much less.

Actor sequitur forum rei. The plaintiff follows the court of the country where the subject of the action is situated.

Actus non facit reum, nisi mens sit rea. The act itself does not make a man guilty, unless he does it with a guilty intention.

Ad colligenda bona. To collect the goods.

Ad hoc. Arranged for this purpose; special.

Ad idem. *See* CONSENSUS.

Ad infinitum. To infinity; without limit; for ever.

Ad litem. For the purpose of the law suit.

Ad opus. For the benefit of: on behalf of.

Ad referendum. For further consideration.,

Ad valorem. Calculated in proportion to the value or price of the property.

Adversus extraneos vitiosa possessio prodesse solet. Possession, though supported only by a defective title, will prevail over the claims of strangers other than the true owner.

A fortiori (ratione). For a stronger reason; by even more convincing reasoning.

Agrément. Approval; consent.

Aliter. Otherwise; the result would be different, if ...; (also, used of a judge who thinks differently from his fellow judges).

Aliud est celare; aliud est tacere; neque enim id est celare quicquid reticeas. Mere silence is one thing but active concealment is quite another thing; for it is not disguising something when you say nothing about it.

Aliunde. From elsewhere; from other sources.

A mensa et thoro. A separation from the 'table and bed' of one's spouse.

Amicus curiae. A friend of the court.

Animo contrahendi. With the intention of contracting.

Animo et facto. By act and intention.

Animo non revertendi. With the intention of not returning.

Animo revocandi. With the intention of revoking.

Animus deserendi. The intention of deserting.

Animus donandi. The intention of giving.

Animus manendi. The intention of remaining.

Animus possidendi. The intention of possessing.

Animus residendi. The intention of residing.

Animus revertendi. The intention of returning.

Animus testandi. The intention of making a will.

Ante. Before; (also used of a case referred to earlier on a page or in a book).

A posteriori. From effect to cause; inductively; from subsequent conclusions.

A priori. From cause to effect; deductively; from previous assumptions or reasoning.

Arguendo. In the course of the argument.

Argumentum ab inconvenienti. An argument devised because of the existence of an awkward problem so as to provide an explanation for it.

Asportatio. The act of carrying away.

Assensus. *See* CONSENSUS.

Assensus ad idem. Agreement as to the same terms.

Assumpsit (super se). He undertook.

Ats. (ad sectam). At the suit of. (The opposite of VERSUS.)

Autrefois acquit. Formerly acquitted.

Autrefois convict. Formerly convicted.

A vinculo matrimonii. From the bonds of matrimony.

Bis dat qui cito dat. He gives doubly who gives swiftly; a quick gift is worth two slow ones.

Bona fide. In good faith; sincere.

Bona vacantia. Goods without an owner.

Brutum fulmen. A silent thunderbolt; an empty threat.

Cadit quaestio. The matter admits of no further argument.

Caeterorum. Of the things which are left.

Capias ad satisfaciendum. A writ commanding the sheriff to take the body of the defendant in order that he may make satisfaction for the plaintiff's claim.

Causa causans (proxima). The immediate cause of something; the last link in the chain of causation.

Causa proxima non remota spectatur. Regard is paid to the immediate, not to the remote cause.

Causa sine qua non. A cause without which an event would not happen; a preceding link in the chain of causation without which the CAUSA CAUSANS could not be operative.

Caveat emptor. The buyer must look out for himself.

Caveat venditor. The seller must look out for himself.

Cessante ratione legis, cessat lex ipsa. When the reason for its existence ceases, the law itself ceases to exist.

Cestui(s) que trust. A person (or persons) for whose benefit property is held on trust; a beneficiary (beneficiaries).

Cestui que vie. Person for the duration of whose life an estate is granted to another person.

Chargé d'affaires ad interim. One charged with affairs in the mean time.

Chose in action. Intangible personal property or rights, which can be enjoyed or enforced only by legal action, and not by taking physical possession (eg debts).

Chose jugée. Thing it is idle to discuss.

Coitus interruptus. Interrupted sexual intercourse, i.e. withdrawal before emission.

Colore officii. Under the pretext of a person's official position.

Commorientes. Persons who die at the same time.

Confusio. A mixture; union. The mixture of things of the same nature, but belonging to different persons so that identification of the original things becomes impossible.

Consensu. By general consent; unanimously.

Consensus ad idem. Agreement as to the same thing.

Consortium. Conjugal relations with and companionship of a spouse.

Contra. To the contrary. (Used of a case in which the decision was contrary to the doctrine or cases previously cited; also of a judge who delivers a dissenting judgment.)

Contra bonos mores. Contrary to good morals.

Contra mundum. Against the world.

Contra proferentem. Against the party who puts forward a clause in a document.

Cor. (coram). In the presence of; before (a judge).

Coram non judice. Before one who is not a judge. Corpus. Body; capital.

Corpus. Body; capital.

Coverture. Marriage.

Cri de coeur. Heartfelt cry.

Cujus est solum, ejus est usque ad coelum et ad inferos. Whosoever owns the soil also owns everything above it as far as the heavens and everything below it as far as the lower regions of the earth.

Culpa. Wrongful default.

Cum onere. Together with the burden.

Cum testamento annexo. With the will annexed.

Cur. adv. vult. (curia advisari vult). The court wishes time to consider the matter.

Cy-pres. For a purpose resembling as nearly as possible the purpose originally proposed.

Damage feasant. *See* DISTRESS.

Damnosa hereditas. An insolvent inheritance.

Damnum. Loss; damage.

Damnum absque injuria. *See* DAMNUM SINE INJURIA.

Damnum emergens. A loss which arises.

Damnum fatale. Damage resulting from the workings of fate for which human negligence is not to blame.

Damnum sine (or absque) injuria. Damage which is not the result of a legally remediable wrong.

De bene esse. Evidence or action which a court allows to be given or done provisionally, subject to further consideration at a later stage.

Debitor non praesumitur donare. A debtor is presumed to give a legacy to a creditor to discharge his debt and not as a gift.

Debitum in praesenti. A debt which is due at the present time.

Debitum in futuro solvendum. A debt which will be due to be paid at a future time.

De bonis asportatis. Of goods carried away.

De bonis non administratis. Of the assets which have not been administered .

De cujus. The person about whom an issue is to be determined.

De die in diem. From day to day.

De facto. In fact.

De futuro. Regarding the future; in the future; about something which will exist in the future.

Dehors. Outside (the document or matter in question); irrelevant.

De integro. As regards the whole; entirely.

De jure. By right; rightful.

Del credere agent. An agent who for an extra commission guarantees the due performance of contracts by persons whom he introduces to his principal.

Delegatus non potest delegare. A person who is entrusted with a duty has no right to appoint another person to perform it in his place.

De minimis non curat lex. The law does not concern itself with trifles.

De momento in momentum. From moment to moment.

De novo. Anew; starting afresh.

Deodand. A chattel which caused the death of a human being and was forfeited to the Crown.

De praerogativa regis. Concerning the royal prerogative.

De son tort. Of his own wrong.

Deus est procurator fatuorum. God is the protector of the simpleminded.

Devastavit. Where an executor 'has squandered' the estate.

Dictum. Saying. *See* OBITER DICTUM.

Dies certus. Day certain, determined.

Dies non (jurisdicus). Day on which no legal business can be transacted.

Dissentiente. Delivering a dissenting judgment.

Distress damage feasant. The detention by a landowner of an animal or chattel while it is doing damage on his land.

Distringas. That you may distrain.

Doli incapax. Incapable of crime.

Dolus qui dat locum contractui. A deception which clears the way for the other party to enter into a contract.

Dominium. Ownership.

Dominus litis. The principal in a suit.

Dominus pro tempore. The master for the time being.

Donatio mortis causa. A gift made in contemplation of death and conditional thereon.

Dubitante. Doubting the correctness of the decision.

Durante absentia. During an absence abroad.

Durante minore aetate. While an infant; during minority.

Durante viduitate. During widowhood.

Ei incumbit probatio qui dicit, non qui negat. The onus of proving a fact rests upon the man who asserts its truth, not upon the man who denies it.

Ejusdem generis. General words following a list of specific things are construed as relating to things 'of the same kind' as those specifically listed.

Enceinte. Pregnant.

En ventre sa mère. Conceived but not yet born.

Eodem modo quo oritur, eodem modo dissolvitur. What has been created by a certain method may be extinguished by the same method.

Eo instanti. At that instant.

Escrow. A document delivered subject to a condition which must be fulfilled before it becomes a deed.

Estoppel. A rule of evidence which applies in certain circumstances and stops a person from denying the truth of a statement previously made by him.

Estoppel in pais. Estoppel by matter or conduct; equitable estoppel.

Et cetera (etc). And other things of that sort.

Et seq (et sequentes). And subsequent pages.

Ex. From; by virtue of.

Ex abundanti cautela. From an abundance of caution.

Ex aequo et bono. According to what is just and equitable.

Ex cathedra. From his seat of office: an authoritative statement made by someone in his official capacity.

Ex comitate et jure gentium. Out of comity (friendly recognition) and the law of nations.

Ex concessis. In view of what has already been accepted.

Ex contractu. Arising out of contract.

Ex converso. Conversely.

Ex debito justitiae. That which is

due as of right; which the court has no discretion to refuse.

Ex delicto. Arising out of a wrongful act or tort.

Ex dolo malo non oritur actio. No right of action arises out of a fraud.

Executor de son tort. One who 'of his own fault' has intermeddled with an estate, purporting to act as executor.

Exequatur. Governmental permission to an official of another state to enter upon the discharge of his functions.

Ex facie. On the face of it; ostensibly.

Ex gratia. Out of the kindness. Gratuitous; voluntary.

Ex hypothesi. In view of what has already been assumed.

Ex improviso. Unexpectedly, without forethought.

Ex officio. By virtue of one's official position.

Ex pacto illicito non oritur actio. No action can be brought on an unlawful contract.

Ex parte. Proceedings brought on behalf of one interested party without notice to, and in the absence of, the other.

Ex post facto. By reason of a subsequent act; acting retrospectively.

Ex relatione. An action instituted by the Attorney-General on behalf of the Crown on the information of a member of the public who is interested in the matter (the relator).

Expressio unius est exclusio alterius. When one thing is expressly specified, then it prevents anything else being implied.

Expressis verbis. In express words.

Expressum facit cessare tacitum. Where terms are expressed, no other terms can be implied.

Extra territorium. Outside the territory; extra territorial(ly).

Ex turpi causa non oritur actio. No action can be brought where the parties are guilty of illegal or immoral conduct.

Faciendum. Something which is to be done.

Factum. Deed; that which has been done; statement of facts or points in issue.

Fait accompli. An accomplished fact.

Falsa demonstratio non nocet cum de corpore constat. Where the substance of the property in question is clearly identified, the addition of an incorrect description of the property does no harm.

Falsus in ono, falsus in omnibus. False in one, false in all.

Fecundatio ab extra. Conception from outside, i.e. where there has been no penetration.

Feme covert. A married woman.

Feme sole. An unmarried woman.

Ferae naturae. Animals which are by nature dangerous to man.

Fieri facias. A writ addressed to the sheriff: 'that you cause to be made' from the defendant's goods the sum due to the plaintiff under the judgment.

Filius nullius. *See* NULLIUS FILIUS.

Force majeure. Irresistible compulsion.

Forum. Court; the court hearing the case.

Forum conveniens. The appropriate court to hear the case.

Forum domicilii. The court of the country of domicile.

Forum rei. The court of the country where the subject of the action is situated.

Fraude à la loi. Evasion of the law.

Fructus industriales. Cultivated crops.

Fructus naturales. Vegetation which grows naturally without cultivation.

Functus officio. Having discharged his duty; having exhausted its powers.

Furiosus. Frantic, mad.

Genus numquam perit. Particular goods which have been identified may be destroyed, but 'a category or type of article can never perish'.

Habeas corpus (ad subjiciendum). A writ addressed to one who detains another in custody, requiring him 'that you produce the prisoner's body to answer' to the court.

Habitue. A frequent visitor to a place.

Ibid. (ibidem). In the same place, book, or source.

Id certum est quod certum reddi potest. That which is capable of being reduced to a certainty is already a certainty.

Idem. The same thing, or person.

Ideo consideratum est per. Therefore it is considered by the court.

Ignorantia juris haud (neminem) (non) excusat, ignorantia facti excusat. A man may be excused for mistaking facts, but not for mistaking the law.

Ignorantia juris non excusat. Ignorance of the law is no excuse.

Imperitia culpae adnumeratur. Lack of skill is accounted a fault.

In aequali jure melior est conditio possidentis. Where the legal rights of the parties are equal, the party with possession is in the stronger position.

In articulo mortis. On the point of death.

In bonis. In the goods (or estate) of a deceased person.

In capite. In chief; holding as tenant directly under the Crown.

In consimili casu. In a similar case.

In custodia legis. In the keeping of the law.

Indebitatus assumpsit. A form of action in which the plaintiff alleges the defendant 'being already indebted to the plaintiff undertook' to do something.

In delicto. At fault.

Indicia. Signs; marks.

Indicium. Indication; sign; mark.

In esse. In existence.

In expeditione. On actual military service.

In extenso. At full length.

In fieri. In the course of being performed or established.

In flagrante delicto. In the act of committing the offence.

In forma pauperis. In the character of a poor person.

Infra. Below; lower down on a page; later in a book. In futuro. In the future.

In futuro. In the future.

In hac re. In this matter; in this particular aspect.

In jure non remota causa sed proxima spectatur. In law it is the immediate and not the remote cause which is considered.

Injuria. A wrongful act for which the law provides a remedy.

Injuria sine damno. A wrongful act unaccompanied by any damage yet actionable at law.

In lieu of. In place of.

In limine. On the threshold; at the outset.

In loco parentis. In the place of a parent.

In minore delicto. A person who is 'less at fault'.

In omnibus. In every respect.

Inops consilii. Lacking facilities for legal advice.

In pari delicto, potior est conditio defendentis (or possidentis). Where both parties are equally at fault, the defendant (or the party in possession) is in the stronger position.

In pari materia. In an analogous case or position.

In personam. *See* JUS IN PERSONAM.

In pleno. In full.

In praesenti. At the present time.

In propria persona. In his own capacity. In re. In the matter of. In rem. *See* JUS IN REM.

In re. In the matter of.

In rem. *See* JUS IN REM.

In situ. In its place.

In specie. In its own form; not converted into anything else.

In statu quo ante. In the condition in which it, or a person, was before.

Inter alia. Amongst other things.

Inter alios. Amongst other persons.

Interest reipublicae ut sit finis litium. It is in the interests of the community that every law suit should reach a final conclusion (and not be reopened later).

Interim. In the meanwhile; temporary.

Inter partes. Between (the) parties.

In terrorem. As a warning; as a deterrent.

Inter se. Between themselves.

Inter vivos. Between persons who are alive.

In toto. In its entirety; completely.

In transitu. In passage from one place to another.

Intra vires. Within the powers recognised by law as belonging to the person or body in question.

In utero. In the womb.

In vacuo. In the abstract; without considering the circumstances.

In vitro. In glass; in a test tube.

Ipsissima verba. 'The very words' of a speaker.

Ipso facto. By that very fact.

Jura. Rights.

Jura mariti. By virtue of the right of a husband to the goods of his wife.

Jus. A right which is recognised in law.

Jus accrescendi. The right of survivorship; the right of joint tenants to have their interests in the joint property increased by inheriting the interests of the deceased joint tenants until the last survivor inherits the entire property.

Jus actionis. Right of action.

Jus cogens. Law obliging.

Jus gentium. The law of nations.

Jus in personam. A right which can be enforced against a particular person only.

Jus in rem. A right which can be enforced over the property in question against all other persons.

Jus naturale. Natural justice.

Jus neque in re neque ad rem. A right which is enforceable neither over the property in question against all the world nor against specific persons only.

Jus quaesitum tertio. A right vested in a third party (who is not a party to the contract).

Jus regale. A right or privilege belonging to the Crown.

Jus spatiandi. A right to stray.

Jus tertii. *See* JUS QUAESITUM TERTIO

Laches. Slackness or delay in pursuing a legal remedy which disentitles a person from action at a later date.

Laesio fidei. Breach of faith.

Laissez faire. 'Let him do what he likes'; permissive.

Lapsus linguae. Slip of the tongue.

Lex actus. The law governing a legal act or transaction.

Lex causae. The law governing the case or a given issue therein.

Lex domicilii. The law of the country of domicile of a person.

Lex fori. The law of the court in which the case is being heard.

Lex loci actus. The law of the country where a legal act or transaction took place.

Lex loci celebrationis. The law of the place where the marriage was celebrated.

Lex loci contractus. The law of the place where the contract was made.

Lex loci delicti commissi. The law of the place where the wrong was committed.

Lex loci situs. *See* LEX SITUS.

Lex loci solutionis. The law of the place where the contract is to be performed.

Lex monetae. The law of the country in whose currency a debt or other financial obligation is expressed.

Lex nationalis. The law of the country of a person's nationality.

Lex patriae. *See* LEX NATIONALIS.

Lex pecuniae. *See* LEX MONETAE.

Lex situs. The law of the place where the thing in question is situated.

Lex successionis. The law governing the succession to a deceased's estate.

Lien. The rights to retain possession of goods, deeds or other property belonging to another as security for payment of money.

Lis alibi pendens. An action pending elsewhere.

Lis pendens. Pending action.

Loc. cit. (loco citato). In the passage previously mentioned.

Locus celebrationis. The place where the marriage was celebrated.

Locus classicus. Authoritative passage in a book or judgment; the principal authority or source for the subject.

Locus contractus. The place where the contract was made.

Locus delicti. The place where the wrong was committed.

Locus in quo. Scene of the event.

Locus poenitentiae. Scope or opportunity for repentance.

Locus regit actum. The law of the place where an act takes place governs that act.

Locus solutionis. The place where a contract is to be performed or a debt is to be paid.

Locus standi. Recognised position or standing; the right to appear in court.

Lucrum cessans. A benefit which is terminated.

Magnum opus. A great work of literature.

Mala fide(s). (In) bad faith.

Malitia supplet aetatem. Malice supplements the age of an infant wrongdoer who would (in the absence of malice) be too young to be responsible for his acts.

Malum in se. An act which in itself is morally wrong, e.g. murder.

Malum prohibitum. An act which is wrong because it is prohibited by human law but is not morally wrong.

Malus animus. Evil intent.

Mansuetae naturae. Animals which are normally of a domesticated disposition.

Mesne. Intermediate; middle; dividing.

Mesne profits. Profits of land lost by the plaintiff while the defendant remained wrongfully in possession.

Mobilia sequuntur personam. The domicile of movable property follows the owner's personal domicile.

Molliter manus imposuit. Gently laid his hand upon the other party.

Mutatis mutandis. With the necessary changes of detail being made.

Natura negotii. The nature of the transaction.

Negotiorum gestio. Handling of other people's affairs.

Nemo dat quod non habet. No one has power to transfer the ownership of that which he does not own.

Nemo debet bis vexari, si constat curiae quod sit pro una et eadem causa. No one ought to be harassed with proceedings twice, if it appears to the court that it is for one and the same cause.

Nemo est haeres viventis. No one

can be the heir of a person who is still living.

Nexus. Connection; bond.

Nisi. Unless; (also used of a decree or order which will later be made absolute 'unless' good cause be shown to the contrary); provisional.

Nisi prius. Cases which were directed to be tried at Westminster only if the justices of assize should 'not' have tried them in the country 'previously'.

Nocumenta infinita sunt. There is no limit to the types of situations which constitute nuisances.

Nomen collectivum. A collective name, noun or description; a word descriptive of a class.

Non compos mentis. Not of sound mind and understanding.

Non constat. It is not certain.

Non est factum. That the document in question was not his deed.

Non grata. Not acceptable.

Non haec in foedera veni. This is not the agreement which I came to sign.

Non omnibus dormio. I do not turn a blind eye on every instance of misconduct.

Non sequitur. It does not follow; an inconsistent statement.

Noscitur a sociis. The meaning of a word is known from the company it keeps (ie from its context).

Nova causa interveniens. An independent cause which intervenes between the alleged wrong and the damage in question.

Novus actus interveniens. A fresh act of someone other than the defendant which intervenes between the alleged wrong and the damage in question.

Nudum pactum. A bare agreement (unsupported by consideration).

Nullius filius. No man's son; a bastard.

Obiter dictum (dicta). Thing(s) said by the way; opinions expressed by

judges in passing, on issues not essential for the decision in the case.

Obligatio quasi ex contractu. An obligation arising out of an act or event, as if from a contract, but independently of the consent of the person bound.

Omnia praesumuntur contra spoliatorem. Every presumption is raised against a wrongdoer.

Omnia praesumuntur rite et solemniter esse acta donec probetur in contrarium. All things are presumed to have been performed with all due formalities until it is proved to the contrary.

Omnis ratihabitio retrotrahitur et mandato priori aequiparatur. Every ratification of a previous act is carried back and made equivalent to a previous command to do it.

Onus probandi. The burden of proving.

Op. cit. (opere citato). In the book referred to previously.

Orse. Otherwise.

Pace. By permission of.

Pacta sunt servanda. Agreements are kept.

Par delictum. Equal fault.

Par in parem non habet imperium. An equal has no authority over an equal.

Parens patriae. Parent of the nation.

Pari materia. With equal substance.

Pari passu. On an equal footing; equally; in step with.

Pari ratione. By an equivalent process of reasoning.

Parol. By word of mouth, or unsealed document.

Participes criminis. Accomplices in the crime.

Passim. Everywhere; in various places.

Pater est quem nuptiae demonstrant. He is the father whom the marriage indicates to be so.

Patrimonium. Beneficial ownership.

Pendente lite. While a law suit is pending.

Per. By; through; in the opinion of a judge.

Per capita. Divided equally between all the persons filling the description.

Per curiam. In the opinion of the court.

Per formam doni. Through the form of wording of the gift or deed.

Per incuriam. Through carelessness or oversight.

Per quod. By reason of which.

Per quod consortium et servitium amisit. By reason of which he has lost the benefit of her company and services.

Per quod servitium amisit. By reason of which he has lost the benefit of his service.

Per se. By itself.

Persona non grata. A person not acceptable.

Persona(e) designata(e). A person(s) specified as an individual(s), not identified as a member(s) of a class nor as fulfilling a particular qualification.

Per stirpes. According to the stocks of descent; one share for each line of descendants; where the descendants of a deceased person (however many they may be) inherit between them only the one share which the deceased would have taken if alive.

Per subsequens matrimonium. Legitimation of a child 'by subsequent marriage' of the parents.

Plene administravit. A plea by an executor 'that he has fully administered' all the assets which have come into his hands and that no assets remain out of which the plaintiff's claim could be satisfied.

Plus quam tolerabile. More than can be endured.

Post. After; mentioned in a subsequent passage or page.

Post mortem. After death.

Post nuptial. Made after marriage.

Post obit bond. Agreement or bond by which a borrower agrees to pay the lender a sum larger than the loan on or after the death of a person on whose death he expects to inherit property.

Post obitum. After the death of a specified person.

Pour autrui. On behalf of another.

Prima facie. At first sight.

Primae impressionis. Of first impression.

Pro bono publico. For the public good.

Procès verbal. Verbal proceedings.

Profit a prendre. The right to enter the land of another and take part of its produce.

Pro hac vice. For this occasion.

Propositus. The person put forward; the person about whom a legal issue is to be determined.

Pro privato commodo. For private benefit.

Pro rata. In proportion.

Pro rata itineris. At the same rate per mile as was agreed for the whole journey.

Pro tanto. So far; to that extent.

Pro tempore. For the time being.

Publici juris. Of public right.

Puisne. Inferior; lower in rank; not secured by deposit of deeds; of the High Court.

Punctum temporis. Moment, or point of time.

Pur autre vie. During the life of another person.

Q.v. (quod vide). Which see.

Qua. As; in the capacity of.

Quaere. Consider whether it is correct.

Quaeritur. The question is raised.

Quantum. Amount; how much.

Quantum meruit. As much as he has earned.

Quantum valebant. As much as they were worth.

Quare clausum fregit. Because he broke into the plaintiff's enclosure.

Quasi. As if; seemingly.

Quasi ex contractu. *See* OBLIGATIO.

Quatenus. How far; in so far as; since.

Qui sentit commodum sentire debet et onus. He who takes the benefit must accept the burden.

Quia timet. Because he fears what he will suffer in the future.

Quicquid plantatur solo solo cedit. Whatever is planted in the soil belongs to the soil.

Quid pro quo. Something for something; consideration.

Qui elegit judicem elegit jus. He who chooses a judge chooses also the law which the judge administers.

Qui facit per alium facit per se. He who employs another person to do something does it himself.

Qui prior est tempore potior est jure. He who is earlier in point of time is in the stronger position in law.

Quoad. Until; as far as; as to.

Quoad hoc. As far as this matter is concerned.

Quo animo. With what intention.

Quot judices tot sententiae. There were as many different opinions as there were judges.

Quousque. Until the time when.

Ratio decidendi. The reason for a decision; the principle on which a decision is based.

Ratione domicilii. By reason of a person's domicile.

Ratione impotentiae et loci. By reason of weakness and of place.

Re. In the matter of; by the thing or transaction.

Reductio ad absurdum. Reduction to absurdity.

Refouler. To return, drive back.

Renvoi. Reference to or application of the rules of a foreign legal system in a different country's courts.

Res. Thing; affair; matter; circumstance.

Res extincta. The thing which was intended to be the subject matter of a contract but had previously been destroyed.

Res gestae. Things done; the transaction.

Res integra. A point not covered by the authority of a decided case which must therefore be decided upon principle alone.

Res inter alios acta alteri nocere non debet. A man ought not to be prejudiced by what has taken place between other persons.

Res ipsa loquitur. The thing speaks for itself, i.e. is evidence of negligence in the absence of an explanation by the defendant.

Res judicata. A matter on which a court has previously reached a binding decision; a matter which cannot be questioned.

Res nova. A matter which has not previously been decided.

Res nullius. Nobody's property.

Respondeat superior. A principal must answer for the acts of his subordinates.

Res sua. Something which a man believes to belong to another when it in fact is 'his own property'.

Restitutio in integrum. Restoration of a party to his original position; full restitution.

Res vendita. The article which was sold.

Rex est procurator fatuorum. The King is the protector of the simple minded.

Rigor aequitatis. The inflexibility of equity.

Sc. *See* SCILICET.

Sciens. Knowing.

Scienter. Knowingly; with knowledge of an animal's dangerous disposition.

Scienti non fit injuria. A man who is aware of the existence of a danger has no remedy if it materialises.

Scilicet. To wit; namely; that is to say.

Scintilla. A spark; trace; or moment.

Scire facias. A writ; that you cause to know.

Scriptum praedictum non est factum suum. A plea that the aforesaid document is not his deed.

Secundum formam doni. In accordance with the form of wording in the gift or deed.

Secus. It is otherwise; the legal position is different.

Sed. But.

Sed quaere. But inquire; look into the matter; consider whether the statement is correct.

Semble. It appears; apparently.

Sentit commodum et periculum rei. He both enjoys the benefit of the thing and bears the risk of its loss.

Seriatim. In series; one by one; point by point.

Serivitium. Service.

Sic. So; in such a manner; (also used to emphasise wording copied or quoted from another source: 'such was the expression used in the original source').

Sic utere tuo ut alienum non laedas. So use your own property as not to injure the property of your neighbour.

Similiter. Similarly; in like manner.

Simplex commendatio non obligat. Mere praise of goods by the seller imposes no liability upon him.

Simpliciter. Simply; merely; alone; without any further action; without qualification.

Sine animo revertendi. Without the intention of returning.

Sine die. Without a day being appointed; indefinitely.

Situs. The place where property is situated.

Solatium. Consolation; relief; compensation.

Sotto volce. In an undertone.

Specificatio. The making of a new article out of the chattel of one person by the labour of another.

Spes successionis. The hope of inheriting property on the death of another.

Spondes peritiam artis. If skill is inherent in your profession, you guarantee that you will display it.

Stare decisis. To stand by what has been dedided.

Status quo (ante). The previous position; the position in which things were before; unchanged position.

Stet. Let it stand; do not delete.

Stricto sensu. In the strict sense.

Sub colore officii. Under pretext of someone's official position.

Sub judice. Under judgment; being decided by the court.

Sub modo. Within limits; to a limited extent.

Sub nom. (sub nomine). Under the name of.

Sub silentio. In silence.

Sub tit. (sub titulo). Under the title of.

Suggestio falsi. The suggestion of something which is untrue.

Sui generis. Of its own special kind; unique.

Sui juris. Of his own right; possessed of full legal capacity.

Sup. *See* SUPRA.

Suppressio veri. The suppression of the truth.

Supra. (Sup.) Above; referred to higher up the page; previously.

Talis qualis. Such as it is.

Tam ... quam. As well ... as.

Tempore mortis. At the time of death.

Tempore testamenti. At the time when the will was made.

Toties quoties. As often as occasion shall require; as often as something happens.

Transit in rem judicatam. A right of action merges in the judgment recovered upon it.

Turpis causa. Immoral conduct which constitutes the subject matter of an action.

Uberrima fides. Most abundant good faith.

Ubi jus ibi remedium. Where there is a legally recognised right there is also a remedy.

Ubi supra. In the passage or reference mentioned previously.

Ultimus heres. The ultimate heir who is last in order of priority of those who may be entitled to claim the estate of an intestate.

Ultra vires. Outside the powers recognised by law as belonging to the person or body in question.

Uno flatu. With one breath; at the same moment.

Ut res magis valeat quam pereat. Words must be construed so as to support the validity of the contract rather than to destroy it.

v. (versus). Against.

Verba fortius accipiuntur contra proferentem. Ambiguous wording is construed adversely against the party who introduced it into the document.

Vera copula. True sexual unity.

Verbatim. Word by word; exactly; word for word.

Via media. Middle way; compromise.

Vice versa. The other way round; in turn.

Vide. See.

Vi et armis (et contra pacem domini regis). By force of arms (and in breach of the King's peace).

Vigilantibus et non dormientibus jura subveniunt (or jus succurrit). The law(s) assist(s) those who are vigilant, not those who doze over their rights.

Vinculum juris. Legal tie; that which binds the parties with mutual obligations.

Virgo intacta. A virgin with hymen intact.

Virtute officii. By virtue of a person's official position.

Vis-a-vis. Face to face; opposite to.

Vis major. Irresistible force.

Viva voce. Orally; oral examination.

Viz. (videlicet). Namely; that is to say.

Voir dire. Examination of a witness before he gives evidence, to ascertain whether he is competent to tell the truth on oath; trial within a trial.

Volens. Willing.

Volenti non fit injuria. In law no wrong is done to a man who consents to undergo it.

Index

The entry numbers refer to the paragraphs, not the pages.

Access, right of. *See also* WAY,
RIGHT OF
estoppel, by, 76
neighbouring land, to, 845 et
seq
order, 845, 846
Accumulation, 498 et seq, 606 et
seq
power for, 195, 500
trust for, 33, 41
Agricultural holding, 702, 779 et
seq, 822, 882 et seq
'farm business tenancy', 882
rent review, 886 et seq
termination, 891
fixtures, removal of, 784, 885
sub-tenancy, 178
Air space,
trespass, 32, 67, 131, 749
Andrews v Partington
rule in, 12
application, 38
Assurance, 39
disentailing, 199

Bequest, 266. *See also* DEVISE
aggregate fund, 12
certainty, 66, 101, 207
Building,
tenant, removal by, 91
Buy, right to, 757 et seq

Charge. *See also* REGISTRATION
Class A, 666
Class C(iv), 50, 125, 205
Class D(iii), 125
covenants, implied, 529
equitable, 53, 445
land, 650 et seq
local, 677 et seq
legal, 62, 471
lien, 53
matrimonial home, 752
priority, 161, 226, 452, 660
undisclosed, 644

Charity. *See also* REVERTER OF
SITES
land, sale of, by, 851, 967
Commons,
inclosure, 510
pasture, of, 245
prescription, 258
registration, 623 et seq
rights over, 509
Constructive trust,
creation, 144, 175, 224
shares under, 85
Consumer credit, 670 et seq
extortionate bargain, 674
Contract, 416 et seq. *See also*
CHARITY
benefit of, 206, 210
land,
charge, 643
gift of, 175
option, 122, 236, 396
sale of, 70, 87, 95, 120,
150, 151, 196, 226, 737,
835
settlement of, 288
title, period of, 642
vendor, duty of, 180
lease, for, 113
underlease, for, 118
Conveyance, 416 et seq, 534
all estate clause, 427
covenants, implied in, 432, 517
general words, 426
minor, to, 967
personal representative, by, 578
self, to, 431
Covenants, 432–439, 907 et seq.
See also CONVEYANCE;
FORFEITURE; LEASE
building scheme, 26, 83, 89,
126
implied, 130, 166, 235, 243,
438, 529, 861 et seq, 909
land, running with, 21, 96, 126,
191, 194, 197, 210